INJURIES, ILLNESSES, & CONDITIONS IN SPORTS MEDICINE

Linda Gazzillo Diaz • Jaclyn Morrissette

Kendall Hunt
publishing company

Kendall Hunt
publishing company

www.kendallhunt.com
Send all inquiries to:
4050 Westmark Drive
Dubuque, IA 52004-1840

PAK ISBN: 978-1-7924-8798-9
TEXT ISBN: 978-1-7924-8799-6

Printed in the United States of America

Contents

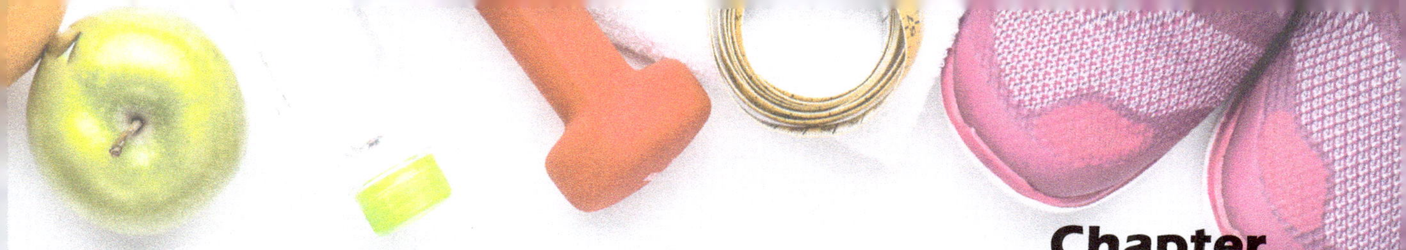

Chapter 1

Legal Issues in Sports Medicine

Chapter Objectives

After you have read this chapter, you will be able to understand:

- Negligence and its four elements.
- The differences between omission and commission.
- The concept of foreseeability, and examples of how harmful acts may and may not be foreseeable.
- Comparative and contributory negligence and how they affect a plaintiff's compensation in a negligence claim.
- The purpose of assumption of risk documents
- Good Samaritan Laws and how they protect the public.
- Defenses against negligence.

In the present day, the potentiality of litigation in the workplace is real. As a sports medicine professional, you are responsible for your patients' wellbeing. However, sports medicine professionals who supervise, instruct, and care for patients are especially at risk for being sued (**Figure 1-1**). As a professional, you must continually be cognizant that providing improper first aid injury and illness care for a patient may result in legal ramifications. These statements are not an attempt to discourage you to assist an injured or ill patient. On the contrary, caring for your injured and ill patients is imperative. However, it is prudent to obtain proper first aid and CPR training and understand the legalities that govern your actions prior to working with and providing care to patients. Knowledge of legal issues affecting you as a sports medicine professional is crucial. With this knowledge, you can guide your actions to provide injured and ill patients' proper care, while protecting yourself as best as possible from litigation.

Figure 1-1 Sports medicine professionals must properly explain and instruct their athletes how to perform skills correctly in order to avoid litigation.

Negligence

The term **negligence** is utilized quite frequently in a variety of contexts. A nurse could be negligent in administering a proper dose of medication to a patient. A physician could be negligent in determining the proper diagnosis of a child's illness. Regardless of how negligence is utilized, the term means that a person did not act as a reasonable, sensible, or prudent, person would (Harrelson, Gardner, & Winterstein, 2017). Negligence is a part of tort law. A **tort** is not a criminal act against someone (Spengler, Anderson, Connaughton, & Baker, 2016). A tort is a civil wrong that occurs to a person's body or property by another person. In tort law, negligence is unintentional harm (Cotton & Wolohan, 2020). For sports medicine professionals who care for patients, negligence can cause injury or illness. A caregiver must act in a reasonable manner when tending to patients. If the caregiver does not act responsibly, then injury or illness can occur to the patient.

For a caregiver (defendant) to be found negligent in a court of law, the injured athlete (plaintiff) has the burden of proving that the defendant did not provide care to the plaintiff as any other reasonable person would. In order for the plaintiff to be awarded damages, usually in the form of money, the plaintiff has to prove that the defendant took part in the four components of negligence. These four components include: (1) the defendant had a duty to the plaintiff, (2) the defendant failed to perform the duty (breach of duty), (3) the defendant's failure to perform the duty was the actual cause of the plaintiff's injury or illness, and (4) the patient sustained injury or illness (i.e. actual damages occurred as a result) (Harrelson, Gardner, & Winterstein, 2017; Pachman & Lamba, 2017). In court, the plaintiff does not have the burden to prove the four elements of negligence by a reasonable doubt as in criminal cases. However, every element must be proven in order for the plaintiff to win the case.

Duty

A patient (plaintiff) can claim that negligence caused their injury or illness; however, for this claim to go forward in court, the defendant (caregiver) had to have a **duty** to the patient (Pachman & Lamba, 2017). In other words, the defendant was liable and responsible for the patient's well-being, and had a special relationship with the patient at the time of injury. Many professionals, including sports medicine professionals, have an inherent duty to patients due to the nature of their employment. For example, collegiate coaches and the National Collegiate Athletic Association (NCAA) have a duty to their student-athletes (Gayles & Blanchard, 2018). Personal trainers have a duty to their clients. Physical education teachers have a duty to their students. These three professionals have a responsibility and duty to the people they serve due to their education, qualifications, and certifications, (Wong, 2010). If the plaintiff cannot prove that the defendant had a duty to the plaintiff, then the case will be dismissed.

Standard of Care

When a defendant has been charged with negligence, the plaintiff must show that not only did the defendant have a duty to care for the plaintiff at the time of injury or illness, but that the defendant did not meet the expected standard of care. The standard of care is the manner in which the defendant acted as compared to other defendants with similar qualifications (Cotten & Wolohan, 2020; Pachman & Lamba, 2017; Pozgar, 2020.) Consider the following scenario: A first aid-certified, physical education teacher conducts an indoor wiffle ball tournament in physical education class. A student participant is injured when a wiffle ball is hit into the student's eye, causing immediate vision problems. The physical education teacher summons the school nurse and simultaneously dials 911 to obtain emergency care for the student. Until Emergency Medical Services (EMS) arrives, the physical education teacher provides first aid to the student.

In this scenario, the court first determines if the physical education teacher had a duty to the student. In this case the court will most likely find that the physical education teacher did have a duty to the student due to the nature of the teacher-student relationship. The court then determines if the physical education teacher's standard of care prior to and after the incident was appropriate for the patient and situation at hand. The court compares the actions of this physical education teacher to other physical education teachers with the same training, qualifications, and certifications. The court's findings determine if the defendant appropriately met the standard of care.

Failure to Act or Breach of Duty

The second step in proving that a caregiver-defendant is negligent is for the patient-plaintiff to show the defendant failed to act and breached their duty to the plaintiff. This failure to act exists if the defendant participated in an act of omission, misfeasance, or commission. Omission, also called nonfeasance, is when a person does not perform an act that they are qualified to do (Cornell School of Law, 2020; Pozgar, 2020; Prentice, 2020).

Consider the following scenario: Athletic trainers are qualified and trained to provide first aid skills. During practice, a football player incurs a deep, large, bleeding, open wound. The athlete informs the athletic trainer. The athletic trainer does not clean or bandage the wound and allows the athlete to continue practice. Days later, the wound is infected, and the athlete sustains a systemic, secondary illness. The athlete's condition resulted from the athletic trainer's lack of first aid care for the wound. In this scenario, the athletic trainer has participated in an act of omission.

Misfeasance occurs when a person is legally able to perform an act that they are qualified to do, but performs the act improperly. As an example utilizing the previous scenario, the athletic trainer tends to the athlete's wound by cleaning it with soap and water. However, the athletic trainer neglects to apply antibiotic ointment or a bandage. The athletic trainer allows the athlete to return to play with an uncovered, open wound. Consequently, the athlete's wound becomes infected. This infection is directly related to the athletic trainer's misfeasance. The athletic trainer was qualified, knowledgeable, and trained to provide proper first aid care for an open wound. The athletic trainer did not apply the appropriate care as required to prevent wound infection, which is an act of misfeasance.

Commission, also referred to as malfeasance, occurs when a person performs an act that they are not qualified to perform on another person. These acts of commission are completely illegal or wrongful (Harrelson, Gardner, & Winterstein, 2017; Prentice, 2020). Utilizing the previous scenario once more, the athletic trainer cares for the athlete's deep, large, bleeding, open wound. However, the athletic trainer decides to inject the wound site with lidocaine and suture the wound instead of referring the patient to a physician or calling 911 for emergency services. The athletic trainer's state's regulations do not allow for athletic trainers to inject lidocaine or suture wounds. Days later, the athlete's wound is infected, and the athlete sustains a systemic illness due to the wrongful care that the athletic trainer provided. In this scenario, the athletic trainer participated in an act of commission.

In any of these scenarios, by the nature of the athletic trainer-athlete relationship, the athletic trainer has a duty to perform proper first aid on their athletes as any other reasonable athletic trainer would. However, the athletic trainer failed to act in a proper manner and could be deemed negligent.

Failure to Act as the Primary Cause of Injury

In order to prove negligence, the plaintiff has the burden to show that the defendant's failure to act in a reasonable manner is the primary cause for the plaintiff's injury or illness (Harrelson,

Gardner, & Winterstein, 2017). The plaintiff has the opportunity to make various claims. A plaintiff can claim that physical, bodily injury or illness resulted from the defendant's failure to act in a reasonable manner. Likewise, the plaintiff can claim that they suffered negative emotional, psychological, or social damages due to the defendant's failure to act. The plaintiff can also claim that they have lost employment and earnings due to the defendant's failure to act (American Academy of Orthopedic Surgeons [AAOS], 2022). In the previous scenarios, the athletic trainer took part in acts of omission, misfeasance, and commission. However, if these acts did not directly cause the illness, then the plaintiff's negligence claim is dismissed. Despite the fact that the plaintiff has experienced injury or illness, often it is very difficult for the plaintiff to prove that the defendant's actions were the proximate cause.

Actual Harm or Damages Occurred

An athletic trainer may have had a duty to their athlete, and breached the duty to provide a reasonable standard of care that caused the athlete's injury or illness, but the athlete must prove that actual harm resulted (Harrelson, Gardner, & Winterstein, 2017). In the previous wiffle ball tournament scenario, the physical education teacher breached their duty to the student, which caused the immediate vision problem. The student sued the physical education teacher for negligence, which caused vision loss. However, if the student's vision returned to normal, then no actual damages occurred. Consequently, the courts most likely dismiss the negligence claim. Even though damages did not occur, the student may attempt to prove that a potential for harm to his eye or vision existed. Negligence claims of what could have occurred, or the potentiality of harm, would not hold up in court. Therefore, this negligence claim of what could have happened to the student's eye would be dismissed.

Foreseeability

Even though a special relationship exists between people, a duty or obligation from one person to another may not exist due to unforeseeable events. Foreseeability is the ability of a person to anticipate danger and resultant harm which could occur to others sharing in the special relationship. Even when a person conducts themself in a reasonable manner, an unforeseeable act can cause harm to another person (Cotton & Wolohan, 2020). When an act is not foreseeable, then the person who performed the act cannot be found negligent. Reflect upon the following scenario: A little league baseball team is playing a game during a partly cloudy day. As usual, throughout the day and immediately prior to the game, both teams' coaching staff and the umpires view the weather forecast. The local meteorologists did not predict rain or stormy weather for this day. The home team school district also utilizes a lightning detector for all outdoor events. The visiting team is in the field. Unexpectedly, lightning strikes an outfielder. The home team coach calls 911 immediately. Despite the coaches' efforts to provide CPR, the player is pronounced dead by EMS. In this scenario, the coaching staffs and the umpires were unable to foresee that lightning, coming from 30 miles away, would strike a player. The coaching staffs and the umpires have been particularly cognizant of the weather report throughout the course of the day and immediately prior to the game. No meteorologists predicted lightning storms on this day, and the working lightning detector did not reveal any threat. This unfortunate event was not foreseeable. Consequently, the coaching staffs and the umpires would not be found negligent. The courts ultimately determine foreseeability in any negligence case. In this particular scenario, it is evident that the coaches and umpires could not foresee the lightning strike, so it is unlikely that they would be found negligent.

Comparative Versus Contributory Negligence

When a defendant is found negligent, the court will determine if **comparative negligence** or **contributory negligence** exists. Although the defendant is deemed negligent, in some cases the plaintiff contributed to the damages that they incurred. Comparative negligence is when the court assigns some fault to both the defendant and the plaintiff. In comparative negligence cases, the court typically assigns blame to both the defendant and plaintiff as a percentage of total fault (Cornell Law School, n.d.). The court determines how much the plaintiff contributed to the negligence. Judgment, in the form of monetary compensation, is then awarded to the plaintiff. Because the plaintiff is to some extent at fault, the compensation will not meet the plaintiff's original demands. Instead, the compensation is a percentage of the demanded award, which is usually derived from the defendant's percentage of fault from the total demanded compensation.

Most states have adopted this principle of comparative negligence; however, in the past, most states utilized the principle of contributory negligence. As with comparative negligence, contributory negligence is found when a plaintiff is deemed to be responsible to some extent for the injury. The major difference between contributory and comparative negligence is how the compensation is awarded. Unlike comparative negligence, if contributory negligence is found, with the plaintiff contributing to the injury to any extent, then no compensation whatsoever is awarded to the plaintiff (Harrelson, Gardner, & Winterstein, 2017). Because the contributory negligence principle seems very unyielding, many states changed their statutes to utilize comparative negligence instead. Only four states, Alabama, Maryland, North Carolina, and Virginia, and the District of Columbia currently utilize contributory negligence principle in court (Cotton & Wolohan, 2020).

Consider the following scenario: A personal trainer works at We R Fit Gym. The personal trainer and client have been working together to increase the client's muscle mass and strength for approximately 1 year. The personal trainer repetitively explains and demonstrates to the client how to utilize the equipment properly and safely. The client understands how to utilize the equipment and does so as taught by the personal trainer. One day, the client comes into the gym for a training session with the personal trainer. The client is angry, and in an unsettled mood. The personal trainer recommends to the client not to train today due to the client's disposition. However, the client willingly and voluntarily participates in the day's training session. Despite some hesitancy, the personal trainer instructs the client to perform the daily training session activities, which are written on the client's chart. The client begins the training session, and the personal trainer assists another client. Without the personal trainer's direction, the client decides not to follow the charted activities. The client proceeds to increase the lumbar spine extension machine resistance. Immediately upon beginning the exercise, the client feels a tearing sensation in at their lower back and experiences excruciating pain. The client reports the event to the personal trainer. The personal trainer immediately calls for an ambulance to transport the client to the emergency room (ER), then cares for the injury. As per the ER physician's prescription, the client must lie in bed to rest their back for a minimum of 1 week . Consequently, the doctor's orders result in the client being unable to work during this time. Due to the nature of his employment, the client does not get paid when he is not working, nor does the client receive worker's compensation.

The client decides to sue the personal trainer for negligence. The client demands monetary compensation in the sum of $100,000 for pain and suffering and loss of wages. In this case, the court considers comparative negligence. The client voluntarily participated in the training session against the personal trainer's professional judgment. The personal trainer previously taught the client how to utilize the equipment properly and safely. The client had always utilized the equipment as instructed for previous training sessions. The personal trainer set up the daily activities as usual, which the client disregarded. Consequently, the client is injured due to lack of judgment and failure to follow the personal trainer's directions. The personal trainer may be found negligent to some extent. The personal trainer did not prevent the client from training on that day due to his angry and unsettled mood. Also, the defendant may be found negligent due to leaving the client temporarily to assist another client, which caused a temporary lack of supervision. However, the court will use the comparative negligence principle and find the client contributed to his injury. In this scenario, the court judges what percentages the defendant and plaintiff were at fault. The court awards a percentage of monetary compensation according to the percentage the defendant was at fault. If the court states that the defendant was 25% at fault and the plaintiff was 75% at fault, then the court would award $25,000 of the $100,000 original demands to the plaintiff.

Vicarious Liability

In the previous scenario the personal trainer's employer, We R Fit Gym, would also be liable for the client's injury, and consequently named in the lawsuit. We R Fit Gym is liable due to vicarious liability. Vicarious liability, also called *respondeat superior*, is when an employer or supervisor is responsible for the employees' negligent acts. This **doctrine** is imposed only if the employee was working in their employment capacity under the employer's direction. If the employee is not working under the employer's direction at the time the negligent injury occurred then the employer is not held liable by vicarious liability (Wong, 2010).

Consider this example: The personal trainer, who works for We R Fit Gym, decides to train a client at home. The personal trainer is training the client on their personal time. The personal trainer is an independent agent in this instance, and is not working for We R Fit Gym. If the client is injured as in the previous scenario, then We R Fit Gym is not held responsible for the personal trainer's negligence. Whenever an employer has a supervisory relationship with its employees, then vicarious liability exists (Pozgar, 2020). Other common organization/supervisor-employee/participant relationships include a school district and a physical education teacher, an athletic director and coaching staff, a strength and conditioning coach and clients, and rehabilitation specialists and patients (Wong, 2010).

Assumption of Risk

In many athletic activities, due to the inherent nature of the activity, the risk of injury is possible. **Assumption of risk** is when a person knowingly recognizes the inherent risk of injury by participating in activity, and then voluntarily participates in the activity. This inherent risk is evident in sports such as football, ice hockey, and rugby, and activities such as skydiving, downhill skiing, and swimming when no lifeguard is present (Decker, 2016). For other activities such as running, weightlifting, and golf, the risk of injury is not as inherently dangerous. Regardless, most patients understand that due to each activity's nature injury can result.

In order to participate in activities, participants voluntarily accept the risk of injury. Assumption of risk is categorized as either implied or expressed. Implied assumption of risk is when a person assumes the inherent danger associated with the activity that they are participating in. Express assumption of risk is when the participant recognizes the potential for harm and signs a waiver or other document relieving the organization from any liability for incurred injury (Pozgar, 2020). In most traditional athletic activities, implied assumption of risk is prevalent. However, the participant must be made entirely aware of all risks involved of the activity regardless of the potential for harm, even if the activity is assumed by most people to be dangerous (Harrelson, Gardner, & Winterstein, 2017). Depending on the events that occur, implied assumption of risk varies in regard to the court's judgment and award. The judgment varies depending on whether the danger is inherent in the activity and the plaintiff willingly participated, or if the defendant was negligent, the plaintiff had knowledge of this negligence, and the plaintiff participated in the athletic activity regardless. If the sports medicine professional, employer, organization, etc. fails to warn the participant of potential harm regardless of the type of activity, the courts may find these entities negligent if damages occur (Harrelson, Gardner, & Winterstein, 2017).

Consider the following scenario: A high school senior football player is preparing for their final season. The athlete and parents sign an assumption of risk waiver. The coaching staff clearly explains the potential for harm to the parents and athlete. The parents allow their child to participate on the football team, and the child voluntarily does so. During a game, the athlete is hit by an opposing player and suffers a season ending knee injury. The player's parents attempt to sue the coach and school district for damages, because the player will no longer be recruited by universities to play football as a scholarship athlete. The coach and university are not found negligent. The injury was a direct result of football, a collision sport, and its inherent dangers. The parents and athlete signed an assumption of risk document, and were clearly warned by the coaching staff about the potential dangers and injury that can occur to athletes from participating on the football team. Consequently, no compensation is awarded to the plaintiff.

Express assumption of risk occurs when a person knowingly and voluntarily participates in activities with inherent danger, but signs a **waiver** or release of liability prior to participation (**Box 1-1**). A waiver is a type of contract presented to a person by an organizing body. Once the participant signs the waiver, the organization (i.e. We R Fit Gym, Physical Therapy Clinics of America, the school district) is released from liability if the participant is injured. The organization's administrators must first consider various issues when developing and instituting waivers. The waivers must be written clearly without fine print to make the patient aware of the inherent risks of injury by participating in the activity. They must be written clearly in a manner and utilize language that the patient fully understands. Common language and not legal jargon must be utilized. The waiver must be written in the patient's first language (i.e. English, Spanish, etc.). The organization should have an attorney, who has legal knowledge regarding athletic participation waivers, review the document before distribution to participants.

When presenting the waiver to a participant, make sure they recognize and acknowledge the activity's inherent risks, and explain the risks to them. Be certain the participant understands injury may occur as a result of participation. They must voluntarily agree to participate in the activity and willingly sign the waiver. These steps must take place for the waiver to be upheld in court (Cotton & Wolohan, 2020; Pozgar, 2020). However, as in all legal cases, the court has the ultimate decision whether or not to uphold the waiver. The court considers if the participant understood the waiver and its contents clearly enough before voluntarily participating. If the patient did not clearly understand the document that they were signing, then the waiver is not enforced, and the organization is held liable for the participant's injury. The court also determines if the participant was coerced or forced to sign the waiver by an employee of the organization. If this is the case, then the waiver is not

Box 1-1 An example of a basic waiver

I,____________________(name), attest that I am voluntarily participating in the activities that We R Fit Gym provides. I entirely understand that there is an inherent risk of injury, including the possibility of disabling injuries and even death, while participating in these activities, and I knowingly and willingly assume this risk. I also attest that I have voluntarily signed this waiver, and was not coerced to do so.

Participant's Signature	Date
Witness's Signature	Date

enforceable. Even if the participant clearly understands the waiver's terms, willingly signs it, and voluntarily participates in the activity, but an employee or participant inflicts careless or deliberate harm to the patient, then the waiver is not enforced, and the organization is held liable for the patient's injury.

Consider a scenario at Physical Therapy Clinics of America. It is winter in the northeast United States. A patient is being rehabilitated by an athletic trainer. On the first day of rehabilitation and prior to beginning any activities, the patient signs a waiver. This waiver releases the clinic from any liability if the patient is injured while participating in rehabilitation activities at the clinic. One snowy day, the patient enters the clinic and begins the rehabilitation session. At the end of the session, the patient exits the clinic through a commonly used exit door. Unknown to the patient, the exit has accumulated a great amount of ice located immediately outside of the door on the sidewalk, which is on the clinic's property. The patient exits the gym, slips on the ice, falls hard on the ground. The patient is rushed to the hospital via ambulance, and is later diagnosed with a broken fibula. Consequently, the injury prevents the patient from being able to work, and is not compensated by their employer while not working. Also due to the nature of the injury, complications, and multiple surgeries, the patient incurs major medical bills that are not entirely covered by the client's medical insurance. The patient sues Physical Therapy Clinics of America for negligence. In the suit, the patient claims the assumption of risk waiver should not be upheld because the waiver was only related to injury during the rehabilitation sessions. The patient demands monetary compensation for salary lost, medical bills, and pain and suffering. In this case, Physical Therapy Clinics of America's waiver that the client voluntarily signed most likely will not be upheld in court. Physical Therapy Clinics of America had the responsibility to keep the gym and the grounds safe for its patrons. Ice had accumulated at the doorway on the clinic's property where the patients exit. The staff was careless and did not remove the ice during the course of the day. Due to the clinic's duty and lack of action to secure the safety and welfare of its patients, Physical Therapy Clinics of America is negligent. Consequently, in this scenario the waiver that the patient signed that releases Physical Therapy Clinics of America's from any liability is upheld and judgment is in the patient's favor.

In most assumption of risk cases when adults have signed waivers, and the requirements necessary to uphold the waiver are in place, the court upholds the waiver. Again, the court determines whether to uphold the waiver on a case-by-case basis. However, it becomes increasingly difficult for the courts to uphold waivers when parents sign waivers on behalf of their minor children. This difficulty occurs because some minor children do not or cannot truly understand the inherent risks of certain activities. Also, the courts have to discern whether or not it is reasonable for the parents to sign a waiver on behalf of their minor children. Parents who sign on behalf of their minor children essentially relinquish their children's rights (Wong, 2010). Ultimately, waivers may or may not be upheld in court. Regardless, organizations that utilize waivers have instituted one means to defend the organizations and their employees against litigation.

Good Samaritan Laws

All 50 states and the District of Columbia have some type of **Good Samaritan Laws.** Good Samaritan Laws are statutes that protect someone from legal liability when they are assisting an injured or ill person. The person being helped is typically a stranger, and requires some sort of first aid care. Often these laws are considered first aid immunity. The Good Samaritan Laws are different among the states, but in general they provide some protection for people providing necessary first aid care to others in emergency and life-threatening situations. In most cases, a caregiver is protected if they provide first aid in an emergency situation, at the immediate emergency location, with good intentions, in a prudent manner, and without any monetary or other compensation (Cotton & Wolohan, 2020).

Even though Good Samaritan Laws exist, in certain situations the person providing first aid (the first aider) is required to obtain consent from the injured person before performing first aid skills. If the victim is a conscious adult, the first aider obtains consent to assist the victim. If the victim is a child and the parent or guardian is present, the first aider must obtain consent from the guardian in order to assist the child. In an emergency situation, if the victim is a minor without a parent or guardian present, or is an unconscious adult, then consent is implied, and the first aider can begin assisting the victim immediately (AAOS, 2022).

How the Good Samaritan Laws are written and the laws' content in each state's statutes determine what first aid actions are considered covered under the laws. A scenario where Good Samaritan Laws often apply, again depending on the state, is as follows: You are a spectator at a junior high soccer game. Parents, family members, and spectators fill the bleachers. During the game, a parent in the stands near you screams. Her husband is apparently unconscious on the bleachers. You go to the woman to see what is wrong. The woman says that her husband was clutching his chest, and then suddenly passed out. You tell a bystander to call for an ambulance immediately. You have had CPR training in the past. You find that he is not breathing and begin CPR immediately. You do not remember the accurate number of breaths and compressions, but you assist the man anyway. Unfortunately, the man does not survive. The woman attempts to sue you in court for your actions, under the pretense that you were not currently certified in CPR and did not remember the exact proper CPR skill set when you provided care for her husband. In this instance in most states Good Samaritan Laws prevail and you are not held responsible for the gentleman's death. Likewise, the court rules that you are not responsible for any compensation to his wife.

Although it is rare for first aiders to be sued in court, the Good Samaritan Laws do not apply in all cases. In some states, the first aider is protected when they participate in ordinary acts of omission; however, in many states, the first aider cannot act in a willful, reckless manner that causes additional injury (AAOS, 2022). Consider the scenario above, but in this case a parent in the stands screams because her toddler son is having trouble breathing. You go to the woman and see that her son is wheezing. The mother tells you that he has not previously been diagnosed with asthma. You also have asthma, and decide to give two puffs of your rescue inhaler to the toddler. The toddler reacts adversely to the medication and his situation becomes worse. He stops breathing and goes unconscious. You call for an ambulance. The ambulance arrives minutes later. The EMTs perform CPR and revive the boy. Unfortunately, he has minor brain damage. In this case, the courts find that the Good Samaritan Laws do not prevail for you since your first aid conduct for the toddler boy was reckless and caused further harm.

If you choose to provide first aid to an injured person, you have the duty to stay with that person until EMTs or another equally or more qualified person assists the victim (AAOS, 2022). However, one issue to consider when deciding to provide first aid care for bystanders is that most states do not have laws which mandate a person has a duty to provide first aid assistance to an injured or ill person in the first place (Pfeiffer & Mangus, 2015; Cotton & Wolohan, 2020). Although no duty may exist, your personal ethics and morals come into play when you witness an emergency situation when a person is seriously injured or ill.

It is extremely important to know the Good Samaritan Laws in your state. Good Samaritan Laws provide you, as a first aider, some protection against lawsuits in emergency situations, so hopefully you and other bystanders are willing to assist the injured and ill victims in these unfortunate situations.

Statute of Limitations

When an injured person decides to file a negligence claim against another person, they do not have an unlimited amount of time to file a lawsuit. The **statute of limitations** is a finite number of years that a person has to file a negligence claim. The statute of limitations is determined by and varies from state to state. In most states, the statute of limitations is from 1 to 6 years. An exception to this rule is when the damages occurred to a minor. In this case, the statute of limitations begins when the child turns 18 years old (Cotton & Wolohan, 2020). Also, in some states the statute of limitations begins when the person has been given notice or has knowledge that the negligent act created the injury or illness. The statute of limitations also begins when a person should have become aware of the injury (Pozgar, 2020). Often, even with each state's designated statute of limitations, the courts have difficulty determining when the statutory period began. The court must determine if the plaintiff knew or should have known that the negligent act caused the injury, and the date when this knowledge occurred. Consider the previous case in which you provided first aid assistance to the toddler boy at the soccer game. Instead of being immediately permanently injured, consider that the toddler boy has no apparent injury or illness after the incident. Years later, when the boy is a 20-year-old adult and attends college, he begins to have migraines, memory loss, a cognitive deficit, and vision problems. His mother tells him what occurred at the soccer game many years before. He decides to file a lawsuit against you for damages that occurred when he was a toddler. The plaintiff sues and demands monetary compensation for medical bills and pain and suffering.

The courts consider a variety of factors in this case. First, as previously determined, the court determines that the Good Samaritan Laws do not prevail in this case. Also, the court considers the state's statute of limitations in regard to the plaintiff's age. The injury occurred when the plaintiff was a minor. In most states the statutory time period begins when the child turns 18 years old. If the statute of limitations is greater than 2 years, then the man can file a lawsuit. If the statute of limitations is less than 2 years, then the man cannot file the lawsuit. The court recognizes that this incident was a probable cause of the injury and illnesses he incurred. However, in this case the court determines that the man should have known of the incident because his parents should have informed him.

Depending on the situation, the statute of limitations can complicate an injured person's ability to sue another person in court. Although each state has its own rules governing statute of limitations for negligence cases, all states do have one aspect in common: If a person attempts to file a lawsuit after the statute of limitations, then the lawsuit will not hold up in court.

Defenses Against Negligence

You can take action to defend yourself against negligence claims. What you do to protect yourself can mean the difference between being found negligent in court and liable for damages, or not. Because you instruct and supervise people on a continual, daily basis, you are responsible for their lives. You have the duty to protect your patients from harm; however, you have to protect yourself in case your patient chooses to sue you for negligence. To best prepare yourself for legal action, take steps shown in **Table 1-1** to make sure you have the best protection against these tortuous claims.

Table 1-1 A checklist for defending yourself against negligence lawsuits

You should complete the following actions as part of your "to do" checklist in order to actively prepare yourself for a defense against a negligence claim:

- Utilize waivers, releases of liability, and assumpton of risk agreements with your patients.
- Utilize contracts that specify the terms of use for the patients at your facility.
- Have all patients complete a medical history questionnaire prior to participation.
- Have every patient complete a preparticipation examination (PPE), performed by a physician (MD or DO).
- Mandate that all patients who have preexisting or questionable injuries and/or illnesses must be cleared for participation by a physician (MD or DO).
- Create, maintain, and practice emergency action plans (EAPs) at your facility.
- Warn the patients of the inherent dangers of the activities.
- Provide proper training and instruction to the patients within your qualifications.
- Supervise the patients appropriately.
- Provide proper, well-fitted, and safe equipment for the patients' use.
- Hire qualified employees to work with the patients.
- Obtain quality professional certifications.
- Participate in continuing education activities.
- Purchase liability and malpractice insurance for yourself and your employees.

> **TIPS FROM THE FIELD**
>
> **Tip 1** All important documents such as the patient's assumption of risk and PPE and medical history questionnaire paperwork must be minimally duplicated and stored in different locations. One copy of the documents should be electronic, in confidential, password protected files on a computer hard drive, in a cloud, and/or a flash drive. The other copy is typically a paper hard copy that is filed by the patient's name in a locked filing cabinet. Some sports medicine professionals choose to have paper copies that are be scanned into the computer, tablet, and/or smartphone and saved as electronic files. Computer software programs also exist to record your patient's information. Access to these confidential documents should be limited to the personnel who would need the information within these documents.

As previously discussed, important defenses from negligence are waivers, release of liability, or assumption of risk agreements. Utilize these documents whenever you are responsible for a person's safety and well-being, and regardless if you are employed by an organization or self-employed. Clear, concise, detailed documentation can assist you in avoiding litigation (Miller-Isaac & Noble, 2015). Similar to these documents are contracts which can also include assumption of risk elements. If you are the owner of We R Fit Gym, you can have each client sign a contract which depicts not only information such as the gym's terms of use and fees required from the client, but also includes assumption of risk elements.

Other documents utilized to avoid negligence claims include preparticipation exams (PPEs), medical questionnaires, emergency medical treatment consent forms, daily treatments and injury reports documentation, emergency action plans, and clear and current policies and procedures (Harrelson, Gardner, & Winterstein, 2017). A PPE along with a medical questionnaire assists you to identify the patient's predisposing medical conditions, both physical and psychological, which could cause injury or illness during participation at your facility. The PPE should be performed, and the medical questionnaire verified by a licensed physician. The physician signs and dates the forms and states whether or not the patient is allowed to fully participate in your organization's activities.

These documents, as well as others utilized for the organization, can be hard copy and/or electronic. The hard copy documents must be in a secured location (i.e. locked file cabinet), and the electronic documents must be backed up and password protected to assure confidentiality. Confidentiality is important in regard to all patients' files. Your patients' personal health information is protected by the Health Insurance Portability and Accountability Act of 1996 (HIPAA). This act prevents patient health information sharing between various entities without the patient's permission. This information includes all medical information. You are not allowed to share your

> **TIPS FROM THE FIELD**
>
> **Tip 2** If the patient has any questionable or previous injuries, illnesses, or conditions, as identified to you by the patient's medical history questionnaire, do not let the patient participate in any activity at your facility. Require the patient to have a PPE and obtain a physician's (MD or DO) clearance for the patient to participate in the activity prior to participation. The physician writes the clearance, or lack thereof, on prescription paper or letterhead. This paperwork is kept in the patient's files.

patient's information with anyone unless the patient signs a waiver giving you permission to disclose your patient's personal health information to specific people. Likewise, you do not have access to your patient's health information from their physician or other health care providers. If the patient needs or wants you to have their health information, they must sign a waiver at their physician or health care provider's offices allowing you to obtain their health information.

TIPS FROM THE FIELD

TIP 3 When you are rehabilitating or training a minor athlete (under the age of 18), regularly communicate with the athlete's parents or guardians regarding the child's progress, changes in their program or activity, and any concerns regarding their child. When you communicate with the parents regarding their child, give them the opportunity to respond to your comments, questions, and concerns. Allow them to ask questions. By communicating with the parents regarding their child, you give them proper notification, warning, and knowledge of the activity and situation at hand.

Review your client's participation forms with them annually at minimum. This regular review is important to determine if the client's medical status has changed. By having your client (or client's parents or guardians if the client is a minor) complete and review these forms, and client's physician verification and medical clearance, you have taken additional steps to protect yourself against a negligence claim.

Another defense against negligence is to always have emergency action plans (EAPs) at your facility. EAPs are written documents which prepare you, the staff, and your patients for various emergencies. By having EAPs, you show your organization's preparedness for your clients' safety and welfare at your facility if an emergency occurs. EAPs specify the course of action by the facility's staff in case of emergencies such as when a person is injured or comes down with illness, a fire breaks out, or an environmental emergency occurs. EAP components include the location of emergency phones and emergency numbers. Staff members have particular roles such as who is responsible for calling 911, who remains with the injured person, and who meets the ambulance upon arrival. The EAP addresses facility access, including how emergency personnel enter and exit, as well as emergency exit routes for each facility area. The EAP delineates who has access to all rooms, fields, gates, and the like while the facility is in use. The location of emergency and first aid supplies and client emergency and health information are noted in the EAP. The personnel involved in instituting the EAPs must understand each EAP's purpose and their role in the EAP. Likewise, the employees must practice each EAP in a simulated manner on a regular, continual basis, annually at

TIPS FROM THE FIELD

TIP 4 If an injury does occur to your client at your facility, make sure you document the incident immediately. Write in detail the day, time, pertinent client information, events that occurred, and care given. Write legibly and clearly in ink, or use a password protected electronic document to document the injury. Do not use white-out or other erasable devices. Sign and date the injury report and keep it somewhere secure. If you are summoned to court by the injured client you can utilize this documentation to recall events and perhaps present it in court.

minimum, and when new employees are hired. This practice will ascertain that the emergency plans run efficiently and appropriately in a real emergency (Harrelson, Gardner, & Winterstein, 2017).

Other than utilizing various forms of documentation, you must perform certain actions to prevent yourself from being sued. If you are a coach, physical education teacher, athletic trainer, sports medicine professional, or someone who works with, instructs, and supervises patients, you have a duty to do the following:

- Warn the patients of the activity's inherent dangers
- Provide proper training and instruction
- Supervise the patients appropriately
- Provide proper equipment for their use
- Hire qualified employees
- Purchase liability and malpractice insurance

As noted previously, informing the patient of the activity's inherent risks includes not only having the patient read and voluntarily sign waivers, but also thoroughly explaining the risks involved and answering any questions that the patient has in regard to the risks. If you are in charge of hiring qualified personnel, consider your state laws and policies of the organization and governing bodies. Depending on your organization, facility, or institution, you may want to consider or be required to hire appropriate sports medicine healthcare personnel. Laws in each state vary, as do the policies within organizations' governing bodies, in regard to the availability of healthcare personnel on site. To protect your organization from negligence lawsuits, you can hire physicians, athletic trainers, physical therapists, psychologists, EMTs, or other sports medicine healthcare personnel to assist in caring for your clients, athletes, and patients. Always make sure your participants are safe and well cared for. At the same time, you will protect yourself from litigation by hiring appropriate personnel.

Once the participant understands the activity's inherent risks and voluntarily signs the waiver, you need to provide them with proper training and instruction. If a client is attempting a new activity, show him how to properly and safely perform the activity. If a client at We R Fit Gym is going to utilize the leg press machine for the first time, demonstrate and clearly explain the purpose of the exercise, how to utilize the machine properly and safely, and what to do if the client has difficulty or pain when completing the exercise. After you have instructed your client to use the equipment properly, continually supervise them to make sure that they are utilizing the proper techniques and performing the activity safely as you instructed.

When the client is working with equipment, or has equipment to wear, it is your responsibility to make sure the equipment is safe, in good working order, properly fitted, and frequently checked and reconditioned according to safety standards. Utilize all equipment as intended by the manufacturer. Any unapproved alterations and/or equipment modifications renders the product unsafe to use by manufacturers' standards. If the client uses this altered product and is injured as a result, the manufacturer is released of liability. The individual who altered the equipment could be held liable for damages.

If you are the employer or the person in charge of hiring staff, hire competent, certified, knowledgeable employees. Thoroughly interview each prospective employee, review the applicants' qualifications, and acquire character references and employment recommendations. If you perform all of these actions, you demonstrate your desire to ensure the health, safety, and welfare of your clients. These actions are extremely important if a client claims that you are negligent.

Various actions that you take to protect yourself from a negligence claim can enhance your personal and professional development as a sports medicine professional. Obtain professional certifications in your field. By obtaining high level, national, professional certifications, you demonstrate that you are knowledgeable and skilled in your field. Some organizations claim to offer respected certification programs. However, in reality the certifications are not highly regarded and are very simple for a candidate to obtain. Investigate and seek out the reputable organizations in your field of work and obtain the corresponding certifications. One well-respected organization is the National Strength and Conditioning Association (NSCA) (www.nsca.com). The NSCA offers a Certified Strength and Conditioning Specialist® (CSCS®) certification. This certification is nationally recognized and challenging to obtain. Candidates must have at minimum a bachelor's degree and pass a rigorous certification exam. The NSCA also offers a NSCA-Certified Personal Trainer® (NSCA-CPT®) certification. Because the NSCA is a highly respected organization in the personal training and fitness field, the certifications that a personal trainer or certified strength and conditioning specialist hold from the NSCA show that the professional has met the stringent education, knowledge, and testing requirements. (Please note that this organization is only one example of highly regarded national organizations that provide additional certifications and credentialing for sports medicine professionals.) If a personal trainer holds additional respectable certifications and credentials, a client can be reasonably assured that he is under the supervision of a highly knowledgeable professional.

Finally, by participating in continuing education activities, you further protect yourself from being found negligent. In professional fields, such as sport medicine, information and practices are continually changing based upon new research activities and conclusions. Professionals must be up to date with the latest information, technology, and best practices. In your field, since you are working with, supervising, teaching, and providing care for people who depend on your expertise, it is imperative to continue your education for as long as you are employed and practicing in your chosen field. If you are well versed, knowledgeable, and utilize current, evidence-based best practices with your patients, you have another defense against a negligence claim. Some professional organizations demand that credential holders complete continuing education and report these activities to the professional organization. For example, once you have earned you athletic training certification credential (ATC) through the Board of Certification, you are required to participate in continuing education activities based on the BOC's continuing education policies (see https://bocatc.org/athletic-trainers/maintain-certification/continuing-education/continuing-education for the BOC's continuing education requirements). This organization's continuing education policy ensures that its credentialed professionals stay abreast of new, evolving information and best practices in athletic training. The continuing education requirements for other professions depend on the profession's and/or professional's affiliation with a national, regional, or state organization as well as individual state rules and regulations. Some of the continuing education activities required include attendance at seminars, workshops, laboratories, and webinars. Continuing education participation can assist you if you are brought to court for a negligence claim. You would demonstrate to the court that you are up to date with the most current information and best practices in your field. You would also explain how you used this knowledge and best practices with your patient. With this continuing education and its application, you have an additional defense in court against the negligence claim.

Even if you take all of the aforementioned actions to prevent and defend yourself against the potential for negligence litigation, you may still be named as a defendant in a negligence claim. What will happen if you are brought to court for a negligence claim? Fortunately, professional liability and malpractice insurance exists that can assist you in a negligence lawsuit. If you are employed by an organization, often your employer provides this insurance at no cost to you. If your employer provides this insurance, obtain a copy of the insurance policy, and investigate the coverage terms. While working under the direction of the employer, this liability and malpractice insurance should minimally provide you legal defense and fees. The insurance policies only provide you with certain monetary limits per lawsuit per year. However, your employer's insurance may not provide you adequate coverage while on the job, and in most instances does not provide you any coverage when working outside your duties for your employer.

Consider another scenario with Physical Therapy Clinics of America. The clinic provides liability and malpractice insurance for all employees. Each physical therapist has $1,000,000 insurance coverage per claim (i.e. lawsuit) per year with a maximum of $3,000,000 total per year. The physical therapist decides to rehabilitate their patient in their home and not as part of Physical Therapy Clinics of America. The patient sustains a significant muscle tear while performing rehabilitation techniques that the physical therapist instructed. Now, the patient is unable to work for weeks due to the injury. The patient files a negligence claim against the physical therapist. The physical therapist does not have any professional liability and malpractice insurance other than the insurance provided by their employer, Physical Therapy Clinics of America. Because the physical therapist was providing care to their patient under their personal business and not as an employee of Physical Therapy Clinics of America, the Physical Therapy Clinics of America liability and malpractice insurance is not applicable to cover the physical therapist for this negligence claim. The physical therapist will have to pay all legal defense fees, among other expenses, which most likely prove to be extremely costly.

As a sports medicine professional, it is wise to purchase personal liability and malpractice insurance for as long as you work with patients. Even if your employer provides this insurance for you, it is always prudent to purchase your own personal liability and malpractice insurance as a supplement to your employer's insurance (Miller-Isaac & Noble, 2015). By having this professional liability and malpractice insurance, you can rest easy knowing that if you find yourself as a defendant in a negligence claim that you have adequate protection and representation.

Summary

As a sports medicine professional, you must be aware and knowledgeable about legal issues that can affect you. You work with and are responsible for people's lives. Consequently, you have a standard to uphold not only in your patients' eyes, but also in the eyes of the courts. If you actively recognize these legal issues, and act as a prudent, responsible professional when working with your patients, you will be on the right track to avoid the courtroom.

Keywords

Negligence When a person did not act as a reasonable, prudent person would, and damages occur to another person or their property.

Tort A civil wrong that occurs to a person's body or property and is not a criminal act.

Duty When a person is liable and responsible for the patient's well-being, due to the special relationship with the patient at the time of injury.

Comparative negligence When the court assigns some fault to both the defendant and the plaintiff.

Contributory negligence Prevents a plaintiff from collecting any damages after an accident if they were careless and partially to blame.

Doctrine A rule or principle of law.

Assumption of risk When a person knowingly recognizes the inherent risk of injury, and voluntarily participates in the activity.

Waiver A type of contract that releases an organization from liability.

Good Samaritan Laws Statutes that protect people from legal liability when assisting injured or ill people in an emergency situation.

Statute of limitations A finite number of years that a person has to file a negligence claim in court. The statute of limitations is determined by and varies from state to state.

Discussion Questions

1. In regard to the four components of negligence, which component(s) do you feel would be the most difficult for a plaintiff to prove in a negligence claim? Why do you feel this way?
2. Describe an example of a foreseeable event in the sports medicine field that could cause harm or damages to another person?
3. Would vicarious liability exist at your place of employment or at your school with a negligence claim? Why or why not?
4. If you came across an injured person who desperately needed first aid, what could you do to protect yourself from being named in a negligence lawsuit?
5. What specific actions can you take during your daily activities and employment to protect yourself from being a defendant in a negligence claim?

CASE STUDY: ONE SEEMINGLY HARMLESS DECISION CREATES SIGNIFICANT LEGAL RAMIFICATIONS

Mike is a new performance enhancement trainer at the Garden State Performance Training Center. He is meeting today with Meredith, who is a new client. Meredith is a 6- foot-tall, 130-pound, 18-year-old, female, collegiate volleyball player who is very athletic and fit. She wants to continue increasing her speed and power especially when she jumps to spike a ball. Mike plans to help her attain her goals. Today she meets Mike at the center to complete the necessary paperwork, including a medical history, insurance, and assumption of risk forms. Mike aspires to begin her first training session after the paperwork has been completed. As per the Garden State Performance Training Center policies, if a new client does not have medical conditions that would prevent her from participating on the same day that she completes the medical questionnaire, then she can begin her first training session immediately. Meredith indicates on her medical questionnaire that she has "heart problems". When Mike questions what the "heart problems" entail, Meredith says "I think my doctor said I have something minor like a heart murmur, but I am not sure." Mike knows that patients with heart murmurs have participated in his strenuous training activities before without any problems. He tells Meredith that he needs a clearance note from her doctor before she participates. Meredith says she just saw her doctor last week when she returned from college, and her doctor said she can participate in all athletic activities. Meredith is anxious to begin her training session today, and knowing that she may not be able to do so is getting her visibly upset. After briefly thinking about the situation, Mike decides to allow Meredith to participate in one session before attaining the medical clearance. After all, Meredith said that last week her doctor allowed her to participate in all athletic activities.

Mike begins the one-hour training session with Meredith. She is performing high intensity vertical jumping and sprinting activities. She seems to be doing very well with the activities, but is breathing very fast and shallow. With approximately 10 minutes remaining in the session, Meredith begins to complain of chest pain and dizziness. Mike immediately stops her session, and asks her what is wrong. Meredith says that she "feels lightheaded and out of breath." She continues to say that her "heart is pounding hard and hurts." Mike notices Meredith's face is pale, and she is unsteady when standing. Mike helps her sit comfortably in a chair, and leaves her briefly to go to the sign-in desk to call 911. When

Mike returns to Meredith she is unconscious and not breathing. Mike begins CPR without any protective barriers. Within a few minutes, the EMTs arrive and take over. They apply an automated external defibrillator (AED) and are able to restart her heart, but Meredith is still unconscious. Mike's supervisor, Pamela, arrives at the scene and asks Mike what happened. The EMTs take Meredith to the hospital via ambulance. Now that the scene is cleared, Pamela orders Mike to come to her office to discuss what happened.

1. How should Mike have handled this situation differently from the beginning, so as to avoid any potential litigation?
2. What legal issues does Mike have to consider in this scenario?
3. Will Mike be liable for any damages resulting from this event?
4. Will the Garden State Performance Training Center be liable for any damages?

References

American Academy of Orthopaedic Surgeons [AAOS]. (2022). *First aid, CPR, and AED advanced* (8th ed.). Emergency Care and Safety Institute.

Cornell Law School Legal Information Institute. (n.d.), *Comparative negligence.* https://www.law.cornell.edu/wex/comparative_negligence

Cornell Law School Legal Information Institute. (2020, June). *Nonfeasance.* https://www.law.cornell.edu/wex/nonfeasance#:~:text=The%20omission%20to%20perform%20a,of%20contract%20and%20tort%20law.

Cotton, D. J., & Wolohan, J. T. (2020). *Law for recreation and sport managers* (8th ed.). Kendall Hunt Publishing.

Decker, K. (2016). The Chase Utley question: A controversial collision between tort law and professional sports. *St. John's Law Review, 90*(3), 745-771.

Gayles, J. G., & Blanchard, J. (2018). Playing outside the lines: Contemporary legal issues in college sports. *New Directions for Student Services, 2018*(163), 23-32. https://doi.org/10.1002/ss.20267

Harrelson, G. L., Gardner, G., & Winterstein, A. P. (2017) *Administrative topics in athletic training* (2nd ed.). SLACK, Inc.

Miller-Isaac, K., & Noble, M. (2015). *Athletic training clinical workbook: A guide to competencies.* FA Davis Company.

Pachman S., & Lamba A. (2017). Legal aspects of concussion: The ever-evolving standard of care. *Journal of Athletic Training, 52*(3), 186-194. https://doi.org/10.4085/1062-6050-52.1.03

Pfeiffer, R. P., Mangus, B. C., & Trowbridge, C. (2015). *Concepts of athletic training* (7th ed.). Jones and Bartlett Publishers.

Pozgar, G. D. (2020). *Legal and ethical issues for health professionals* (5th ed.). Jones and Bartlett Publishers.

Prentice, W. E. (2020). *Essentials of athletic injury management* (11th ed.). McGraw-Hill. Spengler, J. O., Anderson, P., Connaughton, D., & Baker, T. (2016). *Introduction to sports law* (2nd ed.). Human Kinetics.

Wong, G. M. (2010). Essentials of sports law (4th ed.). Santa Barbara, CA: Praeger/ABC-CLIO.

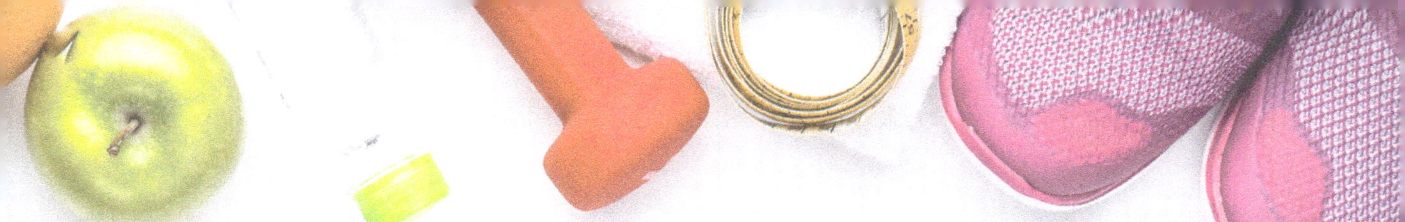

Chapter 2

Wellness, Physical Activity, Exercise, and Fitness

Chapter Objectives

After you have read this chapter, you will be able to understand:

- The definitions and benefits of wellness, physical activity, exercise, and fitness.
- How to prepare your clients, athletes, and patients to incorporate cardiorespiratory and strength training exercise activity into their daily schedule.
- The importance of conditioning principles in exercise programs.
- The FITT principle and how it is incorporated into cardiorespiratory, flexibility, muscular strength, and muscular endurance exercise activities.
- The differences between, and advantages and disadvantages of isotonic and isokinetic exercise.
- Various methods utilized to assist your clients, athletes, and patients in maintaining positive mental health.

Injuries and illnesses cannot always be prevented; however, we can take appropriate action with our athletes to avoid them. Many factors play a significant role in injury and illness prevention, but one of the most important factors is regular participation in wellness, exercise, and fitness activities. As a sports medicine professional, your role is to educate and instruct your athletes how to participate in lifelong, beneficial wellness, exercise, and fitness activities. Since you are their instructor and mentor, you must be a good role model and participate in these activities as well. This chapter focuses on how you and your athletes can properly incorporate wellness, exercise, and fitness into an everyday regimen, in order to promote and maintain a healthy lifestyle.

Wellness, Physical Activity, Exercise, and Fitness

As sports medicine professionals, we continually instill knowledge in our athletes, clients, and patients. We explain and demonstrate the importance of both physical and mental wellness. Wellness is the body's reaction to lifestyle choices. The National Wellness Institute (NWI) defines wellness as "an active process through which people become aware of, and make choices toward, a more successful existence" (National Wellness Institute, 2021). In 1976, Dr. Bill Hettler, the founder of the NWI, created *The Six Dimensions of Wellness Mode*l (see https://nationalwellness.org/resources/six-dimensions-of-wellness/). These dimensions include occupational, physical, social, intellectual, spiritual, and emotional dimensions, which are all connected. When an athlete participates in positive activities within these six dimensions, they will promote a healthy lifestyle.

Participation in physical activity is very important to promote an individual's health. According to the U.S. Department of Health and Human Services National Heart, Lung, and Blood Institute "physical activity is any body movement that works your muscles and requires more energy than resting. Walking, running, dancing, swimming, yoga, and gardening are a few examples of physical activity" (see https://www.nhlbi.nih.gov/health/heart/physical-activity). Along with your muscles, your heart works above resting level during physical activity. The World Health Organization (WHO) states that both moderate and vigorous physical activities have numerous positive effects on a person's health, including improving overall physical and mental well-being (see https://www.who.int/news-room/fact-sheets/detail/physical-activity for additional benefits of physical activity.) The United States Department of Health and Human Services Office of Disease Prevention and Health Promotion has devised *Physical Activity Guidelines for Americans*, which "provides evidence-based guidance to help Americans maintain or improve their health through physical activity" (see https://health.gov/our-work/nutrition-physical-activity/physical-activity-guidelines/current-guidelines). Physical activity is not a regularly scheduled, planned, structured activity. Rather, a person participates in physical activity on a casual basis. Everyone should partake in some form of daily physical activity to enhance their health and promote a good quality of life.

Exercise is a subcategory of physical activity (Dasso, 2019). Like physical activity, exercise raises a person's heart rate, decreases their risk of illness, and promotes and improves their health. However, the term "exercise" should not be utilized interchangeably with the term "physical activity" because exercise entails planned activities in which a person participates on a regular, scheduled basis (Dasso, 2019). Exercise incorporates **aerobic**, endurance, strength, resistance, balance, and flexibility activities (U.S. National Library of Medicine MedlinePlus, 2021). Lifting weights in a gym, running on a treadmill, participating in aerobics and yoga classes, and spinning® are examples of exercise. Daily exercise is imperative to promote an individual's health and wellness.

Depending on an individual's level of activity, they may not be as fit as they should be. Fitness is the body's response to daily exercise. If a person is fit, they will be physically strong and healthy and have enough energy to participate in a multitude of activities with ease and without excessive fatigue. The term "fitness program" is often used to describe the type of exercise program that a person undertakes in order to improve their health. Fitness programs include exercises specifically focused on various components of fitness, which will ultimately promote a healthy lifestyle.

Various components of fitness exist. The components are divided into two categories, which are health-related fitness and skill-related fitness **(Table 2-1)**. Health-related fitness includes muscular strength, muscular endurance, flexibility, cardiorespiratory endurance (also sometimes referred to as cardiovascular endurance), and **body composition** (Hoeger et al., 2022). Each of these health-related fitness components is important in promoting overall physical health. Muscular strength is the muscles' ability to produce force. Muscular endurance is the muscles' ability to produce force over a period of time without undue fatigue. Flexibility is the muscles' ability to lengthen and stretch in order to allow the joints to move through a full range of motion (ROM). Cardiorespiratory endurance is the ability for the heart and lungs to work hard enough for the athlete to meet exercise training demands. Although these health-related fitness components are seemingly different, the components are closely related. Exercises incorporated into common fitness programs should touch on each health-related component of fitness to foster overall health and fitness.

Unlike health-related components of fitness that focus on general physical health, the skill-related components of fitness focus on specific skills during sport activities. These skill-related components of fitness include agility, balance, coordination, power, reaction time, and speed (Hoeger et al., 2022). Agility is a person's ability to change direction very quickly with coordinated body motion. Balance is the ability to hold the body in a stable position. Coordination is when all body parts function together and create smooth motion. Power is the muscles' ability to produce a large amount of force in a short amount of time. Reaction time is how quickly the body responds and the motions that result. Speed is how fast motion occurs

Table 2-1 Health- and Skill-Related Components of Fitness

Health-Related Components of Fitness	Skill-Related Components of Fitness
• Muscular strength	• Agility
• Muscular endurance	• Balance
• Flexibility	• Coordination
• Cardiorespiratory (cardiovascular) endurance	• Power
• Body Composition	• Reaction time
	• Speed

over a distance. Skill-related fitness is crucial for a competitive athlete because they must have enhanced motor skill function for competition. However, anyone who wants to increase or maintain their health, and does not desire or need to enhance athletic skill, should concentrate on the health-related fitness components.

According to the U.S. National Library of Medicine (2021, March 8), if a person participates in 150 minutes moderate-intensity or 75 minutes of vigorous- intensity aerobic exercise each week their fitness level and overall health will improve. However, daily physical activity and exercise are not the only factors that promote fitness. Wellness, accomplished by making healthy lifestyle choices, is highly linked to promote a good quality of life. A person may be physically fit, but if they make detrimental lifestyle choices **(Table 2-2)** these choices ultimately result in poor wellness. People may believe that if they have bad habits or make poor lifestyle choices, they can negate these detrimental effects by taking part in positive lifestyle choices. For example, a person may believe that even though they smoke, with daily exercise they can negate the detrimental effects of smoking and will be well, fit, and lead a healthy life. Unfortunately this is not the case. As sports medicine professionals we must educate our clients about the effects of detrimental lifestyle choices. Ultimately, an individual should adopt positive lifestyle choices and participate in exercise activity. Hopefully by choosing to partake in activities which promote physical and mental wellness, perform daily exercise, and maintain a satisfactory level of fitness, they can live a healthy, long, good quality of life.

Life Expectancy

In today's society, people do not often consider how their current lifestyle will affect their quality and length of life. People tend to live for the moment, and take on destructive habits and lifestyle choices which are detrimental to their health. Some destructive habits include

Table 2-2 Detrimental Lifestyle Choices

The following lifestyle choices are detrimental to a person's health:

- Smoking
- Chewing tobacco
- Drug abuse
- Leading a sedentary lifestyle
- Excessive or improper (i.e. not nutritious) food consumption
- Unwillingness to wear seatbelts
- Excessive alcohol consumption
- Participating in high-risk behaviors (e.g., unprotected sexual activity, careless driving, etc.)
- Participating in violent behaviors (e.g., fighting, gang-related activities, etc.)
- Inadequate hygiene
- Unprotected environmental exposure (e.g., sun, chemicals, pollutants, etc.)
- Unwillingness to manage psychological stress

smoking, excessive alcohol consumption, overeating, and lack of exercise. A **sedentary lifestyle** can also lead to injury, illness, and disease early in life. These lifestyle practices have been linked to illness and diseases, including cancer and heart disease (Center for Disease Control [CDC], 2019). The lack of physical and mental wellness commonly results in a poor quality of life and a shorter life expectancy.

The average life expectancy in the United States in 2020 was projected as 77.3 years for biological men and biological women combined, with 74.5 years for biological men, and 80.2 years for biological women (Aria et al., 2021). Both of these figures have dropped slightly from previous years. However, the average life expectancy is anticipated to rise annually, and is projected to be 85.6 years in 2060 (Medina et al., 2020). However, what truly matters is not a person's **chronological age**, but rather their **biological age**. Biological age is reflected by the age of the cells and organs in the body. Biological age is determined by various factors including an athlete's fitness level, including cardiovascular fitness, muscular strength, and flexibility, along with blood pressure, cholesterol values, skin elasticity, and cognitive ability. An individual who is 50 years old and in exceptional health most likely has a biological age less than their chronological age. On the other hand, an individual who is 50 and in extremely poor health, smokes and is obese may have a biological age that is 20 years more than their chronological age. As sports medicine professionals, we should educate our clients to be more concerned with their biological age rather than their chronological age. They must consider their behaviors while they are young, and recognize that negative behaviors will definitely be a detriment to their future health.

Healthy People 2030

In 1979, the United States Department of Health and Human Services put forth a report titled *Healthy People: The Surgeon General's Report on Health Promotion and Disease Prevention*. Subsequent to that report were the following reports: *Healthy People 1990: Promoting Health/Preventing Disease: Objectives for the Nation*, *Healthy People 2000: National Health Promotion and Disease Prevention Objectives*, *Healthy People 2021: Objectives for Improving Health*, and *Healthy People 2020*. The initiatives, which supplied information for these reports, were created to give goals and objectives to the United States people to "attain, high-quality, longer lives free of preventable disease, disability, injury, and premature death; achieve health equity, eliminate disparities, and improve the health of all groups; create social and physical environments that promote good health for all; promote quality of life, healthy development, and healthy behaviors across all life stages." (Office of Disease Prevention and Health Promotion, 2021a). Unlike previous health goals, which focused on treatment of illness and disease, *Healthy People 2020's* goals focus on community education and measures to prevent illness and disease prevention. The overarching goals are measured and assessed in regard to the progress made.

In August 2020, the Office of Disease Prevention and Health Promotion published *Healthy People 2030* (see https://health.gov/news/202008/healthy-people-2030-here).

Similarly to *Healthy People 2020*, the purpose of *Healthy People 2030* is to set goals and objectives for people in the United States to assist them in achieving personal well-being and living a healthy life (Office of Disease Prevention and Health Promotion, 2021b). The 355 measurable objectives are based upon research and data, including information gathered from the *Healthy People 2020* and previous *Healthy People* initiatives and objectives data. The additional 114 developmental and 40 research objectives are being further studied. Unlike previous initiatives, *Healthy People 2030* objectives addresses emerging health issues such as COVID-19, opioid use disorder, e-cigarette use, and tobacco use in adolescents. The initiative also incorporates social determinants of health and measures of well-being, among other innovative components of health to benefit the United States' people (U.S. Department of Health and Human Services, 2021c).

Benefits of Wellness, Physical Activity, Exercise, and Fitness Programs

Healthy People 2030 aims to educate people on how to obtain and maintain optimal health. The initiative informs them about the benefits of wellness, physical activity, exercise, and fitness programs. These benefits collectively assist a person to live a long, good quality of life. The benefits are not only physical, but include mental benefits as well, which encompass emotional and social benefits. Physical benefits gained from participating in wellness, exercise, and fitness programs include, but are not limited to, the following:

- increased vigor and ability to perform tasks
- increased muscle tone and decreased fat tissue
- increased bone strength, which can decrease the possibility of a person having osteoporosis
- increased heart and lung function, which will increase the efficiency and effectiveness of the cardiorespiratory system
- increased ability for the body to regulate blood sugar and insulin levels, which is crucial for athletes with Type 2 diabetes
- decreased weight, consequently decreasing Body Mass Index (BMI)
- decreased cardiovascular heart disease risk factors
- decrease cancer risk factors
- decreased fatigue in performing exercise and activities of daily living (ADL)
- decreased mental stress, which will decrease anxiety and physical muscle tension
- decreased blood pressure, which will decrease stress on the heart and cardiorespiratory system
- decreased total cholesterol, decreased low-density lipoproteins (LDLs), increased high-density lipoproteins (HDLs), which will help decrease the chance of cardiovascular disease and heart attack.

When an individual begins to participate in wellness, exercise, and fitness programs, they will see and feel the benefits immediately. These benefits may progress slowly or quickly depending on the individual. However, the individual should be assured that they will become healthier with a renewed opportunity to obtain a longer, good quality of life.

Readiness to Participate in a Wellness, Exercise, and Fitness Program

Physical activity is important to everyone's well-being, and certainly assists people in leading a healthier lifestyle. However, many people participate in more structured wellness, exercise, and fitness programs. In order to begin a wellness, exercise, and fitness program, you and your client must evaluate their current status of wellness and fitness. Various reliable resources exist to accomplish this evaluation including, but not limited to, the Physical Activity Readiness Questionnaire for Everyone 2021 (PAR-Q+ 2021), Lifestyle and Health History Questionnaire, Healthstyle: A Self-Test, Body Composition Measurement, and Cardiorespiratory Assessment. The National Academy of Sports Medicine (NASM) has a variety of pre-participation assessment forms available for you on its website (see https://www.nasm.org/resources/downloads).

Physical Activity Readiness Questionnaire for Everyone (PAR-Q+)

One of the most common standardized tools utilized to evaluate an individual's current state of wellness, readiness to participate in exercise, and fitness is the PAR-Q+ **(Activity 2-1)**. The PAR-Q+ is a commonly used questionnaire that people of all ages will take in order to determine their exercise participation readiness. The questionnaire was devised by the Canadian Society for Exercise Physiology. The individual completes the questionnaire, and if they answers "yes" to any question, then a physician examination is necessary before the person begins an exercise program.

TIPS FROM THE FIELD

Tip 1 When meeting with a client for the first time to help them develop an appropriate personal wellness, exercise, and fitness program, give them an assumption of risk form, waivers, medical history, and preparticipation questionnaires. Also have them take a Healthstyle, PAR-Q, and any other wellness and exercise readiness questionnaires or self-tests that are applicable. Have on hand a list of credible, reliable websites for your client's daily reference. For example, many websites offer fitness tracking programs and applications that your client can download to a smartphone or computer. Many smartphones have technology to assist your client in tracking their daily exercise activity, nutrition intake, emotional status, and so on. Some programs and applications are free whereas others are accessible for a fee. Many offer a variety of interactive tools to assist your client in meeting their goals. In this era of increasing technology use, clients may be more inclined to stay focused on a wellness, exercise, and fitness program if they utilize innovative technology tools to record their progress.

Healthstyle: A Self-test

Another means to determine an individual's current health status is the *Healthstyle: A Self-Test*. This self-test was devised by the United States Department of Health and Human Services. The self-test is used as a reliable means to determine if the individual's lifestyle choices put them at risk for illness or disease **(Activity 2-2)**. This test requires the individual to answer a variety of questions. The questions pertain to the following lifestyle choice categories: use of tobacco, alcohol, and other drugs; eating habits; exercise/fitness; stress management; and safety. For each question within the categories, the individual will respond "almost always", "sometimes", and "almost never" in regard to their participation in the activity. Each response is worth a certain number of points. At the end of the self-test, the individual sums up the total number of points in each category. A high score represents the individual's good health in regard to the category. For example, if the individual scores high in the stress management category, you can conclude that the individual is able to handle their stress well. However, if the individual scores low in the eating habits category, then the individual has significantly poor eating habits. This self-test identifies which health-related behaviors and lifestyle choices the individual has under control. The self-test also identifies the behaviors and lifestyle choices which the individual must change in order to obtain overall wellness and a healthier lifestyle. With the self-test results, your expertise and assistance, your client can create wellness goals to incorporate into their wellness, exercise, and fitness program.

Body Composition Evaluation

Skinfold Thickness Measurement

One means for an individual to assess their body composition before beginning a wellness, exercise, and fitness program, is by utilizing skinfold thickness measurements. These measurements give an approximation of the individual's percent body fat content. Skinfold thickness measurements taken throughout the course of the program assists the individual in continually tracking their progress to lose fat and/or gain muscular tissue. The measurement is called a skinfold thickness measurement because the assumption is that approximately 50% of the body's fat lies directly below the skin. To measure skinfold thickness, calipers are necessary. A caliper is a handheld, pressure sensitive measurement tool used to measure body fat **(Figure 2-1)**. You can purchase calipers from various stores, internet websites, etc. Sports medicine professionals should regularly practice taking skinfold measurements to become proficient. Likewise to obtain reliable results, an individual

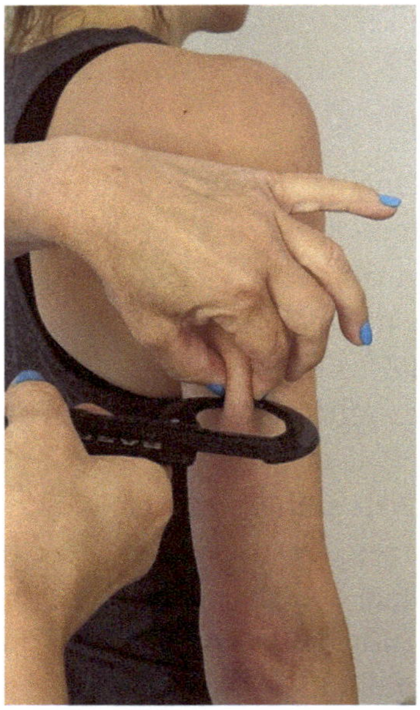

Figure 2-1 Calipers are used to measure skinfold thickness.

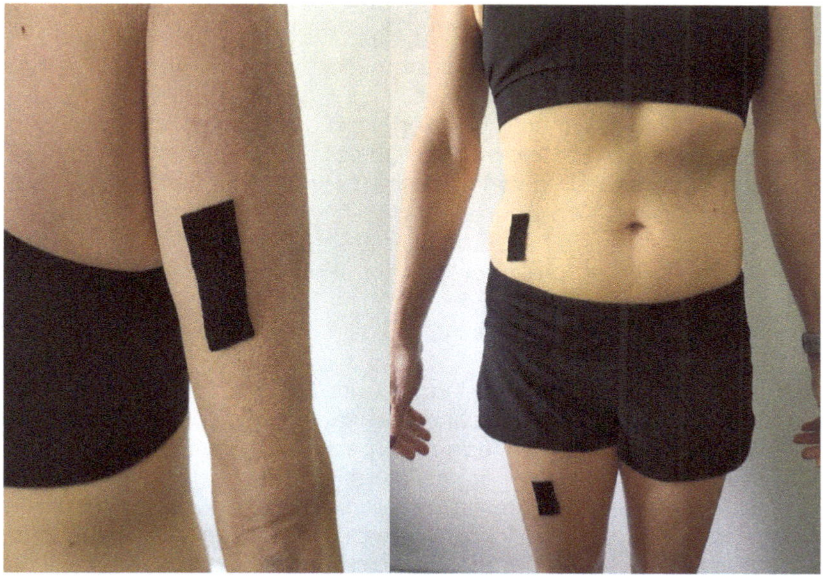

© Linda Gazzillo Diaz

Figure 2-2 Skinfold sites for biological women (3 site)

should have the same sports medicine professional take their measurements every time to accurately compare the measurements from one measurement session to the next.

Skin thickness measurements are taken at different sites on the body. Typically three to nine sites are utilized. For three site measurements, biological women are measured at the middle of the triceps, the superilium (right above the anterior iliac crest by the hip), and the anterior, middle thigh **(Figure 2-2)**. Biological men are measured at the chest between the anterior axillary line and nipple, the abdomen about one inch to lateral to the umbilicus, and the anterior, middle thigh **(Figure 2-3)**.

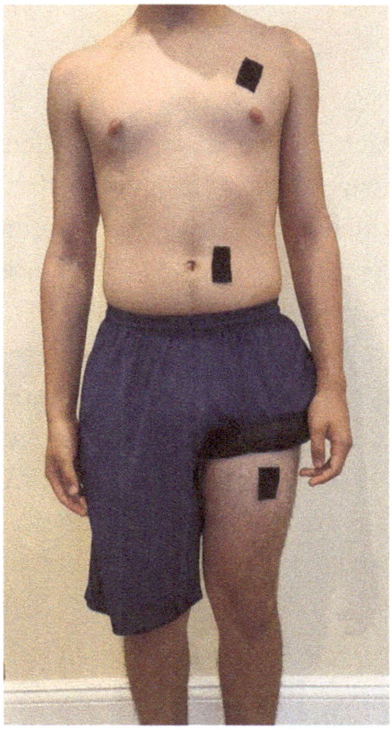

© Linda Gazzillo Diaz

Figure 2-3 Skinfold sites for biological men (3 site)

There are some important considerations and special techniques to take accurate skinfold measurements **(Table 2-3)**. Before taking the skinfold thickness measurements, explain to your client the purpose of the skinfolds and what you will be doing to obtain the measurements. At the first site, gently but firmly grasp the skin and slightly pull it away from the muscle. Then take the calipers and place them perpendicularly to the fold. Take the measurement approximately one-half inch below where you are holding the skin. Take the measurements in each location three times in millimeters, releasing and grasping the skin each time, while

Table 2-3 Techniques for taking skinfold measurements

1. Before measuring, if you prefer, mark the anatomical site with a water-soluble felt-tip pen.
2. Take all measurements on the right side.
3. Grasp the skinfold firmly by the thumb and finger of your left hand and pull away from the body. This is usually easier on thin people. Do not pinch the skinfold too hard. The skinfolds are normally pinched in a vertical rather than a horizontal line.
4. With your right hand, hold the caliper perpendicular with the skinfold, keeping the skin fold dial up so that it can be read. The caliper should be a quarter- to a half-inch away from the thumb and the forefinger so that the pressure of the caliper will not be affected.
5. Do not place the skinfold caliper too far into the skinfold or too far away on the tip of the skinfold.
6. Read the dial 1 to 2 seconds after releasing your grip. Take a minimum of two measurements at each site. Allow at least 15 seconds between measurements to permit the skinfold site to return to normal. If the repeated measurement varies by more than 1 millimeter, take another measurement until there is consistency.
7. Do not take measurements when the skin is moist, because dampness makes it easier to grasp the extra skin and thus obtain larger values. Do not take measurements immediately after exercise because exercise makes the skin moist.
8. Be sure to grasp the same size of skinfold consistently at the same location every time. This requires practice.

recording each measurement. Average the measurements for each location and add together each location's averages. Then take the final calculation and find that number on a skinfold chart or input all information into a percent body fat calculator, such as the calculator provided by the American Council on Exercise (ACE), to determine individual's body fat percentage (see https://www.acefitness.org/education-and-resources/lifestyle/tools-calculators/percent-body-fat-calculator/). According to ACE (n.d.), a body fat percentage for biological women to be considered fit is 21% - 24% and biological men is 14% - 17%. Biological women who have over 32% body fat and biological men who have over 25% body fat are considered obese. Skinfold measurements are only one means for an individual to obtain their body fat percentage prior to beginning a wellness, exercise, and fitness program. This measurement is used continually throughout the program to determine the individual's progress in losing body fat and/or gaining muscular tissue.

Body Mass Index

Another tool which tracks a person's progress to obtain health is Body Mass Index (BMI). BMI evaluates a person's weight relative to height. BMI indicates if a person is underweight, normal, overweight, or obese. A BMI chart assists the person in determining a normal weight for their height. The person identifies their height and weight on the chart, locates the BMI,

BMI	19	20	21	22	23	24	25	26	27	28	29	30	31	32	33	34	35	36	37	38	39	40	41	42	43	44	45	46	47	48	49	50	51	52	53	54
Height (inches)	Body Weight (pounds)																																			
58	91	96	100	105	110	115	119	124	129	134	138	143	148	153	158	162	167	172	177	181	186	191	196	201	205	210	215	220	224	229	234	239	244	248	253	258
59	94	99	104	109	114	119	124	128	133	138	143	148	153	158	163	168	173	178	183	188	193	198	203	208	212	217	222	227	232	237	242	247	252	257	262	267
60	97	102	107	112	118	123	128	133	138	143	148	153	158	163	168	174	179	184	189	194	199	204	209	215	220	225	230	235	240	245	250	255	261	266	271	276
61	100	106	111	116	122	127	132	137	143	148	153	158	164	169	174	180	185	190	195	201	206	211	217	222	227	232	238	243	248	254	259	264	269	275	280	285
62	104	109	115	120	126	131	136	142	147	153	158	164	169	175	180	186	191	196	202	207	213	218	224	229	235	240	246	251	256	262	267	273	278	284	289	295
63	107	113	118	124	130	135	141	146	152	158	163	169	175	180	186	191	197	203	208	214	220	225	231	237	242	248	254	259	265	270	278	282	287	293	299	304
64	110	116	122	128	134	140	145	151	157	163	169	174	180	186	192	197	204	209	215	221	227	232	238	244	250	256	262	267	273	279	285	291	296	302	308	314
65	114	120	126	132	138	144	150	156	162	168	174	180	186	192	198	204	210	216	222	228	234	240	246	252	258	264	270	276	282	288	294	300	306	312	318	324
66	118	124	130	136	142	148	155	161	167	173	179	186	192	198	204	210	216	223	229	235	241	247	253	260	266	272	278	284	291	297	303	309	315	322	328	334
67	121	127	134	140	146	153	159	166	172	178	185	191	198	204	211	217	223	230	236	242	249	255	261	268	274	280	287	293	299	306	312	319	325	331	338	344
68	125	131	138	144	151	158	164	171	177	184	190	197	203	210	216	223	230	236	243	249	256	262	269	276	282	289	295	302	308	315	322	328	335	341	348	354
69	128	135	142	149	155	162	169	176	182	189	196	203	209	216	223	230	236	243	250	257	263	270	277	284	291	297	304	311	318	324	331	338	345	351	358	365
70	132	139	146	153	160	167	174	181	188	195	202	209	216	222	229	236	243	250	257	264	271	278	285	292	299	306	313	320	327	334	341	348	355	362	369	376
71	136	143	150	157	165	172	179	186	193	200	208	215	222	229	236	243	250	257	265	272	279	286	293	301	308	315	322	329	338	343	351	358	365	372	379	386
72	140	147	154	162	169	177	184	191	199	206	213	221	228	235	242	250	258	265	272	279	287	294	302	309	316	324	331	338	346	353	361	368	375	383	390	397
73	144	151	159	166	174	182	189	197	204	212	219	227	235	242	250	257	265	272	280	288	295	302	310	318	325	333	340	348	355	363	371	378	386	393	401	408
74	148	155	163	171	179	186	194	202	210	218	225	233	241	249	256	264	272	280	287	295	303	311	319	326	334	342	350	358	365	373	381	389	396	404	412	420
75	152	160	168	176	184	192	200	208	216	224	232	240	248	256	264	272	279	287	295	303	311	319	327	335	343	351	359	367	375	383	391	399	407	415	423	431
76	156	164	172	180	189	197	205	213	221	230	238	246	254	263	271	279	287	295	304	312	320	328	336	344	353	361	369	377	385	394	402	410	418	426	435	443

Figure 2-4 BMI Chart
Source: Courtesy of the National Heart, Lung, and Blood Institute.

Table 2-4 Classification of BMI values

Classification	BMI
Underweight	Below 18.5
Normal	18.5 – 24.9
Overweight	25.0 – 29.9
Obese	30.0 and above

and determines if their calculation falls within normal BMI ranges **(Figure 2-4)**. A BMI of 18.5 to 24.9 is considered normal **(Table 2-4)**. A normal BMI has shown to decrease risk of illness, disease, and death.

The U.S. Department of Health and Human Services National Heart, Lung, and Blood Institute has calculators and charts for calculating BMI on its website (https://www.nhlbi.nih.gov/health/educational/lose_wt/BMI/bmicalc.htm). By determining their BMI, the individual can set their weight loss goals appropriately, aiming for a BMI within the normal range.

BMI should not be the only tool used to determine risk of illness, disease, mortality, or overall health, due to its notable limitation. BMI calculations do not factor in the body's quantity of muscle. Muscle has a greater density and weighs more than fat. An individual's body may be composed of a large quantity of muscle and very little fat. Consequently, a shorter person who has significant muscular tissue may have a high BMI, which categorizes them as overweight or even obese. Likewise, older people who have lost muscular tissue may have lower than true BMI values. Therefore, BMI should not be the sole predictor of a person's body composition and current health status.

Waist Circumference

If an individual has excessive fat stored in their waist, and has an "apple shaped" body, their risk of illness and disease is heightened. Waist circumference is another quick means to screen your clients when determining their current health status. The CDC (2020) states that a biological man whose waist circumference is more than 40 inches and a non-pregnant biological woman whose waist circumference is more than 35 inches are at a higher risk of acquiring illness and disease due to obesity. Another study found that waist circumference has a strong, conclusive relationship to BMI and occurrence of obesity in individuals (Ahmad et al., 2016). In order to measure waist circumference properly, have your client stand upright and put a cloth tape measure around their waist right above their iliac crests. Make sure that the tape measure is flat and not twisted. The tape measure should be snug, but do not pull it so tight that it pinches or compresses the client's skin. Have your client breathe out and then take the measurement (CDC, 2020). Be certain to utilize this method of body composition evaluation with other assessment tools to determine your client's current health status.

Other Evaluation Processes

Although skinfold thickness, BMI, and waist circumference measurements are common tools utilized to determine an individual's current state of health and risk for illness and disease, other health and wellness predictors must be utilized to gain an overall perspective of the individual's wellbeing. Other more highly accurate tests to determine body composition exist. For example, some testing procedures performed by sports medicine professionals in a clinical or medical setting utilize specialized medical equipment that are not available to the general public. Some specialized tests include Dual-Energy X-ray Absorptiometry (DXA), hydrostatic weighing, air displacement plethysmography (ADP), bioelectrical impedance analysis (BIA), bioimpedance spectroscopy (BIS), 3-D body scanners, and multi-compartment models. More commonly, the methods mentioned in this chapter are performed as quick and easy means to give an approximation of your client's current body composition, which assists in determining overall health status.

Goal Setting

When a person wishes to begin a wellness, exercise, and fitness program, ask them to explain why they desire to participate and what they want to accomplish. Listen to your client, speak with them, and gain a history of how they arrived at this decision. At this point, evaluate their current state of wellness and fitness using the aforementioned self-tests. Assist the individual in assessing the results, and educating and offering suggestions for a healthier lifestyle. The results along with their history will assist you in helping them set long- and short-term program goals.

An individual's long- and short-term goals help guide a wellness, exercise, and fitness program. As a sports medicine professional, you will help your client set goals before they begin a program, and modify the goals as necessary. Goal setting gives an individual motivation and challenges during their journey to achieve better health. Work with your client to help them set reachable goals. Make sure your client does not set unreachable, unhealthy, or inappropriate goals. Long-term goals are general and focus on the program's outcomes. Two common long-term goals individuals make are to lose weight and stop smoking. On the other hand, numerous short-term goals combined together will drive a person to reach their long-term goal. Short-term goals are set with the intent that the individual can reach them within a week or two. Short-term goals are objective, measurable, and challenging, yet obtainable. Examples of short-term goals are to lose 1 to 2 pounds per week and to smoke only 15 cigarettes per day instead of 20 during the week. These short-term goals act as motivators for the individual to continue on their quest for a healthier lifestyle.

Always explain to your client that short-term goals are motivators. Encourage them to give their best effort to reach these goals. Let your client know that during almost every program setbacks occur. For example, the client may only lose one-half of a pound by the week's end. At this point discuss the related short-term goal, the program, and the client's effort in reaching the goal. Assist them in identifying why they did not reach the goal. The short-term goal may have been too difficult for the client, and consequently needs to be modified. The client may have not provided adequate effort to reach the goal. Keep in mind that short-term goals should challenge your client, but if you find they are not reaching the goals on a consistent basis then the goals may be too difficult. As a result, the client can become discouraged and want to give up on their long-term goal. Also if the short-term goals are too easy, your client can get a sense of being infallible. Then the client acquires a sense of being able to conquer all tasks and reaching all short-term goals. Consequently, when your client faces a challenging short-term goal and does not reach it, they will feel defeated. To avoid short-term goal setbacks, keep your client motivated. By creating measurable, challenging, and reachable long- and short-term goals with your client, you can prepare your client to obtain a healthier lifestyle.

Principles of Conditioning

After assisting your client in setting long- and short-term goals, begin to assist them in devising an exercise program. When assisting an individual in devising an exercise program, educate them about the importance of the principles of conditioning. These principles include the following: warm-up/cool-down, motivation, overload, consistency, progression, intensity, specificity, individuality, stress, and safety (Prentice, 2020).

The warm-up prepares the body, in particular the muscles, for exercise. The warm-up should be approximately five to twenty minutes. It should be an active, otherwise known as "dynamic", warm-up that consists of continuous aerobic activity that incorporates the entire body. Examples of aerobic activities include fast walking, jogging, jumping rope, bicycling, and calisthenics. One means to determine that the body and muscles are warmed up enough to begin exercise is if the individual has broken a sweat. The warm-up includes stretching exercises that promote muscle lengthening and flexibility. Stretching principles and exercises are discussed in detail in the flexibility section of this chapter.

After exercise, a cool-down is necessary in order to return the body to a normal state. The cool-down takes place immediately after the exercise activity for approximately five to ten minutes. The cool-down activities include similar aerobic activities as in the warm-up, but at a significantly lower intensity. Muscle stretching during both the warm-up and cool-down promotes flexibility, which increases ROM and function.

Motivation is a principle of conditioning that is a key to success for your clients to progress in becoming healthy. Traditional athletes are typically highly motivated to exercise in order to excel in their sport. However, many other individuals are not as motivated to perform exercise, even if they know exercise will assist them in becoming healthy. Your role as a sports medicine professional is to verbally motivate your client to perform exercise by being their advocate for health. Likewise, modify their exercise activities frequently to make the exercise program continually enjoyable for your client. If your client enjoys participating the exercise program you create for them, most likely they will be motivated to continue, and ultimately see positive results.

When the muscles are subjected to progressively increasing demands, over time the muscles become accustomed to the demands. For example, if you progressively increase the resistance or intensity that your client is utilizing during exercise, the muscles become accustomed to the resistance or intensity. As a result, the muscles become larger and stronger. This principle of conditioning is called overload. Adaptation is similar to overload; however, adaptation deals with other components of fitness and not solely increasing muscles muscular strength. Adaptation is also referred to as the specific adaptations to imposed demands (SAID) principle. The SAID principle means that when the body is presented with a challenge or stressor, over time the body reacts in either a positive or negative manner. For example, if your client wishes to increase joint ROM, which is limited due to decreased muscular flexibility, they must progressively provide a stretch to the affected muscles during each exercise session. The stretch applied is a type of muscular stress. Over time, the muscles adapt and respond to the stress by lengthening, thereby providing the individual with increased flexibility and resultant ROM.

It is important for your client to participate in regular, scheduled, frequent exercise. This consistency of exercise is necessary for your client in order to reap the health benefits resulting from exercise.

Progression describes how the exercise activities are sequenced throughout the duration of the exercise program. By utilizing the principle of progression, the preliminary exercise activities are simple, and then continue to become progressively difficult. The activities begin at a low intensity and increasingly become more intense, but only to a level of what the individual can handle at the time as to avoid injury. An adequate progression is necessary in order to advance the individual's exercise program and meet their fitness goals.

The intensity of exercise is the extent that exercises challenge the individual. When an individual begins an exercise program, the intensity should be low and progress to be higher. The intensity increases as their body becomes accustomed to the intensity. Likewise, as you incorporate new exercises into your client's program, the new exercises are at a low intensity and are increased as tolerated.

Exercise program specificity means that programs must be tailored to the individual's specific needs and goals. The exercise program includes general exercises which benefit their health and others which mimic skills utilized in their chosen activities. For example, if the individual wants to play tennis, then their exercise program should focus on lower body muscular endurance, upper body power in their dominant arm, cardiorespiratory endurance exercises, and agility.

Individuality is the principle of conditioning that goes hand-in-hand with specificity. Individuality takes into consideration each person's activity level, personal characteristics, goals, and body type. Each wellness, exercise, and fitness program must address the differences among individuals' attributes. You will utilize some of the same exercise skills and other programmatic methods for all of your clients. However, you must consider that all clients are not the same and have different needs. Consequently, you must personalize each client's program to assist them in reaching their goals and promote their health gains.

Stress is both physical and mental. You must challenge your clients to perform exercise activities that physically stress their body within their capabilities in order for them to become fit and well. However, you must consider the mental stress that your clients may be experiencing, which can affect their progress. Make sure that your clients have rest time from exercise to not only physically relax their bodies, but also to relax their minds.

As for the principle of conditioning of safety, always make sure the exercise programs do not put the individual in harm's way. They must be able to complete challenging exercise activities with the least possibility of injury, but keep in mind that intense, difficult exercises predispose the individual to harm. Also make sure that the environment is safe prior to beginning the day's session. For example, all equipment must be safety checked regularly, surfaces and equipment cleaned after each use, and all participants must follow standard safety policy and procedures of the facility.

The principles of conditioning must always be taken into consideration when you devise an exercise program for your clients. By utilizing these principles as a framework, you can plan, evaluate, and adjust the athlete's exercise program effectively, and your clients can meet their goals.

The FITT Principle

Assisting your client with their goals and educating them on the principles of conditioning are important tasks to complete before your client begins an exercise program. Along with these tasks, you and your client collaboratively decide what type of exercise program will be most effective in order to achieve their long-term goals. A client who wishes to lose weight, increase muscular tone and strength, and increase heart and lung efficiency requires a combination of cardiorespiratory and strength training exercise. When planning the individual's cardiorespiratory endurance and strength training exercise program, incorporate the FITT principle. FITT stands for Frequency, Intensity, Time, and Type of exercise.

Frequency of exercise is the number of days per week that an individual exercises. In order to increase cardiorespiratory endurance, they should exercise a minimum of three days a week and progress to five days per week. For individuals who wish to lose weight, progressing to five to six days of cardiorespiratory endurance exercise is optimal. In order to increase muscular strength, individuals should strength train three to four days per week. However, the individual should perform the exercises on alternate body areas on alternate days. For example, an individual may work on upper and core body strength on Monday, lower body strength on Tuesday, rest on Wednesday, and then continue the week alternating activities specific to body areas. Some highly competitive athletes participate in more than five days per week of both cardiorespiratory and strength training exercise due to their sport activity demands.

The "I" in FITT is intensity. Intensity is a principal of conditioning, but is also applied to cardiorespiratory exercise programming. During cardiorespiratory exercise, an individual works continuously at percentage of their **heart rate reserve** (HRR). HRR is an individual's maximum heart rate (MHR) minus their resting heart rate (RHR). The target or training heart rate (THR) is a percentage of the HRR. The higher THR indicates a higher intensity. For moderate exercise, individuals will work at 50% to 70% of HRR. For vigorous exercise, individuals will work at an intensity of 70% to 85% of HRR (Mayo Clinic, 2021). Some sedentary or unfit individuals may need to begin cardiorespiratory exercise at 40% to 60% of HRR.

In order to determine your client's MHR, first determine their RHR. The RHR is the number of heart beats per minute when an athlete is at rest. Typically, the best time for the individual to calculate their RHR is in the morning, while they are still lying in bed. They can also take their RHR after sitting or lying still for at least 15 minutes. To find RHR, the individual must find their radial pulse first. The radial artery is located by the wrist and pulsates with each heartbeat. Finding the radial pulse is not difficult. Place your palm up and with your opposing index and middle fingers, place them approximately one inch below the wrist joint on the thumb side of the hand **(Figure 2-5)**. The beating sensation is the radial pulse.

Your client can also take their pulse by utilizing the carotid artery. To find the carotid artery place the index and middle fingers below the chin on the middle of the throat. Then slide the fingers about an inch to the left. The carotid artery pulse will be evident due to its strength **(Figure 2-6)**. Either the radial or carotid pulses are entirely appropriate to utilize when determining RHR and THR. Once your client has found their pulse, have them time how many pulses occur within 15 seconds. Then multiply the number of pulses by four. The final number of pulses is the RHR in beats per minute (bpm). The average person has a RHR of approximately 60 to 100 bpm (Mayo Clinic, 2021). Your client should take their RHR in the same manner (i.e. in bed before waking, sitting at rest for 15 minutes) for three days, and average the three RHR values to determine the true RHR.

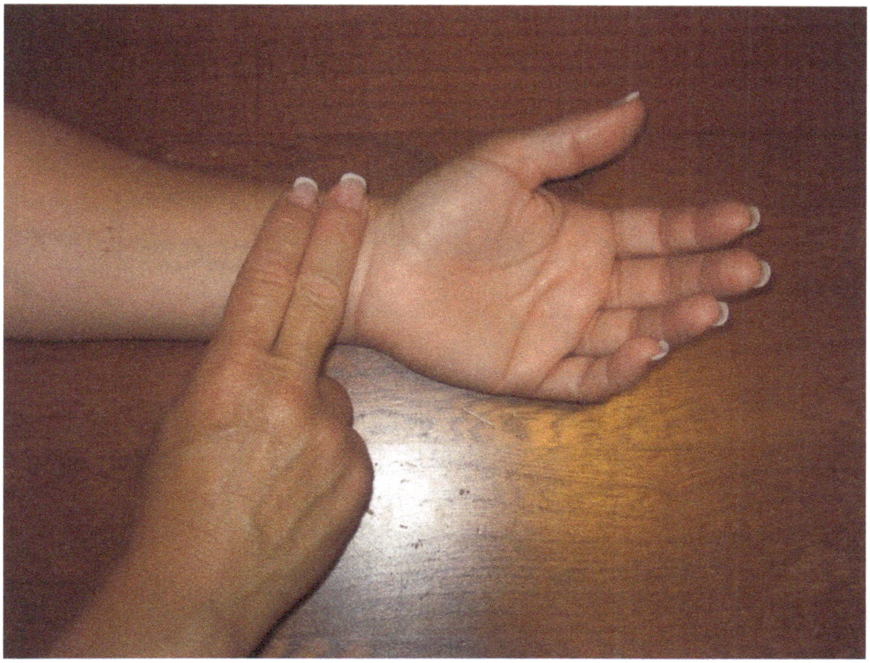

Figure 2-5 Location of the radial pulse

Figure 2-6 Location of the carotid artery pulse.

In order to get your client's lower and upper heart rate training thresholds take the client's RHR, and utilize the Karvonen formula **(Figure 2-7)**. Maximum heart rate (MHR) is calculated first. Maximum heart rate in bpm is determined by taking 220 minus your client's age. Therefore, a 40-year-old's MHR is 220 – 40 = 180 bpm. Then the individual's HRR must be calculated. To calculate the HRR, your client takes their MHR – RHR. If a 40-year-old individual has a RHR of 70 bpm, then their HRR is 180 bpm - 70 bpm = 110 bpm. Finally, to calculate the individual's THR for moderate exercise, the individual takes their (HRR × 0.5) + RHR = the lower value of the THR approximating 50% MHR, and (HRR × 0.7) + RHR = the higher value of the THR approximating 70% MHR. Therefore, a 40-year-old individual with a RHR of 70 bpm, a MHR of 180 bpm, and a HRR of 110 bpm has a lower threshold THR of (110 bpm × 0.5) + 70 bpm = 125 bpm, and a higher threshold THR of (110 bpm × 0.7) + 70 = 147 bpm. When performing cardiorespiratory exercise, the individual's pulse must range between 125 bpm to 147 bpm to get beneficial cardiorespiratory effects. Always have the individual determine their lower and upper THR before beginning a cardiorespiratory exercise program, so they know what THR to achieve during exercise.

\# of beats (pulses) per minute at rest = RHR
220 – age = MHR
MHR – RHR = HRR
[(HRR x 0.5) + RHR] = THR lower threshold for pulse rate for moderate exercise
[(HRR x 0.7) + RHR] = THR upper threshold for pulse rate for moderate exercise

Figure 2-7 Karvonen formula

Once the individual has completed their warm-up and begins the exercise program, have the individual complete approximately 20 minutes of cardiorespiratory exercise before taking their pulse. Inform them to take their pulse while continuing to exercise at a lower intensity, without stopping entirely. If your client stops suddenly during exercise, their blood may pool to the extremities, and they may faint. After taking a pulse, if the individual's heart rate is not within training levels, they can modify the exercise accordingly to meet the desired intensity.

An individual has many commercial heart rate monitor devices available to utilize during exercise to determine if they are meeting their THR. Heart rate monitors are devised within many wristwatches, which can quickly determine an athlete's current heart rate during exercise. Most exercise equipment, such as treadmills, stationary bicycles, and step machines, have heart rate monitors built into the equipment. An individual places their hands on the heart rate monitor, and the machine determines their heart rate while exercising. It is beneficial to use these commercial heart rate monitors because the individual does not need to slow down their exercise, which quickly reduces heart rate, to calculate their heart rate. Utilizing a heart rate monitor during exercise is beneficial because the individual can constantly visualize changes in heart rate while exercising, and immediately modify the work out if necessary.

The third component of the FITT principle is time. Time is the duration of the exercise session. To obtain positive cardiorespiratory effects, an individual must exercise continuously at heart rate training levels for at least 20 minutes when beginning an exercise program, and gradually progress to 60 minutes as their cardiorespiratory endurance increases. Positive cardiorespiratory effects are evident in individuals participating in this continuous exercise for 3 to 5 days per week. However, a 60-minute exercise session is optimal.

The last component of the FITT principle is type. Aerobic activities are a type of exercise activity. The individual must take part in aerobic activities in order to obtain positive cardiorespiratory effects. Aerobic activities that include whole body movements, utilizing both the arms and legs, are most beneficial. Swimming and jogging are two whole body movement, aerobic activities. Riding a stationary bicycle or utilizing a step machine is aerobic and advantageous, but these activities only utilize lower body movements. An upper body ergometer is also an aerobic exercise machine, but the individual utilizes only the upper body **(Figure 2-8)**. Regardless of which machine an athlete utilizes, the individual will gain valuable cardiorespiratory effects. Muscular strength

Figure 2-8 An upper body ergometer (UBE)

training exercises include utilizing free weights, resistance bands, machine and hydraulic weights, and body weight exercises.

Cardiorespiratory Exercise Program Readiness

As a sports medicine professional, evaluate your client's current level of cardiorespiratory fitness before they begin a cardiorespiratory program. The most accurate way to measure cardiorespiratory fitness is to measure your client's maximal oxygen uptake or VO_{2max}. This measure shows how efficiently the cardiorespiratory system utilizes oxygen. The most conclusive VO_{2max} tests are performed under laboratory conditions with expensive equipment by highly trained sports medicine professionals. The most common test has an individual put on a face mask and run on a treadmill. The volume and oxygen concentration of the individual's inspired and expired air can be accurately determined. Many sports medicine professionals to not have access to this equipment and testing. However, you can utilize a few simple tests to estimate your athlete's VO_{2max}. These tests include the Rockport Fitness Walking Test™, the YMCA Step Test, and the Cooper 12-minute run test (Thygerson & Thygerson, 2019).

For both the Rockport Fitness Walking Test™ and the YMCA Step Test, the individual performs cardiorespiratory exercise, takes their pulse, and refers to the respective charts to determine their fitness level. The Rockport Fitness Walking Test™ requires them to walk 1 mile before taking their heart rate, which can be via a heart rate monitor. Then the individual must calculate their VO_{2max} and compare norms by utilizing a chart or use calculators found on the internet (**Activity 2-3**). The YMCA 3-minute Step Test requires the individual to step onto a 12-inch-high stable step or bench. (**Activity 2-4**). To perform the Cooper 12-minute run test, the individual runs as hard as they can on a flat oval track or treadmill for 12 minutes, noting the distance when the time has ended. Afterward, they refer to the Cooper 12-minute run test chart (**Activity 2-5**) to determine their fitness level, and can also determine their VO_{2max} by utilizing the following equations:

Miles: $VO_{2max} = (35.97 \times \text{miles}) - 11.29$

1 mile = 1760 yards

Kilometers: $VO_{2max} = (22.351 \times \text{kilometers}) - 11.288$

Instead of this test, you can use the Cooper 1.5-mile run/walk test, which has virtually the same results for determining VO_{2max} as the Cooper 12-minute run test (Cooper Institute, 2018). The individual runs 1.5 miles and records their time to do so. Again, they will look at a chart or use calculators found on the internet to determine norms and their VO_{2max} (**Activity 2-6**). See https://www.cooperinstitute.org/2018/06/08/50-years-of-the-cooper-12-minute-run for the history of the two Cooper tests. New technology provided in some smart watches allow for VO_{2max} to be estimated by heart rate. Although these tests are not exact determinants of cardiorespiratory fitness, the tests are inexpensive, easy, common tests utilized to give an approximate baseline cardiorespiratory fitness level.

Flexibility

Flexibility is important for your clients who participate in both cardiorespiratory or strength training programs. Flexibility also helps clients maintain adequate blood flow to the working muscles, improves posture, and reduces muscular tension. A flexibility program incorporated in both cardiorespiratory and strength training programs is necessary because flexible muscles allow for more joint ROM, thereby assisting your clients in gaining a full, unrestricted ROM for activity. Consequently, your clients will obtain optimal performance with their exercise activity and ADLs.

It is important to determine your client's current state of flexibility before beginning a cardiorespiratory or strength training program. In order to test your client's current state of flexibility, you can use a variety of methods. The basic and commonly used method is called the sit-and-reach test. This test evaluates general flexibility of the back musculature and hamstrings **(Activity 2-7)**. A shoulder flexibility test **(Activity 2-8)** and additional flexibility tests for various areas of the lower body **(Activity 2-9)** can also assist you and your client in determining their current state of flexibility.

In order to obtain positive effects from a flexibility program, the client first performs a proper warm-up. The warm-up prepares the muscles and tendons for stretching activities. The flexibility program incorporates the FITT principle. The flexibility program frequency for beginners is three days per week and progresses to daily stretching activities. The stretch intensity must be sufficient enough to create muscular tension. The client lengthens the muscles to the point of tightness and discomfort, but not pain. By stretching the muscles to the point of discomfort, the client deforms and elongates the muscle fibers. Explain to your client that performing a stretch to the point of pain is very detrimental. If your client stretches and feels pain, they are actually causing detrimental fiber tearing, creating injury, and causing inflammation as a result.

The stretch duration is important because the muscle fibers must be on a stretch for an adequate time in order to deform and lengthen. Your client should minimally hold the stretch for approximately 10 seconds. Some clients may wish to hold the stretch longer (i.e. 30 seconds). The stretch is repeated at least three times. Each time the muscles are stretched, the muscle fibers become accustomed and adapt to the stretch, and remain at the lengthened state. The client performs additional **repetitions** if they need to obtain further immediate muscular lengthening prior to or after exercise activity. Remind your client to stretch the contralateral muscles so those muscles are equally flexible.

Static, dynamic, or proprioceptive neuromuscular facilitation (PNF) stretching activities are used to promote muscular flexibility. However, the stretching activity utilized is dependent on the client's current flexibility and specific goals. A static stretch is a passive motion. The client places the muscle on tension and lengthens it to the point of discomfort. An example of static stretching is when your client sits on the floor in a hurdler's stretch and leans forward in attempt to put their chest to thigh. This static stretch results in hamstring muscle group elongation. Static stretching is a very common and safe stretching method. Therefore, inflexible clients should begin a stretching program using static stretching.

Once your client has an adequate amount of flexibility resulting from performing static stretching exercises, they can begin dynamic stretching exercises. To perform a dynamic stretch, the client performs active range of motion (AROM), which requires active muscle contractions. Simultaneously, the muscles are lengthened and create muscular tension. An example of a dynamic stretch is a "walking lunge". Your client stands with their feet together, then places one foot forward so their knee is at approximately a 90-degree angle, allowing them to assume a lunge position. They will feel muscular tension and a stretch at the quadriceps and hip flexor muscle groups. Afterwards, they alternate the lower extremities, brings the posterior extremity forward, and assumes the lunge position again. Your client continues the dynamic stretching exercises by alternating right and left lower extremities to perform "walking lunges". They must not bounce when performing dynamic stretching exercises, since the bouncing (ballistic) movements can cause muscle strains.

Your client requires your assistance to properly perform PNF stretching. PNF stretching involves **isometric** and **isotonic contractions** with periods of relaxation and stretching. PNF stretching utilizes the principles of autogenic and reciprocal inhibition. During autogenic inhibition, the **antagonist** isometrically or isotonically contracts. Then the antagonist contraction is released, and the client allows the muscle to relax. Following the muscle relaxation, the muscle is stretched. Reciprocal inhibition differs from autogenic inhibition because the antagonist is stretched simultaneously as the **agonist** is isometrically or isotonically contracted. In order for the agonist to contract, the antagonist must relax. Therefore, the most opportune time to stretch the antagonist is when the antagonist is in a relaxed state.

Three PNF stretching techniques commonly used are hold-relax, contract-relax, and slow-reversal-hold-relax (Houglum, 2016). Hold-relax utilizes autogenic inhibition. The antagonist is first placed on a stretch. Then your client isometrically contracts the muscle against your manual resistance as forcefully as they can. The contraction is held for 10 seconds. Then on your command, the client releases the contraction and allows the muscle to relax. The relaxation phase lasts 10 seconds. After this time, move the client's muscle into a new, elongated position, and hold the stretch for 10 seconds. The entire process is repeated a few times as necessary for the client, and performed on the contralateral side.

Contract-relax also utilizes the principle of autogenic inhibition. The antagonist is first placed on a stretch. Then the client isotonically contracts the muscle against your manual resistance as forcefully as they can. The contraction is held for 10 seconds. On your command, the client releases the contraction, allowing the muscle to relax. The relaxation phase lasts 10 seconds. After 10 seconds, your client minimally contracts the agonist to perform AROM, while you move the muscle into a new, elongated position. The stretch is held for 10 seconds. As with hold-relax, the entire process is repeated a few times as necessary for the client, and performed on the contralateral side.

Slow-reversal-hold-relax utilizes both autogenic and reciprocal inhibition. The antagonist is first placed on a stretch. Then your client isometrically contracts the muscle against your manual resistance as forcefully as she can. The contraction is held for 10 seconds. Then on your command, the client releases the contraction, allowing the muscle to relax. The relaxation phase lasts 10 seconds. After 10 seconds, and on your command, they maximally contract the agonist to perform AROM against your resistance for 10 seconds. Afterwards, they relax the agonist while you move the antagonist into a new, elongated position. The stretch is held for 10 seconds. As with hold-relax and contract-relax, the entire process is repeated a few times as necessary for the client, and performed on the contralateral side. PNF stretching is as effective as static stretching (Lempke et al., 2018), but requires good communication between you and your client. This stretching technique has the potential to cause injury if not performed properly. Consequently, you must demonstrate the techniques before implementation and practice them carefully with your client. Static, dynamic, and PNF stretching methods are effective, valuable means to increase your client's flexibility. Therefore, choose the methods that best meet the client's abilities and goals.

Strength Training

Most athletes incorporate strength training activities into their exercise programs. Strength training activities build muscular strength, endurance, and power. Many principles of conditioning, especially overload, intensity, and progression, come into play when an athlete incorporates strength training into their exercise protocol. Strength training exercises involve resistance, or weight, applied to a muscle or group of muscles. The muscles move the resistance through an AROM. The muscles are overloaded and adapt to the resistance via the SAID principle. The muscles respond to the resistance by becoming larger and stronger. To continue gaining positive strength training benefits, the athlete increases the resistance and exercise intensity in a progressive manner.

Isotonic Exercise

Strength training programs consist of isotonic and isokinetic exercises. Both exercises involve muscular **concentric contractions** and **eccentric contractions**. Isotonic exercise is performed with a fixed resistance through a full or partial ROM. However, the speed of the exercise is variable. For example, if your athlete held a 20-pound dumbbell, the weight of the dumbbell does not change during the exercise. The speed of the exercise is variable, since through the entire ROM the athlete will not move this 20-pound dumbbell at the exact consistent speed throughout (even though they may try to do so).

Isotonic exercises include the use of equipment such as resistance machines, free weights, barbells, dumbbells, sandbag weights, resistance bands, and tubing. The resistance machines, free weights, barbells, dumbbells, and sandbags have the exact weight noted on the equipment. However, resistance bands and tubing do not. Instead, the resistance bands and tubing are color coded with each color signifying the extent of resistance applied. Consequently, the athlete cannot quantify exactly how much resistance they are moving. As a sports medicine professional, you are only able to record your athlete's resistance progression in regard to band or tubing color. Also, when using bands or tubing the resistance is greater at one point of the ROM and less at another due to the band's or tubing's position relative to the body. Regardless of the limitations, resistance bands and tubing are portable, inexpensive, and effective pieces of isotonic equipment utilized to create muscular strength.

Isotonic exercise produces many positive attributes. Isotonic exercise can build strength throughout the entire ROM by varying the resistance applied. The athlete performs the activities at various speeds and directions, which make the exercises functional and applicable to their activities. The athlete moves the resistance in functional patterns, as they would when performing activities such as throwing or kicking. Consequently, isotonic exercise is very appropriate for athletes to gain strength specific to their exercise skills. Resistance machines, commonly found in gyms and fitness centers, are simple and generally safe to utilize with prior, proper instruction. An athlete can very easily perform isotonic exercise at home or while traveling. For example, inexpensive free weights can be purchased to utilize at home, or commercial resistance elastic bands can be packed in a suitcase to utilize when traveling.

Isotonic exercise does have disadvantages. One disadvantage is in regard to **sticking points**. Commonly, while an athlete moves a resistance through a ROM, they come across particular point within the ROM where they experience difficulty and are unable to move the resistance (Kompf & Arandjelović, 2017). At this point in the ROM, the athlete is forced to stop their motion and switch to a lighter weight to complete the ROM. If they try to move the resistance, which too heavy at that sticking point, then injury is probable. Another disadvantage of isotonic exercise is that resistance machines in gyms and fitness centers typically focus on one muscle or muscle group. Consequently, the athlete must use numerous machines in order to build strength throughout the body. These machines take up a large amount of space and are costly. Therefore, people typically do not have each, individual machine

TIPS FROM THE FIELD

Tip 2 If your athlete does not have access to weights or resistance tubing at home, have them use items around the house that can be weighed to continue their isotonic workouts at home. For example, an athlete can take an empty plastic milk gallon jug that has a handle, clean it out, let it dry, and put in sand, rocks, or even water to create the resistance. They can do the same with a tennis ball can. Have the athlete weigh the jug or can to prior to exercise. Depending on how much resistance your athlete uses, they can also utilize other household objects, such as unopened food cans or bungee cords, to complete their workouts. Always remind your athlete that they can use their own body weight to complete isotonic exercise and gain muscular strength.

within their homes. Barbells are simple to utilize; however, an athlete requires assistance from another athlete (called a "spotter"). This assists spotter the athlete by aiding them if they lose grip on the bar and drops it while performing a lift. The spotter also assists them in lowering and placing the barbell correctly back on the rack. This assistance can be viewed as a disadvantage because the athlete may not always have a spotter when performing barbell activities at home or in other venues. As previously mentioned, quantifying resistance with resistance bands and tubing is not possible. Resistance applied to the body segment changes as the resistance band's or tube's position changes. For purposes of recording resistance measures and building strength through a full ROM, resistance bands and tubing may not be the isotonic equipment of choice. In general, despite some disadvantages, isotonic exercise is a very beneficial, common means for an athlete to gain muscular strength.

Isokinetic Exercise

Isokinetic exercise is different than isotonic exercise because the resistance accommodates to the athlete's force output and the speed is fixed. Accommodating resistance means that resistance is placed upon the athlete's extremity throughout the ROM in response to the amount of force the athlete creates against the machine. Therefore, athlete's muscles are overloaded throughout the entire ROM. Specialized, computerized exercise machines, such as a Cybex® and Biodex© dynamometers, are utilized for isokinetic training. As a sports medicine professional in charge of your athlete's exercise programming, you will set the machine for a specific speed prior to exercise. If you want the athlete's extremity to move slowly through a ROM and build muscular strength and increase muscular power, you will set the machine to function at a low speed (i.e. 60 degrees per second). If you want the athlete's extremity to move quickly through a ROM and build muscular strength and increase muscular endurance, then set the machine to function at a high speed (i.e. 360 degrees per second). The number of repetitions and **sets** of the exercises are incorporated into the athlete's program based upon whether the athlete's goal is to increase muscular power or muscular endurance.

Many benefits of isokinetic exercise exist. The athlete is able to gain muscular strength through a full ROM, without any sticking points because the machine accommodates the resistance output based upon the athlete's muscular force output. The machine can be set to allow the athlete to move at a variety of speeds, in order to focus on muscular strength along with muscular endurance or power. The computer software allows the athlete to immediately view their effort on the monitor, as well as the ability to print out, download, and save their progress. As with all exercise methods, disadvantages of isokinetic exercise exist. Many isokinetic machines only allow for straight plane movement and do not simulate functional movements that occur in sport. The machines are large and not portable, so an athlete cannot perform isokinetic exercise at home. Isokinetic machines are also expensive. Some machines, including the accessory equipment needed for the machine, service plans, and annual calibrations, sum to tens of thousands of dollars. When utilizing the machine, a large learning curve exists for the athlete. In order to utilize an isokinetic machine, the sports medicine professional must instruct an athlete on its use as well as have "training" or practice sessions in order to familiarize themselves with the machine. The sports medicine professional must ascertain safe use of the machine and learn its limitations before incorporating it into their athlete's exercise program. Although isokinetic exercise has its disadvantages, it is a valuable and effective means to increase an athlete's muscular strength.

Beginning a Strength Training Program

In order to begin a strength training program, sports medicine professionals must assess their athlete's current state of muscular strength and endurance, which can be done by having the athlete perform a variety of tests. One means to determine your athlete's current state of muscular strength is by the One-Repetition Maximum Test (1 RM) **(Activity 2-10)**. The findings from this test give a baseline to determine the starting resistance for your athlete's strength training program. The Hand Grip Strength Test utilizes a hand-held device called a dynamometer. The athlete grips the dynamometer, applies a full force contraction, and the dynamometer reads the force produced **(Activity 2-11)**. An easy test for muscular endurance is having the athlete perform as many push-ups as they can **(Activity 2-12)**. The YMCA Bench-Press Test is another means to measure muscular endurance, especially for larger athletes **(Activity 2-13)**. The YMCA Half Sit-up Test (Partial Curl-up Test) is also valuable to determine current state of muscular endurance **(Activity 2-14)**. These muscular strength and endurance assessment tests are critical to utilize in determining your athlete's baseline capabilities, and to create an effective, safe strength training program.

When devising an athlete's strength training program you must keep in mind the principles of conditioning. Also remember that one athlete has different goals than another. Although you can incorporate many of the same exercise skills from one athlete's program into another, each athlete must be treated as an individual (the individuality principle of conditioning). Plan the program according to their specific activity needs and goals (the specificity principle of conditioning). As always, the program must be safe for the athlete (the safety principle of conditioning), and include a warm-up and cool-down (the warm-up and cool-down principles of conditioning). An appropriate progression of overload and intensity (the overload and intensity principles of conditioning) is necessary so the athlete's muscles can adapt to the stresses placed on it and benefit from the training (adaptation and the SAID principle).

Along with the principles of conditioning, utilize the FITT principle when creating your athlete's exercise prescription. Devise the athlete's program dependent upon the athlete's goals. Typically, when an athlete begins strength training, they participate three times per week. Upper, lower, and core body activities comprise the program. Typically, an athlete trains one body group each of the three days. Perhaps on Mondays the athlete performs upper body exercises, on Wednesday they perform core body exercises, and on Friday they perform lower body exercises. During the additional two to three days per week, the athlete performs cardiorespiratory activities. The athlete completes flexibility exercises every day.

The exercise intensity must be great enough to progressively overload the muscles. If the specific muscles performing the exercise are not entirely fatigued by the last repetition, then the muscles were not overloaded enough due to the intensity being too low. Consequently, your athlete will not see any exercise benefits. Considering intensity and frequency together is very important to produce strength gains. Research has shown that low load strength training exercises more times per week are not different in results to high load strength training exercises fewer times per week (Thomas & Burns, 2016).

In regard to exercise program time, each exercise session begins with the standard 5 to 20 minute warm-up, and ends with the 5 to 10 minute cool-down. However, the duration for the other exercises varies according to the number of exercises, repetitions, and sets incorporated into the program each day. The number of exercises depend on the muscles and body area targeted for the day (i.e. upper body, lower body, core body). As previously discussed, for muscle endurance typically a higher number of repetitions is warranted, and for muscular power a lower number of repetitions will suffice. Research varies on the optimal number of exercises to complete per muscle group per session. A beginner strength training athlete completes approximately 2 to 3 sets per each different exercise, which focuses on one muscle or muscle group during the strength training session. However for intermediate or advanced athletes, 5 or more sets per each different exercise should be completed for adequate strength gains (Ralston et al., 2017).

The type of exercises includes isotonic and/or isokinetic exercises, utilizing the equipment previously discussed. The athlete can also utilize their own body weight to provide resistance, for example when performing lunges, push-ups, pull-ups, and sit-ups. The exercises should include open kinetic chain (OKC) and closed kinetic chain (CKC) exercises. OKC exercises include isotonic activities with the distal extremity (the hand or foot) moving through space. In OKC activities the hand or foot is not fixed to a surface, such as a table, floor, or wall. Utilizing dumbbells or performing a bench press are examples of OKC upper extremity activities. CKC activities are performed with the distal extremity fixed on a stable object, such as the floor, table, or wall. Lunges or push-ups are examples of CKC activities. OKC activities strengthen muscles around a particular joint, while CKC exercises strengthen muscles throughout the entire extremity. OKC activities are important to incorporate into an athlete's strength training program if the athlete cannot weight bear on either the upper or lower extremity. However, OKC activities are not as safe as CKC activities, since with CKC activities the athlete has entire limb control and can stop the motion immediately, if necessary. Both OKC and CKC exercises are activities which incorporate isometric, isotonic, and isokinetic exercises effectively into your athlete's strength training program.

Guidelines for a Strength Training Program

In order to devise specific resistance exercises to incorporate into your athlete's strength training program, first determine why they want to strength train. The athlete's goals direct you to devise a specific, individual program for them. Ask your athlete if they want to gain muscular strength to perform everyday activities and obtain optimal health, muscular endurance to perform activities for a long period of time, or muscular power to perform forceful activities for a short period of time. All athletes must have some muscular strength to perform ADLs and other physical activities. Some athletes are content with only obtaining this goal. However, many athletes want to continue with strength training and obtain muscular endurance or power capabilities.

The amount of resistance utilized, along with number of repetitions and sets in a strength training program varies depending on your athlete's goals. Experts differ on how many repetitions and sets, and the amount of resistance necessary to obtain desired results. Therefore, after reviewing literature, including recommendations from the National Academy of Sports Medicine (Penney, n.d.), the American College of Sports Medicine (Fiataraone Singh et al., 2019), and The U.S. Department of Health and Human Services (n.d.), the following guidelines can be utilized. As a beginner, to gain optimal muscular strength in order to perform ADLs and promote a healthier lifestyle, the individual should attempt 8 to 12 repetitions and 2 to 3 sets of activity into your athlete's strength training program. A low resistance of approximately 60% to 80% of the athlete's 1 rep maximum (1 RM) is utilized. The rest time between sets is approximately one minute. For an athlete who wishes to gain muscular endurance, they should begin with approximately 12 to 16 repetitions and 3 sets of each activity incorporated into their strength training program. The resistance is approximately 50% to 70% of the athlete's 1 RM, which is a greater resistance than utilized for general muscular strength gains. Rest time is the same as for muscular strength exercises. Approximately 2 to 4 repetitions with 1 to 3 sets are appropriate for gaining muscular power. The athlete uses approximately 70% to 80% of 1 RM of resistance, with a longer rest period of approximately 2 to 5 minutes between sets. Regardless of whether the athlete wants to gain muscular endurance or power, when they are beginning a strength training program, have them perform general muscular strength exercises first. Later, after the muscles **hypertrophy**, then modify your athlete's program to focus on muscular endurance or power.

Mental Readiness

Although determining your athlete's physical readiness for a cardiorespiratory, flexibility, and strength training exercise programs are important, do not forget to make sure your athlete is mentally ready for exercise. If the athlete is not mentally ready for exercise, then injury can result. When taking your athlete's history, you can tell if they are mentally ready for exercise by how they behave and what they say. Watch the athlete's body language, including facial expressions. You know they are mentally ready if they express confidence and a positive attitude. An athlete beginning a new program most often expresses excitement and readiness to make a lifestyle change. They relay to you their motivation along with any anxieties. It is normal for an athlete to state they are anxious. If the athlete shows signs of anxiety or fear, offer suggestions on how to manage stress by performing relaxation techniques. For some athletes exercise itself helps relieve mental stress.

Each individual typically knows what works best to manage their stress. Some examples of stress management and relaxation activities include listening to music, reading, or playing video games. Some athletes receive full body massages to relieve physical tension along with mental stress. Athletes also participate in other exercise activities which focus on body and mind relaxation, such as yoga and tai chi. Even though the athlete participates in these activities, additional stress reduction techniques can be incorporated into an athlete's daily schedule. Three effective stress management methods that can be utilized include imagery, meditation, and Jacobson's muscular relaxation technique.

Imagery

Imagery is a method of visualizing something pleasant that creates positive thoughts. An athlete may start an exercise program to lose body fat. The athlete imagines their body as it will appear when they have reached their goal. Another athlete chooses to picture a place, such as a beautiful, serene island, which creates a calming effect for the athlete. The athlete performs the imagery anywhere, at any time. To get the most beneficial effects, instruct your athlete to perform the imagery alone in a quiet, low-lighted room. Tell them to lay down on a couch, bed, or the most comfortable position, with his eyes closed. The athlete must not be disturbed while performing the activity. The imagery session takes as long as the athlete needs. When they feel a decrease in mental stress that is sufficient, then the imagery was successful, and the session can end.

Meditation

Meditation is similar to imagery in a variety of ways including body positioning and environment. However, meditation requires slow and controlled breathing. The athlete breathes in through the nose and out through the mouth. They focus on a word or phrase to repeat in their mind, with the intent to block all negative or unnecessary thoughts. Have the athlete incorporate meditation into their daily activities. The meditation session should begin at approximately the same time each day and must be uninterrupted for approximately 10 to 20 minutes.

Jacobson's Relaxation Techniques

In the early 1900's, Edmund Jacobson, MD, PhD, created a muscular relaxation technique, which assists in decreasing muscular tension, resulting in a decrease of mental stress (Gessel, 1989). The progressive relaxation techniques consist of voluntary, forceful muscle group contractions. Jacobson wanted his patients to focus on the awareness of muscular tension and then relaxation. He concluded that this awareness decreases physical tension as well as mental tension. The athlete should be in a low-lighted, quiet room in a comfortable position. The exercises begin with the upper extremity. During the first session, the athlete creates a fist, noting the muscular tension produced. Then they voluntarily relax the muscles. The athlete performs subsequent sessions of upper extremity, trunk and core, and lower extremity voluntary muscular contractions. The contractions focus on one group of muscles at a time. Voluntary relaxation follows each contraction. The athlete progresses to eventually complete the muscular contractions and relaxations in a systematic fashion throughout the entire body in one session. These relaxation techniques do not always result in benefits immediately. As the athlete continues to perform these techniques and learns how to listen to their body, the techniques will become very beneficial in managing their mental stress.

Summary

As sports medicine professionals, we have many roles in regard to our athletes, clients, and patients. We guide them to lead a healthy lifestyle. We educate them to understand how wellness, physical activity, exercise, and fitness are beneficial to decrease the likelihood of injury, illness, disease, and death. We recommend many helpful, and potentially lifesaving, tools to begin a wellness, physical activity, exercise, and fitness program. The roles we assume are imperative to create a better quality of life for our athletes, clients, and patients.

Keywords

Body composition The amount of lean soft tissue, including muscle and fat, in the body.

Sedentary lifestyle A lifestyle without regular physical activity or exercise.

Chronological age The actual number of years that an athlete has been living.

Biological age The age an athlete is classified as when factoring in their overall health as compared to athletes who are their chronological age.

Aerobic Means that the body, in particular the cardiorespiratory system, utilizes oxygen.

Heart rate reserve The difference between an athlete's RHR and MHR. The heart rate reserve is used to calculate the THR for the athlete during cardiorespiratory exercise.

Isometric contraction When the muscle contracts and creates tension. The muscle does not cause movement, shorten, or lengthen.

Isotonic contraction When the muscle contracts and creates tension while moving through a partial or full ROM.

Antagonist The muscle to be stretched.

Agonist The muscle which is contracted and opposes the antagonist.

Concentric contraction When the muscle contracts and shortens. An example would be when the biceps brachii in the upper body in lifting an object, while the athlete is flexing his elbow, and in the gastrocnemius in the lower body when the athlete is pushing off his toes during jumping.

Eccentric contraction When the muscle contracts and lengthens. An example would be when the biceps brachii in the upper body assists in lowering an object, while the athlete is extending his elbow, and in the hamstrings in the lower body when the athlete is slowing down during running.

Sticking points Specific locations within the ROM when the athlete is unable to move the resistance because the resistance is too great, the muscle is too weak, or both.

Repetitions How many times the exercise, stretch, etc. is performed.

Sets A series of repetitions. An athlete may perform 10 repetitions in one set. In this case, three sets make up 30 repetitions.

Hypertrophy When a muscle increases in size due to progressive overload of the muscle by increasing the resistance.

Discussion Questions

1. Name the health-related components of fitness. Name the skill-related components of fitness. What do each of these components measure? Why are the health-related components of fitness important for all individuals?
2. What tools can an individual utilize to determine their current health status and to predetermine their readiness for exercise?
3. What are the principles of conditioning? Describe how each principle of conditioning is incorporated into an individual's exercise program.
4. What assessment tests are utilized to determine the individual's current state of cardiorespiratory, flexibility, and muscular strength? Why is it important to assess the individual's current state of cardiorespiratory, flexibility, and muscular strength prior to devising their exercise program?
5. What does FITT stand for and how is this principle utilized for cardiorespiratory, flexibility, and muscular strength exercise programs?
6. Name different methods of how to promote an individual's mental health.

CASE STUDY: FITNESS WISHES, BUT DANGEROUS HEAT!

It is a sunny Saturday afternoon. Dan, a 35-year-old man, wants to become more fit in order feel better physically and mentally. In order to become more fit and decrease his mental stress, Dan knows that he needs to lose some weight and become physically active. Dan is 5'9" tall and weighs 270 pounds. Therefore, his BMI is 40, which means Dan is considered obese. Although Dan is taking an active role to become healthier, he smokes approximately one pack of cigarettes per day. Dan admits that he is not ready to quit smoking. He figures the exercise will negate the detrimental effects of smoking and make him healthier.

Dan wants to take advantage of the beautiful weather and decides to begin his fitness program by exercising outside today. Dan has not participated in any exercise for approximately one year. He takes part in casual physical activity, but realizes he needs

(continued)

CASE STUDY: FITNESS WISHES, BUT DANGEROUS HEAT! (*CONTINUED*)

to have structure with his exercise program. Dan set a goal to progress and increase the exercise activity intensity as his body allows, and as a result, he will lose fat tissue. He also wishes to overload his muscles to make him stronger. He is hoping that exercise will alleviate some of his mental stress. To get back into shape, he wants to incorporate jogging into his exercise protocol. Dan figures that he can exercise approximately 30 minutes or so a day to start, and then increase the exercise duration over time.

After taking care of a few chores around the house, and having another cigarette, Dan gets dressed in sweatpants and a t-shirt, laces up his sneakers, and heads outside. Dan will jog slowly, since he has not jogged in a long time. Since he decided to jog slowly, he believes a warm-up or stretching is not necessary. Dan heads out to jog to the park, which is about 2 miles from Dan's house. Dan plans on running from his house to the park and back for a total of 4 miles. He figures it will take him approximately 40 minutes or so to jog this distance. After all, over a year ago when he was more physically fit he remembered that he could run a 6-minute mile; however, Dan knows he must take the jog slow. He also believes he will be able to jog the 4 miles without stopping.

A half mile into his jog, Dan begins to become thirsty. He realizes that he has not eaten or drank anything since breakfast, and does not have any water or electrolyte drinks with him. Dan figures that he will be fine, and instead of turning around and going back to his house he decides to continue jogging to the park. Dan reaches the mile mark in 15 minutes. It is taking him longer to run than he thought it would. At this point Dan is extremely thirsty, is sweating profusely, has labored breathing, and is becoming extremely tired. However, Dan continues on, figuring that the thirst, sweat, breathing, and fatigue are side effects from lack of conditioning. Shortly into his second mile, Dan begins to get a headache. He becomes increasingly nauseous and dizzy, and his breathing is becoming more difficult. Again, Dan continues to jog. Dan reaches the park and turns around. He now is into his third mile and begins to become uncoordinated, weak, and disoriented.

At this point, the discomfort is too much for Dan. He sees a park bench up ahead, jogs to the bench, immediately stops jogging, and sits on the bench to rest. While he is sitting down his calf and hamstring muscles begin to cramp in his right leg. He begins to feel very ill. His breathing is extremely fast and shallow. Dan feels like he cannot catch his breath. A woman walking her dog by Dan notices that he does not look okay. She walks over and asks him what is wrong. She notices that he is profusely sweating, and his face is very pale. Barely able to speak due to his breathing difficulty, he tells her how he feels. She asks him for permission to assist him with his condition and he welcomes the help.

1. How much weight would Dan have to lose to maintain a BMI that is considered normal?
2. How do you think the detrimental lifestyle choice of smoking has affected Dan's ability to jog the 4 miles?
3. Should Dan have warmed up and stretched prior to exercise? If so, what exercises should Dan have incorporated into his warm-up?
4. What should Dan have considered in regard to the FITT principle, since this is the first time he has exercised in approximately one year?
5. What should Dan have done to better prepare for his jog?
6. If you were Dan's sports medicine professional, what would you do to devise a proper wellness, exercise, and fitness program for Dan?

References

Ahmad, N., Adam, S. I., Nawi, A. M., Hassan, M. R., & Ghazi, H. F. (2016). Abdominal obesity indicators: Waist circumference or waist-to-hip ratio in malaysian adults population. *International Journal of Preventive Medicine*, *7*(1), 82. https://doi.org/10.4103/2008-7802.183654

American Council on Exercise (ACE). (n.d.). *Percent body fat calculator : Skinfold method.* Retrieved August 5, 2021 from https://www.acefitness.org/education-and-resources/lifestyle/tools-calculators/percent-body-fat-calculator/

Arias, E, Tejada-Vera, B., Ahmad, F., and Kochanek, K. D. (2021, July). *Provisional life expectancy estimates for 2020.* Center for Disease Control (CDC).Retrieved August 4, 2021 from https://www.cdc.gov/nchs/data/vsrr/vsrr015-508.pdf

Center for Disease Control (CDC). (2019, December 9). *Know your risk for heart disease.* Retrieved August 4 2021, from http://www.cdc.gov/heartdisease/behavior.htm

Center for Disease Control (CDC). (2020, September 17). *Assessing your weight.* Retrieved August 6, 2021 from https://www.cdc.gov/healthyweight/assessing/index.html

Cooper Institute (2018, June 8). *50 years of the of the Cooper 12-minute run.* Retrieved August 16, 2021 from https://www.cooperinstitute.org/2018/06/08/50-years-of-the-cooper-12-minute-run

Dasso, N.A. (2019). How is exercise different from physical activity? A concept analysis. *Nursing Forum, 54*(1), 45-52. https://doi.org/10.1111/nuf.12296

Fiataraone Singh, M., Hackett, Daniel, Schoenfeld, B., Vincent, H. K., & Wescott, W. (2019, July 31). *ACSM guidelines for strength training.* American College of Sports Medicine. Accessed on August 20, 2021 from https://www.acsm.org/blog-detail/acsm-certified-blog/2019/07/31/acsm-guidelines-for-strength-training-featured-download

Gessel, A. H. (1989). *Edmund Jacobson, M.D., Ph.D.: The founder of scientific relaxation.* Retrieved August 20, 2021 from http://www.progressiverelaxation.org/

Hoeger, W. W. K., Hoeger, S. A., & Hoeger, C. I. (2022). *Lifetime physical* fitness *and wellness: A personalized approach* (16th ed). Cengage Learning.

Houglum, P. A. (2016). *Therapeutic exercise for musculoskeletal injuries* (4th Ed.)Human Kinetics.

Kompf, J., & Arandjelović, O. (2017). The Sticking Point in the Bench Press, theSquat, and the Deadlift: Similarities and Differences, and Their Significance forResearch and Practice. *Sports medicine (Auckland, N.Z.)*, *47*(4), 631–640. https://doi.org/10.1007/s40279-016-0615-9

Lempke, L., Wilkinson, R., Murray, C., & Stanek, J. (2018). The effectiveness of PNF versus static stretching on increasing hip-flexion range of motion. *Journal of Sport Rehabilitation, 27*(3), 289-294. Retrieved August 17, 2021 from https://journals.humankinetics.com/view/journals/jsr/27/3/article-p289.xml

Mayo Clinic. (2021, June 17). *Exercise intensity: How to measure it.* Retrieved August 10, 2021 from https://www.mayoclinic.org/healthy-lifestyle/fitness/in-depth/exercise-intensity/art-20046887

Medina, L., Sabo, S., & Vespa, J. (2020, February). *Living longer: Historical and projected life expectancy in the United States, 1960 to 2060.* U.S. Census Bureau. Retrieved August 4, 2021 https://www.census.gov/content/dam/Census/library/publications/2020/demo/p25-1145.pdf

National Wellness Institute. (n.d.). *The six dimensions of wellness.* Retrieved August 2, 2021, from https://nationalwellness.org/resources/six-dimensions-of-wellness/

Office of Disease Prevention and Health Promotion (2021a, June 23). *About healthy people.* Retrieved August 5, 2021 from http://www.healthypeople.gov/2020/about/default.aspx

Office of Disease Prevention and Health Promotion (2021b, June 23). *Healthy people 2030 framework.* Retrieved August 5, 2021 from https://www.healthypeople.gov/2020/About-Healthy-People/Development-Healthy-People-2030

Office of Disease Prevention and Health Promotion. (2021c, August 2) *Healthy people 2030 questions and answers.* Retrieved August 5, 2021 from https://health.gov/our-work/healthy-people/healthy-people-2030/questions-answers

Penney, S. (n.d.). *Fitness: How much activity is enough?* National Academy of Sports Medicine. Accessed on August 20, 2021 from https://blog.nasm.org/fitness/fitness-how-much-activity-is enough#:~:-text=The%20weekly%20recommendation%20for%20resistance,at%20least%20twice%20per%20week

Prentice, W. (2020). *Essentials of athletic injury management* (11th Ed.). McGraw-Hill.Ralston, G. W., Kilgore, L., Wyatt, F. B., & Baker, J. S. (2017). The effect ofweekly set volume on strength gain: A meta-analysis. *Sports Medicine (Auckland,N.Z.), 47*(12), 2585–2601. https://doi.org/10.1007/s40279-017-0762-7

Thomas, M. H., & Burns, S. P. (2016). Increasing lean mass and strength: A comparison of high frequency strength training to lower frequency strength training. *International Journal of Exercise Science, 9*(2), 159–167.

Thygerson, A. L. & Thygerson, S. M. (2019). *Fit to be well* (5th Ed.). Jones and Bartlett Learning.

U.S. Department of Health and Human Services National Heart, Lung, and Blood Institute. (n.d.). *Assessing your weight and health risk.* Retrieved August 6, 2021 from https://www.nhlbi.nih.gov/health/educational/lose_wt/risk.htm

U.S. Department of Health and Human Services National Heart, Lung, and Blood Institute. (n.d). *Physical activity and your heart.* Retrieved August 3, 2021 from http://www.nhlbi.nih.gov/health/health-topics/topics/phys/

U.S. Department of Health and Human Services Office of Disease Prevention and Health Promotion. (n.d.). *Physical activity: Current guidelines.* Retrieved August 3, 2021 from https://health.gov/our-work/physical-activity/current-guidelines

U.S. National Library of Medicine MedlinePlus. (2019, May 8). *Definition of health terms: Fitness.* Retrieved August 4, 2021 from https://medlineplus.gov/definitions/fitnessdefinitions.html

U.S. National Library of Medicine MedlinePlus. (2021, March 8). How much *exercise do I need?* Retrieved August 4, 2021 from https://medlineplus.gov/howmuchexercisedoineed.html

U.S. National Library of Medicine MedlinePlus. (2021, August 2). *Exercise and physical fitness.* Retrieved August 4, 2021 from https://medlineplus.gov/exerciseandphysicalfitness.html

World Health Organization. (2020, November 20) *Physical activity.* Retrieved August 4, 2021 from https://www.who.int/news-room/fact-sheets/detail/physical-activity

Activities

Activity 2-1 PAR-Q+

Please visit the following link to view PAR-Q+ assessment:
http://eparmedx.com/wp-content/uploads/2022/01/ParQ-Plus-Jan-2022-Fillable.pdf

Activity 2-2 Healthstyle: A Self-test

This self-test, which is a modified version of the one developed by the U.S. Public Health Service, assesses several health-related behaviors. Although these behaviors apply to most individuals, pregnant individuals, and people with chronic health concerns should follow the advice of their physicians. Answer each of the following questions by circling the number of the response that applies best to you. Add the number of points under each health-related behavior category to obtain a score for that category. Use the scoring guide at the end of the test to determine the level of risk you are incurring by your health-related behavior.

Tobacco, Alcohol, and Other Drugs			
If you have never used tobacco products, enter a score of 10 for this section, and skip questions 1 and 2.			
	Almost always	**Sometimes**	**Almost never**
1. I avoid using tobacco products.	2	1	0
2. I smoke only low-tar cigarettes.	2	1	0
Smoking Score:			
3. I avoid drinking alcoholic beverages, or I drink no more than one or two drinks per day.	2	1	0
4. I avoid using alcohol or other drugs (especially illegal drugs) as a way of handling stressful situations or problems in my life.	2	1	0
5. I avoid driving while under the influence of alcohol and other drugs.	2	1	0
6. I am careful not to drink alcohol when taking certain pain medications or when pregnant.	2	1	0
7. I read and follow the label directions when using prescribed and over-the-counter drugs.	2	1	0
Alcohol and Other Drugs Score:			
Eating Habits			
8. I eat a variety of foods each day, including fruits and vegetables, whole-grain products, lean meats, low-fat dairy products, seeds, nuts, and dry beans.	3	1	0
9. I limit the amount of fat that I eat, especially animal fats such as cream, butter, cheese, and fatty meats.	3	1	0

(continued)

Eating Habits *(Continued)*			
	Almost always	**Sometimes**	**Almost never**
10. I limit the amount of salt that I eat, by avoiding salty foods and not using salt at the table.	2	1	0
11. I avoid eating too much sugar, by eating few sweet snacks and limiting sugary soft drinks.	2	1	0
Eating Habits Score:			
Exercise/Fitness			
12. I maintain a body weight that is reasonable for my height.	3	1	0
13. I do vigorous exercise (for example, running, swimming, or brisk walking) for at least 30 minutes at least three times per week.	3	1	0
14. I do exercises to enhance my muscle tone and flexibility (for example, yoga or calisthenics) for 15 to 30 minutes at least three times per week.	2	1	0
15. I use part of my leisure time participating in individual, family, or team activities that increase my level of physical fitness (for example, gardening, bowling, or golf).	2	1	0
Exercise/Fitness Score:			
Stress Management			
16. I take time every day to relax.	2	1	0
17. I find it easy to express my feelings.	2	1	0
18. I recognize and prepare for events or situations that are likely to be stressful.	2	1	0
19. I have close friends, relatives, or others I can talk to about personal matters and contact for help when needed.	2	1	0
20. I participate in hobbies that I enjoy or group activities such as religious or community organizations.	2	1	0
Stress Management Score:			
Safety			
21. I wear a seat belt while riding in a motor vehicle.	2	1	0
22. I obey traffic rules and speed limits while driving.	2	1	0
23. I have a working smoke detector in my home.	2	1	0

Safety (*Continued*)			
	Almost always	**Sometimes**	**Almost never**
24. I am careful when using potentially harmful products or substances, such as household cleaners, poisons, and electrical devices.	2	1	0
25. I avoid smoking in bed.	2	1	0
Safety Score:			

What Your Scores Mean

Scores of 9 or 10 for each section: Excellent! Your responses show that you are aware of the importance of this area to your health, and that you are practicing good health-related habits. As long asyou continue to do so, this area of health should not pose a risk.

Scores of 6 to 8 for each section: Your health practices in this area are good, but there is room for improvement. Look at the items that you answered with "Sometimes" or "Almost Never." What lifestyle changes can you make to improve your score and reduce your risk?

Scores of 3 to 5 for each section: Your health-related behaviors are risky. What lifestyle changes can you make to improve your score in this area of health and reduce your risk?

Scores of 0 to 2 for each section: You may be taking serious and unnecessary risks with your health and, possibly, the health of others. What lifestyle changes can you make to improve your score and reduce your risk?

Source: Healthstyle: A self-test. Hyattsville, MD: U.S. Public Health Service, 1981.

Activity 2-3 Rockport Fitness Walking Test™

This activity assesses cardiorespiratory (aerobic) fitness. To perform the test, you need a watch with a second hand to record your time, and to wear good walking shoes and loose clothes to walk in. You should have your physician's consent before undertaking this exercise test.

Instructions

1. Find a measured track or measure 1 mile using your car's odometer on a level, uninterrupted road.
2. Warm up by walking slowly for 5 minutes.
3. Walk 1 mile as fast as you can, maintaining a steady pace. Note the time that you began walking.
4. When you complete the mile walk, record your time to the nearest second and keep walking at a slower pace. Count your pulse for 15 seconds and multiply by 4, then record this number. This gives your heart rate per minute after your test walk.
   Heart rate at the end of 1-mile walk in beats per minute
   Time to walk the mile in minutes

5. Remember to stretch once you have cooled down.
6. To find your cardiorespiratory fitness level, refer to the appropriate Rockport Fitness Walking Test™ charts based on your age and sex. These show established fitness norms from the American Heart Association.

Please visit this site to evaluate your results:
https://www.verywellfit.com/rockport-fitness-walking-test-calculator-3952696

Activity 2-4 YMCA 3-minute Step Test

Complete the PAR-Q+. Do not take the test if you have joint problems in your ankles, knees, or hips, or if you are obese.

Preparation

You will need the following:

- 12-inch-high sturdy bench
- Metronome (or some other cadence timing sound device)
- Stopwatch, watch, or clock with a second hand

Warm up for 5 minutes before taking the test. Practice before, but you should be well rested with no prior exercise of any kind for several hours before the test.

Procedure

1. Set the metronome at 96 beats per minute (four clicks of the metronome equals one step cycle: up—1, 2; down—3, 4).
2. Step up and down on the 12-inch bench for 3 minutes.
3. After the 3 minutes of stepping, sit down and within 5 seconds count your radial pulse for 1 full minute.
4. See the following table for your fitness rating.

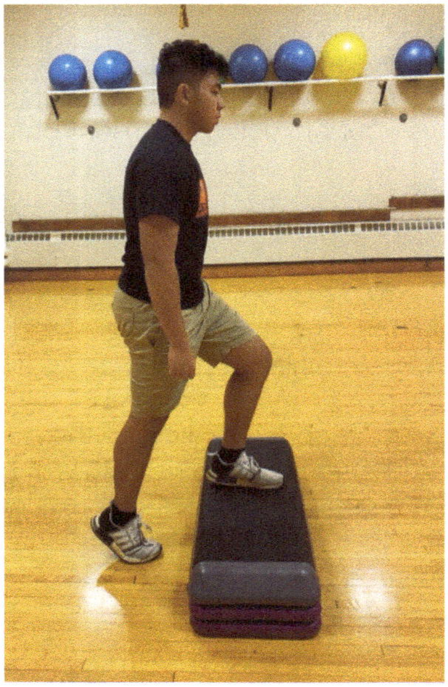

3 Minute Step Test to Estimate the Quality of VO_{2max} by Utilizing Age, Gender, and Heart Rate (bpm)				
	Quality of VO_{2max}			
Men Aged	**Excellent to Good**	**Above Average to Average**	**Below Average to Poor**	**Very Poor**
18-25 years	<84	85–100	101–119	>119
26-35 years	<85	86–102	103–121	>121
36-45 years	<88	89–105	106–124	>124
46-55 years	<93	94–111	112–126	>126
56-65 years	<94	95–109	110–128	>128
65+ years	<92	93–110	111–126	>126
	Quality of VO_{2max}			
Women Aged	**Excellent to Good**	**Above Average to Average**	**Below Average to Poor**	**Very Poor**
18–25 years	<93	94–110	111–131	>131
26–35 years	<92	93–110	111–129	>129
36–45 years	<96	97–112	113–132	>132
46–55 years	<101	102–118	119–132	>132
56–65 years	<103	104–118	119–135	>135
65+ years	<101	102–121	122–133	>133

Activity 2-5 Cooper 12-minute Run Test Results Chart

For biological females in yards

Age	Excellent	Above Average	Average	Below Average	Poor
20–29	>2950	2410 – 2950	1970 – 2410	1640 – 1970	<1640
30–39	>2730	2190 – 2730	1860 – 2190	1530 – 1860	<1530
40–49	>2520	2080 – 2520	1640 – 2080	1310 – 1640	<1310
50+	>2410	1860 – 2410	1530 – 1860	1200 – 1530	<1200

For biological males in yards

Age	Excellent	Above Average	Average	Below Average	Poor
20–29	>3060	2620 – 3060	2410 – 2620	1750 – 2410	<1750
30–39	>2950	2510 – 2950	2080 – 2510	1640 – 2080	<1640
40–49	>2730	2300 – 2730	1860 – 2300	1530 – 1860	<1530
50+	>2620	2190 – 2620	1750 – 2190	1420- 1750	<1420

For biological females in meters

Age	Excellent	Above Average	Average	Below Average	Poor
20–29	>2700	2200 – 2700	1800 – 2199	1500 – 1799	<1500
30–39	>2500	2000 – 2500	1700 – 1999	1400 – 1699	<1400
40–49	>2300	1900 – 2300	1500 – 1899	1200 – 1499	<1200
50+	>2200	1700 – 2200	1400 – 1699	1100 – 1399	<1100

For biological males in meters

Age	Excellent	Above Average	Average	Below Average	Poor
20–29	>2800	2400 – 2800	2200 – 2399	1600 – 2199	<1600
30–39	>2700	2300 – 2700	1900 – 2299	1500 – 1999	<1500
40–49	>2500	2100 – 2500	1700 – 2099	1400 – 1699	<1400
50+	>2400	2000 – 2400	1600 – 1999	1300 – 1599	<1300

Activity 2-6 Cooper 1.5-mile Run/Walk Test

The 1.5-mile run/walk test is recommended for those who are motivated, experienced in running, and in good condition before taking the test. Do not take the test unless you can already jog nonstop for 15 minutes. It is not recommended for the following people:

- Those failing the PAR-Q+
- Sedentary people older than 30 years of age
- Severely deconditioned people
- Those with joint problems
- Obese individuals

Sedentary individuals (especially those older than 30 years of age) should participate in a walking/running program for 1 to 2 months before taking the test. For those in hot or cold environments, do not take this test unless you have been exercising in these conditions.

Preparation

You will need the following:

- Stopwatch, watch, or clock with a second hand
- Oval running track
- Appropriate running shoes and clothing

Warm up for 5 to 10 minutes before the test.

Procedure

1. Complete a 1.5-mile distance in the shortest possible time. If outdoors, the test should be conducted in favorable weather conditions. Physically fit individuals can cover the distance either by running or jogging. Less fit individuals can run and jog, but may need to walk some of the time.
2. Attempt to keep a steady pace throughout the test.

3. When completed, record the time (minutes and seconds) it took to complete the 1.5-mile distance.
   Time to finish the 1.5-mile distance:
4. Visit this site to find your fitness rating:
   https://canadacollege.edu/fitnesscenter/assess-1-mile.php

Activity 2-7 Sit-and-Reach Test

Precautions

1. Warm up.
2. Stop the test if pain occurs.
3. Do not be competitive. This is a test to help assess your spine/back flexibility, not a game. Do not perform fast, jerky movements.
4. If any of the following apply, seek medical advice before performing tests:
   - You are presently suffering from acute back pain
   - You are currently receiving treatment for back pain
   - You have had a surgical operation on your back
   - A health-care professional told you to never exercise your back

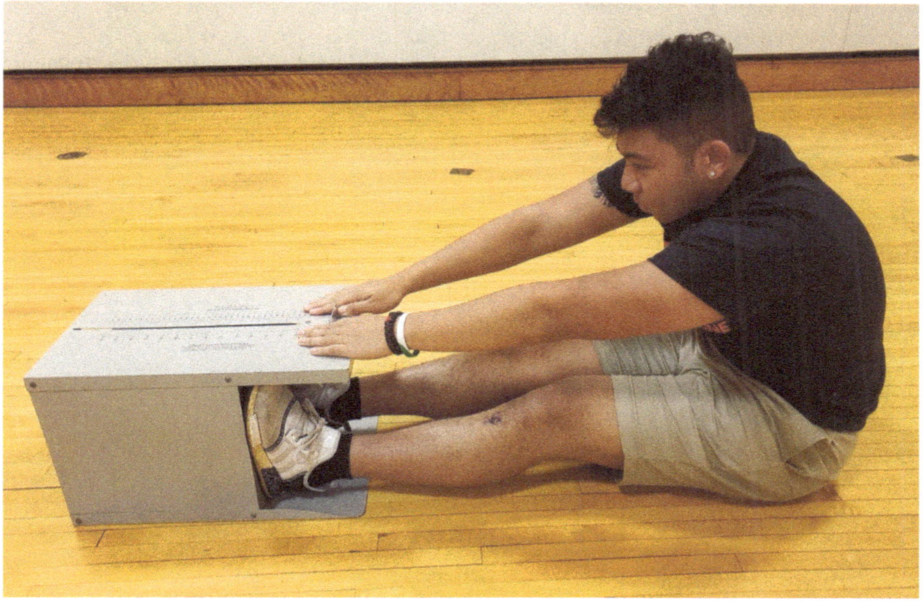

Procedure

Step 1: Sit on the floor with your legs straight, knees together, toes pointing upward toward the ceiling, and soles of your feet flat on the box.

Step 2: Keep hands flat on the box, with your thumbs by the movable ruler.

Step 3: Slowly stretch forward without bouncing or jerking. Move the ruler with your thumbs slowly and stop when tightness or discomfort occurs in the back or legs. Record the distance at the tip of the middle finger in centimeters (cm).

Step 4: Repeat this test two more times (three times total) and average the distance.

Below is normative data (cm) for the sit and reach test for biological males and biological females by age.

	AGE									
CATEGORY	**20–29**		**30–39**		**40–49**		**50–59**		**60–69**	
SEX	**M**	**F**	**M**	**F**	**M**	**F**	**M**	**F**	**M**	**F**
Excellent	40	41	38	41	35	38	35	39	33	35
Very Good	39	40	37	40	34	37	34	38	32	34
	34	37	33	36	29	34	28	33	25	31
Good	33	36	32	35	28	33	27	32	24	30
	30	33	28	32	24	30	24	30	20	27
Fair	29	32	27	31	23	29	23	29	19	26
	25	28	23	27	18	25	16	25	15	23
Needs improvement	24	27	22	26	17	24	15	24	14	22

M, biological male; F, biological female.
[a]Note: These norms are based on a sit-and-reach box in which the zero point is set at 26 cm. When using a box in which the zero point is set at 23 cm, subtract 3 cm from each value in this table.

Activity 2-8 Shoulder Flexibility Test

Precautions

- Briefly warm up with a few minutes of stretching.
- Avoid rapid or jerky movements during the test.

Procedure

Step 1: Bring the right hand around to the back of the neck.
Step 2: Bring the left hand around to the small of the back.
Step 3: Try to touch the fingertips of both hands behind the back.
Step 4: Have someone measure the distance between the fingertips.
Step 5: Do the test the other way, left hand to the back of the neck, right hand to the small of the back.
Step 6: Try to touch the fingertips of both hands behind the back.
Step 7: Have someone measure the distance between the fingertips.

Flexibility is rated as per the following:

Excellent: fingers overlap
Good: fingers touch
Average: fingers are less than 2 inches apart
Poor: fingers are more than 2 inches apart

Activity 2-9 Additional Lower Body Flexibility Tests

These additional tests can be used to evaluate an athlete's general lower body flexibility.

While performing the flexibility tests, the athlete may feel some discomfort due to the muscular stretch. This sensation is entirely normal, and the athlete's flexibility may be evaluated at the point of discomfort. However, keep in mind that while performing these flexibility tests, under no circumstances should the athlete experience any pain or abnormal sensations. If the athlete experiences pain or abnormal sensations, the flexibility test must stop immediately. After performing the flexibility tests, the athlete's muscles are considered "flexible" or "inflexible." For purposes of this activity, the term inflexible means that the athlete has the potential to increase the muscles' flexibility.

Iliopsoas and Rectus Femoris (Hip Flexor Muscles)

Directions:

- Have the athlete lie on their back on a table with their knees bent at a 90-degree angle over the edge.

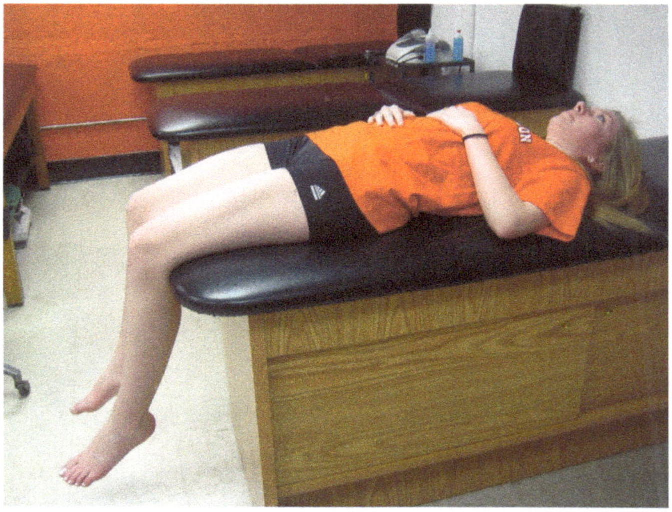

- Instruct the athlete to flex their hip and raise one leg up to their chest with their knee flexed.
- Tell the athlete to grasp their thigh and hold their leg with both hands in this position.
- Evaluate their flexibility.
- Repeat with the other leg.

Results:
While grasping their thigh:

- The athlete has flexible hip flexors if their opposite thigh remains flat on the table and their knee remains flexed.
- The athlete has an inflexible iliopsoas if their opposing hip flexes.
- The athlete has an inflexible rectus femoris if their opposing knee extends.
- The athlete has both an inflexible iliopsoas and an inflexible rectus femoris if both the opposing hip flexes and the knee extends simultaneously.

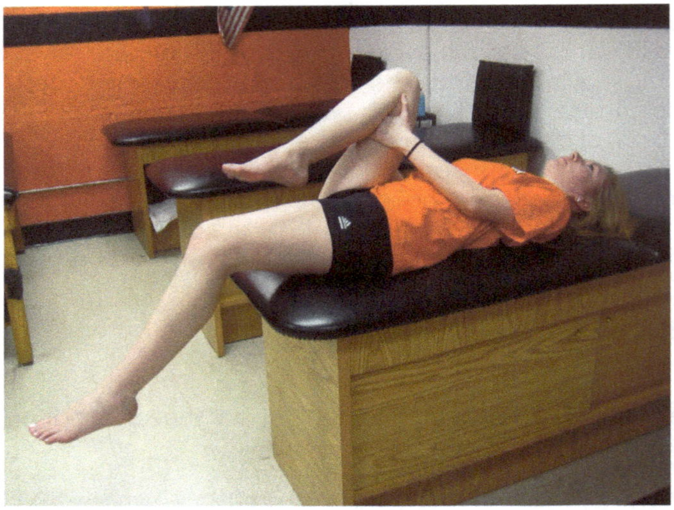

Vastus Medialis, Vastus Intermedius, Vastus Lateralis, and Rectus Femoris (Quadriceps Muscle Group)

Directions:

- Have the athlete lie on their stomach and relax their legs.

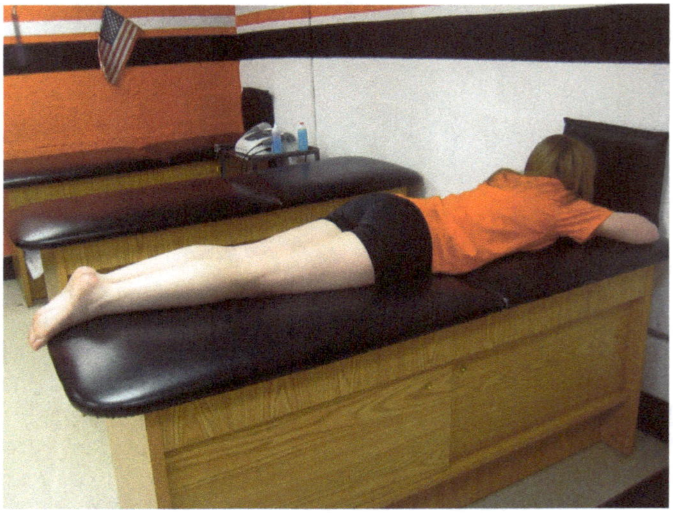

- Firmly grasp one ankle and passively flex their knee to the point where you feel resistance and the athlete feels a stretch.
- Evaluate their flexibility.
- Repeat with the other leg.

Results:

- The athlete has a flexible quadriceps muscle group if their heel touches their buttocks.

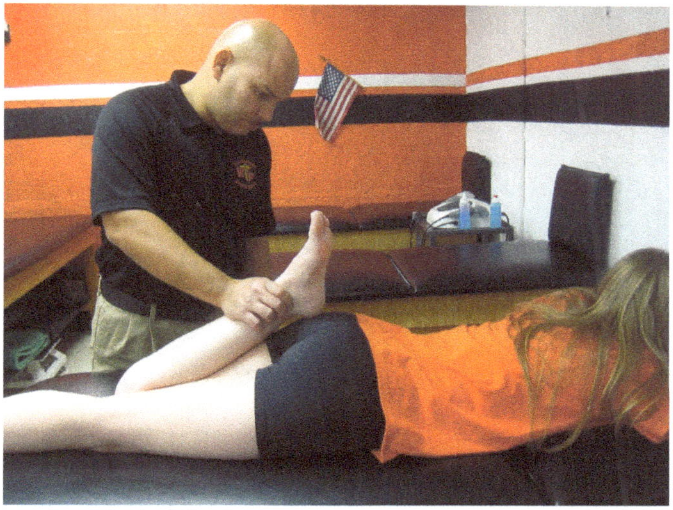

- The athlete has an inflexible quadriceps muscle group if their heel cannot touch their buttocks.

Semitendinosus, Semimembranosus, and Biceps Femoris (Hamstring Muscle Group)

Directions:

- Have the athlete sit in a "modified hurdler's position," with one leg extended and the other with the sole of the foot touching the opposite knee's medial side. The athlete's legs will appear like a forward or backward number 4.

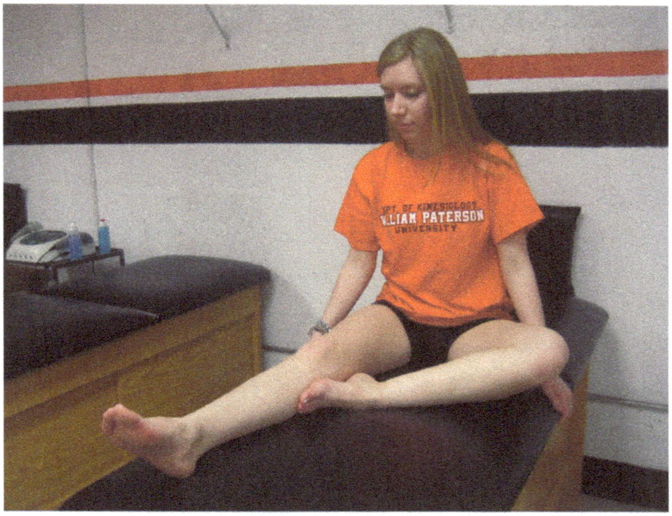

- Have the athlete reach forward toward the extended leg, in an attempt to rest their chest on their thigh and touch their toes.

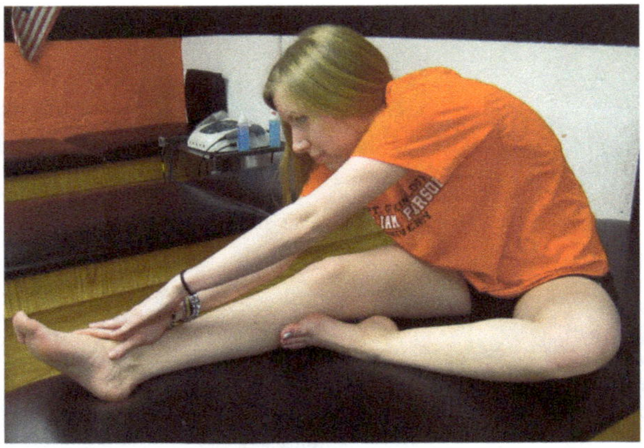

© Linda Gazzillo Diaz

- Evaluate their flexibility.
- Repeat with the other leg.

Results:

- The athlete has a flexible hamstring muscle group if she is able to place their chest to their thigh and/or touch their toes.
- The athlete has an inflexible hamstring muscle group if she is not able to place their chest to their thigh and/or touch their toes.*

*An athlete's upper or lower extremity length, not hamstring muscle group flexibility, may prevent them from touching their toes. If this is the case, then evaluate their hamstring muscle group flexibility by determining if they can bring their chest to rest upon their thigh.

Iliotibial Band

Directions:

- Have the athlete lie on their side on a table, with their hips and knees flexed to 90 degrees and relaxed.

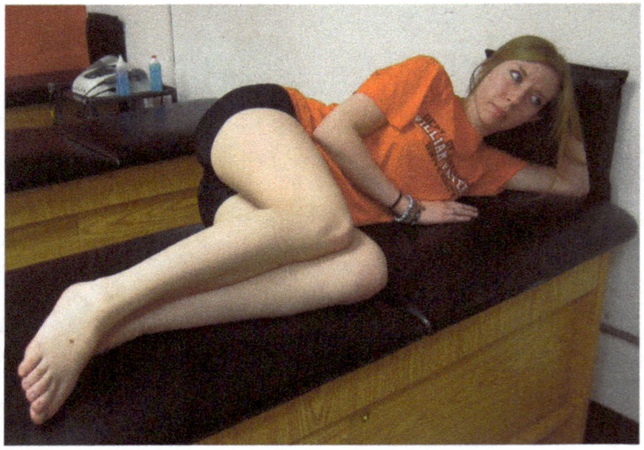

© Linda Gazzillo Diaz

- Stand by the table, facing the athlete's back.
- Grasp the athlete's upper ankle with one hand and stabilize their hip with your other hand.

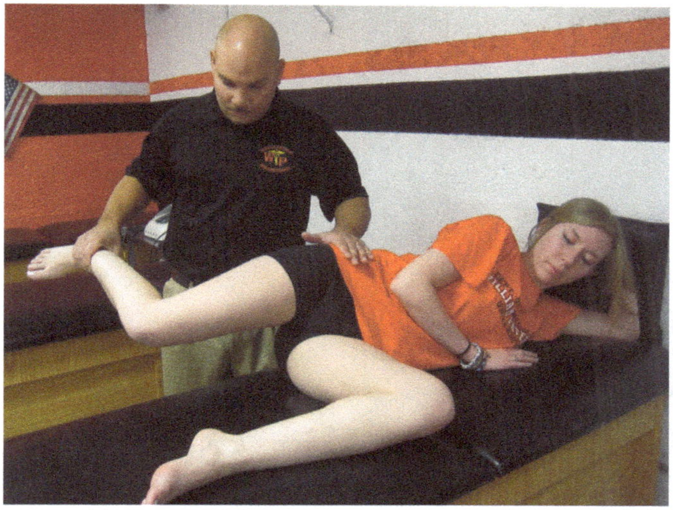

- Utilizing passive motion, slightly extend the athlete's hip, while the knee remains flexed, and the hip stabilized.
- Carefully allow their leg to drop.
- Evaluate their flexibility.
- Repeat with the other leg.

Results:

- The athlete has a flexible iliotibial band if, when the upper leg is dropped, it falls to the table.

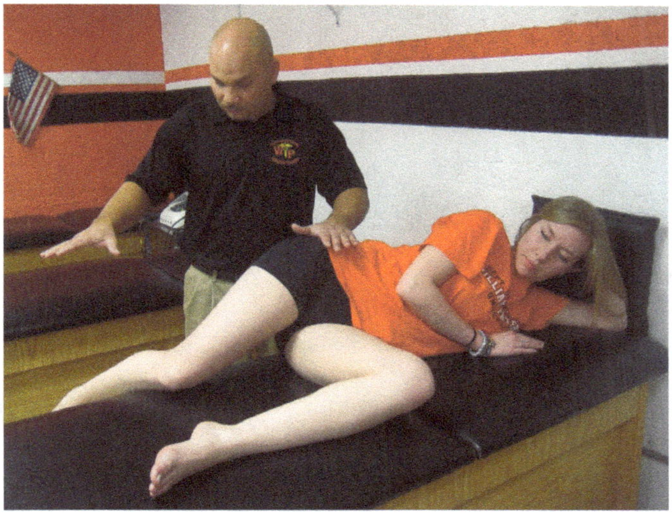

- The athlete has an inflexible iliotibial band if, when the upper leg is dropped, the leg does not fall to the table and remains suspended in air (abducted).

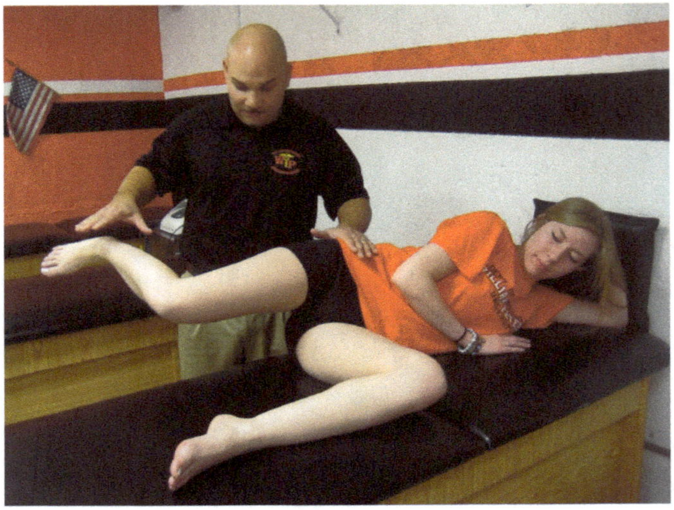

Gracilis and Adductor Muscle Group (Groin Muscles)

Directions:

- Have the athlete sit on the floor with the soles of their feet together and their knees bent in a "butterfly position."

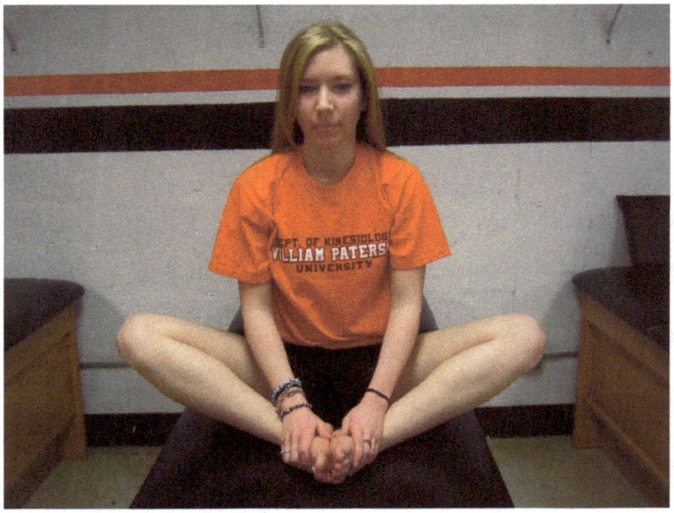

- Passively abduct their hips by slowly pushing their knees toward the floor until you feel resistance and the athlete feels a stretch.

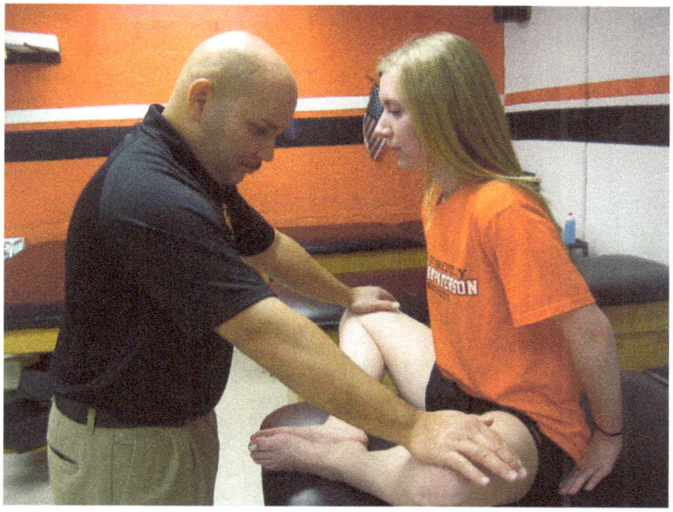

- Evaluate the flexibility of both legs.

Results:

- The athlete has flexible groin muscles if their knees can be moved to become parallel to the floor.
- The athlete has inflexible groin muscles if their knees cannot be moved to become parallel to floor.

Gastrocnemius and Soleus (Calf Muscles)

Directions:

- Have the athlete sit on a table with their legs straight and knees extended.

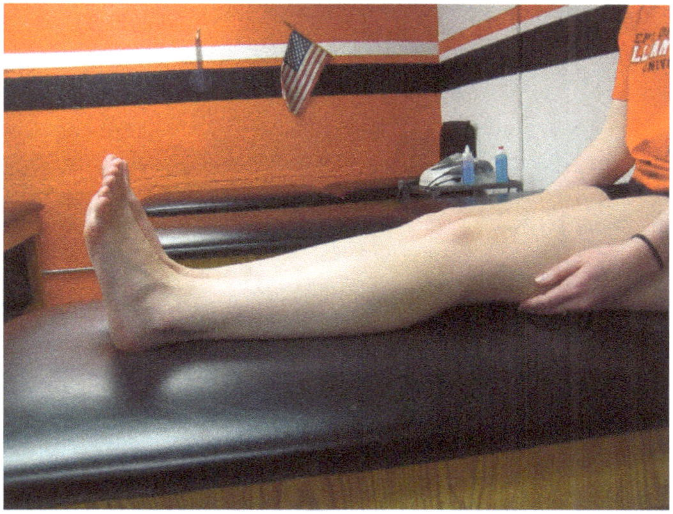

- Their ankles and feet should be in neutral positions, so it appears as if their ankles are at 90-degree angles.
- Stabilize their distal lower leg with one hand while grasping their foot with the other.
- Passively move their ankle so their toes are pointed toward their knees (dorsiflexion).

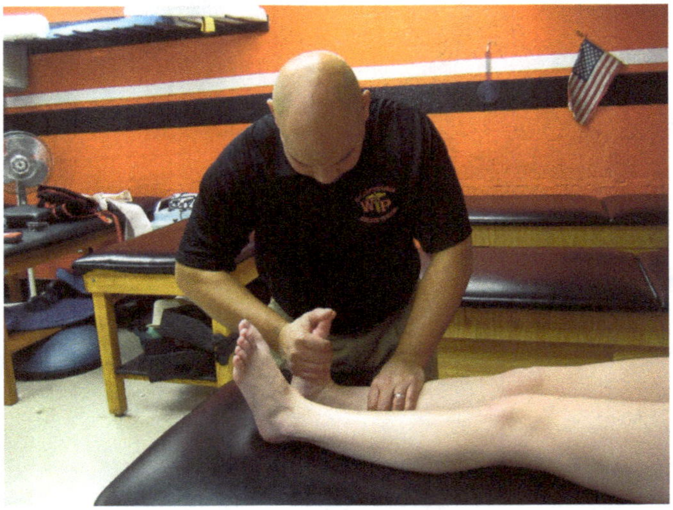

- Evaluate their flexibility.
- Repeat with the other ankle.

Results:

- The athlete has flexible calf muscles if their ankle can be passively moved into dorsiflexion approximately 15 degrees past the starting, neutral position.
- The athlete has inflexible calf muscles if their ankle cannot be passively moved into dorsiflexion approximately 15 degrees past the starting, neutral position, and/or if the athlete's knee flexes when the ankle is passively moved.

Activity 2-10 One-Repetition Maximum Test (1 RM)

The one-repetition maximum (1 RM) test for muscular strength is not recommended for older individuals and unconditioned individuals because of possible injury. The 1 RM test should be used only after several weeks of strength training. Muscular strength can be measured by the 1 RM test, which measures the maximum amount of weight that can be lifted one time.

Preparation

You will need the following:

- Barbell and various weights with collars
- One or two spotters for safety
- The bench press, shoulder press (military press), and arm curl are the most common methods for assessing muscular strength. Warm up by performing the selected lift to be used several times.

Procedure

- For the selected muscle group to be tested, choose a starting weight that you can lift without a great deal of stress. Then, gradually add weight until you reach the maximum weight that you can lift one time. Rest 2 to 3 minutes between each trial or new attempt to lift the new weight.
- If you can lift the weight more than once, add more weight until you reach a level of resistance that can be performed only once.
- Compute your strength score by dividing your 1 RM weight (in pounds) by your body weight (in pounds) and then multiply by 100.

$$\frac{\text{1 RM weight (lb)}}{\text{body weight (lb)}} \times 100 = \text{muscle strength score}$$

Please visit this website to assess your score:
https://www.topendsports.com/testing/tests/1rm-bench-press.htm

Activity 2-11 Hand Grip Strength Test

Preparation

You will need the following:

- Hand-held dynamometer
- Dry hands

Hand-held dynamometer

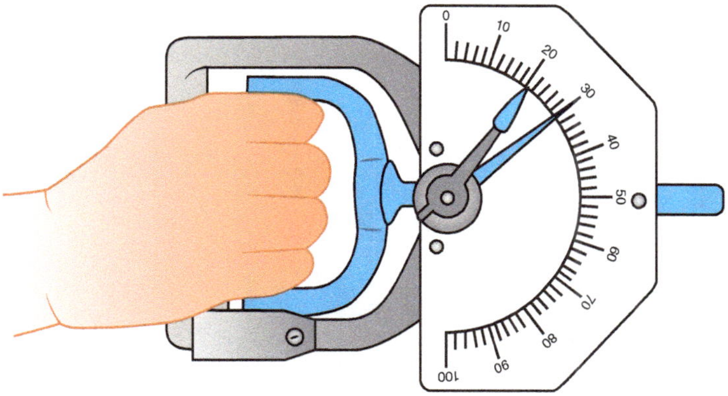

Procedure

- Adjust and comfortably place the dynamometer in the hand to be tested. The second joint of the hand should fit snugly under the handle, which is gripped between the fingers and the palm at the base of the thumb.
- Bend forward slightly, with the hand to be tested out in front of your body. Neither the hand nor the arm should be touching the body or any other object. The arm can be slightly bent.
- During the test, an all-out effort should be given for between 2 and 3 seconds. No swinging or pumping of the arm is allowed. The dial can face you.

- The score comes from the sum of both hands, based on the best of two to four trials each.
- See the following table for your fitness level.

Please visit the following site to assess your grip strength results:
https://www.topendsports.com/testing/tests/handgrip.htm

Activity 2-12 Push-up Test for Muscular Endurance

Preparation

- Use a large space on the floor, clear of obstructions.
- Warm up for 3 to 5 minutes before starting. Give yourself a couple of minutes to recover after warm-up before beginning the test.

Procedure

Biological Men

- Assume the standard position for a push-up, with the body rigid and straight, toes tucked under, and hands about shoulder-width apart and straight under the shoulders.
- Lower the body until the elbows reach 90. Some individuals prefer to place an object such as a paper cup beneath to touch.
- Return to the starting position with the arms fully extended.
- The most common error is not keeping the back straight and rigid throughout the entire push-up.
- Perform as many push-ups as you can without stopping.

Biological Women
Biological women should use the modified push-up position to assess their upper body endurance. The test is performed as follows:

- Directions are the same for biological women as for biological men, except biological women should perform the test with the knees remaining on the floor. Make sure that your hands are slightly ahead of your shoulders in the up position so that when you are in the down position, your hands are directly under the shoulders.
- Keep the back straight and rigid throughout the entire push-up.
- Perform as many push-ups as you can without stopping.

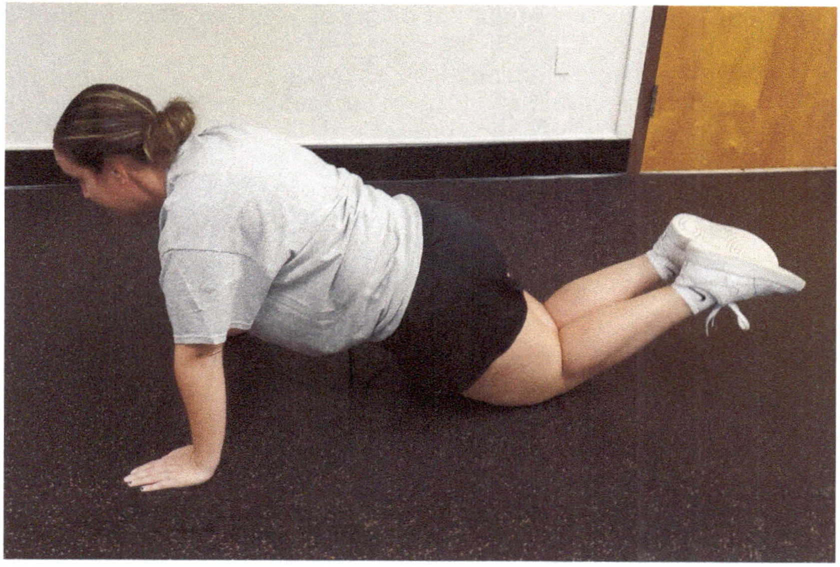

Please visit the following site to assess your results:
https://www.topendsports.com/testing/tests/home-pushup.htm

Activity 2-13 YMCA Bench-Press Test

The YMCA developed a bench-press test for muscular endurance, using a standardized weight. This test offers several advantages, but it discriminates against lighter individuals.

Preparation

You will need the following:

- Barbell with weights and collars to hold them in place
- For the test, men use an 80-pound barbell and women use a 35-pound barbell
- Another person to "spot" for you
- Flat bench
- Metronome set for 60 bpm (or some other cadence timing sound device)

Warm-up should include doing a few bench presses with a small amount of weight to practice bench pressing. Give yourself a couple of minutes to recover after warm-up before beginning the test.

Procedure

- Lie on the flat bench with your feet on the floor.
- Your spotter hands the barbell to you. The down position is the starting position (elbows flexed, hands shoulder-width apart, palms facing up).
- Press the barbell upward to fully extend (straighten) the elbows. After each extension, the barbell is returned to the original down position with the bar touching the chest. Do not bounce the bar on your chest. Do not arch your back.
- Keep up with the rhythm of the metronome—lift the barbell on one beat and lower it on the next. Your spotter counts the number of bench presses you perform (each time the barbell is in the down position); each click represents a movement up or down for 30 lifts per minute.

- Perform as many reps as you can without stopping, and keep with the rhythm. Stop the test when any of these occur:
  (1) you are unable to reach full extension of the elbows,
  (2) you are unable to keep up with the rhythm of the metronome, or
  (3) you are unable to do any more bench presses.

Please visit the following site to assess your results:
https://www.trainermetrics.com/fitness-assessment-calculations/bench-press-ymca/

Activity 2-14 YMCA Half Sit-up Test (Partial Curl-up Test)

Preparation

You will need the following:

- Ruler for measuring 3 inches
- Stopwatch, watch, or clock with a second hand
- Adhesive tape
- Metronome (or some other cadence timing sound device)

Sit on a mat or carpet with your knees bent 90 degrees (your feet must remain flat on the floor). Extend your arms so that both hands' longest fingertips touch a strip of tape placed on the floor perpendicular to the body. A second strip of tape is placed on the floor 3 inches toward the feet and parallel to the first. Alternatives to the two tape marks are a 3-inch-width piece of cardboard or two pieces of athletic tape (each is 1.5 inches and can be applied next to each other or a yardstick or similar piece of wood used for the mark nearest the feet).

- Warm-up should include a few sit-ups. Give yourself a couple of minutes to recover after warm-up before beginning the test.
- Set the metronome for 50 bpm.

Procedure

- While lying on the mat or carpet, the curl-up is done by raising your trunk (e.g., curling upward) with arms straight. Fingers slide along the floor until your longest fingertip of each hand touches the second strip of tape or object and then returns to the starting position. You then curl down so that your upper back touches the floor.
  Keep the 90-degree bend in your knees. Your feet should not be held down.
- Perform curl-ups to the rhythm of the metronome—curl up on one beat and down on the second beat.
- Perform as many curl-ups as you can without stopping and keep with the rhythm. Stop the test when either of these occurs:
  (1) You are unable to keep up with the rhythm of the metronome or
  (2) you are unable to do any more curl-ups.

At the end of the test, check your fingertip position. If the fingertips do not touch the near side of the line, your score is not accurate.

- See the following table for your fitness level.

Please visit the following site to assess your results:
https://exrx.net/Calculators/CurlUp

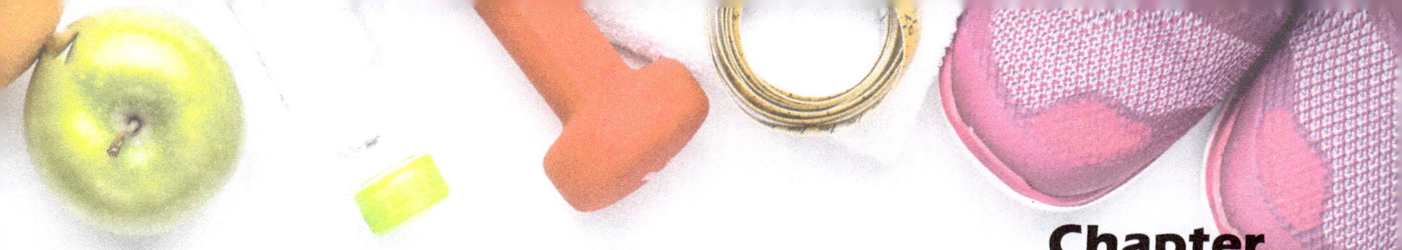

Chapter 3

Nutrition and Supplementation

Chapter Objectives

After you have read this chapter, you will be able to understand:

- The roles of macronutrients and micronutrients in the body.
- The illnesses and diseases that can overcome an individual who does not consume the proper macronutrients.
- The most commonly deficient minerals in the body.
- The various considerations when beginning a weight management program.
- Eating disorders, including the signs, symptoms, and effects.
- What constitutes the female athlete triad.
- The purpose of supplements and nutritional ergogenic aids.

The old saying goes "you are what you eat". This saying is very true. The variety and quantity of food we eat not only physically shapes our bodies, but also affects the possibility of acquiring a serious illness or disease. An individual who wishes to become healthy, increase performance, and reduce possibility of illness and disease has to participate in a wellness, exercise, and fitness program in order to achieve their goals. However, an integral component of this program includes the individual undertaking a proper nutritional program. When an individual consumes proper **nutrients**, their bodily functions are optimal, and a healthy lifestyle is facilitated. Nutrients also assist in preventing disease, which help maintain the individual's wellness. Proper nutrients incorporated into an individual's daily dietary plan is beneficial to promote a long, healthy, and good quality of life.

Nutrients

Our bodies require a variety of nutrients in order to ensure optimal function. These nutrients include macronutrients and micronutrients. Macronutrients include the required basic food components in our everyday **diet**. These macronutrients are carbohydrates, fats, proteins, and water. Vitamins and minerals are micronutrients, which are substances found in the macronutrients. Unlike macronutrients, our bodies do not require micronutrients in large quantities. Micronutrients are considered essential nutrients since our bodies cannot produce them. Consequently, eating a variety of food containing micronutrients is imperative. Both macro- and micronutrients are key nutritional components essential to keep our bodies healthy.

Macronutrients

The four macronutrients include carbohydrates, fats, proteins, and water. Each macronutrient contributes to facilitate optimal bodily function.

Carbohydrates

Carbohydrates (CHO) are the body's main energy source. Athletes need CHO for their bodies to produce enough energy to participate in ADLs and activities such as running, bicycling, and other endurance-type exercises. Consuming enough quality CHO promotes adequate energy, which can maximize an athlete's performance.

CHO are made of carbon, hydrogen, and oxygen, along with water. Two forms of CHO, complex and simple CHO, are broken down by the body to form glucose. Glucose is also known as "blood sugar", which is the body's primary energy source. The liver stores glucose for future energy needs in the form of glycogen. Complex CHO are starches such as pasta, brown rice, grains, **legumes**, vegetables, and fruits. Simple CHO include white rice and bread, processed foods, desserts, and candy. Complex CHO are better to eat than simple CHO since they are healthier and contain fiber (fiber is discussed later in this chapter). Some simple CHO do not have any nutritional value nor vitamins or minerals. These simple CHO are considered "empty calories". Likewise, processed simple CHO, such as plain bagels, white bread, and white potatoes including french fries, have a drastic negative effect on blood sugar levels. Complex CHO take longer for the body to break down than simple CHO, and do not cause as much of a rapid increase in **insulin** as simple CHO does. The continual rapid increase in blood sugar can predispose an athlete to acquire **Type II diabetes**.

Each CHO has its own glycemic index. Glycemic index is utilized to determine the best CHO choices for the individual, so blood sugar levels are not drastically and suddenly increased. A food with a glycemic index of 70 or higher is considered a high glycemic index food, 56 to 69 is considered a medium glycemic index food, and 55 or below is low glycemic index food (Dansinger, 2021). Individuals should attempt to include low glycemic index CHO into their diet, since the low glycemic CHO are better for the individual's body and overall health.

Typically, complex CHO, especially those made of whole grains, have a low glycemic index. Low glycemic index foods have proved to decrease the potential of heart disease. (**Table 3-1**).

Glycemic load is another measurement utilized when referring to CHO and its effect on raising blood sugar levels. The higher the glycemic load, the greater detrimental effect the food has on blood sugar and insulin levels. A glycemic load of 20 or higher should be avoided, because it raises blood sugar levels quickly. Foods with a glycemic load of 10 or less are beneficial to consume. To calculate the glycemic load multiply the glycemic index by the grams of CHO in the food, and then divide this number by 100. The resultant figure categorizes the CHO food with a glycemic load. Examples of foods and beverages with a glycemic load of 10 and under (per serving) include the following: an apple, one slice of whole wheat bread, couscous, skim milk, and tomato juice. Examples of foods and beverages with a glycemic load of 20 and over (per serving) include the following: raisins, a frozen, white bagel, instant oatmeal, white rice, and apple juice.

Cholesterol is a fat-like substance that is made by the body, found in the body's cell walls, and carried through the blood. Cholesterol assists the body in digestion, as well as hormone and vitamin D production (U.S. National Library of Medicine, 2020). Although the body produces adequate amounts of cholesterol, many foods contain cholesterol, including egg yolks, meat, seafood, and whole milk products. If an individual eats a significant amount of high cholesterol foods, cholesterol will build up in the arteries. Along with the cholesterol, calcium, fat, and other substances build up inside the arterial walls. This substance is called plaque. Over time, the inside of the artery decreases in size due to the increasing amount of plaque, which results in reduced blood flow. This condition is called atherosclerosis (**Figure 3-1**). When atherosclerosis occurs in the **coronary arteries**, the heart does not get adequate amounts of oxygen. As a result, the individual may experience a heart attack.

Lipoproteins carry cholesterol through the blood. Low-density lipoproteins (LDL) and high-density lipoproteins (HDL) are two predominant lipoproteins. The LDL are the "bad" cholesterol, which build up in the bloodstream, stick to the arterial walls, and cause heart disease. HDL are the "good" cholesterol that help decrease the LDL in the blood. High glycemic index foods increase **triglycerides** while decreasing the body's HDL (U.S. National Library of Medicine, 2020). High triglycerides and low HDL cholesterol put an individual at risk for heart disease.

Whether an individual consumes complex or simple CHO, if excessive CHO are ingested and not utilized for energy during exercise, then CHO eventually is converted into fat. Therefore, an individual cannot solely eat CHO without exercising daily. One gram of CHO has only 4 calories. The recommended daily allowance (RDA) for CHO for adult athletes is approximately 45% to 65% of total caloric intake (Mayo Clinic, 2020). Complex CHO starches and any natural sugar simple CHO should comprise most of an individual's diet. Natural sugar simple CHO foods include milk, fruits, and vegetables.

Dietary fiber is another CHO. Dietary fiber is necessary for the individual's diet, but it is different than complex and simple CHO. Dietary fiber is not broken down and utilized as an energy source. However, it is imperative in assisting with digestion, preventing constipation, helping to make an individual feel full when eating, and helping them maintain an optimal

Table 3-1 Glycemic index and glycemic load of common foods

Food Glycemic Index (Glucose = 100)		Glycemic Index (White Bread = 100)	Glycemic Index Category*	Serving Size (g)	g CHO/ Serving	Glycemic Load
White bread, Wonder	73±2	105±3	High	30	14	10
White rice, boiled	64±7	91±9	High	150	36	23
Couscous	65±4	93±6	High	150	35	23
Gatorade	78±13	111	High	250 mL	15	12
Ice cream	61±7	87±10	High	50	13	8
Sweet potato	61±7	87±10	High	150	28	17
Baked potato, russet	85±12	121±16	High	150	30	26
Cranberry juice cocktail	68±3	97	High	250 mL	36	24
Grapenuts	71±4	102±6	High	30	21	15
Cornflakes	81±3	116±5	High	30	26	21
Blueberry muffin	59	84±8	High	57	29	17
Power bar	56 ±3	79±4	Med	65	42	24
Honey	55±5	78±7	Med	25	18	10
White rice, long grain	56 ±2	80±3	Med	150	41	23
Coca-Cola	58±5	83±7	Med	250 mL	26	16
Sweet corn	54 ±4	78±6	Med	80	17	9
Carrot	47±16	68±23	Med	80	6	3
New potato	57±7	81±10	Med	150	21	12
Banana	52±4	74±5	Med	120	24	12
Orange juice	50±4	71±5	Med	250 mL	26	13
Chickpeas	28 ±6	39±8	Low	150	30	8
Kidney beans	28±4	39±6	Low	150	25	7
Xylitol	8±1	11±1	Low	10	10	1
Lentils	29±1	41±1	Low	150	18	5
Chocolate cake, frosted	38±3	54	Low	111	52	20

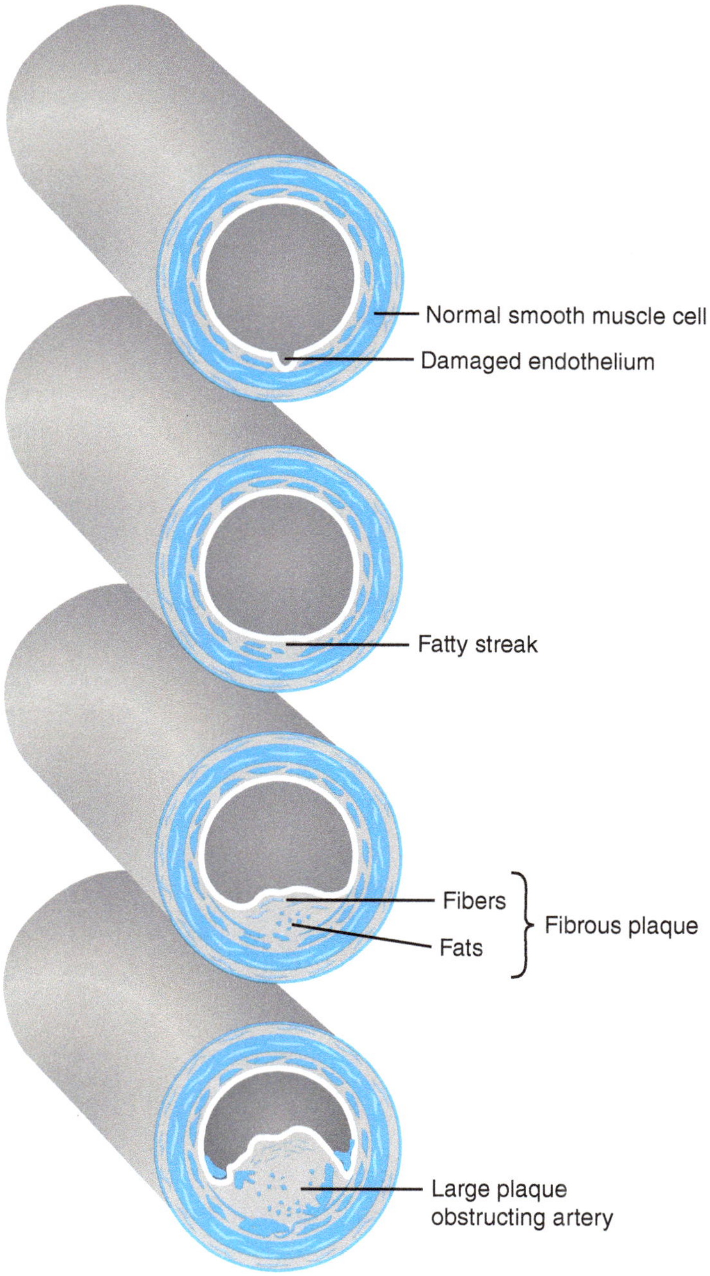

Figure 3-1 Plaque buildup in arteries is called atherosclerosis.

weight. Adequate dietary fiber has also been linked to a decrease in the potential of acquiring Type 2 diabetes, heart disease, constipation, and diverticulitis, or large intestine inflammation. Fiber is classified as soluble and insoluble. Soluble fiber helps slow down digestion, assists in moving food through the digestive system, and assists in lowering cholesterol (MayoClinic, 2021). Foods containing a considerable amount of soluble fiber include legumes, lima beans, peas, lentils, beans, broccoli, nuts, almonds, sunflower seeds, whole-grain cereal, oatmeal, rye and pumpernickel breads, prunes, oranges, apples, and pears. Foods that contain insoluble fiber include carrots, celery, corn, asparagus, whole grain pasta, bread, apples, grapes, and pears (**Table 3-2**). Individuals can also take fiber supplements, which come in forms such as powders mixed with liquid, gummy chews, or tablets. Some fiber supplements have added vitamins and minerals such as vitamin D, vitamin B complex, and calcium. Children ages 1 to 18 years require 14 to 31 grams of fiber per day depending on age and gender. Women under the age of 50 years should consume approximately 25 to 28 grams of fiber per day, while men under the age of 50 years tend to need more fiber than women and should consume 31 to 34

Table 3-2 Sources of fiber

The National Academy of Sciences' Institute of Medicine gives the following daily total fiber recommendations for adults:

	Age 50 and younger	**Age 51 and older**
Men	38 grams	30 grams
Women	25 grams	21 grams

Foods with Soluble and Insoluble Fiber

Soluble Fiber	***Insoluble Fiber***
• Apples	• Whole grain
• Oranges	• Whole wheat breads
• Pears	• Barley
• Peaches	• Brown rice
• Grapes	• Bulgur
• Prunes	• Whole-grain breakfast cereals
• Blueberries	• Wheat bran
• Strawberries	• Seeds
• Seeds and Nuts	• Vegetables:
• Oat bran	• Carrots
• Dried beans	• Cucumbers
• Oatmeal	• Zucchini
• Barley	• Celery
• Rye	• Tomatoes
• Vegetables	

Foods with High Fiber

Vegetables Serving Size Total fiber (grams)	***Fruits Serving Size Total fiber (grams)***	***Legumes, Nuts & Seeds Serving Size Total Fiber (grams)***	***Grains, Cereal & Pasta Serving Size Total Fiber (grams)***
Peas 1 cup 8.8	Apple, with skin 1 medium 4.4	Cashews 18 nuts 0.9	Bread, mixed grain 1 slice 1.7
Potato, baked with skin 1 medium 4.4	Apricots, dried 10 halves 2.6	Peanuts 28 nuts 2.3	Bread, whole-wheat 1 slice 1.9
Corn 1 cup 4.2	Raisins 1.5 ounce box 1.6	Pistachio nuts 47 nuts 2.9	Bread, rye 1 slice 1.9
Popcorn, air-popped 3 cups 3.6	Orange 1 medium 3.1	Almonds 24 nuts 3.3	Oatmeal 1 cup 4.0
Tomato paste 1/4 cup 3.0	Peaches, dried 3 halves 3.2	Baked beans, canned 1 cup 10.4	Bran flakes 3/4 cup 5.1
Carrot 1 medium 2.0	Blueberries 1 cup 3.5	Lima beans 1 cup 13.2	Spaghetti, whole-wheat 1 cup 6.3
Pear 1 medium 5.1	Pear 1 medium 5.1	Black beans 1 cup 15.0 Lentils 1 cup 15.6	

Data from Institute of Medicine, Food and Nutrition Board. Dietary Reference Intakes for Energy, Carbohydrate, Fiber, Fat, Fatty Acids, Cholesterol, Protein, and Amino Acids. © 2005 by the National Academy of Sciences, National Academies Press, Washington, DC.; U.S. Department of Agriculture, Agricultural Research Service. USDA National Nutrient Database for Standard Reference, Release 25.2012.

grams per day. Adults over 50 years old require less fiber than adults under 50 years old, with only 22 grams for women and 28 grams for men. (U.S. Department of Agriculture and U.S. Department of Health and Human Services, 2020).

Fats

Fat in the body serves a variety of purposes. Fat helps insulate and cushion the body's organs. It is utilized as an energy source when glycogen is not available. Fat assists fat soluble vitamins to dissolve in the body. It also assists in hormone production. At 9 calories per gram, fat is the densest macronutrient. Although fat has benefits, too much fat in the diet can prove to be harmful and should only comprise approximately 25% to 35% of nutrient intake per day. For the average adult on a 2,000-calorie diet, approximately 56 grams to 77 grams of fat per day is sufficient. Excess intake has shown to increase the chance of an individual acquiring Type 2 diabetes, heart disease, and cancer. Individuals who regularly consume an excessive amount of fat are predisposed to becoming obese as well as have high LDL cholesterol levels.

Certain types of fat cause adverse conditions, illnesses, and diseases. Two detrimental fats are classified as saturated and trans fat. Saturated fat is solid at room temperature. Examples of saturated fat foods include animal fats, beef, lard, butter, whole milk products, avocados, and coconut. In excess, these fats increase LDL cholesterol, which increases the likelihood that an individual will acquire heart disease. Trans fat sources are also found in saturated foods, but are also created during food processing. Trans fats are found in cooking oil, butter, margarine, animal meats such as beef and pork, fast food such as French fries, and frozen food such as pizzas, cereals, potato chips, cookies, cakes, and candy. Trans fats can cause similar adverse conditions as saturated fats, which include a decrease in HDL cholesterol and an increase in LDL cholesterol. These effects can precipitate heart disease. Therefore, individuals should limit or even avoid both saturated and trans fats in their diet.

Not all fat is bad, however. Some fats are healthier than others and can promote a healthier diet. The healthier fats are classified as monounsaturated and polyunsaturated fats **(Table 3-3)**. These fats are liquid at room temperature and include oils such as olive, vegetable, canola, and sunflower oil. Monounsaturated fats can improve cholesterol levels, which helps decrease the chance of an individual acquiring heart disease. Monounsaturated fats also assist in regulating blood sugar levels, especially for an individual with Type 2 diabetes. Polyunsaturated fats are

Table 3-3 Fat content of various food

Food Item	Serving Size	Total Fat (grams)	Saturated Fat (grams)	Monounsaturated Fat (grams)	Polyunsaturated Fat (grams)
Grains					
Oatmeal, dry	1/2 cup	2.5	0.5	1.0	1.0
English muffin	1 muffin	1	0.1	0.2	0.5
Pasta, cooked	1 cup	0.9	0.1	0.1	0.4
Brown rice	1 cup	1.8	0.4	0.6	0.6
Whole wheat bread 1 slice	1.2	0.3	0.5	0.3	
Whole wheat pita	1 pita (61/2")	1.7	0.3	0.2	0.7
Blueberry muffin, made from a mix	1 muffin	6.2	1.2	1.5	3.1
Biscuit	1.2 oz	4.6	0.9	2.8	0.2
Fruits/Vegetables					
Pear	1 medium	1	<0.1	0.1	0.2
Orange	1 medium	0	0	0	0
Watermelon	1 cup	0.7	0.1	0.2	0.2
Banana	1 medium	0.5	0.2	<0.1	0.1

Food Item	Serving Size	Total Fat (grams)	Saturated Fat (grams)	Monounsaturated Fat (grams)	Polyunsaturated Fat (grams)
Spinach, raw	1/2 cup	0	0	0	0
Broccoli, cooked	1/2 cup	0.1	<0.1	<0.1	<0.1
Carrots, cooked	1/2 cup	0.1	<0.1	<0.1	<0.1
Avocado	1 medium	27	5.3	14.8	4.5
Milk/Alternative					
Skim milk	8 oz	0.5	0.4	0.2	<0.1
1% milk	8 oz	2.6	1.6	0.7	0.1
2% milk	8 oz	4.7	2.9	1.4	0.2
Whole milk	8 oz	8	5.1	2.4	0.3
Cottage cheese, 2%	1/4 cup	4.4	2.8	1.2	0.1
Swiss cheese	1 oz	8	5.0	2.1	0.3
Soy milk	8 oz	5	0.5	1.0	3.0
Meat and Beans/Alternative					
Ground beef, lean	3 oz	13.2	5.2	5.8	0.4
Chicken with skin	3 oz	9	2.4	3.4	1.9
Chicken without skin	3 oz	3.1	0.9	1.1	0.7
Turkey, white meat, without skin	3 oz	3	1.0	0.6	0.9
Turkey, dark meat, without skin	3 oz	6	2.2	1.5	2.0
Pork chop	3 oz	6.9	2.5	3.1	0.5
Salmon, pink	3 oz	4	1.0	0.8	0.6
Orange roughly	3 oz	1	<0.1	0.5	<0.1
Veggie burger	1 patty	0.5	0.1	0.3	0.2
Almonds	1 oz	15	1.1	9.5	3.6
Oils					
Margarine, stick	1 T	11	2.1	5.2	3.2
Butter	1 T	12	7.2	3.3	0.4
Olive oil	1 T	14	1.8	9.9	1.1
Salad dressing, ranch	2 T	18	2.5	NA	NA
Salad dressing, reduced calorie ranch	2 T	5	0.4	NA	NA

classified as either Omega-6 or Omega-3 polyunsaturated fats. Omega-6 polyunsaturated fats include oils such as soybean, corn, and safflower oil. Omega-3 polyunsaturated fats include fish such as salmon and trout, walnuts, flaxseed, and oils such as soybean and canola oil. Both Omega-6 and Omega-3 polyunsaturated fats provide the essential fatty acids the body needs to function. Polyunsaturated fats can decrease the possibility of developing Type 2 diabetes and high blood pressure. Omega-3 polyunsaturated fats can possibly decrease the risk of coronary artery disease. Educate your clients to consume monounsaturated and polyunsaturated fats instead of saturated and trans fats within their diet whenever possible.

In recent years, a high-fat and low-CHO diet, otherwise known as a ketogenic diet (keto diet), has become popular. The purpose of this diet is to put the body in ketosis, which is when the body burns fat instead of CHO. Studies have shown that ketogenic diets have been beneficial in improving glycemic control and insulin sensitivity for Type 2 diabetics (Saslow et al., 2017), treating obesity (Ludwig, 2020), decreases in triglycerides, increases in HDL, and weight loss in the short term (Batch et al., 2020). However, some negative effects, such as increased LDL, could cause cardiovascular issues. Unfortunately, research on the detrimental and long-term effects on ketogenic diets is limited (Batch et al., 2020; Ludwig, 2020). Consequently, individuals who wish to consume a ketogenic diet should first have a thorough discussion with their physician regarding the diet and how it relates to their current health.

Proteins

Proteins are called the "building blocks" of the body. Proteins are a component of almost every part of the body including the organs, tissues, and cells. They function to repair cells and tissues, and assist in growth and development. After proteins are ingested, they are digested and broken down into amino acids. Twenty amino acids exist which are classified as essential, nonessential, and conditional amino acids (Medline Plus, 2019). Nine essential amino acids are necessary for proper body function. These amino acids are not produced by the body and must be supplied by daily food intake. Nonessential amino acids are created in the body by protein and essential amino acid breakdown. Consequently, unlike essential amino acids, nonessential amino acids are plentiful in the body. Conditional amino acids are supplied by protein-rich food, and are necessary in higher than normal quantities when an individual is experiencing illness and/or stress.

Adults need approximately 10% to 35% of protein in their daily diet (MedlinePlus, 2019). Endurance athletes and body builders may need a greater amount of daily protein due to the utilization, breakdown, and repair of muscle tissue **(Table 3-4)**. Most often these athletes consume enough protein in their diet, whereas protein supplements are not necessary. Proteins contain 4 calories per gram, which is the same as CHO. Good sources of proteins and amino acids include meat, fish and shellfish, milk products, eggs, nuts (kidney, black, garbanzo, pinto beans, peanuts, walnuts, and almonds), legumes, and fortified soy products (U.S. Department

Table 3-4 Daily protein recommendations

Type of Athlete	Daily Grams of Protein/ Kilogram Body Weight	Percentage of Total Calories Contributed by Protein
Sedentary individual	0.8g/kg	12 – 15%
Strength athlete	1.4 – 2.0 g/kg	15 – 20%
Endurance athlete	1.2 – 2.0g/kg	12 – 18%
Team sport athlete	1.2 – 1.6 g/kg	12 – 16%
Weight gain/loss	1.6 – 2.0 g/kg	16 – 20%

of Agriculture and U.S. Department of Health and Human Services, 2020) (See https://www.nal.usda.gov/sites/www.nal.usda.gov/files/protein.pdf for additional sources of protein.) An individual should be careful not to eat excess meat or eggs, since meat contains a large quantity of fat and egg yolks are high in cholesterol. Instead, individuals should choose leaner cuts of red meat, pork, or chicken, and trim off excess fat, to obtain an appropriate amount of protein while limiting the amount of fat from these sources. An individual who chooses to eat egg whites instead of the entire egg including the yolk will take in beneficial protein without cholesterol. Vegetarians, also called vegans, may not get enough of essential proteins since they do not eat meat, fish, and other animal products (Mariotti & Gardner, 2019). They may need to take protein supplements in liquid, gel, powder, or bar form. Vegetarians must consume a variety of plant-type proteins to supply the body with enough essential amino acids.

Protein is a crucial macronutrient, which promotes an individual's health. Proteins assist with tissue and cell repair, facilitate body growth and development, and maintain a properly working immune system. Like high-fat low-CHO diets, some individuals choose to consume a high-protein low-CHO diet. This diet requires the individual to consume 30 to 50 percent of total calories from protein. Individuals who consume a greater percentage of protein with reduced CHO have lost weight more rapidly in the short term (6 to 12 months) than individuals eating the recommended daily percent of CHO. Larger quantities of protein in the diet as compared to CHO helps curb appetite and improves triglyceride levels. Although it seems that this type of diet is beneficial, individuals who have kidney disease may exacerbate their condition due to the demands on the kidneys to rid the body of protein. Also, a high-protein diet may predispose an individual to cardiovascular disease, and nutritional deficiencies (Zeratsky, 2020). As with high-fat, low-CHO diets, more research must be performed to validate the short- and long-term effects of high-protein low-CHO diets.

Since athletes typically consume enough daily protein, a severe protein deficiency, called kwashiorkor, is rare for this population. Most cases of kwashiorkor occur to infants and children in poverty-stricken countries where their inhabitants do not have access to adequate protein (Benjamin & Lappin, 2021). In the United States, it is suspected that almost half of the elderly nursing home inhabitants are protein deficient (Kaneshiro & Zieve, 2020). If an individual has a protein deficiency, the signs and symptoms of illness include, but are not limited to, fatigue, skin pigmentation, a decrease in muscle mass, a distended abdomen, diarrhea, swelling, rash, and irritability. If you suspect an individual has a protein deficiency, refer them to a physician for a full physical exam and blood tests.

In some cases individuals consume excess daily protein, often in the form of bars, shakes, and powders. Many people believe that since protein helps repair muscles and assists in growth and development, consuming excess protein will create even more muscle. In reality, an excessively high protein diet causes the kidneys to work harder than they should to excrete waste, which can result in kidney damage. Likewise, high protein diets may also contain high amounts of fat, which can cause illnesses or diseases previously mentioned. Although protein is an important nutrient to incorporate in your athlete's daily diet, always educate them about the consequences of excess protein intake.

Water

Water is a very important macronutrient that comprises approximately 60% of body weight. It is crucial for body organ and cellular functions. Water dissolves minerals and other nutrients in the body so they can be utilized. Water prevents constipation, alleviates heat from the body via perspiration, flushes out waste products from the kidney and liver, lubricates joints, and moistens tissues. Water is vital for proper body functioning. Consequently, without water the body can only sustain itself for approximately 3 days.

Individuals must drink plenty of water each day in order for the body to function properly. According to the United States Anti-Doping Agency (USADA) (2021), when an individual is thirsty, they have already lost approximately 2% of their body weight or more. This water weight loss can detrimentally affect an individual's performance. The amount of water an individual drinks per day varies, and is dependent on the individual's age, health, and activity level. According to the National Academies of Sciences, Engineering, and Medicine's "Dietary Reference Intakes for Water, Potassium, Sodium, Chloride, and Sulfate" (2005), the standard daily water consumption is at least 15.5 cups (3.7 liters) for men and 11.5 cups (2.7 liters) per women. This consumption includes both water, beverages containing water, and food. Food and drinks with high water content include milk, soup, leafy green lettuce, watermelon, cantaloupe, grapefruit, strawberries, tomatoes, cucumbers, carrots, celery, and broccoli. Many of these foods have other nutritional benefits, including preventing illnesses and diseases. Keep in mind that fluids containing **caffeine** are not as beneficial compared to decaffeinated drinks because caffeine is a diuretic, and the individual may become dehydrated.

Many individuals choose to consume electrolyte (sports) drinks instead of water. Electrolyte drinks have the following functions: electrolyte replacement, hydration, prevent dehydration, facilitate post-exercise recovery, and supply energy (Orrù et al., 2018). Electrolyte drinks are comprised of water, electrolytes, such as sodium, chloride, and potassium, CHO, sweetener, and flavoring. Some electrolyte drinks include caffeine, which should be avoided before, during, and immediately after exercise. Likewise, children should avoid these caffeinated sports drinks entirely due to potential health risks (Pound et al., 2017). Some electrolyte drinks contain a large quantity of CHO and simple sugars which provide energy. However, when an electrolyte drink is composed of a large quantity of CHO and the athlete drinks it the body focuses on breaking down the CHO prior to delivering the water to the body. This process results in delayed hydration. Many of the sports drinks that have added sugar have a very high glycemic index. Consequently upon consumption, blood sugar fluctuations and insulin spikes will result.

Some companies make lower CHO electrolyte drinks with only 6 to 8 percent CHO, which is optimal (USADA, 2021). Many electrolyte drinks are sweetened with sucralose, aspartame, stevia, or erythritol instead of sugar. These drinks may be a better choice for some individuals. For example, individuals who are diabetic and/or overweight can gain benefits of these sugar-free electrolyte drinks without ingesting excess and sugar and calories. Children can drink these sugar-free electrolytes without consuming empty calories. However, keep in mind that studies have shown that children who participate in normal play and physical activity do not benefit much from sports drinks (Pound et al., 2017). Regardless, the water and electrolyte content in these drinks is certainly beneficial for competitive athletes.

An individual knows they are properly hydrated if they are urinating frequently and the urine is a light yellow to clear color. If their urine is dark yellow and has a foul odor, then the individual is dehydrated. Some vitamins and supplements turn an individual's urine a dark yellow. Therefore, you will have to discuss with the individual what they are consuming to determine if the individual is truly dehydrated. Other signs and symptoms of dehydration include dry mouth, thirst, fatigue, headache, lack of or no sweating, constipation, rapid breathing and heart rate, and low blood pressure. If the individual experiences sign and symptoms of dehydration, they need to hydrate immediately. If it appears that their body is not readily responding to hydration attempts or is experiencing shock, call 911 since the individual is in a life-threatening situation.

When exercising, individuals must always have water, decaffeinated drinks containing water, or electrolyte drinks on hand to replenish the water loss from perspiration. Typically, exercising athletes should drink four to eight ounces of water every 15 to 20 minutes of exercise. This consumption varies depending on the intensity of exercise, the ambient temperature and relative humidity, and the individual's age, health, and fitness level. Water is essential to the body, and individuals must always have adequate water content in the body to continue to perform ADLs and exercise.

Micronutrients

Vitamins

Vitamins are organic compounds that do not supply energy and are not made by the body. Two categories of vitamins exist, which are fat-soluble vitamins and water-soluble vitamins. Fat-soluble vitamins are A, D, E, and K. These vitamins require fat in the body to assist in breaking down and dissolving the vitamins. The body does not readily eliminate fat-soluble vitamins. The fat-soluble vitamins not utilized by the body are not eliminated in urine.

Consequently, if fat-soluble vitamins are regularly consumed in excess, then toxicity results. Unlike fat-soluble vitamins, water-soluble vitamins breakdown and dissolve in water. The water-soluble vitamins include vitamin C and the B-complex vitamins. The eight B-complex vitamins include thiamine (B_1), riboflavin (B_2), niacin (B_3), pyridoxine (B_6), cobalamin (B_{12}), folate, panthothenic acid, and biotin (Thygerson & Thygerson, 2019).

Vitamins are imperative for a variety of bodily functions. Individuals must consume a variety of foods containing many different vitamins. If they do not consume all of the vitamins the body needs, then vitamin deficiency may result **(Table 3-5)**. If an individual has a deficiency, they may require vitamin supplements specifically to address the deficiency. An individual who eats a well-rounded diet, including a variety of plant and animal foods, most likely does not need vitamin supplementation. However, it is a very common practice for people of all ages to take a daily multivitamin in order to give them the proper vitamin RDA. Pediatricians recommend that children take a daily children's multivitamin since their bodies are growing. Many adults and children have erratic and unhealthy eating habits and do not consume all vitamins in the quantity necessary per day. Consequently, daily vitamin supplementation for these people is necessary. Pregnant women are directed by their physicians to take a daily multivitamin, along with extra supplementation of folic acid. Vitamin supplementation may also be recommended by an individual's physician due to conditions or deficiencies that the individual may have. For example, the B complex vitamins can potentially help fight heart disease. Therefore, physicians often recommend that individuals who have atherosclerosis should supplement their diets with extra B vitamins. Although vitamin supplementation seems to be an easy means to obtain the RDA of necessary vitamins, remind your clients that vitamin supplementation should not replace healthy eating.

Table 3-5 Major vitamins necessary for bodily functions

Vitamin	Major Functions	Rich Food Sources	Deficiency Signs/Symptoms	Toxicity Signs/ Symptoms
A and provitamin A (beta-carotene)	Vision in dim light, growth, reproduction, maintains immune system and skin, antioxidant	Liver, milk, dark green and leafy vegetables, carrots, sweet potatoes, mangos, oatmeal, broccoli, apricots, peaches, romaine lettuce	Poor vision in dim light, dry skin, blindness, poor growth, respiratory infections	Intestinal upset, liver damage, hair loss, headache, birth defects, death (betacarotene is less toxic than vitamin A)
D	Bone and tooth development and growth	Few good food sources other than fortified milk and eggs	Weak, deformed bones (rickets)	Growth failure, loss of appetite, weight loss, death

Vitamin	Major Functions	Rich Food Sources	Deficiency Signs/Symptoms	Toxicity Signs/ Symptoms
E	Antioxidant: protects cell membranes	Vegetable oils, whole grains, wheat germ, sunflower seeds, almonds	Anemia (rarely occurs)	Intestinal upset, bleeding problems
C	Scar formation and maintenance, immune system functioning, anti oxidant	Citrus fruits, berries, potatoes, broccoli, peppers, cabbage, tomatoes, fortified fruit drinks	Frequent infections, bleeding gums, bruises, poor wound healing, depression (scurvy)	Diarrhea, nosebleeds, headache, weakness, kidney stones, excess iron absorption and storage
Thiamine	Energy metabolism	Pork, liver, nuts, dried beans and peas, wholegrain and enriched breads and cereals	Heart failure, mental confusion, depression, paralysis (beriberi)	No toxicity has been reported
Riboflavin	Energy metabolism	Milk and yogurt, eggs and poultry, meat, liver, wholegrain and enriched breads and cereals	Enlarged, purple tongue; fatigue; oily skin; cracks in the corners of the mouth	No toxicity has been reported
Niacin	Energy metabolism	Protein-rich foods, peanut butter, wholegrain and enriched breads and cereals	Skin rash, diarrhea, weakness, dementia, death (pellagra)	Painful skin flushing, intestinal upset, liver damage
Vitamin B6	Protein and fat metabolism	Liver, oatmeal, bananas, meat, fish, poultry, whole grains, fortified cereals	Anemia, skin rash, irritability, elevated homocysteine levels	Weakness, depression, permanent nerve damage
Folate (folic acid)	DNA production	Leafy vegetables, oranges, nuts, liver, enriched breads and cereals	Anemia, depression, spina bifida in developing embryo, elevated homocysteine levels	Hides signs of vitamin B12 deficiency; may cause allergic response
B12	DNA production	Animal products	Pernicious anemia, fatigue, paralysis, elevated homocysteine levels	No toxicity has been reported

Minerals

Not only do micronutrients include vitamins, but they also include minerals. Minerals are inorganic substances, which are required daily for adequate body function. Similar to vitamins, minerals do not supply energy, but are important in many body functions. Minerals assist with function and production of enzymes, hormones, body fluids, the heart, hair, teeth, and bones. Macrominerals are essential micronutrients which are needed by our bodies in large amounts. These macrominerals include calcium, magnesium, potassium, sodium, phosphorous, sulfur, and chloride. Trace minerals are required by our bodies in small quantities. Trace minerals include iron, selenium, copper, zinc, iodine, cobalt, manganese, and fluoride. Not one food contains all of the important minerals that the body requires. Therefore, the athlete's diet must include various foods in order to obtain all necessary minerals. Minerals are found in foods such as bananas, leafy green vegetables, spinach, legumes, milk and dairy products, salt, whole grains, and red meat. Similar to vitamins, if the body is deficient of minerals then illness can result **(Table 3-6)**.

Sodium is an important mineral which assists in nerve function. However, sodium is over consumed by the public. Individuals typically overindulge in salty foods such as fast food, potato chips, frozen, processed foods, lunch meats, and condiments. Many individuals add sodium in the form of table salt to their food, which also creates excess sodium in their diet. In October 2021, the U.S. Department of Health and Human Services Food and Drug Administration (FDA) published recommended voluntary sodium reduction goals, including maximum limits, for corporations that produce processed, packaged, and prepared foods (See https://www.fda.gov/media/98264/download). The FDA created these recommendations in attempt to begin lowering the American public's sodium consumption. According to the *Dietary Intakes for Sodium and Potassium, Sodium: Dietary Intakes for Toxicity* (2019) *and Dietary Guidelines for Americans 2020-2025* (2020), excess sodium can cause a multitude of illnesses and conditions. Excess sodium can cause hypertension, which can lead to heart problems and stroke. Excess sodium has also been shown to lead to osteoporosis, fluid retention, kidney stones, and even death. An individual's typical diet contains a sufficient amount of sodium, therefore added sodium is not recommended.

Unlike sodium, which is overconsumed, the *Dietary Guidelines for Americans 2020-2025* (2020) state that calcium and potassium are two underconsumed minerals. Calcium helps bone strengthening, muscles contractions, and nerve conduction. Calcium sources include milk and dairy products, soy, broccoli, spinach, and calcium-fortified foods such as orange juice. Although calcium is important for all adults and children, it is of particular importance to women. As women age, their bones tend to become weakened, which predisposes the bones to fracture. The bones also lose their density, leading to osteoporosis. If women consume the RDA of calcium throughout their lives, then the risk of bone weakening and loss will

Table 3-6 Essential minerals necessary for bodily functions

Mineral	Roles	Rich Food Sources	Deficiency Signs/ Symptoms	Toxicity Signs/ Symptoms
Calcium	Builds and maintains bones and teeth, regulates muscle and nerve function, regulates blood pressure and blood clotting	Milk products; fortified orange juice, tofu, and soy milk; fish with edible small bones such as sardines and salmon; broccoli; hard water	Poor bone growth, weak bones, muscle spasms, convulsions	Kidney stones, calcium deposits in organs, mineral imbalances
Potassium	Maintains fluid balance, necessary for nerve function	Whole grains, fruits and vegetables, yogurt, milk	Muscular weakness, confusion, death	Heart failure
Sodium	Maintains fluid balance, necessary for nerve function	Salt, soy sauce, luncheon meats, processed cheeses, pickled foods, snack foods, canned and dried soups	Muscle cramping, headache, confusion, coma	Hypertension
Magnesium	Regulation of enzyme activity, necessary for nerve function	Green, leafy vegetables, nuts, whole grains, peanut butter	Loss of appetite, muscular weakness, convulsions, confusion, death	Rare
Zinc	Component of many enzymes and the hormone insulin, maintains immune function, necessary for sexual maturation and reproduction	Meats, fish, poultry, whole grains, vegetables	Poor growth, failure to mature sexually, improper healing of wounds	Mineral imbalances, gastrointestinal upsets, anemia, heart disease
Selenium	Component of a group of antioxidant enzymes, immune system function	Seafood, liver, and vegetables and grains grown in selenium-rich soil	May increase risk of heart disease and certain cancers	Hair and nail loss
Iron	Oxygen transport involved in the release of energy	Clams, oysters, liver, red meats, and enriched breads and cereals	Fatigue, weakness, iron-deficiency anemia	Iron poisoning, nausea, vomiting, diarrhea, death

be minimized. Potassium is important for adequate nerve conduction, muscle contraction, blood pressure and heart rate regulation, and cellular fluid maintenance. Sources of potassium include vegetables, such as raw spinach, sun-dried tomatoes, green beans, and mushrooms, and fruits, such as bananas, oranges, peaches, and apricots. Individuals deficient in potassium can become weak and hypertensive. They can experience muscular cramping and irregular heartbeats. Potassium deficiency can even cause death.

Iron is an important trace mineral. Iron's primary function is blood and hemoglobin. The body readily absorbs iron from animal sources such as lean beef, chicken, fish, and eggs. Plant-based iron sources include legumes, spinach, whole-grains, and fortified cereals. The body does not absorb iron plant-based sources as well as animal-based sources. Consequently, vegetarians may require iron supplements. As with other minerals, iron deficiency can occur. Babies, toddlers, preschoolers, teenage girls, women, including menstruating and pregnant women, and the elderly are commonly iron deficient. If an individual has an iron deficiency, their red blood cells cannot contain an adequate amount of oxygen. Consequently, the individual experiences a variety of symptoms including fatigue, mental problems, sleep difficulties, pale skin, and **anemia**. Iron deficient individuals may need to take iron supplements. If an individual experiences any iron deficiency symptoms, refer them to a physician for evaluation.

MyPlate.gov

In 2021, the United States Department of Agriculture comprised a tool called "MyPlate" (See https://www.myplate.gov/). This symbol depicts the necessary proportions of food groups that Americans should consume daily **(Figure 3-2)**. Fruits and vegetables should be plentiful and varied in the diet, whole grains should be at least 50% of total grains, proteins should be low fat, and dairy products should be consumed with each meal in order to consume proper calcium RDA. If an individual incorporates MyPlate into their daily food regime, they will ingest all required macro- and micronutrients.

Dietary Reference Intake and Recommended Daily Allowance

In 1997, the term dietary reference intake (DRI) was devised as another means to describe dietary intake. According to the National Institutes of Health Office of Dietary Supplements (http://ods.od.nih.gov/health_information/dietary_reference_intakes.aspx) DRI includes various reference measurements utilized to determine if the general population is meeting intake requirements. DRI measures include recommended daily allowance (RDA), adequate intake (AI), and tolerable upper intake level (UL). Recommended daily allowance (RDA) is the amount of a nutrient that a healthy person's body requires per day in order to function properly and remain healthy. AI is the amount of a nutrient that an athlete must consume to

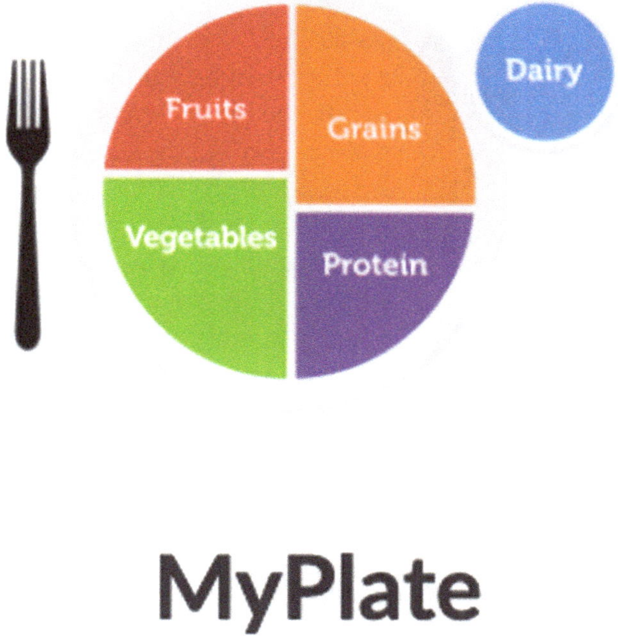

Figure 3-2 MyPlate
Source: USDA.gov

be healthy. UL is the highest amount of a nutrient that an athlete can consume without any detrimental effects. DRI is used by United States governmental agencies as a scientific means to research and determine these values for specific foods, and then to report the findings to the public.

RDA is utilized to determine nutrients' recommended daily value (RDV). The RDV is used as the basis for the percent daily value (%DV) as printed on the nutrition fact label on food and supplement packaging **(Figure 3-3)**. This %DV indicates the nutrient values and percent of total RDV for each nutrient for a 2,000 calorie per day diet. Individuals can utilize the %DV on nutrition fact labels to determine if they are consuming an adequate amount of required nutrients per day and how well they are meeting the governmental recommendations.

TIPS FROM THE FIELD

Tip 1 Your client may not be aware of the best foods to include in their diet. Likewise, they may not know how to utilize the valuable information listed on the nutrient labels. Once you have assisted them in setting their goals and devised their daily nutrient requirements, take your client to the grocery store. Show them the various foods that would qualify under each section of MyPlate. Then show them how to utilize the nutrient information and %DV on nutrient fact labels. Once you educate your client to incorporate this information into their dietary plan, over time they will be able to make healthy food choices on a regular basis without assistance.

Figure 3-3 Nutrition fact label

Weight Loss and Weight Gain

To facilitate their health, an individual must manage their weight. An individual must be motivated to keep their body weight at normal values. Some individuals need or desire to lose fat or gain lean muscle mass. As previously discussed, various means to manage and to determine proper weight exist, which include utilizing RDA, MyPlate, exercise, and BMI. In order to begin a weight maintenance program, your client must understand that for each pound of fat they want to lose their weekly caloric intake must decrease by 3,500. Expending calories will assist in meeting this goal. To gain lean muscle mass, your client must increase their caloric intake by adding protein to their diet. Likewise, exercise, in particular strength training exercise, will assist them in meeting their weight goals.

A safe, realistic weight loss or gain goal would be one to two pounds per week. In order to make this weight management program work, the individual must incorporate good nutrition and eating habits along with daily exercise. For weight loss, reducing calorie intake alone is not successful long term. The individual will lose weight at first, but then plateau. Regular exercise must be incorporated into the individual's weekly schedule otherwise they most likely will gain the weight back. Likewise, exercise alone will not help an individual lose weight, especially if they do not change their eating habits. If an individual wishes to gain lean muscle tissue, consuming extra calories without strength training exercise will not produce desired results.

When your client wants to begin a weight management program they must set long- and short-term goals. Help them be realistic when creating weight management goals. Determine how much weight your client wants to lose or gain. Have them complete a daily food diary of their current consumption for approximately one week, including a calculation of calories ingested and expended. This food diary is very important for you to review with your client in order to create short-term goals, and determine what dietary changes must be made. Once you have created a weight management nutrition plan with your client, advise them to keep a food diary. Once they have reached their weight goal, this food diary will assist them in continuing a nutritionally balanced diet. A significant amount of research is available for you to review in regard to the best dietary plan for your client. As previously mentioned, low CHO, high protein, and high fat dietary plans may work for some individuals. On the contrary, endurance athletes most likely need high CHO, low protein, and low-fat dietary plans, due to the amount of CHO burned during endurance exercise. Although these dietary plans are at opposite ends of the diet spectrum in regard to their macronutrient content, dietary programs in between exist. Your client may inquire about a certain dietary program that they have read or heard about. Assist them in determining the dietary program's safety and effectiveness by researching the information utilizing reputable, research-based sources. If you cannot provide the athlete with this information, or need additional assistance, contact a registered dietician who is an expert in this area.

TIPS FROM THE FIELD

Tip 2 When your client is beginning a nutritional program, ask them how they would feel most comfortable keeping track of their nutrient intake. If your client tracks their food intake each day, there is a better chance for them to stick to their nutritional plan versus if they do not track their food intake. Have a variety of paper tracking documents as well as website and electronic application programs available for your client to try. Review the various tracking programs first so you have an idea of which ones would be best for your client. Determine the ease of use, if the application specifically tracks what your client needs, and the cost for these online tools. Many programs are free, but others require a monthly, yearly, or one-time fee. Whichever your client chooses, make sure they have some means to track their progress on a daily basis.

Eating Disorders

When the term "eating disorder" is mentioned, anorexia nervosa and bulimia nervosa often come to mind. Although these illnesses are eating disorders, binge eating disorder is also an eating disorder that affect individuals, including athletes. Bulimia nervosa and binge eating disorder are related to obesity in that they can contribute to obesity and vice versa (da Luz et al., 2018). Likewise, obesity and all three eating disorders can be caused by psychological, social, and emotional issues manifested within the athlete. When an eating disorder affects an athlete, their performance declines and their physical and mental health is not optimal. Unless the athlete seeks medical assistance to combat the eating disorder, significant illness, disease, and death may result.

As previously discussed, obesity is defined as an individual having a significant amount of body fat and weight for their height, as compared to a healthy, normal weight individual. Obese individuals have a BMI of over 30. Obesity does not have a single cause, rather it results from a myriad of factors. If an individual has poor nutritional habits and consumes more calories than they expend during exercise, then over time they will gain weight and could become obese. An individual who has low self-esteem, emotional issues, and trauma in their life may rely on food as a comfort and become obese. Also, a medical condition called hypothyroidism and certain prescription medication such as corticosteroids may cause an individual to gain significant weight. If an individual becomes obese and remains in that state, they can acquire a variety of illnesses. Obese athletes are prone to the following conditions and illnesses including, but not limited to, heart disease, stroke, cancer, high cholesterol, high blood pressure, Type 2 diabetes, **gout**, sleep apnea and other respiratory problems. In order to assist an individual in lowering her weight, refer them to a physician for evaluation, a registered dietician for consultation, and a psychologist or counselor for therapeutic sessions.

Whereas an obese individual has a high amount of body weight due to body fat, an individual with anorexia nervosa is extremely thin. Anorexia nervosa begins when the individual's mental and emotional issues result in self-starvation. Anorexia mostly effects girls in their teens and women in their 20s (U.S. Department of Health and Human Services Office on Women's Health, 2018a). Males, especially wrestlers who need to continually manage their weight for athletic participation, also can become anorexic. Various situations exist as to why an individual becomes anorexic. An individual may feel out of control with some issue or event in their life. However, they feel they can control the amount of food they consume. The individual may believe they are fat, which often occurs due to outside influences. These influences can include peer, coach, or public pressure to be thin (i.e. magazines, advertisements, social media). Consequently, the individual severely limits the amount of nutrients that they consume. As a result, they become significantly underweight. Signs and symptoms of anorexia nervosa include, but are not limited to, significant underweight appearance, fatigue, constipation, amenorrhea, thinning and falling out hair, soft hair covering the body, dry skin, dizziness, fainting, low blood pressure, and arrhythmias. The individual also exhibits behavioral signs of anorexia such as social withdrawal, depression, a preoccupation with and denial of food, and fear of gaining weight (U.S. Department of Health and Human Services Office on Women's Health, 2018a). The individual visualizes themselves as being fat, even though they are not. They tend to wear large bulky clothes to hide their drastic weight loss. If an individual does not get professional assistance to deal with their mental, emotional, and physical condition, they will succumb to a variety of illnesses such as anemia, electrolyte imbalance, osteoporosis, kidney failure, heart attack, and even death.

Bulimia is an eating disorder when an individual binges and purges typically in secret. The individual binges by eating thousands of calories of food and then purges or eliminates the food by induced vomiting and/or utilizing laxatives. The individual may also attempt to avoid gaining weight by excessively exercising. Bulimia has many of the same characteristics as anorexia nervosa. Bulimic individuals typically are females of the same age groups as anorexic females. Similar to anorexia nervosa, bulimia is a mental and emotional illness as well as a physical illness (U.S. Department of Health and Human Services Office on Women's Health, 2018b). A bulimic individual tends to binge and purge food in secret, is preoccupied with food, and is overly concerned with their weight. Unlike anorexic athletes, bulimic individuals are approximately their normal weight. Signs and symptoms of bulimia include tooth and fingernail decay, gum disease, depression, anxiety, obsessive-compulsive disorder, and fainting. If a bulimic individual does not seek professional help, they may succumb to an electrolyte imbalance, osteoporosis, arrhythmias, esophageal ulcers, kidney damage, and even death.

Binge-eating disorder is similar to bulimia since the individual consumes large quantities of food in one sitting on a regular basis, but they do not purge after eating. Individuals who tend to binge-eat typically are depressed, anxious, and have other mental and emotional issues. The food acts as a comfort for the individual. The individual eats secretively and even when they do not feel hungry. They consume food until their stomach is painfully full. The individual wants to stop binging but feels like they are incapable to stop (Mayo Clinic, 2018). They become upset and unhappy with themselves after binging. The individual remains at their normal weight for a period of time, but with continued binging they gain weight and may become obese.

Although obesity and anorexia is evident by the physical appearance of the athlete (if the anorexic is not wearing large, bulky clothing), bulimia and binge-eating are typically not as evident. If you suspect your athlete has an eating disorder, obtain guidance from professionals as how to handle the situation and approach the athlete. Since we often have a trusting, respectful relationship with our athletes, they may communicate to you that they have an illness and ask for help before discussing their condition with anyone else. However, if you suspect that your athlete has an eating disorder, you must approach their situation very delicately. First speak to a professional for advice on how to properly approach and assist the athlete. Expect the athlete to be defensive. Do not attack the athlete and bluntly accuse them of having an eating disorder. You may need to discuss other topics with the athlete and transition into a conversation regarding their performance in relation to their weight and eating habits. You could discuss reevaluating their exercise and nutritional goals. Show them care and compassion during your communication. Listen to everything your athlete has to say and do not pass judgment. Hopefully the athlete verbally communicates their feelings in regard to their illness and desires assistance. Offer them support and encouragement. Assure them that they can confide and trust you to help. Athletes may not realize or deny that they have an eating disorder, or believe their eating behavior is normal. If this is the case, consult an eating disorder expert for advice on how to handle the situation and get the athlete professional treatment.

Female Athlete Triad

The female athlete triad occurs when a biological female athlete is suffering from disordered eating (typically anorexia nervosa or bulimia nervosa), amenorrhea, and osteoporosis **(Figure 3-4)**. These three conditions combined can be severely damaging to the athlete's body. Due to an athlete's exercise regimen, hormonal imbalance, and changes in body weight due to the eating disorder, amenorrhea occurs. Osteoporosis is bone weakening and loss. This condition occurs due to hormonal imbalances and prolonged amenorrhea (Hobart & Smucker, 2000). Consequently, the female athlete triad is a detrimental cycle of these three conditions, which continues until the athlete receives treatment. If you suspect that your athlete is affected by the female athlete triad, refer her to a physician, a psychologist, and a registered dietician for evaluation and treatment.

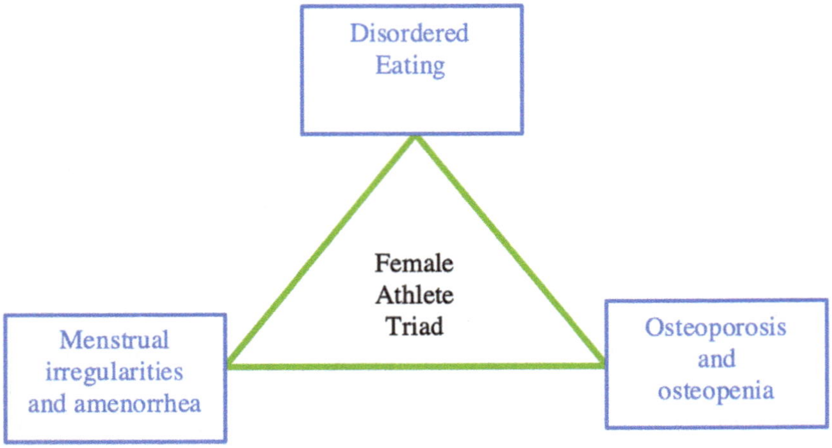

Figure 3-4 The female athlete triad

Supplements and Nutritional Ergogenic Aids

Dietary supplements are non-food substances that individuals add to their diet. These supplements not only include vitamins and minerals as previously discussed, but also include herbs, botanicals, amino acids, and metabolites. Athletes take supplements for a variety of reasons. Competitive athletes want any advantage they can to triumph over their competitors. Many athletes believe that by taking supplements they can obtain this advantage. Athletes consume supplements such as protein and whey, and other supplements that assist them in gaining muscle mass. Some athletes, most notably female athletes, consume weight loss, vitamin, mineral, and energy enhancement supplements (Fink & Mikesky, 2021).

Supplement manufacturers advertise that their products have nutrient value, health benefits, and cause structural and functional improvements (Fink & Mikesky, 2021). Since supplements are not drugs, the manufacturers cannot claim supplements have a pharmacological use or can cure illness or disease. Over the counter (OTC) and prescription drugs are put through mandatory, rigorous testing for safety or effectiveness by the Food and Drug Administration (FDA). Supplements are not tested or regulated by the FDA. The FDA does not put supplements' ingredients through testing, nor does the organization evaluate proper dosage, side effects, labeling, etc. before the supplement is available to consumers. Therefore, supplements could contain ingredients not listed on the label. This fact could pose significant problems and health risks for individuals. Additional ingredients not listed on the label could interfere with other supplements and OTC or prescription drugs that the individual is taking. Supplements may also interfere or exacerbate an individual's medical condition. Some supplements may have ingredients that are banned by the United States Anti-Doping Organization (USADA), the National Collegiate Athletic Association, governmental agencies, and other organizations.

In this case, an athlete may be found positive for banned substances during an employment or athletic activity drug test.

Athletes must take precautions when utilizing supplements, and truly understand what substances they are ingesting. USADA (2019) has recommended that athletes use NSF Certified for Sport® supplements, which can reduce the risk of athletes ingesting a banned or illegal substance. The athletes should also have the supplements tested by a third-party laboratory testing organization. Also have them consult their physician regarding the supplements that they wish to take, prior to taking them, especially if they have a medical condition. The physician can determine if the supplements are contraindicated due to the athlete's conditions and medications. Along with these measures, the athlete should do as much research as possible to determine if the supplement is safe and beneficial to consume.

Most supplements do not give athletes a competitive advantage. Likewise, some supplements do not create the effects that the manufacturers claim. However, many supplements do have performance enhancement effects. These performance enhancing supplements are considered nutritional ergogenic aids. Nutritional ergogenic aids are made from nutrients produced by the body or found in food. Two examples of commonly used nutritional ergogenic aids include creatine and caffeine.

Creatine is made by the body from amino acids. In addition, individuals typically consume creatine by eating high protein foods including meat and fish. Creatine is a natural ergogenic aid because it increases energy and ability to exercise longer, while decreasing fatigue and recovery time. Creatine is beneficial in increasing performance particularly for short term high intensity exercise (Kreider et al., 2017). Creatine monohydrate is the most common creatine supplement, which comes in pill and powder form. This form of creatine is utilized due to its efficacy. However, some side effects of utilizing supplemental creatine include water retention in the muscles, muscle cramping, and diarrhea. Regardless, creatine has been widely researched and consistently proven to work as a relatively safe ergogenic aid.

In moderate quantities, caffeine also acts as a natural ergogenic aid. However, caffeine is different than creatine because is not produced by the body, and must be consumed from drinks such as coffee, tea, soda, energy drinks, and food such as chocolate and kola nut. Caffeine is a central nervous system stimulant and can assist an endurance athlete to continue with activity for a longer duration. The athlete also has more energy at the end of exercise activity than without consuming caffeine. Caffeine increases the athlete's metabolism, which assists in expending more calories. Also, caffeine releases stored fat into the blood, which is utilized as an energy source during exercise. These functions make caffeine a valuable aid to many athletes. Although the World Anti-Doping Agency (WADA) banned the use of caffeine from 1984 to 2004, the NCAA is presently the only athletic organization that restricts caffeine use. Consequently, collegiate athletes must be mindful of the quantity of caffeine ingested prior to competition. Many other nutritional ergogenic aids are used by both endurance and strength and power athletes. These ergogenic aids have a range of effectiveness from low to high. Some supplements have no side effects, while some have significant side effects that can be severely detrimental to the athlete's body. If an athlete wishes to utilize a nutritional ergogenic aid supplement, assist them in researching the supplements, have the supplements tested, and refer the athlete to a physician who can assist the athlete in determining if the supplement is safe for consumption.

Summary

In order for individuals to be healthy, not only do they have to participate in a wellness, exercise, and fitness program, but they also have to focus on proper nutrition. We must assist our athletes in devising the best, most effective, practical dietary plan that they can utilize to facilitate a good quality of life.

Keywords

Nutrients Substances in food that nourish the body, provide it with energy, and promote its proper function and growth.

Diet The food and drink that we consume each day. A "diet" is also referred to a program or plan that an individual follows when he is attempting to modify their weight.

Legumes Pod-type foods including, but not limited to, beans, lentils, peas, soy, and peanuts.

Coronary arteries Supply the heart with oxygenated blood.

Triglycerides A type of fat found in your blood. Excess sugar in the blood or unnecessary calories consumed which are not burned off with physical activity are converted into triglycerides.

Insulin A hormone which is released when an increase in blood glucose exists. The hormone transports blood glucose into the body cells to be utilized for energy.

Type 2 diabetes The inability for the body to utilize or make insulin properly. Consequently, sugar remains in the blood. If the sugar level is not regulated, over time an individual can succumb to eye conditions including blindness, foot conditions including ulcers, kidney damage, heart attack, and stroke. Individuals who are overweight and obese are predisposed to Type 2 diabetes.

Diuretic A substance that causes the kidneys to produce urine, which consequently increases the urination rate. Other than prescription and over-the-counter diuretic drugs and caffeine, parsley, watermelon, grapes, celery, and asparagus are some examples of natural diuretics.

Anemia When a decreased amount of hemoglobin and/or red blood cells exist in the body. Consequently, since hemoglobin carries oxygen in the red blood cells, if an individual has anemia they will have a decreased oxygen supply in the body.

Gout Caused by crystallized uric acid in the blood. The crystals move into the joints and body tissues, especially in the foot. This condition creates painful arthritis and is often recurrent.

Discussion Questions

1. What are the differences among CHO, fats, and proteins? What is the role of each macronutrient?
2. Why is water important for an athlete to drink during exercise and on a regular, daily basis?
3. Why are vitamins and minerals important for an individual to consume? If an individual is vitamin and mineral deficient, what can occur to their body?
4. What are some considerations before beginning a weight management program?
5. What are the prevalent eating disorders, their causes, and signs and symptoms? What illnesses or diseases can an athlete acquire if they have an eating disorder?
6. What are natural ergogenic aids and how can they assist an athlete in increasing their performance?

CASE STUDY: A NEW BEGINNING

Rebecca is a 45-year-old English teacher at Old State High School. She is well respected by her peers, administrators, and students alike. Rebecca has been married for 10 years, and has two children. She is financially secure, has many friends, and is an active participant in her community's activities. Rebecca's family, friends, and coworkers believe that she is happy due to her outgoing personality. Rebecca could not ask for her life to be any better except for one aspect, which is that she is obese.

Rebecca played basketball in college and was in the best physical shape of her life. However, once she graduated from college and stopped playing basketball, she no longer exercised on a regular basis. Her weight began to increase slowly and steadily. Now after 24 years, she fights a battle with her weight every day. Rebecca's obesity makes her extremely unhappy inside.

Recently, Rebecca went to her physician for her annual physical. She was diagnosed with Type 2 diabetes, high LDL cholesterol, and high triglycerides. Her blood pressure was elevated. Rebecca never had these conditions before. She realized that her health is failing. The physician said that she had to make a conscious decision to help herself and improve her health.

The day after her physical, Rebecca woke up feeling sullen and depressed. She stepped on the scale. The scale displayed a weight of 230 pounds. Rebecca looked at herself in the mirror. She finally decided to dedicate herself to leading a healthy lifestyle and lose weight. At 5 feet 10 inches tall with a BMI of 33, she knows she has to lose 60 pounds to get down to a normal, healthy weight. In order to lose weight, Rebecca knows that she must begin to exercise regularly and also consume nutritious foods.

Since Rebecca played college basketball, she has a basic idea of how to create a personalized exercise program. However, Rebecca admits that she knows little about healthy eating. Rebecca has two young children, and she works full time. Consequently, she barely has time to cook. Her diet consists mostly of fast and processed foods, as well as large quantities of empty calorie foods such as cakes, cookies, and potato chips. Rebecca tends to drink a few cans of sugared soda along with caffeinated coffee daily. Since Rebecca is not knowledgeable about how to create a healthy, nutritious diet plan,

(continued)

she makes an appointment with a Registered Dietitian, Ms. Tully. Rebecca is certain that Ms. Tully will help her reach her goals, and is excited to begin a new, healthy lifestyle.

1. How much weight should Rebecca plan on losing per week?
2. What information should Ms. Tully provide to Rebecca in regard to daily and weekly caloric requirements?
3. How should Ms. Tully formulate Rebecca's daily diet in regard to quantity and type of CHO, protein, and fat?
4. What suggestions can Ms. Tully give Rebecca in types of foods that she should each in each category of macronutrients? What foods should Rebecca avoid?
5. What information should Ms. Tully give Rebecca in regard to the importance of dietary fiber? What foods should Rebecca eat that are high in fiber?
6. What foods can Ms. Tully suggest for Rebecca to eat that would help fight against Type 2 diabetes, high LDL cholesterol, and high triglycerides?
7. Should Ms. Tully suggest that Rebecca take vitamin and mineral supplements? Why or why not?
8. Why would Ms. Tully tell Rebecca to avoid drinking sugared soda and caffeinated coffee? What should Rebecca drink instead?

References

Batch, J. T., Lamsal, S. P., Adkins, M., Sultan, S., & Ramirez, M. N. (2020). Advantages and disadvantages of the ketogenic diet: A review article. *Cureus, 12*(8), e9639. https://doi.org/10.7759/cureus.9639

Benjamin, O., & Lappin, S.L. (2021, July 22). *Kwashiorkor*. StatPearls. https://www.ncbi.nlm.nih.gov/books/NBK507876/

Dansinger, M. (2021, February 7). *How to use the glycemic index*. WebMD. https://www.webmd.com/diabetes/guide/glycemic-index-good-versus-bad-carbs

da Luz, F. Q., Hay, P., Touyz, S., & Sainsbury, A. (2018). Obesity with comorbid eating disorders: Associated health risks and treatment approaches. *Nutrients, 10*(7), 829. https://doi.org/10.3390/nu10070829

Fink, H. H., & Mikesky, A. E. (2021). *Practical applications in sports nutrition* (5th Ed.). Jones and Bartlett Publishers.

Hobart, J. A., Smucker, D. R. (2000). The female athlete triad. *Am Fam Physician, 61*(11), 3357–3364.

Kaneshiro, N. K. & Zieve, D. (2020, January 1). *Kwashiorkor*. MedlinePlus. https://medlineplus.gov/ency/article/001604.htm

Kreider, R.B., Kalman, D.S., Antonio, J. et al. (2017). International Society of Sports Nutrition position stand: safety and efficacy of creatine supplementation in exercise, sport, and medicine. *Journal of the International Society of Sports Nutrition,* 14(18). https://doi.org/10.1186/s12970-017-0173-z

Ludwig D. S. (2020). The ketogenic diet: Evidence for optimism but high-quality research needed. *The Journal of Nutrition, 150*(6), 1354–1359. https://doi.org/10.1093/jn/nxz308

Mariotti, F., & Gardner, C. D. (2019). Dietary protein and amino acids in vegetarian diets-A review. *Nutrients, 11*(11), 2661. https://doi.org/10.3390/nu11111266

Mayo Clinic (2018, May 5). *Binge-eating disorder.* Retrieved October 23, 2021, from https://www.mayoclinic.org/diseases-conditions/binge-eating-disorder/symptoms-causes/syc-20353627

Mayo Clinic (2020, April 17). *Carbohydrates: How carbs fit into a healthy diet.* Retrieved September 11, 2021, from https://www.mayoclinic.org/healthy- lifestyle/nutrition-and-healthy-eating/in-depth/carbohydrates/art-20045705

Mayo Clinic (2021, January 6). *Dietary fiber: Essential for a healthy diet.* Retrieved October 26, 2021, from https://www.mayoclinic.org/healthy-lifestyle/nutrition- and-healthy-eating/in-depth/fiber/art-20043983

Medline Plus (2019). *Protein in diet.* Retrieved September 13, 2021, from https://medlineplus.gov/ency/article/002467.htm

National Academies of Sciences, Engineering, and Medicine. (2005). *Dietary reference intakes for water, potassium, sodium, chloride, and sulfate.* The National Academies Press. https://doi.org/10.17226/10925

National Academies of Sciences, Engineering, and Medicine; Health and Medicine Division; Food and Nutrition Board; Committee to Review the Dietary Reference Intakes for Sodium and Potassium. (2019). *Dietary reference intakes for sodium and potassium. Sodium: Dietary Reference Intakes for Toxicity*. (M. Oria, M. Harrison, & V.A. Stallings, Eds). National Academies Press.

Orrù, S., Imperlini, E., Nigro, E., Alfieri, A., Cevenini, A., Polito, R., Daniele, A., Buono, P., & Mancini, A. (2018). Role of functional beverages on sport performance and recovery. *Nutrients, 10*(10), 1470. https://doi.org/10.3390/nu10101470

Pound, C. M., Blair, B., & Canadian Paediatric Society, Nutrition and Gastroenterology Committee. (2017). Energy and sports drinks in children and adolescents. *Paediatrics & Child Health, 22*(7), 406–410. https://doi.org/10.1093/pch/pxx132

Saslow, L. R., Mason, A. E., Kim, S., Goldman, V., Ploutz-Snyder, R., Bayandorian, H., Daubenmier, J., Hecht, F. M., & Moskowitz, J. T. (2017). An online intervention comparing a very low-carbohydrate ketogenic diet and lifestyle recommendations versus a plate method diet in overweight individuals with Type 2 diabetes: A randomized controlled trial. *Journal of Medical Internet Research, 19*(2), e36. https://doi.org/10.2196/jmir.5806

Thygerson, A. L. & Thygerson, S. M. (2019). *Fit to be well* (5th Ed.). Jones and Bartlett Learning.

U.S. Department of Agriculture and U.S. Department of Health and Human Services. (2020). *Dietary guidelines for Americans, 2020-2025, 9th Edition.* Retrieved October 10, 2021, from https://www.dietaryguidelines.gov/sites/default/files/2020-12/Dietary_Guidelines_for_Americans_2020-2025.pdf

U.S. Anti-Doping Agency. (2021). *2020 Fluids and hydration.* Retrieved September 17, 2021, from https://www.usada.org/athletes/substances/nutrition/fluids-and- hydration

U.S. Anti-Doping Agency. (2019). *Supplement risk and NSF Certified for Sport®*. Retrieved October 25, 2021, from https://www.usada.org/athlete-advisory/supplement-risk-nsf-certified-for-sport/

U.S. Department of Health and Human Services Office on Women's Health. (2018a, August 28). *Anorexia nervosa.* Retrieved October 23, 2021, from https://www.womenshealth.gov/mental-health/mental-health-conditions/eating- disorders/anorexia-nervosa

U.S. Department of Health and Human Services Office on Women's Health. (2018b, August 28). *Bulimia nervosa.* Retrieved October 23, 2021, from https://www.womenshealth.gov/mental-health/mental-health-conditions/eating- disorders/bulimia-nervosa

U.S. National Library of Medicine, MedlinePlus. (2020, February 10). *Cholesterol*. Retrieved October 26, 2021, from https://medlineplus.gov/cholesterol.html

Zeratsky, K. (2020, July 2). *Are high-protein diets safe for weight loss?* Mayo Clinic. https://www.mayoclinic.org/healthy-lifestyle/nutrition-and-healthy-eating/expert-answers/high-protein-diets/faq-20058207

Bloodborne Pathogens

Chapter
4

Chapter Objectives

After you have read this chapter, you will be able to understand:

- The similarities and differences among the three most common bloodborne pathogens, which include hepatitis B virus (HBV), hepatitis C virus (HCV), and human immunodeficiency virus (HIV).
- How bloodborne pathogens are transmitted between individuals.
- The signs and symptoms of bloodborne pathogen infection.
- How an individual develops acquired immune deficiency syndrome (AIDS).
- The Occupational Safety and Health Administration (OSHA) bloodborne standard.
- How to protect yourself and your patients from contracting bloodborne pathogens.

Sports medicine professionals work closely with clients, patients, and athletes on a daily basis. Although they do not commonly come in contact with their patients' blood or bodily fluids, potential exposure to and transmission of blood borne pathogens exists. Consequently, we must make every attempt to prevent bloodborne pathogen infection. This chapter gives an overview of three most common bloodborne pathogens, including how to protect yourself from infection.

Three Common Bloodborne Pathogens

According to the United States Department of Labor's Occupational Safety and Health Administration (OSHA) (1991), bloodborne pathogens are microorganisms in the blood that cause disease. These pathogens are also found in some bodily fluids such as vaginal secretions, semen, cerebrospinal fluid, synovial fluid, saliva in dental procedures only, and any other bodily fluid where blood is present. Sweat, urine, feces, vomit, and general saliva do not contain bloodborne pathogens unless blood is visibly present.

As sports medicine professional, we must take an active role in preventing transmission of bloodborne pathogens in the workplace. One means to acquire blood borne pathogens is through **direct contact** with another person's infected blood or the bodily fluids previously noted. At some point during your professional career, one of your clients will have an open, bleeding wound. If your client sustains this type of injury under your supervision, you are responsible to provide first aid. Always consider that your clients may have acquired bloodborne pathogens. Treat them appropriately while protecting yourself from infection.

One means to protect yourself from bloodborne pathogen infection is to assume that all individuals are passive carriers. A passive carrier means that an individual can be infected with a bloodborne pathogen, transmit it to other individuals, and infect them even though the infected individual does not exhibit any signs or symptoms of illness at the time of transmission. Since you must assume all individuals are passive carriers, appropriately utilize personal protective equipment (PPE) at all times when providing first aid. PPE includes items such as disposable latex gloves, protective eye wear, and disposable face masks and gowns. Individuals can be passive carriers of the three most common bloodborne pathogens, which include Hepatitis B (HBV), Hepatitis C (HCV), and Human Immunodeficiency Virus (HIV). Consequently, be aware that these bloodborne pathogens may be prevalent during your employment activities as sports medicine professionals.

Hepatitis B Virus

Hepatitis B virus (HBV) is a bloodborne pathogen that originally was thought to be found only in blood, and transferred only via open wounds, contaminated needles, and blood transfusions. However, HBV is also found in other bodily fluids such as semen, vaginal fluid, synovial fluid, and cerebrospinal fluid. HBV is also found in saliva; however, it is in low concentrations and transmission is unlikely (Wang, 2021). As sports medicine professionals, our primary concern regarding HBV in our daily employment activities is coming in contact with significant quantities of our patients' blood. Likewise, HBV exists in dried blood for approximately one week and can still cause infection (World Health Organization, 2021). Therefore, dried blood found on towels in your facility's locker room dirty laundry bin, or on the bathroom sink after an athlete has shaved may contain HBV for up to one week. Another cause for concern is that patients can be HBV passive carriers for years, and infect others without knowledge of doing so.

When an individual is infected with HBV, the virus travels to the liver where it multiplies. During this time, some of the virus' coating is released into the blood. A blood test confirms if the **antigen** and antibodies are in the blood. Signs and symptoms may occur between 60 to 150 days, which include continual fatigue, weakness, loss of appetite, and nausea (CDC, 2020a). The individual complains of a constant headache and abdominal pain. They may have a fever, and exhibit **jaundice**, dark colored urine, and light-colored stools (World Health Organization, 2021) **(Figure 4-1)**. An individual with these signs and symptoms may not recognize that they have been infected with HBV since many mimic flu signs and symptoms. If an individual approaches you with questions regarding their symptoms, or you notice they are exhibiting signs of illness, immediately refer them to a physician to obtain a correct

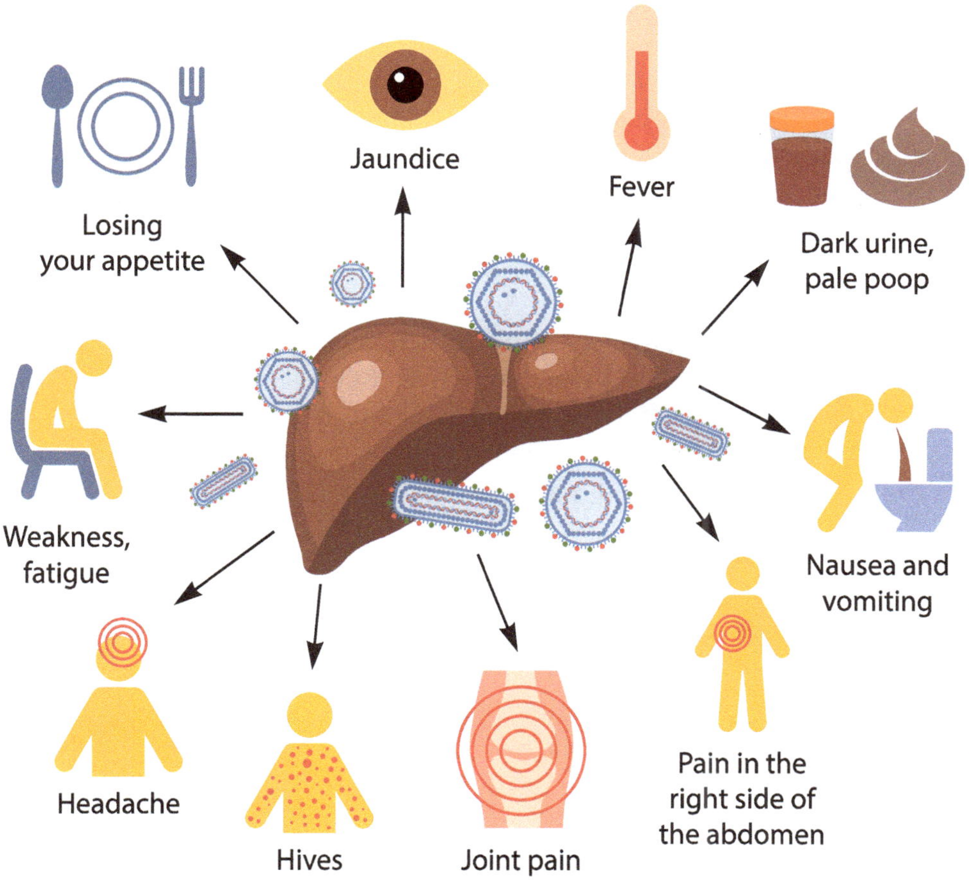

© Olga Bolbot/Shutterstock.com

Figure 4-1 Signs and symptoms of Hepatitis B

diagnosis and treatment. Fortunately for many individuals who are infected with HBV, the body eliminates the virus, and they undergo no further illness (Mejia et al., 2020). For some athletes, the HBV turns into a chronic infection without signs and symptoms for years. Over time, the chronic HBV infection destroys the liver, causing liver **cirrhosis** or cancer, then death. If infected, an individual can take oral antiviral medication in attempt to suppress the virus as well as reduce the incidence and/or progression of liver cirrhosis and cancer (World Health Organization, 2021).

The incidence of HBV infection in the United States has remained steady between 2011 and 2018 (CDC, 2020a). However, sports medicine professionals and other individuals can actively take measures to prevent infection. Depending on their work environment, sports medicine professionals must abide by OSHA workplace practices, which can protect them from infection. Also, the CDC (2020a) recommends that children are given their first dose of a Hepatitis B vaccine at birth. Various elementary and secondary schools, along with higher education institutions require students to be vaccinated in order to attend. Many sports medicine professionals who were not inoculated at birth are being proactive and have their primary care physician inoculate them. Also like some schools, some employers require Hepatitis B vaccination for their sports medicine employees as a condition of employment. If you work in a facility where your role is to provide first aid or medical care to athletes, or you handle blood or other potentially infectious material (OPIM), then OSHA regulations require your employer to offer you the series of HBV vaccinations at no cost to you and pay the cost for the vaccine (OSHA, 1991).

The vaccine consists of three doses. If an infant is given the first dose at birth, then the second dose is given 1 month after the first, and third dose is given 6 months after the first (CDC, 2020a). The vaccine is approximately 98% to 100% effective against acquiring the virus (World Health Organization, 2021). A month or two after the last dose, a blood test is necessary to determine if an individual's body has produced an adequate number of antibodies. If a person is vaccinated and HBV does enter their body, the antibodies fight against the virus and destroy it. Consequently, if their blood contains enough antibodies then they will be immune to HBV.

Hepatitis C Virus

According to Denault and Gardner (2021), Hepatitis C virus (HCV) is "the most commonly reported bloodborne infection in the United States and a serious public health problem". HCV is found in the blood and passed between individuals via openings in the skin, such as open wounds, or mucous membranes. HCV is most commonly passed by sharing contaminated needles during illicit injectable drug use. The primary concern for sports medicine professionals in the workplace is HCV exposure and transmission via their patients' open bleeding wounds. According to the Center for Disease Control (2020b), HCV can live outside the body for a maximum of 4 days. Many HBV infection signs and symptoms are the same for HCV infection. HCV infection first produces flu-like symptoms such as loss of appetite, vomiting, nausea, fever, and fatigue. Additional signs and symptoms include jaundice, joint pain, dark urine, and clay-colored stools (Mayo Clinic, 2021) **(Figure 4-2)**. However, in approximately half of HCV cases the athlete is asymptomatic (Mayo Clinic, 2021), consequently most individuals do not recognize that they have been infected with HCV. If individuals have symptoms, they most likely assume they have the flu and ignore the possibility of HCV infection.

HCV positive individuals must be continually under a physician's care, and have their blood tested regularly to determine if the HCV is adversely affecting the liver. Unlike HBV, no

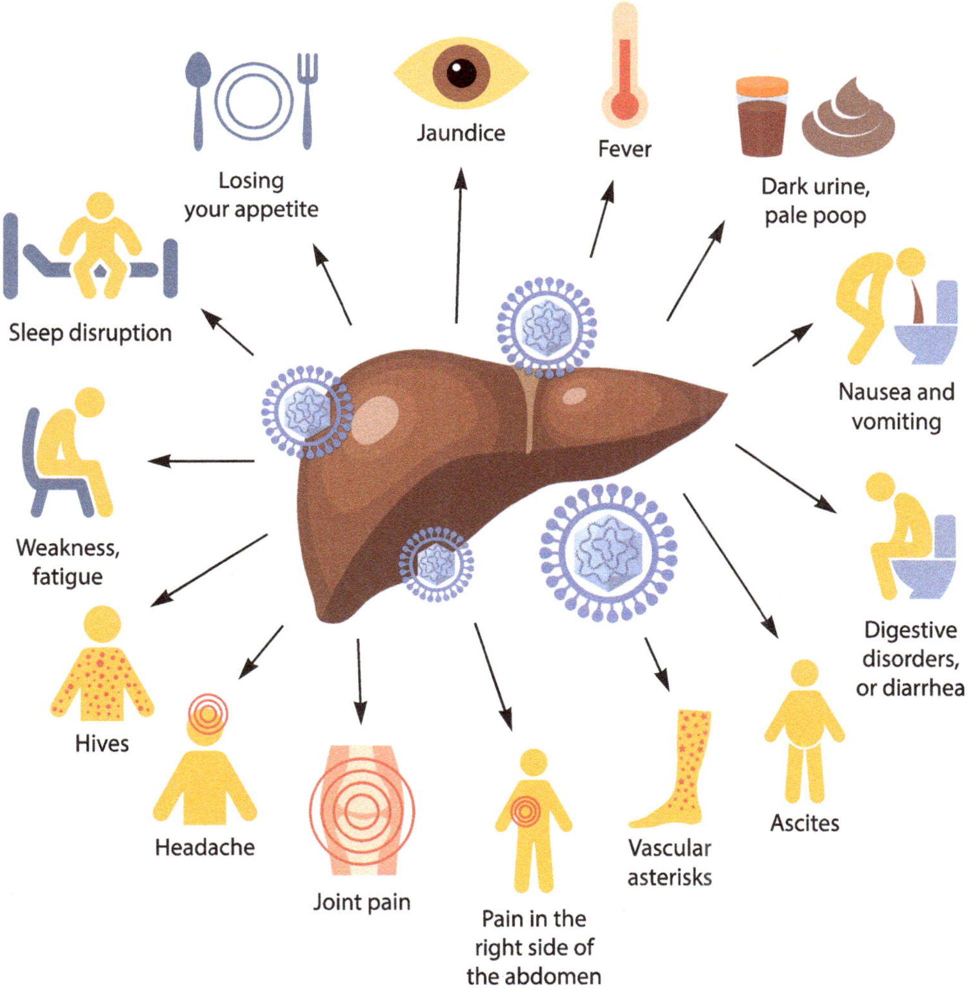

Figure 4-2 Signs and symptoms of Hepatitis C.

vaccine for HCV exists. However, the infected individual will be prescribed daily antiviral oral medication, which can rid the virus from the individual's body within two to six months (Mayo Clinic, 2021b). However in many cases, an individual has chronic HCV infection and as a result develops serious liver disease such as cirrhosis or liver cancer. For people with these chronic HCV infections, it will take decades after infection for the liver to develop these serious diseases.

Human Immunodeficiency Virus

Human immunodeficiency virus (HIV) is the virus which causes acquired immune deficiency syndrome (AIDS). HIV is found in blood and bodily fluids such as semen, vaginal fluid, and cerebrospinal fluid. HIV does not exist in sweat, saliva, or tears. Therefore, sports medicine professionals who work with sweaty athletes daily (in particular personal trainers, strength and conditioning specialists, and athletic trainers) do not need to worry about HIV transmission when coming in contact with athletes' sweat. HIV is less likely to be transmitted than HBV and HCV (Denault & Gardner, 2021). Unlike HBV and HCV, HIV cannot live outside the body or in dried blood for more than a few hours. Therefore in these instances, HIV is not transmissible. However, similarly to HBV and HCV, HIV enters the individual's body via an open wound or mucous membrane by direct contact with HIV-infected blood. After entering the body, HIV invades white blood cells called CD4+ T **lymphocytes**, which play a key role in an individual's immune system. HIV lives in these cells, replicates, and spreads throughout the body. Consequently, after the T cells are destroyed by HIV, the body cannot protect itself against illness and disease. Over time the individual's immune system is destroyed.

Similarly to an individual whose blood tests have affirmed HBV or HCV infection (referred to as HBV or HCV "positive") an HIV positive individual can be a passive carrier and transmit the virus to non-infected individual. The HIV positive individual can also be infected for many years before they exhibit signs and symptoms of illness. In many cases, the athlete exhibits signs and symptoms of HIV infection that mimic the flu for about a week or two. The athlete experiences fatigue, fever, night sweats, joint pain, headaches, nausea, weight loss, and small infections **(Figure 4-3)** If your athlete complains of these signs and symptoms or you identify that they are ill while at your facility, discontinue his activity and refer them to a physician for evaluation.

In order to determine if an individual is infected with HIV, a blood test is performed to test for the actual virus, antigens/antibodies, or antibodies. A "window period" is the timeframe in which the virus, antibodies, or antigens can be detected in the blood. According to the CDC (2021b), depending on the type of HIV test performed the window period varies. A nucleic acid test (NAT), also called a HIV viral load test, tests for the actual virus in the blood and has a window period of 10 to 33 days after exposure. An antigen/antibody test has a window period of 18-45 days. An antibody test has a window period of 23 to 90 days. If an

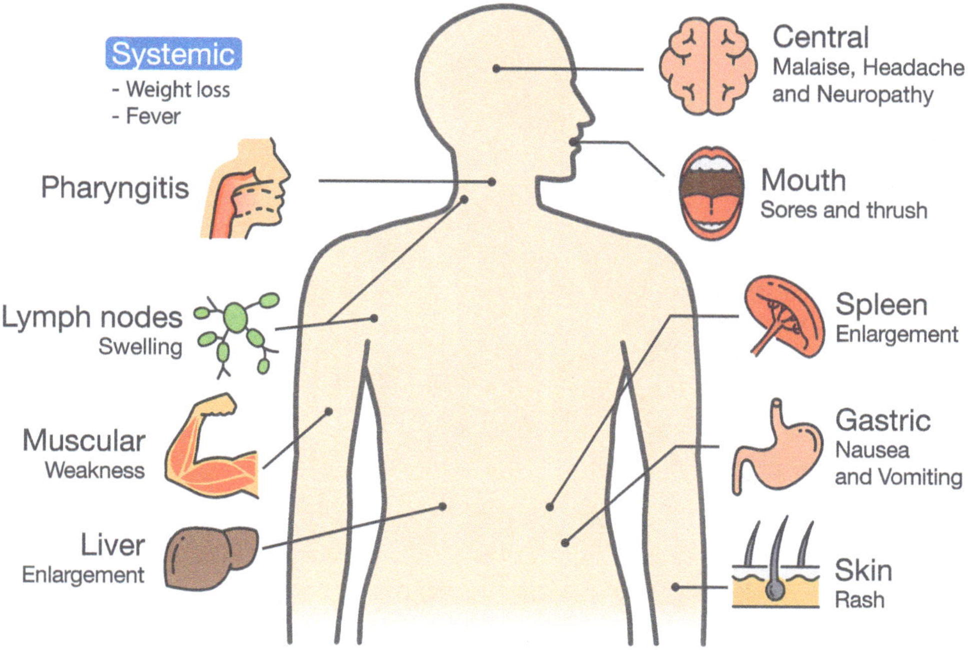

Figure 4-3 Signs and symptoms of HIV infection

individual believes they have been exposed and tests negative within the window period, they should be tested again after the window period.

Fortunately in recent years antiretroviral therapy (ART), which includes at least three HIV medications prescribed to assist a HIV positive individual in decreasing their viral load. The ART must start immediately after HIV diagnosis, and the medications must be taken daily. This therapy has the potential to suppress the virus so that it is undetectable in a NAT. Consequently with ART, the individual has less potential to transmit HIV to others, and can promote a healthier life for themselves (CDC, 2021).

Acquired Immunodeficiency Syndrome

Without ART, HIV eventually weakens the individual's immune system and causes acquired immunodeficiency syndrome (AIDS). The length of time for an HIV infected athlete to develop AIDS varies among individuals, but it can be up to 8 to10 years (Mayo Clinic, 2020). Prior to being diagnosed with AIDS, the individual experiences stages of HIV illness. These stages include primary infection (acute HIV infection) and then the clinical latent infection (chronic HIV) stage. Finally, the individual progresses to the symptomatic infection stage where AIDS is diagnosed **(Figure 4-4)**. During the primary infection (acute HIV infection)

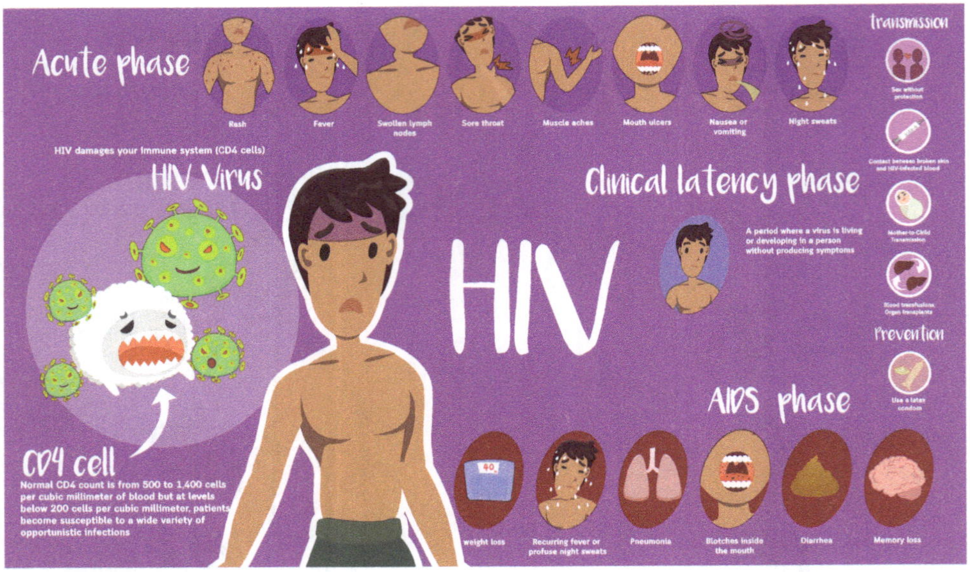

Figure 4-4 The stages of HIV infection progressing to AIDS

stage, the individual exhibits many flu-like signs and symptoms previously mentioned. In the clinical latent infection (chronic HIV) stage the athlete is symptom-free. A blood test confirms a decrease in the T cells. In both the primary infection (acute HIV infection) and clinical latent infection (chronic HIV) stages the individual may not have significant symptoms, be a passive carrier, and unknowingly transmit the virus to others. The third stage is the symptomatic stage. In this stage a blood test reveals a severe decrease in T cells. The athlete exhibits significant weight loss and signs and symptoms of **opportunistic infections**. AIDS is diagnosed when the HIV has significantly destroyed the individual's T cells as determined by a blood test. The individual has signs and symptoms of the disease including severe weight loss, fatigue, nausea, vomiting, weakness, and diarrhea. They may develop disorders such as stomach ulcers, pancreatitis, esophagitis, and skin infections.

Once the individual has been diagnosed with AIDS, their body will not be able to fight any opportunistic infections due to the significant immune system damage. Usually, when a bacterium, virus, fungus, parasite, or other pathogen enters a healthy individual's body, their immune system fights off the pathogen, destroys it, and eliminates it from their body. When an individual has AIDS, the immune system cannot fight even the most common pathogens as a healthy individual's immune system does. Opportunistic infections thrive in their body and take over the systems. Consequently, the pathogen creates deadly illness and disease. Common opportunistic infections include Kaposi sarcoma and other cancerous tumors, pneumonia, and tuberculosis (Mayo Clinic, 2020). Kaposi sarcoma, which is caused by a herpes virus, is the most common type of cancer that affects an individual with AIDS. This cancer forms

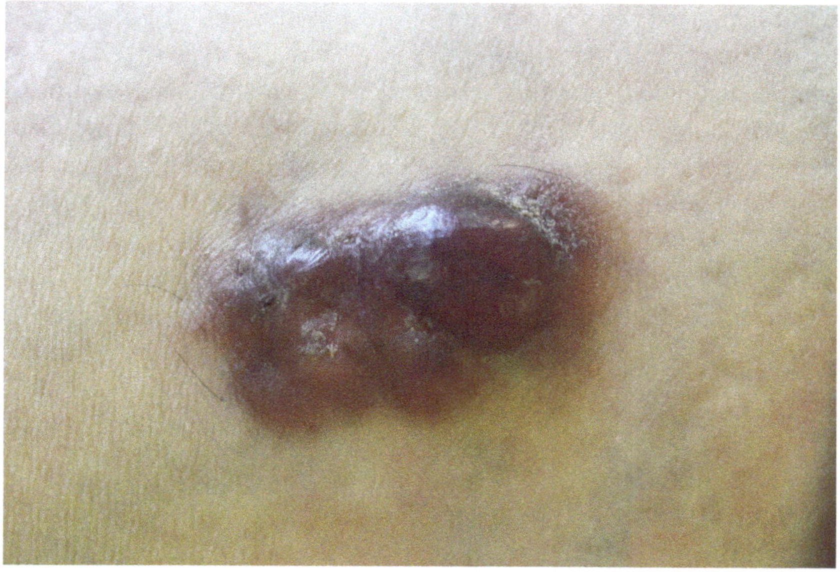

Figure 4-5 Kaposi sarcoma

under the skin and in the mouth, throat, nose, and organs, causing lesions with a reddish-purple appearance, which may be painful **(Figure 4-5)**. From initial AIDS diagnosis and without ART, an individual's life expectancy is approximately 3 years (CDC, 2021b). Presently, no vaccine exists for HIV, nor is there a cure for AIDS.

Exposure and Transmission of Bloodborne Pathogens

Some individuals participate in high-risk activities, which include having unprotected sexual intercourse and sharing contaminated needles. During these activities, **exposure** to bloodborne pathogens may occur. With sexual intercourse, the bloodborne pathogens are exposed to and transmitted through the mucous membranes. When an infected user injects drugs, the needle will most likely contain a minute amount of infected blood. When a non-infected individual shares the same needle, bloodborne pathogens may be transmitted directly into the non-infected individual's bloodstream. These high-risk activities do not occur in a sports medicine professional's daily employment. However, we have to consider that we do not know what high-risk activities our athletes with whom we work participate in on their personal time.

In the sports medicine field, unless a professional is handling blood on a daily basis, the potential for exposure to bloodborne pathogens is minimal. Typically, an exposure incident occurs if an infected athlete's blood comes in direct contact with a non-infected individual's skin, eyes, nose, mouth, mucous membranes, or non-intact skin. The following scenario depicts an exposure incident. You are an athletic trainer at a wrestling tournament. One of your wrestlers sustain a significant nosebleed during practice. With your nitrile gloves on, you assist the athlete by providing first aid to stop the bleeding. Suddenly, they sneeze in front of you. The nasal discharge and blood sprays onto your face, and into your eyes and nasal passageways. Although you do not know if the athlete is infected with a bloodborne pathogen, this situation is an exposure incident. Although uncommon and unusual, a sports medicine occupational (workplace) exposure can realistically occur.

Even though you or your athlete may be exposed to bloodborne pathogens, transmission does not necessarily occur. The infected blood must actually enter another uninfected individual's body via openings in the skin, eyes, nose, mouth, or mucous membranes. The bloodborne pathogens must enter the individual's bloodstream, and the virus must attack and take over a healthy, host cell to begin replicating. This sequence of events is considered bloodborne pathogen transmission.

OSHA Bloodborne Pathogen Standard

In 1991, the Occupational Safety and Health Administration (OSHA) Bloodborne Pathogens Standard 29 CFR 1910.1030 (OSHA, 1991) was publicized. The OSHA Bloodborne Pathogens Standard was instituted to protect all employees, including sports medicine professionals, who may be exposed to bloodborne pathogens or other OPIM, while on the job. The regulations were set forth to designate specific procedures to prevent bloodborne pathogen exposure in the workplace. Also, the standard defines what to do if an exposure incident occurs, as well as your employer's role in reporting and following up with the exposure.

The OSHA standards regulate your employers' actions regarding bloodborne pathogen training for employees, **work practice controls**, employee medical history, and status reviews. If you are an employer, you must abide by the OSHA standards, and implement them appropriately and effectively for your employees' and clients' safety. All employees that have the potential to come in contact with bloodborne pathogens must go through bloodborne pathogen training when they are first hired and annually thereafter (Denault & Gardner, 2021). According to the OSHA standards, the training must be provided by the employer during work hours at no cost to the employee. The training includes information on bloodborne pathogens, exposure, transmission, and prevention.

Work practice controls include procedures that sports medicine professionals practice in order to prevent bloodborne pathogen exposure and transmission. Work practice controls include washing hands after removing gloves, using eyewash stations if necessary, and disposing of needles, scalpels, and the like into sharps containers. In any area where a possibility for bloodborne pathogens or OPIMs exists, eating, drinking, smoking, applying cosmetics, and handling contact lenses is prohibited (OSHA, 1991). Also, sports medicine professionals must make every attempt to prevent spraying or splattering of their patients' blood. On a minimally annual basis, employers must reevaluate the work practice controls. The organization must ascertain that it is taking all precautions to prevent bloodborne pathogen and other OPIM exposures.

Universal Precautions

In order to prevent bloodborne pathogen transmission, sports medicine professionals must follow universal precautions. Universal precautions are standardized, sequenced actions utilized by sports medicine professionals when assisting a bleeding patient or when OPIMs exist. Universal precautions are not necessary when dealing with sweat, tears, vomit, or spit, unless blood appears in these bodily fluids. Universal precautions include the utilization of PPE. PPE must be included in your facility's first aid kit, which must be readily accessible to all employees. Necessary first aid kit materials include disposable gloves, a face mask, protective eyewear, sterile roller gauze and pads, breathing barriers for administering CPR, and hand sanitizer **(Table 4-1)**.

Table 4-1 Items that should be in a workplace first aid kit
• Adhesive bandages (different sizes)
• Latex, vinyl, and/or nitrile disposable gloves
• Sterile gauze pads (different sizes)
• Sterile nonstick pads (different sizes)
• Sterile roller gauze (different widths and lengths)
• Antibiotic ointment
• Antiseptic skin wipes
• Porous cloth tape
• Waterproof tape
• Scissors
• Tweezers
• Spray foaming wound soap
• Saline
• Hand sanitizer
• Biohazard bags
• Cotton swabs
• Tongue depressors
• Triangular bandages
• Moldable splints
• Elastic bandages
• CPR mask
• Protective face mask
• Protective eyewear/goggles
• Mini flashlight and batteries
• Emergency number card

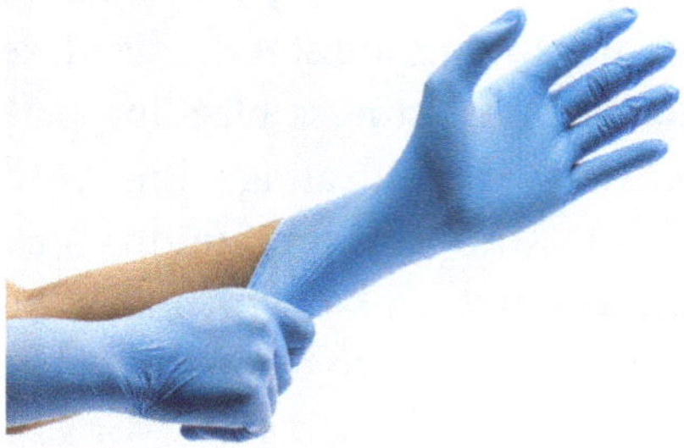

Figure 4-6 When dealing with your patient's blood be certain to put latex, vinyl, or nitrile gloves on first.

Before touching a bleeding athlete put on latex, nitrile, or similar protective gloves (**Figure 4-6**). In situations where a large quantity of blood or the potential for blood to spurt, spray, or splatter exists, such as if an athlete is severely cut, vomiting blood, or has an open fracture, wear face and body protection (mask and gown, respectively). When you are finished providing first aid to the athlete, dispose of the bloody materials properly. If the first aid materials you utilize, such as gauze, bandages, gloves, etc., are classified as **regulated waste** place them in a properly labeled biohazard container or bag (**Figure 4-7**). You should keep biohazard bags in your first aid kit and have biohazard receptacles in your facility. If the materials are not considered regulated waste, then place them in regular garbage. Never reach into a biohazard container or bag to remove any materials. Once you are finished with the first aid care, carefully and properly remove your gloves (**Figure 4-8**). When you remove your gloves, do not touch your skin with a bloody glove. Make every attempt to remove the gloves inside out with a clean portion of the glove. Immediately after removing the gloves and placing them in the proper receptacle, wash your hands with soap and water. If soap and water are not available, use a hand sanitizer or other commercially prepared sanitizing lotion, gel, or towelette. As soon as you can, wash your hands with soap and water.

Figure 4-7 Place regulated waste in a biohazard container or bag.

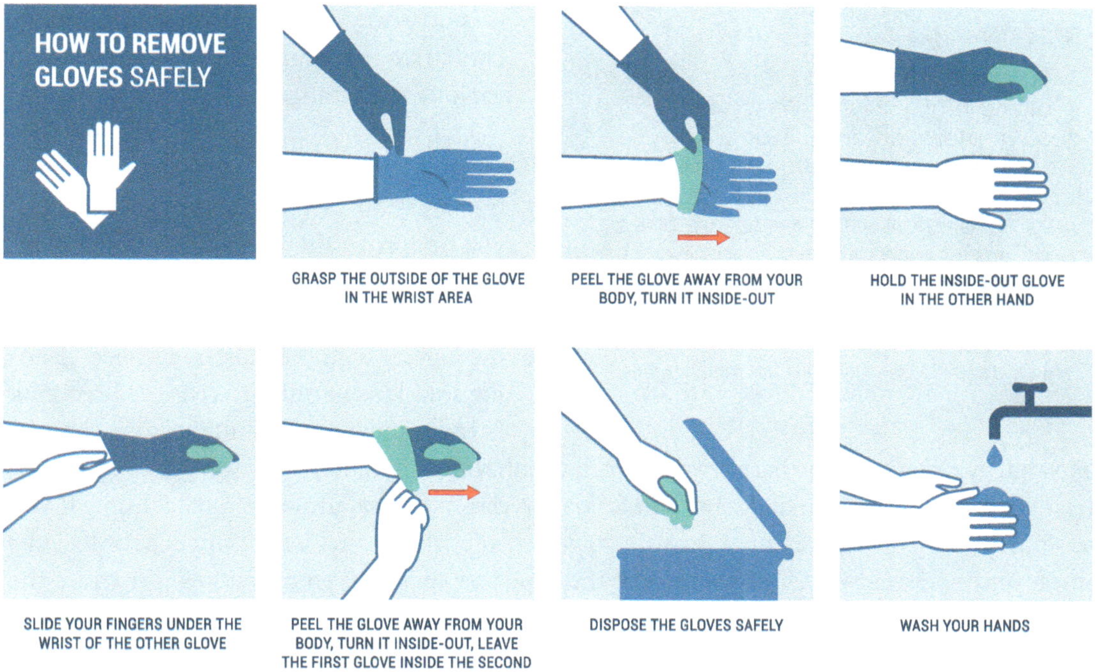

Figure 4-8 Remove your gloves carefully and safely after providing first aid care.

Universal precautions also include cleaning all surfaces that have been exposed to blood and OPIM. Always wear disposable gloves when cleaning surface areas where blood was located. All contaminated items, equipment, floors, etc. must be disinfected as well. Many commercial liquid disinfectant cleaning solutions are available which destroy HIV, HBV, HCV, other viruses, and bacteria when used as directed. Many of these commercial cleaning agents are utilized effectively for daily equipment cleaning. According to the CDC (2021a), a bleach and water solution of one-third cup bleach and one gallon of room temperature water is effective. Since the bleach and water solution loses its effectiveness in 24 hours, the solution must be prepared daily. A bleach and water solution

TIPS FROM THE FIELD

Tip 1 Keep a small storage bag in your car which contains the following contents: at least three pair of disposable latex, vinyl, or nitrile gloves, a few packages of 4" x 4" sterile gauze, a large gauze roll, and a CPR pocket mask. If you have to provide first aid to control bleeding or administer CPR and have access to your car, the basic, appropriate PPE items are available for use. These PPE items are crucial to assist you in preventing bloodborne pathogen transmission. Check the gloves and pocket mask periodically. Changes in temperature detrimentally affect the materials over time. For example, hot temperatures and direct sunlight cause nitrile glove disintegration. Over time in extreme temperatures, latex gloves can stick together and become weak, causing rips and holes. The CPR pocket mask material can break down as well. Frequently check the mask to make sure that it does not have any cracks, is still supple, and air is still in the bladder

> **TIPS FROM THE FIELD**
>
> **Tip 2** For some individuals, latex is an allergen. A latex allergy exhibits mild to severe signs and symptoms on an individual's skin. The mild signs and symptoms can include redness, itchiness, pain, hives, or a rash after wearing latex gloves. More severe allergic reactions include difficulty breathing, chest tightness, and other signs of anaphylactic shock. If you or your patients are allergic to latex, utilize nitrile or vinyl disposable gloves, which cause less allergies for individuals.

is not always the cleaning solution of choice since it breaks down and discolors various materials.

Universal precautions require use of breathing barriers in order to prevent transmission of bloodborne pathogens. If you perform CPR, utilize a breathing mask as a barrier whether or not the athlete has open bleeding facial wounds. Do not clean the barrier with the aforementioned cleaning solutions in order to reuse it. Breathing barriers must only be utilized one time on one athlete. Dispose of the barrier properly in a biohazard container.

Reporting exposure incidents and follow up care is part of universal precautions. If you or your client experiences an exposure incident, report the incident immediately to your employer or supervisor. Once you report the exposure incident, your employer provides the individual with an immediate medical evaluation, provided they give their consent to be evaluated. Your employer bears the cost of blood testing, counseling, and follow up care, and also investigates the exposure incident, including how and why it occurred. It is your employer's responsibility to determine if any workplace controls must be modified. The employer also investigates what steps can be taken at the facility to prevent a future exposure.

Summary

The bloodborne pathogens HBV, HCV, and HIV are three serious viruses that cause significant disease and potentially death. Sports medicine professionals must take an active role in preventing bloodborne pathogen exposure and transmission. Throughout your career, instances will arise requiring you to provide first aid to a bleeding individual. Be certain to utilize universal precautions and PPE when dealing with blood and OPIM. If we consistently and carefully utilize universal precautions when dealing with bloodborne pathogens, we can promote a decline of HBV, HCV, and HIV transmissions in the future.

Keywords

Direct contact When a person has come in contact with another person's infected blood.

Antigen A substance that, when introduced in the body, stimulates the immune system to produce antibodies. Antibodies assist the body to destroy foreign substances such as bacteria.

Jaundice A yellowing of the skin and white of the eyes that can occur with liver inflammation, infection, or disease.

Cirrhosis An irreversible liver disease that occurs over time. The liver tissue is replaced with scar tissue and eventually liver function terminates.

Lymphocytes White blood cells in the body that assist the immune system to fight illness and disease.

Opportunistic infections Illnesses or diseases that invade the body of an individual who has AIDS. Some opportunistic infections include herpes simplex virus, encephalopathy, Kaposi sarcoma, lymphoma, tuberculosis, and pneumonia. Typically in healthy people, these illnesses or diseases can be eliminated by the body or be cared for with medical treatment. However, without treatment including daily medication, HIV will completely destroy individual's immune system. Consequently, their body cannot fight these illnesses or diseases. Eventually, the individual succumbs to the illness or disease and dies.

Exposure Contact with blood or other potentially infectious materials (OPIM) or bodily fluids via mucous membranes, eyes, nose, mouth, non-intact skin, or injection into skin or mucous membranes.

Work practice controls Policies and procedures that an employer creates to assist sports medicine professionals in reducing the chances of bloodborne pathogen exposure in the workplace.

Regulated waste Defined by OSHA is "liquid or semi-liquid blood or other potentially infectious material (OPIM); contaminated items that would release blood or OPIM in a liquid or semi-liquid state if compressed; items that are caked with dried blood or OPIM and are capable of releasing these materials during handling; contaminated sharps; and pathological and microbiological wastes containing blood or OPIM" (OSHA, 1991).

Discussion Questions

1. As discussed in this chapter, sports medicine professionals must be aware of which three common bloodborne pathogens?
2. Bloodborne pathogens are found in what bodily fluids?
3. What are the different ways that a sports medicine professional can contract a bloodborne pathogen in the workplace?
4. What is a passive carrier?
5. Which of the three bloodborne pathogen infections is preventable via immunization?
6. What are the stages of HIV infection which eventually lead to AIDS?
7. HBV, HCV, and HIV have many similar signs and symptoms. Describe the signs and symptoms that are <u>different</u> among the three bloodborne pathogens.
8. Name some of the OSHA universal precautions that a sports medicine professional must follow when treating an athlete with a bleeding wound or when OPIM are present.
9. What are your employers' responsibilities if you or your patient experience an exposure incident in the workplace?
10. What are some PPE that you must use when providing first aid care to a bleeding athlete?

CASE STUDY: WHAT A BLOODY MESS!

Ms. Anderson is a physical education teacher at Welcoming High School. She has just completed a week of teaching her freshmen students a volleyball unit, including skills, etiquette, and modified rules, in preparation for a class volleyball tournament. Today the boys and girls begin the tournament in class. Ms. Anderson stresses to the students that as a safety precaution they must adhere to the modified rules she has previously taught and explained to them. In particular, she emphasizes that students are not allowed to spike the ball in her physical education class. Ms. Anderson instituted this rule in attempt to prevent any unnecessary harm to students who do not possess the skills, strength, and experience to properly defend a spiked volleyball.

To begin the tournament, Ms. Anderson divides the class into four, equally skilled teams. All four teams play at once on two courts. The first day of the tournament went smoothly and the students appeared to have a great time. However, on the second day of the tournament a student named George becomes agitated due to his team's poor performance. He feels that he is doing all of the work to score points for his team. George also believes his teammates are not contributing as much as he was. George expect much more of his teammates and he becomes incredibly mad. At this point, he cannot control his anger. It is George's turn to rotate into the attack line. George's teammate sets the ball close to the net right by George. George spikes it with extreme force into the opposing court. The ball hits his opponent, Monica, squarely in the face. She immediately begins to bleed profusely from both nostrils. George immediately helps Monica and gets blood all over his hands.

Monica's teammates yell for Ms. Anderson, who is settling a scoring issue on the adjoining court. Ms. Anderson goes over to see what all of the commotion is about. When she arrives, Monica is sitting on the gymnasium floor with both hands covering her nose and mouth. There is a small pool of blood beneath her, and blood all over her hands. George is crouching next to Monica and is helping her. He has Monica's blood all over his hands. Ms. Anderson asks Monica and George what happened, and if there is anything else wrong other than her bloody nose. Monica states that she is very dizzy and her vision is a bit blurry. Ms. Anderson asks a student, John, to run to get the school nurse. In the meantime, Ms. Anderson begins to panic because she knows that she needed to stop Monica's bleeding. The only items Ms. Anderson has in her pocket are tissues.

1. What should Ms. Anderson do first?
2. Should Ms. Anderson consider Monica a bloodborne pathogen passive carrier? Why or why not?
3. What universal precautions should Ms. Anderson take to protect both her and Monica from bloodborne pathogen transmission?
4. What should be done about the pool of blood on the gymnasium floor?
5. How should Ms. Anderson have been more prepared for this bleeding incident?
6. What PPE should Ms. Anderson have on-site in the gym?
7. Since George had Monica's blood on his hands, is Ms. Anderson required to report this as an exposure incident?

References

Center for Disease Control and Prevention (CDC). (2021a, July 22). *Cleaning and disinfecting with bleach and water.* Retrieved March 14, 2022, from https://www.cdc.gov/healthywater/hygiene/disinfecting-bleach.html

Center for Disease Control and Prevention (CDC). (2021b, May 20). *Living with HIV.* Retrieved March 13, 2022, from https://www.cdc.gov/hiv/basics/livingwithhiv/treatment.html

Center for Disease Control and Prevention (CDC). (2020a, July 28). *Hepatitis B questions and answers for healthcare professionals.* Retrieved March 12, 2022, from https://www.cdc.gov/hepatitis/hbv/hbvfaq.htm#treatment

Center for Disease Control and Prevention (CDC) (2020b, July 28). *Hepatitis C questions and answers for the public.* Retrieved March 12, 2022 from, https://www.cdc.gov/hepatitis/hcv/cfaq.htm?CDC_AA_refVal=https%3A%2F%2Fwww.cdc.gov%2Fhepatitis%2Fc%2Fcfaq.htm#A3

Denault, D., & Gardner, H. (2021, October 19). *OSHA bloodborne pathogen standards.* StatPearls [Internet]. https://pubmed.ncbi.nlm.nih.gov/34033323/

Mayo Clinic. (2021a, February 13). *HIV/AIDS.* Retrieved March 13, 2022, from https://www.mayoclinic.org/diseases-conditions/hiv-aids/symptoms-causes/syc-20373524

Mayo Clinic. (2021b, August 31). *Hepatitis C.* Retrieved March 12, 2022, from https://www.mayoclinic.org/diseases-conditions/hepatitis-c/symptoms-causes/syc-20354278

Mejia, A., Nemer, J.A., & Elling, B. (2022). *Bloodborne and airborne pathogens (8th Ed.)* Jones and Bartlett Learning.

Occupational Safety and Health Administration (OSHA). (1991). *Standard 29 CFR 1910.1030.* Retrieved March12,2022,fromhttps://www.osha.gov/laws-regs/regulations/standardnumber/1910/1910.1030

Wang, E. (2021, September 22). Hepatitis B Foundation. *Your sexual health and Hepatitis B!* https://www.hepb.org/blog/sexual-health-hepatitis-b/

World Health Organization (WHO). (2021, July 27). *Hepatitis B.* https://www.who.int/news-room/fact-sheets/detail/hepatitis-b

Chapter 5

Wound Care and Bandaging

Chapter Objectives

After you have read this chapter, you will be able to understand:

- The various types of wounds that an individual can sustain.
- The signs, symptoms, and differences between external and internal bleeding.
- How to provide first aid care for open and closed wounds.
- How to apply dressings and bandages.
- When to refer an individual with an open wound or internal bleeding to a physician or the emergency room (ER).

Wounds are extremely common soft tissue injuries that frequently occur to people. Undoubtedly, a time will come when you must provide first aid care for an individual, who has sustained a wound at your facility. You will have to determine the wound type and severity. Many wounds are minor and can be adequately treated without advanced medical care; however, you will have to determine if referral to a physician or emergency medical services (EMS) is warranted. Determining whether a wound is life threatening is imperative for an individual's survival. It is crucial that you recognize the types of wounds, mechanisms of injury, and signs and symptoms You must know how to provide adequate first aid care for wounds, which most often includes applying dressings and bandages. Also, when treating or in close proximity to an individual's open bleeding wound, you must recall the Chapter 4 information and always use universal precautions. This chapter offers you useful information regarding wounds that will certainly assist you in your sports medicine practice.

Bleeding

Capillaries, veins, and arteries are the three blood vessels in the body. Although capillary, venous, and arterial bleeding are all similar in that blood exits the damaged blood vessel, other signs of bleeding for each vessel are dissimilar. Capillaries are the smallest and most numerous of the three types of blood vessels, while arteries are the largest. Capillary bleeding is the most common type of bleeding that will occur to your clients (American Academy of Orthopaedic Surgeons [AAOS], 2022). Capillary blood seeps out from a wound very slowly, and usually in smaller amounts in comparison to venous and arterial bleeding. The blood appears to be red. Common mechanisms of injury causing capillary bleeding can be when an object scrapes or causes a minor cut on the skin's surface. Typically the wound will slowly bleed, and in most cases, the capillary bleeding will not be difficult to control with first aid skills.

Unlike capillary bleeding, venous and arterial bleeding are rare and occur only with severe, traumatic mechanisms of injury. Although venous and arterial bleeding are both notably serious, arterial bleeding typically leads to fatalities or neurological dysfunction (Hartkamp et al., 2017). Venous blood flows out of the body comparable to how water flows out of a garden hose. It exits the blood vessel in a steady manner and commonly in large quantities. These factors make venous bleeding difficult to control. Due to the carbon dioxide in venous blood, the blood is darker red than capillary blood. On the other hand, the high oxygen content in arterial blood causes this blood to be much brighter red than capillary blood. Arterial blood does not seep out like capillary blood, nor does it continuously and steadily pour out like venous blood. Instead, arterial blood shoots out of the blood vessel with each heartbeat. Each time the heart beats, a large quantity of blood exits the artery with significant force. The arterial blood exiting the wound is plentiful and difficult to stop with common first aid skills. Immediate surgery is necessary to treat a severed artery (Guven & Kafadar, 2020). Whenever you recognize venous or arterial bleeding, summon advanced medical care at once by calling 911, and treat the individual for **shock**. Venous and arterial bleeding is life-threatening. Therefore, act immediately and quickly to help save your patient's life (**Figure 5-1**).

Often venous and arterial bleeding occur simultaneously due to the veins' and arteries' close proximity. If one vessel is damaged, it is highly probable that the other vessel is damaged as well. Consider how arterial and venous bleeding occurs simultaneously in the following

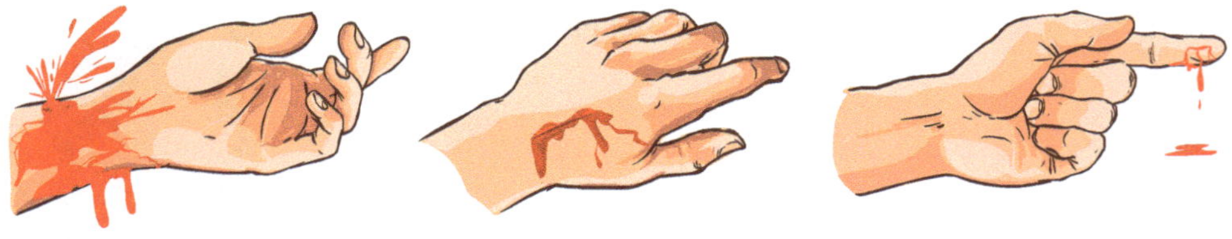

Figure 5-1 Arterial, venous, and capillary bleeding

scenario. Two collegiate ice hockey players are racing for the puck. Both players checked each other and lost their balance. One player's skate strikes the front of the other player's neck and lacerates the skin and underlying tissues. As the injured player stands up and exits the ice to sit down on the bench, the athletic trainer looks at the players on the ice. The athletic trainer looks at the blood's appearance on the ice and immediately knows the athlete has a life-threatening injury. On the ice are two trails of blood. One trail appears as a dark red, steady line from where the athlete was injured and continues all the way to the bench. The other trail appears in spurts or sprays over the ice. A spray of bright red blood follows a void area, and alternates blood and void the entire distance to the bench. It is evident that the athlete has both his jugular vein and carotid artery injured by the skate. These two blood vessels are located in the neck in close proximity to each other. The vein expels dark red blood in a continuous stream, while the artery expels blood with each heartbeat which created the bright red blood spray followed by a void, then another blood spray, and so on. This venous and arterial external bleeding is a life-threatening, medical emergency. EMS must be summoned immediately to transport the injured athlete to the emergency room. While waiting for the ambulance, the athletic trainer must provide appropriate first aid to the athlete. Appropriate first aid is discussed later in this chapter.

You can easily determine what type of bleeding an individual is experiencing by remembering characteristics of capillary, venous, and arterial bleeding. By knowing the manner in which the blood is exiting the wound, the quantity of blood produced, and its color, you can decide if the bleeding is capillary, venous, or arterial. Make this determination immediately, so you can provide appropriate first aid skills, and know whether to summon EMS.

External and Internal Bleeding

Regardless of whether a capillary, vein, or artery is bleeding, the blood exits the body, remains in the body, or possibly both simultaneously. When blood exits the body either from the skin via an **open wound** or another opening in the body, such as the nose, mouth, or ears, then the bleeding is considered external bleeding. An example of external bleeding is when a person is playing basketball at your gym and is hit in the nose by the ball. As a result, capillaries are damaged in his nasal passageway, their nose begins to bleed, and the blood exits through their nostrils. You can easily determine if a person is bleeding externally due to the visible blood. However, internal bleeding is very different. Internal bleeding occurs when a blood vessel is damaged and releases blood inside the body. The blood does not exit through any wound or opening in the body and remains within the skin. Internal bleeding occurs with various injuries and illnesses. Injuries caused by a direct blow often bleed internally. Often you cannot see signs of internal bleeding. Ecchymosis, or a black and blue skin color caused by internal bleeding, may be present. Usually the area that is injured and is bleeding is painful, tender to the touch (point tender), and rigid. An example when internal bleeding occurs is when your client drops a free weight on their foot and hours later ecchymosis appears (**Figure 5-2**). Because the

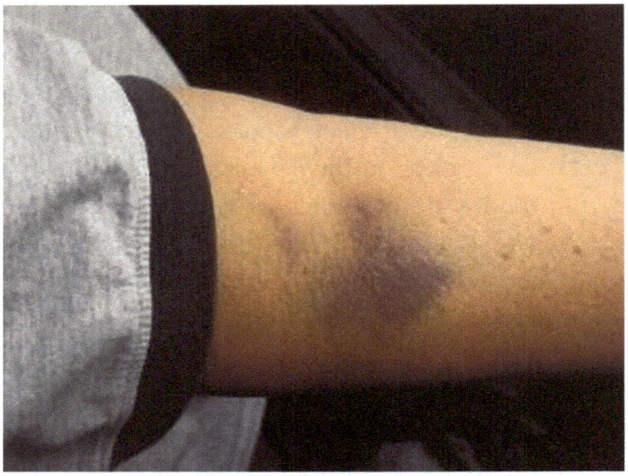

Figure 5-2 Ecchymosis is a sign of internal bleeding.

bleeding in this **closed wound** occurs within the underlying tissues and an open wound does not exist, signs of bleeding, such as ecchymosis, may not be apparent. Consequently, it may be difficult to determine if your client is significantly injured when they have a closed wound and internal bleeding.

Open Wounds

Open wounds are a commonality in our everyday life. Minor open wounds occur frequently when we sustain a paper cut, a pinprick, or blacktop skin abrasion. We can experience more severe open wounds from objects such as glass breaking the skin, a steering wheel during a car accident, or a knife while cutting food. Whether these open wounds are simple, complex, or life threatening, they are classified to help you determine the first aid necessary and whether referral to advanced medical care is warranted. The six classifications of open wounds include abrasions, incisions, lacerations, punctures, avulsions, and amputations.

Abrasions

Abrasions occur when the skin comes in contact with a surface or object which rubs against the skin (**Figure 5-3**). The rubbing removes minute portions of the skin, leaving an open wound. The surfaces that rub against the skin and cause abrasions are most often rough surfaces, such as blacktop, concrete, and sand. Picture a softball player wearing their standard uniform which includes shorts and high socks. When their teammate hits the ball, they run and slide into second base. An abrasion occurs as a result of the rubbing of the grainy sand on the lateral side of their unprotected knee. Smooth surfaces such as a tiled or gymnasium

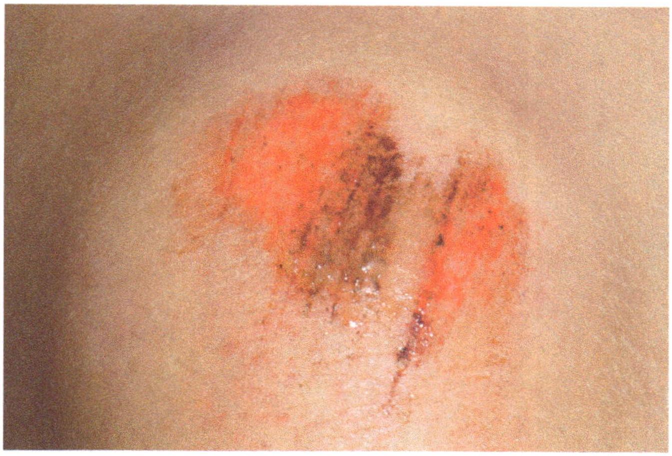

© Jarretera/Shutterstock.com

Figure 5-3 An abrasion

room floor can also cause abrasions. Think about a middle school physical education class having scooter races. A student is lying on their stomach on the scooter and is pushing it with their hands and feet. Suddenly, while going fast down the floor, they fall off the scooter. Their forearm forcefully rubs against a portion of the floor, and they consequently sustain an abrasion on their forearm.

Abrasions are typically painful. The patient usually feels a stinging or burning sensation. These wounds are also prone to infection due to dirt carrying bacteria that becomes imbedded into the wound, coupled with lack of bleeding (Lloyd Jones, 2007). To an extent, blood coming out of a wound actually helps eliminate some dirt, bacteria, and other small foreign debris from a wound. Generally speaking, because abrasions do not bleed a lot, they have a greater potential for infection than other wounds which tend to bleed more readily.

Incisions

Incisions are open wounds that appear to have smooth edges (**Figure 5-4**). Sharp objects, such as smooth blade knives and glass, can cause incisions. These objects may cause incisions that appear to be superficial, but in reality are very deep (Lloyd Jones, 2007). Paper cuts are incisions that are superficial; a smooth blade knife can cause a very deep incision. Often the object causing the incision may be so sharp that the individual does not even feel the object strike the skin. Consider the following scenario: Your client has just completed a workout and is standing next to you in We R Fit Gym. They are drinking orange juice in a glass from the snack bar. They suddenly drop the glass on the tile floor, which shatters next to you. You immediately close off the area and clean up the glass so other clients do not get injured. Due to the hectic scene, you did not notice that your lateral lower leg is bleeding from an incision caused by the shattered glass. You did not have any pain, and noticed the incision due to the

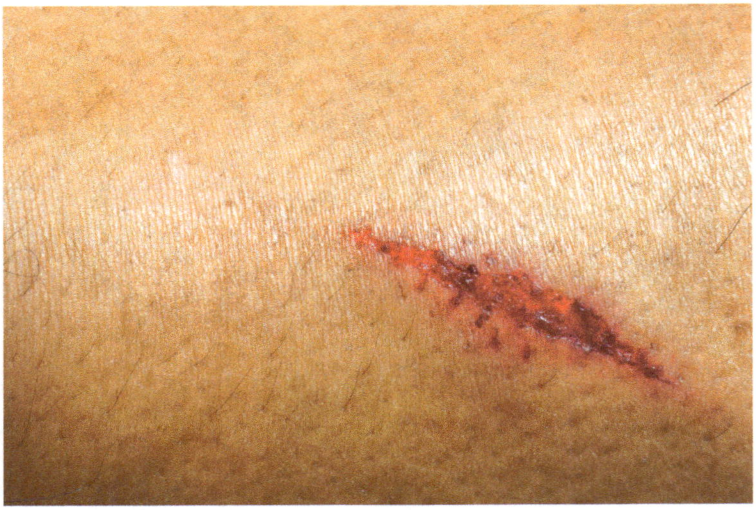

Figure 5-4 An incision

feeling of blood slowly dripping down your leg. Superficial incisions can cause minimal to no pain. Deep wounds usually cause sharp and throbbing pain. Incisions tend to bleed significantly, depending on their length, depth, and location. The quantity of blood can be minimal to immense. Incisions to the scalp tend to bleed enormously due to the vast quantity of capillaries in the tissue. Also, the skin may not **approximate**. The cut edges may seem to pull away from each other.

Lacerations

Lacerations are very similar to incisions because they may be superficial or deep, with minimal or immense bleeding (**Figure 5-5**). These wounds can be caused by sharp objects striking the skin, or by an object crushing, pulling, or grinding against the skin. Consider the following scenario: After one training session with your client, they decide to run on their own. They go to the local high school and run around the track. As part of their workout your clients run up and down the metal stadium bleachers. While running up the bleachers, they do not plant their foot well, slip, and fall. They hit their shin as they fall down. The metal stadium bleacher causes a crushing, grinding force against the skin which pulls the skin apart, creating a laceration. The appearance of lacerations differs from incisions. Whereas an incision's skin has straight, clean edges, a lacerated skin appears jagged and uneven. Consequently, like an incision, the edges may not approximate. The cut edges may seem to pull away from each other. Due to the skin's jagged edges, skin may also appear missing. As with incisions, the pain varies depending on the laceration's size and depth. Other than with the wound's appearance, lacerations and incisions have similar characteristics.

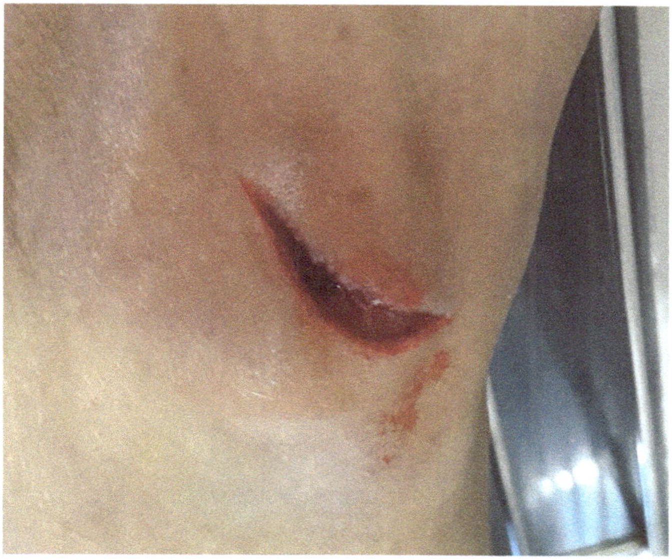

Figure 5-5 A laceration

Punctures

Punctures occur when an object penetrates the skin (**Figure 5-6**). An object can be small like a splinter, or large like a knife. When an object punctures the skin, it may fall out of or remain in the wound. Some objects protrude from the wound. Most puncture wounds are not life-threatening, but secondary complications, such as infection, can occur (Baddour & Brown, 2019). In general, puncture wounds do not bleed much in comparison to incisions and lacerations. However, as with other wounds, punctures cause pain. The pain may be dull, aching,

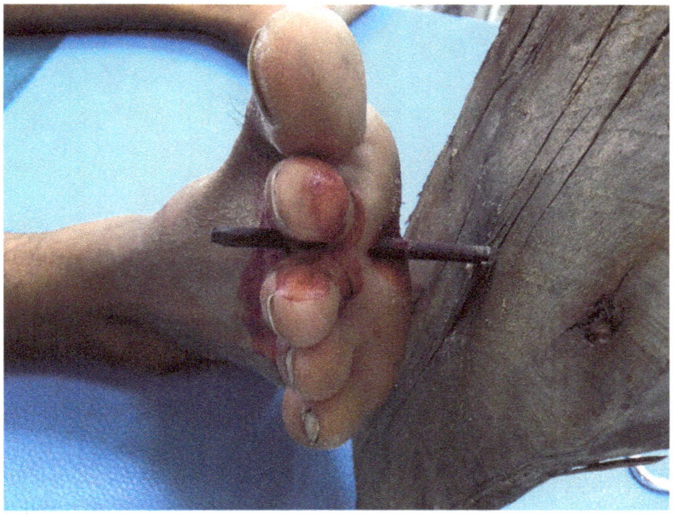

Figure 5-6 A puncture

or sharp. The amount of pain produced often indicates the extent and depth of the injury (McDevitt & Gillespie, 2008). The object's size determines not only the depth of injury, but also the extent of injury. A large puncturing object, such as knife, undoubtedly causes greater trauma, bleeding, and pain than a smaller object, such as a pin. Swelling and ecchymosis may also arise around the wound. Many puncture wounds occur to the foot because we bear weight and put pressure on our feet when we stand, walk, and run. Common objects that cause punctures to the feet include glass, nails, and shells on the beach. Puncture wounds also commonly occur to the fingers and hands since we use implements, equipment, and objects during the course of the day. Typical objects that puncture hands and fingers include pins, needles, wood (splinters), nails, and fishhooks.

Avulsions

Avulsions are wounds where the skin is torn, and some tissue is actually ripped off (**Figure 5-7**). The mechanism of injury is a traumatic event. For example, people should not wear jewelry, in particular earrings and rings, during activity. Some activities in which wearing jewelry would not be recommended due to potential avulsion injury include lifting weights, contact sports, yard work, construction, or equipment use. These activities, as well as others not mentioned in this text, can cause jewelry to be ripped from the body and pull tissue off. This type of avulsion injury causes significant pain and bleeding. Stitching and/or surgery may be necessary to repair the tissues. Consequently, if an individual has sustained an avulsion, call 911 immediately and treat them for shock.

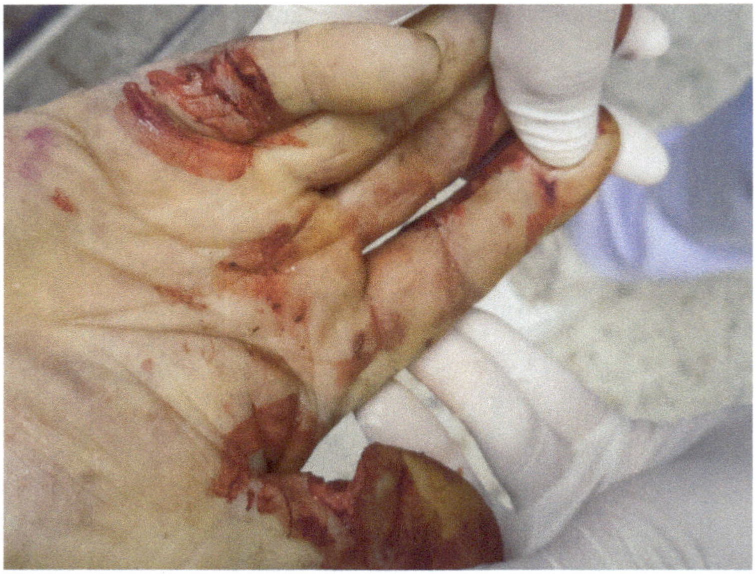

Figure 5-7 An avulsion

Amputations

Similar to avulsions, amputations occur when a significant traumatic force entirely cuts off a part of the body (**Figure 5-8**). Amputations occur as a result of a traumatic force. Usually these wounds occur to smaller body parts, such as fingers, toes, and earlobes. However, in some major traumatic events, such as automobile accidents, loss of a limb is very possible. Objects causing amputations include knives, saws, mechanical power equipment, and glass. To prevent amputations, individuals must use these objects correctly, pay attention to warning labels and directions, and avoid utilizing defective equipment.

Signs and symptoms of amputations include minor to major bleeding, which depends on the size and location of the body part that has been amputated; significant pain; shock; and the severed body part (MedlinePlus, 2020). In the case of amputations, shock occurs due to the significant external bleeding. Because blood is exiting the body at the open wound, oxygen is not distributed as needed to the brain and vital organs. If the patient is in shock for a period of time, death can result.

In some cases, amputated body parts can be reattached by surgeons. In other cases, as determined by physicians, the limb may not be able to be reattached. Also, the physician may

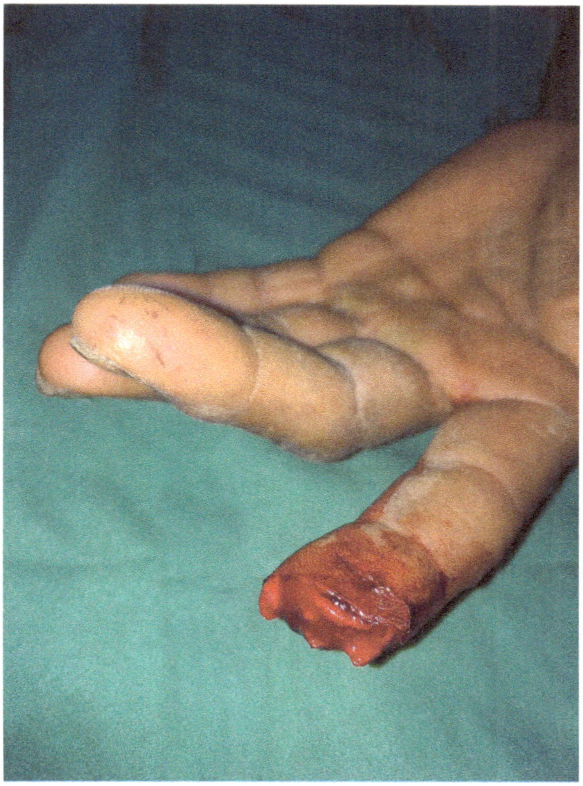

Figure 5-8 An amputation

determine that for adequate healing and to obtain better functional capabilities, the patient is better off with a **prosthesis** rather than reattachment of the amputated body part.

Infection

With any open wound, a possibility of infection exists (**Figure 5-9**). Infection results from improper initial treatment and inappropriate continual care of a wound. Also, debris, bacteria, or other pathogens that were initially in or remain in the wound can cause infection. Regardless of the type of open wound, the penetrating object may have debris, bacteria, or other pathogens on it. Therefore, any open wound can become infected. Punctures are particularly prone to infection. Debris or a pathogen on the puncturing object can be pushed far down into the puncture hole. Because small punctures, in particular, bleed minimally, the pathogen remains in the puncture. If the puncture is not cleaned properly, the pathogen remains in the wound. Over time, the pathogen creates infection. Wound infection signs and symptoms vary. Common signs and symptoms include pus discharge, swelling, and redness in and around the wound. A patient with an infection may also complain of pain at the wound, general body fatigue, and fever. Usually an infected wound does not appear to progress through the healing process. If your patient's wound is infected, refer your patient to a doctor.

One notable bacterium that causes infection, and even creates a life-threatening illness for your patients, is the bacterium that causes tetanus. It is a fallacy that only puncture wounds can cause the tetanus infection. Likewise, it is false that only rusty metal objects carry the bacteria. On the contrary, the bacteria causing tetanus can enter the body via any open wound and any object. Typically, tetanus bacteria are found on dirty objects. Within 1 to 3 weeks from when the tetanus bacteria enter the body, a first signs of infection appears.

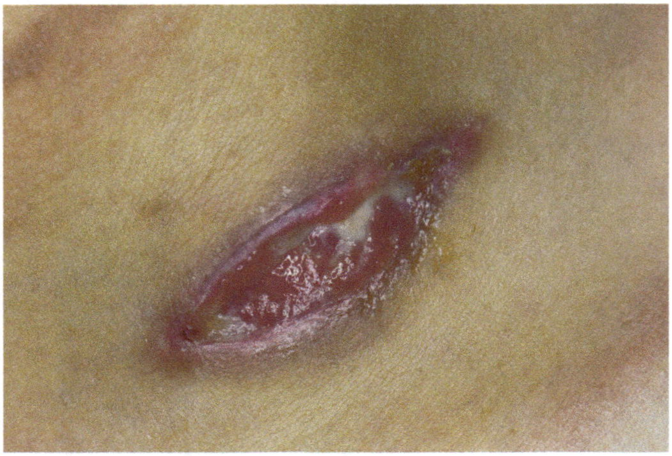

Figure 5-9 An infected wound

This sign is called "lockjaw", which is a serious facial muscle spasm. Along with lockjaw, other immediate signs of infection include fever, sweating, and irritability. Soon thereafter, the spasms occur to other muscles. These spasms can cause muscle ruptures, fractures, and breathing difficulty (MedlinePlus, 2019). The potential for significant, life-threatening illness from tetanus is why vaccination for tetanus, as well as get a **booster vaccination** every 10 years, is imperative.

First Aid for External Wounds

External, open wounds require appropriate first aid care. If proper first aid is not rendered, then proper wound healing does not occur. Likewise, to complicate matters, without proper first aid and wound healing, possible wound infection can occur. Many sports medicine professionals have formal basic or advanced first aid training and know how to provide proper first aid for wounds. If you do not have formal first aid training, you can and should heed general guidelines to provide your patient with adequate, appropriate care.

When providing first aid care for open, bleeding wounds, the first step you take is to stop the bleeding. In order to stop the bleeding, put on gloves and then apply direct pressure to the wound with a clean, preferably sterile, dressing. These dressings, such as gauze sponges or squares, must be in your organization's first aid kit (**Figure 5-10**). The dressings will become saturated with blood with venous, arterial, and severe capillary bleeding. If saturation occurs, keep the dressings on the wound and add additional dressings on top. Do not remove any dressings, otherwise bleeding most likely will resume. Continue to provide direct pressure over the wound. Have someone call 911, and comfort your patient by talking to them. If a wound exhibits only minor

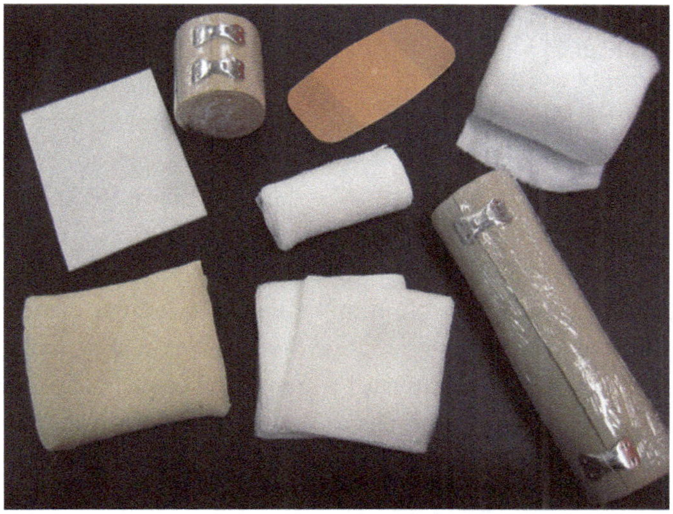

Figure 5-10 Various dressings must be included in your first aid kit.

TIPS FROM THE FIELD

Tip 1 When providing first aid care for an open wound, take all necessary first aid supplies out of the first aid kit before providing care. One mistake that a caregiver could make is to have gloves on, touch the bleeding wound, then with the bloody gloves put their hands back into the first aid kit. The caregiver would contaminate the entire first aid kit with blood, and possibly bloodborne pathogens. If you care for an open wound and forget to take an item out of the first aid kit, properly take off the gloves, dispose of them appropriately, retrieve the materials you need from the first aid kit, apply new gloves, and then care for the bleeding wound. Try to avoid this delay in care by removing all necessary first aid items before touching the bleeding patient. Taking time to think about what materials you need will assist you in providing efficient and timely first aid care. Often you will have a coworker or bystander able to assist you in retrieving materials from the first aid kit and handing them to you for application. For example, taking off the wax-lined tabs on adhesive bandages is difficult because the adhesive sticks to the gloves. Your coworker, who is not wearing gloves, could easily prepare these bandages and materials for you. Be careful not get blood on your coworker when obtaining the materials from them. Have your coworker put the items down for you to take, as to prevent any exposure from your coworker.

capillary bleeding, the dressings most often do not become saturated. Slowly and carefully remove the dressings, dispose of them properly, and continue with your first aid skills. At any time if the dressings stick to the wound, do not attempt to remove them. However, if you must remove the dressing to bandage the area, wet the dressings with small amounts of water or saline until the dressings are loosened, then remove them. If you are not able to remove the dressings easily, continue with your first aid skills and refer the patient to a physician. Remember when applying dressings; do not put direct pressure on an impaled object, on a wounded eye, or a fracture (AAOS, 2022). Also, especially with a potential underlying fractured bone, minimize movement of the area and stabilize it; otherwise, further injury can result. Fortunately, the majority of minor open wounds stop bleeding within about 5 minutes. Shock typically does not result from minor bleeding; however, keep in mind that some patients are not able to tolerate the sight of blood, and will go into shock.

After the bleeding has stopped, continue to provide care to your patient by cleaning the wound. For major wound bleeding, cleaning the wound is not a priority. With major bleeding, your patient needs immediate advanced medical care before they go into shock from loss of blood. Therefore, EMS must be summoned immediately. In contrast for minor wound bleeding, clean the wound immediately to remove bacteria, pathogens, and debris, as well as promote proper healing. Once the bleeding has stopped, carefully remove the dressings and gently wash the wound with antibacterial or ordinary soap and clean water. In place of soap and water, you can also use a commercially prepared cleaning agent. Over the years, various companies have created wound **antiseptics** in various forms including liquids, gels, ointments, and aerosols. Some research has shown that utilizing these commercially prepared wound cleaning agents produces better wound healing and decreasing healing time as compared to using soap and water (Kramer et al., 2018). One benefit of having these agents in a first aid kit is that they are readily available for immediate wound cleaning, especially when soap and water are not accessible. While cleaning the wound, carefully observe the wound to see if any debris is in the wound. If debris is embedded in the wound, do not remove it. Continue to clean the wound and flush it with water, then dress and bandage the wound, and call for medical assistance.

TIPS FROM THE FIELD

TIP 2 You can "double glove" when providing first aid care. *Double glove* means to apply two gloves on each hand before touching the bleeding patient. If you need to take off your gloves in order to go back into your first aid kit because you forgot to take out an item (as described in Tip 1), or need additional items, you take off the outer layer gloves and have the second layer underneath.

Many different dressings have been created and are useful for providing wound care. Some dressings are formulated not to stick to the wound, while others have **antimicrobial** agents incorporated into the dressing to help prevent infection. Specialized dressings exist and are often used by sports medicine professionals. One specialized dressing is an occlusive dressing, which is a nonabsorbent dressing that creates a film over the wound. Occlusive dressings are built to seal out debris, air, moisture, bacteria, and other pathogens. Hydrocolloid dressings contain particles that combine with the blood from the wound and form a gel that creates a moist environment and promotes healing. Butterfly bandages or Steri-Strip™ skin closures hold the wound edges together. Some specialized dressings are very expensive. Some wounds require these specialized dressings, and others only require basic gauze and nonadherent dressings.

When using sterile gauze or a non-adherent dressing, choose the appropriate dressing size to completely cover the wound. For very minor wounds, a typical commercial adhesive bandage, which contains a non-adherent dressing, most often will suffice. Prior to applying the adhesive bandage, apply an antibacterial ointment to the wound, as per the directions on the product package. This ointment helps seal out any debris or pathogens from getting into the wound. Once you have placed the ointment on the wound with a cotton tipped applicator and applied the dressing, you may or may not need to apply a roller gauze bandage. Typically, if the patient is continuing activity or if the wound is minor yet large, then placing a roller gauze bandage on the wound is purposeful (**Figure 5-11**).

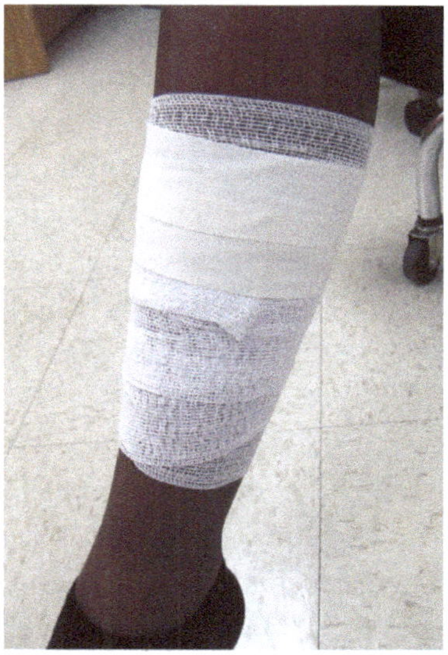

Figure 5-11 Apply a roller gauze to secure dressings.

The roller gauze bandage holds the dressing in place during activity. To apply the roller gauze to an extremity,

begin at the furthest end of the wound closest to either the hand or foot. Unroll the roller gauze upwards toward the head. As you unroll the roller gauze bandage, unroll it so it overlaps by about half the width of the previously applied roller gauze bandage. As you unroll the roller gauze, do not wrap the wound and extremity too tightly, which may cut off circulation, or too loosely, which may cause the roller gauze to fall off. Completely cover the wound. When you are finished, you may have excess roller gauze. Cut the excess roller gauze with safety, blunt tipped scissors. Place elastic or paper tape on the unsecured end of the roller bandage. Apply enough tape to secure the roller gauze bandage and keep it from falling off. Once the roller gauze bandage has been applied, ask your patient if it feels comfortable, is not too tight or loose, and does not restrict movement.

When you are applying the roller gauze bandage, and once you have finished, check the patient's circulation to make sure it is normal. Do so by comparing the color of your patient's hands and feet, depending on where the roller gauze bandage has been applied. The color and temperature should be the same on the contralateral extremities. Also, check the patient's capillary refill. With two of your fingers, press the fingernail or toenail bed on the extremity with the open wound. The nail bed color should be pink without pressure, and change to white with pressure. Upon releasing your pressure, the nail bed should immediately turn back to pink. This refill of blood into the nail bed demonstrates adequate circulation through the extremity to the fingers and toes. If the patient is responding well to your first aid treatment, consider whether you need to refer them to the ER for stitches.

To Stitch or Not to Stitch?

Before you dress and bandage an open wound, inspect it carefully and ask yourself "Does this wound need stitches?" You can utilize a few criteria to determine whether to refer your patient to a physician for stitches. Whenever an individual has a laceration or incision on the face, hands, or head, you must refer them to their physician or the ER immediately for stitches. Even if the wound is minor in these areas, stitches are necessary to help minimize scarring. Also, if the wound is very severe or greater than an inch long, the damaged ends do not approximate, it does not stop bleeding in a short amount of time, or you can see the underlying tissues in the wound, then the individual must be

TIPS FROM THE FIELD

TIP 3 Have the person assist you as much as possible when providing first aid for their bleeding wound. When an individual approaches you for help, hand them something clean, such as a towel, T-shirt, or sweatshirt to hold over the wound and apply direct pressure to it. If you have sterile gauze readily available you can give them the gauze to hold over the wound. Do not hand the item or dressing to the bleeding patient. They may grab the item or dressing with a bloody hand, which may touch you. Instead, put the item down on his lap if they are sitting, or on a table or hard, non-fabric chair, which can be easily cleaned. By putting the item down and having the individual pick it up to use, you will not have contact with the individual's blood. In the meantime, while the individual is applying their own direct pressure with a dressing, access your first aid kit, put on gloves, and get the first aid materials prepared.

referred to the ER for stitches right away (Prentice, 2021). The stitches help slow the bleeding significantly, assist with proper healing, and minimize skin scarring (**Figure 5-12**). Whenever in question as to whether or not the individual needs stitches, refer them to a physician.

Additional Considerations With Open Wounds

Certain open wounds call for special first aid care. When dealing with a puncture wound, do not remove any large object that is protruding from or inside the wound. Objects such as nails, knives, and glass are examples of protruding objects. The protruding object may have severed an artery or vein. Leaving the object in place may prevent significant bleeding by blocking off a major blood vessel. If the object is removed, further tissue damage may occur. Any object protruding from the eye should not be removed. For a small puncture object, such as a common splinter or a bee stinger, carefully help your patient to remove the object if you feel comfortable doing so, with tweezers or the side of a credit card, respectively. For larger objects that must not be removed, take special care not to move the object and keep the patient as still as possible. Call 911 immediately for help. In the meantime, place bulky dressings and bandages around the object to stabilize it and minimize bleeding. For an eye puncture, use dressings and bandages around the object to keep it still. Since eyes move together, to minimize movement of the injured eye and the protruding object bandage both eyes. Stay with the individual in order to comfort them, to treat them for shock, to give cardiopulmonary resuscitation (CPR) if necessary, and to afford the emergency medical technicians (EMTs) details of the injury when they arrive.

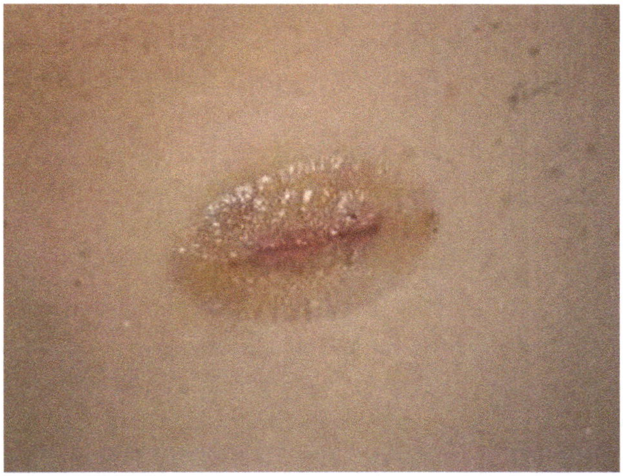

Figure 5-12 In place of common stitches, physicians can use other materials on the wounds, such as DERMABOND®, as seen in this picture.

TIPS FROM THE FIELD

Tip 4 If your patient has a nose bleed, you can utilize many effective, commercially prepared nose bleed materials. These materials come in a variety of forms including powder and granules. However, a very effective means to stop the bleeding is to utilize a small piece of a cut, regular sized tampon and insert it into the bleeding nostril. A tampon's size, absorbency, and ability to assist in clotting are perfect for bleeding nostrils. After you take the tampon out of the packaging, estimate the size of the tampon needed in order to fit only part-way up the patient's nostril. Cut the tampon at its width before you place it in the patient's nostril. When you cut the tampon, make sure it is long enough so some of the tampon sticks out of the nostril, because you want the tampon to be easy to grasp to remove it. When you insert the tampon, make sure it is far enough in so it will not fall out. Do not insert the tampon too far up the nostril since it could get lodged in the cavity and cause further injury. If both nostrils are bleeding, put a piece of cut tampon in each nostril. You may want to put a regular sized tampon or two, along with blunt tipped medical scissors, in your workplace first aid kit in case you must assist a patient with a nosebleed.

When dealing with an avulsion, provide first aid care as discussed, but also consider how washing the wound in running water and soap would affect the individual. Consider the following scenario: You are working in We R Fit Gym and overseeing the weight training floor from your office. One of your clients is performing upper body weightlifting with free weights. Suddenly, you hear a deafening scream. You run onto the floor and see your client holding his severely bleeding hand. You approach them and ask what happened. Your client said that they finished the set and was attempting to put the free weight back onto the rack. Your client was not paying attention and put the weight down on their third and fourth fingers. Their fingers became caught between the free weight and the metal rack. The weight was so heavy that it crushed two fingers. When your client pulled their fingers from under the weight, they noticed the fingers were severely cut, and skin was avulsed. Your client looked at their fingers and immediately went into shock. In this scenario, would you wash the wound? In this case, washing his fingers under running water would probably complicate the injury and make it worse. The force of the water could very well cause more harm and perhaps amputate the fingers. To provide your client with immediate care, call 911. Then control bleeding, bandage the wounds, and treat your client for shock.

Hopefully, your clients will never have an amputation. However, if they do you must think about what you should do with the amputated body part. If an amputation exists, call 911, then dress and bandage the wound while treating for shock. If possible, retrieve the amputated body part and place it in a plastic bag. Place this bag in another plastic bag containing ice. Inform the EMTs that you have the body part and make sure it accompanies the patient to the hospital. The physicians might be able to reattach the amputated body part.

Closed Wounds

Unlike open wounds, which bleed externally, closed wounds bleed internally. Internal bleeding does not necessarily mean that the bleeding occurs deep down in the tissues; rather, the bleeding can occur at the epidermal and upper tissue layers. Also, internal bleeding can occur within solid and hollow internal organs in the thorax and abdomen. The blood does not break through the skin with internal bleeding. Similarly to open wounds, closed wounds exist on a continuum from minor bleeding to life-threatening bleeding.

Typical minor internal bleeding is due to ruptured capillaries. A simple contusion is an example of a closed wound with minor internal bleeding. Contusions are caused by a direct blow of an object to your client's body. The object can be propelled at your client, your client can run into an object, or both the object and your client can be moving and collide together. Internal bleeding can occur in your gym as per the following scenario: Your client is walking to the locker room while talking to a workout partner. They are not paying attention and bumps their forearm into the stationary bicycle handlebar. They feel immediate pain, which quickly subsides. The next day, they notice minor ecchymosis in the area. Your client has sustained a contusion with minor internal bleeding.

An example of a major closed wound in which internal bleeding occurs is when an abdominal organ is injured. Usually these closed wounds occur due to a significant blunt force trauma to the abdomen. The force causes a contusion or even laceration of the organ. Significant abdominal internal bleeding typically causes abdominal muscle **rigidity** and **guarding**. Consider the following scenario: You are coaching high school baseball. Your centerfielder sees the batted ball approaching him high in the air. He runs to the ball. At the last second, he realizes he is too short and will not catch the ball. He dives for the ball. When he dives, his gloved arm buckles underneath him. His elbow is bent and forcefully moves backward into his abdomen. Within minutes, he exhibits signs of shock. He has a lacerated spleen, which is bleeding profusely. This spleen injury and associated internal bleeding is life-threatening.

First Aid for Closed Wounds

When your patient sustains a closed wound at your facility, provide immediate first aid care. First, ask your patient what happened to cause the wound, which helps you determine the mechanism of injury. Attempt to identify symptoms of injury. Ask them how they are feeling, to describe the pain, and note any abnormal sensations. Determine signs of injury by looking at the wound and the patient in general. Is there ecchymosis or deformity at the impact site? Are they holding the area to support or protect it? Do they move the injured area freely? Does their face look pale or blue? Do they have breathing difficulty or are breathing more rapidly than usual? The mechanism of injury, along with the signs and symptoms of injury, assist you in determining

TIPS FROM THE FIELD

Tip 5 If a patient complains of pain in an area such as the abdomen, chest, or musculature, it is imperative to find out the specific details of the mechanism of injury. If your patient says they were kicked, hit, punched, or had some other kind of blunt force trauma to the area, then assume they have internal bleeding. The bleeding may be minor or severe. Regardless, when you suspect internal bleeding, refer your patient for a medical evaluation or phone 911 in emergent situations.

whether the wound is minor or life-threatening. If blunt force trauma was applied to the thorax or abdomen, check for signs of shock, including rapid breathing and pulse, and treat as necessary. As with any life-threatening injury, be prepared to call 911 and provide CPR. Likewise, if you cannot determine the severity of the closed thoracic or abdominal wound, always call 911 immediately, treat for shock if signs and symptoms exist, monitor the patient's airway, breathing, and pulse, and use RICE, which stands for rest, ice, compression, and elevation, if the circumstances allow. If you have determined that the closed wound is minor, such as a mild contusion, use RICE. Refer your patient to their physician for further evaluation. Do not forget to obtain a physician's medical clearance from your patient before allowing them to resume participation, treatment, or rehabilitative services at your facility.

Applying Bandages for Closed Wounds

When your patient sustains a minor closed wound that causes mild to moderate pain or disability, wrap the area with an elastic bandage to provide support and compression to the area (**Figure 5-13**). This elastic bandage, also called an elastic wrap, relieves some pain until the

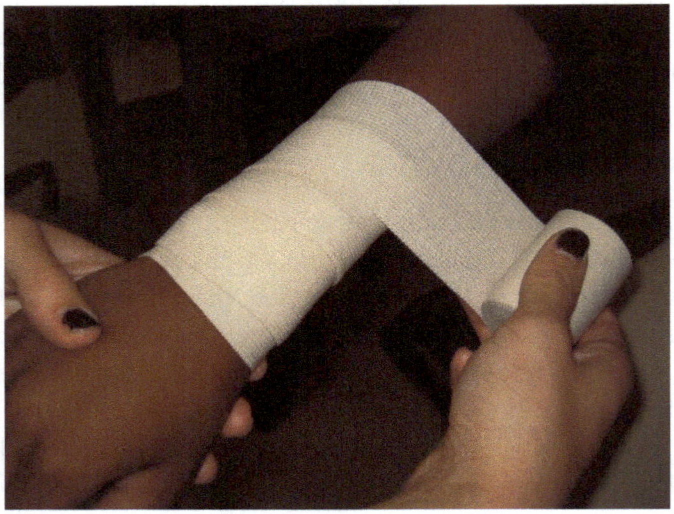

Figure 5-13 Elastic bandages can help minimize pain and provide support to an injured area until the patient can see a physician.

patient is examined by their physician. Elastic wraps are not necessary for significant, major closed wounds because you must call 911 and treat the patient as previously discussed. Elastic wraps typically are a brownish color and come in various widths, including 2-inch, 4-inch, and 6-inch, and lengths of 5-yards or 10-yards. You can always cut the wrap with blunt tipped scissors to obtain the appropriate length if you need to do so. Keep a variety of elastic bandages in your organization's first aid kit or supply cabinet. Before beginning to wrap the injured body part, choose the appropriate size bandage. Typically, 2-inch width and 5-yard length wraps work well for wrist injuries. For patients with large thighs, 6-inch width and 10-yard length wraps are best.

When beginning to wrap the closed wound, start distally, or furthest away from the head. Therefore, if you are wrapping the upper arm, start by the elbow and wrap upward toward the shoulder. If you are wrapping the calf, start by the ankle and move toward the knee. Wrap the elastic bandage in the same manner as you wrap a roller gauze bandage. Overlap the bandage by half of the width of the previously applied wrap. Avoid leaving the skin exposed, which occurs when the wrap is not applied properly. Holes or "windows" in the applied wrap will not provide the appropriate compression for the patient and can more easily slide off. As you apply the wrap, smooth it out with your available hand to prevent any bumps in the wrap, which also prevent proper compression. Pull the wrap so it has tension, but not so tight that it cuts off circulation to the extremity. When you have covered the injured area once, any leftover wrap can continue to be applied, or you can cut off the remainder with blunt tipped scissors. Secure the elastic bandage with the clips provided with the wrap, or athletic tape secured around the wrap's loose end. While you are applying the wrap, ask the patient if it is comfortable, and watch for signs of decreased circulation. After you finish applying the wrap, check for proper circulation as when applying a roller gauze bandage.

Summary

Open and closed wounds will most likely be common injuries occurring to your clients while participating in activities at your facility. Fortunately, these wounds are not often severe, and only require minimal first aid care until your client can see their physician. Frequently, your client will not need to see a physician and can continue participation safely. However, sometimes a patient will be severely injured at your facility and require advanced medical care. Your role in these instances is to recognize that a significant injury exists, call 911, and provide immediate first aid care to your client until EMTs arrive. Always remember when dealing with open wounds to follow universal precautions and Occupational Safety and Health Administration (OSHA) standards. When in doubt about a client's needs advanced medical care, call 911.

Keywords

Shock A life-threatening condition that occurs when oxygenated blood in the body is not getting to the vital organs, including in the chest, abdomen, and brain.

Open wound A cut in the skin through which external bleeding occurs.

Closed wound An injury to the tissues underlying the skin. Unlike open wounds, bleeding occurs but does not exit the body.

Lateral A structure's location furthest away from the midline when the body is bisected into right and left halves through the umbilicus.

Approximate When the damaged, cut portions of the skin of an open wound fall back in line and close proximity.

Prosthesis A synthetic body part that is custom made to replace an amputated body part.

Booster vaccination A dose of the antigen administered to the body, after the original vaccination was given, in order for the body to create additional antibodies to fight against infection.

Antiseptics Substances that assist in cleansing a wound and destroying pathogenic bacteria that may have entered the wound.

Antimicrobial A substance that attempts to kill pathogens such as bacteria, viruses, and fungi.

Rigidity Occurs as a result of an abdominal organ injury. The abdominal muscles become stiff upon palpation.

Guarding Occurs when an abdominal organ is injured. The abdominal muscles spasm and become tense in order to protect the injured abdominal organs from further injury.

Discussion Questions

1. What are the three primary types of blood vessels in the body? What are the characteristic differences in how they bleed?
2. Name six signs and symptoms of an infected open wound.
3. Describe how you provide first aid for your patient with a minor open bleeding wound.
4. Why is it important to leave large, impaled objects in the wound?
5. Describe different methods to check for circulation after applying a bandage.
6. Under what circumstances must you refer an individual to a physician or the ER for stitches?
7. What are some ways a bystander can assist you when providing first aid care for your injured patient's open wound?
8. Describe the mechanism of injury for closed wounds. When can a closed wound be life-threatening?

CASE STUDY: TO PLAY OR NOT TO PLAY

It is Friday night at North Hudson High School. The school is wrestling their rivals, South Hudson High School, for the conference championship. North Hudson is down by two points with only the 150-pound weight class left to wrestle. Diego is North Hudson's senior star wrestler and the reigning county champion at 150 pounds. The match is running smoothly, and Diego is beating his opponent by 6 points with one period remaining. As long as he continues to wrestle smart he should win and take home the conference championship for his school.

The wrestlers start the period in neutral position. The referee blows their whistle, and the wrestlers aggressively approach each other and begin to wrestle. Within the first 10 seconds, the wrestlers simultaneously go for a shot and butt heads. There is a loud thud, and both wrestlers fall to their knees. Immediately, blood starts to pour down from Diego's forehead onto his face. His blood drips all over the wrestling mat. He is in significant pain. He places his hands on the wound as a reaction to the pain and in order to control the bleeding. Diego stands up steadily, and begins to turn toward his coach. Diego's coach, Coach Cornell, immediately runs out onto the mat with the team's medical kit to help Diego.

Unfortunately, no other medical personnel are at the wrestling meet, so Coach Cornell must provide first aid to Diego. He hands Diego a towel from the bench to place over his cut, and begins to put on a pair of latex gloves. Afterwards, Coach Cornell slowly removes the towel from Diego's wound to examine the injury. Coach Cornell sees a deep 1-inch horizontal laceration just above the outer edge of Diego's left eyebrow. The two cut skin edges are not approximating and seem to have been torn away from each other. Coach Cornell recognizes that the bleeding has stopped. Coach Cornell asks Diego "How are you feeling?" Diego says, "I feel okay." Coach Cornell asks, "Do you have any head, neck, or back pain or vision difficulty?" Diego responds "No, but some blood ran into my eye." He adamantly tells Coach Cornell that he wants to stay on the mat and finish the match to win the county championship for his team. Diego says "Coach, just bandage me up and put me back in!"

1. Should Coach Cornell allow Diego to continue wrestling? Why or why not?
2. What should Coach Cornell do to control the bleeding?
3. What types of dressings and bandages should he apply in attempt to protect against infection and to keep the wound closed?
4. Should Coach Cornell advise Diego's parents to transport Diego to the hospital? Why or why not?

References

American Academy of Orthopaedic Surgeons [AAOS]. (2022). Advanced First Aid, CPR, and AED eBook (8th Ed.). Sudbury, MA: Jones and Bartlett Publishers.

Baddour, L. M., & Brown, A. M. (2019). Infectious complications of puncture wounds. *UpToDate.*

Guven, C., & Kafadar, H. (2020). Evaluation of extremity vascular injuries and treatment approaches. Nigerian Journal of Clinical Practice, 23(9), 1221. Doi: 10.4103/njcp.njcp_656_18

Hartkamp, N.S., Petersen, E.T., Chappell, M.A., Okell, T.W., Uyttenboogaart, M., Zeebregts, C.J., Bokkers, R.P. H. (2017). Relationship between haemodynamic impairment and collateral blood flow in carotid artery disease. Journal of Cerebral Blood Flow & Metabolism, 38(11), 2021–2032. doi: 10.1177/0271678X17724027

Kramer, A., Dissemond, J., Kim, S., Willy, C., Mayer, D., Papke, R., Tuchmann, F., Assadian, O. (2018). Consensus on Wound Antisepsis: Update 2018. *Skin Pharmacology and Physiology*, 31, 28-58. doi: 10.1159/000481545

Lloyd Jones, M. (2007). Repair of minor wounds. *Practice Nurse,* 33(12), 31-34.

MedlinePlus. (2020). *Traumatic Amputation.* Retrieved October 24, 2021, from http://www.nlm.nih.gov/medlineplus/ency/article/000006.htm

MedlinePlus. (2019). *Tetanus.* Retrieved October 24, 2021, from https://www.medlineplus.gov/ency/article/000615.htm

Prentice, W.E. (2021). *Principles of athletic training: A competency-based approach (17th Ed.).* New York: McGraw-Hill.

Chapter 6

Emergency Care

Chapter Objectives

After you have read this chapter, you will be able to understand:

- The components of an emergency action plan.
- The steps involved in taking a primary survey.
- The differences among cardiac arrest, heart attack, and angina.
- The signs, symptoms, and management of a stroke.
- How to assist an individual who is having a seizure.
- The different types of shock and how they affect the body.
- The differences among hypoglycemia, hyperglycemia, and diabetic ketoacidosis.
- The signs and symptoms of heat and cold related illnesses, and the appropriate treatment.

No matter where you work or what activities you participate in, emergency situations will arise. Emergency situations that occur to individuals can include life-threatening or **limb-threatening** injuries and illnesses. Although you will rarely experience emergency situations while supervising your clients, when emergencies arise you have a duty to provide care to them. Therefore, you must have adequate knowledge signs and symptoms of life-threatening or limb-threatening injuries and illnesses, along with knowing how to provide proper emergency care for your clients.

Emergency Action Plan

In order to provide appropriate emergency care, you must first create, practice, and implement an emergency action plan (EAP) for your facility. An EAP is a crucial component of any organization's policies and procedures. An EAP includes written procedures with specific actions to assist you in responding to an emergency in a safe, timely, efficient, and proper manner. The EAP must be communicated to all personnel on a regular and perhaps annual basis, and when new personnel are hired as well. EAP components include first responder and other personnel roles, activation of the EMS system, availability of emergency equipment, and delivery of emergency care.

The EAP designates that the first person on the scene of an emergency is considered the "first responder" who activates the EAP. The first responder provides immediate care to the injured individual, commands the scene, and gives direction to other personnel who can help. Other personnel at the scene assist the first responder in a variety of activities. These personnel have duties which include assisting the first responder with providing care, activating the EMS system by calling 911, obtaining emergency equipment, controlling bystanders, unlocking any entrances for EMS access to the facility, and meeting the ambulance at a designated area. The specific employee roles depend on various factors such as the organization type, user population, and venue demographics.

Activation of the EMS system begins when the first responder instructs another employee or bystander to call 911. The EAP will designate the imperative information that the caller must give to the dispatcher. This information includes the type of emergency, the number of injured people, the extent of injuries, and the care being provided. The caller should also tell the dispatcher the best way to enter the venue and access the injured person, while also informing the dispatcher that someone will be waiting for EMS at the entry point.

Emergency equipment utilized to care for injured individuals should always be on site and easily accessible. Emergency equipment at your facility should include, but should not limited to, an automated external defibrillator (AED), wheelchairs, crutches, vacuum, air, and other splinting materials, and fire extinguishers. As part of EAP training, employees must be instructed how to utilize the emergency equipment properly. Any new employees must be taught how to utilize the equipment immediately upon hire. Have the equipment calibrated and checked for safety annually (i.e. AED) or as required by the manufacturer.

Delivery of emergency care is the last component of the EAP. The care provided assists in stabilizing the individual until EMS arrives. Your goal is to provide the individual with the best possible care and chance for survival. Typically the first responder provides and commands individual's care. However, if another person present is more experienced or holds higher credentials to provide care (i.e. a physician, EMT), then that person should be the primary care provider. The first responder can, however, continue to activate the EAP. When an EAP is in place, and regularly communicated to and practiced by all personnel, they have appropriate direction to properly handle an emergency.

Safety First

Even though you have a duty to provide care for your clients in an emergency situation at your place of employment, always put your safety first. If your client is in an environment that is unsafe for you to enter, then you do not enter the area. For example, consider the following scenario. At We R Fit gym, you pass by the locker room door and see your client lying on the ground. They appear unconscious. As you enter the room you smell an unusual odor. What do you do? At this point, you must not enter the room. The odor may be a poisonous substance that can cause you to become another unconscious victim. Instead, call 911 immediately. In sports medicine professions, unsafe environments in your place of employment could include a building fire, a poisonous gas or substance leak, or an armed assailant. In these or any other dangerous environments, you will want to desperately help your clients. However, do not be brave and take the chance to enter the scene or you may become another victim. Your role in these situations is to activate the EAP and make sure 911 is called immediately.

The Primary Survey

Before providing emergency care to an individual, always complete an initial evaluation. The initial evaluation is known as a primary survey. A primary survey is performed to determine if your client is experiencing a life-threatening injury or illness which warrants emergency care. Some injuries and illnesses which are considered emergency situations include unconsciousness, traumatic spine injuries, stroke, cardiac arrest, heart attack, shock, choking, asthma attacks, seizures, and diabetic emergencies.

An Unconscious Athlete

The primary survey begins by first determining if the individual is unconscious. Unconsciousness can occur in physical activity when your client has had some type of bodily trauma that affects the brain causing it not to function properly. Some illnesses and injuries which can cause unconsciousness include head injuries, shock, cardiac arrest, and heat stroke. An example of how your client can become unconscious in your facility is as follows: Your client is playing a competitive racquetball game in We R Fit gym. During a long rally, they run to return the ball, and does not realize where their body is relative to the wall. As your client strikes the ball, their body's momentum is so great that they cannot stop, and strikes their head hard onto the wall. This blunt force trauma to the head causes your client to be, as some people say, "knocked out". Being knocked out is a layman's term for being rendered unconscious. Immediately upon becoming unconscious, your client falls to the ground, lies motionless, and is unaware of their surroundings. Although you call your client's name and tap their shoulder in attempt to arouse them, your client is not able to respond to your verbal or tactile (touch) stimuli.

Two stimuli that can be used to arouse your client from an unconscious state is your voice and touch. When an individual is lying motionless, determine if they are unconscious by approaching them while shouting his name and "are you okay?" At the same time, gently tap their shoulder to see if they respond. By no means shake the individual since they may have a spinal injury. If you shake or move an unconscious individual with a spinal injury, you can do further harm. Make sure your client stays as still as possible.

You may say to yourself "How do I know if an athlete has a spinal injury?" Well, you may not always know. However, suspect your client has sustained a spinal injury if they fall from a significant height such as a ladder that is taller than they are, if they have a traumatic accident such as a car accident, or sustains a direct blow to the head by an object or another person. Also, if you did not see your client go unconscious, but is motionless and lying on the floor, always suspect that they have a spinal injury. Consequently, maintain their head, neck, and spine in a straight orientation, called in-line stabilization, at all times **(Figure 6-1)**. In-line stabilization means that you are keeping the head, neck, and spine in line with each other as if the person was standing or lying flat on their back.

Regardless of whether or not the individual has a spinal injury, once you determine that they are unconscious, immediately send someone to summon Emergency Medical Services (EMS). If no one is around to call for you and you do not have your cell phone on you, position your client in the modified HAINES position (High Arm IN Endangered Spine position), call 911, then return to them and continue care (**Figure 6-2**). The purpose of the modified HAINES position is to attempt to maintain an open airway while you have left to phone 911. This position is an appropriate recovery position for keeping the spine in a neutral position as much as possible when you must leave the unconscious individual to summon advanced medical care. In the modified HAINES position, if the individual vomits, the vomit will drain from the mouth instead of blocking the airway. To put your client in this position, have them lie on their side with their head resting on an outstretched arm, the spine straight, and knees flexed. In this position, monitor your client's breathing. If their breathing stops then carefully roll them on their back, maintaining in-line stabilization, and administer CPR until EMS arrives and takes over.

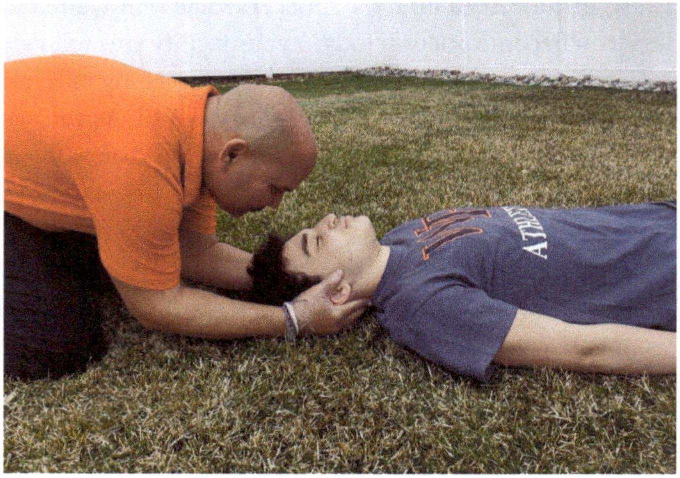

Figure 6-1 In-line stabilization must be used when you suspect your athlete has sustained a spinal injury, or are unsure if they do.

Figure 6-2 The modified HAINES position

Check for Breathing

After you have determined whether or not the individual is unconscious, check them to see if they are breathing. If your client is lying face down, tilt your head to the side, put your face by their nose and mouth, and see if you can hear or feel breaths. If possible, check to see if their chest is rising and falling, which would indicate that they are breathing. Put your hand gently on your client's back to see if you can feel their thorax expanding with each respiration. If they are breathing, stay close to your client's face and monitor breathing until advanced medical personnel arrives. If you cannot tell if your client is breathing then you must log roll them onto their back.

To log roll the individual, it would be beneficial to have additional coworkers or bystanders assist you (**Figure 6-3**). When you log roll a person, it is important to keep

Figure 6-3 Log rolling an individual

the head, neck, and spine in a straight orientation. When log rolling your client, their head and neck must move as a unit with the spine at all times. If you are the first person to approach your client, take the lead at their head and stabilize their head and neck. In order to stabilize the head and neck, place your hands on either side of the head, keeping in mind that your arms will shift position as you roll the individual. Sometimes it is easier to cross your arms and then place your hands on either side of their head. Make sure you cross your arms in a manner so when you have rolled your client on their back, your arms end up straight and in a comfortable position to continue to maintain in-line stabilization. Your assistants are positioned on one side of the individual, at the arms, hips, and thighs, and one person is at the feet. Direct your assistants as to which direction to roll the individual. Roll them opposite the resting direction of their face. Then utilize a command such as "ready, set, roll" or "on three, one, two, three" and tell your assistants before you roll the individual the command to roll. Direct your assistants to keep the individual's body in line at all times. This log roll technique is not easy. All employees must work together efficiently and successfully in these cases. Consequently, your organization should make in-line stabilization and log rolling an individual a regular part of your organization's employee EAP training.

Once your client is on their back, check for breathing again **(Figure 6-4)**. If you are stabilizing the head and neck, then it is better for one of your coworkers to check to see if the individual is breathing. You do not want to remove your hands from the unconscious individual's head and neck because movement can occur.

If you are the only person around to assist your client, and you cannot tell if they are breathing while lying on their stomach, log roll them by yourself while maintaining in-line stabilization. Get on the side of your client in the direction opposite their face. Kneel as close to them as much as possible by placing your knees so they touch their side, and sit on your heels. Place the hand which is closest to his head on the back of your client's neck, and grasp the neck firmly. Place your other hand at your client's hip which is farthest away from you. Maintaining in-line stabilization, roll them toward you, onto your thighs, and then carefully and slowly move backward on your knees to allow your client to rest on the ground. At this point when they are face up, you must continue your primary survey.

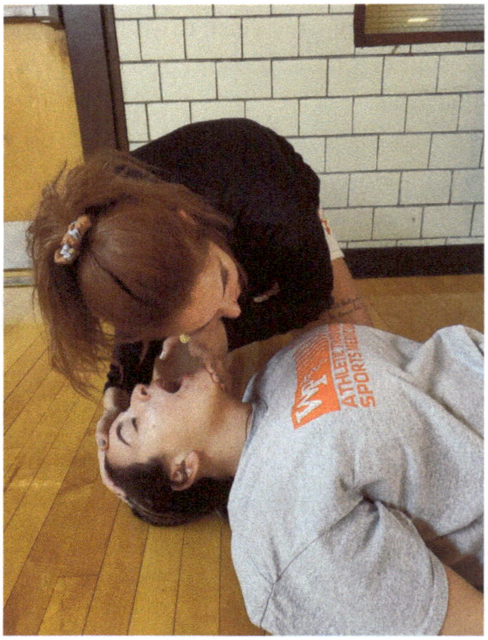

© Linda Gazzillo Diaz

Figure 6-4 Check to see if the unconscious individual is breathing.

Check for Severe Bleeding

Severe bleeding can be the cause of the individual's unconsciousness. Severe bleeding can also make an unconscious individual's situation worsen rapidly due to the lack of oxygenated blood to the brain and internal organs. As you determine if the individual is unconscious by checking for unresponsiveness, you must examine them from head to toe to check for severe bleeding (**Figure 6-5**). While you are checking their breathing, look to see if there is blood around their body, on their clothes, or on the surrounding ground. If you see external bleeding consider that internal bleeding may be occurring as well. If your client is severely bleeding, and you have someone available to assist you, have them use PPE, or clean clothing, blankets, or towels and put pressure on the bleeding site in attempt to stop or slow down the loss of blood. If you are alone, then your priority is to check for breathing and determine if your client needs cardiopulmonary resuscitation (CPR).

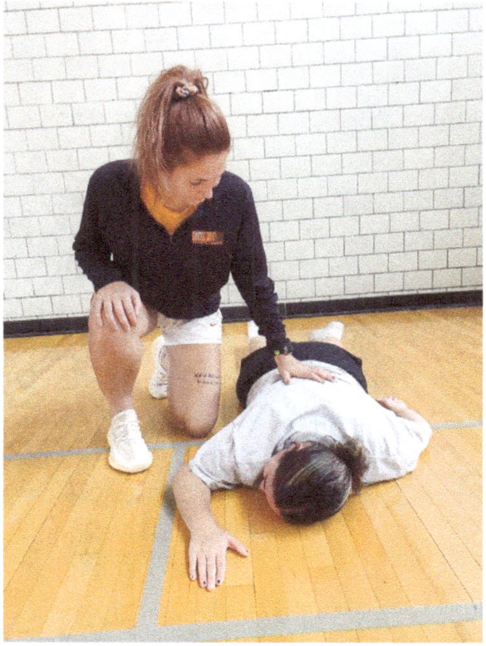

Figure 6-5 Check the individual from head to toe to see if they are severely bleeding.

Cardiopulmonary Resuscitation (CPR)

Although CPR instruction is not a part of this textbook, it is critical to address the importance of CPR in emergency care. CPR is a technique used to potentially save the life of an individual who is experiencing **cardiac arrest** by manually forcing the heart to pump oxygenated blood to the brain and vital organs. If oxygenated blood is reaching the brain and vital organs, then the individual's tissues can be sustained for a short period of time.

Conventional CPR and Hands-Only CPR are the two types of CPR utilized (American Heart Association, 2022b). Conventional CPR is performed by healthcare providers and other trained individuals, including sports medicine professionals. Conventional CPR includes rescue (mouth-to-mouth) breathing along with chest compressions. Rescue breathing entails placing your mouth over the individual's mouth by utilizing a breathing barrier such as a disposable pocket mask, and breathing your oxygenated air into the individual (**Figure 6-6**). Breathing barriers are imperative during rescue breathing to prevent disease transmission and to promote adequate oxygen entering into the individual's respiratory tract (**Figure 6-7**). Along with rescue breathing, you compress the chest 30 times at

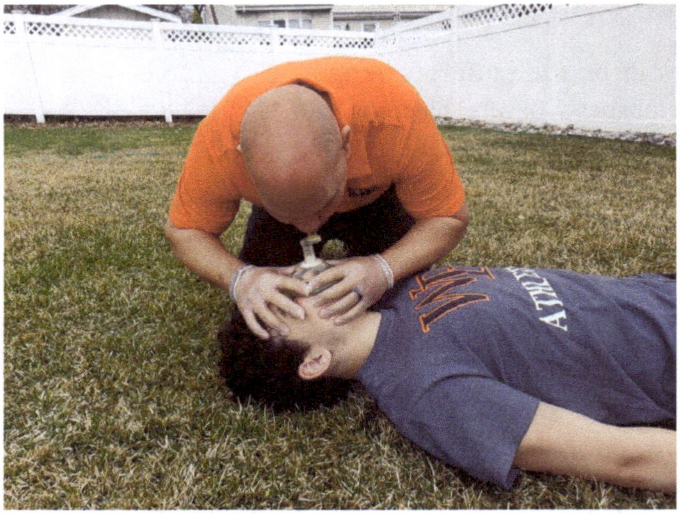

Figure 6-6 Utilize a breathing barrier such as a pocket mask to deliver breaths.

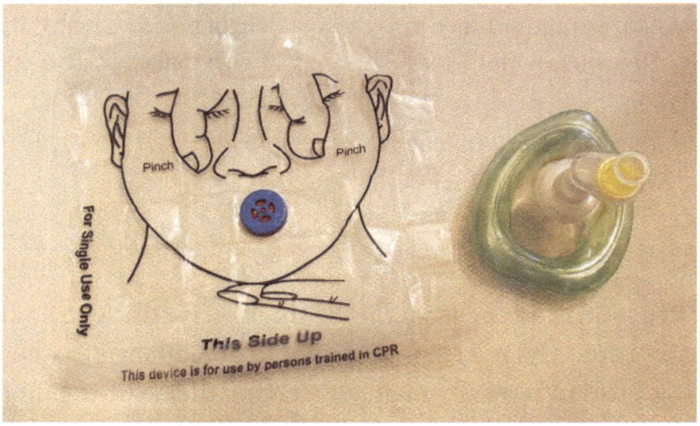

Figure 6-7 Various breathing barriers exist and should be a part of your first aid kit.

the mid-sternum in order to compress the heart between the sternum and the vertebrae (**Figure 6-8**). The series of compressions and breaths result in oxygenated blood moving through the adult athlete's body.

Hands-Only CPR is utilized by bystanders or the general public who are untrained in conventional CPR, including by individuals who witness a person collapse with no warning (American Heart Association, 2022b). Unlike conventional CPR, Hands-Only CPR requires only chest compressions. No rescue breaths are given. A rescuer will "push hard and fast" in the center of the chest. Similarly to conventional CPR, with Hands-Only CPR, the heart mechanically pumps blood throughout the body. However, since you are not performing rescue breaths, no additional oxygen is being introduced into the individual's blood. Only the oxygen that was in the blood when the individual ceased breathing remains in the body. Even though no additional oxygen is entering the individual's blood, the mechanical circulation of the blood throughout the body can increase the individual's chance of survival as compared to not performing CPR at all.

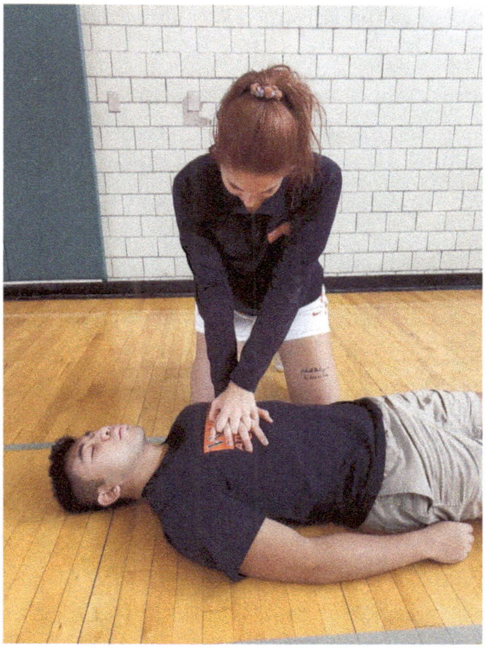

© Linda Gazzillo Diaz

Figure 6-8 CPR compressions are performed mid-sternum.

Regardless of whether you administer conventional or Hands-Only CPR, continue CPR until the individual begins to breathe, you are too tired to continue, advanced medical personnel arrive, an AED is brought to the scene, another trained person takes over for you, or the scene becomes unsafe for you to continue (AAOS, 2022). Since you work regularly with individuals in sports medicine and related professions, becoming certified to perform conventional CPR is imperative. Some employers will require you to initially obtain and then maintain CPR certification as a condition of hire. You have a legal duty to assist your clients at your facility and perform CPR if needed. However, outside of your facility and employment duties, even if you are not certified in CPR and you witness an athlete suddenly collapse, you can assist and individual in cardiac arrest. You can perform Hands-Only CPR or at the very least call 911. If you perform conventional or Hands-Only CPR even if you have not obtained CPR certification, you will be protected by the Good Samaritan Laws as previously discussed.

Automated External Defibrillators

CPR as a lifesaving technique which manually forces an individual's heart to pump oxygenated blood to the brain and vital organs. However, in most circumstances for adults CPR alone cannot restart the heart and make it beat on its own. The use of an automated external defibrillator (AED) is absolutely necessary to restart the heart, make it beat in a normal fashion, and consequently distribute blood and oxygen throughout the body. When adults go unconscious due to the heart not functioning properly, the heart is most likely not beating normally and cannot sustain a normal rhythm. Most likely something is wrong with the heart's electrical conductivity. The heart may be in ventricular tachycardia or ventricular fibrillation, and therefore cannot pump blood throughout the body. Ventricular tachycardia is when the heart beats very fast at approximately 100 beats per minute or more. Also, the heart will have a few irregular beats in a row (Medline Plus, 2022). Ventricular fibrillation can also occur, especially after a person has a heart attack (Mayo Clinic, 2021b). Ventricular fibrillation is when the heart beats with an unusual, irregular rhythm, or fibrillates. In this instance, adequate blood and oxygen cannot get to the brain and vital organs.

A heart attack is different than cardiac arrest in that the individual is experiencing part of the heart dying, but they are still breathing. In adults, a heart attack can result in cardiac arrest which typically involves ventricular tachycardia or ventricular fibrillation. The only means to correct ventricular tachycardia or ventricular fibrillation is to utilize an AED. The AED's purpose is to briefly stop the heart's electrical system in order for it to reset itself, and then beat normally. AEDs are mounted on many buildings' walls including hospitals, airports, restaurants, schools, shopping malls, and movie theaters **(Figure 6-9)** . The chance of survival for an individual in cardiac arrest is significantly increased when AED use is initiated immediately after the individual succumbs to cardiac arrest as compared to individuals with delayed defibrillation (i.e. waiting for EMS to arrive on the scene to administer the AED) (American Heart Association, 2018).

Utilizing an AED is simple. Once the AED's power button is pressed and the AED turns on, the AED verbalizes step-by-step instructions. The AED begins by directing you to place the adhesive, conduction pads in the correct areas on the individual. Each adhesive pad is attached to a wire and an adapter which is plugged into the AED. To make it easy for you to place the pads, the adhesive pads have pictures depicting where the pads must be placed on the individual. Then the AED directs you to plug in the adapter (if it is not permanently attached). The AED verbalizes when it is analyzing the heart's rhythm. It also states whether or not to

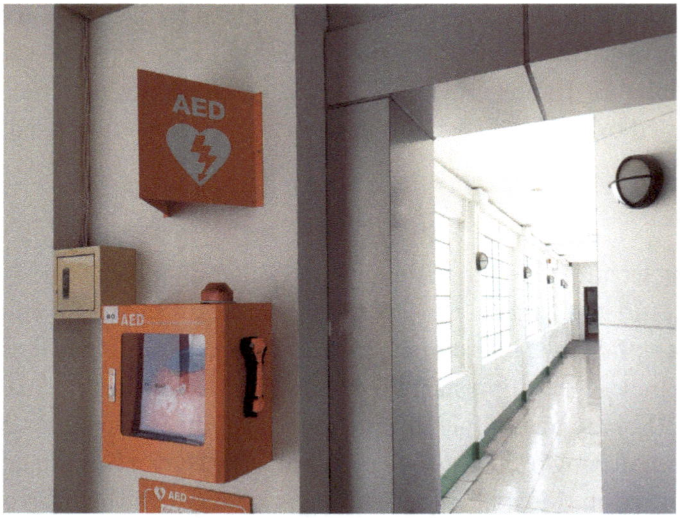

Figure 6-9 AEDs are commonly seen mounted on walls in buildings.

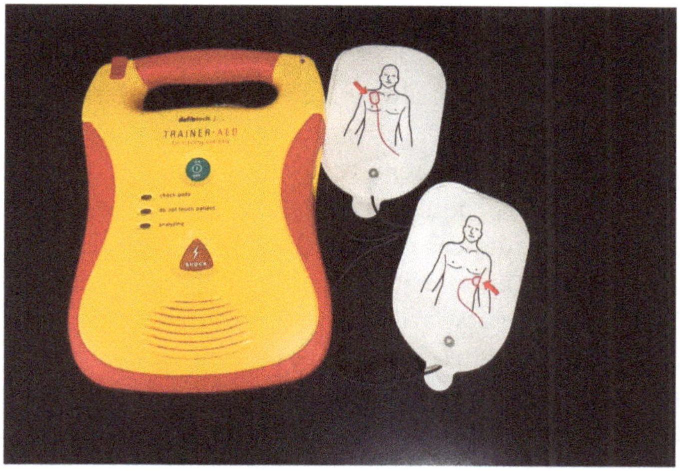

© Linda Gazzillo Diaz

Figure 6-10 An automated external defibrillator (AED) trainer is used to train individuals on proper use. The trainers are identical to a real AED.

deliver a shock (by pressing the shock button), or simply continue to administer CPR. It is extremely important that that no one, not even yourself, is in contact with the individual while a shock is being delivered. If someone is touching the individual while they are being shocked, the shock may not be effective. Also, the person touching the individual will also be shocked, and possibly sustain a significant injury.

As part of being trained and certified in conventional CPR certification, you will be trained and certified to use an AED as well **(Figure 6-10)**. CPR and AED certification courses are offered by a variety of national organizations, including but not limited to the American Heart Association, the American Red Cross, and the National Safety Council. Sports medicine professionals who work with clients, patients, athletes, and other individuals should become certified in CPR and AED even if the certifications are not required by their employers. As with CPR, Good Samaritan Laws will protect the layperson to an extent when utilizing an AED on an individual in cardiac arrest. In 2000, the Cardiac Arrest Survival Act (CASA) was passed into federal law which provides some immunity for laypersons using an AED on a cardiac arrest victim (H. Rept. 106-634, 2000). Therefore, do not be afraid to utilize an available AED on an individual in cardiac arrest.

The Primary Survey and Athletic Equipment

At some point, you may have to perform a primary survey on an athlete who is wearing equipment. For example, football, hockey, and lacrosse players wear helmets and shoulder pads which can be a hindrance to you when completing a primary survey and determining if a person needs CPR. Nevertheless, in life threatening situations a primary survey must be performed regardless of the equipment worn.

Sports medicine personnel should always gain access the athlete's airway as a priority (Courson et al., 2020), whether or not the athlete is unconscious. To access the athlete's airway, the facemask must be immediately removed or lifted upward by its hinges to allow for rescue breathing if warranted. Depending on the helmet, specialized tools such as pruners, cordless screwdrivers, and other devices which can cut through or remove the clips holding the facemask on the helmet are necessary. Be cognizant of the helmets your athletes wear and the tools required for emergency face mask removal. Practice removing the facemask in simulated situations. Your goal is to remove the facemask quickly and safely, while minimizing any movement of the head or cervical spine. At all times while caring for an athlete wearing a helmet, the first responder maintains stabilization of the athlete's head and spine. If the athlete is in respiratory distress and/or to administer rescue breathing to them and the facemask cannot be removed in a timely manner, then the helmet must be removed (Courson et al., 2020).

If the athlete is wearing shoulder pads with a jersey and you must perform CPR it is imperative to cut the jersey, shoulder pad laces, and remove any VELCRO® attachments at the chest. You will then open the pads enough to access the chest. The chest must be exposed in order to appropriately place your hands on the sternum to perform CPR and for the AED pads to be placed appropriately on the athlete. Research has shown that for football and men's lacrosse equipment, it is recommended that helmets and shoulder pads are removed for more effective CPR, while maintaining spinal stabilization (Clark et al, 2018; Mihalik et al., 2016). Simultaneous removal of the helmet and shoulder pads takes significant training and practice. Consequently, the sports medicine personnel team should frequently practice this skill in simulated manner to be properly prepared to give proper care to an athlete in need.

Life-Threatening Situations

As a sports medicine professional, at some point in time you will likely have a client experience a life-threatening illness or injury in your presence. Hopefully, you will have CPR and AED training and knowledge, as well as immediate access to an AED, to assist you in proper lifesaving efforts for your client. By simply and properly recognizing life-threatening situations, calling EMS, and keeping your client comfortable and stable, you will give them the best chance to survive. Even though these actions may seem trivial, and you want to do more to help the athlete, these actions can save their life. Some life-threatening situations warranting advanced emergency care include heart attack, stroke, seizures, choking, shock, asthma attack, diabetic emergencies, and environmental emergencies.

Heart Attack

A heart attack is caused by the same heart condition as cardiac arrest, but as noted previously, an individual who has a heart attack does not necessarily succumb to cardiac arrest. Similar to cardiac arrest, a heart attack occurs when over time portions of the heart muscle die. The heart dies due to coronary artery disease. Coronary arteries deliver oxygenated blood to the heart. In coronary artery disease, plaque has built up in the coronary arteries and cause blockage. This blockage causes insufficient oxygenated blood flow to the portion of the heart muscle tissue affected by the blocked coronary arteries. Consequently, that portion of the heart tissue dies due to lack of adequate oxygen (**Figure 6-11**).

An individual experiences heart attack signs and symptoms as a portion of the heart muscle dies. These signs and symptoms include chest pain, shoulder pain, jaw pain, the feeling of indigestion, nausea, sweating, shortness of breath, and dizziness. Some signs and symptoms are very noticeable, and others are mild. Likewise, the signs and symptoms vary among

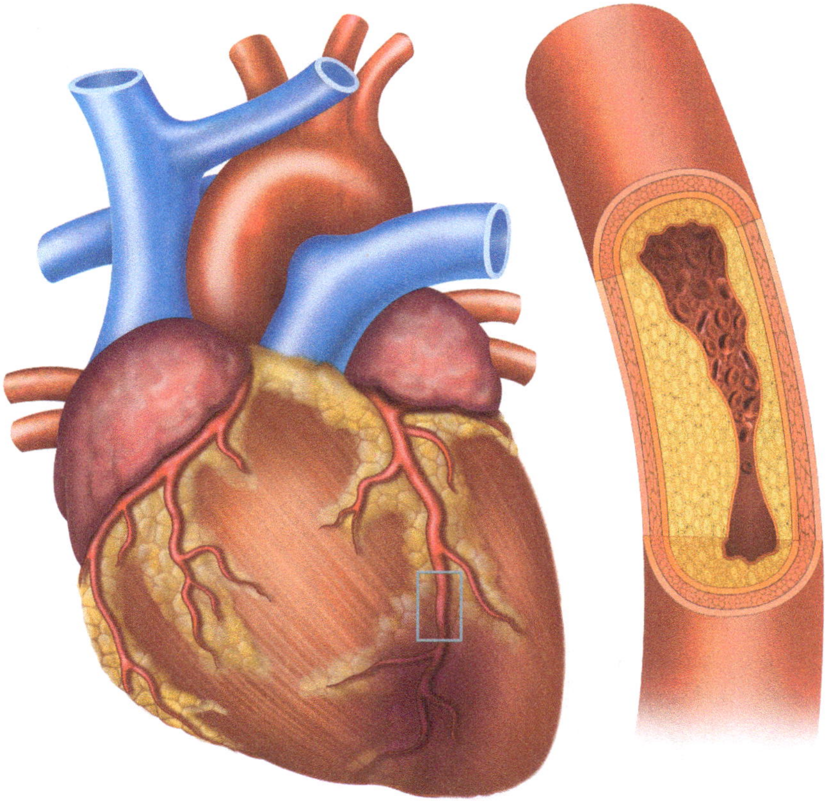

Figure 6-11 Coronary artery disease is a main cause of heart attack.

individuals. For example, one person who experienced a heart attack may describe the pain by stating that it feels like "an elephant is sitting on my chest", whereas another individual may describe the symptoms as it only "felt like constant indigestion". Biological women often have more subtle signs of heart attack, including nausea and vomiting, lightheadedness, fatigue, shortness of breath, back and/or jaw pain, and sweating (American Heart Association, 2022a). If signs and symptoms are subtle or mimic indigestion, individuals may not to recognize that they are having a heart attack. If an individual exhibits any of these signs and symptoms, or complains about pain without having undue cause for the occurrence (i.e. shoulder pain when a shoulder injury has occurred), suspect that they are having a heart attack.

When you are with an individual who is experiencing heart attack signs or symptoms, have them sit down and relax in whatever position is comfortable and make sure they are breathing normally and call 911 immediately. While waiting for EMS to arrive, ask them if they have a heart condition such as **angina** and if they take prescribed medication to make the symptoms subside. Their physician may have prescribed medication such as nitroglycerine when an angina episode occurs. If this is the case, assist them in taking their medication. If they have not been prescribed medication, have them swallow or chew an aspirin to help increase blood flow to the heart and decrease heart damage during a heart attack.

Even if you are unsure if an individual is having a heart attack, calling for advanced medical care is crucial for the individual's survival. Any delay in help can be fatal. Also keep in mind that until EMS arrives you must always be prepared to administer CPR and utilize an AED if the individual suddenly goes into cardiac arrest.

Stroke

Similar to blocked coronary arteries of the heart, a lack of arterial blood flow sometimes occurs to the brain. When the brain's arteries are blocked or bleeding internally, then an individual may suffer a cerebrovascular accident (CVA). A CVA is most commonly known as a stroke. Stroke signs and symptoms include weakness, **paralysis**, numbness, or tingling on one side of the body, vision problems, slurred speech, sudden headache, dizziness, confusion, and chest pain (Mayo Clinic, 2022b) (**Figure 6-12**).

An individual can suffer a stroke with no warning, and some stroke signs and symptoms can mimic other conditions. Therefore, attempt to detect signs and symptoms of a stroke quickly in order to obtain advanced medical care in a timely manner. First, ask the individual if they have lost any feeling or has any weakness in their face, arms, or legs. Have them make facial expressions, such as smiling and frowning, and see if their face droops or is unable to perform the expressions. Then have the individual close their eyes while you lightly touch their arms, fingers, and legs, while asking them if they can feel your touch. If they say that they can feel your touch, ask them to describe the location. This test determines if the individual has sensation in those areas. Next, determine if the individual can perform various motions. Instruct them to raise their arms up over their head. While sitting in a chair, have them flex

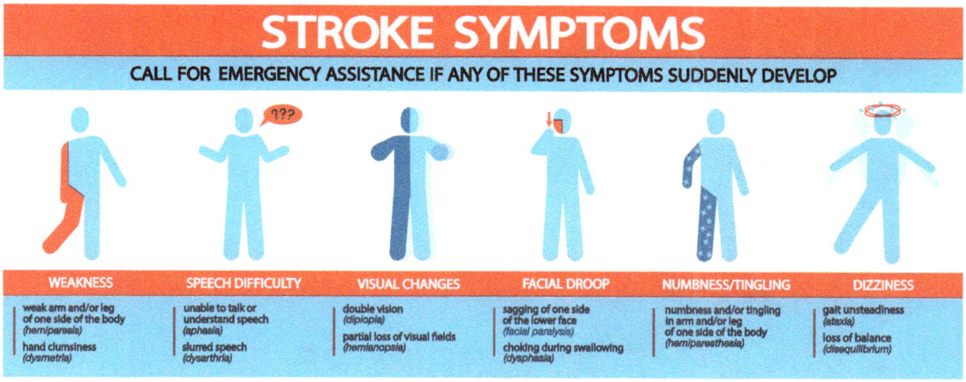

Figure 6-12 Signs and symptoms of a stroke

and extend their knees. If the individual is not able to perform these upper and lower body movements, ask them what they believe is preventing them from moving these areas (i.e. pain, weakness, muscle tightness). Throughout this entire process evaluate their speech, to determine if it is slurred, and their memory. If the individual exhibits these signs or symptoms, then suspect that they have experienced a stroke. You must act quickly and call 911 without delay. Have them rest in a comfortable position and monitor their breathing until advanced medical help arrives.

Seizures

Another emergency situation occurs when an individual experiences a seizure. Seizures are caused by unexpected, abnormal, electrical discharges from the brain and spinal cord. When a person is seizing, a change in behavior or abnormal, uncontrollable motor function results. Sometimes they experience an **aura** which indicates a seizure is forthcoming. Focal and generalized seizures are the two different groups of seizures (Medline Plus, 2021) **(Figure 6-13)**. Focal seizures occur in one area of the brain, while generalized seizures occur in both sides of the brain. Both groups of seizures are further broken down into types of seizures within each group.

Focal seizures include simple, complex, secondary generalized, and unknown onset seizures. Simple focal seizures cause signs and symptoms of twitching and changes in sensation (i.e. changes in smell or taste) (CDC, 2020). Simple focal seizures may occur prior to a complex focal seizure. An individual having a complex focal seizure may stare into space and have some unusual repetitive movements (i.e. eye and lip movements). Secondary generalized seizures begin on one side of the brain (focal seizure) and then move to both sides of the brain (generalized seizure).

Generalized seizures include absence and tonic-clonic seizures. The mildest seizures are absence or petit mal seizures. Absence seizures have subtle signs and symptoms. Consequently, it is not as easy to determine if an individual is experiencing an absence seizure.

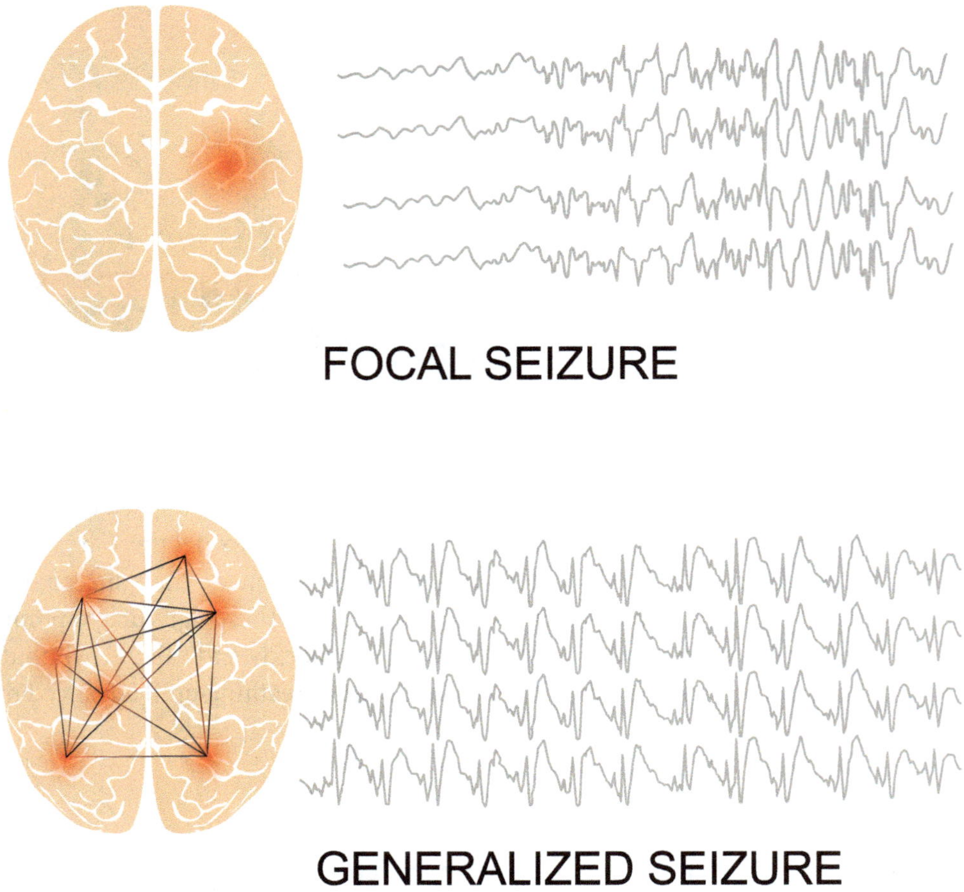

Figure 6-13 Focal versus generalized seizures

Absence seizures are more common in children, ages 4 to 12 years, than adults (Albuja & Khan, 2021). During an absence seizure, the individual appears to be staring at an object and daydreaming with a dazed look on their face. For a short amount of time they will be unable to respond to your voice, as they are oblivious to their surroundings. Usually as children get older, the absence seizures will stop. Allow the absence seizure to run its course. The seizure usually resolves in less than 15 seconds (Albuja & Khan, 2021). Attempt to arouse the individual by talking to them, call their name and say "are you okay?" Do not shake them, but stay with them until the seizure is over, and comfort them once they become aware of their surroundings. Advanced medical care is rarely necessary to treat an individual who has experienced an absence seizure, since emergency situations do not typically result. However, refer them to their physician for a thorough examination.

Tonic-clonic, or grand mal, seizures are also generalized seizures, which are very severe. Signs and symptoms of a tonic-clonic seizure are very recognizable. Although the individual's eyes may be open, they are not aware of their surroundings and may go unconscious. The individual will not be able to respond to your verbal or **tactile** commands. Their eyes may appear to roll into the back of their head, their teeth may be clenched, and they will be breathing very rapidly. During a tonic-clonic seizure, the individual's muscles, including facial muscles, are maximally contracted throughout the seizure. They may also have muscle jerks, convulsions, and fall to the ground. The individual might bite their tongue causing it to bleed, and lose bladder or bowl control during the seizure. You will have to wait for the seizure to run its course, and it may continue for a few minutes. When the seizure is over the individual will slowly regain consciousness. They will be dazed, confused, unaware of what happened, and possibly embarrassed, anxious, irritable, and sullen.

You play an important role in assisting an individual having a seizure (**Figure 6-14**). Recognizing the signs and symptoms of a seizure are important in order to prepare for what will follow. Protect the individual and bystanders from harm as best you can. Have bystanders move away from the seizing individual. If the individual is experiencing a tonic-clonic seizure have bystanders clear the area of objects such as tables, chairs, equipment, and anything that could harm the seizing individual should they fall or move into them. Immediately designate someone to call 911. Allow the seizure to run its course. Do not restrain the individual, shake

Figure 6-14 What to do if a person is having a tonic-clonic seizure

them, or put anything in their mouth. Restraining the individual can cause further harm to the individual, yourself, or bystanders. Loosen any of the individual's tight clothing if possible. If the individual is seizing on the ground, place something soft, such as a sweatshirt, pillow, or rolled towel, under their head so they do not forcefully hit their head on the floor causing a head injury. Stay with them during the course of the seizure, noting how long the seizure lasts. The seizure's duration is important information to give the EMS personnel when they arrive on the scene.

When the seizure is over, be mindful that the individual may or may not be conscious. Monitor their breathing at all times. Often the individual's breathing after a tonic-clonic seizure may be very faint, so make sure their airway is open and are breathing normally. If the individual is conscious, they may be embarrassed, confused, or disoriented. Talk to them, comfort, and reassure them that you are there to help them and EMS is on the way. Stay with the individual until EMS arrives. Whether they are unconscious, or conscious and breathing after the seizure is over, the best position to place the individual in is the modified HAINES position.

Choking

When a conscious person has food, drink, or any other object in their mouth the possibility of choking is real. Choking occurs when the object goes into the trachea and blocks air flow. For example, a person can choke when they are eating and talking at the same time. When an individual is conscious and coughing or talking due to an object entering their airway, then they are getting sufficient oxygen to supply the brain. Encourage them to continue coughing. By having them cough, the object may dislodge from the airway and be expelled. However, if the person cannot cough or talk, or has a high-pitched wheeze or squeal sound coming from them, then the airway is sufficiently blocked.

According to the American Red Cross (n.d.) the best course of action for assisting a choking individual is giving 5 back blows and 5 abdominal thrusts. Ask the individual "are you choking". If they nod "yes", then ask if you can assist them. If they nod again, then they have given you consent to help. Stand to their side with your arm across their chest for support. Bend them over slightly at their waist. Deliver 5 back blows between the individual's shoulder blades with the heel of your hand **(Figure 6-15)**. Then deliver 5 abdominal thrusts. Stand and position yourself behind the individual. Wrap your arms around their waist. Put your thumb into your fist with one hand. Find the individual's navel and place the thumb side of your fist slightly above the navel. Place your other hand over your fist and deliver slow, controlled, strong thrusts to the individual's abdomen. Deliver the 5 abdominal thrusts in and upward to the abdomen as single attempts **(Figure 6-16)**.

Continue alternating between 5 back blows and 5 abdominal thrusts until the object is expelled and the individual is able to breathe, or until the individual goes unconscious. If the object is expelled and the individual is able to breathe, monitor their breathing. If they are

© pixelaway/Shutterstock.com

Figure 6-15 Back blows

© pixelaway/Shutterstock.com

Figure 6-16 Abdominal thrusts

having any difficulties breathing or any pain results from the choking incident, then call 911 immediately. If the individual goes unconscious while choking, have someone call 911 immediately and begin CPR until EMS arrives.

If the food or object does not dislodge after a short period of time, the individual will not have enough oxygen supplied to the brain. Consequently, they will go unconscious and still be choking. To assist an unconscious choking adult, begin CPR. Compress the chest hard and fast 30 times at a rate of 100 compressions per minute, then look in the mouth to see if the object has been dislodged. If the object is in the mouth remove it with a finger and attempt to deliver 2 rescue breaths utilizing your pocket mask. If you do not see an object in the person's mouth, deliver 2 rescue breaths then continue with 30 compressions. This cycle of 30 compressions, object check, and 2 rescue breaths continues until the individual begins to breathe, another qualified person or EMS arrives to take over for you, an AED is delivered to the scene, you are too exhausted to continue, or the scene becomes unsafe (American Red Cross, n.d.).

Shock

At any point in time when an injury or illness occurs, a life-threatening condition called shock can result. Shock is the body's reaction to the loss of or diminished blood flow to the body. Blood is shunted away from the body's core. Consequently, hemoglobin in the red blood cells is unable to supply the brain and vital organs with oxygen. If shock is not treated immediately, then your patient can die.

Various types of shock can occur to your patient. A common type of shock which occurs as a result of injury is hemorrhagic shock. For example, hemorrhagic shock occurs when a vein or artery is severed, and the person is bleeding externally or internally. The shock causes a decreased quantity of blood in the circulatory system. Therefore, adequate blood and oxygen is not delivered throughout the body to sustain proper function.

Hypovolemic shock occurs with a loss of body fluids. If your patient has an illness which involves severe diarrhea and vomiting, dehydration may occur. If they are not taking in adequate fluids to replenish the fluids they have lost, hypovolemic shock may occur due to the dehydration.

During and after an individual has a heart attack they can experience cardiogenic shock. When a heart attack occurs diminished oxygenated blood flows throughout the body. This diminished blood flow with insufficient oxygen leads to shock.

Psychogenic shock is brought on by witnessing or hearing about a drastic event. As a result, the individual experiences various emotions such as fear or grief. These emotions can cause them to go into shock. For example, your client is lifting weights at We R Fit Gym. They decide to perform cleans as part of their work out, and increases the weight from the previous session. As your client lifts the bar, they cannot handle the increased weight and their right shoulder dislocates. Your client looks at their severely deformed shoulder, and due to the pain they are overcome with fear. Your client immediately goes into psychogenic shock. In this case, your client's blood vessels quickly become dilated, resulting in blood moving away from the brain and vital organs which diminishes the organs' oxygen supply.

Neurogenic shock typically occurs when an individual experiences severe spinal cord trauma. This trauma results in spontaneous **autonomic nervous system** (ANS) dysfunction. Signs of neurogenic shock include hypotension, or low blood pressure, bradycardia, and neurological disruption. The hypotension causes blood to move toward the extremities and away from the brain and core body. For example, a wide receiver is running a pattern across the middle of the field. They jump up for a high pass. While airborne, a defender hits the receiver's legs, causing them to spin and flip over in the air. When the receiver lands, their head hits the turf, and they sustain a cervical spinal cord injury. Due to the nature of the injury, the ANS signals to the blood vessels are disrupted and the athlete immediately goes into neurogenic shock.

Septic shock occurs when an individual has a significant bacterial infection. Although rare, fungus can also cause septic shock. The infection precipitates a series of events that result in lack of blood flow, which creates a lack of oxygen to the tissues. As with other types of shock, the heart has to work much harder in order to increase the blood flow and oxygen to the tissues. These events cause tissue death and possibly the individual's death, as septic shock has a high mortality rate (Mahapatra & Heffner, 2021).

Anaphylactic shock is caused when an **allergen** enters the athlete's body. Common allergens include various nuts, especially peanuts, bee stings, shellfish, medications, latex, and dairy products. The effects of anaphylactic shock range from mild to life-threatening. A mild reaction includes hives or a rash appearing on the skin. However, in severe cases, the blood vessels dilate, become permeable, and release blood and fluid into the body. Swelling, most often around the face and neck, occurs as a result. Also, the respiratory passageways become swollen, which results in breathing difficulty. Consequently, within minutes the individual cannot breathe and, if the condition is not treated quickly, they will quickly go unconscious and die.

Most types of shock have similar signs and symptoms. The most common signs and symptoms include a glassy-eyed stare, disorientation, agitation, irritability, confusion, nausea, thirst, pale, moist, and cool skin, sunken eyes, a rapid, weak pulse, decreased blood pressure, increased respiration rate, and dilated pupils. Certain types of shock also have very specific signs and symptoms. A sign of an athlete experiencing cardiogenic shock is neck vein protrusion (NIH, n.d.). Septic shock will also result in fever and red skin (Mahapatra & Heffner, 2021). A person in anaphylactic shock will exhibit signs and symptoms including a red rash, hives, constriction of the throat which causes breathing difficulty, low blood pressure, weak, rapid pulse, and fainting (AAAAI, n.d.).

After you have recognized that a person is experiencing shock, regardless of what type of shock they are experiencing, immediately call 911 and provide care until EMS arrives. Signs and symptoms of shock can be reversed if proper and immediate treatment is given. However, if an individual has been in shock for some time and immediate care is not provided, then death can occur. When you identify that an individual is in hemorrhagic, hypovolemic, neurogenic, or psychogenic shock help them lie down comfortably on their back with her feet raised, in attempt to redistribute blood to the core body. If the individual has a lower body injury such as a dislocation or fracture, or has sustained a spinal injury, do not raise the feet as you may cause further harm. Do not move the individual otherwise. Since the blood has shunted away from the core of the individual's body, they may shiver and feel cold. Keep the individual warm by putting a blanket, a jacket, or any soft material over them **(Figure 6-17)**. They may feel thirsty, but do not give them anything to drink by mouth since they most likely

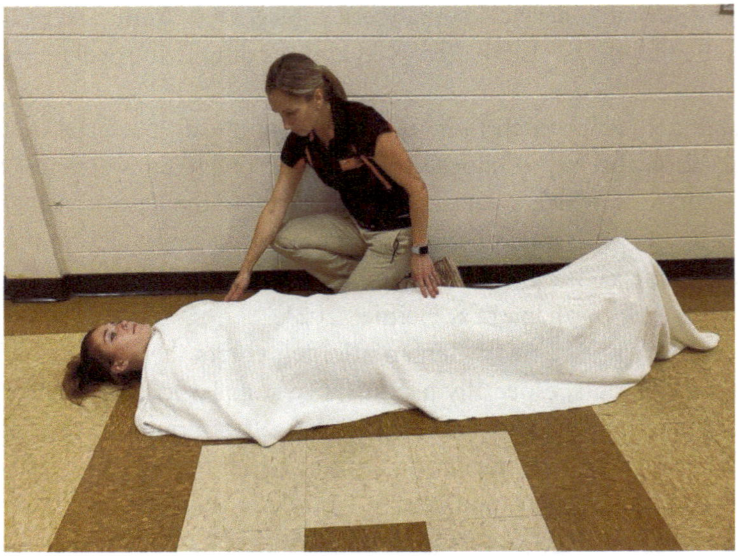

Figure 6-17 Cover the individual with a blanket if they are in shock and feel cold.

will not be entirely coherent, and you do not want them to choke. If the person is bleeding, put an absorbent material (gauze pads, sweatshirt, towel, etc.) over the wound and apply pressure to slow down bleeding. While you are providing care, talk to and comfort the individual. Reassure them that they will be okay, and talk to them about other topics in order to take their mind off of the injury, illness, and the situation at hand.

If you suspect an individual is in cardiogenic shock, be prepared to administer CPR if they go into cardiac arrest. For anaphylactic shock, ask the individual if they have an epinephrine auto-injector (one common brand is the Epi-pen®) and if so, assist them in obtaining and administering it to themself immediately **(Figure 6-18)**. Regardless of what type of shock the individual is experiencing, their life is on the line. You must react immediately, summon advanced medical care, provide care until EMS arrives, and always be prepared to administer CPR.

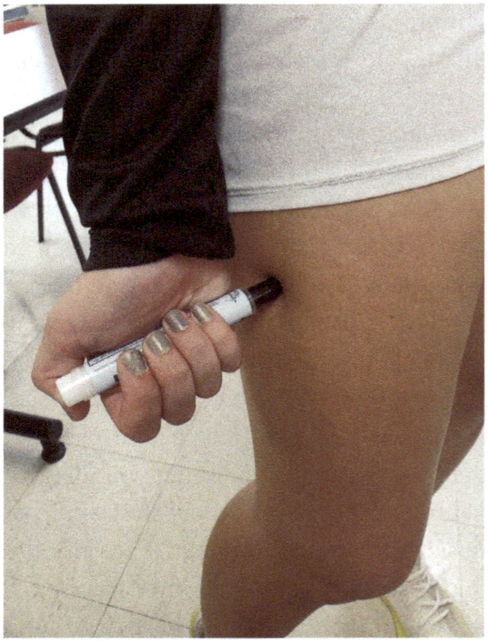

Figure 6-18 If an individual is in anaphylactic shock, assist them in administering their prescribed epinephrine auto-injector.

Asthma Exacerbations

Many athletes have a respiratory tract condition called asthma. Asthma is a chronic condition which occurs when the respiratory tract becomes inflamed and the bronchi become constricted. Typically asthma attacks, also called asthma exacerbations, occur due to an allergen or another substance affecting the athlete which, as a result, detrimentally affects the respiratory tract. Allergens and other substances which trigger asthma attacks include air pollution, smoke, aerosols, perfume, and other strong-smelling substances, dust, medication, pet dander and fur, food, exercise, and various emotions (AAAAI, 2020).

Physiologically, asthma can occur due to inflammation, bronchospasm, or both. An allergen enters the respiratory tract, and an inflammatory response is triggered. Airway inflammation of the bronchi and bronchioles occurs, as well as creation of mucous in these passageways, which cause decreased airflow. Acute attacks have a rapid onset and cause the bronchi and bronchioles to spasm. The smooth muscle lining of these passageways become constricted due to the muscles contraction, which also decreases airflow (**Figure 6-19**). Since the air entering the respiratory tract is decreased, oxygen exchange in the lungs is also decreased. Consequently, asthma attacks are life-threatening.

Since asthma attacks are life-threatening it is crucial to recognize the signs and symptoms immediately. Common signs and symptoms of an asthma attacks include wheezing, shortness of breath, increased respiratory rate, coughing, chest tightness, headache, and nausea. Since

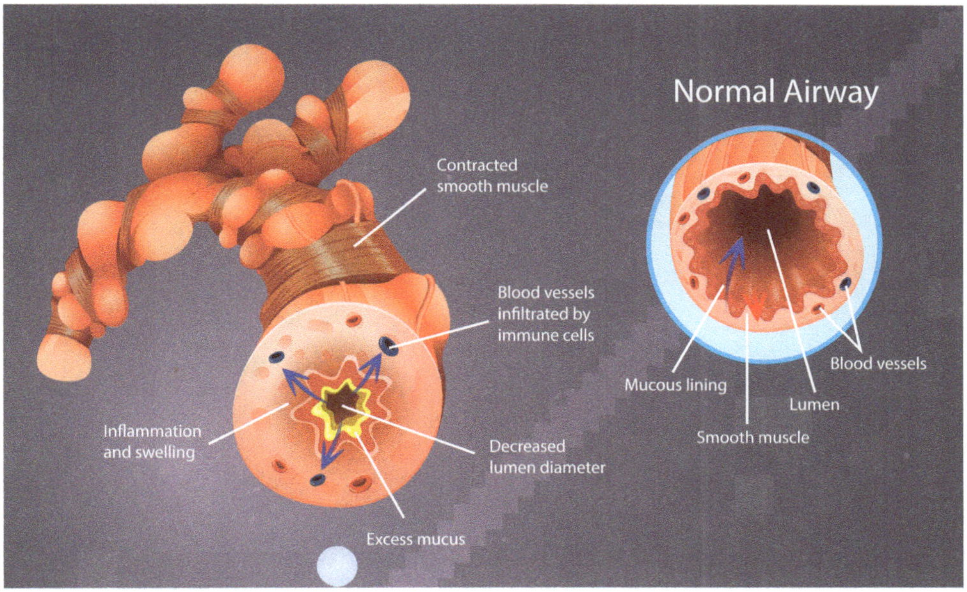

Figure 6-19 Inflammation and creation of mucus occurs with bronchial asthma.

the athlete is experiencing the effects of reduced airflow into their respiratory tract, they most likely will be anxious, nervous, and unsettled.

Proper immediate care for an athlete having an asthma attack is essential. First, ask the athlete if they are asthmatic. If they respond "yes", then ask if they have medication with them. Most medications that help treat acute asthma attacks are referred to "rescue inhalers". These rescue inhalers are quick-relief medications. They are metered dose inhalers (MDIs), which expel a specific dose of prescription medication **(Figure 6-20)**. When taken properly, the MDIs typically alleviate acute asthma attack signs and symptoms. In most instances these MDIs work very quickly to normalize the athlete's respiratory rate and quality. If your athlete says they have a MDI, assist them in obtaining the medication and have them administer it as prescribed **(Figure 6-21)**. If the medication does not relieve the symptoms shortly after administration, call 911.

If the athlete does not have the MDI available, attempt to calm them down, put them in the most comfortable position to facilitate breathing, and have them take slow, regulated, deep breaths. If the signs and symptoms do not subside within a couple of minutes, then call EMS. Also, if at any time the athlete's lips, face, or nails skin turn **cyanotic**, then calling 911 is imminent. If the athlete is unaware if they are asthmatic and has an attack, then treat them in the same manner as an asthmatic athlete who does not have a MDI. Asthma can

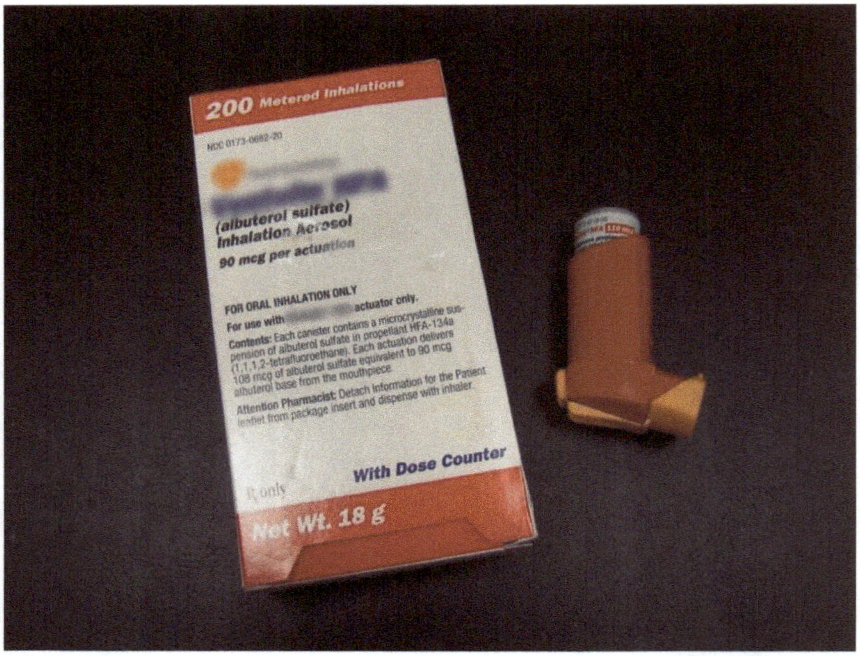

Figure 6-20 Quick-acting "rescue" inhalers are prescribed to athletes to curtail asthma attack signs and symptoms.

© Linda Gazzillo Diaz

Figure 6-21 When your athlete is having an asthma attack, have them administer their prescription asthma medication.

be life-threatening due to insufficient oxygen to the brain and vital organs. Consequently, when your athlete experiences an attack, take a brief, thorough history and treat the athlete without delay.

Diabetic Emergencies

Diabetes mellitus (usually referred to as "diabetes") is a disease in which high levels of sugar exist in the blood. The three common types of diabetes include Type 1, Type 2, and gestational diabetes. Type 1 diabetes (previously called juvenile or insulin-dependent diabetes) is often diagnosed in children. The exact cause is unknown. However, with Type 1 diabetes the pancreas produces little or no insulin because the body destroys the insulin producing beta cells in the pancreas (Mayo Clinic, 2021a). Consequently, glucose builds up in the bloodstream instead of moving into the body's cells. The individual may experience signs and symptoms including thirst, hunger, unexplained weight loss, frequent urination, blurred vision, and wounds that are slow to heal (CDC, n.d.). In order for the individual with Type 1 diabetes to have proper breakdown of sugar and for the body to function properly, the individual must self-administer insulin and monitor their blood glucose daily.

Type 2 diabetes (previously referred to as adult-onset diabetes) is the more common than Type 1 diabetes. Most often Type 2 diabetes occurs within adults; however children, especially obese children, can be affected by Type 2 diabetes. Individuals with Type 2 diabetes cannot utilize insulin properly, due to the body's cells being resistant to insulin and/or the pancreas not producing enough insulin **(Figure 6-22)**. Consequently, sugar builds up in the blood stream. These individuals have similar signs and symptoms as individuals with Type 1 diabetes as well as tingling in their feet or hands (American Diabetes Association, n.d.). Individuals who are predisposed to Type 2 diabetes are most often obese, sedentary, older adults, who have poor diets. As with individuals with Type 1 diabetes, individuals with Type 2 diabetes must monitor their blood sugar levels daily. However, individuals with Type 2 diabetes may not need supplemental insulin in order to manage or treat their condition. Over time, a proper diet and adequate exercise may be sufficient enough to control the individual's blood sugar levels at a normal range. If this treatment is not working to normalize the individual's blood sugar levels, then their physician may prescribe insulin.

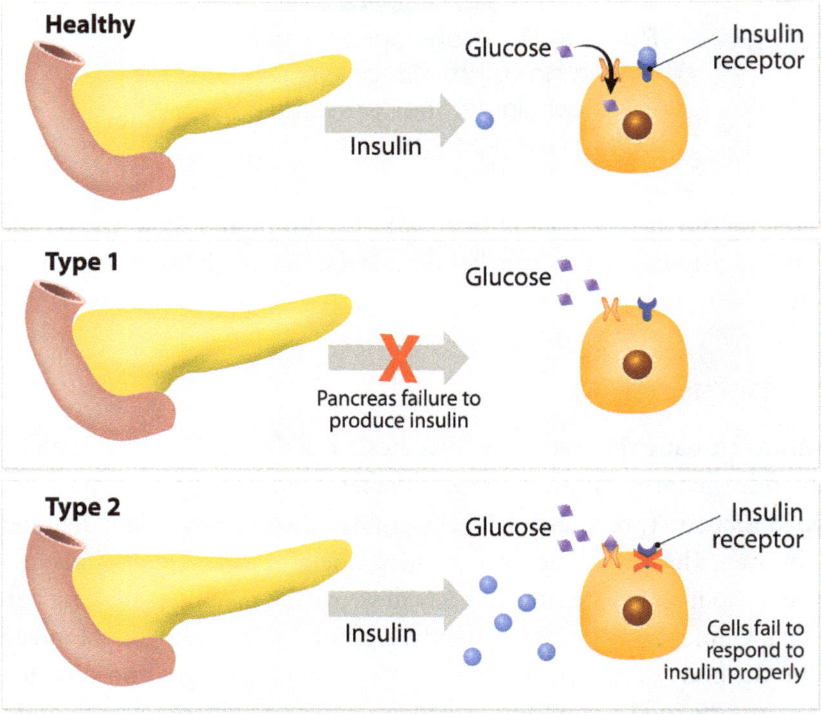

Figure 6-22 For an individual with diabetes mellitus, the pancreas does not produce enough insulin or the body's cells do not respond to the insulin being produced.

Gestational diabetes occurs when hormones produced during pregnancy decrease the ability of the body to utilize insulin. Pregnant women who do not have diabetes can acquire gestational diabetes. Testing is done around the end of the second trimester of pregnancy. Signs and symptoms of gestational diabetes are usually nonexistent. Regardless, pregnant women with gestational diabetes should test their sugar levels, eat nutritious foods, have pregnancy wellness physicals, and exercise (CDC, 2021).

Without adequate treatment for both Type 1 and Type 2 diabetes, various secondary illnesses including, but not limited to, eye conditions, including retinopathy, glaucoma, cataracts, blindness; foot conditions, including decreased circulation, nerve damage, ulcers; hearing loss, kidney disease, stroke, and skin disorders (**Figure 6-23**). Gestational diabetes must be

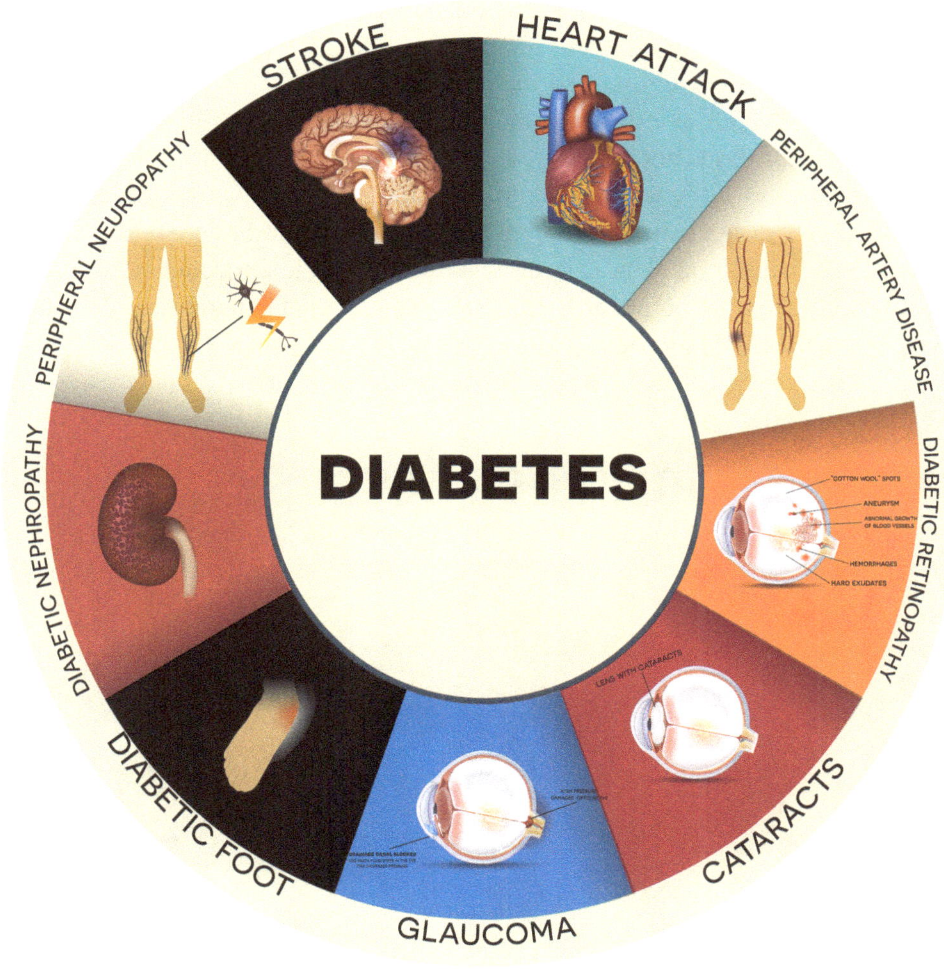

Figure 6-23 Diabetes can cause a multitude of secondary illnesses and/or complications.

addressed as well, otherwise the baby may be larger than normal, be born before term, have low blood sugar, and potentially acquire Type 2 diabetes later in life (CDC, 2021).

Whether an athlete has Type 1 or Type 2 diabetes, detrimental conditions can result. Hypoglycemia, hyperglycemia, and diabetic ketoacidosis (diabetic coma) are three potentially life-threatening conditions that can occur to a diabetic athlete **(Figure 6-24)**. A diabetic athlete can experience hypoglycemia or low blood sugar. A diabetic athlete who engages in intense exercise should eat a nutritious snack containing complex carbohydrate and protein before exercise (Prentice, 2021). During exercise, the athlete's body will break down glycogen. If the athlete does not eat a snack before exercise, then the body's sugar level will be very low. Consequently, the athlete's insulin will be high, which is called insulin shock. Likewise, if a Type 1 diabetic athlete administers their daily insulin, but does not eat an appropriate quantity of food during the day, the athlete's insulin level will be high and blood sugar levels will be low. Signs and symptoms of hypoglycemia include dizziness, confusion, weakness, fatigue, headaches, increased respirations, and tremors (Prentice, 2021).

Hyperglycemia or high blood sugar occurs when excess sugar is in the blood, insulin levels are too low, or insulin is not being used properly. When an individual consistently has hyperglycemia, they most likely will be diagnosed as having diabetes. If an athlete is already diagnosed with Type 1 diabetes and they forget to take their insulin or do not take as much as they are prescribed, their blood glucose levels will become elevated throughout the course of the day due to the intake of carbohydrates. Signs and symptoms of hyperglycemia include glucose in the urine as measured by chemstrips **(Figure 6-25)**, glucose in the blood as measured

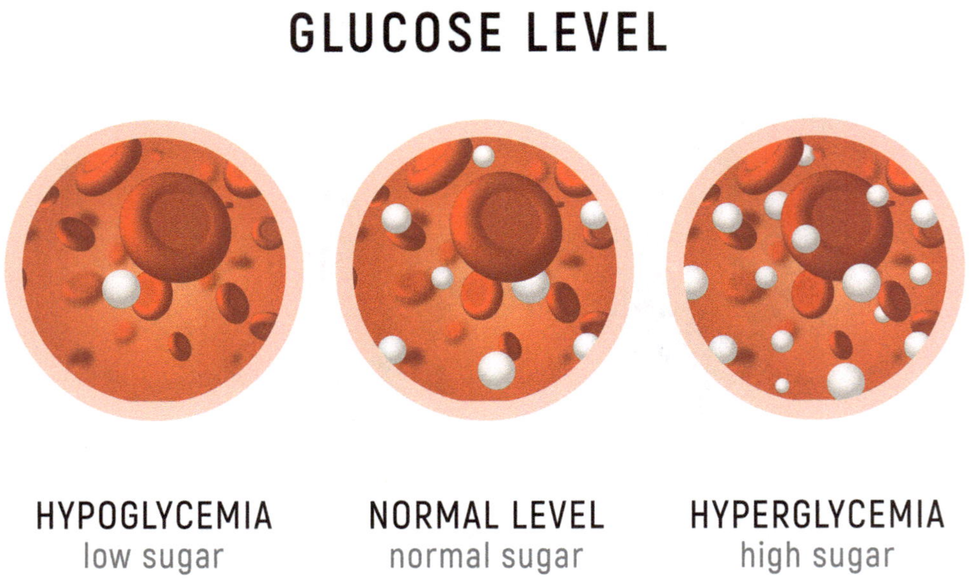

Figure 6-24 Hypoglycemia, normal blood sugar, and hyperglycemia

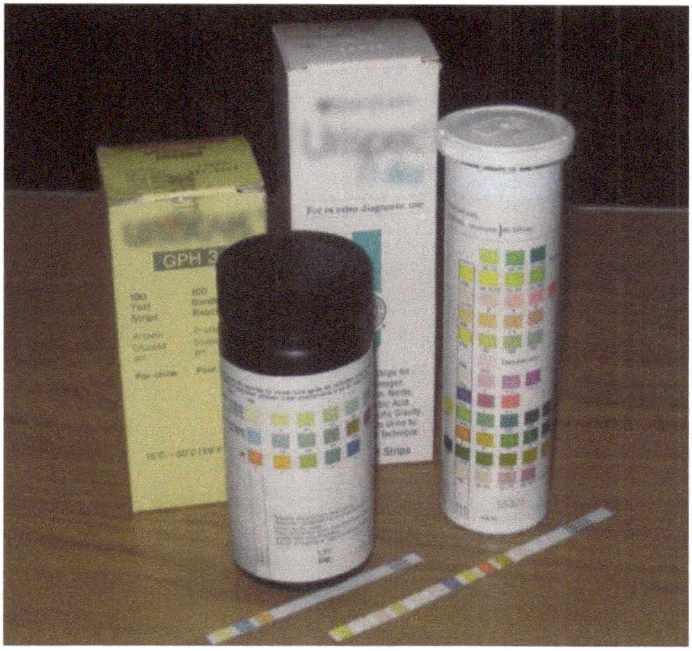

© Linda Gazzillo Diaz

Figure 6-25 Chemstrips can determine if sugar (glucose) is in an athlete's urine.

by self-monitoring blood glucose equipment, blurred vision, and increased appetite, thirst, and urination.

Hyperglycemia can lead to a life-threatening condition called diabetic coma, also more commonly known as diabetic ketoacidosis (DKA) (Gosmanov et al., 2021). Diabetic ketoacidosis occurs when the athlete's blood glucose levels remain high and the athlete's body is unable to effectively utilize the glucose for energy. Consequently, the body uses fat as an energy source instead of glucose. The athlete will exhibit signs and experience symptoms of hyperglycemia, along with a fruity-smelling breath due to the production of ketones. Ketones are chemicals created by the body when fat is broken down and utilized by the body as an energy source. Other signs and symptoms of diabetic ketoacidosis include fatigue, breathing difficulty, muscle aches, and nausea and vomiting.

Whenever you recognize that your athlete is exhibiting signs and symptoms of diabetes mellitus, take their history and ask them if they are diabetic, if you do not know already. If the athlete has not been diagnosed as diabetic, then recommend they promptly see their physician to be examined. When an athlete exhibits signs and symptoms of hypoglycemia, hyperglycemia, or diabetic ketoacidosis, the athlete's immediate treatment varies. In order to treat an athlete experiencing hypoglycemia, have them ingest a small amount of simple sugars. Give the athlete a small spoonful of granulated sugar, a few sips of orange juice, or glucose tablets or

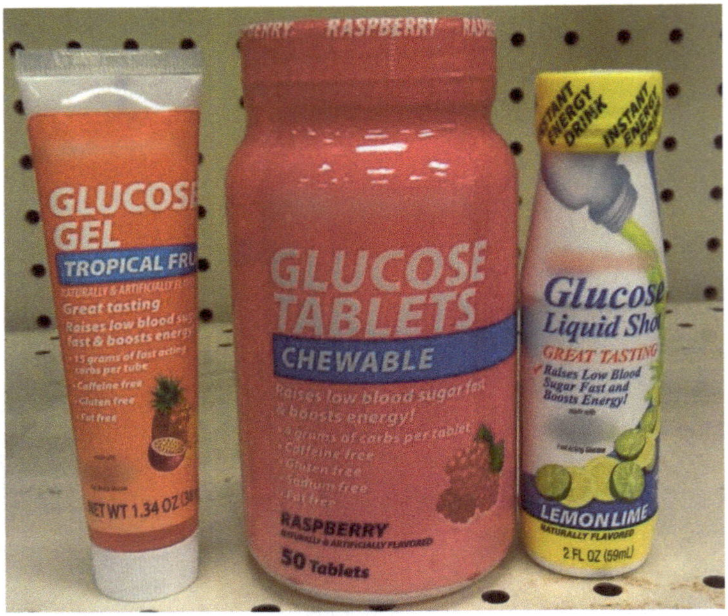

Figure 6-26 Glucose gel, tablets, and liquid can assist in returning a hypoglycemic athlete to a normal state.

gel, provided they are completely coherent **(Figure 6-26)**. Once the sugar is in their body, the hypoglycemia signs and symptoms should decrease rapidly, and the athlete should return to a normal state very quickly. If the athlete does not progressively return to a normal state within a few minutes, then immediately refer the athlete to their physician, or call 911.

If a diabetic athlete is experiencing hyperglycemia, ask them if they have taken their insulin that day. If the athlete has not taken their insulin and have it with them, then have them administer it immediately. If the athlete does not have insulin with them or does not take insulin, then refer her to a physician immediately. Athletes who continuously have bouts of hyperglycemia must be put on a strict exercise and diet regimen and insulin may be prescribed to control the high blood sugar.

If at any time you smell a fruity scent from your athlete's breath, or you see signs of diabetic ketoacidosis, give them water to drink to begin body cell rehydration, and have them administer their insulin. Call 911 to summon EMS without delay because diabetic ketoacidosis can result in coma or death if not treated immediately.

Environmental Emergencies

Individuals frequently exercise indoors, such as in gyms or clinics. To keep your clients motivated and interested in exercise, not only can you vary their specific exercises, but you can change their exercise environment. When working with clients outdoors, educate them in regard to heat and cold related illnesses, along with the danger of lightning.

Heat related illnesses typically occur outdoors when the environmental temperature and **relative humidity** is high **(Figure 6-27)**. When the relative humidity is high, the air carries a large quantity of water molecules. During exercise, our muscles and core body create heat. As the environment increases in temperature, our core body temperature increases also. In order to eliminate heat, and maintain a safe core body temperature, the body sweats. The sweat is dissipated into the air by evaporation of the water molecules in sweat. The environment can readily accept these water molecules provided that the air is not saturated with water already. Less sweat evaporation will occur as the relative humidity increases. Consequently, your client's body will not sufficiently eliminate heat. They will be in danger of succumbing to heat related illness. The hot, humid environment predisposes an individual exercising outdoors to various heat related illnesses including heat syncope, heat cramps, rhabdomyolysis, heat exhaustion, and heat stroke.

Figure 6-27 Prior to exercising outdoors, be certain to check the ambient temperature and relative humidity.

Heat syncope occurs when an individual is exercising in the hot, humid environment, becomes dizzy, lightheaded, and as a result suddenly faints (NIOSH, 2018b). Fainting typically occurs due to blood vessel vasodilation, blood pooling at the extremities, and dehydration. When an individual faints and falls to the ground, the blood is then redistributed to the vital organs and brain. After fainting, the individual typically returns to full consciousness within a short amount of time. After noticing that your client has fainted, approach them immediately and perform a primary survey. Make sure that they have no life-threatening conditions If so call 911 and provide immediate care. Remove the individual from the environment and bring them to a cool environment such as a room with fans or air conditioning. Have them sit comfortably, while drinking plenty of cool water or low carbohydrate drinks to rehydrate. Your client should revert back to their normal state shortly with rest, external cooling of the body, and rehydration.

Heat cramps are involuntary, painful muscle spasms which occur typically at the gastrocnemius or abdominal muscles while exercising in a hot, humid environment. As with heat syncope, heat cramps can be a result of dehydration and/or a lack of electrolytes in the body. The individual will be sweating, fatigued, and have muscle pain and cramping. At this point, care for your client by having them rest in a cool environment. Give them water or electrolyte drinks to rehydrate. Assist your client in massaging and gently performing static stretches for the involved muscles. You can also apply ice or perform ice massage on the painful muscles.

Once your client is rehydrated and the pain and cramps are alleviated, then they can return to activity with caution.

Rhabdomyolysis (rhabdo) is a condition that may occur when an individual exercising for an extended period of time in a hot environment, whereas significant dehydration, electrolyte loss, and/or core body elevation exists. The condition involves muscular breakdown, rupture, and death (NIOSH, 2018b). When muscle tissue dies, skeletal proteins enter into the bloodstream. Rhabdo is a potentially life-threatening situation, due to the possible kidney failure and heart rhythm disruption. Signs and symptoms of rhabdo include tea colored urine, muscle cramps or pain, and weakness, while some individuals are asymptomatic for a few days after injury (Torres et al., 2015). Since rhabdo is potentially life-threatening, it is a medical emergency. Call 911 immediately to summon advanced medical care for your client. Have them stop all activity, rest, and drink water or an electrolyte drink to rehydrate while waiting for EMS to arrive.

Heat exhaustion is a more serious heat related illness than heat syncope or heat cramps. After exercising in the hot, humid environment for a period of time without rehydrating, the individual loses a significant amount of water and electrolytes (salt). If they do not continuously replace the fluids and electrolytes, then they may succumb to heat exhaustion. Signs and symptoms of heat exhaustion are profuse sweating, pale, clammy, moist skin, rapid, weak pulse, increased respirations, lightheadedness, and dizziness (NIOSH, 2018b). The core body temperature is elevated but less than 105° F (Casa et al., 2015). To care for a person experiencing heat exhaustion, immediately move them to a cool area, preferably one with air conditioning and/or fans. Remove all sweaty clothes, except for undergarments in order to be discreet, to allow for the surrounding air to cool the skin and for evaporation of sweat to occur. Have them lie on their back with their legs raised. Apply ice packs or ice towels to the individual's body, especially at the neck, armpits, and groin. Have them rehydrate by drinking water or electrolyte drinks. The *National Athletic Trainers' Association Position Statement: Exertional Heat Illnesses* states that in order to effectively determine and monitor an individual core body temperature when the possibility of heat exhaustion exists, you must utilize a rectal thermometer (Casa et al., 2015). However, you must be appropriately trained on how to use a rectal thermometer to determine accurate core body temperature. If you are not trained to use a rectal thermometer properly, utilize an infrared thermometer **(Figure 6-28)** to monitor your client's core body temperature, and determine if your efforts to decrease core body temperature are working. Once your client has returned to a normal state, have them rest for the remainder of the day. Refer the athlete immediately to a physician or call 911 if your client does not show improvement within 30 minutes of treatment (Casa et al., 2015) and/or has more than one bout of heat exhaustion. Regardless, you should refer your client to a physician to be examined and cleared for physical activity participation.

Heat exhaustion can progress to a more serious, life-threatening condition called heat stroke. Heat stroke occurs when the body is not able to regulate the core temperature due to excessive heat production, inability to sweat, or decreased evaporation of sweat (Casa et al., 2015).

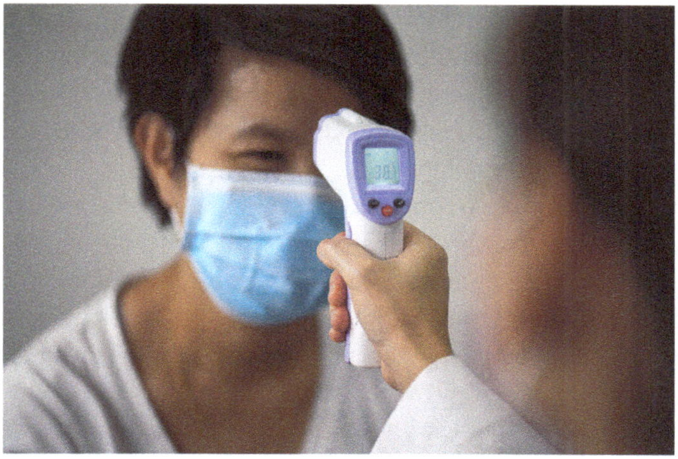

Figure 6-28 Infrared thermometer

The individual is severely dehydrated, with a rapid, strong pulse, and rapid, increased respirations. The skin appears hot, red, and dry; however, an individual who has just been sweating may still have residual sweat on their body **(Figure 6-29)**. The individual is extremely disoriented, and does not respond to your questions or commands. The individual can become unconscious, and their core body temperature is over 105° F. Heat stroke is a medical emergency. The individual's core body temperature must be decreased immediately, and then they must be transported to a hospital via EMS. Call 911 and provide immediate care. Similar to heat exhaustion, move them to a cool environment, preferably with air conditioning. Do not give them any fluids by mouth. Other than their undergarments, remove clothing. Place the individual in a cold immersion tub up to their neck, making sure that they do not slip under water. If the individual has equipment on, which is difficult to remove and delays cooling, put them in the tub with the equipment on

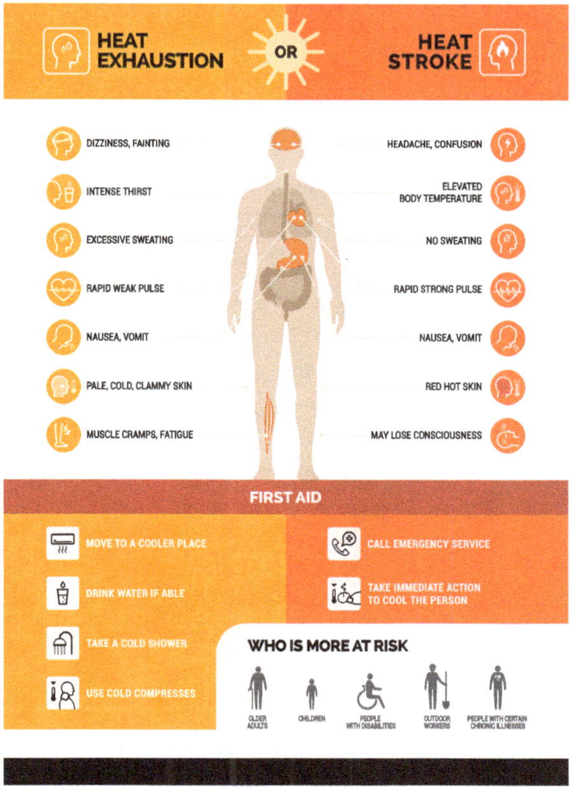

Figure 6-29 A comparison of heat exhaustion and heat stroke signs and symptoms, immediate first aid care, and risk factors.

and then remove the equipment while in the tub (Casa et al., 2015). Monitor the individual's core body temperature with a rectal thermometer (if trained) or an infrared thermometer. When the core body temperature decreases to 102° F, then the individual must be transported via ambulance to the hospital for further treatment. Heat stroke can cause death, so you must provide this emergency care to your client without haste.

Educate your client on preventative measures so they are not afflicted with a heat related illness. Your client should be certain that they are hydrated before, during, and after exercise. They should drink approximately 8 ounces of water or electrolyte fluid every 15 minutes. Advise them to wear light colored and textured clothing which wicks sweat and heat away from the body. The individual should exercise during the morning or evenings when the environment is less hot and humid. The individual should avoid outdoor exercise when the heat index is high **(Figure 6-30).** Have them acclimatize their body by spending short amounts of time exercising each day in the hot, humid environment. In time, the individual's body becomes accustomed to working in this environment, which assists in preventing heat related illness. Overall, in order to prevent heat related illness the individual must be cautious and adjust their behaviors if they wish to successfully exercise outdoors in a hot, humid environment **(Figure 6-31).**

As with heat related illnesses, individuals can sustain cold related illnesses when exercising outdoors. Cold related illnesses include chilblains, trench foot, frostbite, and hypothermia.

NWS Heat Index — **Temperature (°F)**

Relative Humidity (%)	80	82	84	86	88	90	92	94	96	98	100	102	104	106	108	110
40	80	81	83	85	88	91	94	97	101	105	109	114	119	124	130	136
45	80	82	84	87	89	93	96	100	104	109	114	119	124	130	137	
50	81	83	85	88	91	95	99	103	108	113	118	124	131	137		
55	81	84	86	89	93	97	101	106	112	117	124	130	137			
60	82	84	88	91	95	100	105	110	116	123	129	137				
65	82	85	89	93	98	103	108	114	121	128	136					
70	83	86	90	95	100	105	112	119	126	134						
75	84	88	92	97	103	109	116	124	132							
80	84	89	94	100	106	113	121	129								
85	85	90	96	102	110	117	126	135								
90	86	91	98	105	113	122	131									
95	86	93	100	108	117	127										
100	87	95	103	112	121	132										

Likelihood of Heat Disorders with Prolonged Exposure or Strenuous Activity

Caution | Extreme Caution | Danger | Extreme Danger

Figure 6-30 Individuals should use a heat index chart to determine if it is safe to exercise outdoors.
Source: National Weather Service (https://www.weather.gov/media/unr/heatindex.pdf)

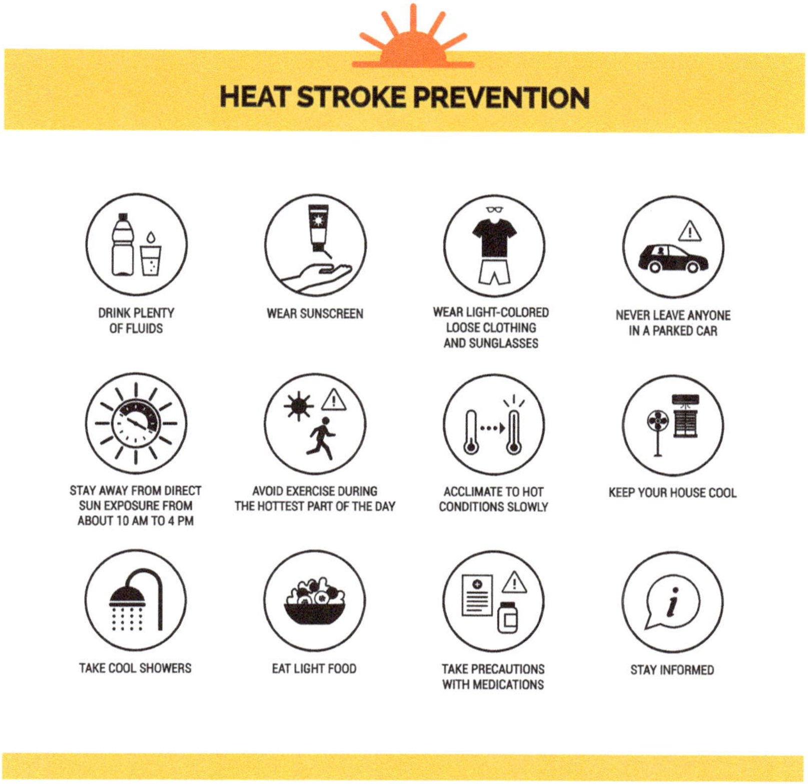

Figure 6-31 Measures to prevent heat stroke and other heat-related illness
Source: NOAA.gov

Although, low environmental temperatures can cause cold related illnesses, if the environmental conditions are also wet (i.e. rain or snow) and windy then the chances of an athlete sustaining a cold related illness is more probable than with cold air alone. Consequently, individuals should take precautions in exercising in the cold as they would in the heat.

Normal body temperature is approximately 98.6° F. In order for the body to create heat in cold temperatures, the body shivers. When the body temperature drops even slightly from the norm, then shivering occurs. Along with shivering, the body attempts to protect itself by shunting blood away from the extremities. The blood moves toward the trunk, vital organs, and brain in attempt to provide adequate oxygen to these areas. Since the blood is moving away from the extremities, areas such as the fingers and toes, and unprotected areas such as the nose and ears are susceptible to chilblains, trench foot, and frostbite. When the body temperature decreases further, to about 95° F, then the body becomes hypothermic (Mayo Clinic, 2022a).

Chilblains (also called pernio) occur when skin tissue is repeatedly subjected to cold temperatures ranging from freezing to 60° F (NIOSH, 2018a). The capillaries in the skin, most often in the nose, cheeks, earlobes, fingers, and toes become damaged. The affected area

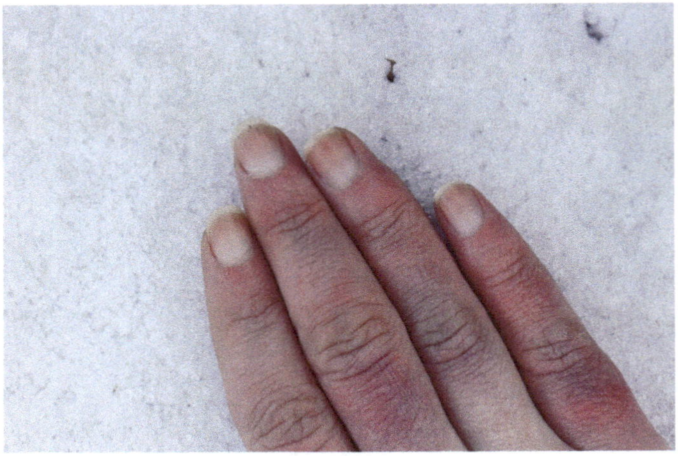

Figure 6-32 Chilblains of the fingers

becomes red, itchy, swollen, and blisters may develop **(Figure 6-32)**. To treat chilblains, remove the patient from the cold, remove cold clothing covering the affected area, and slowly rewarm the area. Warm the tissues by putting them in proximity to warm air (blowing on them), a warm object (by a heating element), or in the armpits (an area of core body warmth). Do not vigorously rub or itch the area, otherwise further skin damage may occur. If attempts to rewarm do not return the tissue to normal temperature and sensation, the individual must seek medical care immediately.

Trench foot occurs in the same temperatures causing chilblains; however, as per its name, trench foot occurs to the feet. When the feet are exposed to a cold, wet environment for a prolonged time, they lose heat. The body will conserve heat by increasing blood flow to the core, resulting in decreased blood flow to the feet. Likewise, the feet will lose oxygen from the lack of blood flow to the area, causing the tissue to show signs and symptoms of redness, pain, numbness, swelling, blistering, and gangrene (NIOSH, 2018a) **(Figure 6-33)**. The immediate treatment for trench foot is the same as chilblains. If the individual notes gangrene on the toes or foot, they must seek medical attention immediately.

Frostbite involves the same areas as chilblains such as the ears, nose, fingers, toes, and cheeks; however, it can affect the superficial and deep tissues. Superficial frostbite begins when ice crystals form in the tissues, which become frozen. The individual's skin appears waxy and bluish color due to the lack of oxygen. The individual complains of tingling, stinging, or numbness, and loss of function due to tissue stiffness. if the individual does not get out of the cold environment then deep frostbite can occur. With deep frostbite, the tissues are entirely numb, and the affected areas are no longer painful. The tissues are extremely hard and cannot be moved either actively or passively. Blisters typically begin to form on the skin. The individual must get out of the cold environment and rewarm the area immediately. Help them remove any wet, cold clothing, and put on dry clothing. Cover the individual with warm blankets **(Figure 6-34)**.

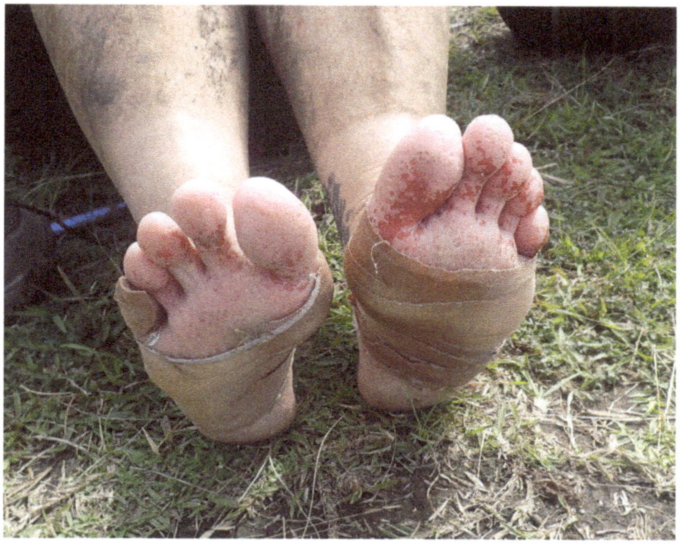

Figure 6-33 Trench foot

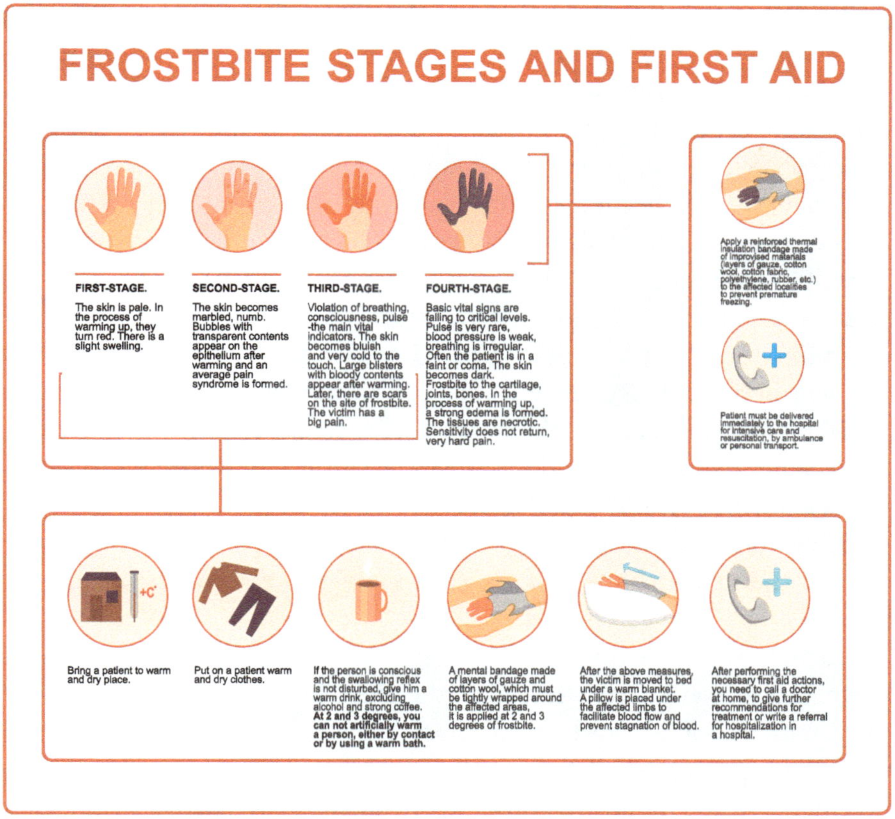

Figure 6-34 Stages and treatment for frostbite

TIPS FROM THE FIELD

Tip 1 If you have an asthmatic client who utilizes a rescue inhaler (MDI), ask if they have an extra MDI to keep locked up at the facility, depending on your facility's policies. For example, many public schools allow or require a student-athlete to have an additional prescribed inhaler stored in the Nurse's or Athletic Trainer's Office in a locked medicine cabinet. This additional inhaler must be labeled with the student-athlete's full prescription including their name, medication, dosage, and prescribing doctor on the box and MDI. If your facility is not able to maintain clients' MDIs (which is usually the case in gyms, clinics, etc.), then direct your client to keep a MDI with them at all times, with their personal belongings, during exercise. Having the medication on hand while exercising is imperative for your client in case they experience an asthma attack.

Place the frostbitten body part in warm, but not hot, water, or in the armpits to warm the area. Do not rub the area or use a heating pad, heat lamp, fireplace, or the like as a source of heat since the tissues are numb as further tissue damage can result (NIOSH, 2018a). If blisters are present, dress the blisters with non-adherent gauze pads and dressings, in order to prevent infection and the tissues from sticking to each other. While you are treating the individual for frostbite, call 911 to have them transported to an emergency room for immediate advanced medical treatment.

Hypothermia is the most severe of the cold related illnesses. This life-threatening illness occurs with prolonged exposure to the cold environment, and as a result the body temperature decreases to 95° F (Mayo Clinic, 2022a). The body conserves heat and oxygen in the blood by decreasing blood flow to the extremities and increasing it to the brain and vital organs. The blood vessels become constricted, and the individual begins to have significant nervous system and brain dysfunction. They become confused, disoriented, and lethargic. The individual's speech is slurred, vision is impaired, and gait and body movement are uncoordinated. The body tissues are blue, hard, and stiff. The individual experiences intense shivering until the body temperature falls to 86° F when shivering stops. Eventually if they do not get out of the cold environment and get advanced medical care immediately, then the individual's heart rhythm will become dangerously irregular, and breathing rate and quality will be significantly decreased. Ultimately without emergency care, a hypothermic individual will go unconscious, enter into a coma, and die. Therefore, your first priority is to get them out of the cold, into a warm area, and call 911. Lay the individual down and attempt to rewarm them by removing cold, wet clothing and replacing them with many layers of warm blankets or coats over their entire body. Stay with the individual and be prepared to give CPR if necessary.

In order to prevent cold related illnesses, suggest to your clients to avoid exercising outdoors in extremely cold, wet, windy weather. If your client insists on exercising in wet, windy, and cold conditions, educate them to wear appropriate clothing that insulates their body. Many exercise clothing companies have formulated fabrics which assist in keeping the body warm in the cold. Layered clothing keeps heat around and insulates the body. If the individual

Wind Chill Chart

Temperature (°F)

Wind (mph) Calm	40	35	30	25	20	15	10	5	0	-5	-10	-15	-20	-25	-30	-35	-40	-45
5	36	31	25	19	13	7	1	-5	-11	-16	-22	-28	-34	-40	-46	-52	-57	-63
10	34	27	21	15	9	3	-4	-10	-16	-22	-28	-35	-41	-47	-53	-59	-66	-72
15	32	25	19	13	6	0	-7	-13	-19	-26	-32	-39	-45	-51	-58	-64	-71	-77
20	30	24	17	11	4	-2	-9	-15	-22	-29	-35	-42	-48	-55	-61	-68	-74	-81
25	29	23	16	9	3	-4	-11	-17	-24	-31	-37	-44	-51	-58	-64	-71	-78	-84
30	28	22	15	8	1	-5	-12	-19	-26	-33	-39	-46	-53	-60	-67	-73	-80	-87
35	28	21	14	7	0	-7	-14	-21	-27	-34	-41	-48	-55	-62	-69	-76	-82	-89
40	27	20	13	6	-1	-8	-15	-22	-29	-36	-43	-50	-57	-64	-71	-78	-84	-91
45	26	19	12	5	-2	-9	-16	-23	-30	-37	-44	-51	-58	-65	-72	-79	-86	-93
50	26	19	12	4	-3	-10	-17	-24	-31	-38	-45	-52	-60	-67	-74	-81	-88	-95
55	25	18	11	4	-3	-11	-18	-25	-32	-39	-46	-54	-61	-68	-75	-82	-89	-97
60	25	17	10	3	-4	-11	-19	-26	-33	-40	-48	-55	-62	-69	-76	-84	-91	-98

Frostbite Times: 30 minutes / 10 minutes / 5 minutes

$$\text{Wind Chill (°F)} = 35.74 + 0.6215T - 35.75(V^{0.16}) + 0.4275T(V^{0.16})$$

Where, T= Air Temperature (°F) V= Wind Speed (mph)

Effective 11/01/01

Figure 6-35 In cold climates, have your client look at a wind chill chart prior to determining if it is safe to exercise outdoors.
Source: NOAA.gov

gets too warm while exercising, they can remove clothing to regulate body temperature. All extremities, as well as the head, must be adequately covered. Also, make sure that your client continually hydrates when exercising in cold environments as they would in hot, humid environments. Proper hydration assists the individual's body to maintain its water balance and proper blood flow to the extremities and core. Also, prior to exercise, your client should review the ambient temperature and wind chill to see if cold related illnesses are imminent **(Figure 6-35)**.

Lightning is a potentially fatal environmental hazard for athletes who exercise outside. The National Weather Service (n.d.) reports approximately 30 lightning deaths per year, with two-thirds of those deaths to individuals participating in outdoor recreational activities. Therefore, athletes must avoid exercising outside when a thunderstorm is approaching. Educate your athletes to utilize weather channels or technological applications to determine if a thunderstorm is probable prior to exercising outdoors. Explain to them what action to take if they are caught outside and an unexpected thunderstorm is approaching. They must move quickly indoors into an enclosed building. If a building is not nearby, then the athlete should get into their car with the windows closed. If the athlete is outside without any shelter, they should squat down low, in the position similar to that of a baseball catcher with their head down. This position makes the athlete less likely to be struck by lightning. If an individual

> **TIPS FROM THE FIELD**
>
> **Tip 2** If you do not have a cold immersion tub accessible for cooling an athlete who is experiencing heat stroke, an effective means to bring down the body temperature is by utilizing " ice towel buckets". Have bath-sized towels in a bucket with ice and water. If an athlete is experiencing heat stroke, take towels out of the bucket, slightly wring them out, and spread them out on the athlete. Then if needed, pour ice all over the towels. With the cold, wet towels on the athlete with the ice applied, the ice will more readily adhere to the towels and consequently cool the athlete faster than if you apply loose ice to the athlete's skin. This care should be administered while waiting for advanced medical personnel to arrive on the scene. You can use ice towels on an athlete experiencing heat exhaustion as well, but the additional ice poured onto the towels may not be necessary to decrease the athlete's core body temperature.

is struck by lightning, you must summon EMS immediately. You can touch them as their body will not carry an electrical charge (National Weather Service, n.d.). Check to see if they are conscious, and be prepared to administer CPR if they are not breathing and do not have a pulse.

You can determine approximately how far away the thunderstorm is from your location by utilizing "flash-to-bang" method. Begin counting when you see a flash of lightning until you hear the corresponding bang of thunder. Then divide the number of seconds by five. The result is how many miles the lightning is away from your location. If the bang of thunder occurs before 30 seconds, then you must take shelter immediately. Outside activity should not be resumed until 30 minutes after the last sound of thunder (National Weather Service, n.d.). The flash-to-bang method is a very basic method to determine when a lightning strike is imminent. If you will be working outside with your athletes on a regular basis, consider purchasing a lightning detector. This electronic equipment can detect lightning up to 40 miles away, which gives you ample time to get indoors. Effective, accurate lightning detectors can be costly, but are well worth the expense since it potentially saves lives.

Summary

At some point in your sports medicine career, you will most likely have an athlete who sustains a life-threatening injury and/or illness. Your role as a sports medicine professional is to readily recognize the signs and symptoms of these life-threatening injuries and illnesses and provide care without delay. In these situations, you must provide emergency care without delay. Summoning EMS and treating the athlete appropriately is imperative in order to give them the best chance of survival.

Keywords

Limb-threatening When an individual sustains a significant injury resulting in loss of motor function and/or sensation of the arm(s) or leg(s).

Cardiac arrest When an individual's heart is significantly damaged, it will no longer function properly and stops beating.

Angina Occurs when a part of the heart does not get enough oxygenated blood. The athlete feels similar pain as an individual who is experiencing a heart attack, but most often not as severe.

Paralysis The inability to move a body part, with or without an inability to feel sensation.

Aura An abnormal feeling of the mind and body which may come directly before an individual experiences a seizure.

Tonic A state where the muscles are in constant contractions.

Clonic A state where the muscles rapidly and forcefully contract and then reflexively relax.

Tactile Refers to the sense of touch.

Autonomic nervous system Controls automatic bodily functions such as the abdominal organs, pupils, heart rate, breathing, digestion, and other unconscious or involuntary functions of the body.

Allergen A substance or object that causes sensitivity or an allergy.

Cyanotic A blue color which occurs when lack of oxygen and increased carbon dioxide is present in the tissues.

Relative humidity The amount of water molecules in the air, which is designated by the percent of air saturation.

Discussion Questions

1. What is the purpose of a primary survey? What must you determine when performing a primary survey on an individual?
2. Describe four different types of injuries or illnesses that would cause an individual to become unconscious?
3. Describe how you would use an AED on an individual that is in cardiac arrest.
4. What is a stroke? Describe the signs and symptoms of a stroke.
5. When faced with an individual who is having a grand mal seizure, how should you care for the individual to minimize the potential for injury?
6. Describe in detail how you would care for a conscious, choking adult?
7. Name the different types of shock that commonly occur to individual. How must you care for an individual in shock? When must you summon EMS when a person is in shock?
8. What are the different types of diabetic emergencies?
9. Describe the various types of heat related illness that an individual can succumb to when exercising. What are the signs and symptoms for the different types of heat related illnesses? How would you treat each of the heat related illnesses? What measures can be taken by the individual to prevent heat related illness?

CASE STUDY 1: CLASSROOM SEIZURE

Derek is a healthy sixteen year-old at Anywhere High School. He is a star member of the varsity soccer team who trains year-round. Derek has no health issues and no history of any ailments in his family. During health class, Derek is watching a video with his classmates when suddenly he slumps to the side of his desk and begins to have a tonic-clonic, grand mal seizure. His head and upper and lower body begin to shake uncontrollably. The students that are sitting near Derek panic, rush out of their seats, and run to the front of the room near the teacher. Ralph, Derek's best friend, runs over to him and grabs Derek from the back, holding Derek's arms tightly to prevent him from falling to the floor. While restraining Derek, Ralph gets hit in the nose by the back of Derek's head, giving Ralph a nose bleed. Ralph lets go of Derek who immediately falls out of the chair, hitting his head on one of the desks as he falls to the floor. After about one minute, the seizure subsides and Derek's body relaxes.

Upon coming out of the seizure, Derek finds himself lying on the classroom floor. He is groggy and anxious. Derek sees his classmates and teacher hovering over him. He looks around in confusion. He does not know what happened to him and why he is lying on the floor. Derek complains that he feels tired, his head and body are sore, and does not remember what just happened. The teacher helps Derek up and sit in a chair. She calls the nurse, who then calls 911. Derek is quickly transported to the hospital for further evaluation.

1. What should the teacher have done to ensure that all of the students, including Derek, were safe from harm during the seizure?
2. Was it appropriate for Ralph to restrain Derek? Why or why not?
3. When and how should have Ralph's bloody nose been treated?
4. Why was Derek sore and tired after the seizure?
5. What were the proper steps that should have been taken to give Derek appropriate care during and after the seizure?

CASE STUDY 2: SHOCK IN THE GYM

On an early Saturday morning in We R Fit Gym, a 30-year-old client, Tom, was completing his usual workout. He was performing three sets of ten repetitions of bilateral bicep curls using 65-pound dumbbells. When Tom completed the exercise sets he went to put the dumbbell weights back on the rack. However, due to the sweat dripping down his arms and on his hands, his right-hand lost grasp of the dumbbell. Tom dropped the dumbbell onto the top of his foot, and screamed due to the excruciating pain. The surrounding clients were alerted by Tom's screams and summoned the personal trainer, Mary, who was nearby on the floor. When Mary arrived, Tom was sitting in a chair with his sneaker and sock off of his injured foot, crying and grabbing his foot. Immediately, Mary noticed that Tom had significant foot deformity and bleeding. It appeared that two metatarsal bones were protruding from Tom's foot.

Within seconds, Tom began to become agitated. His face turned pale, and his eyes became glassy. When Mary asked him what happened, Tom seemed disoriented and confused. Tom answered Mary and said that his foot was broken. Tom continued to say that he was cold and thirsty. Upon hearing that Tom was thirsty, another client gave him a water bottle to drink from. After looking at his deformed, bleeding foot, Mary panicked. She then became agitated, irritable, and shaken up, as she did not like the site of blood and did not know what to do to help Tom. Another personal trainer, Dave, went over to Tom to see what the commotion was all about. When Dave arrived, he saw that not only was Tom in distress, but now his coworker Mary was also. He realized that both Tom and Mary will be in grave danger if someone did not take immediate action. Consequently, Dave called 911 immediately. Then Dave assisted Tom by walking with him to the front entrance to wait for the ambulance.

1. Other than Tom's fractured foot, what condition are Tom and Mary suffering from?
2. How should the two victims be treated prior to the arrival of EMS?
3. Could Mary's condition have been prevented? If so, what could have been done?
4. What actions were taken by all parties involved in this emergency situation that were improper and could have made the situation worse?

References

Albuja, A.C., & Khan, G.Q. (2021, Dec 13). Absence seizure. StatPearls [Internet]. https://www.ncbi.nlm.nih.gov/books/NBK499867/

American Academy of Allergy, Asthma, & Immunology (AAAAI). (n.d.). *Anaphylaxis symptoms & diagnosis.* Retrieved on March 20 2022, from https://www.aaaai.org/conditions-treatments/allergies/anaphylaxis

American Academy of Allergy, Asthma, & Immunology (AAAAI). (2020, September 28). *Asthma triggers and management.* https://www.aaaai.org/Tools-for-the-Public/Conditions-Library/Asthma/Asthma-Triggers-and-Management-TTR

American Academy of Orthopaedic Surgeons [AAOS]. (2022). *Advanced first aid, CPR, and AED, (8th Ed.).* Jones and Bartlett Learning.

American Diabetes Association. (n.d.). *Diabetes symptoms.* Retrieved March 21, 2022, from http://www.diabetes.org/diabetes-basics/symptoms/

American Heart Association. (2022a). *Warning signs of a heart attack.* Retrieved March 19, 2022, from https://www.heart.org/en/health-topics/heart-attack/warning-signs-of-a-heart-attack

American Heart Association. (2022b). *What is CPR?* Retrieved March 16, 2022, from https://cpr.heart.org/en/resources/what-is-cpr

American Heart Association. (2018, February 26). Cardiac arrest survival greatly increases when bystanders use an automated external defibrillator. *ScienceDaily.* Retrieved March 15, 2022, from www.sciencedaily.com/releases/2018/02/180226085812.htm

American Red Cross. (n.d). *Adult ready reference card.* Retrieved March 20, 2022, from https://www.redcross.org/content/dam/redcross/atg/PDFs/Take_a_Class/Adult_Ready_Reference_Card.pdf

Casa, D.J., DeMartini, J.K., Bergeron, M.F., Csillan, D., Eichner, E.R., Lopez, R.M., Ferrara, M.S., Miller, K.C., O'Connor, F., Sawka, M.N., & Yeargin, S.W. (2015). National Athletic Trainers' Association position statement: Exertional heat illnesses. *Journal of Athletic Training*; *50*(9), 986–1000. https://doi.org/10.4085/1062-6050-50.9.07

Center for Disease Control and Prevention (CDC). (2020, September 30). *Types of seizures.* Retrieved March 20, 2022, from https://www.cdc.gov/epilepsy/about/types-of-seizures.htm

Center for Disease Control and Prevention (CDC). (2021, August 10). *Gestational diabetes.* Retrieved March 21, 2022, from https://www.cdc.gov/diabetes/basics/gestational.html#:~:text=Gestational%20diabetes%20is%20a%20type,pregnancy%20and%20a%20healthy%20baby

Clark, M. D., Davis, M. P., Petschauer, M. A., Swartz, E. E., & Mihalik, J. P. (2018). Delivering Chest Compressions and Ventilations With and Without Men's Lacrosse Equipment. *Journal of athletic training, 53*(4), 416–422. https://doi.org/10.4085/1062-6050-91-17

Courson, R., Ellis, J., Herrins, S.A., Boden, B.P., Henry, G., Conway, D., McNamara, L., Neal, T.L., Putukian, M., Sills, A.K., & Walpert, K.P. (2020). Best practices and current care concepts in prehospital care of the spine-injured athlete in American tackle football. *Journal of athletic training, 55*(6), 545–562. http://doi.org/10.4085/1062-6050-430-19

Gosmanov, A.R., Gosmanova, E.O., & Kitabchi, A.E. (2021). Hyperglycemic crises: Diabetic ketoacidosis and hyperglycemic hyperosmolar state. In K.R. Feingold, B. Anawalt, A. Boyce, et al., Eds. Endotext [Internet]. MDText.com, Inc. Available from: https://www.ncbi.nlm.nih.gov/books/NBK279052/

H. Rept. 106-634. (2000, May 23). *Cardiac arrest survival act of 2000.* Retrieved on March 16, 2022, from https://www.congress.gov./congressional-report/106th- congress/house-report/634.

Mahapatra, S., & Heffner, A.C. (2021, June 24). Septic Shock. *StatPearls [Internet].* StatPearls Publishing. https://www.ncbi.nlm.nih.gov/books/NBK430939/

Mayo Clinic. (2022a, March 5). *Hypothermia.* Retrieved on March 25, 2022, from https://www.mayoclinic.org/diseases-conditions/hypothermia/symptoms-causes/syc-20352682

Mayo Clinic. (2022b, January 20). *Stroke.* Retrieved March 19, 2022, from https://www.mayoclinic.org/diseases-conditions/stroke/symptoms-causes/syc-20350113

Mayo Clinic. (2021a, March 27). *Type 1 diabetes.* https://www.mayoclinic.org/diseases-conditions/type-1-diabetes/symptoms-causes/syc-20353011

Mayo Clinic. (2021b, June 2). *Ventricular fibrillation.* Retrieved March 16, 2022, from http://www.mayoclinic.com/health/ventricular-fibrillation/DS01158

Medline Plus. (2022, February 18). *Ventricular tachycardia.* Retrieved March 16, 2022, from http://www.nlm.nih.gov/medlineplus/ency/article/000187.htm

Medline Plus. (2021, August 17). *Understanding different types of seizures.* Retrieved March 19, 2022, from https://magazine.medlineplus.gov/article/understanding- different-kinds-of-seizures

Mihalik, J.P., Lynall, R.C., Fraser, M.A., Decoster, L.C., De Maio, V.J., Patel, A.P., Swartz, E.E. (2016). Football Equipment Removal Improves Chest Compression and Ventilation Efficacy. *Prehosp Emerg Care, 20*(5):578–85. https://doi.org/10.3109/10903127.2016.1149649

National Heart, Lung, and Blood Institute (NIH). (n.d.). *Cardiogenic shock.* Retrieved on March 20, 2022, from https://www.nhlbi.nih.gov/health-topics/cardiogenic-shock

National Institute for Occupational Safety and Health (NIOSH). (2018a, June 6). *Cold stress – cold related injuries: Types of cold-related illnesses.*Retrieved March 25, 2022, from https://www.cdc.gov/niosh/topics/coldstress/coldrelatedillnesses.html

National Institute for Occupational Safety and Health (NIOSH). (2018b, June 6). *Heat stress – heat related illness.* Retrieved on March 23, 2022, from https://www.cdc.gov/niosh/topics/heatstress/heatrelillness.html#:~:text=Heat%20syncope%20is%20a%20fainting,dehydration%20and%20lack%20of%20acclimatization.

National Weather Service. (n.d.) *Lightning safety and outdoor sports activities.* Retrieved on March 25, 2022, from https://www.weather.gov/safety/lightning-sports

Prentice, W.E. (2021). *Principles of athletic training: A guide to evidence-based clinical practice, 17th Ed.,* McGraw-Hill Education.

Torres, P. A., Helmstetter, J. A., Kaye, A. M., & Kaye, A. D. (2015). Rhabdomyolysis: pathogenesis, diagnosis, and treatment. *The Ochsner journal, 15*(1), 58–69.

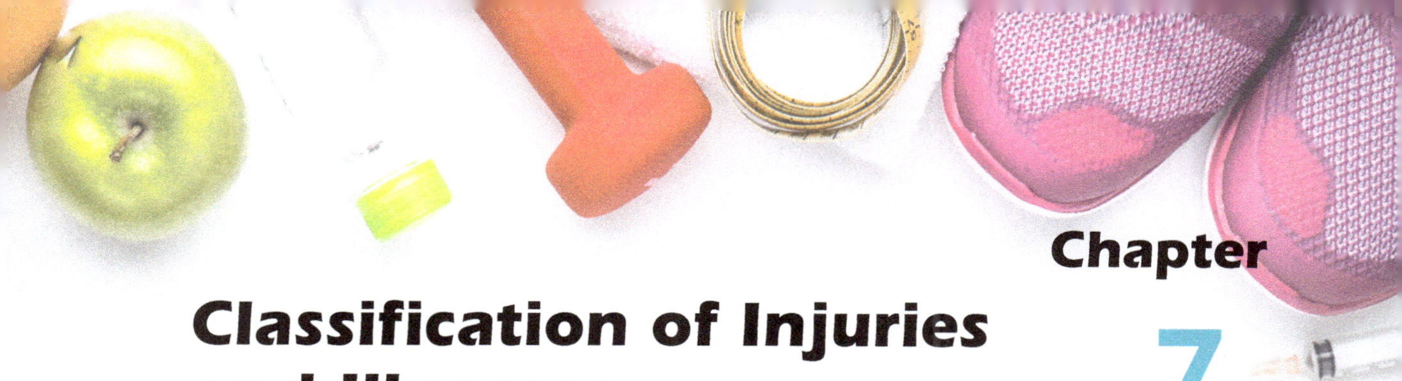

Chapter 7

Classification of Injuries and Illnesses

Chapter Objectives

After you have read this chapter, you will be able to understand:

- The various mechanisms of tissue injury.
- The healing process, including the phases of healing.
- Signs and symptoms of injury and illness.
- The differences between acute and chronic injuries.
- Various classifications of injuries and illnesses.
- The microorganisms that cause illnesses.

Numerous types of injuries and illnesses exist. An individual can experience an injury or be overcome by an illness that can be minor or severely disabling. Whether an injured individual has a broken bone, a muscular injury, or a skin infection, the body must heal in order to return to its original state. The healing process is a systematic means for tissue to respond to the injury and allow the body to resume normal function. This chapter explains the tissue response to injury and introduces you to the general classifications of injuries and illnesses. By understanding these general classifications, you will be able to identify various types of injuries and illnesses. Likewise, you will be prepared for the subsequent chapters which give detailed information regarding specific, common injuries and illnesses that occur to individuals of all ages.

Mechanism of Injury

Various mechanisms of injury for injuries and illnesses exist. A mechanism of injury is the cause of the injury or the manner in which the injury occurs. Compressive, tensile, and shear forces are three very common mechanisms of injury for both soft tissue and bony injuries (**Figure 7-1**).

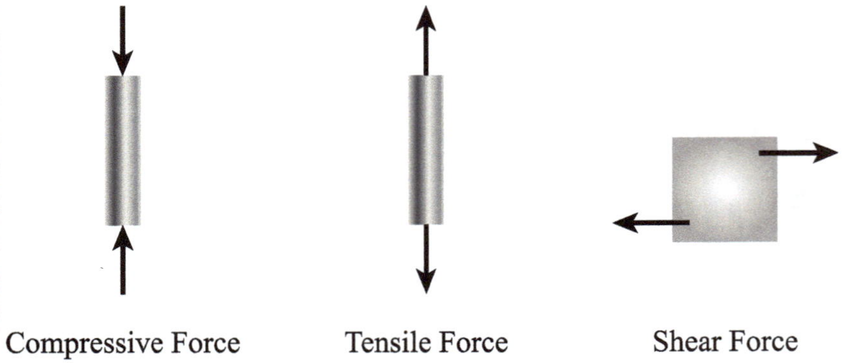

Figure 7-1 Compressive, tensile, and shear forces are common mechanisms of injury.

Compression forces occur when tissue is crushed between two or more objects. For example, during a workout a weightlifter drops a weight on their foot. Their foot is compressed between the weight and the floor. Consequently, the weightlifter sustains a metatarsal fracture due to a compressions mechanism of injury. Tensile forces cause a structure to be pulled apart from either one or both ends. The tissue is stretched beyond the anatomical limit, which is the maximal length the tissue can withstand, and as a result the tissue tears. For example, an athlete "twists" his ankle in a manner that stretches a ligament. The ligament cannot withstand the force and the ligament tears. The mechanism of injury in this example is a tensile (or separation) force placed on the tissue. A shear force occurs to the body when one or more forces move across the tissues. These forces typically move in opposite directions. For example, if a soccer player kicks their opponent's thigh while wearing cleats, the cleats move across the thigh and shear the skin. Consequently, a skin wound, such as an abrasion or laceration, can occur.

Regardless of the mechanism of injury, the severity of injury is determined by many factors. Severity is determined by the intensity, or amount, of force that is applied. Greater forces cause greater severity of injury than milder forces. The amount of force along with the speed of the object striking the body can determine severity of injury. For example, if a baseball player at bat is hit by a 95 mile per hour (mph) versus 70 mph pitch from the mound, the severity of injury caused by the 95-mph pitch will be greater. The size and hardness of the object striking the body also determines severity of injury, with larger, harder objects causing greater injury than smaller, softer objects. An individual's age, size, and physical condition also play a role in extent of injury. These factors are only a few of the many factors which come into play in determining severity of injury.

The Healing Process

After an injury occurs to an individual, the healing process begins. The healing process is imperative because it is a means to repair tissues, return the body back to its uninjured state, and restore the body's equilibrium. The three phases of the healing process include the inflammatory

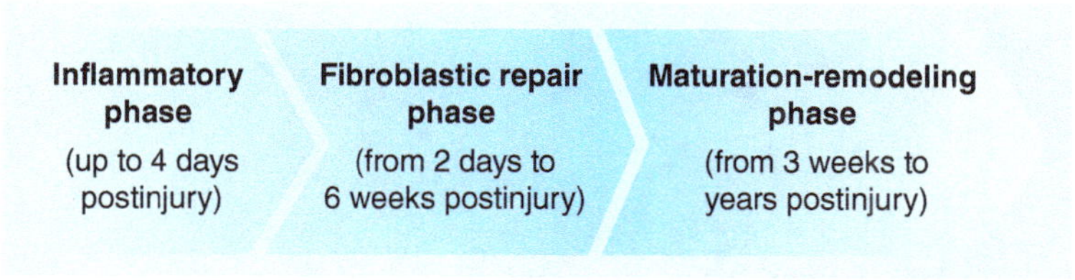

Figure 7-2 The three phases of healing overlap each other.

phase, the fibroblastic repair phase, and the maturation-remodeling phase (Prentice, 2021). These phases occur in a continuum, and overlap each other (**Figure 7-2**). The three phases do not have a rigid time frame when one phase ends and the subsequent phase begins. However, the completion of each phase is imperative for the tissue to heal properly. When the healing process is complete, the individual should be able to obtain normal, pre-injury function.

The Inflammatory Phase

The inflammatory phase is the first phase in the healing process for **acute injuries**. This phase can arguably be considered the most important phase. If the inflammatory phase does not properly follow an intended course of events, then the damaged tissue will not move on to the fibroblastic phase. This lack of progression can cause further injury, in particular **chronic injury** which is discussed later in this chapter.

The inflammatory phase begins at the time of injury with hemostasis, which is the body's ability to stop blood flow (Houglum, 2016). Immediately when tissue and blood vessels are damaged vasoconstriction occurs. Vasoconstriction is when the blood vessels' lumen, or opening, becomes narrowed and smaller in diameter. Vasoconstriction often takes place for an extremely short amount of time, which is typically five to ten minutes (Prentice, 2021). During this time, blood flow is slowed to the injured area. After vasoconstriction occurs, then vasodilation begins.

Vasodilation is when the blood vessels' openings become larger in diameter. The vasodilation occurs during the beginning stages of the inflammation phase. The damaged tissue, cells, such as white blood cells or mast cells, and enzymes release chemical mediators which cause the vasodilation (Prentice, 2021). Two chemical mediators that are seemingly detrimental to an individual, yet important to the healing process, are histamine and bradykinin. Histamine causes vasodilation, which increases blood flow to the injured area. Histamine causes redness, an increased temperature at the injured site, and blood vessel permeability. Like histamine, bradykinin is a vasodilator, creates blood vessel permeability, and also causes pain at the injured site and surrounding areas (Houglum, 2016).

When the blood vessels are vasodilated and their walls are permeable, the damaged red and white blood cells and the plasma fluid in the blood exit the blood vessels. Plasma fluid and cells that accumulate in the injured area outside the blood vessels is called **exudate**. How

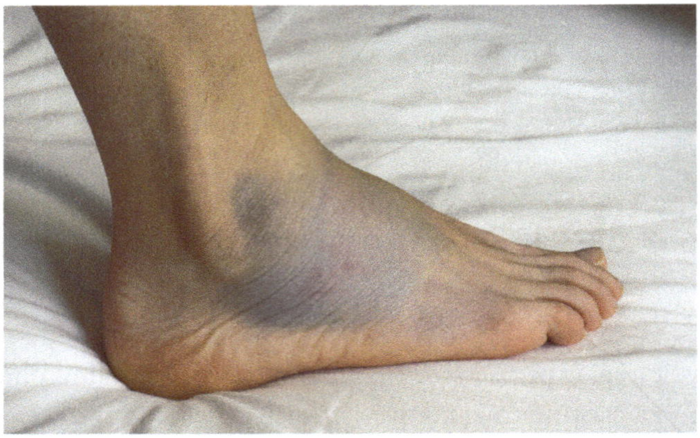

Figure 7-3 Ecchymosis is a sign of injury, which often occurs in the inflammatory phase.

much exudate is formed depends on factors such as the extent of injury, chemical mediators released, and blood vessel permeability. The exudate becomes viscous and remains stagnant in the injured area. Due to its viscosity, the exudate creates the appearance of swelling, and the capillary permeability with resultant bleeding and effusion causes **ecchymosis (Figure 7-3)**. As the exudate increases, the pressure increases at the injury site. The pressure causes cellular death due to lack of oxygenated blood flow to the area. Also, pressure on nerve endings causes pain at the injury site. The exudate also prevents the veins from functioning properly. Usually the venous system brings waste, including carbon dioxide, damaged cells, and extracellular fluid through the circulatory system to clean up the injured area after trauma. However, this restoration cannot occur until other chemical mediators are released.

Heparin, serotonin, leukotrienes, and prostaglandins are chemical mediators that assist in returning the area to its pre-injury state (Prentice, 2011). Heparin is an anticoagulant, which assists the exudate from being less viscous. This chemical mediator thins out the exudate which makes venous return possible. Serotonin assists the blood vessels to vasoconstrict and become less permeable. Consequently, the amount of fluid and cells exiting the blood vessels is minimized. Leukotrienes and prostaglandins both impede inflammation and decrease swelling.

At the end of the inflammatory response phase and in response to other chemical mediators, phagocytes accumulate at the injury site and debride the area. Phagocytes include cells such as leukocytes, neutrophils, and macrophages. They function to remove the waste materials, damaged cells, and foreign matter from around the injured tissues (Denegar, 2015). Platelets, which are sticky substances that attach to the exposed collagen fibers on the blood vessels' walls, assist the phagocytes. The platelets create a plug which limits the inflamed area size.

At this time thromboplastin is released from the damaged cells. Thromboplastin initiates a series of events, which causes the clot to be formed. The existence of thromboplastin makes prothrombin change to thrombin, which is the sticky substance comprising the clot. A clot begins to form approximately 12 hours after injury and is completely formed within two days (Prentice, 2021). The clot, like the platelet plug, limits the size of the inflamed area, and prevents further blood flow to the injured area. As the clot forms, phagocytes continue to debride the area.

The inflammatory phase of healing is characterized by specific signs and symptoms of inflammation. Signs of inflammation are characteristics that are physically observable. Symptoms of inflammation are characteristics that are not physically observable, but are subjective and reported by the individual. Signs of inflammation include redness **(Figure 7-4)**, swelling **(Figure 7-5)**, increase in tissue temperature, and loss of function. The predominant and most common symptom of inflammation that the individual experiences is pain. As the inflammatory phase comes to an end and the second phase of healing begins, these signs and symptoms of inflammation notably subside. The inflammatory phase can take up to four days to complete before the fibroblastic repair phase commences (Prentice 2021).

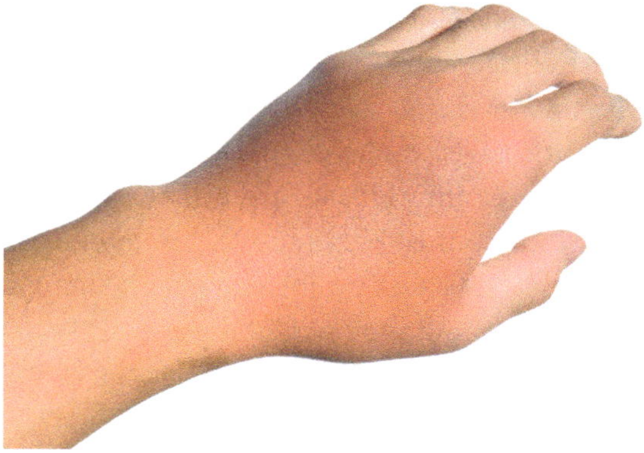

Figure 7-4 Skin redness is a sign of inflammation.

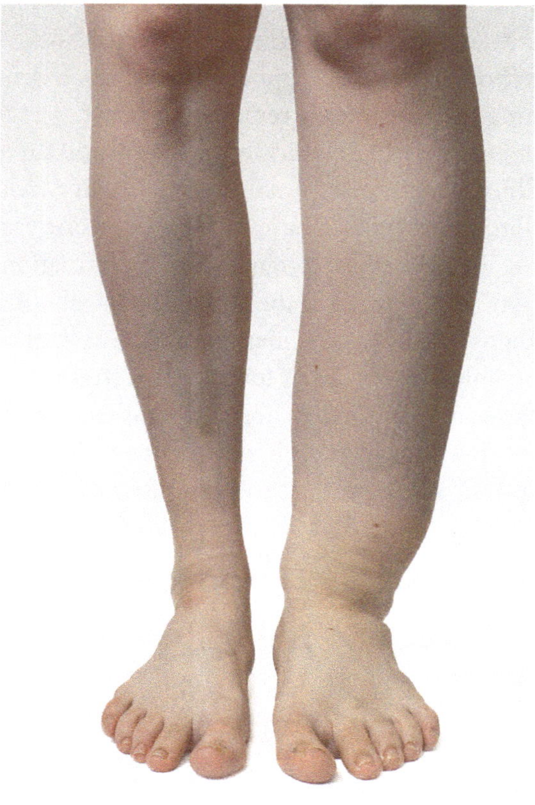

Figure 7-5 Swelling from edema is a sign of inflammation.

The Fibroblastic Repair Phase

The end of the inflammatory phase overlaps with the beginning of the fibroblastic repair phase. The fibroblastic repair phase has a longer duration than the inflammatory phase, and can take up to six weeks to complete (Prentice, 2021). This phase of healing is characterized by a decrease in signs and symptoms of inflammation, continuation of phagocytic activity, fibroblastic activity, and formation of collagen tissue and a fragile scar.

By the time the fibroblastic repair phase begins, the signs and symptoms of inflammation have decreased. New capillaries form at the injury site which brings oxygenated blood to the area, while phagocytes continue to rid debris from the injured site. Consequently, pressure decreases, which in turn decreases pain and swelling at the site. With decreased pain and swelling, the individual is able and willing to move the area. This voluntary movement increases range of motion (ROM), which is the amount of available motion, at the injured area. Fibroblasts are cells which have the ability to form collagen fibers. They are located in connective tissue and migrate to the injured area. The fibroblasts begin to create a loose meshwork of unorganized **collagen** at the injury site (Wallace et al., 2021). The collagen creates a fragile scar at the site of the previously formed clot. Over weeks, the collagen begins to reform and strengthen as the fibroblasts decrease in number, and thus begins the maturation-remodeling phase.

The Maturation-Remodeling Phase

During the fibroblastic repair phase, collagen is laid down in a disorganized fashion which creates a fragile scar. However, as stress is applied to the area, then the collagen lines up parallel to how the stress is applied. This collagen scar tissue fibers' organization occurs in the beginning the maturation-remodeling phase. The maturation-remodeling phase is the final phase of healing, which typically begins around three weeks post-injury, and overlaps the end of the fibroblastic repair phase. The maturation-remodeling phase is significantly longer than the fibroblastic repair phase, as it can take one year to complete (Wallace et al., 2021).

As the phase progresses, scar formation continues. A continuation of wound contraction, which began at the end of the fibroblastic repair phase, occurs as well. Stress on the scar aligns the scar tissue fibers parallel to each other and the lines of stress. This stress creates more organized scar tissue. However, this stress must be applied in a manner which does not disrupt the scar. If too much stress exists, then scar disruption occurs and the healing process takes much longer than originally planned. Over time, the collagen fibers become more organized, and the scar continues to strengthen and decrease in size (Houglum, 2016).

Bone Healing Versus Soft Tissue Healing

Bone healing is similar to soft tissue healing in regard to the events that occur in the inflammatory phase. However, once the fibroblastic repair phase begins, bone healing is different than soft tissue healing. During the fibroblastic repair phase, osteoblasts from the surrounding bone move to the break, or fracture, in the bone. These osteoblasts, which are a type of fibroblast, form a callus at the injured site (**Figure 7-6**). The callus is a combination of collagen and cartilage, which fills in the break in the bone. Over time, as with soft tissue healing in the maturation-remodeling phase, this bony callus becomes hard and strong. A physician determines if the fractured bone is immobilized for days, weeks, or months, and what type of immobilization is necessary. The physician makes this determination depending on various factors which include the severity of the fracture, secondary injuries and

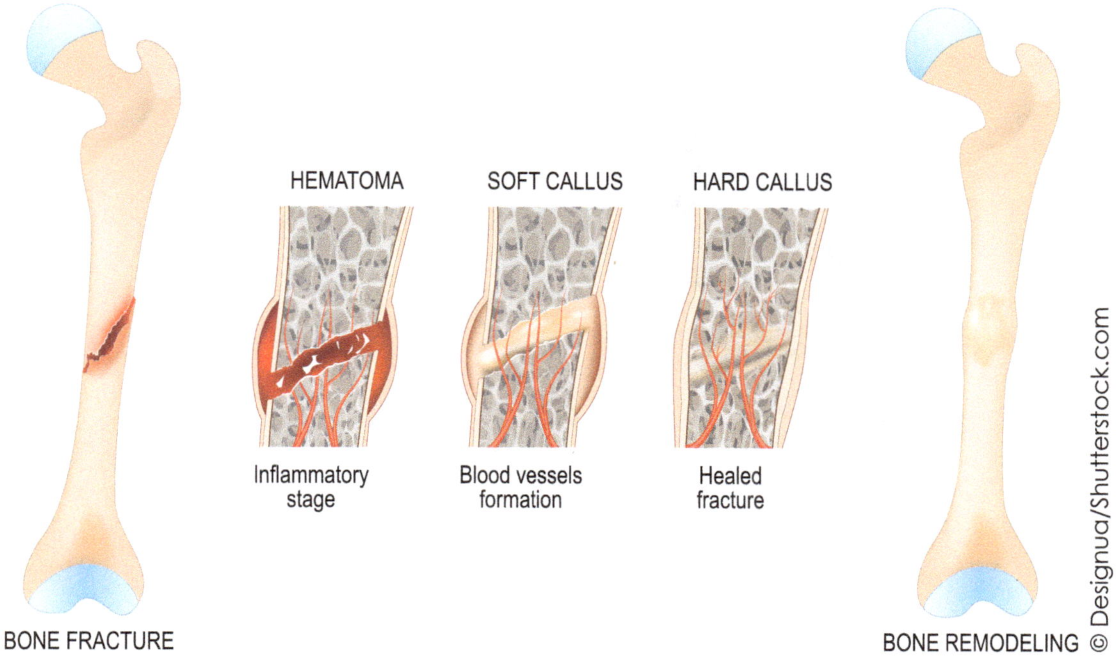

Figure 7-6 Bone healing after a fracture

complications, bone(s) injured, and the athlete's age and health. With proper treatment of the fracture, the injured site will heal and become continuous with the surrounding bone.

Signs Versus Symptoms

Every injury has typical signs and symptoms. Signs of injury are physically observable characteristics of injury. Signs are also objective, which means that you are able to see a sign of injury as another person would. The injured individual's perception cannot change the signs of the injury that you see. Unlike signs of injury, symptoms are characteristics of injury that are not physically observable. Instead, symptoms are subjective to the injured person. You cannot see the symptoms that an injured individual experiences. Since you cannot see symptoms, you can only take the injured individual's word that the symptom exists. Both signs and symptoms are equally important to determine what type of injury an individual has sustained, and to consequently render the proper treatment.

Numerous, common signs and symptoms of injury exist. Some typical signs include differences in tissue temperature, asymmetry, and misalignment as compared to the opposite, uninjured or **contralateral** side, ecchymosis, swelling, deformity (**Figure** 7-7), redness, hives, **crepitus**, and loss of function. Some common symptoms include pain, soreness, fever, nausea, **tinnitus**, headache, and numbness. Signs and symptoms of injury are often the same for various injuries, which makes it sometimes difficult to determine the individual's injury or illness.

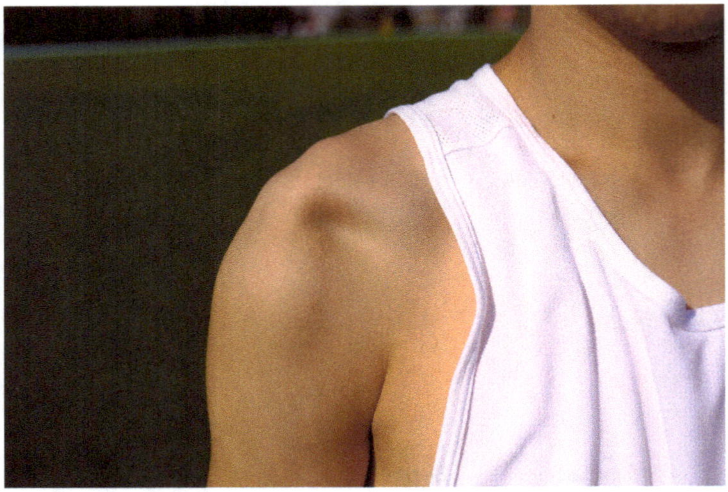

Figure 7-7 Deformity is a common sign of injury for dislocations and fractures.

Acute Versus Chronic Injuries

An acute injury occurs when the body is suddenly afflicted by trauma or damage to its tissues. Consequently, acute injury initiates immediate inflammatory phase events. Acute injuries have a specific, sudden mechanism of injury. An individual can typically describe and pinpoint the exact time the injury occurred. For example, an individual at We R Fit Gym drops a weight on their foot. They can describe the exact moment of injury to you. The injury is acute because a specific, sudden mechanism or cause of injury occurred. Likewise, immediately upon dropping the weight on their foot the healing process begins.

Chronic injuries are unlike acute injuries because with many chronic injuries the individual cannot identify a specific, sudden mechanism of injury. Also, the signs and symptoms of chronic injuries develop more slowly than with acute injuries. For example, an individual at We R Fit Gym complains of diffuse pain at both shoulders which has been increasing for three weeks. They cannot recall any specific day or time when inflammation, including signs and symptoms of injury, began. This scenario is very typical when an individual has a chronic injury.

Another, common reason why an injury is deemed chronic is due to the individual having an acute injury and not receiving proper treatment. If acute injuries are not treated appropriately, they do not heal properly. The injury does not move through the healing process continuum as it should. Consequently, the injury becomes chronic. This process often occurs with mild to moderate injuries. For example, some athletes who sustain acute mild to moderate sprains and strains commonly learn to adapt to or ignore the associated discomfort and other inflammatory signs and symptoms. The athlete continues to participate in activities instead of obtaining proper treatment for the acute injury. In most cases this continued participation hinders the healing process and prolongs the inflammation as well as signs and symptoms.

Consider the following scenario: During a Friday night championship game, a basketball player goes up for a lay-up and on their way down they land with their foot on another player's foot. The athlete inadvertently twists their ankle into inversion, which creates a mild sprain of their anterior talofibular ligament on the lateral side of the ankle. The athlete experiences immediate pain and disability. Almost as quickly the pain appears, it subsides, and the athlete is able to run down the court to play defense. The athlete's team wins the game. The athlete is so excited and does not pay attention to their acutely injured ankle. The weekend arrives and the athlete has mild ankle pain, swelling, and no loss of motion. The athlete continues to perform activities of daily living, including participating in Saturday morning basketball practice. The athlete decides not to see a physician for evaluation, nor did they obtain any first aid treatment to the injured ankle. This scenario is typical for how an athlete's acute injury, due to lack of or improper treatment, can easily predispose an acute injury to become a chronic injury.

TIPS FROM THE FIELD

Tip 1 Remember that each athlete has a different tolerance to and perception of pain. When you ask the athlete how much pain they are experiencing, ask them to rate their pain on a scale of 1 to 10, with 1 being the least pain they have ever experienced and 10 being the most pain that they have ever experienced. Then after they have given you their rating, ask them to describe the circumstance or scenario in which they felt that level of pain before. This information can give you an idea of the severity of injury.

Another reason why an injury becomes chronic is due to an athlete's inability to recognize they have a subacute or overuse injury and seek treatment. A subacute injury exhibits very minimal signs and symptoms as compared to an acute injury, and is usually caused by microtraumas to a body structure. Overuse injuries occur from repetitive motions, and over time the structure is damaged. Since chronic injuries do not have a specific, identifiable, sudden mechanism of injury, it is often difficult for an athlete to recognize or even admit that an injury exists.

Consider another scenario: A baseball pitcher constantly throws overhead. This constant throwing puts a significant amount of stress on the shoulder musculature and tendons. After every practice and game, the athlete believes the shoulder soreness is due to high intensity throwing. They do not consider that their shoulder is injured. Therefore, the athlete does not mention the soreness to the athletic trainer. Three weeks later, the athlete goes to the athletic trainer and explains that on some days, during and after throwing, their shoulder "feels fine" and on other days it is "extremely painful". The athlete now complains of loss of motion and strength. Although the athlete is now in the fibroblastic repair phase of healing, they are still experiencing symptoms of injury that are consistent with the inflammatory phase. The athlete may not have experienced a sudden acute mechanism of injury, but instead sustained small, subacute injuries that occurred over time. Unfortunately, now the baseball player has sustained a chronic shoulder injury.

Many chronic injuries occur because the acute inflammatory process did not progress through to the fibroblastic repair phase as it should have (Prentice, 2021). Often, for the chronic injury to heal properly a physician or qualified allied health care person must take an aggressive treatment approach to promote proper healing. Chronic injuries are often difficult to heal due to the repetitive microtraumas that have occurred, resistance to physical and pharmacological treatments (Prentice, 2021). Consequently, chronic injuries may take many months or even years to heal.

In many instances, chronic injuries can be avoided if athletes closely listen to their bodies and seek treatment from sports medicine professionals for their acute injuries. Educate your athletes to report any acute inflammatory signs and symptoms of injury to their physician or another sports medicine professional, such as an athletic trainer, immediately upon recognizing them. Even if the athlete experiences mild signs and symptoms, they must receive care to promote the healing process and in attempt to avoid chronic injury.

Classification of Injuries

Various body structures are commonly injured due to external and internal forces placed on and created by these anatomical structures. Consequently, your clients are predisposed to injury at some point in their lives. After reading this chapter, you will be able to classify the type of injury your client has experienced. Along with acute and chronic injuries, experts have classified injuries into two additional categories based on the tissue type involved. These categories are soft tissue injuries and bone injuries. Soft tissue and bone injuries are acute and chronic and further broken down into numerous classifications. Common soft tissue injuries include sprains, strains, tendinopathies, muscle spasms, contusions, bursitis, and skin wounds. Common bone injuries include fractures, apophysitis, exostosis, and joint injuries.

Soft Tissue Injuries

Sprain

A sprain is an injury that occurs to a ligament when the ligamentous fibers are stretched or torn. A sprain occurs typically due to a sudden, acute mechanism of injury such as a twisting (shear) or pulling apart (tension) of a joint. A joint is the articulation between two or more bones, which are held in close proximity to each other by ligaments. A ligament can be stretched or completely torn (ruptured). However, not all fibers in a single ligament are always ruptured. A single, injured ligament may have intact, stretched, and torn fibers at the same time. As with other acute injuries, when a sprain occurs the healing process begins. The signs and symptoms of inflammation develop immediately after injury. During the healing process, scar tissue fills the space where the ligament tear occurred. The ligament and the scar tissue have plastic qualities. Plasticity means that the tissue does not have elasticity. Elasticity means that tissue can be stretched, deform, and then return to its original length. However, when a plastic structure such as a ligament is stretched then the ligament remains at that stretched length. This fact is the same for scar tissue laid down during the ligament healing process. After injury, the damaged ligament and resultant scar tissue are not strong enough to withstand significant stress. Consequently, it is very common for an individual to have subsequent injuries occur to the same ligament.

A sprain is classified by using terminology describing its degree of severity. In 1964, the American Medical Association (AMA) charged a Subcommittee on Classification of Sports Injuries with creating standardized athletic injury nomenclature. The Subcommittee finalized the content in 1966, and the publication, *Standard Nomenclature of Athletic Injuries*, was published by the AMA soon thereafter (AMA, 1966). Since that time, the medical field has utilized this nomenclature as a standard for explaining the severity of injuries.

A sprain's severity of injury is classified by three degrees or grades of injury. These degrees are first-, second-, and third-degree (also stated as Grade 1, Grade 2, and Grade 3 respectively) (Schultz et al., 2016) (**Figure 7-8**). The severity of injury increases with first-degree being the least severe to third-degree being the most severe. If an individual has a first-degree sprain, their ligaments are stretched, but ligamentous fibers are not torn. These sprains exhibit mild signs and symptoms of inflammation, which include a slight increase in tissue temperature, minimal skin redness at the injured site, mild or no loss of motion, mild swelling, discomfort to mild pain, and mild stiffness due to edema. Second-degree sprains occur when many of the ligament's fibers are complete torn, yet some remain intact, to create a partially torn ligament. Second-degree sprains exhibit moderate signs and symptoms of inflammation. An individual with a second-degree sprain experiences a definitive increase in tissue temperature, skin redness at the injured site, moderate loss of motion, moderate swelling, significant pain, and joint instability. Third-degree sprains are the most severe sprains. These sprains are often referred to as "ruptured" ligaments, because the ligament is completely torn. Consequently, the inflammatory signs and symptoms of third-degree sprains are severe. Third-degree sprains exhibit a greater localized increase in temperature than a second-degree sprain, notable redness, and significant loss of motion, swelling, pain, and joint instability. Regardless of the degree of injury, when an individual suffers a sprain they will adversely be affected to some extent. Your role is

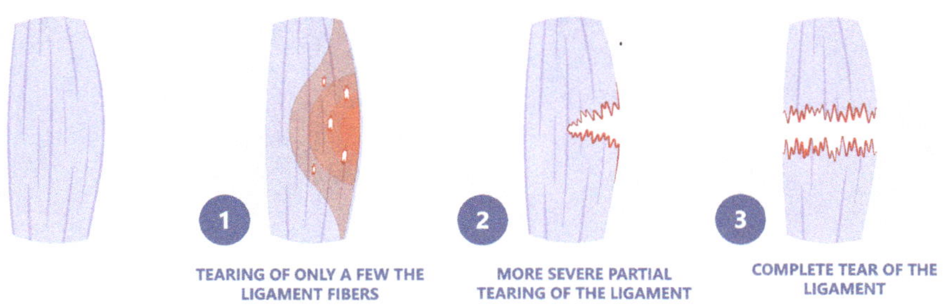

© Pepermpron/ Shutterstock.com

Figure 7-8 Grades of ligament sprains

to provide immediate, proper care and medical referral for an individual with a sprain. You will learn all immediate injury treatment and referral information for sprains later in this text.

Strain

A strain is an injury to a muscle, tendon, or to the musculotendinous junction where the muscle and tendon meet (Schultz et al., 2016). The muscle and tendon fibers may be stretched or torn. Not all fibers in one muscle or tendon are necessarily affected. Unlike ligaments which are plastic, muscles and tendons are elastic. A muscle or tendon can be stretched and return back to its original length. Of course, if a muscle or tendon fibers cannot withstand the amount of stress applied and is stretched beyond its anatomic limit, then it will rupture. The common mechanisms of injury for a strain include a sudden stretch or a quick, forceful muscle contraction. Strains are similar to sprains because both are classified by the three degrees previously described. First-, second-, and third-degree strains all have similar inflammatory signs and symptoms as sprains in regard to pain, redness, swelling, and loss of function **(Figure 7-9)**.

To determine if the injury is a sprain or a strain, you can keep one rule of thumb regarding ligaments in mind. Ligaments are not contractile tissues, but muscles and tendons are. Therefore, if an individual has sprained a ligament, the pain most likely is more pronounced when the joint is passively moved versus actively moved. With passive motion, no muscle contraction occurs. The joint is separated, and the bony joint surfaces are moved apart. Since ligaments attach bones at joints, this passive motion and joint surface distraction consequently stretches the ligament, resulting in pain. When a muscle or tendon is injured, pain is more

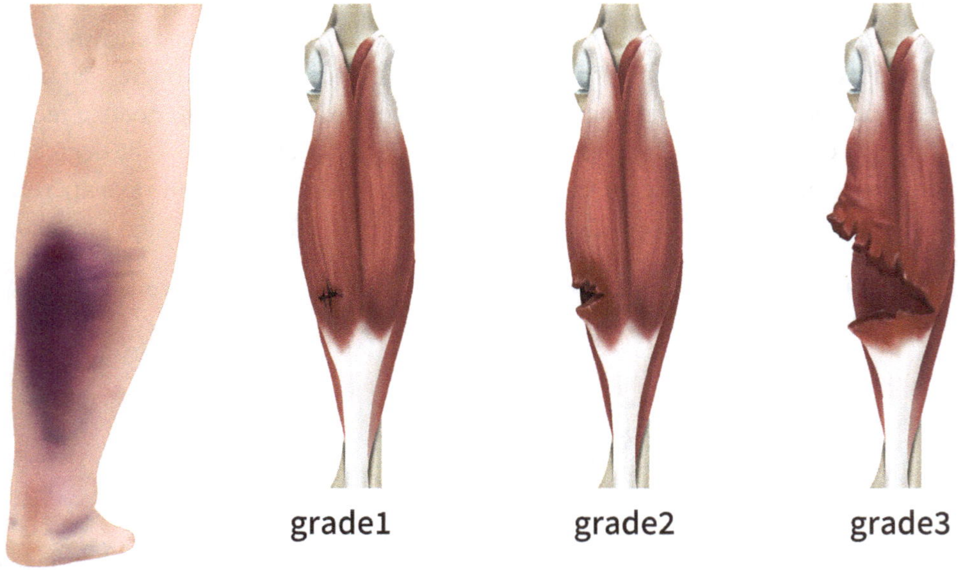

Figure 7-9 Grades of strains at the gastrocnemius

pronounced with active movement. Active movement occurs when muscles contract to move the joints through a range of motion (ROM). The concentric (shortening) or eccentric (lengthening) muscle contraction causes pain. This rule of thumb is not always full-proof, since at times, sprains and strains can occur simultaneously.

Tendinopathy

Tendinopathy is the common term describing injury and degeneration to tendons (Scott et al., 2015). The injuries include tendinitis, tenosynovitis, and tendinosis (**Figure 7-10**). Tendinitis is an inflammatory condition of the tendon, while tenosynovitis is an inflammatory condition of the synovial sheath which surrounds the tendon. Tendinosis is tendon degeneration, and can result from tendinitis if proper treatment is not obtained. As a result, the tendon does not heal and degenerates, causing the tendinosis.

Signs and symptoms of tendinopathies include pain during activity which decreases after activity, crepitus, loss of motion, swelling, and **point tenderness**. The mechanism of injury for tendinitis and tenosynovitis can be acute or chronic. Acute mechanisms of injury include

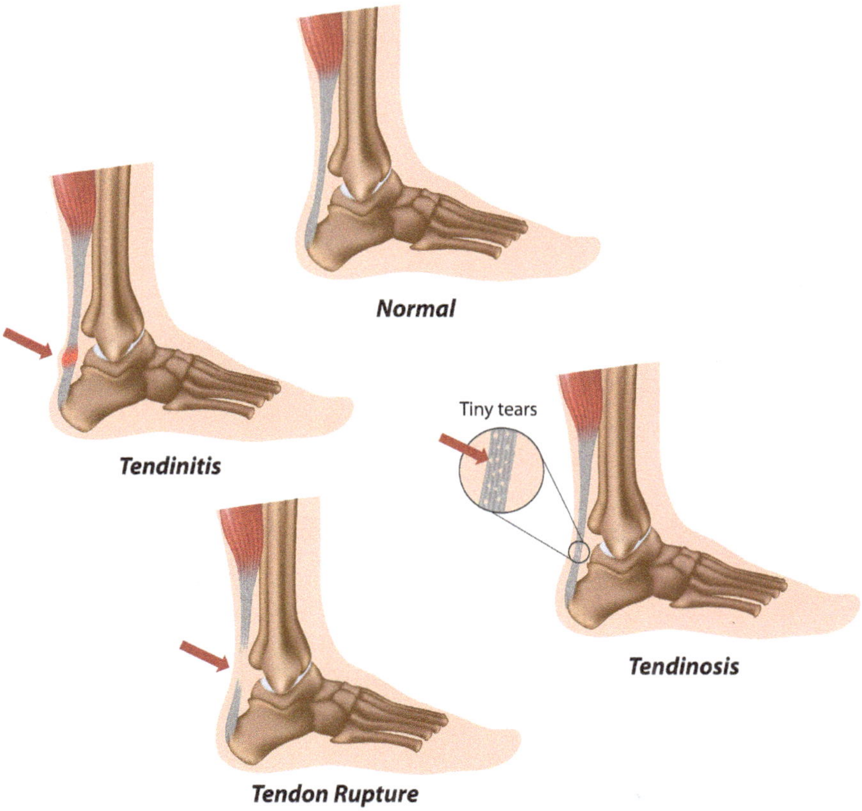

Figure 7-10 Microtrauma can cause tendons to be inflamed, degenerate, and rupture.

TIPS FROM THE FIELD

Tip 2 Athletes who have injuries in the fibroblastic repair phase of healing are able to participate in limited activities (with a physician's direction and/or clearance note). However, if they have any signs or symptoms of inflammation, including soreness, before, during, or after activity, then their activity must be modified or reduced further. In some cases you may need to stop activity that entails that area. For example, if your athlete has a lower body injury, you can have your athlete perform upper body activities until the signs and symptoms from the lower body injury subside.

a sudden contraction or stretch of the tendon, which is similar to the mechanism of injury for a strain. More commonly the mechanism of injury for tendinitis and tenosynovitis is **microtrauma**, which occurs due to repetitive overuse. During muscular contraction activity, athletes create continuous, repetitive joint movements. Some athletes must move their extremities in a more repetitive fashion than others by nature of their sport. For example, swimmers and baseball players have repetitive shoulder motion during activity. They tend to perform at a high level of intensity in order to gain optimal performance. The intensity, quantity, duration, and repetition of tendon function all play a part in injury. If athletes do not adequately rest between practice and competition sessions, seek treatment for any mild signs and symptoms of injury, and vary their activity in regard to intensity, duration, and function, then microtraumas can result and cause tendinopathy.

Muscle Spasm

Muscle spasms, or muscle cramps, are involuntary muscle contractions. The muscles become stiff and hard, which results in pain and loss of motion. Various mechanisms of injury for muscle spasms exist. A direct blow to a muscle, a sudden, forceful movement, in particular an unexpected stretch, or overuse of a muscle, especially when the muscle is fatigued, can cause a muscle spasm. When a joint, muscle, or bone is injured, the surrounding muscle involuntarily contracts in order to protect the injured area from further harm. If an athlete stretches their hamstrings to the point where the muscle group cannot tolerate the stretch, the muscles spasm to protect against further injury. If a boxer is struck in the abdomen by an opponent, and an internal organ is injured, the abdominal muscles involuntarily contract in response to pain, and become hardened in order to protect the internal organs from further injury. This reflexive involuntary muscle spasm is referred to as muscle guarding.

Muscle spasms can occur if a body part remains in a still position over time. For example, if an individual sleeps in the same, and potentially awkward, position for hours, spasms may occur in the neck muscles. Muscle cramping can also occur from dehydration and lack of electrolytes in the body. If an athlete does not hydrate enough or ingest adequate electrolytes before exercise, they may succumb to muscle cramping. This muscle cramping particularly occurs when exercising in a hot and humid environment due to the loss of water and electrolytes when an individual sweats and does not rehydrate. If you educate your athletes on proper hydration before, during, and after activity, you can prevent this heat related muscle cramping from occurring.

Contusions

A bruise is another name for a contusion. The mechanism of injury for a contusion is a compression force. Typically this force originates from an object compressing a muscle against the underlying bone (Prentice, 2021). The direct blow from the object crushes the muscle fibers causing injury to the muscle fibers, the capillaries, and underlying structures. The object causing injury can be stationary, such as a weight rack that your client walks into. The object can also be moving, such as a batted baseball. The contusion's severity depends on numerous factors. The size and speed of the object striking the muscle as well as the size, thickness, and strength of the muscle can affect the severity of injury. In regard to object's speed, an object traveling at high speed and striking the body would cause a more severe contusion than the same object traveling at a lower speed. Also, if an athlete has strong, large, hypertrophied muscles, then these muscles can withstand greater compression forces as compared to muscles that are weak, small, and atrophied.

Once a muscle is contused, inflammation begins. Signs and symptoms of a contusion are the same as with sprains and strains. Pain, redness, increase in tissue temperature, swelling, and loss of function are the typical signs and symptoms of inflammation exhibited immediately after injury. Hematomas, blood from damaged, bleeding tissues and capillaries, can accumulate around the muscle and under the skin. The hematomas can sometimes be visible if they form at the skin surface. These hematomas cause ecchymosis **(Figure 7-11)**. Whenever a severe contusion with significant signs and symptoms occurs to your athletes, suspect that the underlying bone, internal organs, or structures other than the muscle are also injured. Consequently, refer your athlete to a physician for evaluation.

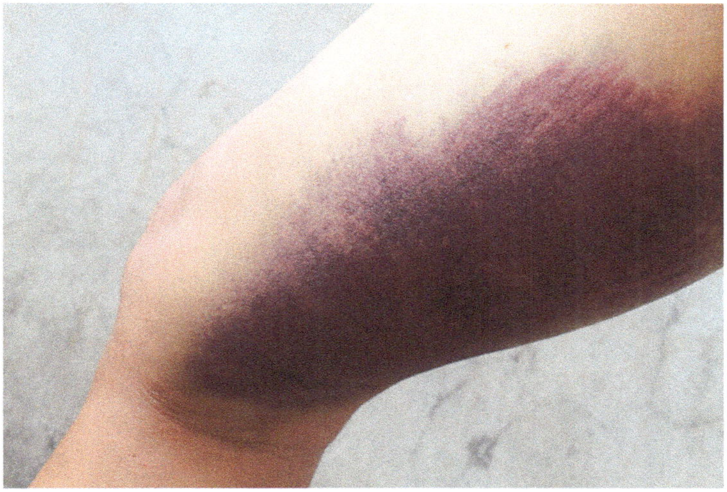

Figure 7-11 Hematomas can form in the muscle when an individual has a contusion, and result in ecchymosis at the skin surface.

Bursitis

Bursae are fluid-filled sacs located throughout the body. They assist shock absorption and decrease friction between various anatomical structures in the body such as ligaments, tendons, bones, and skin. Commonly injured bursae include the prepatellar bursa which is located between the skin at the knee and patella **(Figure 7-12)**, the olecranon bursa which is located between the skin and the olecranon of the elbow **(Figure 7-13)**, and the trochanteric bursa which is located at the hip between the greater trochanter and the gluteal muscles **(Figure 7-14)**.

Bursae can be injured by an acute or chronic mechanism of injury. Acute bursitis is caused by a direct, forceful blow to the bursa. For example, a common mechanism of injury for acute olecranon bursitis is a direct blow to the elbow while in maximal flexion against a nonyielding object such as a wall. The injured bursa immediately fills with fluid and appears

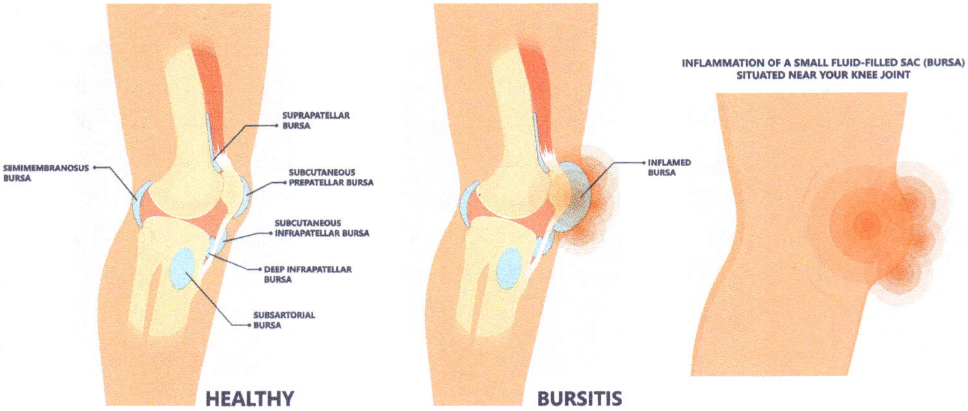

Figure 7-12 Prepatellar bursitis of the knee

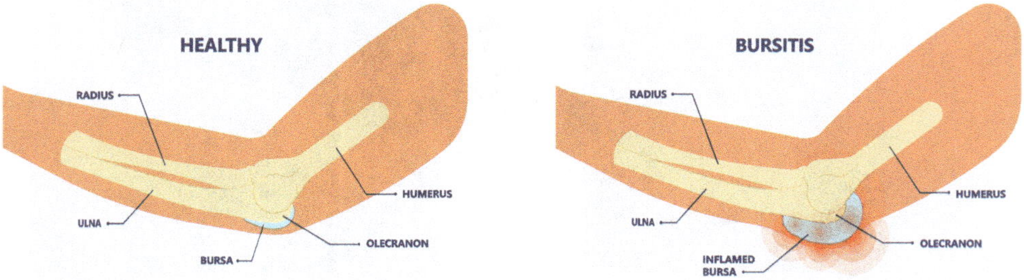

Figure 7-13 Olecranon (elbow) bursitis

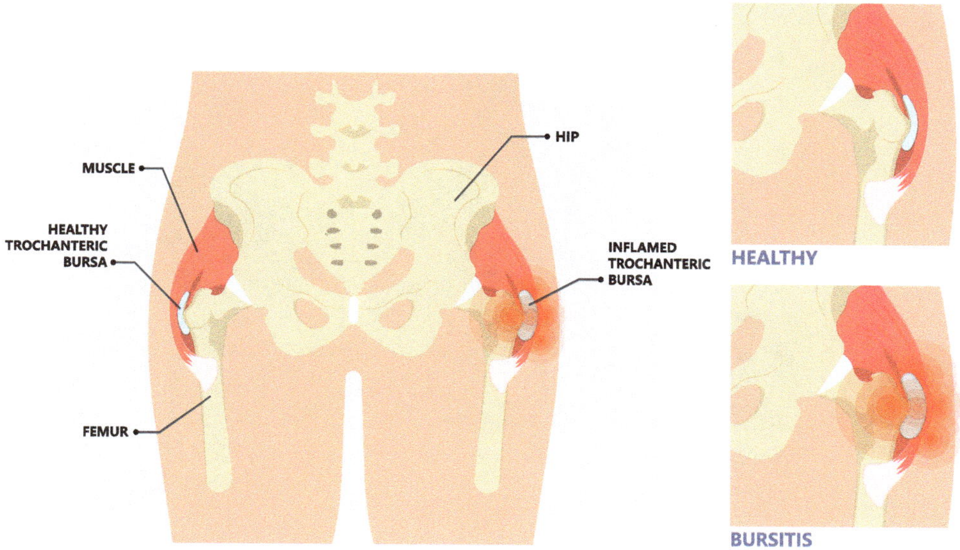

Figure 7-14 Trochanteric bursitis at the hip

very swollen. The individual experiences pain and loss of function at the area. Interestingly enough, they may not have point tenderness when touching the swollen bursa, but most likely has pain when touching the bone under and around the bursa. The bursa may feel like a ball of encapsulated jelly, which can be moved back and forth without eliciting pain. The individual may not be willing to move the elbow joint due to pain. Likewise, they might not be able to move the joint due to the swelling and the significantly larger bursa taking up space and stretching the skin, thereby preventing movement.

Consider the following scenario: An ice hockey player is competing in a game. They skate after the puck at full speed with their stick in hand. Their opponent checks the athlete into the boards. At that moment, their elbow is flexed, and their elbow pad slides just enough for their olecranon to strike the boards. The athlete feels immediate pain and disability. A few minutes later, as the athlete returns to the bench, their pain has decreased. However, they are unable to flex their elbow. The olecranon bursa is approximately the size of a golf ball, and the elbow appears deformed **(Figure 7-15)**. The athlete touches the bursa and moves it around without much pain. When the athlete touches the underlying olecranon, he has significant point tenderness. This point tenderness suggests that the direct blow against the boards may have caused a fracture to the underlying bone. Consequently, the athlete was treated and referred by the athletic trainer to a physician for X-rays.

Bursae can also be injured by a chronic type mechanism of injury. This mechanism of injury includes overusing a muscle or tendon, and repetitive friction over a bursa. In these cases, the signs and symptoms of injury are similar as with acute bursitis. However, the signs

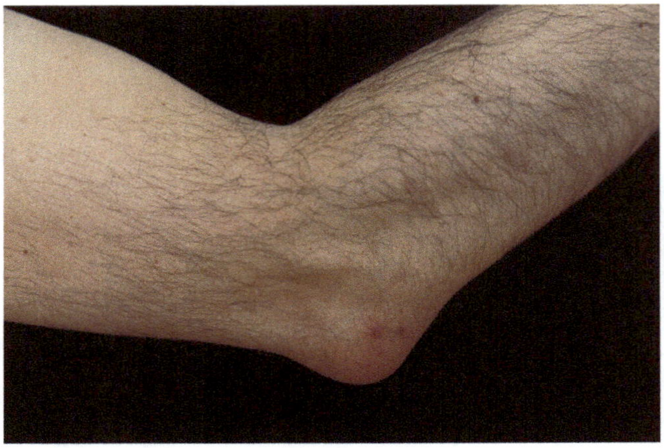

Figure 7-15 Acute olecranon bursitis will appear deformed.

and symptoms appear slowly, perhaps over hours or days. Also, typically the immediate swelling after an acute bursa injury is more pronounced and appears localized. With chronic bursa injuries, the swelling is more generalized. An individual could have chronic bursitis due to repetitive activities over a period of time. For example, your client begins an intense running program in preparation for a 5K. Their body, in particular their hips, are not accustomed to this intense training. Over a period of days, your client begins to feel discomfort and tenderness at the hip joint while they run. They do not tell you about their symptoms, nor do they seek treatment. As a few weeks go by, their pain slowly increases while exercising, moves to the thigh area, and continues as a dull ache when at rest. Symptoms continue to increase as the days and intensity progress. After sitting for extended periods of time, walking upstairs, and lying on the affected side, the pain worsens. Their hip function deteriorates, and one day they walk into We R Fit Gym with a slight limp. You observe your client's function and approach them. They finally report their symptoms to you. As a sports medicine professional, you have your client rest for the day, give your client ice to treat the area, and refer them to a physician. The physician diagnoses your client with chronic hip bursitis, and recommends that your client take a break from their running program until the chronic hip bursitis signs and symptoms subside.

The soft tissue injuries discussed are some of the most common soft tissue injuries that individuals will experience. The severity varies immensely from individual to individual and injury to injury. The injury may be so mild that the individual is able to continue activity participation. On the other hand, the injury may be so severe that they are not capable or allowed to participate for a period of time. No two soft tissue injuries are the same, and your clients may experience more than one soft tissue injury simultaneously. Regardless of which soft tissue injuries your clients experience, your role in educating and providing immediate care and referral is imperative to their well-being and return to full pre-injury function.

Bone Injuries

Fractures

Most likely at some point during your career, one of your athletes will sustain a fracture. Fractures are disabling to an athlete for a variety of reasons. When an athlete breaks a bone, the bone is immobilized with a splint or cast for a period of weeks to allow proper healing. Sometimes it is necessary to perform surgery to assist in realigning the broken bones into their proper position. Fractures typically do not occur as a single injury. Often another injury exists along with the fracture, such as a ligament rupture, muscle contusion or strain, joint dislocation, and nerve and/or blood vessel injury. Mechanisms of injury for fractures include compression, tensile, and shear forces. The signs and symptoms of fractures include the typical signs and symptoms of inflammation, including pain, swelling, loss of function, redness, and an increase in temperature. Other signs and symptoms include crepitus, deformity, joint locking due to bony fragments lodged in the joint space, and loss of sensation due to nerve injury at and furthest away from the injury site.

Fractures are classified as closed or open, displaced or non-displaced, and complete or incomplete. Most fractures are closed fractures. A closed fracture occurs when the broken bones do not protrude through the skin. When the broken bones protrude through the skin, the bones create an open wound. The fracture is classified as an open or compound fracture **(Figure 7-16)**. These fractures are more troublesome than closed fractures due to

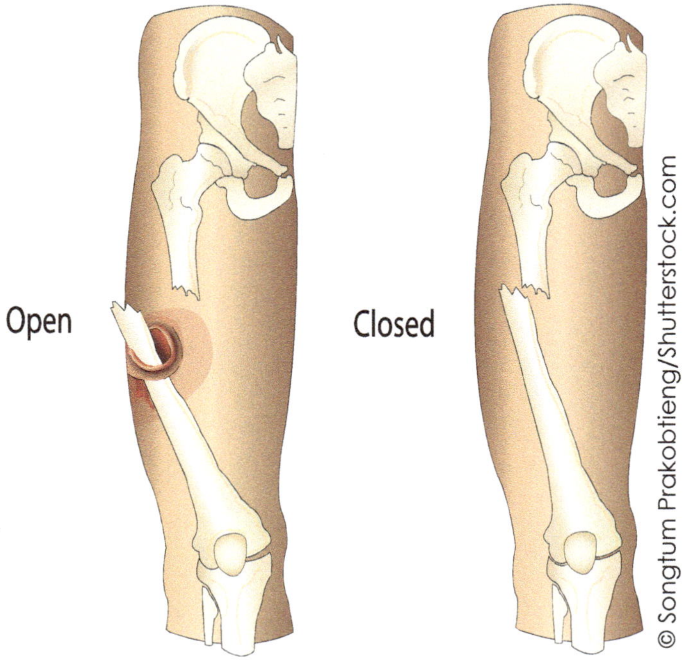

Figure 7-16 An open and closed fracture

the open wound that is created by the fractured bones. The open wound is susceptible to infection, which could become **systemic** and potentially fatal. Likewise, significant external bleeding may occur which can also be fatal. Fractures are also classified as displaced or non-displaced. If the ends of the fractured bones are not in proper alignment with each other, then the fracture is displaced. If the ends of the bones remain in alignment then the fracture is non-displaced. Displaced fractures are often more severe and have the potential to cause additional trauma due to bone movement. When the fractured bones have been pushed out of alignment, more opportunity for injury to other structures, including nerves and blood vessels, exist. When fractures are open they are also displaced. Closed fractures can be displaced or non-displaced. Fractures can occur through the entire bone creating two or more separate pieces, which is called a complete fracture. An incomplete fracture is when the fracture line does not pass through the entire bone, which leaves part of the bone intact.

Specific terminology is used to describe the type of fracture line. Some of the more common fractures are classified as transverse, oblique, greenstick, comminuted, compression, spiral, avulsion, stress, or epiphyseal fractures (Schultz et al., 2016) (**Figure 7-17**). A transverse fracture is a complete fracture with fracture line that is perpendicular to the long axis of the bone (**Figure 7-18**). An oblique fracture line is similar to the transverse fracture line except that it runs on a diagonal to the bone's long axis (**Figure 7-19**). A greenstick fracture typically occurs in young children whose bones are not completely finished growing and have not entirely hardened. These fractures are incomplete fractures. The side opposite where the force was applied is broken, but the side where the force was applied is intact (**Figure 7-20**).

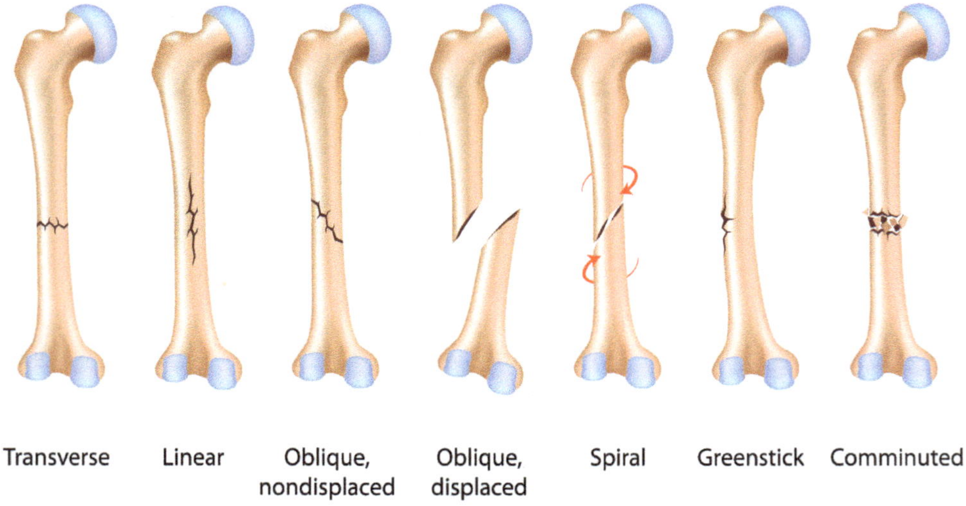

Figure 7-17 Types of bone fractures

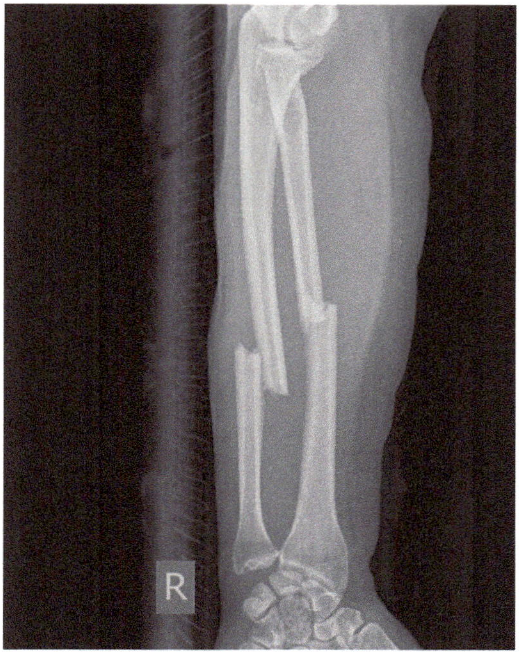

Figure 7-18 A transverse displaced fracture of the ulna

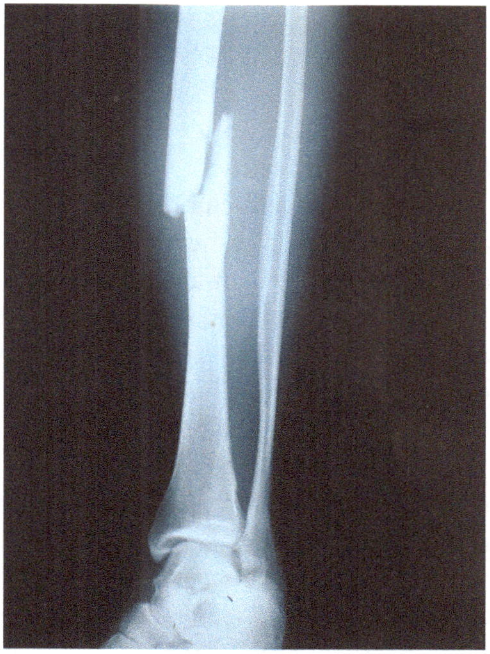

Figure 7-19 An oblique fracture of the tibia

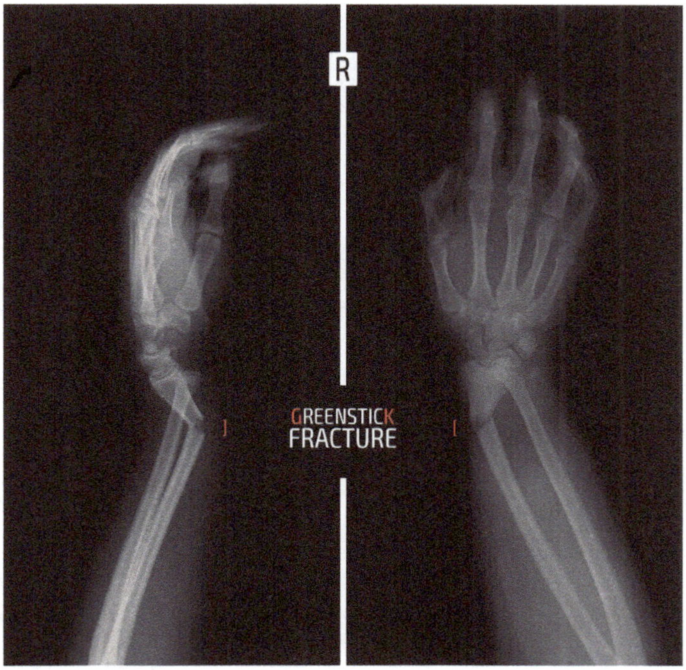

Figure 7-20 A greenstick fracture of the radius

A comminuted fracture is a complete fracture with numerous tiny pieces **(Figure 7-21)**. These fragments can dislodge from the space and move around among the tissues or within joints and cause further damage.

Compression fractures occur when stress is applied to the ends of the long bones. This type of fracture can occur if an individual jumps or falls from a great height, such as a tall ladder or building roof. The compressive forces from the ground and the individual's body on the femur or tibia can cause the compressive fracture. Likewise, this same mechanism of injury can cause a compression fracture of the spinal vertebrae **(Figure 7-22)**.

Spiral fractures occur as a result of torsion and compression forces. These forces are directed along the long axis of the bone, and create a spiral fracture line appearance **(Figure 7-23)**. Consider how a spiral fracture can occur to a football player during a game. The athlete is running with the ball and when tackled puts their hand out to catch themselves. The force causes his hand to be strike the ground, creating a compressive force among the ground and upper extremity bones. Likewise, during the tackle, the athlete's body, including the shoulder joint, rotates which creates torsion. Consequently, a spiral fracture occurs to the humerus.

Avulsion fractures occur when a piece of bone is pulled off of a bone by a ligament or tendon **(Figure 7-24)**. When a tensile stress occurs to a joint, the ligament or tendon sometimes cannot withstand the force, and instead of a sprain or strain (respectively) occurring, the ligament or tendon pulls the bone from its attachment creating a fracture. Often avulsion fractures are difficult to distinguish from a sprain or a strain at the ligament's or tendon's insertion, respectively. Ultimately, when an avulsion fracture is suspected, refer the athlete for X-rays to obtain a correct diagnosis.

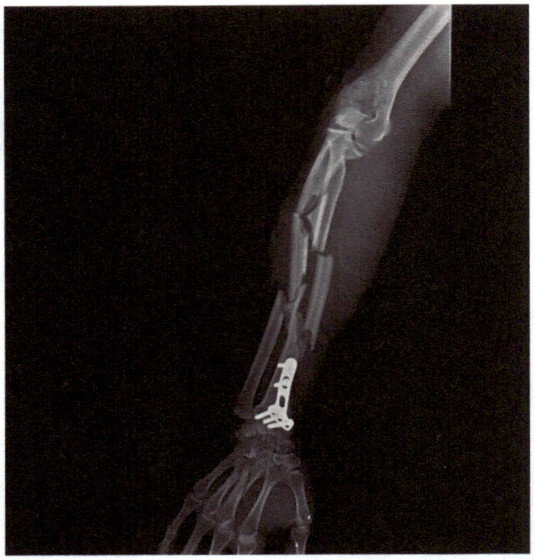

Figure 7-21 A comminuted fracture of the radius and ulna

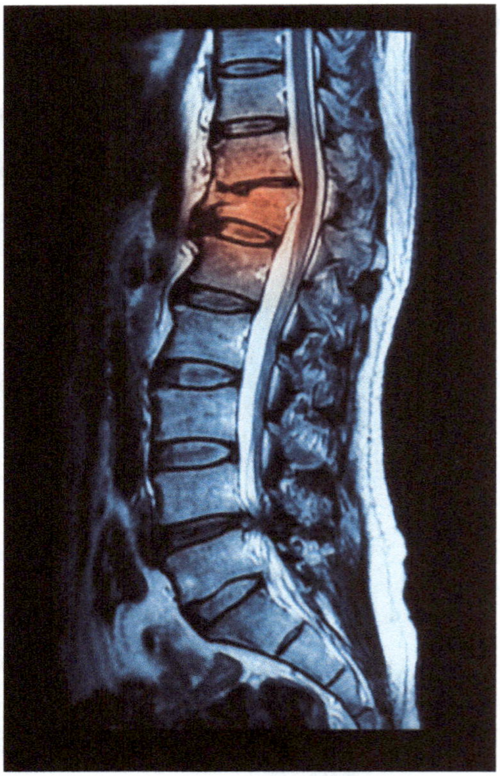

Figure 7-22 A compression fracture of the first lumbar vertebrae (L1)

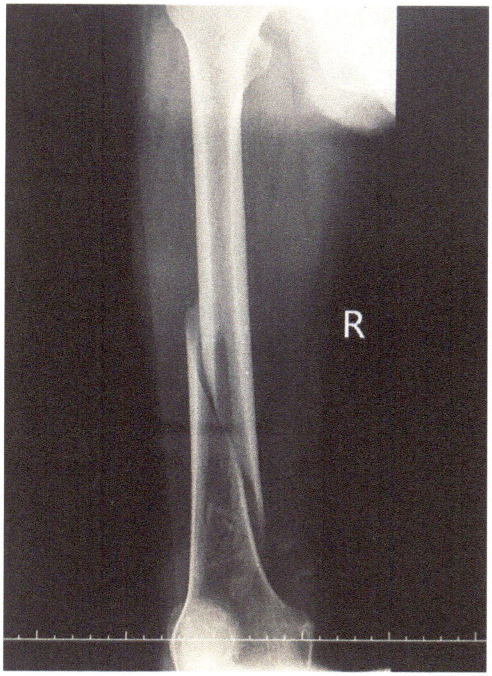

Figure 7-23 A spiral fracture of the femur

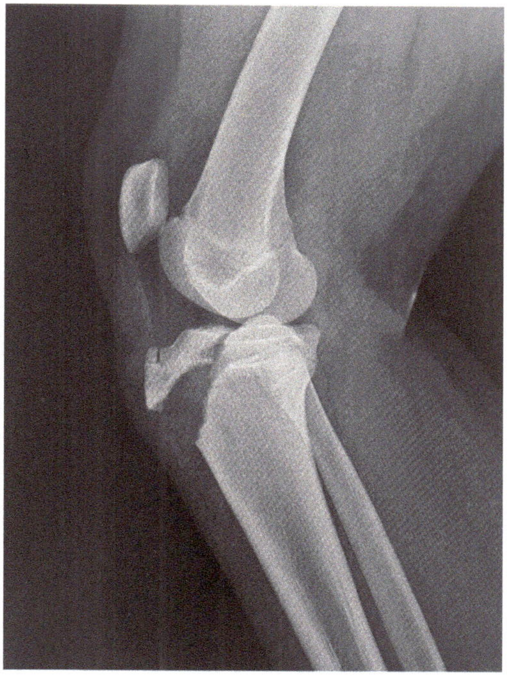

Figure 7-24 An avulsion fracture of the tibial tubercle

A fracture that occurs from repetitive or atypical stress over a period of time is referred to as a stress fracture. Stress fractures typically occur in weight bearing bones due to the force continually and repetitively placed on it by the athlete contacting the ground or another surface. Therefore, these fractures are not considered to have an acute, traumatic mechanism of injury. Most stress fractures occur to the lower extremities, such as the metatarsals, tibia, femoral neck, and pubis, due to the constant pounding during running or jumping activities **(Figure 7-25)**. The muscles and bone cannot readily dissipate the constant, repetitive force. Over time, which could be many weeks, the bone gradually weakens and breaks down (Schultz et al., 2016). Symptoms will appear slowly, with pain at first only during activity and subsiding with rest. Gradually, a dull pain may occur even at rest and point tenderness over the stress fracture site will exist. Sometimes the athlete has a dull aching pain at night that wakes them. They often are able to function, but pain causes their function to decline. If you suspect your athlete has a stress fracture, stop the athlete's training activities, and refer them to a physician for evaluation. The physician will most likely order X-rays, although when viewing an X-ray, stress fractures are not visible unless it has already healed. On an X-ray the healed stress fracture appears as a stark white line on the bone.

Epiphyseal fractures occur at the end of a bone where new bone is formed **(Figure 7-26)**. This bone formation occurs during a child's growing years. Once an adult has stopped growing, then the epiphyseal plates, or growth plates, close and solidify. When a child sustains

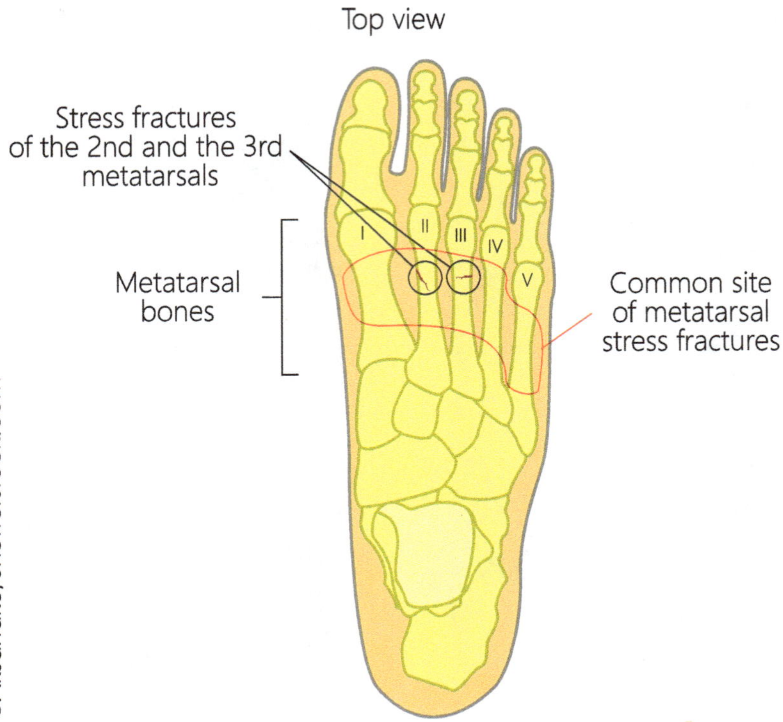

Figure 7-25 Stress fractures commonly occur to the metatarsal bones.

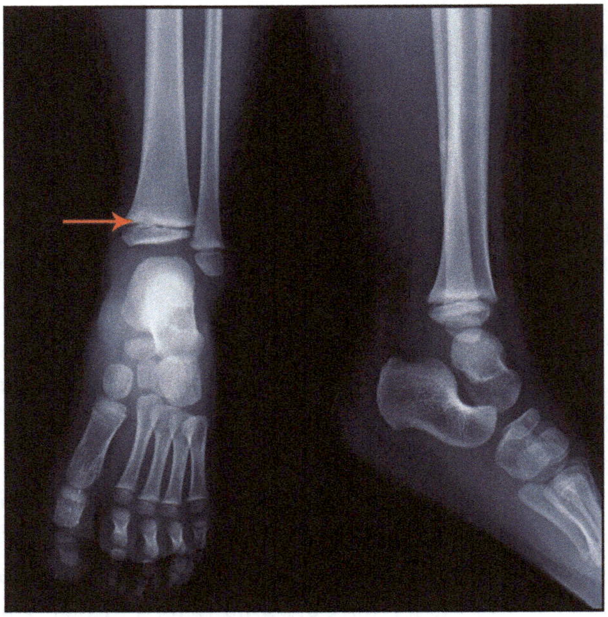

Figure 7-26 An epiphyseal fracture of the tibia

a fracture at the epiphyseal plates, the fracture can be extremely detrimental to their limb growth. Depending on the severity of the fracture, the fracture may disrupt the osteoblast (bone forming) and osteoclast (bone break down) activity. Consequently, the bone may stop growing and close prematurely, creating a shortened limb as compared to the contralateral limb. Any mechanisms of injury previously discussed can cause an epiphyseal fracture, and the signs and symptoms are similar to other fractures. Epiphyseal fractures may occur as stress fractures or acute, traumatic fractures. All acute fractures are medical emergencies. Therefore, to ensure proper athlete care, your primary role in treatment of the athlete's acute fracture is summoning emergency personnel immediately.

Joint Injuries

Injuries to the joints are common. Not only can the ligaments and tendons that cross over joints become injured, but the bony articulation at the joint can be damaged. Stresses placed on the joint from bodily movements and outside forces can cause dislocations and subluxations, which are two common joint injuries.

Dislocations

Dislocations, or luxations, are acute joint injuries, which occur when one end of a bone is forced out of its normal position relative to the other bone. The mechanisms of injury for a dislocation are a direct blow to the joint by an outside force or a force created by the individual's body along with the bones moving in an atypical manner. Some joints are more easily dislocated than others. The glenohumeral (shoulder) **(Figure 7-27)**, patella-femoral (kneecap)

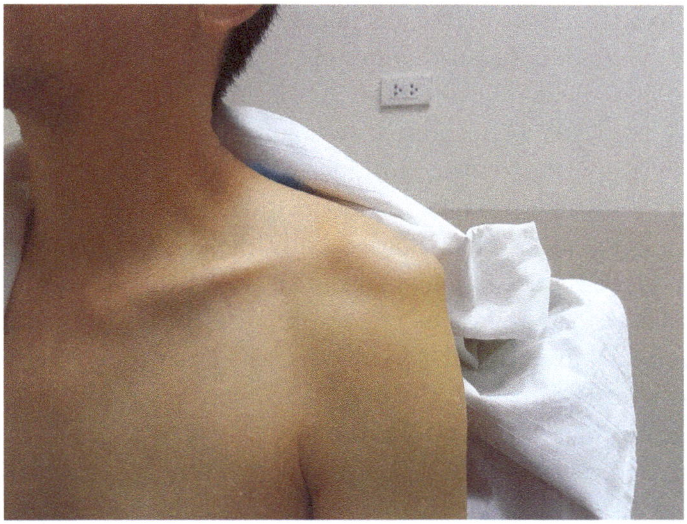

Figure 7-27 A dislocated shoulder

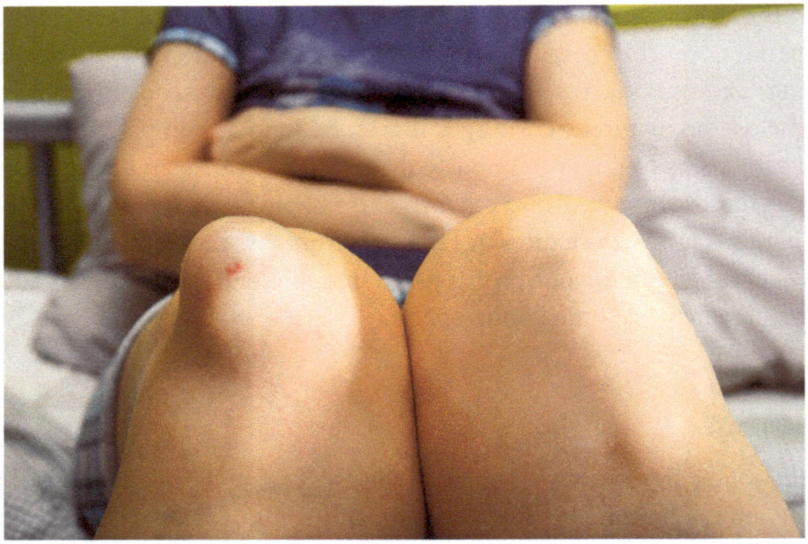

Figure 7-28 A dislocated patella

(Figure 7-28), and phalangeal joints (fingers) **(Figure 7-29)** are most frequently dislocated. Signs and symptoms of dislocations are readily apparent. Obvious deformity is a very prevalent sign exhibited when a dislocation occurs. The bone protrudes from its normal position creating disfigurement. Swelling may or may not be present. The individual cannot move the joint since the bones are out of place. The individual has significant pain and some sensation loss in their fingers or toes depending on where the dislocation occurs. Picture a quarterback preparing to throw the football with their arm in a cocked position. Suddenly, the opposing lineman goes for the ball and tackles the quarterback. The opponent's force pushes the quarterback's arm in a posterior, or backwards, position which results in a shoulder dislocation. In another scenario, a basketball player attempts to catch a ball, which forcefully hits the tip of their finger. The ball forces their finger to move out of alignment. The distal phalange dislocates and moves on top of the middle phalange.

Unfortunately, once an individual dislocates a joint for the first time, the chance of the same joint dislocating again is increased. Additional dislocations are possible due to the joint structures, including the capsule, ligaments, tendons, and muscle, being significantly stretched and injured during the first dislocation. Consequently, the bones that comprise the joint are not held as tightly in place as prior to injury. The force necessary to dislocate the same joint a second time does not have to be as great as with the initial injury (Schultz et al., 2016). Keep in mind that the force needed to cause a dislocation can also cause a concurrent fracture, along with nerve and blood vessel damage at the injury site. Since secondary injuries are possible with dislocations, dislocations must be treated as medical emergencies. Only physicians and athletic trainers, who have a written plan of care and proper training by their supervising physician, are qualified to relocate the bones. Never put the bones back into normal alignment, as

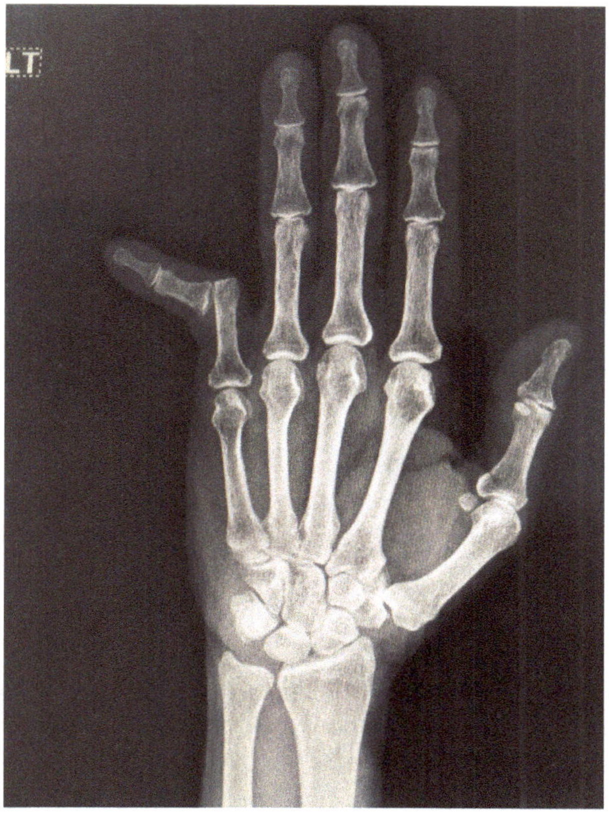

Figure 7-29 A dislocation of the 5th finger

you can do further harm to the joint and affected bones. Instead, splint the dislocated bones, check for a pulse, treat the individual for shock if warranted, and call your local emergency number immediately.

Subluxations

Subluxations occur when a bone within a joint moves out of normal alignment and then spontaneously moves back into normal position. The movement out of normal joint alignment occurs due to an external force, such as a direct blow from an object, or an internal force, such as a forceful muscle contraction. Unlike dislocations, subluxations can be acute or chronic. The mechanism of injury for an acute subluxation is the same as the mechanism of injury for a dislocation. An example of an acute subluxation is when the quarterback's humeral head rapidly moves out of normal joint position, but instead of remaining out of the joint as with a dislocation, the humeral head moves immediately back into normal joint position on its own. This injury is classified as acute due to the traumatic mechanism of injury. Similarly to a dislocation, the possibility for future subluxations exists. After an athlete sustains their first, acute subluxation, they may have repetitive subluxations of the same joint. These recurrent subluxations are classified as chronic subluxations. Along with the glenohumeral joint, chronic subluxations often occur at the patellar-femoral joint. The signs and symptoms of subluxations include pain, point tenderness, loss of function, swelling, and possible loss of sensation. Unlike dislocations, since a subluxed joint returns to normal alignment, you will not see deformity. However, since the joint was out of normal alignment temporarily, consider that secondary injury may have occurred. Therefore, in order for your athlete to obtain proper care, refer your athlete for immediate physician evaluation.

The Body's Response to Illness

Individuals are prone to various illnesses. The healthier the individual is psychologically and physically, the less chance they will acquire an illness. However, illnesses cannot entirely be prevented. A variety of common causes of illness exist. Some of these causes include nutritional deficiencies, lack of exercise, impaired immunity, mental stress, heredity, toxins, and microorganism infection (Neighbors & Tannehille-Jones, 2019).

Over time, lack of exercise, or even a lack of minimal physical activity, decreases bodily function, causing weakened muscle and bones, and immune system deterioration. Consequently, the individual's immune system cannot fight infection properly and illness results.

Mental stress can increase to the point where the body can no longer tolerate the stress. Again, the immune system weakens, and illness can invade the body.

Hereditary illness is due to abnormalities in an individual's chromosomes in utero. These chromosome abnormalities may not cause illness until later in life, or perhaps not at all (Neighbors & Tannehille-Jones, 2019).

Toxins are poisonous substances produced by a living cell that enters an athlete's body and causes illness. A bee creates venom, which is a toxin, as a defense mechanism. Venom is released when the bee stings a person. For some individuals, this sting may be deadly since the venom released causes an individual to go into anaphylactic shock. Anaphylactic shock occurs to an individual when they are severely allergic to a toxin. The toxin causes swelling in and constriction of the air passages, which result in the individual's inability to breathe and get oxygen into their body. Consequently, anaphylactic shock is a serious medical emergency.

Microorganisms can cause illness and infection. The three microorganisms

TIPS FROM THE FIELD

Tip 3 When speaking with your client regarding their injury, in order to determine the mechanism of injury always ask the question "What happened?" even if you saw the injury occur. Obtaining their subjective opinion and feelings regarding the injury is important. Do not assume you know exactly what happened and how the injury occurred because you witnessed it happen. On the same lines, to determine whether the injury is acute or chronic, ask your client "When did it happen?" The answer to this question gives you a good idea as to the acute or chronic classification of the injury.

that commonly cause illness are bacteria, viruses, and fungi. These microorganisms enter the body are the predominant causes everyday illnesses.

TIPS FROM THE FIELD

TIP 4 If you are unsure if your patient has sustained a stress fracture, immediately have your patient stop any sign and symptom-provoking activities, and refer them to a physician for evaluation. Do not forget to get a clearance note from the patient's physician prior to allowing them to return to activity.

Bacteria are cells which reproduce in the body and produce systemic illnesses and localized infections. When an illness affects the entire body, it is a systemic illness, while a localized illness or infection is when the bacteria effects only a particular area. Many types of bacteria exist. Some bacteria are very strong and difficult to eliminate from the body, such as methicillin-resistant *Staphylococcus aureus* (MRSA) **(Figure 7-30)**, while others are more easily destroyed, such as *Campylobacter* which causes food poisoning (Reisner & Reisner, 2022). Bacteria cause common illnesses and infections such as acne, sinus infections, strep throat, meningitis, gastroenteritis, and Lyme disease. Fortunately for individuals, antibiotics can be utilized when necessary to break down the bacteria and return the individual's body to a normal state.

Viruses are smaller microorganisms than bacteria. However, unlike bacteria viruses must attach to a host cell in the individual's body in order to live. (Neighbors & Tannehille-Jones, 2019). Viruses can replicate and mutate, which makes it extremely difficult to destroy the

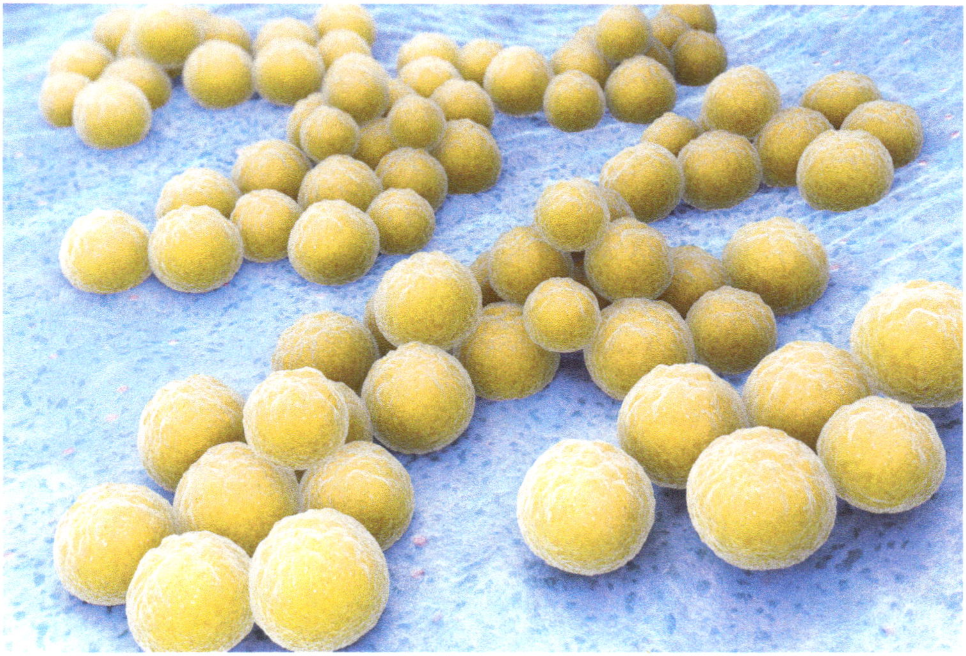

© Tatiana Shepeleva/Shutterstock.com

Figure 7-30 Methicillin-resistant *Staphylococcus aureus* (MRSA) is a bacterium that is difficult to treat by antibiotics.

TIPS FROM THE FIELD

Tip 5 If your client has any skin lesions that appear as pustules, rashes, hives, or any unusual, unfamiliar markings, immediately have your client see a doctor. Your client must not be permitted to participate in activities with your organization or in your facility until they have received written clearance from her physician and provided it to you. The skin lesion may be infectious and contagious. Immediately disinfect any object and area that your client has contacted, since the microorganism causing the potential infection could be transferred to your other clients or anyone in your facility.

virus with any medicinal agent. Antibiotics and other drugs are not able to destroy the virus as effectively as destroying bacteria. Consequently, over the counter (OTC) and prescription drugs are utilized to alleviate the individual's signs and symptoms. The individual's immune system attempts to fight the virus, break it down, and eliminate it from the body, but the viral illness must run its course. Common viral illnesses include herpes simplex 1 virus (cold sores), conjunctivitis (pink eye), rhinoviruses (common colds), and human papillomavirus (warts) (Mayo Clinic, 2022) **(Figure 7-31)**. Fortunately, vaccines exist that can assist an individual from becoming ill from certain viruses. Some common immunizations include those for hepatitis B virus (HBV), influenza (flu), and measles, mumps, and rubella (MMR). In response to these immunizations, the body creates antibodies. These antibodies fight the virus, and the athlete does not acquire or decreases the extent of the illness or infection.

Fungi are plantlike organisms that thrive in dark, moist environments. Many fungal infections occur on the skin and remain localized, such as tinea corporis (ringworm), tinea cruris (jock itch), tinea pedis (athlete's foot), and *Candida albicans* (yeast infection) **(Figure 7-32)**. Although rare, fungal infections can become significant systemic illnesses. Usually, normal bodily bacteria prevents fungi from causing a systemic illness, such as a pulmonary fungal infection. However, if bacteria are not functioning properly, then acute systemic fungal illness can occur (Reisner & Reisner, 2022). Fungal infections can be treated by antifungal oral and topical medications.

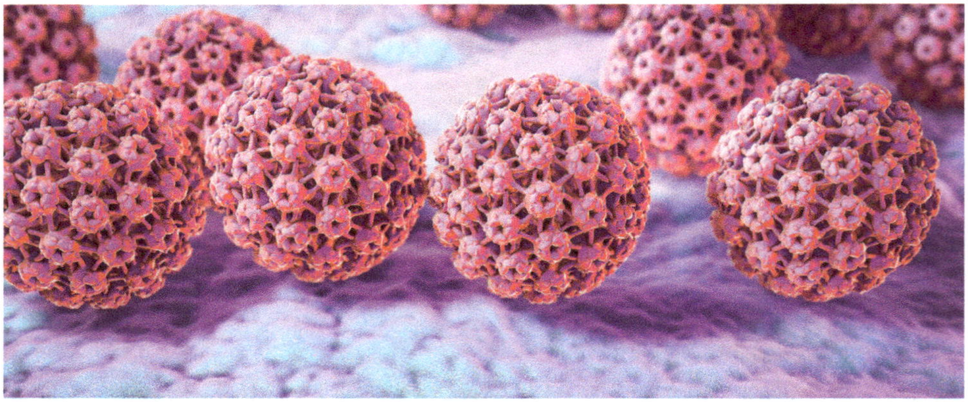

Figure 7-31 A type of human papillomavirus causes warts.

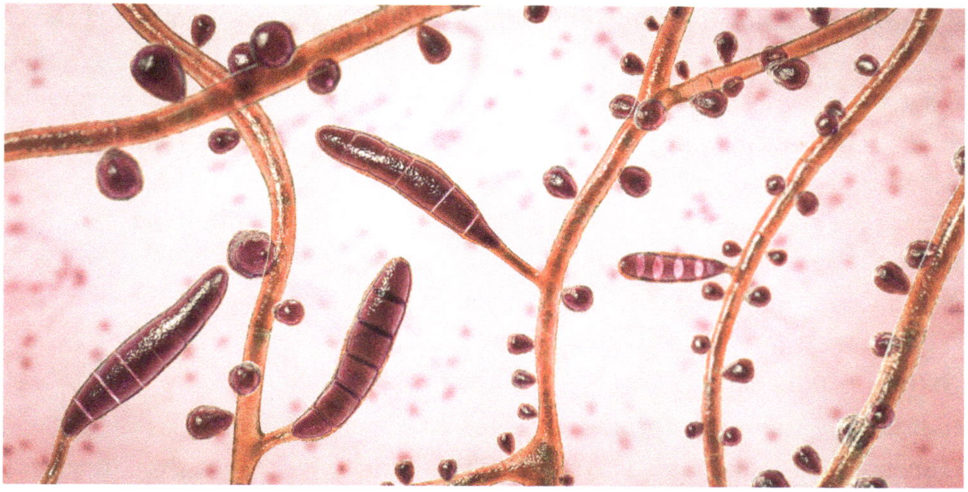

Figure 7-32 Fungal infections are typically local infections affecting one area of the body, such as the feet for *Trichophyton rubrum.*

Regardless of the microorganism, many bacteria, viruses, and fungi are contagious. A contagious microorganism is one that can be spread from person to person, by direct contact, such as touching the infected area, or indirect contact, such as the transference through water molecules in saliva or a sneeze. If an individual has a contagious illness, the duration of time in which the person can pass on the illness to others varies depending on the microorganism. Common contagious illnesses and infections include the flu, pink eye, ringworm, herpes, and COVID-19.

Summary

The healing process and classification of injuries and illnesses, including mechanisms and signs and symptoms of injury are important to know in order to determine the extent of injury. This information will assist you as a sports medicine professional in providing patient care. Subsequent chapters describe specific injuries and illnesses in detail, as well as provide you with information regarding first aid treatment and referral for your patients.

Keywords

Acute injury When the body is suddenly afflicted by trauma or damage to its tissues, which consequently initiates inflammation.

Chronic injury When an injury is no longer acute, yet remains in the later inflammatory phase or early fibroblastic repair phase of the healing process.

Exudate Formed by plasma fluid and cells, and is located in the space outside of the blood vessels.

Ecchymosis A black and blue, bruise-like color which can occur with internal bleeding.

Collagen A strong protein which comprises bone, soft tissue including skin, cartilage, and other connective tissues.

Contralateral The opposite side of body symmetrical to the injured side. If the injury is at the right knee, then the contralateral side is the left knee.

Crepitus A crackling or grating sensation that you and an athlete may feel during movement or palpitation when a structure is injured.

Tinnitus Ringing in the ears.

Point tenderness Discomfort or pain when an injured area is touched.

Microtraumas Small injuries to the tendon fibers which collectively, over time create a chronic injury. Both improper and proper muscular-tendonous mechanics or function can cause microtrauma.

Systemic Throughout the entire body.

Discussion Questions

1. What are the key events that occur in the three phases of healing?
2. What is the difference between a sign and symptom of injury and illness?
3. What are differences between sprains and strains? What can you do to preliminarily determine if an athlete has a sprain or a strain?
4. How can an injury go from being acute to chronic? What classifies an injury as being chronic?
5. Why are compound fractures medical emergencies? Why could the athlete's life be threatened if they have a compound fracture?
6. Why is it important that sports medicine professionals do not reduce a dislocated joint? What could happen to the athlete if an untrained person relocates the bones?
7. What is bursitis and how can it affect an individual's performance?
8. What microorganisms cause illness and how do they differ? What general treatments can be utilized to rid the organisms from the body and/or decrease signs and symptoms of illness?

CASE STUDY: LISTEN TO YOUR BODY

Megan is a 15 year old, slender cross country runner at Ocean Crest High School. Megan has just won the county championship meet, and as a result has an automatic entry into the state championship meet which takes place in one month. The state championship meet distance is twice as long as any other meet Megan has ever participated in. Likewise, it takes place on unfamiliar terrain for Megan, which includes rugged, steep hills. To prepare for this meet Megan's coach, Mr. Roberts, instructs her to train five days per week. He says that he will run with her each day, as he aspires to motivate and push Megan to her training limit.

Megan's training intensity is significantly increased as compared to her previous training for the county championship. She runs farther each day on various surfaces including dirt, blacktop, and all-weather track. Megan begins training up and down hills, which she is not accustomed to doing. After a few days of intense training, as a gift her mother purchases Megan new running sneakers which she wears the next day to train. Megan sees that she is progressing just after a few days of vigorous training. She thinks to herself that if she also runs on weekends, she will improve faster and become better. Consequently, Megan decides to train on her two days off, making her training schedule seven days per week. She does not schedule any rest days.

After about two weeks of training, during her workouts Megan begins to experience some discomfort in the bottom of her right foot. She believes that the discomfort will go away on its own. Megan is afraid to tell her mother or coach about the discomfort because she is fearful that they would not allow her to continue the seven days per week training. Megan tries to ignore the discomfort and work through it. A few days after her discomfort began, the discomfort turns into a dull, aching, constant pain after the workouts. The pain is not only considerably worse after workouts, but then Megan begins to experience aching on the bottom of her right foot even when her foot is at rest while sitting or lying down.

One day during a workout, the pain is so bad that it begins to affect her gait and she starts to limp. Megan is not able to put her right foot flat on the ground and instead walks on her right foot's toes. At this point, she still tries to complete the workout, but due to the pain the workouts suffer considerably. Megan cannot run at all and complete the workout. She cannot tolerate the pain and finally realizes that her foot is not getting any better. She immediately tells her coach and mother about what has occurred over the last three weeks. The next day, her mother takes her to the doctor who says that Megan cannot run for a month or more, which prevents her from competing in the state championship meet.

1. What type of injuries could Megan have?
2. What factors led to Megan's injury?
3. What could Megan have done when she first began to train for the state championship meet in attempt to prevent this injury?

References

American Medical Association (AMA) Committee on the Medical Aspects of Sports,Subcommittee on Classification of Sports Injuries. (1966). *Standard nomenclature of athletic injuries.* American Medical Association.

Denegar, C. R. (2015). *Therapeutic modalities for musculoskeletal injuries, 4th Ed.* Human Kinetics Publishers.

Houglum, P. (2016). *Therapeutic exercise for musculoskeletal injuries, 4th Ed.* Human Kinetics Publishers.

Mayo Clinic (2022, March 8). *Germs: Understand and protect against bacteria, viruses and infections.* Retrieved on April 3, 2022, from https://www.mayoclinic.org/diseases-conditions/infectious-diseases/in-depth/germs/art-20045289

Neighbors, M. & Tannehille-Jones, R. (2019). *Human diseases.* Cengage.

Prentice, W. E. (2021). *Principles of athletic training: A guide to evidence –based clinical practice, 17th Ed.* McGraw-Hill.

Reisner, E. & Reisner, H. (2022). *Crowley's an introduction to human disease: Pathology and pathophysiology correlations, 11th Ed.* Jones and Bartlett Learning.

Schultz, S.J. & Houglum, P.A. & Perrin, D.H. (2016) *Examination of musculoskeletal injuries, 4th Ed.* Human Kinetics Publishers.

Scott A., Backman, L.J, & Speed, C. (2015). Tendinopathy: Update on pathophysiology. *Journal of Orthopaedic & Sports Physical Therapy, 45*(11), 833–841. https://www.jospt.org/doi/10.2519/jospt.2015.5884

Wallace,. HA., Basehore, B.M., & Zito, P.M. (2021, November 15). *Wound healing phases.* StatPearls [Internet]. https://www.ncbi.nlm.nih.gov/books/NBK470443/

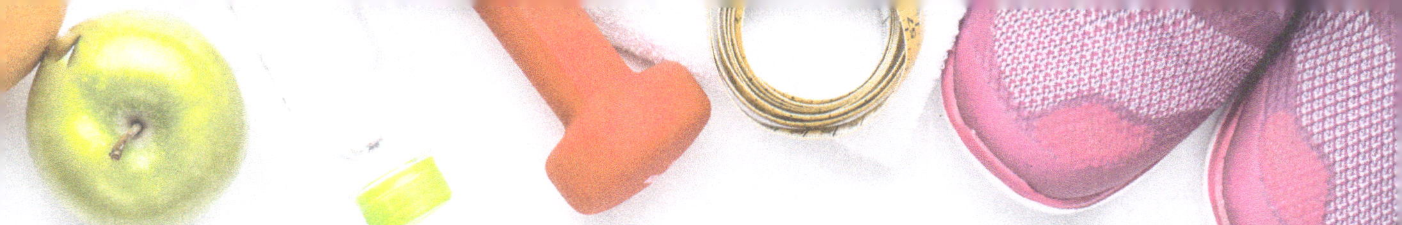

Chapter 8

Basic Injury Examination and Care

Chapter Objectives

After you have read this chapter, you will be able to understand:

- The differences between a primary survey and a secondary survey.
- The components of a basic injury examination.
- The HOPS process.
- When and how to properly move an injured or ill patient.
- How to utilize RICE for patient injury care.
- When to refer a patient for further medical evaluation or to summon EMS.

The Basic Injury Examination

The primary survey is the first step in the evaluation process that you take to care for your patients when they have sustained an injury and illness. If your patient experiences a life-threatening emergency, you will be able perform a primary survey and obtain advanced emergency medical care. However, your care will go beyond the primary survey. Once you have ascertained that your patient has no apparent life-threatening conditions, is conscious and breathing, or is not in shock or bleeding severely, you continue to care for the patient by performing a basic injury examination, otherwise known as the secondary survey. The basic injury examination is a step-by-step, organized process that helps you determine the non-life-threatening conditions that exist. By performing the secondary survey, you will be able to conclude the patient's specific injury or illness, the appropriate immediate care, and whether medical referral or emergency care is warranted.

Severity, Irritability, Nature, and Stage of Injury

The secondary survey helps you to pinpoint the severity, irritability, nature, and stage (SINS) of the patient's injury or illness (Schultz, Houglum & Perrin, 2015). The *severity* of the injury is the degree or extent of structural damage. For example, ligaments can be sprained and muscles can be strained to various degrees. Grade 1, or first-degree, is considered a mild injury. Grade 2, or second-degree, is considered a moderate injury. Grade 3, or third-degree, is considered a severe injury. With Grade 3 injuries, there is an increased possibility that the patient will need to be referred to a physician or emergency medical personnel.

Irritability is determined by what the patient tells you in regard to their symptoms. The extent of pain and the actual injury determine the injury's irritability. Ask the patient if they have pain. If they say yes, then ask them to describe the pain. They may describe the pain as sharp, dull, burning, aching, tingling, or radiating. The description can lead you to determine the type of injury. For example, sharp pain is indicative of a fracture. Dull and aching pain occurs with a muscle strain or ligament sprain. Burning, tingling, and radiating pain are signs of a neurological injury. Utilize a pain scale to quantify how much pain they are experiencing. An appropriate way to determine the patient's extent of pain is to ask "On a scale of 1 to 10, with 10 being the most pain that you have ever experienced, rate your pain right now." Be sure to ask what caused the most pain that they have ever experienced. By identifying the circumstances in which they were in the most pain, you can compare the pain from the past experience to the present injury or illness. This comparison gives you an idea of the patient's pain tolerance. Keep in mind that each patient has a different perception of pain. Some patients have a high pain tolerance whereas others do not. Regardless of the patient's pain tolerance, the higher the patient's pain scale rating, the more irritable the patient's injury or illness is.

In its basic form, the *nature* of the injury or illness is a description of the injury or illness that has afflicted the patient. This description commonly involves the damaged structure or structures and the injury's classification. Ligaments, muscles, and bones are commonly injured anatomical structures. Sprains, strains, contusions, dislocations, and fractures are some injury classifications, whereas illnesses are classified as bacterial, viral, or fungal infections.

The *stage* of the injury is described by three common injury classifications - acute, subacute, and chronic injuries. Similar to the phases of inflammation, the stages of injury are in a continuum and overlap each other. There is no definitive beginning or end of each stage; however, guidelines for the duration of each injury stage exist.

Acute injuries are caused by a traumatic event, which results in sudden inflammation to the injured area. The patient exhibits signs and complains of symptoms of injury consistent with inflammation. These signs and symptoms last from a week to a month. An example of an acute injury is when one of your clients approaches you limping in We R Fit Gym. They say that they were just participating in a kickboxing class and experienced a tearing sensation in their hamstring. Now they are in significant pain. You can see their hamstring is swollen and that they have loss of motion. This hamstring injury was caused by a single, traumatic event which resulted in spontaneous signs and symptoms of inflammation. This hamstring injury is considered an acute injury.

After the acute stage, the injury moves into the subacute stage. When a patient has a subacute injury, the injury has afflicted the patient for a month or so. Although signs and symptoms of inflammation significantly decrease in this stage, they often still exist and are bothersome. Think about the following scenario: You are training a client to participate in a marathon. They have been running on their own on the streets in their neighborhood. Three weeks ago, they sustained a Grade 2 lateral ankle sprain when they slipped on some gravel and inverted their ankle. Once their injury was no longer acute, they continued to train with you. For the past few training days, they have complained of dull pain, minor loss of motion and strength, and slight swelling after their training sessions. Their injury is clearly in the subacute stage.

The last stage of injury is the chronic stage. Chronic injuries typically have a long **onset**. The patient is not able to participate in activity at their desired level for many months due to the signs and symptoms that accompany the injury (Prentice, 2021; Shultz et al., 2015). A chronic injury requires intervention and rehabilitation, and takes an atypical amount of time to heal. A common chronic injury is lateral epicondylitis, which is otherwise known as tennis elbow. The injury occurs over a long duration due to repetitive stress to the wrist extensor muscles that originate at the lateral epicondylitis of the elbow. The patient has signs and symptoms including intermittent pain, muscle weakness, and loss of function. The injury remains chronic for months, affects athletic participation, and interferes with activities of daily living (ADLs). Continual treatment and rehabilitation must be applied before the chronic injury starts to heal.

History, Observation, Palpation, and Special Tests

When performing a basic examination on your patient, the goal is to attempt to identify the specific injury or illness in order to provide the patient with proper care and/or referral to a physician or emergency medical personnel. Regardless of the stage or severity, carefully detect as many details of the patient's condition as possible. Perform your exam in an organized manner in order to accurately determine your next course of action on the patient's behalf. One organized way to perform your basic examination is by using the acronym HOPS, which stands for history, observation, palpation, and special tests.

History

History is the first component of HOPS. The history helps you to obtain the patient's perspective on the injury. In this part of the secondary survey, you will gain the patient's subjective point-of-view and information regarding the injury from their personal experience.

The history consists of a variety of questions that you ask the patient. These questions should be general at first and become more specific to uncover injury details as you find out more information regarding the patient's condition. The questions must be as open-ended as possible, allowing for the patient to fully describe their condition in detail. Consequently, try to avoid questions that only require the patient to answer "yes" or "no". For example, one question you must ask the patient is if they have pain. Avoid asking a yes or no question, such as "Do you have pain?" The patient will most likely respond only with yes or no. You can add to your question to get a detailed response; for example, you could ask "Do you have pain and if you do, please describe how the pain feels." The patient's descriptive answer gives you some details about the extent of injury. Also, try not to lead the patient with your questions, which will solicit an unnatural response. For example, if you need to ask questions regarding the location of pain, instead of asking the patient, "Do you have pain here?" while you point to the area where you believe their pain exists; ask them "Show me where you have pain." A variety of questions can be posed to the patient regarding their injury, with the primary questions directed toward the **mechanism of injury** and their symptoms **(Table 8-1)**. After you pose one question, their answer will assist you in formulating the subsequent question. As they answer each question, think about their response. Ask yourself how the response relates to the injury. Use this information, along with previous responses, to formulate additional questions related to and expanding upon the previous ones. This method of questioning will aid you in gaining detailed information, or assist you in redirecting your questions onto a different topic related to

Table 8-1 History questions

Some questions to ask your patient when completing the history portion of the basic examination include:

- What happened?
- When did the injury occur?
- Did you hear any unusual sounds when the injury occurred? If so, please explain what you heard.
- Did you have any unusual sensation or lack of sensation at the time of injury or currently?
- Describe your symptoms. How do you feel?
- Do you have pain? If so, where is the pain?
- On a scale of 1 to 10, with 10 being the worst pain you have ever experienced, rate your pain. What is the worst pain you have ever experienced?
- Describe your pain. Is the pain burning, tingling, aching, radiating, dull, or sharp?
- Are you able to move the body part without pain?
- Do you feel joint instability, locking, or catching?
- What movements or positions increase and decrease your symptoms?
- Have you ever injured this body part before? If so, what happened? What did you do to treat and rehabilitate the previous injury?
- Are you taking any medication? If yes, what are the medications and what conditions do they treat?

their injury symptoms. Taking a thorough history is similar to trying to figure out a puzzle with clues given to you by the patient. At all times during the history, try to encourage the patient to talk freely, share their experience, and express their feelings in regard to the injury in detail.

> **TIPS FROM THE FIELD**
>
> **Tip 1** Even if you witnessed how the patient's injury occurred, and you immediately visualize the injured structures, your first question to the patient should always be, "What happened?" It is important to obtain the patient's own perspective and description of how the injury occurred. As observers, we may not see the exact mechanism of injury. Likewise, the patient may have injured more than one structure, which may not be evident immediately. Therefore, we must determine first and foremost what happened to cause the patient's injury.

When you listen to the patient's responses, carefully listen to their tone of voice, which can indicate pain perception, fear, anger, anxiety, and many other emotional responses to the injury. Your line of questioning may be short or long depending on a variety of factors. Your history will often be short if you are able to quickly determine the SINS of injury. Also, if you quickly determine that the individual is in serious distress, then your history will be very brief but direct. For example, brevity is necessary in situations where the individual has sustained a dislocated joint, a fracture, or shock, so you can provide immediate and necessary emergency care. Your history may be much longer if they do not exhibit significant distress or evident signs and symptoms, such as with a chronic injury like shoulder tendinitis. Over time, you will learn which pertinent questions to ask an injured patient dependent on their specific situation. These pertinent questions assist you in obtaining information you need to make an informed decision regarding their care. Often, after taking a detailed history you will have a good, possibly definitive, idea of the injury that the patient is suffering.

At times, the patient will not be able to give you a thorough history or respond to your questions at all. The patient may be unconscious, in shock, or severely injured or ill and is unresponsive. In these cases, you must ask bystanders and witnesses various questions relating to the patient's injury or illness. Witness accounts can be invaluable in helping you determine the SINS of injury and what patient care must be provided.

Observation

It may seem that the history ends at some point during the examination, but it actually does not. You continue to ask the patient questions throughout the entire basic examination process as you discover more pertinent information regarding the injury. As you are taking the patient's history, you also take part in the observation process. The observation is also referred to the inspection. Whereas the history is subjective because the patient tells you how the injury occurred and the symptoms they are experiencing, the observation is objective and identifies the irrefutable signs of injury. Any observer can find the signs of injury. Various signs of injury that you would observe the patient for include, but are not limited to, bleeding; ecchymosis;

red, pale, blue, and other skin color variations and discolorations; bulges, divots, or other lack of **continuity** in muscles; deformity; malalignment; asymmetry; body and limb posture; swelling; patient grasping the injury; inability to move the body part; breathing rate and quality; lack of coordination and balance; and abnormal **gait (Table 8-2)**. By observing their body language and facial expressions, you can determine various emotions, such as anxiety, fear, and apprehension, and their extent of pain, visualized by the patient wincing.

You always want to observe and examine the patient bilaterally, meaning that you observe both the injured and uninjured extremities. For example, if the patient's right knee is injured, you examine the patient's left knee as well. For other body parts, such as the face or abdomen, visualize the patient cut in half into two equal right and left sides from the head, down the bridge of the nose, through the sternum, and the umbilicus. This division creates two symmetrical left and right halves of the body, and is called the sagittal plane. By looking at the patient in this manner, you can compare the right and left sides of the entire body for signs of injury. Typically, the uninjured area is examined first to get a baseline, or what is normal, for the patient. If in the unusual chance that the patient has the same or similar injury to both sides (i.e. bilateral lateral ankle sprains), then compare injury to injury while questioning the patient as to what is a "normal" appearance for the body part.

Although most often you start the examination by taking the patient's history first, sometimes you begin the observation step in HOPS prior to the history, such as when the injured patient is walking toward you, or you are approaching the patient. For example, you are working in We R Fit Gym and suddenly you hear a large crash. Immediately, you start to run toward the sound. On the other side of the room, you see an injured client lying on the mat. As you approach the person, you see them writhing in pain on the floor by the weight rack. They are grasping their right knee. They are screaming loudly and clenching their teeth. Their knee is deformed. In this case, your observation begins before the history. You observe the client

Table 8-2 Observable signs of injury

Signs of injury that may be present when an individual is injured include:

- Redness, ecchymosis, or discoloration of the skin
- Warm skin
- Swelling
- Deformity
- Postural malalignment
- Unusual body position
- Asymmetry
- Abnormal gait
- Facial apprehension
- Abnormal sounds
- Athlete inability to move the area
- Abnormal movements
- Muscular incontinuity

before you are able to ask your history questions. Once you finally reach the client, you say "What happened?" In this instance, the observation in the basic injury examination began before the history portion. As your line of questioning continues, the observation also continues. The history and observation portions are perpetuated throughout the entire secondary survey.

Palpation

When you have completed the majority of your observation, you move on to palpation, or touching, the injured area. Before you touch your patient, ask for their permission to allow you to touch the injured area, the surrounding tissues, and the **contralateral** side as part of your basic examination. You must be discrete and professional at all times. Do not stray from palpating the injured area and surrounding areas. If at all possible, palpate the patient's injury with another person present. Palpate the uninjured side first. This contralateral palpation is important for a variety of reasons. When you palpate the contralateral, uninjured side first, your patient knows what to expect and how you will palpate the injured area. Also, by palpating the uninjured side first, you attempt to earn your patient's trust, if you have not earned it already. Palpating the uninjured side first also helps you to determine what is normal, or a baseline, for your patient's injured side. Along with your observation, contralateral side palpation helps you determine the injured structures by comparing the injured side after the uninjured side via the use of touch.

When you palpate, be cognizant as to what structures you are palpating. Picture the structures in your mind when you are touching the patient's skin. If you are palpating the quadriceps, visualize the tendons' origins and insertions under your fingers. Imagine each muscle as you palpate the muscle bellies. Recognize all anatomical structures and their location, including the bony and soft tissues, as you palpate. Also, distinguish what is abnormal for the patient. If you find an abnormal bony or soft tissue structure as compared to the contralateral side, this may indicate structural injury. Likewise, various signs of injury can be determined when palpating the anatomical structures. You will feel for signs of injury including, but not limited to, tissue continuity (including divots, bumps, and bulges), **crepitus**, skin temperature differences (including warm skin indicating inflammation or cold skin indicating lack of blood flow to the area), **muscle guarding**, **muscle spasm**, **point tenderness**, and **edema**.

TIPS FROM THE FIELD

Tip 2 During your palpation, you may have some difficulty trying to determine if the patient has any signs of injury. In this case, while you are palpating a structure, briefly close your eyes. By removing one of your senses, your sense of touch becomes more acute. This method can assist you in feeling for signs of injury. Obviously, if the patient is in significant distress, you must not break eye contact with them. You need to visualize the patient and their condition at all times. However, the skill of closing your eyes briefly during palpation, to use your fingers as your eyes, is acceptable when the patient requires a basic examination for a seemingly chronic condition or when they are not in distress.

Touch and feel both bony and soft tissues in an organized manner. Start furthest away from and gradually work toward the injured area, palpating the injured area last. The manner in which you palpate the uninjured side is exactly how you should palpate the injured side. It is recommended to palpate the structures in the same order on the injured side as you do on the uninjured side, in order to continue in an organized fashion and not mistakenly forget to palpate a structure. You must palpate all bones and soft tissue. When you palpate, begin with a light touch, using your finger pads and not the tips of your fingers, especially if you have long fingernails. Hard and pointy fingernail touch may be very uncomfortable to the patient, potentially causing the patient to lose trust in you for causing discomfort or even pain. If the patient is able to tolerate light touch, then you can gradually increase your pressure as they can tolerate.

Some circumstances would prevent you from palpating the injury. If the patient has an open wound, a rash, hives, or unidentified skin lesion, then by no means palpate the area, even if you are wearing gloves. It is contraindicated to palpate over open wounds due to the potential of increase bleeding, trauma, or introducing infectious substances into the wound. Do not palpate over a skin condition because you may spread the infection on the patient or have it transmitted to you. Other times when you would not palpate the injury would be if it occurred in an area such as the breasts on a female, the groin or buttocks on both males and females, and any other area for which you or the patient may feel uncomfortable. Do not forget to always be discrete and to have the patient give you consent to palpate before you do so. If at all possible, you need the patient to discreetly expose the injured area and the contralateral side not only to observe and compare the areas, but to palpate both areas for differences in bone and soft tissue. Patients commonly wear clothing such as bathing suits, sports bras, t-shirts, and shorts during activity. Consequently, it is often easy to visualize both the uninjured and injured body parts.

Remember to always obtain permission to touch the patient before you do so. Also, at all times, palpate the patient in a public area, while being discreet and exemplifying professionalism. Explain to the patient what you are going to do even before palpating the uninjured side. If at any time the patient does not want you palpate the area or no longer wants you to palpate, stop immediately and refer the patient to a physician or emergency personnel if their injury or illness warrants advanced medical referral. The principles of palpation are discussed in **Table 8-3**.

Special Tests

Special tests refer to various testing procedures used to examine, rule out, and confirm the extent of the patient's joint and muscular function; strength; vital signs, including circulation, respiration rate, and blood pressure; and peripheral nerve function. During your basic examination, after you have palpated the injured and surrounding area bilaterally, you begin to determine the patient's active and passive range of motion (ROM). Active ROM (AROM) is

Table 8-3 Principles of palpation

The following various principles of palpation will assist you during the basic examination:

- Obtain permission from the patient to touch the injury and surrounding area. Do not touch the patient if she does not give you permission.
- Explain to the patient the purpose of palpation.
- Explain to the patient what structures you will palpate.
- Ask the patient to bear the area as necessary to allow you palpate and visualize the skin surface.
- Demonstrate to the patient how you will palpate the injured body part by palpating the contralateral side first.
- Utilize your finger pads and palms of the hands to palpate.
- Begin with light pressure, and then gradually increase pressure as the patient tolerates.
- Tell the patient that if she has any pain or other symptoms during palpation, to inform you immediately.
- Palpate the uninjured side in an organized manner, and visualize the structures that you are palpating as you touch them.
- Palpate the injured side in the same manner as the uninjured side.
- Always palpate the patient with another person present.
- Be discreet and do not have the patient remove any clothing that would put you or the athlete in an awkward or unprofessional situation.
- Do not palpate the area if a rash, lesions, hives, open wounds, or the like exist, even if you are wearing gloves.
- If at any time the patient asks you to stop palpation, immediately stop your exam and refer the patient to a physician or EMS.

the amount of joint motion that the patient creates by contracting their muscles voluntarily. Passive ROM (PROM) is the available amount of motion around a joint without muscular contraction. PROM is involuntary motion, which is created when you move the patient's joint while the muscles are relaxed. Regardless of whether you are checking AROM or PROM, you always check the patient's ROM first on the contralateral side to determine what is the patient's normal motion. By checking the uninjured side first, you also familiarize the patient with what active and passive testing you will perform on their injured extremity.

To begin determining the patient's ROM, you first determine the extent of the patient's AROM. During AROM, the patient controls the motion by voluntarily contracting their muscles. If the patient experiences any pain during the AROM, they are able to stop the motion and further pain. Before the patient performs the AROM, explain what you want them to do and then demonstrate the motion. If you want the patient to perform active hip flexion, lie down on your back on a table or mat. Show them how to flex the hips, one at a time, with their uninjured side first (**Figure 8-1**). Move through the entire available ROM, and then have the patient do the same. Tell them in advance that if any motion is painful, or they have difficulty in completing the motion for any reason, they should stop the motion. Then immediately ask them where the pain is, or what is the difficulty in moving the joint through an AROM. After they perform AROM on both sides, you can then determine if they have any deficits. You can

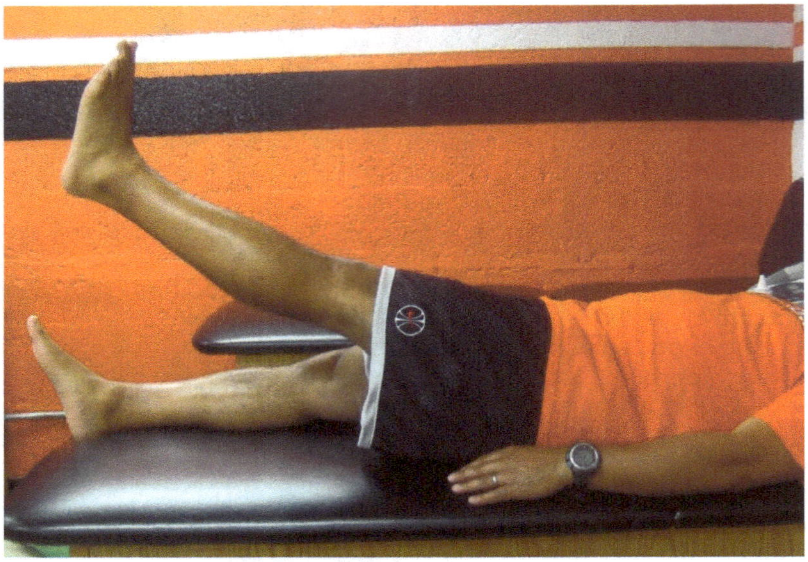

Figure 8-1 AROM of hip flexion

also use a **goniometer** to determine the actual, numerical degrees of motion as compared to researched norms and the patient's contralateral side (**Figure 8-2**). Using a goniometer takes significant instruction and practice to yield accurate results. Consequently, further discussion of goniometry is not purposeful for this text.

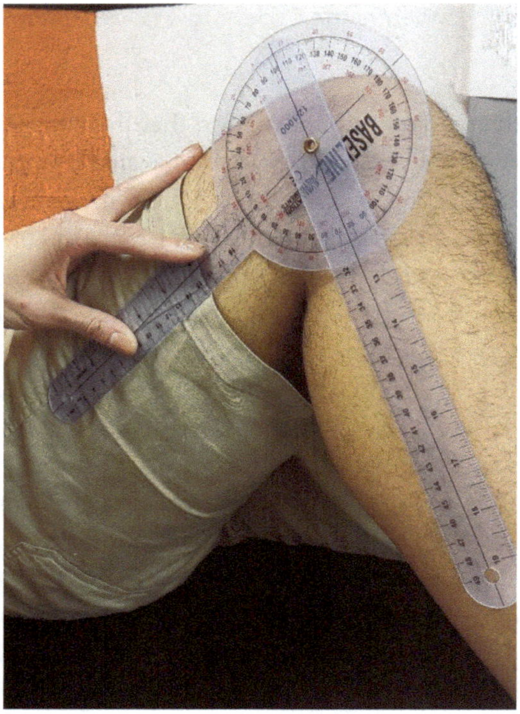

Figure 8-2 A goniometer is an objective means to quantify a patient's ROM.

As the patient performs AROM, observe various characteristics regarding the patient's motion. Look at the fluidity of the motion and determine if it is smooth throughout the entire ROM. If the patient is having a hard time actively moving the joint due to pain or other issues, the patient's motion may be choppy or stop at different points throughout the range. Also, by observing the patient's facial expressions, you can tell if the patient is experiencing pain or having difficulty moving the body part. If the patient has no pain or difficulty with active ROM throughout the entire range, you can conclude that the muscles and tendons acting on the joint are intact and most likely not injured.

Once you have determined if the patient can actively move the affected joint and contract the surrounding muscles, you can test the patient's PROM. First, have the patient relax in a comfortable position. Place the patient in a chair or have them lie on a table or a mat on the floor. The other joints and limbs must be as stable as possible. Moving the limb when the patient is lying on a treatment table or the floor, or sitting in a chair is easier than if they are standing or unsupported. The position that you place your patient depends on the body part being moved. For example, if you are going to passively move the patient's knee into flexion and extension, have them sit on the edge of a table or in a chair, feet dangling off the edge, and knee bent at a 90-degree angle. This position can also be used to test knee joint AROM.

In order to test the patient's PROM, attempt to move the distal limb. In the case of knee extension, stabilize the thigh by having the patient seated on a table with their legs hanging off the edge. For knee flexion, have the patient on their stomach. Your hand stabilizes the thigh while you grasp the distal tibia. Tell the patient to relax and not contract their muscles while you move the tibia. Then, move the knee joint throughout a full ROM by moving the tibia **(Figure 8-3)**. As you are moving the joint through a PROM, note the smoothness of the motion; the patient's facial expressions, which can indicate apprehension or pain; joint instability; and any abnormal qualities of motion such as catching, grating, clicking, or popping. Move the patient's joint as far as the joint is able without the patient experiencing pain. If at any time the patient complains of pain, instability, or an abnormal or lack of sensation, immediately stop performing the passive motion. If the patient complains of pain around the joint surface when PROM is being performed, then the ligaments or other non-contractile soft tissues around the joint may be injured. If the patient complains of muscular pain when PROM is being performed, then the muscles may be inflexible, stiff, or strained. At this point, since pain or other signs and symptoms of injury exist, refer the patient to a physician for further evaluation.

In order to further test muscular integrity and strength, you would perform manual muscle testing (MMT). MMT entails the patient performing AROM while you are applying

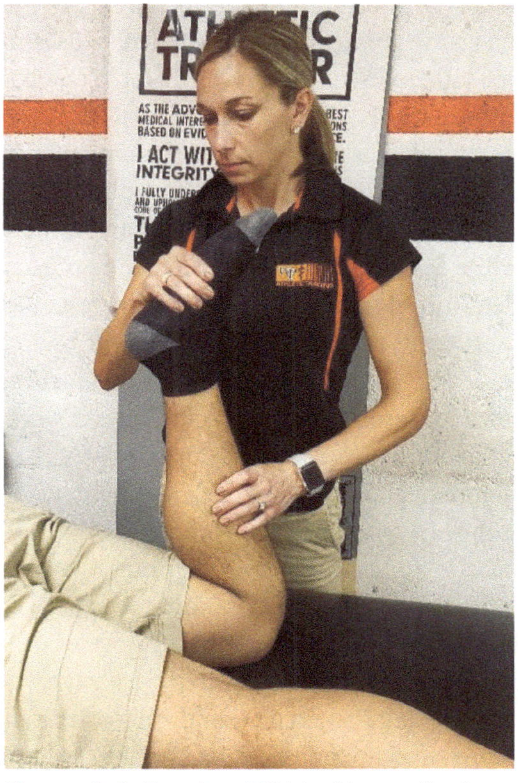

Figure 8-3 Passive ROM of knee flexion

resistance to the distal moving limb and tests muscles that act on the joint. Using the knee joint as an example, the quadriceps muscle group as a whole is strength tested when performing knee extension and the hamstring muscle group is strength tested with knee flexion. Of course you can isolate an individual muscle at any joint by knowing the muscle's action and the appropriate position to isolate the muscle. In order to perform MMT, begin with the contralateral side and place the joint and body segments in the same position as you have the patient placed in during an AROM test. Then have the patient move through an AROM. Afterwards, place your hand at the same location on the moving limb as during PROM. Instruct the patient to perform AROM while you apply moderate resistance to the distal segment. Allow the patient to go through the entire ROM. Do not apply too much resistance to prevent the patient from moving the joint. While the patient is moving the contralateral side, note the quality of movement, and the muscles' ability to create force against your resistance.

After performing the MMT on the uninjured side, perform MMT on the injured side, exactly as it was performed on the uninjured side. Compare the two sides to determine if the injured side is weaker than the uninjured side. When you apply resistance, you can tell if any bilateral muscular force production variations exist. If the uninjured side moves more smoothly through a full ROM and with greater force output against the same resistance as compared to the injured side, then the injured side most likely has a muscular injury such as a strain, or a neurological injury. A neurological injury, such as a neuropraxia, which is caused when nerves are stretched, causes nerve conduction disruption. This disruption prevents the muscle from creating force and contracting preventing the muscle from moving the joint through a full ROM, or any ROM in some cases. If you find a discrepancy in movement quality or muscular strength accompanied by pain or other significant signs and symptoms of injury, then refer the patient to a physician.

AROM and PROM are means to determine the quantity and quality of joint motion, while MMT will help you determine muscular strength. These special tests also assist you in determining the patient's pain. The tests identify injury signs and symptoms in regard to the inert or non-contractile structures around the joint, as well as the muscles during motion, muscular contraction, and force production. Always keep in mind when performing special tests you need to explain to the patient what you are going to do, demonstrate the tests on another patient or colleague, and perform these motions on the patient's contralateral side first. Before beginning, tell them that if any motion is painful they must inform you immediately. If they have difficulty in completing the AROM or MMT for any reason, tell them to stop the motion and describe the symptoms. Continue with your HOPS sequence as appropriate.

In the basic examination, the special tests also include checking the patient's vital signs, including circulation, respiration rate, and blood pressure. For musculoskeletal injuries, checking the patient's circulation, by evaluating their pulse distal to the injured area is important. By checking the circulation distal to the injury, you determine if adequate blood flow is being supplied to the injured area and the rest of the extremity that is lower, or distal, to the injury. Compare pulses bilaterally. While comparing both sides, determine the pulse rate and quality to see if they are equal. The pulse rate, or heart rate, is the number of pulses per minute. For an adult, the average pulse rate at rest, taken in the morning before rising, is 60 to 100 beats per minute (bpm). For an elite or well-trained athlete or client, the average heart rate may be as low as 40 bpm (Laskowski, 2020). The quality of pulse is a description of the pulse strength during palpation. The pulse may be weak, strong, or nonexistent as compared to the uninjured side. A weak or nonexistent pulse means the patient does not have adequate blood flow to the distal extremity. A weak pulse also can indicate various illnesses such as shock or heat exhaustion. A nonexistent pulse could also indicate that the person has succumbed to cardiac arrest. A strong pulse can indicate an illness such as heat stroke.

Taking a pulse is not difficult. Find the artery distal to the injury and palpate it with your second and third fingers. Do not use your thumb since it has a pulse of its own and you may mistake your pulse for the patient's. Most often you can palpate pulses bilaterally at the same time. For example, if the patient has an upper extremity injury, the radial pulse is most commonly used to check circulation. The radial pulse is located over the radial bone on the lateral side of the wrist, approximately an inch from the wrist joint **(Figure 8-4)**. You can easily palpate and evaluate both pulses simultaneously. You can also take a pulse at the brachial artery if the injury is at the shoulder. The brachial artery is located at the inside of the upper arm between the biceps brachii and triceps brachii muscles. This artery is not often utilized for taking a pulse as compared to the radial pulse, since the radial pulse is more easily accessible and at the most distal portion of the upper extremity; however, the brachial pulse is easily identifiable. If the lower extremity is injured, check the patient's

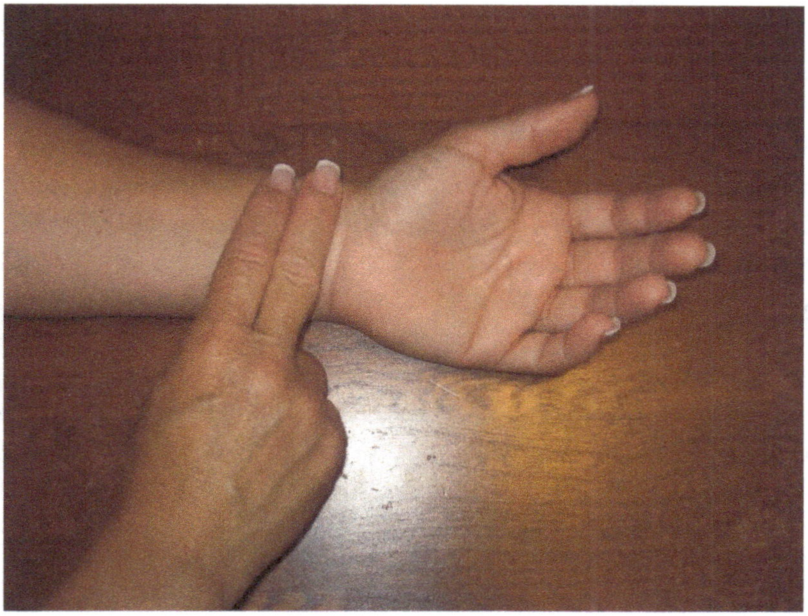

Figure 8-4 Taking radial pulse

circulation at the popliteal, posterior tibial, or dorsal pedal (also called the dorsalis pedis) arteries. Choose the artery that is distal to the injury. The posterior tibial artery and dorsal pedal arteries are most commonly used to examine lower extremity pulses. The posterior tibial artery is found on the medial side of the ankle between the medial malleolus and the Achilles' tendon. This artery is easily found due to its location; however, the dorsal pedal artery is not as easily palpated (Mowalvi, Whiteman, Wilhelmi, Neumeister, & McLafferty, 2002). The dorsal pedal artery is located between the first and second metatarsals on the top of the foot by the carpal bones.

After finding the artery upon palpation, take the pulse rate by counting the beats per minute while watching the second hand on a clock or wristwatch for 10 seconds. Then multiply the number of beats by six. The resulting number is the patient's heart rate in beats per minute (Laskowski, 2020). You can take the pulse rate for a longer duration (i.e. 30 seconds then multiply by 2 or for 60 seconds) to obtain a more accurate reading. The pulse quality is subjective. Attempt to determine whether the pulse quality is the same or varies. The pulse may be slow, normal, fast, weak, or bounding as compared to the uninjured side. If pulses are not equal in rate or quality, among the injured and uninjured sides, then refer the patient for further medical evaluation. In cases of common illnesses, the pulse quality and rate should be identical and normal on both sides. In the case of shock or heat stroke the quality and rate is not normal. With shock, the pulse is rapid and weak, and during heat stroke the pulse is rapid and strong. For musculoskeletal injuries, if the distal pulses are equal in rate and quality, then adequate blood flow and oxygen is being supplied to the injured area. Having some knowledge regarding normal pulse quality is important to determine if the patient needs immediate emergency care when they have sustained an injury or illness.

You can also check circulation to the distal extremities by checking capillary refill. The patient's nail beds are normally a pink color. To check capillary refill, gently squeeze the nail bed of the fingers or toes, depending on the extremity that is injured, one at a time for a few seconds. The nail bed turns white, indicating lack of blood flow to the area. Let go of the pressure and the nail bed's pink color should return immediately. The pink color indicates adequate blood flow to the extremity. Check capillary refill for each finger and toe on the affected limb. If the pink color does not return quickly or at the same rate as compared to the contralateral side, then the patient may have inadequate blood flow to the extremity.

Respiration rate is easily determined by counting the number of breaths per minute. An adult who is at rest has an approximate respiratory rate of 15 to 20 breaths per minute. An exercising athlete or client may reach 25 breaths per minute. An ill patient at rest, including a patient in shock or respiratory distress, may reach 20 respirations per minute.

Blood pressure (BP) is the force blood creates on artery walls as it moves through the circulatory system. BP is measured in millimeters of mercury (mmHg) and is recorded as systolic pressure over diastolic pressure. Systolic pressure is the force of blood on artery walls as the heart beats; diastolic pressure is the force of blood on artery walls as the heart is at rest in between beats. The average, normal adult has a BP less than 120/80 mmHg, which is verbalized as "120 over 80" (Whelton et al., 2018). This BP means the person has 120 mmHg systolic pressure and 80 mmHg diastolic pressure.

Taking an accurate BP requires a lot of practice. In order to take a BP, you need a stethoscope and a sphygmomanometer, also called a BP cuff, or an automatic BP monitor. You can purchase this equipment at various commercial drug stores or through health-related supply companies on the Internet. Sports medicine professionals most often utilize a BP cuff, which is inflated and deflated manually, along with a stethoscope to take a patient's BP **(Figure 8-5)**. Patients who monitor their own BP typically utilize automatic BP monitors since these machines are simple to use **(Figure 8-6)**. To begin using either device, have the patient's biceps brachii and elbow exposed. Place the BP cuff snugly around the patient's biceps brachii muscle approximately one inch from the antecubital fossa on the anterior elbow. When utilizing an automatic monitor, follow the directions that accompany the device, which may include a setting for appropriate inflation. In most cases, the patient presses the Start button, which causes the monitor to automatically inflate and then deflate the BP cuff. The monitor then displays the patient's BP.

When utilizing a BP cuff and stethoscope, place the BP cuff around the biceps brachii so the gauge and bulb tubes are anterior to the elbow. Place the bell of the stethoscope on the brachial artery, slightly superior to the antecubital fossa. Once you hear the "whooshing" sound of the blood flowing through the artery, make sure the bulb valve is shut and inflate the BP cuff by repetitively squeezing the bulb. Inflate the BP cuff so the pin on the gauge reaches approximately 30 mmHg higher than the patient's normal systolic BP. At that point, the whooshing sound made by the blood flow ceases. Slowly open the valve so the gauge pin drops approximately 2 mmHg per second. Watch the gauge carefully. When you hear the first

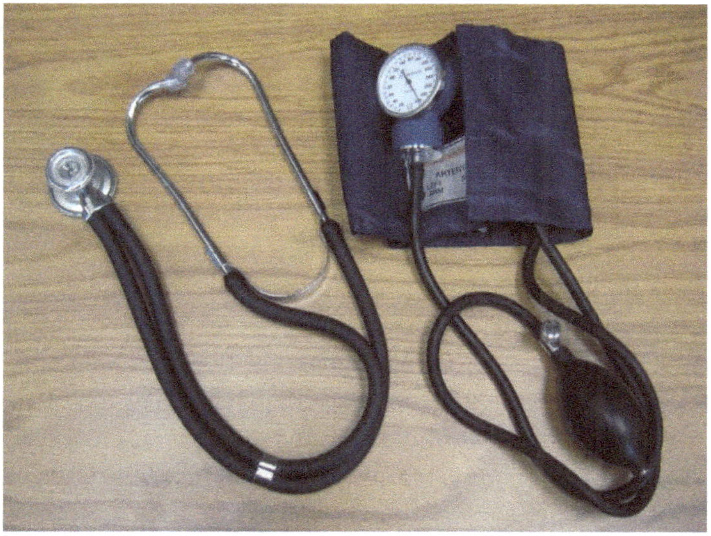

Figure 8-5 Blood pressure cuff and stethoscope

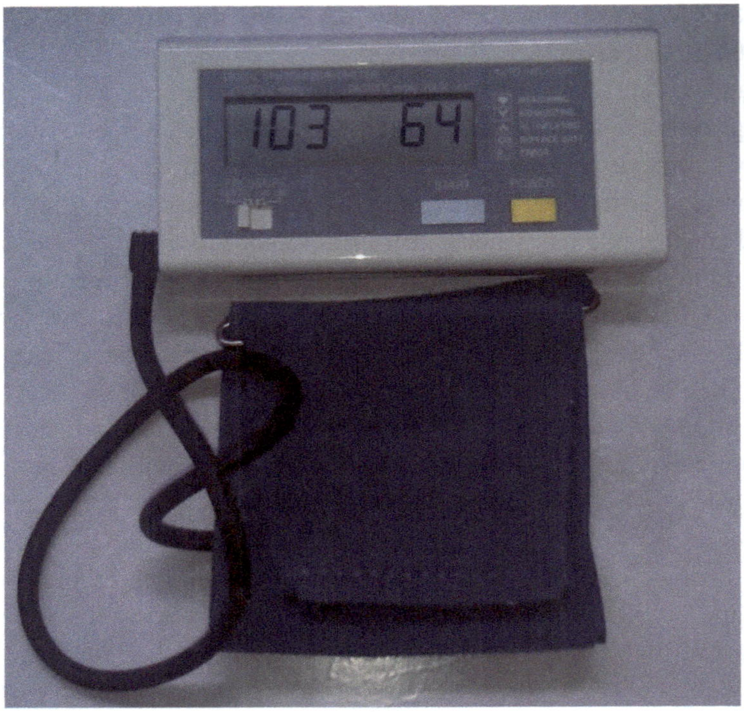

© Linda Gazzillo Diaz

Figure 8-6 Automatic Blood pressure monitor

"thump" record the number displayed on the gauge at that moment as the systolic BP. Continue to slowly open the valve and watch the gauge. The number on the gauge when the last thump occurs is the diastolic BP. Record the systolic BP over the diastolic BP. To determine the accuracy of the reading, take the patient's BP three times with 1 minute of rest in between readings. Once you become proficient in taking a BP, you can obtain an accurate reading with one attempt.

Evaluating a patient's neurological function is extremely important to determine the appropriate course of patient care. Detailed tests exist to evaluate a patient's neurological function for all parts of the body, including the brain and spinal cord, which make of the central nervous system (CNS), and the peripheral nerves. These detailed tests are beyond the scope of this text; however, you can perform generalized tests to evaluate the patient's neurologic function, which can be compromised due to injury. The peripheral, or spinal, nerves arise out of the spinal cord at the cervical, thoracic, lumbar, and sacral vertebrae **(Figure 8-7).** Each nerve has a motor and a sensory branch. Therefore, an individual spinal motor nerve innervates a specific muscle or group of muscles, while an individual spinal sensory nerve innervates an area of the skin. Normally when a patient sustains a common injury such as a sprain or a strain, evaluating the patient's neurological function is not necessary. However, you evaluate the patient's peripheral nerves if they complain of symptoms such as tingling, numbness, or strange sensations at or around the injured area, muscular weakness, or loss of muscular function (Starkey & Brown, 2015).

A quick and easy means to determine if the patient's spinal motor nerves are functioning appropriately is to have the patient perform AROM and MMT testing. You test the injured area as well as the nerves around the injured area. For example, if the patient complains of "pins and needles" or tingling from their elbow down to their fingers, test the patient's peripheral motor nerves from the shoulder to the fingers. Have the patient shrug and abduct their shoulders, flex and extend their elbows and wrists, and flex, adduct, and abduct their fingers. Then have the patient perform these motions while you apply resistance. Determine if the patient can perform the movement normally, has difficulty doing so, or has muscular weakness. If the patient has any deficits, then the possibility that a peripheral motor nerve injury exists. In order to test the peripheral sensory nerves, ask the patient to close their eyes. Touch them on both sides of their body with a soft touch and then a hard touch. You can perform this touch either on one side than the other or simultaneously. Ask them if they can feel your touch on both sides equally, and if the sensation is soft or hard. Also, ask them to distinguish between two points on their skin. In order to complete this task, have the patient close their eyes. Put two fingers, spread at least an inch apart, on the same area of the skin. Ask the patient if they can distinguish between the two points. If the patient complains of paresthesia or numbness, or is unable to distinguish between the two points, then a sensory spinal nerve may be compromised. After this finding, refer them to a physician for further evaluation. Again, to determine if an injury exists, always compare both the uninjured and injured sides.

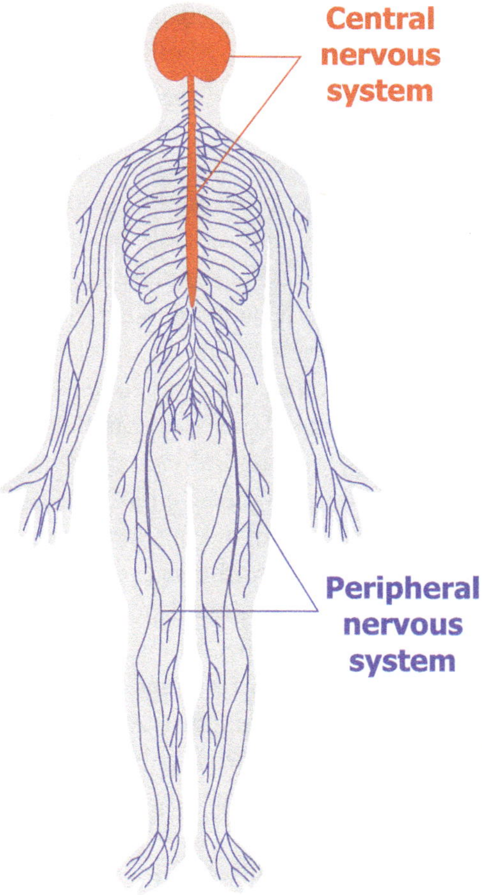

© Systemoff/Shutterstock.com

Figure 8-7 The peripheral nerves arise from the CNS and function to provide sensation and motor function to the body.

Safely Moving an Injured Patient

For acute injuries, if possible, attempt to keep the injured individual at the location where the injury occurred and perform the basic examination. After performing the basic examination, you will determine if the individual should be moved from the area. If you must move the acutely injured individual before performing the basic examination, determine how to do so safely without causing further injury or exacerbating symptoms. In certain instances it is evident that you must move the person. For example, if they injure themselves in the gym and is in the middle of client foot traffic, then you may need to move them, provided it is safe to do so. If an athlete is injured on a playing field in the middle of competition, you may want to move them as long as it is safe to do so. In any situation, you do not move the injured person if moving them may complicate the injury. In some situations you do not move them at all. For example, if the individual is in a life-threatening situation and is not breathing, then leave them where they are and perform CPR. Also, if they have a fractured bone, do not move them.

When you suspect someone has a spinal injury, such as when a blow to the head, neck, or spine occurred and they complain of numbness or an inability to move a portion of the body, or any time an individual is unconscious, they must not be moved and is transported via spine board to the hospital. Placing an injured person on a spine board appropriately is a difficult task. Staff at your facility must practice this skill on a regular basis to ensure the spine boarding is performed properly and assuring patient safety. For some sports medicine professionals, spine board practice is not practical. Likewise, many organizations, such as gyms or Little League, for example, do not have a spine board on site. Therefore, if you suspect your athlete has a spinal injury, stabilize the head and neck and have someone phone 911. Continue to stabilize the head and neck until the EMTs arrive and physically take over for you. The EMTs are highly trained in moving an injured person onto a spine board for transport. The EMTs may ask you to assist in this task, because depending on the technique used a minimum of five people are necessary to appropriately and safely place a patient on a spine board (Prentice, 2021). Do not remove your hands from the patient's head until directed by an EMT.

In many situations when the patient is injured, you can move the patient. A patient with minor to moderate injuries can be moved. If an individual sustains a Grade 1 ankle sprain during an aerobics class, you can move them out of the aerobics studio and into an employee office for evaluation. If a client has a Grade 2 strain of their quadriceps muscles while performing squats, you can move them away from the flow of client traffic into a safe and non-congested area. If the individual can walk without pain or exacerbating symptoms, have them walk to a comfortable area for evaluation. If the individual is in pain, unable to walk, or in a location where they or bystanders would be unsafe if they remained, then you must decide how to properly and safely move them.

If the individual cannot ambulate on their own, or has pain or exacerbated symptoms of injury, then help the individual to move from the area. Some means to move an injured person include ambulatory aid, manual conveyance, or spine board transport (Prentice, 2021). Provide ambulatory assistance to a individual who can fully or partially weight bear and walk on their own. Typically, you provide ambulatory assistance if they have some pain or discomfort in the lower extremity, as with a Grade 1 or Grade 2 ankle sprain, or is unsteady or dizzy, perhaps due to an illness or concussion. In order to provide ambulatory assistance, you need to be approximately the individual's height. You can assist them to ambulate by yourself, but if you have another person assist you, the move will be easier.

If you are working with another person, position yourselves on either side of the individual. Put your arm closest to the individual around their waist. The individual's arm closest to you would be placed around your shoulders **(Figure 8-8)**. It may be beneficial to hold their arm around your shoulders to make sure it does not slip off while ambulating. Then, instruct them to take slow steps to your destination. If you are much shorter or taller than the individual, you may have a difficult time providing ambulatory assistance. Consequently, have other teammates, clients, colleagues, or others who are the approximate height of the person assist them. In this case, before the caregivers move the patient, demonstrate and describe to the caregivers how to position themselves and support the patient during ambulation. If you are the only person available to provide ambulatory assistance, position yourself on the individual's injured side. Instruct them to slightly lean in your direction, and use your body and legs almost as a crutch for their injured lower extremity. Before moving the patient, always make sure you instruct them that if they experience any pain or an increase in symptoms while moving to immediately stop and tell you what they are experiencing.

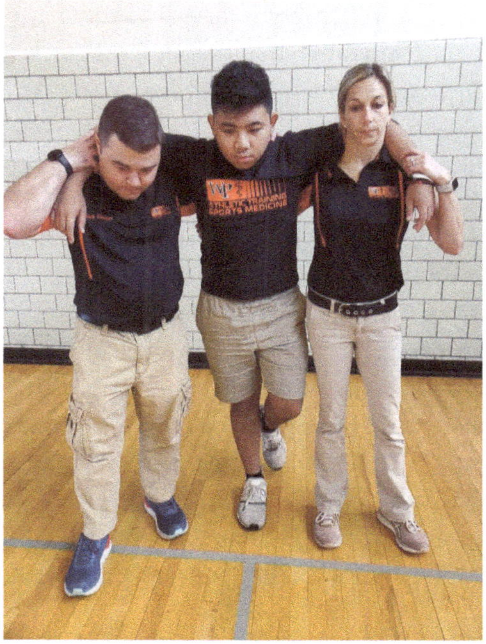

Figure 8-8 If the patient can partially weight bear, then ambulatory assistance can be utilized to move the patient.

Another means to move an injured person is by manual conveyance. Manual conveyance, which can be used with someone who cannot bear weight on their lower extremity or cannot walk on their own. Also, if the individual begins to walk with ambulatory assistance and finds that they are in great pain or their symptoms increase, then manual conveyance is warranted. Two caregivers are always needed to move a person by manual conveyance. Position the individal between you and the other caregiver. Place your arms closest to the individual around their waist as with ambulatory assistance. Then with your other arm, put your forearm under their thighs. Your assistant takes the same position with the injured person on the opposite side. Both of you should grasp hands underneath the individual's thighs. Tell the individual to slowly lean back take a seated position in you and your assistant's arms

(Figure 8-9). Slowly carry and move them to a safe area. If possible, demonstrate this technique to the injured person first by utilizing another, uninjured person who has previously been moved by manual conveyance. If the demonstration is not possible, then carefully describe what you intend to do. Manual conveyance is an appropriate means to move an injured person, but often can be difficult to perform. If the distance to move the individual is very long, the caregivers can become tired and lose their grasp. Likewise, if the caregivers are significantly smaller than the injured person, or not strong enough to carry them the distance, then manual conveyance may not be feasible. In the case when manual conveyance is not possible, but you must move the injured person, you will have to summon EMS.

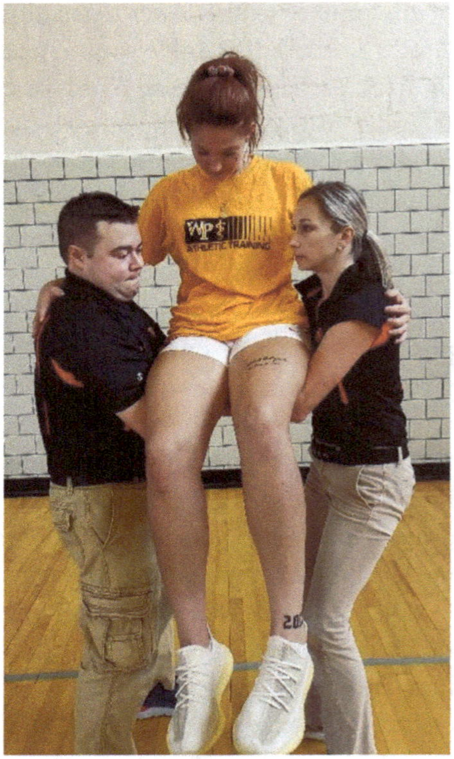

Figure 8-9 The proper position to provide manual conveyance

Providing Care

Now that you have completed your basic examination and moved the injured person safely, you can assist in providing necessary care. Patient care involves basic first aid skills, as allowed by your state's statutes. Depending on the credentials, licenses, and the like that you hold and the state in which you work, the patient care you are able to provide varies. In most circumstances, you can do no wrong if you provide basic first aid and CPR as instructed in formal classes by nationally recognized organizations such as the American Heart Association, the American Red Cross (ARC), the Emergency Care and Safety Institute (ECSI), and the National Safety Council. These organizations offer first aid and CPR courses to become certified in these skills. Even if you are not certified in first aid when you provide proper first aid to an injured patient, your state's Good Samaritan Laws protect you.

When you care for an injured patient, start by utilizing the RICE principle. RICE stands for rest, ice, compression, and elevation. Rest is symbolized by the R in RICE. When a patient is injured, they must rest the injured body part and the adjacent tissues to avoid further injury and promote healing. In order to properly rest the body part, the patient should not move it. To rest the upper extremity from the shoulder down to the fingers, apply a triangular bandage or splint. To rest the lower extremity from the hip down to the toes, apply a splint or commercial brace.

You can also fit the patient for and teach them how to use crutches or a cane if they need to rest the lower extremity and cannot fully weight bear. Crutches can also be used while the patient is partial weight bearing, but they must bear most of their weight on the uninjured lower extremity. You can easily learn how to fit crutches for a patient. Aluminum crutches typically have the patient's height on the crutch post for easy adjustment. Position the crutches with the patient standing so the crutch tips are approximately 2 inches in front of the patient's toes and 6 inches laterally to the patient's feet. The axillary crutch pads must be approximately 2 to 3 inches below the axilla. The patient's body weight is borne by their hands and not by the axilla. The elbow should be at approximately 30 degrees of flexion (Starkey, 2013). In order to ambulate, the patient moves the crutches forward approximately 6-12 inches. They step forward to the crutches with their uninvolved extremity, then move the crutches forward once again.

If a patient can bear a significant amount of weight on the injured lower extremity without pain or other symptoms, the patient can use a cane instead of crutches. To teach a patient to use a cane, have them place the cane handle in the hand opposite the injured lower extremity. The elbow is bent and the cane tip rests by the foot in a similar manner as with crutches. Instruct the patient to move the cane tip forward with the injured lower extremity (Starkey, 2013). The cane acts as a support for the injured lower extremity as it moves forward and bears weight while walking.

Resting the injured body part will have the chance to heal properly. Rest is particularly important for an acute injury in the inflammatory phase. However, too much rest for long periods of time can be detrimental. Consider a patient with a relatively minor biceps brachii strain. For the first day post-injury, the patient complains of pain and weakness while raising their arm. Consequently, you place a sling on the patient's upper extremity with their elbow in 90 degrees flexion in order to rest the biceps brachii muscle for the day. The next day the patient says they still have pain, so you leave the sling on for another day. After the second day you remove the sling. The patient has significant difficulty and pain when attempting to extend their elbow and move their shoulder due to the muscles becoming shortened, contracted, and stiff. In this scenario, too much rest was detrimental. As a rule of thumb, if the patient needs a sling, splint, brace, crutches, or a cane as part of injury care, fit the patient with the device to make them comfortable and refer the patient to a physician for medical evaluation.

Ice is the I in RICE. When the patient is injured, ice facilitates the healing process by decreasing nerve conduction, which decreases pain signals to the brain, acting as an anesthetic and decreasing capillary permeability and vasodilation, which in turn may decrease swelling (Pfeiffer, Mangus, & Trowbridge, 2015). Ice, in the form of ice cubes or crushed ice, is one type of cold therapy. Other forms of cold therapy used for athletic injuries include ice cups, ice baths, and cold whirlpools. Ice cubes placed in a bag is a very common and typically safe cold therapy utilized for injuries such as sprains, strains, and contusions. Care must be taken when applying ice on an injured medial elbow or lateral knee, because superficial nerves are located at these areas. If ice is left on these structures too long, the nerve can become damaged. To prepare an ice bag, put enough ice in the bag to cover the injured area. Do not make the bag too heavy or excessive weight will be applied to the injury and the patient may be very uncomfortable. The ice bag can be applied directly to the skin, unless during questioning you find the patient has loss of sensation, **Raynaud's syndrome**, or any allergy to cold. In these cases, do not apply the ice and refer the patient for medical evaluation. Secure the ice bag with an elastic wrap or any commercial ice wrap.

You may have heard to apply ice for "20 minutes on and 20 minutes off". However, this guide is often not appropriate for injured areas. This process could actually cause more harm than good. For example, in small areas such as the fingers or hand or over a superficial nerve such as the ulnar nerve leaving ice on for 20 minutes and the reapplying after 20 minutes lapses with the ice off can potentially cause freezing of the tissues. Ice is generally applied on the average between 5 and 20 minutes, until the area on the patient is numb. The duration of application depends on factors such as the treatment area size and the tissue depth. For example, the wrist does not have a large quantity of muscle, fat, or other soft tissue and is a smaller area as compared to the gastrocnemius muscle. Consequently, you apply ice for a shorter amount of time, perhaps 5 minutes, as compared to the gastrocnemius, for which ice can be applied for perhaps 15 minutes. At first, the ice makes the patient's soft tissues feel cold. Afterwards, the patient feels burning, then aching, and finally numbness. Once the area is numb, you must remove the ice bag. The ice can be reapplied when the patient has full feeling, the skin has returned to normal color at the injured site, and the tissues are entirely rewarmed.

During the course of the ice application, frequently ask the patient how they are feeling. If a patient has never had ice applied to their body before, check the skin occasionally by briefly removing the ice bag. As the ice is applied and the skin turns cold, the skin changes from pink to red. However, if the skin becomes red, raised, and warm, the patient most likely has an allergy to the ice, cold, and/or bag material. In this case, remove the ice immediately, and monitor the patient to make sure they do not have any other signs or symptoms of an allergic reaction, such as anaphylactic shock. Also, refer the patient to a physician for evaluation to be certain that the patient does not have any underlying issues causing the unusual reaction. If at any time the patient has unusual sensations, begins to feel ill, or has any other abnormal reaction to the ice application, remove the ice bag and begin to take a basic examination.

For injury care, it is important that you have access to ice or cold therapy agents. Most athletic facilities have access to ice. Clinic, hospitals, and similar facilities typically have access to ice via an ice machine. Ice can be made, and reusable, commercial, cold therapy packs can be stored in a freezer. If you do not have a freezer or ice machine available, then cold chemical packs are useful. By squeezing the chemical pack and shaking the contents, the chemical pack turns cold and provides similar effects as ice. When using these chemical cold packs, be careful when applying them to the patient. They should not be placed directly on the patient's skin. The chemical cold packs can get tissues extremely cold and freeze the skin, especially upon direct application to the skin. If the pack is punctured and the chemicals leak out, the patient may sustain a chemical burn. Also, the chemicals may not mix properly and the bag will not get cold. Squeeze the chemical cold pack and shake it as per the directions on the pack. Then place the chemical cold pack into a sealed plastic bag to prevent chemicals from spilling through the bag and onto the skin. Place a minimum one layer of toweling on the injured area before placing the pack on the patient. For those facilities that have access to fallen snow, use snow instead of ice. Snow is an excellent cold therapy agent because you can easily mold and conform it to the injured body part. Place the snow in a sealed plastic bag and use it as you would ice.

Utilizing ice cups are also beneficial due to the cold and massaging effects. To create an ice cup, place cold water in a small paper cup approximately three-quarters full. Put the cup in the freezer and wait until the ice is completely frozen before use. When the water is frozen, carefully rip the top of the cup to expose approximately 1/2 inch of ice. Using a towel to soak up any dripping water, rub the exposed ice on and around the injured area. You should move the cup in small circles or straight lines, for approximately 5-10 minutes, or until the area is numb (**Figure 8-10**). To obtain a massaging effect, you can press deeper into the tissues as tolerated. Ice cup massage, as with any other ice application, should not be done directly over superficial nerves, such as the ulnar nerve or the common peroneal nerve.

A question that many people ask is "When can heat be applied to an injured area instead of ice?" The answer is that when an injury is in the first phase of healing (the inflammatory phase) ice must always be applied. Consequently, ice should be applied for the first

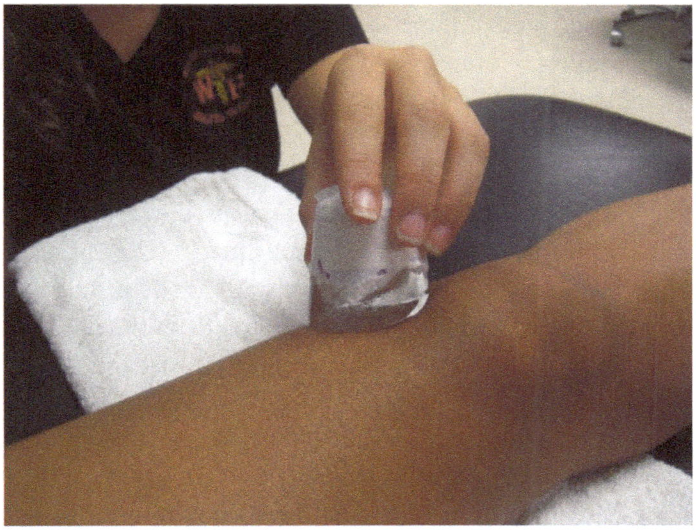

Figure 8-10 Ice cup massage

TIPS FROM THE FIELD

Tip 3 In order to deliver the cold from an ice bag fast to the patient's tissues, and to provide compression at the same time, take an elastic bandage and wet it with cold water. Wring the elastic bandage and roll it back up. Apply the damp elastic bandage to the patient's injured area as you would apply any other elastic bandage. Afterwards, place the ice bag on top of the damp elastic bandage and over the injured area. Secure the ice bag with another dry elastic bandage or a commercial ice bag wrap.

48 to 72 hours after injury. If heat is applied, in the form of either a dry or moist heating pad or any other heating element, then blood vessel vasodilation at the injury site will occur. The heat creates increased vascular permeability and edema, and results in increased swelling. These heat effects will cause the healing process to slow down and possibly exacerbate the injury. In most circumstances, it is appropriate to apply heat to the injured structures after the inflammatory phase is over. When the patient states their symptoms are subsiding and you observe decreasing signs of injury, then most likely heat can be safely applied. If at any time you are unsure if it is appropriate to apply heat, simply continue with ice application. Ice application is appropriate and beneficial throughout all phases of healing.

The purpose of compression, the C in RICE, is to mechanically put pressure on and compress the injured area to assist in supporting the injured and surrounding structures. Compression can also aid in moving edema out of the injured area, which additionally promotes an optimal healing environment for the injured tissue. Compression is most often applied to an acute injured area with an elastic bandage. A patient with a Grade 2 ankle sprain, for example commonly has significant ankle swelling. Applying a compression wrap to the ankle, starting from the metatarsal heads and ending at the Achilles' tendon origin, can provide support to the injured and surrounding structures, whether or not the patient is full weight bearing. The compression also forces the edema out of the interstitial areas, which promotes healing. Compression is also applied with commercial neoprene sleeves. These sleeves are made for various body parts including the thigh, knee, and elbow. To assist in preventing swelling due to increased edema, compression is critical in the RICE process.

Elevation is the E in the RICE principle. Elevation is used to assist in decreasing edema at the injured site, which results in decreased swelling. By placing the injured area higher than the heart, gravity helps the circulatory system to transport waste products and fluid out of the injured area. If waste products and fluid are eliminated from the area, healing can be facilitated. For example, if the patient's ankle is injured apply an ice bag securely to the patient's ankle. Have the patient lie on a treatment table or floor with the affected ankle raised up with their heel on the wall, if feasible. You can also have the patient lie down and their lower extremity supported and raised up 12 inches to have the extremity above the level of the heart **(Figure 8-11)**. Utilizing RICE can certainly assist the patient's injury to heal properly and return them to full, pre-injury activity.

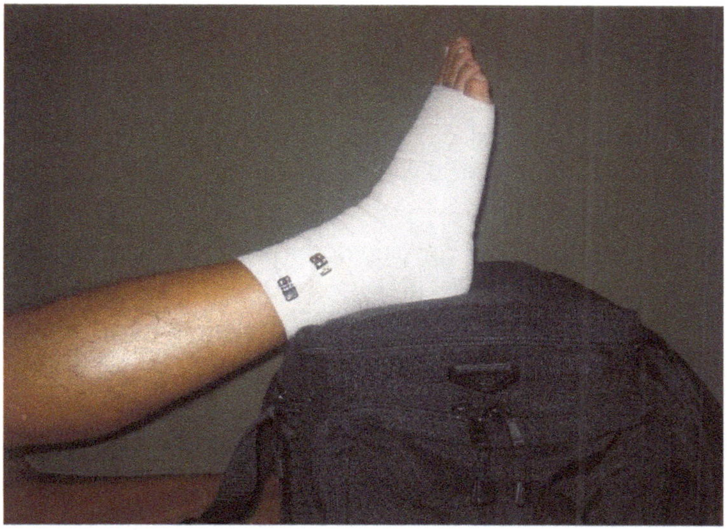

© Linda Gazzillo Diaz

Figure 8-11 Elevation of the injured ankle

Summary

Once the primary survey has been completed, the basic examination is a means to determine what non-life-threatening injuries or illnesses a patient has sustained. The basic examination's history, observation, palpation, and special tests are integral to determining not only what is wrong with the patient, but also how to provide proper first aid treatment. What you find in your basic examination will also assist you to determine whether the patient should be moved and referred to a physician or EMS. Although you may not be formally trained in first aid or injury evaluation, by performing a basic examination you can afford your patients immediate assistance with their injuries.

Keywords

Onset When the injury begins and becomes apparent to the patient. Injuries may have a short, long, or insidious (gradual and undetected) onset.

Mechanism of injury How the injury or illness occurred, which can be determined by asking the patient "What happened?"

Continuity In muscles, this is when the tissue feels the same to the touch throughout the tissue's entire length and width.

Gait The manner in which the patient is walking or running.

Contralateral The corresponding structure on the opposite side of the body.

Crepitus A crackling sound.

Muscle guarding An involuntary muscular response that occurs when the muscles around an injured are become tight and rigid in order to protect an injured area from further injury. Muscle guarding typically is not painful to the patient.

Muscle spasm An involuntary muscular response that occurs when the muscles suddenly contract and shorten. Muscle spasm typically is painful for the patient, and the patient cannot relieve the spasm voluntarily.

Point tenderness A sign of injury. When you palpate the patient's injury, and the patient claims the area you touched was painful, then that area is considered point tender.

Muscle guarding is a muscular response which occurs when the muscles around an injured area become tight and rigid in order to protect an injured area from further injury. Muscle guarding is not typically painful to the patient.

Edema Fluid that accumulates in bodily spaces due to injury or illness. Edema creates the appearance of swelling, especially at the joints and around soft tissue structures.

Goniometer A protractor-type device that is used to measure angles and joint range of motion.

Raynaud's syndrome A condition in which the patient has significant lack of blood circulation to the fingers and toes. It is brought on by exposure to cold.

Discussion Questions

1. Explain what SINS stands for and how you incorporate this principle into a basic injury examination.
2. Why is taking the patient's history so important during the basic examination? What history questions are imperative to ask first during the questioning process?
3. When does the basic examination observation begin? What are some observable signs of injury?
4. What signs of injury can you identify during palpation? Why do you palpate the contralateral side first prior to the injured side? How can you build a foundation of trust with your patient prior to and during palpation?
5. What are the similarities and differences of performing active, passive, and resistive ROM (MMT) with your patient? What do you looking for when evaluating the patient's joint motion and muscular strength?
6. Describe how you properly move an injured or ill patient?
7. What does RICE stand for and what are some principles of each RICE component?

CASE STUDY: A THOROUGH BASIC EXAM...OR NOT?

Karen is a healthy sixteen-year-old softball pitcher with no prior medical history of injury or illness. Today, Karen joins her 12 teammates for a softball game against their league rivals. During the fourth inning, Karen pitches a fastball to the batter who swings and hits a line drive right back at her. She tries to catch the ball but misses it, and gets hit in the abdomen with the ball. Karen immediately falls to the ground in pain. The coach runs out to check on Karen and finds her rolling from side to side on her back. Karen holds her arms in a crossed position over her abdomen to try and ease the pain. After about 1 minute, the coach gets her to calm down enough so that she could take a basic examination and try and figure out the SINS of the injury.

The coach begins her basic examination with the patient's history. She asks Karen the following questions: "What happened? Where are you hurt? What does the pain feel like?" Barely able to speak due to the pain and anxiety she is experiencing, Karen answers, "I was hit with the ball in the stomach" as she clutches the left side of her upper abdomen. Karen describes the pain as a sharp and says through the tears, "It really hurts!" While observing Karen, the coach sees that she is doubled over in pain. She asks her to point exactly where the pain is located. Karen, unable to stand up, slightly pulls up her shirt and clutches her upper left portion of her abdomen. The coach looks at her abdomen and notices that the injured area is slightly swollen and red. Suddenly, Karen says, "Coach I feel sick to my stomach." The coach noticed that Karen was beginning to turn pale. She put the back of their hand to Karen's forehead, which felt cold and clammy. Karen tells her coach that the pain is spreading up into her shoulder and she feels faint. The coach asks Karen, "Can I touch your abdomen and feel the area where you were hit?" Karen gives her coach permission to gently feel her stomach and notices that the area feels very rigid and warm. As the coach palpates her abdomen Karen yells out in pain. Karen's right wrist and finds that Karen has a rapid and weak radial pulse. At this point, Karen seems to be calming down, but is still holding her abdomen in significant pain while sitting on the ground. The coach is not sure what to do next. The coach does not want to further delay the game, so she helps Karen stand up and walk by herself to the dugout to relax. As the game continues, the coach keeps a watchful eye on Karen.

1. What should be the coach's next course of action to assist Karen?
2. Did the coach complete a thorough secondary survey? If no, then what else should the coach done to complete a thorough basic examination?
3. What injuries may Karen have sustained?
4. At any time during this scenario was Karen in a life-threatening situation, warranting the coach to take a primary survey?
5. What could Karen's coach have done to help improve Karen's condition?
6. Should the coach activate the EMS system? Why or why not?

References

Laskowski, E.R. (2020). Heart rate: What is normal? Retrieved July 12, 2021, from https://www.mayoclinic.org/healthy-lifestyle/fitness/expert-answers/heart-rate/faq-20057979

Mowalvi, A., Whiteman, J., Wilhelmi, B.J., Neumeister, M.W., & McLafferty, R. (2002). Dorsalis pedis arterial pulse: Palpation using a bony landmark. *Postgrad Med, 78*, 746-747. doi:10.1136/pmj.78.926.746

Pfeiffer, R. P., Mangus, B. C., & Trowbridge, C.A. (2015). Concepts of athletic training *(7th ed.)*. Sudbury, MA: Jones and Bartlett Learning.

Prentice, W.E. (2021). *Principles of athletic training: a competency-based approach (17th ed.)*. Champaign, IL: McGraw-Hill.

Schultz, S. J., Houglum, P. A., & Perrin, D. H. (2015). *Examination of musculoskeletal injuries (4th ed.)*. Champaign, IL: Human Kinetics.

Starkey, C. (Ed.). (2013). *Athletic training and sports medicine an integrated approach* (5th ed.). Burlington, MA: Jones and Bartlett Learning & American Academy of Orthopedic Surgeons.

Starkey, C., & Brown, S.D. (2015). *Examination of orthopedic and athletic injuries* (4th ed.). Philadelphia: FA Davis.

Whelton, P. K., Carey, R. M., Aronow, W. S., Casey, D. E., Collins, K. J., Dennison Himmelfarb, C., ... & Wright, J. T. (2018). 2017 ACC/AHA/AAPA/ABC/ACPM/AGS/APhA/ASH/ASPC/NMA/PCNA guideline for the prevention, detection, evaluation, and management of high blood pressure in adults: a report of the American College of Cardiology/American Heart Association Task Force on Clinical Practice Guidelines. *Journal of the American College of Cardiology*, 71(19), e127-e248. doi:10.1016/j.jacc.2017.11.006

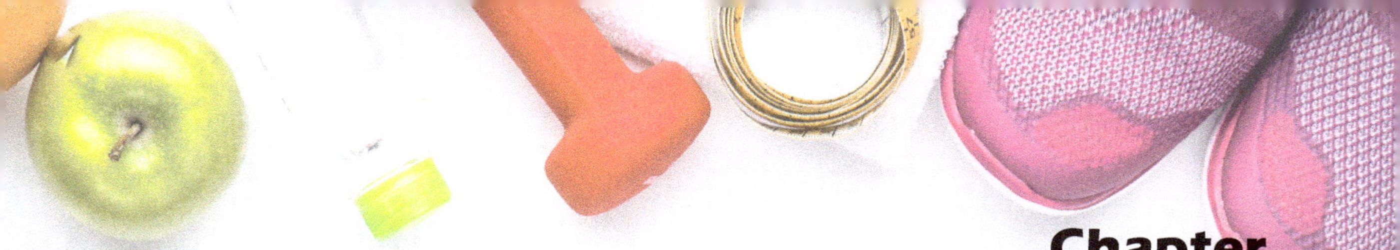

Chapter 9

The Head and Face

Chapter Objectives

After you have read this chapter, you will be able to understand:

- The mechanisms of injury, and signs and symptoms of a mild traumatic brain injury.
- The differences among intracerebral, epidural, and subdural bleeding.
- The emergent care for traumatic brain injury.
- The various facial fractures and specific signs and symptoms for each.
- The eye, nose, and ear injuries that require immediate emergency medical care.
- The various sideline and computer program tests that help you to determine if a patient has a concussion.
- How to determine whether an individual has uncomplicated epistaxis versus a brain injury.

Injuries to the head and face occur frequently, especially in activities where contact occurs among participants. Many of these injuries are severe and can be life threatening. Therefore, treat the person as if they have a cervical spine injury and maintain in-line stabilization until you determine that they have not sustained such an injury. Also, it is common practice to wear gloves when caring for an individual with a head or face injury, regardless of whether blood is present. Any possible contamination (e.g., dirt in the individual's eyes or mouth) must be avoided. As a sports medicine professional, your role is to determine the mechanism, or cause, of injury, recognize the signs and symptoms, provide immediate care to the individual, and identify if the injury warrants immediate medical referral. The care you give could save the person's life.

Injuries to the Head

Mild Traumatic Brain Injury (Cerebral Concussion)

Mild traumatic brain injury (MTBI) is also known as a cerebral concussion. The brain is jarred in the skull, which results in altered consciousness and neurological deficits. The injury is typically not life-threatening. For this reason, the injury is classified as a mild traumatic brain injury; however, the injury can be very serious and result in long-lasting signs and symptoms.

Mechanism or Cause of Injury

MTBI can be caused by a direct blow to the head, such as when a person hits their head against the wall when playing racquetball, or by a fall or force to the **core body**, which causes the jolting or jarring of the brain. As a result, the brain is damaged when it hits the skull. The impact force does not need to be significant for MBTI to occur.

The forces are either linear or rotational. A linear force involves a direct blow to the head. Typically, a blow to the forehead causes the brain to accelerate then decelerate. Coup and contrecoup injuries result. A coup injury occurs when the brain injury occurs at the impact site, while a contrecoup injury occurs on the opposite side of the impact. A contrecoup injury occurs because the brain is basically "floating" inside the skull **(Figure 9-1)**. A rotational force typically occurs with a blow to the side of the head. The cervical spine and head suddenly and violently rotate, causing a shearing brain injury. When the impact is one side of the head, the brain then moves to the opposite side of the skull and forcefully hits the skull bones, which results in the brain injury.

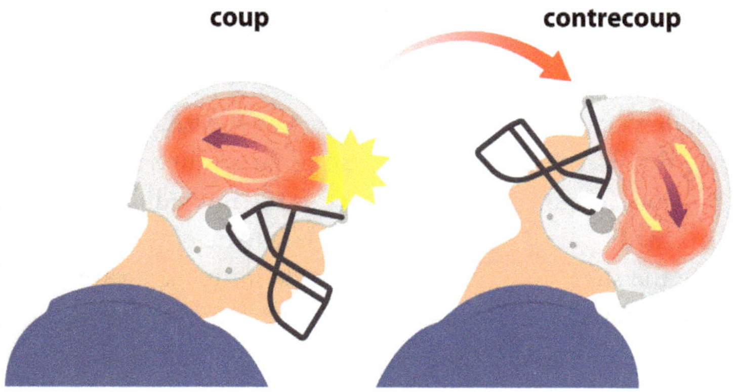

Figure 9-1 A coup and contrecoup injury to the brain

Signs and Symptoms

Signs and symptoms of MTBI can occur immediately or be delayed. The signs and symptoms can also last a very short amount of time (hours to days) or be prolonged (weeks or months). MBTI signs and symptoms include headache, tinnitus, nausea or vomiting, and sleepiness. The patient may have impaired cognitive or mental function, **retrograde amnesia**, **post-traumatic amnesia**, and inability to concentrate. Balance and coordination problems, along with changes in emotions, including sadness and irritability, may exist. They may complain of visual disturbances including blurred vision, **diplopia**, and **photophobia**. The patient may also have unequal pupil size. The eyes may be unable to move at the same rate or in a specific direction (up, down, or side-to-side). The patient may or may not have experienced loss of consciousness. They may say that they "blacked out" or "saw stars," which is indicative of a brief, temporary loss of consciousness.

Immediate Care

If you suspect that an individual has sustained a MTBI, remove them immediately from activity and have them rest. If you are unsure whether they have sustained a MBTI, perform some of the sideline tests noted in Tip from the Field 1. These tests will assist you in confirming if the individual has sustained a MTBI. For MTBI, and all injuries and illnesses where the individual is a minor, contact the parents or guardians immediately to inform them of their child's injury. Tell them what care you are presently giving their child, and if they need advanced medical care. When caring for an adult, ask them whether they wish you to inform anyone of their situation. If the individual has any MTBI signs and symptoms, refer them to a physician immediately for evaluation. Do not have them drive to the physician's office or ER. Instead, have another valid driver (i.e., parent, sibling, family member, or close friend) transport the individual. Call 911 if the individual has no means to get to his physician or ER, if the individual has suffered any loss of consciousness, or if the individual's signs or symptoms rapidly worsen.

When the individual returns to your facility, you cannot let them participate even if they claim their signs and symptoms of MTBI have resolved. You must abide by your employer's local, state, federal, and governing body protocols, as well as require written return to activity verification from the individual's physician for continued participation at your facility. Under no circumstances should you allow the individual to participate in activity without this written clearance.

As part of the patient's MTBI evaluation, the physician and other experts in the field of concussion management complete a variety of mental and physical tests. With this information, the patient's physician gives the patient a proper return to play timeline with guidelines. If the physician does not give you written return to activity guidelines, ask the patient for permission to contact the physician in order to obtain the patient's limitations for participation. Your patient will have to sign a Health Insurance Portability and Accountability Act (HIPAA) form

TIPS FROM THE FIELD

Tip 1 When you suspect a MTBI, you should test your patient's cognitive function to determine the extent of injury. Some quick "sideline" cognitive function tests include asking the patient to state the alphabet or the months of the year backwards. The "serial 7s" test has the patient add the number 7 then adding 7 and adding another 7, etc. (7+7=14+7=21 and so on) to test cognition. You can tell the patient 4 words to remember, then after five minutes ask the patient to repeat the words. You should ask them questions regarding orientation such as "Where are you?" and "Who is your competitor?" If the patient is not able to perform these tasks at a normal rate of speed or cannot perform them correctly, then you must suspect that the patient has a MTBI.

You can also administer the King-Devick test on the sidelines. You will write down a list of single digit numbers on an index card that the patient will read. As the patient reads the digits, if it takes a progressively longer time for the patient to read one number to the next then that is a positive sign that the patient has a concussion.

Other concussion testing involves athletes to perform various computerized programs. One such test is the popular Immediate Post-concussion Assessment and Cognitive Testing (ImPACT™) program (http://www.impacttest.com/) which is utilized to test athletes who have the potential of having a concussion. The test is given to the athletes as a baseline prior to injury, immediately after injury, and then throughout the healing process as one measure for return-to-play guidelines. Since this test is highly effective in determining and monitoring a patient's MTBI, the ImPACT™ test has been at the forefront of concussion testing in recent years at all levels of competition. Although the simple sideline tests for MTBI are effective in determining if a patient has sustained a MTBI, computerized testing is something you and your organization should consider if you work for an organization which works with athletes of all ages who are at a high risk of MTBI.

in the physician's office to give you access to their medical information. Likewise, ask the physician for information as to the appropriate intensity, frequency, and type of activities for the patient, which activities should be avoided, and the duration of the protocol. Be certain to utilize your expertise and judgment, along with research and the patient's needs, to determine the patient's return to play activities. The *National Athletic Trainers' Association Position Statement: Management of Sport-Related Concussion* thoroughly describes MTBI with proper concussion management and detailed return to activity guidelines (Broglio et al., 2014).

Prevention

Prevention of MTBI includes having an athletic participant wear appropriately fitted and safe equipment, such as headgear and helmets, during activities as required. Mouth guards can assist in minimizing MTBI injury by distributing forces away from the head when the jaw has succumbed to a direct blow. Mouth guards can be purchased over the counter or be custom made. An athletic participant needs a mouth guard with a secure fit to protect against injury. Some over-the-counter mouth guards are moldable (utilizing hot water) to fit the participant's teeth. Custom-made mouth guards can be made by a dentist. These mouth guards provide the best fit, allow for the most nondisruptive breathing, and are generally most comfortable for the participant. Athletes must be taught how to properly perform their skills and adhere to their instructors' directions while participating in activities, so they do not get hurt. Activity areas must be kept safe and free from potential hazards (Center for Disease Control [CDC], 2021).

Second Impact Syndrome

Second impact syndrome occurs when a patient's brain rapidly swells, bleeds significantly, and herniates due to a second cerebral concussion, typically while the patient was still experiencing signs and symptoms of the previous cerebral concussion. Brain herniation occurs when the brain tissue is forced out of normal position due to brain swelling and increased skull pressure. In severe cases, death can occur within 2 to 5 minutes, with no time for advanced medical personnel to assist the injured patient (May, Foris, & Donnally, 2021).

Mechanism or Cause of Injury

Second impact syndrome can occur from a blow or jarring force to the head. The patient still is experiencing signs and symptoms when the second impact occurs. When the second impact occurs, the patient is experiencing signs and symptoms from a previous concussion. The second blow or jarring force does not need to be as forceful as the first concussive blow to the head to cause injury. The impact may be extremely mild, which may not raise a concern at the time.

Signs and Symptoms

Athletes experiencing second impact syndrome produces signs and symptoms of injury that include those of a MTBI, such as headache, nausea or vomiting, fatigue, disorientation, memory problems, and loss of consciousness.

Immediate Care

Due to the life-threatening nature of second impact syndrome, call 911 immediately. Monitor the patient and make sure their airway is open and that they are breathing. If they are not breathing, administer cardiopulmonary resuscitation (CPR). Maintain in-line stabilization until emergency medical services (EMS) arrives, and do not move the patient unless absolutely necessary (i.e., your lives are in danger). If the patient vomits while you are maintaining in-line stabilization, roll the patient on their side as a unit with the assistance of bystanders and clear their airway. Make sure the patient is breathing on their own. Again, if they are not breathing, then you must administer CPR. For these severe injuries, always treat the patient for shock.

Prevention

The first course of action to prevent second impact syndrome is to not allow a concussed patient to return to activity who has not been cleared by their physician (as discussed with MTBI). A patient may feel that their concussion has resolved because they no longer have signs and symptoms of MTBI at rest. However, if when exercising, the concussion signs and symptoms reappear, then the patient should not participate in athletic activities. If you suspect the patient is experiencing MTBI signs and symptoms, even though they have been formally cleared by their physician, remove the patient from activity immediately. Refer the patient back to their physician right away, and do not allow them to participate until cleared again by the physician.

Cerebral Contusion (Intracerebral Bleeding)

A cerebral contusion is a brain injury in which the brain is bruised, intracerebral bleeding occurs, and blood leaks into the brain tissue. More than one area of bleeding can occur in the brain, depending on where the contusion occurs. The bleeding may be superficial or deep.

Mechanism or Cause of Injury

A blow to the head from an object, a motor vehicle crash, or a fall with the head striking the floor or a stationary object can cause a cerebral contusion. The cerebral contusion may be a coup or contrecoup injury.

Signs and Symptoms

Blood vessels are torn and swelling occurs with a cerebral contusion, so many of the neurological deficits seen in MTBI and second impact syndrome occur. The patient may have emotional changes, including irritability, agitation, or restlessness. They may complain of headache, dizziness, or nausea. The patient may vomit, have memory difficulty, amnesia, loss of motor function and coordination, and sensory deficits. The signs and symptoms may last for hours or, in more severe cases, for weeks. Severe contusions may cause brain herniation and death.

Immediate Care

If you suspect that your patient has a mild cerebral contusion, refer them to a physician for immediate evaluation. If the patient shows significant signs and symptoms of a cerebral contusion, or his injury status is progressively decreasing, you must call 911 immediately. Maintain in-line stabilization if the patient shows neurological or functional impairment. The patient must be transported immediately to the emergency room. Monitor the patient's airway and breathing, and be prepared to give CPR if necessary. If the patient vomits, clear his airway as previously discussed. Make sure that the patient's parents or guardians are notified if the patient is a minor.

Prevention

In attempt to prevent cerebral contusion, the patient must wear protective headgear appropriate for the athletic participant's activity. Make sure the participant follows safety rules when participating in activities where the potential for a blow to the head exists (i.e., no diving into the shallow end of a pool). Likewise, make sure your participant is aware of their surroundings at all times when participating in these activities.

Epidural Hematoma

An epidural hematoma is a traumatic brain injury that occurs when an artery or vein is damaged, and blood accumulates between the skull and the dura mater (the outer most membrane of the brain) **(Figure 9-2)**. The blood accumulates rapidly, within a few minutes to hours post-injury. Most injuries occur to younger people versus adults because the dura mater is not attached as well to the skull bones in children and teenagers as it is in adults.

Mechanism or Cause of Injury

A direct blow causing a skull fracture can cause an epidural hematoma. Often the injury occurs in car and motorcycle accidents. Epidural hematomas are not as common in athletic activities.

Signs and Symptoms

The signs and symptoms of an epidural hematoma are similar to MTBI and other head injuries. The patient may complain of a severe headache, dizziness, confusion, and nausea. You may see that the patient has one dilated pupil on the side of the injury (Khairat & Waseem, 2021). It is common that the patient will have loss of consciousness, then become alert, then become unconscious again.

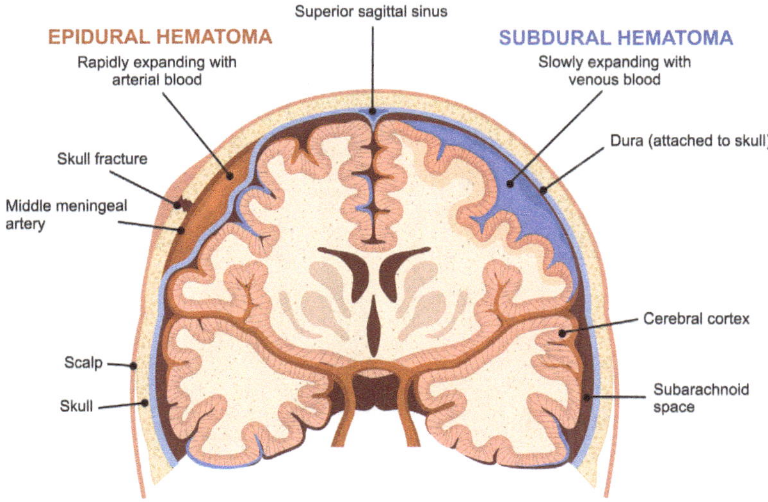

Figure 9-2 An epidural hematoma occurs between the dura mater and the skull, whereas a subdural hematoma occurs between the dura mater and the brain.

Immediate Care

This injury is a medical emergency. Rapid hemorrhage and swelling on the brain cause drowsiness that can progress to coma and death. Consequently, care must be immediate. Your role is to summon EMS and take care of any life-threatening conditions. Maintain head and neck in-line stabilization. The patient may vomit; if so, while maintaining in-line stabilization, log roll the patient on their side and clear their airway. Make sure they are breathing, and administer CPR if necessary. Once the patient is transported to the ER, they will most likely have emergency surgery to drill a hole in the skull, which relieves pressure in the brain (Abdelmalik, Draghic, & Ling 2019). Even though the patient receives immediate care, it is common for future complications from the injury to arise, such as loss of function and seizures.

Prevention

Prevention of epidural hematomas is the same course of action as for MTBIs and cerebral contusions. An athletic participant must wear appropriate head protection, wear seat and other belts securely during activity (i.e. race car driving), perform their skills properly, follow safety rules, and pay attention to their surroundings including any potential dangers to the participants' head.

Subdural Hematoma

A subdural hematoma is a rapid accumulation of blood on the brain. The blood fills in the brain tissue quickly and compresses the brain **(Figure 9-3)**. Subdural hematomas are either acute or chronic. An acute subdural hematoma is life-threatening, whereas a chronic subdural hematoma may not be life-threatening. This injury is one of the most serious brain injuries. The mortality rate for subdural hematoma victims is approximately 60% (Meagher & Young, 2018). Even if treated, a subdural hematoma can cause future neurological complications.

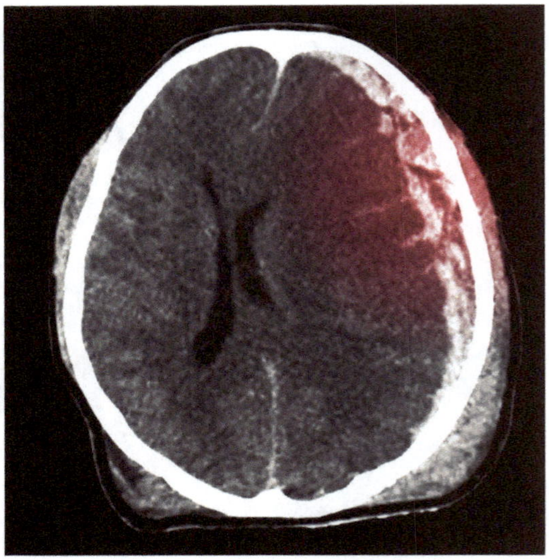

Figure 9-3 Subdural hematoma

Mechanism or Cause of Injury

An acute subdural hematoma is caused by a serious head injury. Chronic subdural hematomas most often occur with a very mild head injury to an elderly person or someone who is taking **anticoagulant drugs**.

Signs and Symptoms

With an acute subdural hematoma, the blood fills the brain rapidly, which causes immediate signs and symptoms of injury. With a chronic subdural hematoma, the blood fills the brain much slower than with an acute subdural hematoma. Consequently, the signs and symptoms of a chronic subdural hematoma may not occur for days. Many of the same signs and symptoms of injury occur with both acute and chronic subdural hematomas, as with the other brain injuries. The patient may have the following signs and symptoms of injury: a headache, confusion, slurred speech, loss of balance, loss of consciousness, disorientation and confusion, memory loss, visual problems, weakness, fatigue, nausea, and vomiting. Elderly patients with a chronic subdural hematoma will show significant mental decline, including loss of memory, over a few days.

Immediate Care

If you suspect a subdural hematoma, you must summon EMS immediately. With a head injury of this severity, assume that the patient may also have a spinal injury. Therefore, keep their head and neck still and maintain in-line stabilization until EMS arrives. Always monitor the patient's airway, breathing, and circulation (ABCs) and be prepared to administer CPR if necessary. The patient may vomit; if they do, maintain in-line stabilization, log roll the patient as a unit, clear their airway, and determine if they are breathing. If they are not breathing, administer CPR.

Prevention

As with other head injuries, instruct your patient to take precautions to avoid the potential of sustaining a subdural hematoma. Your patient must abide by safety measures at all facilities and venues, wear appropriately fitted headgear and safety belts for activities as required, and pay attention to their body while participating in activities to avoid falls.

Skull Fractures

Although the skull bones are particularly strong in adults, skull fractures can occur in conjunction with one of the other traumatic head injuries. These fractures are particularly serious if the skull bones enter into the brain tissue. Various types of skull fractures exist including a simple, linear, depressed, and compound fracture (Medline Plus, 2019). A simple fracture is a break in the skull without any further damage to the skin or underlying structures (i.e., brain, meninges). A linear fracture is classified as a break in a line-type fashion without any other damage to the underlying structures. The bone does not splinter and is not otherwise deformed. A depressed fracture is classified by crushing of the skull bones, which become impacted down into the brain tissue. A compound fracture is when the skull bones break through the skin and cause external bleeding.

Mechanism or Cause of Injury

Skull fractures can occur with any head injury where there is a significant blow to the head. Although this severe head impact does not happen commonly in general exercise and athletic activities, the mechanism of injury likely occurs more frequently in contact sports such as boxing, ice hockey, and football, even though in some of these sports athletes wear headgear. Skull fractures are more often as a result of in car and motorcycle accidents, falling from a height, and been a part of a physical attack (i.e., fist fighting).

Signs and Symptoms

Patients with skull fractures may experience any signs and symptoms of head injuries previously discussed. Additional signs and symptoms that may exist with a skull fracture include external head bleeding, bruising behind the ears (Battle's sign) **(Figure 9-4)** or under the eyes (raccoon eyes) **(Figure 9-5)**. Also, cerebrospinal fluid (CSF), a clear fluid mixed with blood, may come out of the ears or nose. CSF bathes the brain and spinal cord. If CSF is coming from the ears or nose, then the skull injury is significant and most likely a depressed fracture.

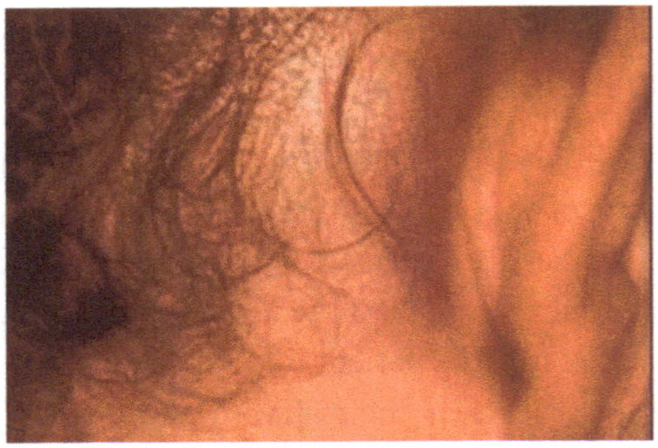

Figure 9-4 Battle's sign is indicative of a brain hemorrhage.
Source: medlineplus.gov

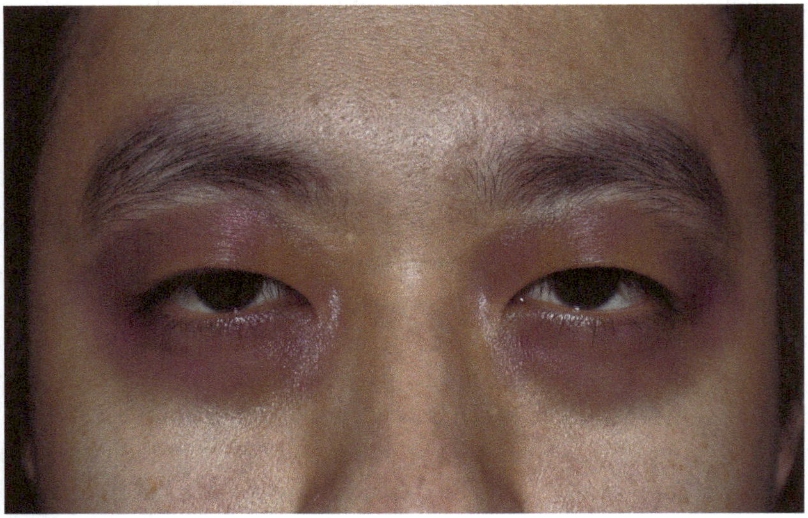

Figure 9-5 Raccoon eyes are a sign of a brain hemorrhage.

Immediate Care

Skull fractures are serious, potentially life-threatening injuries. Therefore, call 911 immediately. If the person is unconscious, maintain in-line stabilization and check their airway and breathing. Administer CPR if they are not breathing. If the injury is a compound fracture, apply gloves, and then place bulky sterile gauze dressings, a clean cloth, or any clean, absorbent items on the wound site. Be very careful not apply pressure to the injured area. Pressure on the injured area may force the fractured bones into the brain tissue. If the dressings become saturated, do not remove them. Instead, place more clean dressings on top of the saturated dressings. If you remove the saturated dressings, the bleeding may resume if you have previously stopped it, or continue to flow and lead to greater blood loss. If an object is protruding from the skull, do not remove it. Attempt to stabilize the object by placing clean bulky dressings around the object, and keep it still until EMS arrives. Do not move the patient unless a dire emergency presents itself in which your life or the patient's is in grave danger. If the victim vomits, log roll them while maintaining in-line stabilization in order to clear the airway. After their airway is clear, log roll them onto their back and check to see if they are breathing. If they are not breathing, administer CPR. Monitor the patient closely until EMS arrives.

TIPS FROM THE FIELD

TIP 2 In order to determine if the fluid coming from the nose is only blood from a minor nosebleed, or if it is CSF along with blood which would indicate a head or brain tissue injury, you can examine the fluid on a piece of gauze. Put on gloves and take a piece of gauze that has blood from the nose on it and put it aside. CSF and blood are like oil and vinegar, in that CSF separates from blood. The CSF will be apparent as a straw-colored "halo" or a ring surrounding the blood spot on the gauze. If CSF is present, then the injury is a medical emergency, and you must call 911 to summon EMS.

Prevention

As with other head injury prevention tactics, athletic participants must be aware of their surroundings when participating in activities, abide by activity and facility rules, and wearing appropriate headgear, equipment, and seat and safety belts.

Lacerations and Incisions

Scalp lacerations and incisions, as well as lacerations to the brain tissue, can occur with athletic activity **(Figure 9-6)**. The scalp has many blood vessels. Consequently, a very minor scalp laceration or incision may bleed significantly. This bleeding creates the appearance of a major wound. Whenever the scalp is bleeding, suspect an additional head injury involving the brain. Lacerations to the brain (cerebral lacerations) can occur if a skull bone is fractured and splinters or is depressed.

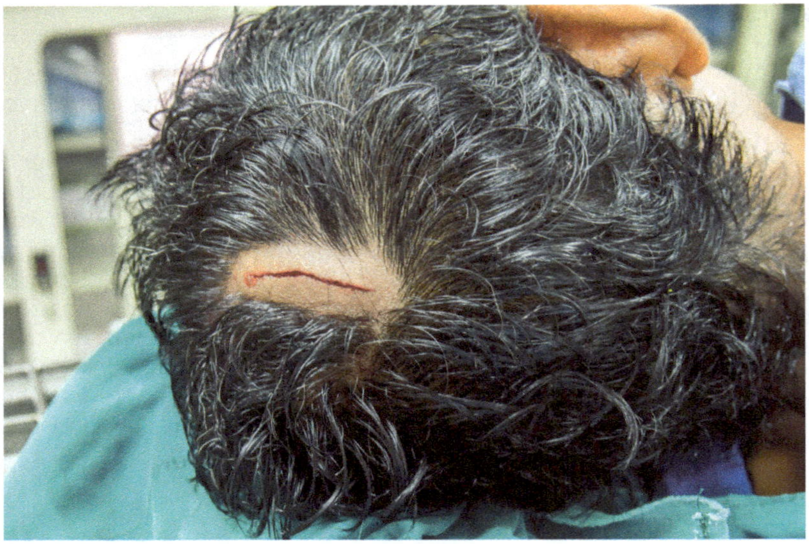

Figure 9-6 Scalp laceration

Mechanism or Cause of Injury

Scalp wounds and cerebral lacerations typically occur due to a direct blow to the head by an object to the head.

Signs and Symptoms

Other than bleeding, a protruding object and other signs and symptoms of head injuries may exist. The predominance of signs and symptoms will help you determine if the injury is a scalp wound versus a cerebral laceration. If the signs and symptoms are similar to those of head injuries, then the wound may be a cerebral laceration. If the patient is bleeding, no other signs or symptoms exist, and the mechanism of injury was a mild force, then the wound is most likely a surface laceration or incision.

Immediate Care

Whether the wound is a surface laceration or incision, immediately control bleeding. Utilize your personal protective equipment (PPE) and apply gentle pressure on the wound to stop the bleeding, without pressing down into the skull. Utilize clean, bulky dressings (sterile dressings if available), and hold it on the wound. As previously mentioned, apply additional dressings if the blood soaks through the first dressings. Do not remove the saturated dressings. If you suspect a cerebral laceration, provide immediate care as per the other severe head injuries. Call 911 immediately, maintain in-line stabilization, be ready to give CPR if necessary, and monitor the patient for consciousness, airway, and breathing until EMS arrives. If the patient's only sign of injury is bleeding, indicating a superficial laceration or incision, after about 15 minutes of applying gentle pressure on the wound, remove the dressing and see if the bleeding has stopped. If the bleeding has not stopped, then continue applying gentle pressure for another 15 minutes. Repeat the application of pressure dressings until the bleeding has stopped. If the bleeding does not stop, or other signs and symptoms of injury arise, then call 911 immediately. However, once the bleeding has stopped, bandage the wound.

Many scalp lacerations and incisions may need sutures if the wound is deep, or the skin edges do not approximate (i.e. come in line together). Sutures are also useful to secure the wound because Steri-Strips ™, butterfly, or other wound closing bandages are difficult to use on the scalp due to the patient's hair. A liquid bandage can be useful for these lacerations. Liquid bandages are clear, adherent gels or sprays that are applied directly to the wound. These liquid bandages are sold over-the-counter and are commonly utilized by physicians in place of sutures. The benefits of liquid bandages are that they seal the wound shut, prevent pathogens from entering the wound, and maintain an environment conducive to healing. Most often, the patient needs to see a physician immediately to have a liquid bandage or sutures applied.

Prevention

Athletic participants can prevent scalp lacerations and incisions and cerebral lacerations by wearing appropriate protective head equipment, performing proper activity skills, and being aware of their surroundings.

Migraines

Migraines are severely painful headaches. Many individuals will experience intense throbbing in the head. According to the Mayo Clinic (2021), these headaches typically occur with nausea, vomiting, sensitivity to light and sound, and visual disturbances. The migraine can last for hours to days. The extent and frequency of the migraine varies from person to person.

Mechanism or Cause of Injury

Migraines in biological women can be caused by hormone imbalance, especially estrogen. Some people may also be genetically predisposed to migraines (Ling et al., 2019). Additionally, various triggers can bring on migraines, including stress, sleep deprivation, intense physical activity for which the a person is not accustomed, foods and substances including chocolate, caffeine, and alcohol, and environmental changes such as going to a higher or lower altitude where pressure changes, or changes in weather. Smoking also triggers migraines (Hagen et al., 2018).

Signs and Symptoms

Migraines can arise suddenly and affect an individual in an instant. An individual may have indications a couple days before the migraine attacks that warn them the migraine is coming. Indications that the person is going to be inflicted by a migraine include hyperactivity, irritability, depression, food cravings, and either constipation or diarrhea. Individuals may also experience an aura before the migraine. An aura may include visualizing spots or flashes of light in their vision, vision loss, speech difficulty, and tingling in the hands or feet. Each of these symptoms may last up to a half an hour. The typical migraine signs and symptoms include throbbing pain in the head, which occurs on one or both sides, sensitivity to light and sound, lightheadedness, disturbed vision, and nausea and vomiting.

Immediate Care

When a client or athlete complains of a migraine, have them stop activity and rest. If they have experienced migraines before and have already been evaluated by a physician for migraines, they will most likely know what to do to alleviate the migraine and/or administer medication. If the individual has never experienced a migraine, then assist them in alleviating the symptoms. A migraine can be eliminated if they lie down in a quiet room with their eyes closed. If they know what triggered the migraine, make sure the trigger is removed or stopped (e.g., if the person is intensely exercising or drinking caffeinated coffee, have them stop exercising and drink noncaffeinated beverages immediately). Refer the individual to their primary care physician or neurologist for evaluation. The physician can give them medication to reduce the incidence of or prevent migraines. The individual also should participate in stress reduction activities if stress is a trigger for their migraines.

Do not let the individual drive if they are experiencing a severe migraine that does not allow normal function or is disturbing their vision. Instead, have a valid driver take the individual to their physician or the ER if necessary. If the individual experiences the migraine with neck stiffness, severe vomiting or diarrhea, a fever, neurological deficits, or any other significant worrisome signs and symptoms, summon EMS. In these cases, the migraine may be indicative of a more severe illness or condition.

Prevention

In order to prevent migraines, the individual must be aware of the triggers that cause their migraines and eliminate them if possible. If stress is a trigger, they should participate in mental stress reduction exercises and physical stress reduction techniques such as body massages, physical activity, and exercise. The individual should get plenty of sleep, and avoid caffeine, alcohol, and smoking. Medications can be prescribed by a physician that are either pain-eliminating medications, which are utilized if an individual sustains a migraine, or preventative medications, which are used to deter migraines. If the individual has been prescribed migraine medication by their physician, the individual must take the prescription as directed.

Injuries to the Face

Facial injuries occur to the face, eyes, nose, and ears. These injuries occur most frequently during activities where the face is unprotected. These injuries can be minor, such as an insignificant nosebleed, to severe, such as an orbital fracture. In some instances, depending on the severity, irritability, nature, and stage (SINS) of the injury, the injury may be treated with first aid; however, in other instances EMS must be summoned for advanced medical care.

Facial Injuries

Facial Fractures Including Zygomatic, Maxilla, and Mandible Fractures

Fractures to the bones of the face typically occur to the zygomatic bone (cheekbone), maxilla (the mid-portion of the face above and around the top lip), and mandible (jawbone). Although the mechanism of injury may be the same for these facial bone fractures, some signs and symptoms of injury vary.

Mechanism or Cause of Injury

Most facial fractures occur in motor vehicle crashes, sport activities, falls, and physical assaults. The specific mechanism of injury is a direct, traumatic impact to the face.

Signs and Symptoms

Some signs and symptoms are similar for all facial areas whereas others are specific to the fractured bone. Common signs and symptoms of facial fractures include pain, deformity, ecchymosis, swelling, inward depression of the bone, and lacerations. Specific signs and symptoms of a zygomatic fracture include visual disturbances, cheek flatness, abnormal sensations, and blood in the eye on the injured side **(Figure 9-7)**. A patient with a maxillary fracture has **malocclusion**, visual disturbances, clear fluid coming from the nose, and difficulty breathing. Mandible fractures cause jaw pain and bruising under the tongue. Malocclusion may be a sign of injury for a mandible fracture as well as a maxillary fracture.

Immediate Care

Any suspected fracture to the face warrants immediate medical care. Summon EMS immediately because facial fractures can disrupt breathing or vision. Likewise, the patient may go into shock. Keep the patient as still as possible and treat them for shock. You can gently apply a small

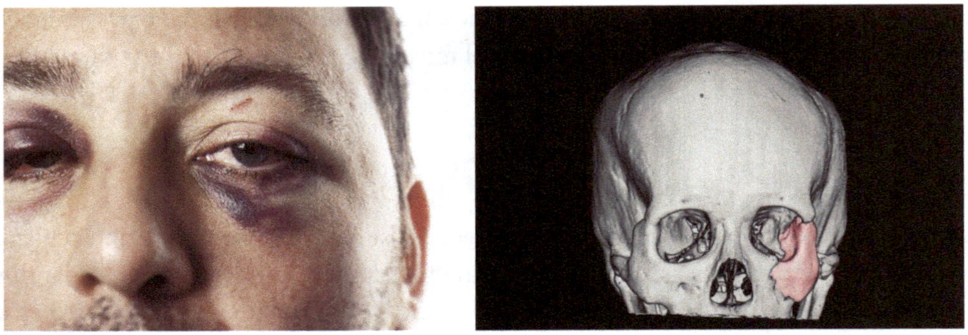

Figure 9-7 When fractured, the bones of the face show varying signs of injury. A zygomatic fracture exhibits ecchymosis and flattened cheekbone.

ice bag to the area, while being careful not to cause further harm by moving or applying pressure to the fractured bones. If the patient has sustained a laceration that is bleeding, use your PPE and gently place clean dressings, preferably sterile gauze, on the open wound to control the bleeding. If the patient has **epistaxis**, control the bleeding by placing gauze or an absorbent dressing up the patient's bleeding nostrils and gently pinch the area just below the bridge of the nose. Have the patient keep their head forward when he has a nosebleed. If they lean their head backward, they may swallow blood (See the section on "Epistaxis (Nosebleed)" for further information on treating nosebleeds). Remain with the patient and monitor them until EMS arrives.

Prevention

Preventing facial fractures includes wearing appropriate face masks, as worn during ice hockey and football activities, as well as avoiding any direct trauma to the face, such as a hit by a fist. Make sure your athletic participant is aware of any safety measures and policies that they must take when participating in physical activity.

Lacerations and Incisions

Facial lacerations and incisions occur to an unprotected face. Lacerations and incisions may be superficial or deep. Deep lacerations and incisions may involve the underlying structures such as muscles, tendons, nerves, and blood vessels. As with any other open wound, significant bleeding and infection are two primary concerns when a person has sustained a laceration or incision.

Mechanism or Cause of Injury

Trauma from impact or a direct blow to the face can cause a laceration or incision. Another mechanism of injury is from an object rubbing and compressing against the skin, such as another athletic participant's fingernail, jewelry, or exercise equipment. Often, the skin is lacerated in conjunction with another injury such as a facial fracture.

Signs and Symptoms

The typical signs and symptoms of open wounds are present for facial lacerations and incisions. Bleeding, pain, swelling, point tenderness, ecchymosis, and redness are some of the signs and symptoms of injury. If the wound becomes infected, then additional signs of fever, increasing redness at the wound site, and pus discharge will be evident.

Immediate Care

Sometimes wounds heal with excessive scaring or keloids, whether or not appropriate care was rendered **(Figure 9-8)**. The scarring would potentially alter the patient's facial appearance. Therefore, proper treatment for facial wounds is critical. To begin caring for the facial wound, put on gloves to stop the bleeding utilizing sterile gauze and direct pressure on the wound site. Once the bleeding has stopped, clean the wound with soap and water. Bandage the wound and refer the patient to a physician or the ER to be sutured. You can apply ice to the area to decrease pain and swelling. Keep in mind that lacerations and incisions must be sutured to encourage proper healing, avoid infection, and avoid undue scar tissue. Refer the patient to their physician's office or to the ER to have the wound sutured immediately. Depending on the extent of the wound, the physician may prescribe antibiotics, pain medication, and/or a tetanus vaccination.

Prevention

In order to prevent lacerations and incisions to the face, your athletic participant must protect their face by wearing facial equipment such as face masks **(Figure 9-9)**, goggles, and the like are required for the particular activity. The patient should pay particular attention to objects

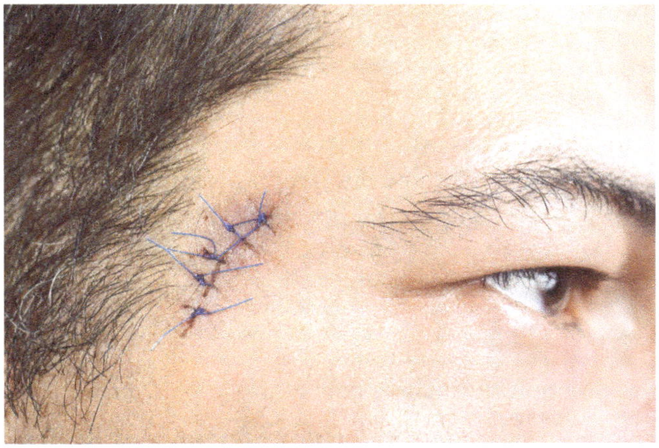

Figure 9-8 Facial laceration should be sutured to ensure proper healing and minimal scarring.

Figure 9-9 Equipment that has cages, such as an ice hockey helmet, will protect the face from injury.

that can strike the face during activity, including implements such as racquetball rackets, hockey sticks, or balls, weights, and so on. Athletic participants need to be cognizant and be aware of their surroundings.

Temporal Mandibular Joint (TMJ) Dysfunction

The temporal mandibular joint (TMJ) is located in front of the ears, and can be palpated when opening and closing the jaw. Similarly to any other joint, the TMJ can become inflamed and painful with overuse. Although rare, the joint can also be dislocated.

Mechanism or Cause of Injury

TMJ dysfunction is common in people who open and close their mouths often, such as frequent chewing gum, or keep it in an open position for a period of time, such as when mouth breathing while sleeping. A direct blow to the jaw or TMJ can also create inflammation or dislocation.

Signs and Symptoms

TMJ dysfunction signs and symptoms include pain at the joint, decreased jaw motion, inability to close the mouth (predominantly with a dislocation), joint clicking and popping, and jaw and face musculature stiffness. The jaw may also appear to be positioned off-center to the face.

Immediate Care

If the TMJ dysfunction is acute, have the patient rest the jaw by not chewing gum, talking, or opening the mouth. Apply ice to the TMJ. The patient can take over-the-counter non-steroidal anti-inflammatory drugs (NSAIDs), such as ibuprofen or naproxen, for pain and inflammation. If the signs and symptoms do not subside with discontinuation of the causative factor and treatment, or the patient has frequent bouts of TMJ pain, clicking, popping, and stiffness, then refer them to a physician for evaluation. The physician may give the patient prescription anti-inflammatory drugs for TMJ dysfunction flare-ups, as well as have the patient obtain a custom-made mouthpiece to wear while sleeping, while also deterring clenching and grinding of the teeth, which can precipitate TMJ dysfunction. Facial massage also decreases facial muscular tension, which is affects the TMJ. If the TMJ is dislocated, care for the patient by calling 911, checking breathing, treating for shock, splinting the area around the head and jaw, and applying ice.

Prevention

TMJ dysfunction can be prevented if a patient pays particular attention to what he does with his jaw in regard to opening and closing it frequently. The patient should avoid chewing gum and hard foods that cause continual and forceful mouth opening and closing. If the patient yawns frequently due to fatigue, they should make a conscious effort to get more sleep. The patient should avoid clenching their teeth, and alleviate any stress by utilizing stress reduction techniques and massage.

Eye Injuries and Conditions

Orbital Fracture

Six bones around the eye that make up the orbit - the frontal, lacrimal, ethmoidal, sphenoid, maxilla, and zygomatic bones. An orbital fracture is break in any of these bones. Blowout fractures are fractures to the thin, bony orbital floor.

Mechanism or Cause of Injury

Orbital fractures are caused by a direct blow to the bones surrounding the eye. A significant amount of force is required to break the bones around the orbit. Consequently, if the orbit is fractured, suspect that the patient has sustained a head injury also. The bones can be broken via impact from a baseball, a fist, a crash, a dumbbell, or any hard object that impacts the orbit with force. A mechanism of injury for a blowout fracture is considered indirect because the object causing the trauma does not directly strike the floor of the orbit. A common mechanism of injury for a blowout fracture is when the orbit is struck by an object that is larger than the eye itself, such as a baseball. As a result of the impact force, the orbital floor breaks.

Signs and Symptoms

Signs and symptoms of orbital fractures will vary depending on which of the six orbital bones is fractured (**Figure 9-10**). If the zygomatic bone is fractured, then the patient will have a flat cheek on the injured side. If the frontal bone is fractured, the bone will be flat, or may have a lump at the injured area due to swelling. Patients with orbital blowout fractures will also experience diplopia, sensation problems below the affected eye, and the inability to look upward. For all orbital fractures, the patient can experience signs and symptoms such as a sunken or bulging eye, the inability to look in various directions, blurred vision, swelling, deformity, raccoon eyes, and bleeding from lacerations.

Immediate Care

Fractures of the orbit are medical emergencies. Call 911 immediately to summon EMS. While you are waiting for EMS to arrive, treat the patient for shock and control any bleeding. Carefully and gently put a small ice pack on the area but not directly on the eye. If you utilize a small ice bag to alleviate pain and swelling, do not press hard on the area because you do not want to move the fractured bones and cause further harm. Also, remember that the eyes move simultaneously, so if one eye is injured and the other eye moves, the patient's injured eye can be further harmed. Therefore, if the patient is having pain when moving the eyes, bandage both eyes to prevent the eyes from moving.

Prevention

Educate your patient on the importance of wearing protective eye wear while participating in activities. Individuals are often not required to wear goggles when playing racquetball, but the

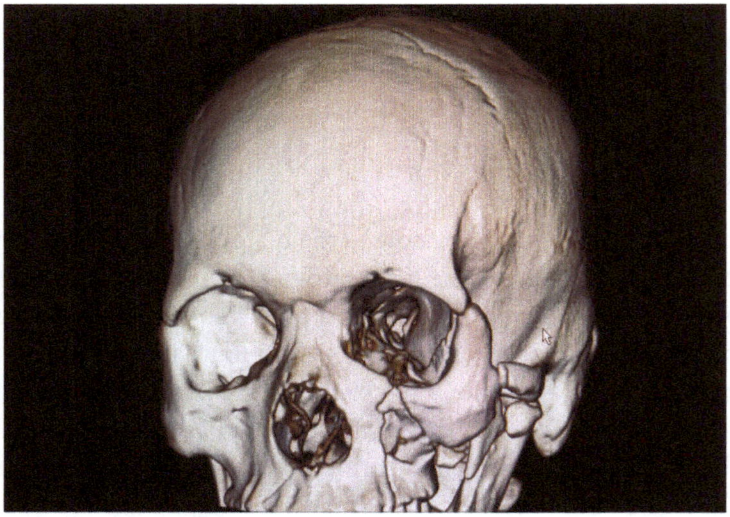

Figure 9-10 Orbital, zygomatic, and maxilla fracture

goggles can prevent the ball from striking the orbital area and causing a fracture. Face shields can also assist in the prevention of work-related orbital fractures from flying objects. Provide the recommendation that all individuals should wear seat and safety belts, even in the back seat of motor vehicles, to avoid or diminish the severity of facial injuries during accidents.

Hyphema

A hyphema is blood that accumulates in the anterior chamber of the eye. The anterior chamber is the area between the cornea and the iris (**Figure 9-11**).

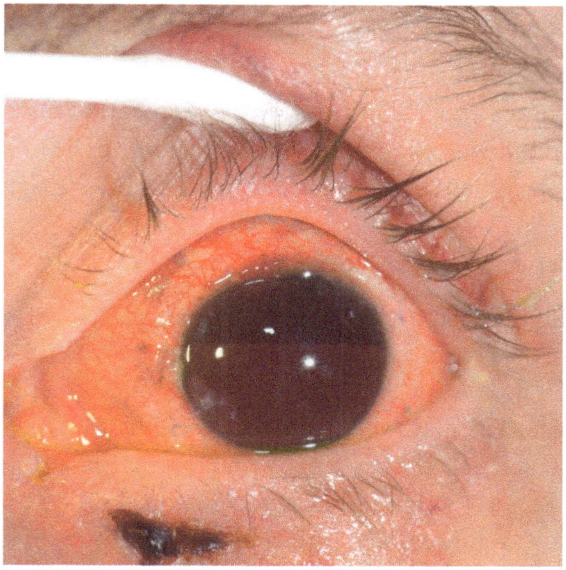

Figure 9-11 Hyphema

Mechanism or Cause of Injury

The typical mechanism of injury is a direct blow to the eye. An object, such as a finger, fist, stick, or athletic implement, strikes the eye causing trauma. A hyphema can also be caused by an individual striking their head or eye on an object, such as the ground, due to a fall.

Signs and Symptoms

The primary sign of injury is blood accumulating in the eye's anterior chamber. The blood may not accumulate immediately, but can develop over a couple of days as inflammation progresses. If the injury is significant, the blood accumulates in the anterior chamber, and fills from the bottom up due to gravity. Consequently, the blood may rise to the pupil. The blood can block some or all vision, depending on the how much blood accumulates in the anterior chamber. The individual would see the red color from the blood in front of the pupil. The individual will have pain, light sensitivity, and blurred vision.

Immediate Care

A hyphema necessitates urgent medical care. Refer the individual to their ophthalmologist immediately. If the individual is unable to be evaluated by their physician, have them transported to the ER by calling 911, and treat them for shock.

Prevention

Appropriate safety eyewear can prevent a hyphema. Also, individuals should be aware of their surroundings, so they can potentially minimize the incidence of unfortunate falls or accidents.

Retinal Detachment

The retina is tissue in the back of the eye that helps us to see images that pass through the eye's cornea and lens. The retina passes the image to the optic nerve. The image is then transmitted to the brain, which allows us to visualize the image. The retina can become separated from its attachment on the back of the eye and cause significant visual problems.

Mechanism or Cause of Injury

Retinal detachment can be caused by a variety of mechanisms of injury. In addition, certain people are at risk for retinal detachment. Retinal detachment appears to be hereditary. Therefore, a person is at risk for retinal detachment if they have an immediately family member who has had a detached retina. Individuals who are older, have very bad nearsightedness, uncontrolled diabetes, chronic retinal inflammation; or previous retinal surgery are also at more at risk for retinal detachment (National Eye Institute, 2020). Individuals can experience retinal detachment if they have a hole in their retina. Fluid leaks out of the hole and causes a bubble to form under the retina. Consequently, the retina is pulled off its underlying structural attachment **(Figure 9-12)**. The retina can be detached by direct trauma to the orbit or a blow to the head, which causes a concurrent MTBI.

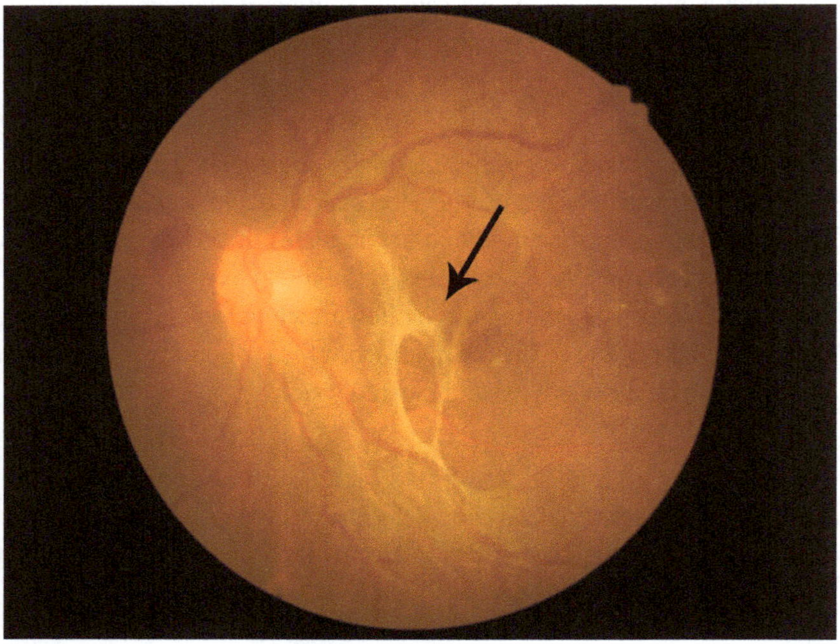

Figure 9-12 Retinal detachment

Signs and Symptoms

A person who is experiencing retinal detachment will complain of bright flashes of light, floating spots in their field of vision, blurred or partially lost vision, and visualization that a black curtain is coming down in front of their eye.

Immediate Care

If an individual complains of these symptoms, refer them to an ophthalmologist for further evaluation. The individual must see their physician within 24 hours after symptoms appear. The individual cannot drive while experiencing these symptoms, so another valid driver must take them to the physician. The physician will perform various eye tests, including those to check retina function, visual acuity, the ability to detect various colors, and pressure within the eye. Surgery to repair the retina will often be necessary. However, depending on the area and extent of injury, surgery may not be a viable option.

Prevention

If a person is at risk for retinal detachment, they should take every effort to minimize the potential for acquiring this condition. Obviously, an individual cannot affect their heredity, but they can be proactive in decreasing other risk factors. For example, if a person is diabetic, they should carefully control their disease with diet, exercise, and prescribed insulin. Age is a risk factor for retinal detachment, but if a person takes good care of their body, including yearly eye exams, and has a good quality of wellness and fitness, age-related risk factors can be minimized. Also, wearing protective eyewear during athletic participation, as appropriate for the specific activity, can reduce risk of injury.

Corneal Abrasion

The cornea is the clear, glass-like portion of the anterior eye. With the lens, the cornea helps focus images onto the retina.

Mechanism or Cause of Injury

Corneal abrasions can occur by various mechanisms of injury. Commonly, corneal abrasions occur due to something scraping the cornea. An object enters the eye and then the individual rubs the eye, which causes the scratch or abrasion. Even an object as small as a grain of sand or dust can cause corneal damage. Contact lenses can scrape his cornea during application and removal. Chemicals, eye drops, and contact solutions can cause corneal abrasion, especially if these liquids cause an allergic reaction in the eye.

Signs and Symptoms

Individuals with corneal abrasions complain of pain and the sensation of an object is in the eye. Their eye will be teary, red, and bloodshot, especially from rubbing the eye. They will complain of blurred and decreased vision, and sensitivity to light.

Immediate Care

Immediately discourage the individual from rubbing their eye, because this action can cause further harm. Attempt to determine if an object in the eye, and if so, carefully remove it (see the following section, "Foreign Object in the Eye"). Even if you remove the object, the individual may continue to complain that something is still in their eye. Whether or not a minute object is in the eye, refer them to an ophthalmologist or ER for treatment. The physician will determine if the cornea has an abrasion by using **fluorescein** strips on the eye (**Figure 9-13**). The physician most likely will give the patient eye drops or ointments and pain medication to heal the abrasion and decrease pain. If the patient wears corrective lenses, they will be directed to wear glasses instead of contacts until the abrasion has healed.

Prevention

In order to prevent corneal abrasions, an individual must wear appropriate protective eyewear when performing daily activities. Contact lenses must be fitted properly for each patient. When working with any chemicals, protective eye should be worn, if possible, and conscious effort should be taken to keep the chemicals away from eyes.

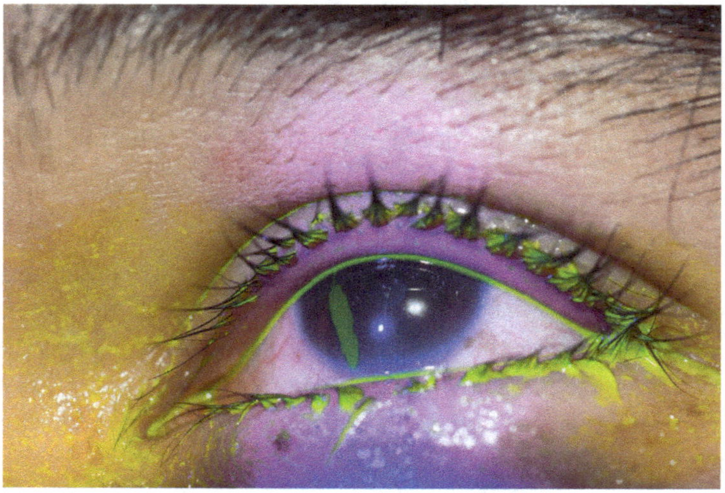

Figure 9-13 Corneal abrasion shown after utilizing a fluorescein strip

Foreign Object in the Eye

Foreign bodies in the eye can range greatly in size. Consequently, the foreign body can create a significant range of injury severity. Obviously, a larger foreign body in the eye, such as a nail protruding from the eye, causes significantly more damage than a grain of sand. If the object is small and in the eyelid, such as an eyelash or a small flying insect, then attempt to remove the object; however, if the object is larger and/or protruding from the eyeball, do not want to remove the object. Removing the object would cause further harm.

Mechanism or Cause of Injury

Foreign bodies can enter the eye when an object flies into the eye, such as a flying insect, or is thrown into the eye, such as sand. An object can touch the eye, such as a finger that has dirt or dust on it, and then transfer the object to the eye. If an object, such as a nail, is shot at the eye, then the object can protrude from the eyeball, causing extensive injury.

Signs and Symptoms

The patient will complain of many of the same signs and symptoms as exist with a corneal abrasion. If the object is large, it will protrude from the eyeball, or the eyelid will involuntary remain open.

Immediate Care

Care is very different if the foreign object is small, and can be removed without creating further harm to the patient, as compared to a large object in the eye that may be protruding from the eyeball. In order to remove a small object from your patient's eye, first wash your hands and then put on non-powdered gloves. In a well-lighted area, have your patient sit in a chair so you can look down into their eyes. Check the eye by gently pulling their upper eyelid up, trying to invert it if possible, while the patient looks down. Then pull the lower eyelid down, inverting it again, while the patient looks up. If you see the object, then have the patient tilt his head to the same side as the injured eye, then the irrigation fluid and the object may be flushed into the other eye. You can use an eyedropper or the tip of the saline bottle to irrigate the eye. Do not touch the tip of the eyedropper or bottle to the eye, because this action can injure the eye and contaminate the eyedropper and bottle. Once the object is out of the eye, have the patient irrigate their eye again to make sure all debris is out of the eye, and to cleanse the area.

Most foreign objects in the eye will be small and can be carefully removed. Rarely will large objects protrude from the eyeball or be stuck in the eye. If you cannot remove the object due to its size or potential for further injury, the patient's eye is still painful after removing the object, their vision is significantly disturbed, or the object is protruding from the

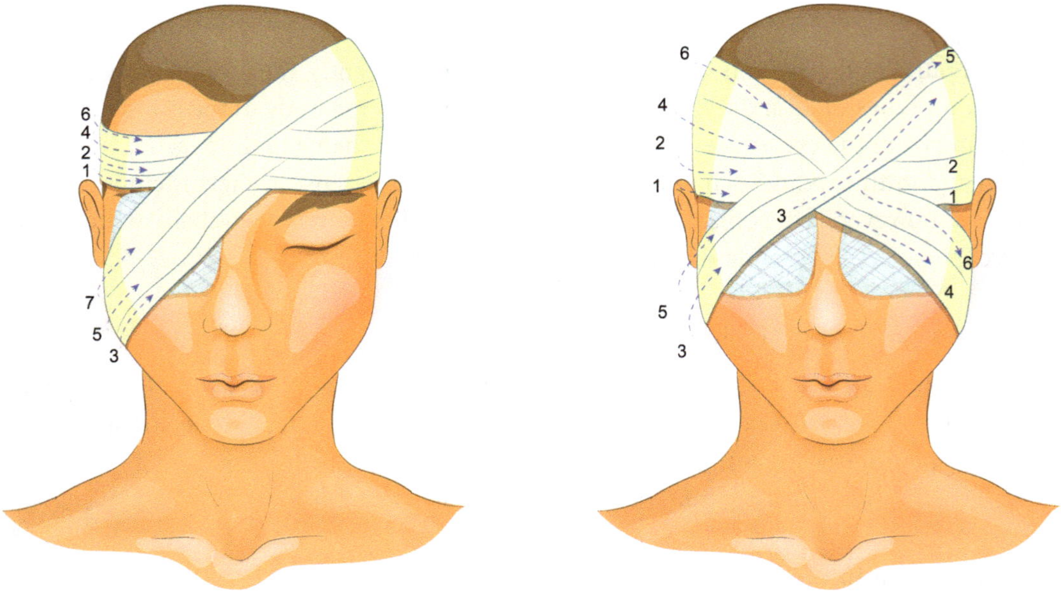

Figure 9-14 Bandage application on one or both eyes

eyeball, then call 911 for the patient to be transported to the ER via ambulance. While waiting for the ambulance, keep the patient still. Do not remove the protruding object. Instead, apply bulky dressings and bandages around the protruding object to keep it still. Because the eyes move (or track) simultaneously in regard to speed and direction, bandage both eyes to prevent the injured eye from moving **(Figure 9-14)**. Monitor the patient for signs and symptoms of shock.

Prevention

To avoid getting a foreign body in the eye, protective eyewear should be worn during activities, if warranted. If an individual is outside, they can also protect their eyes by wearing sunglasses. A simple way to prevent small foreign objects in the eye is to avoid touching the eyes with unclean hands.

Conjunctivitis (Pink Eye)

Conjunctivitis, or pink eye, is an inflammation of the lining of the eye, which is called the conjunctiva. Pink eye often occurs often in children, and is a highly contagious condition. Usually pink eye occurs in one eye, but because it is highly contagious, it can easily spread to the other eye.

Mechanism or Cause of Injury

Various causes of conjunctivitis exist, but the condition typically stems from a viral infection. Conjunctivitis is also caused by bacteria, fungi, allergies, chemicals, and contact lenses.

Signs and Symptoms

A patient experiencing conjunctivitis will have a significant amount of redness or a pink color in the sclera (or white portion) or their eye. They will complain of an itching eye, pain, blurred vision, and sensitivity to light. The patient may have significant eye discharge that dries and becomes crusty overnight and keeps the eyelid from opening properly **(Figure 9-15)**.

Immediate Care

The patient must not be allowed to participate in activity at your organization while they are contagious. Refer them immediately to a physician. In the meantime, the patient can apply warm compresses to the infected eye to alleviate some discomfort. The physician will examine the patient's eye. The treatment varies depending on the type of conjunctivitis. Viral conjunctivitis heals on its own. Most physicians prescribe eye drops for both viral and bacterial conjunctivitis because the viral infection could create a bacterial infection. Allergic conjunctivitis is typically treated with allergy medication. Do not allow the patient to return to activity until they are under a physician's care, no longer contagious, and presents you with a physician's clearance note for return to participation.

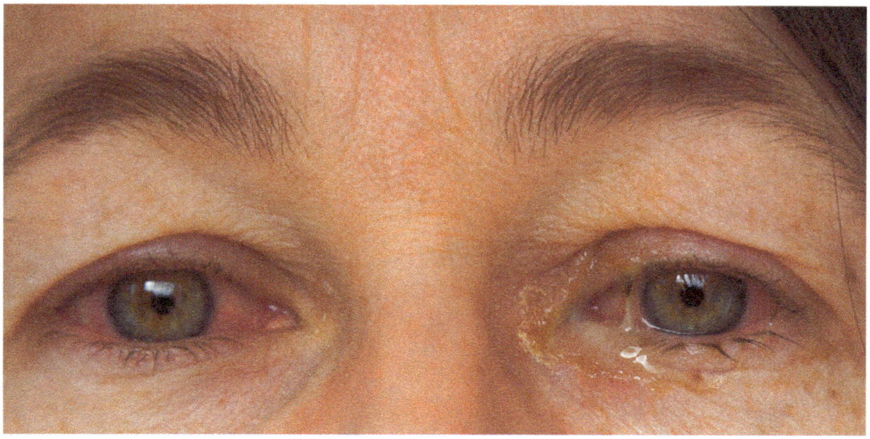

© Anita van den Broek/ Shutterstock.com

Figure 9-15 Signs and symptoms of pink eye, or bacterial conjunctivitis, include reddening of the conjunctiva, itching, and discharge

Prevention

Prevention of conjunctivitis typically starts with good hygiene. Frequent hand washing, and laundering clothes, towels, and bed linens will help prevent conjunctivitis. Individuals should not share towels, cosmetics, contact lenses, or any object that comes in contact with the eye with other athletes. Make sure previously used eye cosmetics and contact lenses are disposed of appropriately and new, uncontaminated ones are used after they recover from the illness.

Stye

A stye is an inflamed sebaceous, or oil, gland in the eyelid, located where the eyelash protrudes (**Figure 9-16**).

Mechanism or Cause of Injury

Bacteria that enter into the gland and causes inflammation. Typically, the stye forms in a few days.

Signs and Symptoms

A stye appears as a red bump that resembles a pimple, which will be point tender and swollen. The individual may feel like something is in their eye, and the eye may tear and be sensitive to light.

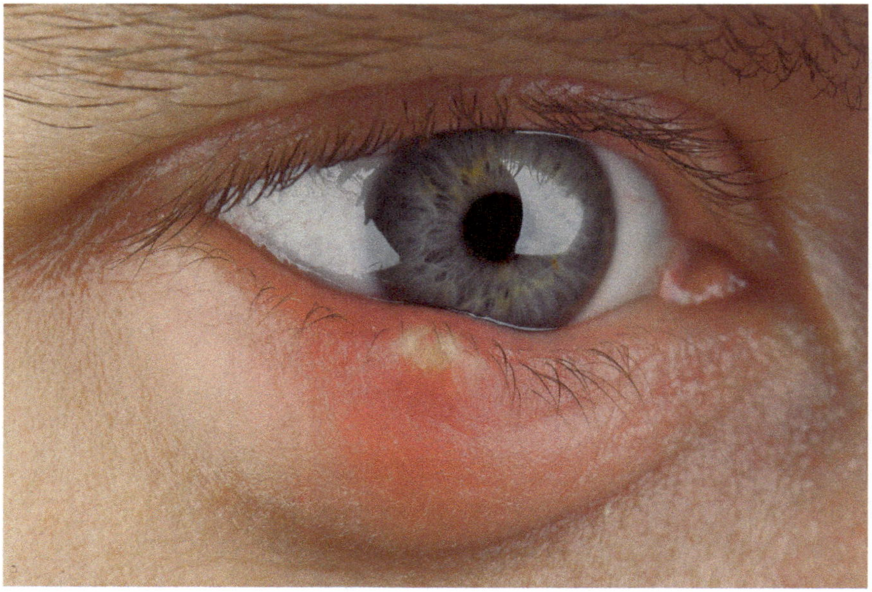

Figure 9-16 Stye

Immediate Care

Typically, styes spontaneously drain without treatment and the eyelid will return to a normal state. The individual can apply warm compresses to the eye to alleviate any discomfort. They must not squeeze the stye because it may cause further harm. Advise the individual that if the stye does not resolve itself in a week's time, proceeds to worsen, or exhibits other signs and symptoms such as bleeding, blurred or blocked vision, or extreme sensitivity to light, then they should see their physician for treatment. Often, antibiotic ointment is prescribed to treat the inflammation.

Prevention

The best prevention to avoid acquiring a stye is similar to preventing a foreign body in the eye. Make sure the individual practices frequent, proper hand and face washing, and avoids putting any unclean objects near the eyes.

Ear Injuries and Conditions

Tympanic Membrane (Eardrum) Rupture

The purpose of the tympanic membrane, or eardrum, is to vibrate when sound strikes it. The vibrations travel to the bones behind the eardrum in the middle ear. The vibrations continue on to the inner ear, in order for the nerves to stimulate the brain and process the sound. A ruptured eardrum means there is a perforation in the tissue that forms a hole. Because the ruptured eardrum is unable to vibrate properly, the transmission of vibrations is affected, which subsequently is detrimental a person's ability to hear.

Mechanism or Cause of Injury

A tympanic membrane rupture is caused by a direct blow to the ear, an ear infection, a foreign object in the ear, a change in pressure, or an extremely loud noise.

Signs and Symptoms

A patient with a ruptured tympanic membrane has a visible hole in the tissue **(Figure 9-17)**, hearing difficulties or loss, discomfort or pain, and possible leakage of fluid or pus (in the case of an ear infection) or blood (in the case of an object forced into the ear).

Immediate Care

Make sure the patient does not get water in the ear, if possible. They can apply warm compresses on the ear to alleviate pain. Refer the patient to a physician for evaluation. The physician may give the patient antibiotics to prevent infection (or to treat an ear infection), and pain

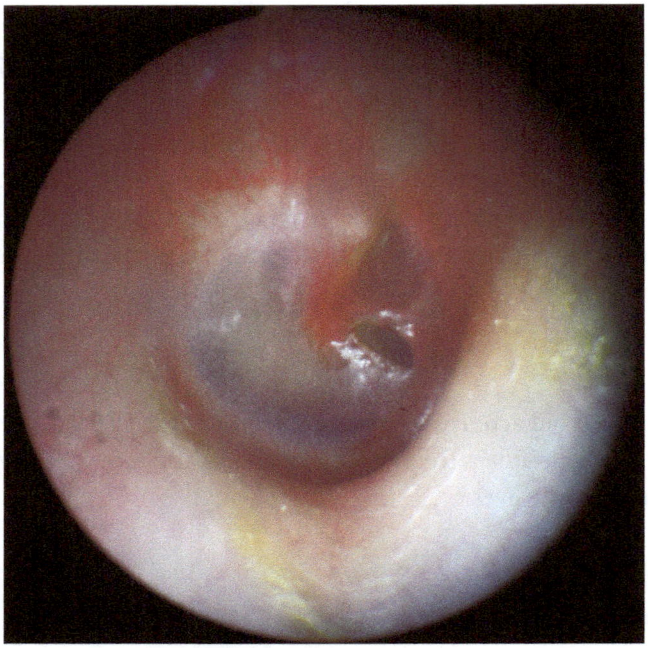

Figure 9-17 A tympanic membrane (eardrum) rupture

medication. Most eardrums will heal without treatment within a couple months, and hearing will be restored to normal.

Prevention

Prevention of a tympanic membrane rupture takes a commonsense approach. Avoid putting any foreign objects in the ear, such as cotton swabs, which can be utilized for cleaning the ear into the external acoustic canal by the eardrum. Explain to your patients to avoid changes in pressure where the pressure will not be equalized (for example, ascending from deep water quickly, or in an airplane without equalized cabin pressure). Earplugs and noise reduction protective earwear are necessary if the patient is in an area with extremely loud noise. Educate your patients not to slap or hit someone's ear. Finally, recommend to your patient to dry the inside of the ear after bathing or swimming. Residual water in the ear can make a great breeding area for bacteria. The bacteria can cause an ear infection, which may lead to a tympanic membrane rupture. To dry the external acoustic canal, utilize a gentle cool hair dryer on low speed held far enough away from the ear so the patient does not blow the air too forcefully into the ear.

Auricular Hematoma (Cauliflower Ear)

Auricular hematoma, or cauliflower ear, is a deformity of the outer ear cartilage that occurs over a period of time. A hematoma in the outer ear is formed, followed by scar tissue. The outer

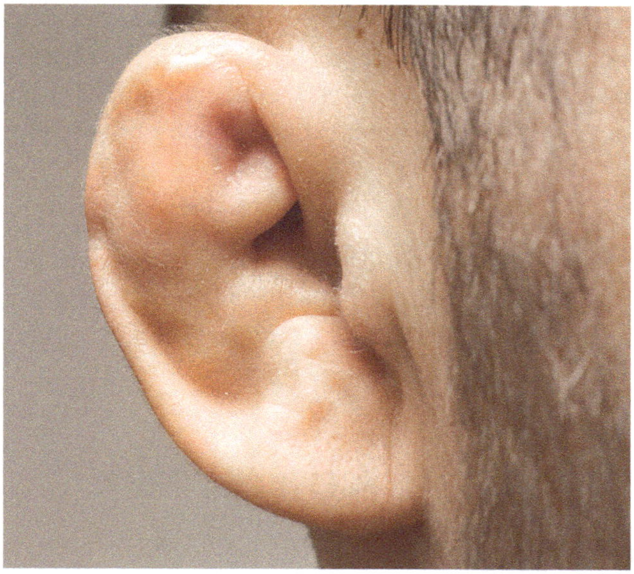

Figure 9-18 Cauliflower ear can be prevented if the patient wears protective headgear.

ear tissue is deprived of oxygenated blood due to the injury. The tissue begins to shrink, becomes bumpy, and takes on the appearance of a cauliflower **(Figure 9-18)**.

Mechanism or Cause of Injury

The mechanism of injury for cauliflower ear is a constant friction of the outer ear, on a surface such as a wrestling mat, while the individual is not wearing protective ear wear. Direct, blunt trauma can also cause cauliflower ear, if the trauma is great enough to cause a hematoma that is not treated or does not heal properly. Some individuals have their outer ear cartilage pierced. If the piercing causes a hematoma to form, the individual may acquire cauliflower ear.

Signs and Symptoms

An individual with cauliflower ear may complain of pain, tinnitus, hearing loss, visual disturbances, and headache. The signs of cauliflower ear include the cauliflower deformation appearance, warmth at the area due to inflammation, swelling, and facial swelling.

Immediate Care

In order to care for cauliflower ear, have the individual apply ice and manual compression to the area. The individual should be examined by their physician. Depending on the severity of the cauliflower ear and how long the individual has had the condition, the physician may drain the fluid from the ear. After the hematoma has been drained, the physician applies a compression bandage on the area to keep fluid from reentering the site. The physician often prescribes antibiotics to prevent possible infection, as well as pain medication. The sooner cauliflower ear is treated, the greater possibility that the outer ear will not be permanently deformed.

Prevention

To prevent cauliflower ear, the individual must wear appropriate protective ear wear, headgear, and helmets while participating in activities where the outer ear. If the patient's ear is inflamed, the patient should immediately put ice and compression on the area to prevent cauliflower ear.

Otitis Externa (Swimmer's Ear)

Otitis externa or swimmer's ear is an infection of the outer ear canal.

Mechanism or Cause of Injury

If water that remains in the outer ear canal after bathing or swimming is not removed or dried, it will sit in the canal. Eventually, bacteria grow in the moist skin environment. Also, if an individual puts an object in their ear and scratches the skin, then bacteria can grow in the skin openings, causing infection.

Signs and Symptoms

An individual with swimmer's ear may not experience significant signs and symptoms at first. However, the signs and symptoms develop over time if the infection is not treated. The individual first experiences itching and mild discomfort. The outer ear canal may be red from inflammation, and possibly a slight discharge may exude from the canal **(Figure 9-19)**. These signs and symptoms will progressively increase if the infection is not treated. Pus may drain from and block the canal, which would prevent proper hearing. More significant signs and symptoms exist if the infection is allowed to continue without treatment. The individual may experience severe pain, redness and swelling, fever, swollen lymph nodes, and complete blockage of the outer ear canal, which prevents hearing.

Immediate Care

If the signs and symptoms of swimmer's ear are mild, refer the individual to a physician. If they are experiencing severe signs and symptoms, then call EMS immediately. The infection is treated with antibiotics for a bacterial infection, or an antifungal drug for a fungal infection. The physician may also prescribe steroids for the inflammation and ear drops to assist in healing the outer ear canal.

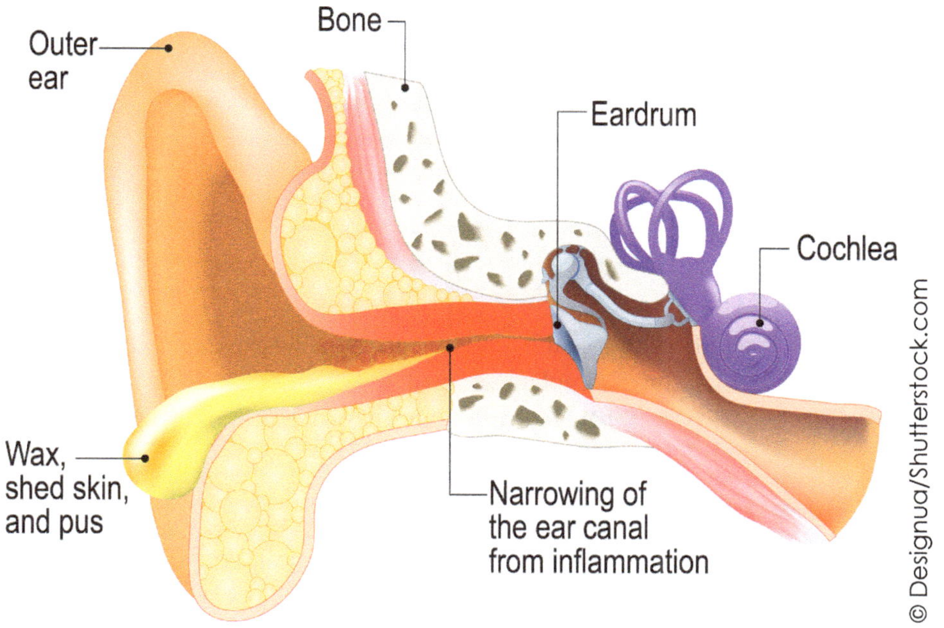

Figure 9-19 Otitis externa (Swimmer's ear)

Prevention

Advise your clients to keep their outer ear canals dry after swimming or bathing. To dry the external acoustic canal, they can utilize a gentle cool hair dryer on low speed held far enough away from their ear, so they do not blow the air too forcefully into the ear. Special over-the-counter eardrops or a combination of white vinegar and rubbing alcohol can help dry out the ear. However, if your client has scrapes in the canal, white vinegar and rubbing alcohol will burn the skin and cause pain and should not be utilized. Your client can utilize earplugs specifically made for swimmers to prevent water from entering the outer ear canal. Tell your clients not to put anything into their outer ear canal, including cotton-tipped swabs.

Otitis Media (Middle Ear Infection)

The middle ear is the portion of the ear from the tympanic membrane to the inner ear. The middle ear contains the three small bones in the body, the malleus, incus, and stapes. Sound vibrations from the tympanic membrane are transferred to these bones and then are transferred to the inner ear. Otitis media is a middle ear infection that occurs most often in babies and children.

Mechanism or Cause of Injury

Bacteria or viruses trapped in the middle ear cause the infection. An individual who has a cold with nasal passageways and Eustachian tubes inflammation is predisposed to a middle ear infection because the inflammation does not allow the fluid to drain well. Consequently, the fluid backs up into the Eustachian tubes and resides in the middle ear. The bacteria then grow in this stagnant fluid and cause the infection.

Signs and Symptoms

Due to the inflammation, the individual has significant pain, a sore throat, and fluid drainage from the ear. The individual may complain of muffled hearing due to the inflammation and fluid in the middle ear **(Figure 9-20)**. Children may also complain of difficulty sleeping, and exhibit a low-grade fever of 100° F.

Immediate Care

Usually middle ear infections heal without treatment after a few days. The individual can typically wait to see a physician for 48 to 72 hours after they become symptomatic in order to see if the infection resolves on its own. In the meantime, the individual can place a warm compress on the ear. If the individual has drainage from their ear, refer them to a physician

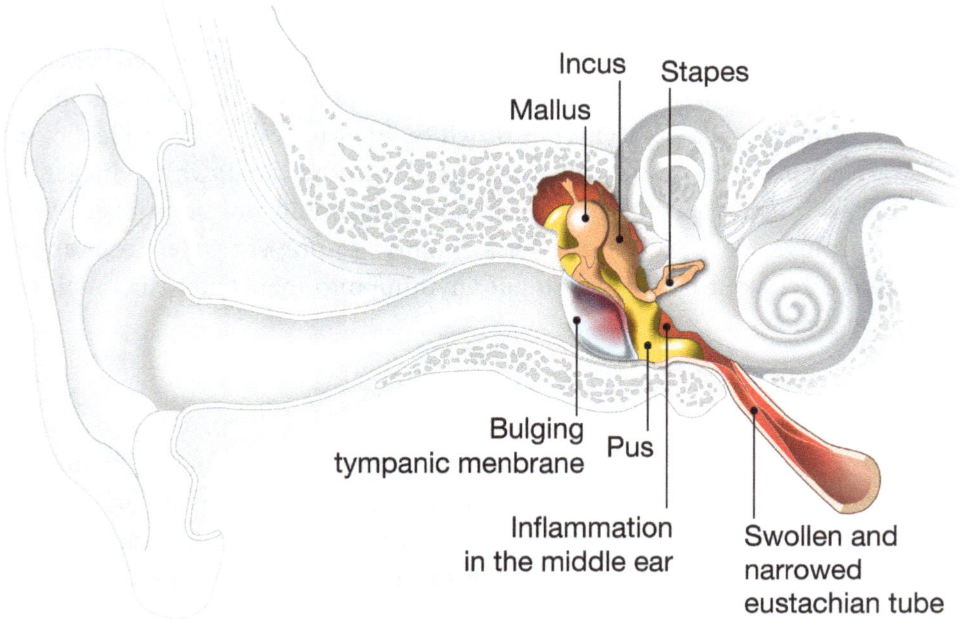

Figure 9-20 Otitis media

immediately. Even though the middle ear infection may heal on its own, the individual often needs evaluation and treatment from a physician. The physician may prescribe antibiotics and pain medication to treat the infection.

Prevention

To prevent otitis media, recommend to your patient to get their flu vaccination annually. Encourage your patient to quit smoking and avoid secondhand smoke, which can irritate the passageways. Also, your patient should attempt to avoid colds by washing hands regularly.

Nasal Injuries and Conditions

Nasal Fractures

In athletic activity, a nasal fracture is a common facial injury. Other facial bones are often fractured along with the nasal bones. Likewise, due to the mechanism of injury, a separated septum can also occur with a nasal fracture. Whenever a nasal fracture exists, always consider that the patient may have a head and neck injury due to the forceful mechanism of injury.

Mechanism or Cause of Injury

Nasal fractures occur from blunt force trauma to the nasal bones. An object, such as a thrown ball or an opponent's elbow or fist, can strike the nose with enough force to break it **(Figure 9-21)**.

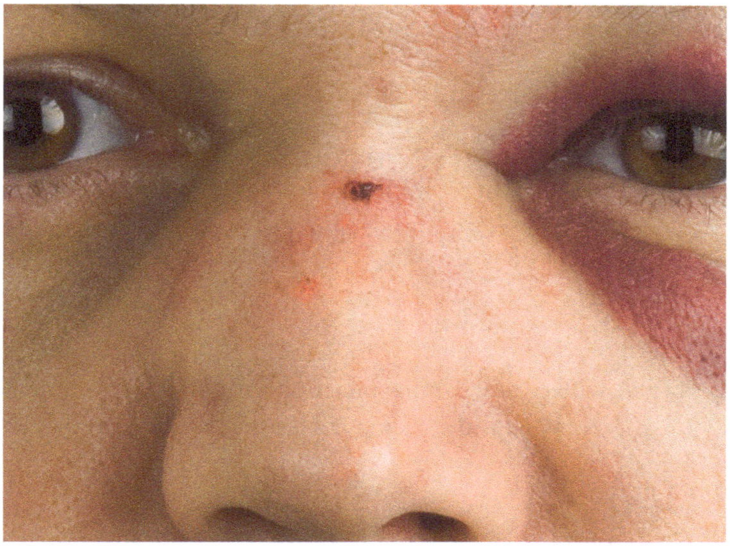

Figure 9-21 A fractured nose can be caused by a straight on or lateral direct blow.

Signs and Symptoms

The patient complains of pain and difficulty breathing from the nose. Epistaxis, deformity, point tenderness, and swelling are present.

Immediate Care

Have the patient sit comfortably with their head leaning forward slightly. Tell the patient to breathe out of their mouth. Keep the patient calm and treat them for shock if necessary. Provide the patient with a small bag of ice to place gently on the injured area. They must not apply too much pressure with the ice bag; otherwise, they may move the broken bones and cause further harm. If the patient has epistaxis, then treat them accordingly (see the following section, "Epistaxis (Nosebleed)"). Never attempt to straighten the nose and do not move the patient if they show signs of a head or neck injury. In the case of a head or neck injury, maintain in-line stabilization on the patient, and call 911.

Prevention

Nasal fractures can be avoided by wearing protective face guards as appropriate for the activity. Recommend to your patient that they wear seat and safety belts.

Epistaxis (Nosebleed)

Typically, epistaxis is not a serious injury unless it is due to a nasal fracture or a head injury. An uncomplicated nosebleed is one that was not caused by any physical trauma to the nose, head, or face. This type of nosebleed can be controlled quickly, and the patient can return to activity. Usually bleeding comes from one nostril unless the bleeding is severe, then the blood can flow into the other nostril.

Mechanism or Cause of Injury

Many causes for a nosebleed exist. Direct trauma, allergies, dry nasal passages, continual inflammation from colds, picking the nose, and drug use (from drugs snorted up the nose) can cause epistaxis.

Signs and Symptoms

Signs and symptoms of a nosebleed are external bleeding from and difficulty breathing through the nose. The patient may have pain and swelling if a direct blow caused the nosebleed.

Immediate Care

For an uncomplicated nosebleed, have the patient sit up and pinch their nose just below where the bone meets the cartilage. Put on your protective gloves and obtain an absorbent material such as gauze, nose plugs, or commercial nosebleed clotting materials. Carefully insert the

Figure 9-22 Care for a nosebleed includes pinching the nose just below where the bone meets the cartilage and carefully inserting the absorbent material into the bleeding nostril.

absorbent material into the patient's bleeding nostril **(Figure 9-22)**. Make sure that the end of the absorbent material is partially protruding from the nostril so it can be removed easily. Have the patient hold a small bag of ice on the nose to decrease any pain, swelling, and bleeding. The patient continues to pinch their nose with the absorbent plug inserted for about 5 to 10 minutes.

After 5 to 10 minutes, remove the plug with a gloved hand and see whether the nostril has stopped bleeding. If the bleeding has stopped, have your patient clean up their face, hands, and any other areas that have blood on them. Remove your gloves, dispose the bloody materials properly, and wash your hands thoroughly. Make sure that you inform your patient not to blow his nose or breathe up deeply through the nose for a few hours after the nosebleed. These actions may disrupt the blood clot in the nasal passageway and restart bleeding. If the bleeding has not stopped after the 5 to 10 minutes of care, apply another absorbent nose plug and have the patient pinch and apply ice to the nose again for another 5 to 10 minutes. If after this time the nose still continues to bleed, then summon EMS. If at any time that you believe the nosebleed was due to a head injury or some other condition that is potentially life-threatening, or the patient has a potential neck injury, treat these injuries appropriately and summon EMS immediately. For recurrent nosebleeds, you should refer your patient to their physician. The physician may **cauterize** the blood vessels that cause the recurrent bleeds.

Prevention

As with nasal fractures, wearing protective face guards can prevent nosebleeds caused by direct trauma. Your patient should take allergy medicine, irrigate the nose with saline regularly, and utilize humidifiers in the home if their nasal passages are dry and susceptible to bleeding. Patients should not pick their nose or put any foreign objects, including drugs, up their noses.

Deviated Septum

The septum is the portion of the nose that separates the two nostrils on the inside of the nasal cavity. A deviated septum can be a significant injury. When the septum blocks one side of the nasal cavity, breathing difficulties can exist **(Figure 9-23)**.

Mechanism or Cause of Injury

A deviated septum is caused by a direct blow to the nose due to participating in contact sports, falls, and accidents. A patient can also be born with a deviated septum.

Signs and Symptoms

A patient with a deviated septum may have frequent nosebleeds, breathing difficulty due to the septum occluding one side of the nasal cavity, nasal and facial pain, sinus infections due to poor drainage of nasal fluid, and snoring or loud breathing through the nose while sleeping.

Immediate Care

If the individual's nose is bleeding, treat the nosebleed as previously discussed. Whether or not the individual's nose is bleeding, refer them to a physician for evaluation. The physician may prescribe nasal sprays such as steroids, antihistamines, and nasal decongestants to alleviate

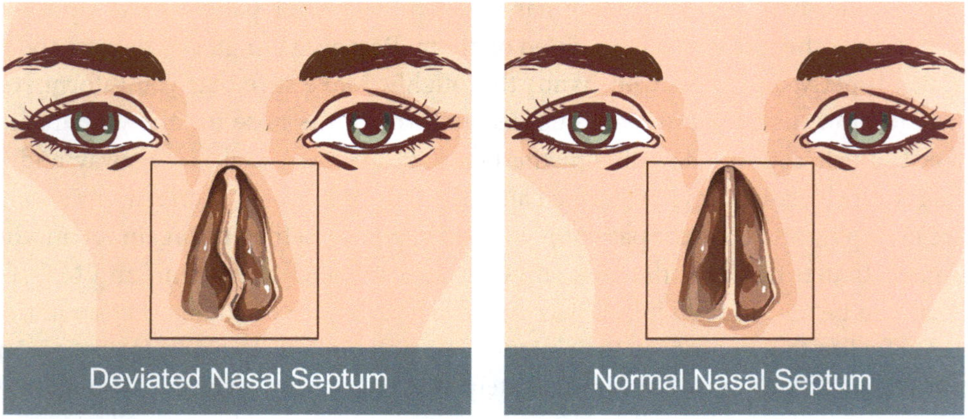

Figure 9-23 A normal versus deviated septum

signs and symptoms of inflammation and promote nasal fluid drainage. If the individual continues to have difficulty breathing, the physician may surgically repair the deviated septum by placing it in the middle of the nose. The physician may also choose to reshape the nasal bones along with centering the septum to make a sufficient passageway for air in both nostrils.

Prevention

It is impossible to prevent a deviated septum that occurs to individuals at birth. In order to prevent a deviated septum from a direct impact, the individual should wear protective face gear, and seat and safety belts as necessary.

Tooth Injuries

As with other bony injuries, fractures, subluxations, luxations, and avulsions can occur to the teeth. Some of these injuries require immediate medical attention, while others are not as urgent.

Fractures

Tooth fractures can be minor when the break runs through the enamel, which is the outermost layer of the tooth. More significant breaks run through the enamel and dentin (the layer of the tooth inside the enamel) **(Figure 9-24)**. An even more significant fracture is when the break

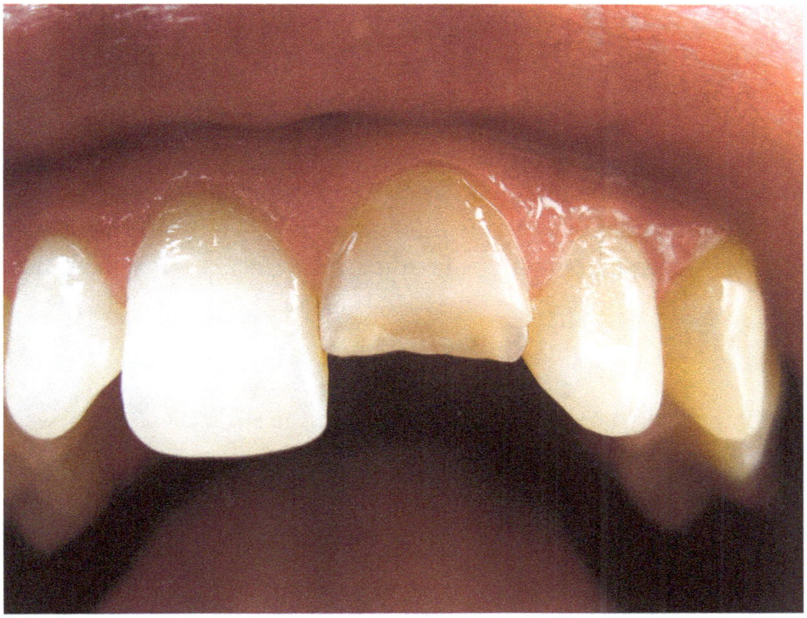

Figure 9-24 Tooth fracture

is through the enamel, dentin, and interior pulp (which is inside the dentin) of the tooth. A severe fracture occurs when the break crosses through the root, which is the portion of the tooth in the gum.

Mechanism or Cause of Injury

Tooth fractures can be caused by a direct blow or falling on the face or mouth. Fractures can also occur by biting down on or chewing hard food, candy, or the like.

Signs and Symptoms

The patient will have pain if a direct blow hits his face or mouth, but he may not have pain if they bite down on a hard object and only fractures the enamel and/or dentin. They may become sensitive to cold or pressure when chewing food. If the pulp or root is fractures, the patient will definitely feel pain. The tooth will be jagged and sharp to the patient's tongue or finger when touched. The patient will be bleeding if they have lacerations to the face, mouth, or gums. Some tooth displacement may be visible.

Immediate Care

A fracture of the enamel, dentin, and pulp is not a medical emergency. The patient can put some sugarless gum on the jagged edges until they are able to see a dentist. If they are bleeding or have any other facial, head, or neck injuries, appropriately treat those injuries first. For minor fractures, the dentist will recreate the tooth. Significant pulp fractures may need a root canal to save the tooth. For fractures to the root, the dentist may need to pull the tooth and replace it with a prosthetic tooth.

Prevention

Athletic participants should wear mouth guards whenever possible during activity where the potential for tooth injury exists. A properly fitted face mask should also be worn in sporting activities that requires the equipment to help reduce the incidence of tooth injury.

Subluxation

A tooth subluxation occurs when it is knocked loose in the socket, but does not fall out. The front teeth are the most commonly affected.

Mechanism or Cause of Injury

A tooth can be subluxed by a traumatic direct blow to or fall on the tooth.

Signs and Symptoms

Usually bleeding occurs to some extent with a subluxation. The patient most likely experiences some pain and tenderness around the gum line, especially when touched with the finger. The gum line will also be swollen.

Immediate Care

The patient must first rinse the mouth out with clean, cool water. Whether the tooth is a baby (primary) or adult (secondary) tooth, instruct the patient to hold the tooth in place and in proper alignment with a clean finger. Apply ice over the mouth. The patient should carefully bite down on some rolled up sterile gauze to help keep the tooth in place. Also have them place sterile gauze at the injured site to stop the bleeding. The socket will eventually close up around the tooth, which makes the tooth stable. If the tooth is very mobile, or you cannot stop the bleeding, refer the patient to the dentist or ER immediately.

Prevention

Prevention for subluxations of the tooth is the same as for fractures of the tooth.

Luxation

A tooth displacement is a luxation. The displacement can be in any direction. A tooth fracture may occur with a luxation. The front teeth are the most commonly affected.

Mechanism or Cause of Injury

The mechanism of injury is the same for a luxation as for a subluxation, which is usually a direct blow to or fall on the face, mouth, or teeth.

Signs and Symptoms

Luxation signs and symptoms are similar to subluxations of teeth, except displacement will be visible. The tooth can be displaced either outward toward the lips, inward toward the tongue, or to either side. The gums at the site of the luxated tooth will be swollen.

Immediate Care

The patient must first rinse the mouth out with clean, cool water. With clean fingers, the patient should then attempt to carefully and slowly move the tooth back into its normal position and alignment with the neighboring teeth. The patient needs to see a dentist immediately. Primary teeth will either be removed or repositioned and splinted as per the dentist's recommendations.

Secondary teeth will be repositioned and splinted. Antibiotics are necessary to avoid infection, and pain medication can also be utilized.

Prevention

Prevention of tooth luxations is the same as for fractures of the tooth.

Avulsion

A tooth avulsion occurs when the tooth is knocked out of the socket (**Figure 9-25**). This injury typically occurs to young children.

Mechanism or Cause of Injury

The cause of a tooth avulsion is the same as a subluxation and luxation. Significant trauma is necessary to cause the avulsion. Therefore, determine that the patient does not also have a face, head, or neck injury, which must be treated as the priority for care.

Signs and Symptoms

Tooth avulsions will exhibit an empty socket where the tooth was knocked out. The socket will often bleed and be swollen. The patient will have a significant amount of pain, even if they did not experience another injury to the face, head, or neck.

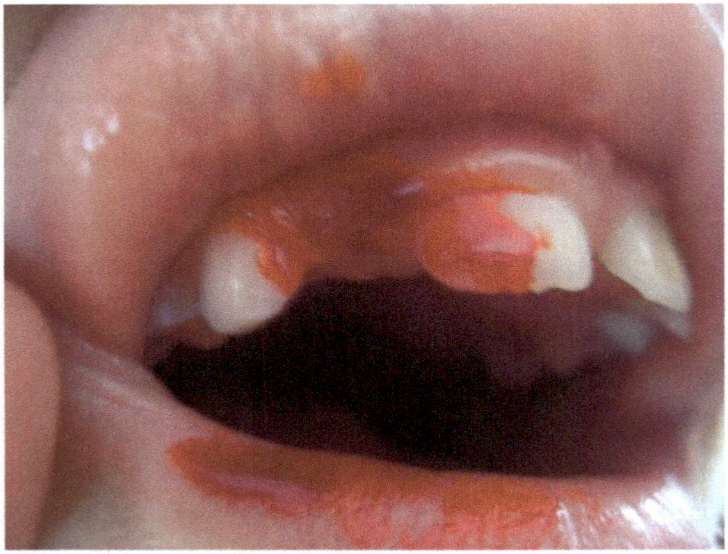

Figure 9-25 A tooth avulsion is when a tooth is knocked out of its socket.

Immediate Care

If an individual has knocked out a primary or secondary tooth, they should make every attempt to replace the tooth. Without touching any exposed root or pulp, the individual must clean the tooth first by rinsing it under water. The individual should not scrub the tooth while rinsing it. Then, they replace it in the socket while looking in a mirror in order to visualize proper positioning and alignment. The individual should see their dentist or go to the ER immediately for evaluation, even if they have properly replaced the tooth. If the individual cannot put the tooth in the socket, have them put the tooth in saline, milk, or another tooth-saving solution that is sold over-the-counter by commercial vendors. The individual must see their dentist or the ER immediately in attempt to save the tooth's life. If the tooth is dry for 15 minutes, then the root covering dies and tooth replantation is not possible. The dentist will most likely apply a splint to the tooth once it is replaced. For avulsed secondary teeth, the dentist will perform a root canal at a later date in attempt to save the tooth. With severe tooth injuries, the individual may go into shock. Consequently, be prepared to treat shock if you see the signs and symptoms arise.

Prevention

Prevention for subluxations of the tooth is the same as for tooth subluxations and luxations.

Summary

Injuries and illnesses to the head and face may be minor, such as TMJ dysfunction or an uncomplicated nosebleed, which do not require urgent care. Head and face injuries may also be significant, such as with MTBI and most head injuries, and require immediate advanced medical treatment. With any traumatic head or face injuries, you must consider the possibility of a neck injury, neurologic disruption, skull and/or brain bleeding, shock, or unconsciousness. Consequently, with head and face injuries, always be prepared for and know how to provide immediate care for any life-threatening situations that arise.

Keywords

Core body The area of the body not including the upper and lower extremities. The core body includes the spine, chest, abdominal, and pelvic cavities.

Retrograde amnesia The inability to remember events that occurred before the MTBI occurred.

Post-traumatic amnesia The inability to remember events that occurred after the MTBI injury occurred.

Diplopia Double vision.

Photophobia Sensitivity to light.

Anticoagulant drugs Drugs that an individual would take in order to thin the blood in order to prevent blood clotting. An individual who sustains an injury to the blood vessels would bleed much more than if they were not taking anticoagulants.

Malocclusion The inability to bring the teeth together in a normal, aligned fashion.

Epistaxis A nosebleed.

Fluorescein An orange dye that is on a type of strip of paper that is put onto the cornea by a physician. The dye covers the cornea, then the physician looks at the cornea under a blue light. Any areas of the cornea that are green indicate that an abrasion exists.

Cauterize To burn tissue with electricity or a laser in order to assist in the healing process. In the case of epistaxis, the blood vessels that continue to bleed would be cauterized in the nose.

Discussion Questions

1. What are some cognitive and neurological signs and symptoms that occur to a patient who has sustained a MTBI?
2. Which type of bleeding in the skull creates a rapid deterioration of cognitive and neurological function in a patient?
3. Other than typical signs and symptoms of fractures, what are some signs and symptoms specific for each fractured facial bone?
4. In regard to a migraine, what is an aura?
5. What treatment is appropriate for TMJ dysfunction?
6. What are the differences between otitis externa and otitis media?
7. What should you do to treat epistaxis? When should you call 911 for an individual has epistaxis?
8. What are the differences among a tooth fracture, subluxation, luxation, and avulsion? How should you treat each injury?

CASE STUDY: ROCK WALL STUMBLE

Dennis, a 35-year-old healthy and fit man, wakes up one Saturday morning excited to go rock climbing with his friends at Northern State Park. When he looks out the window it is pouring rain. He turns on the TV and the weather forecast calls for intermittent heavy rain all day. Dennis calls his friends, and they decide it would be safer to climb indoors at the local Northern State Rock Walls gym. Dennis packs his climbing gear. He has climbed the Northern State Rock Walls gym before. For this climb, Dennis and his friends will attempt the 55-foot wall, which is reserved for elite climbers. Although Dennis has never attempted this height before and knows it is challenging, he believes it will be nowhere near as dangerous as climbing at Northern State Park. He is anxious and excited to climb today.

The friends arrive at the gym and climb for an hour. Dennis has successfully climbed once already. It is now Dennis' turn to climb again. He chooses a route with a small buttress on it, figuring it would be a good challenge. Dennis has no problem clearing the buttress, but just as he is about to continue ascending he loses his grip and falls just below the buttress. Dennis' momentum makes him swing under the buttress. As he swings, he loses control and hits his head extremely hard against the wall and protruding rocks. Rick, Dennis' friend who is belaying Dennis, lowers Dennis to the ground and asks him if he is okay. Dennis was wearing his helmet as required by the gym; however, he tells Rick that he saw stars and his head is throbbing and hurts. Dennis continues to say that he feels "foggy" and is nauseous. His friends tell him to shake it off, and get up and climb the wall again. At first, Dennis does not want to go back up the wall because he starts to feel dizzy, but he succumbs to the peer pressure and begins to climb again.

As he ascends the wall and reaches the top, the dizziness gets worse, and he begins to have significantly blurred vision. Suddenly, Dennis begins to vomit. Rick belays Dennis down and his friends suggest he no longer climbs and rests for the remainder of the 3-hour session. Dennis has never suffered a rock-climbing injury like this before, and he has no idea what is happening to him.

1. What injury or injuries may Dennis have?
2. What are some other signs and symptoms of injury that might arise?
3. What course of action should Dennis' friends take to care for Dennis?
4. What type of cognitive evaluation testing can Dennis' friends perform to determine Dennis' extent of injury?
5. Should Dennis go to the hospital? Why or why not?

References

Abdelmalik, P.A., Draghic, N., & Ling, G.S. (2019). Management of moderate and severe traumatic brain injury. *Transfusion*, 59(S2):1529-1538. doi: 10.1111/trf.15171.

Broglio, S.P., Cantu, R.C., Gioia, G.A., Guskiewicz, K.M., Kutcher, J., Palm, M., & McLeod, T.C. (2014). National Athletic Trainers' Association Position Statement: Management of Sport Concussion. *Journal of Athletic Training*, 49(2), 245-265. doi: 10.4085/1062-6050-49.1.07

Center for Disease Control (CDC) (2021). *Heads Up: Brain Injury Safety Tips and Prevention.* Retrieved July 16, 2021, from https://www.cdc.gov/headsup/basics/concussion_prevention.html

Hagen, K., Åsberg, A. N., Stovner, L., Linde, M., Zwart, J.-A., Winsvold, B. S., & Heuch, I. (2018). Lifestyle factors and risk of migraine and tension-type headache. Follow-up data from the Nord-Trøndelag Health Surveys 1995–1997 and 2006–2008. *Cephalalgia*, 38(13), 1919–1926. doi: 10.1177/0333102418764888

Khairat A, & Waseem M. (2021, August 2). *Epidural hematoma. In: StatPearls* [Internet]. StatPearls Publishing. https://www.ncbi.nlm.nih.gov/books/NBK518982/

Ling, Y.H., Chen, S.P., Fann, C.S.J., Wang, S.J., & Wang, Y.F. (2019). *TRPM8* genetic variant is associated with chronic migraine and allodynia. *Journal of Headache Pain*, 20, 115. doi: 10.1186/s10194-019-1064-2

May, T., Foris, L.A., & Donnally, C.J. (2021). Second impact syndrome. StatPearls [Internet]. Retrieved October 29, 2021, from https://www.ncbi.nlm.nih.gov/books/NBK448119/.

Mayo Clinic (2021). *Migraine*. Retrieved July 16, 2021, from https://www.mayoclinic.org/diseases-conditions/migraine-headache/symptoms-causes/syc-20360201

Meagher, R. J. & Young, W. F. (2018). *Subdural hematoma*. Retrieved July 16, 2021, from http://emedicine.medscape.com/article/1137207-overview

Medline Plus. (2019). *Skull fracture*. Retrieved July 16, 2021, from http://www.nlm.nih.gov/medlineplus/ency/article/000060.htm

National Eye Institute. (2020). *Retinal Detachment*. Retrieved July 16, 2021, from https://www.nei.nih.gov/learn-about-eye-health/eye-conditions-and-diseases/retinal-detachment

Chapter 10

The Upper Extremity

Chapter Objectives

After you have read this chapter, you will be able to understand:

- The various injuries and conditions that a patient can sustain to the shoulder, elbow, forearm, wrist, hand, and fingers.
- Various acute and chronic upper extremity injuries.
- The upper extremity injuries which necessitate calling 911 versus those which only require referral to the individual's physician.
- The upper extremity injuries and conditions require surgery and subsequent rehabilitation in order to restore extremity function.

The upper extremity includes the shoulder, upper arm, forearm, wrist, hand, and fingers. This chapter discusses common upper extremity injuries that may occur to your patients. Many mechanisms of injury are similar regardless of which area of the upper extremity is injured. However, the severity, irritability, nature, and stage (SINS) of injury vary depending on the injury, and whether the injury is classified as acute or chronic. Some injuries require immediate referral to emergency medical services (EMS) whereas others do not necessitate urgent care. Fortunately, injuries to the upper extremity are not often life-threatening.

Injuries to the Shoulder and Upper Arm

Some individuals think the shoulder is only comprised of the ball-and-socket glenohumeral (GH) joint. The GH joint is a prominent part of the shoulder; however, the shoulder is also comprised of the humerus, clavicle, and scapula bones, as well as the scapulothoracic (ST), sternoclavicular (SC), and acromioclavicular (AC) joints. These bones and joints work together for proper shoulder function. When one structure is injured, shoulder function will be hindered.

Fractures

Fractures to the shoulder typically occur to the clavicle and humerus, with the most common fractures occurring to the clavicle. Bones tend to fracture where they change shape and are weakest. Therefore, the clavicle fractures most often at the middle one-third of the bone. The humerus usually fractures below the head of the humerus at the proximal end of the bone. Both fractures can be displaced.

Mechanism or Cause of Injury

A common mechanism of injury for a clavicle or humerus fracture is falling on an outstretched arm. Visualize an individual who falls and tries to catch themselves. Their elbow is straight, and their wrist is extended as their palm strikes the ground. The forces from the fall, their body weight, and the ground's reaction forces can cause injury from the fingers, up the extremity, to the sternoclavicular joint. Another mechanism of injury for a clavicle and humerus fracture is a direct blow to the bone or to the tip of the shoulder. The direct blow creates vibrations that travel through the upper extremity, reaching the humerus and clavicle, and cause the bone to break.

Any type of fracture can occur to the humerus. Transverse fractures are common (**Figure 10-1**). The humerus can sustain a spiral fracture when the hand is firmly fixed on a stable surface, such as the floor, but the individual's body moves. This motion causes a twisting of the humerus, which causes the spiral fracture. A humerus compression fracture can occur when the patient's palm lands on the ground with the elbow extended. This mechanism of injury is called a fall on an outstretched arm or hand, which is also referred to as FOOSH.

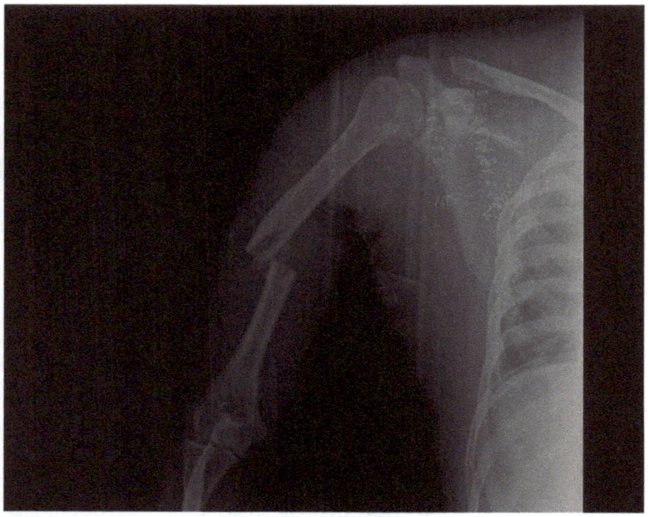

Figure 10-1 A displaced, transverse fracture of the humerus

Signs and Symptoms

Signs and symptoms of a clavicle and humerus fracture are pain, deformity (such as a prominent bump with clavicle fractures), loss of function or complete inability to move the GH joint, point tenderness, ecchymosis, and swelling. Often, humerus fractures are not displaced and no visible deformity is present.

Immediate Care

If you suspect a clavicle or humerus fracture, tell the individual to remain still and not to move their arm. Have them sit in a comfortable position supporting the arm. Call 911, or have someone else call for you, so the individual can be transported to the emergency room (ER). Splint the arm by putting it in a sling, while keeping it still as possible **(Figure 10-2)**. You can also apply an elastic bandage around the arm and splint it to the individual's body to make the arm immovable. If these splinting materials are not available, you are not trained to properly apply splints, or you are uncomfortable with splint application, then instruct the individual to remain completely still and assist them while you wait for EMS to arrive. EMS personnel will appropriately splint the injured area. You can apply a small bag of ice on the injured area. The bag of ice must not move the bones or cause undue weight on the injured area, or it will result in pain or harm. If you see the patient is going into shock, which is common with shoulder fractures, then treat the patient immediately.

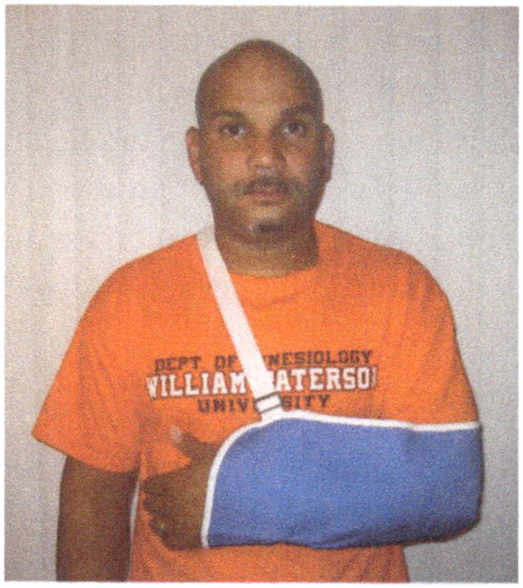

Figure 10-2 A sling can easily be applied to support many upper extremity injuries.

After sustaining a clavicle fracture, the patient will wear a "figure 8" brace **(Figure 10-3)** for 3-8 weeks (American Society for Surgery of the Hand [AASH], 2007). The brace puts a slight traction on the bones. The two broken clavicle pieces straighten out so the ends are in line with each other, which promotes healing. The physician rarely needs to perform surgery to secure a broken clavicle.

Figure 10-3 A patient will wear a figure 8 brace to assist clavicle fracture healing.

For a humeral fracture that is non-displaced and remains in normal alignment, the physician will have the patient wear a sling for approximately 4 weeks before range of motion (ROM) rehabilitation can begin.

If the humerus fracture is displaced and the ends of the broken bones are not aligned, then surgery may be the only viable option for proper healing (AASH, 2007).

Prevention

In attempt to prevent clavicle or humerus fractures, athletes must wear properly fitted shoulder pads, especially in contact activities such as ice hockey, football, or lacrosse. Athletes should also learn how to fall properly, by rolling, instead of falling on an outstretched arm. This skill is commonly executed by volleyball players. Emphasize to the individual to utilize correct form and skills when performing their activities. They must always be aware of their surroundings, as well as body positioning during activity, in order to prevent falls. To keep bones strong, these individuals must have a good supply of calcium and vitamin D in their diet, in conjunction with performing weight bearing activities. Strong bones can minimize the potential risk of fracture.

Dislocations and Subluxations

A dislocation, or a luxation, and a subluxation of the GH joint are similar because these injuries both involve displacement of the humeral head from its normal position in the joint relative to the glenoid fossa. With a dislocated GH joint, the humeral head moves out of normal alignment and remains in that position. With a GH subluxation, the humeral head moves out of normal alignment and then spontaneously reduces back into normal alignment. Dislocations to the GH joint occur in an anterior, inferior, and posterior manner, with an anterior dislocation being the most common (Abrams & Akbarnia, 2021) **(Figure 10-4)**. Anterior and posterior dislocations are characterized by the head of the humerus protruding from the joint anteriorly and posteriorly, respectively. Posterior dislocations occur when the head of the humerus is displaced back toward the scapula. An inferior dislocation occurs when the head of the humerus protrudes inferiorly into the axilla. Once the individual has sustained a GH dislocation or subluxation, chances are that the individual will sustain another dislocation or subluxation or dislocation in the future. After a dislocation or subluxation, the individual's ligaments and joint capsule are permanently stretched, allowing for joint laxity. Therefore, the individual needs to undergo rehabilitation to strengthen the surrounding muscles to keep the head of the humerus in place during GH motion.

Although the injury is rare, the SC joint can also be dislocated or subluxed. Typically the sternum moves posteriorly with an SC joint dislocation or subluxation. With these injuries, keep in mind that the heart is behind the sternum and may also have been injured. Also, a posterior SC joint dislocation can cause damage to the blood vessels, respiratory difficulty, and other serious complications including death (Edwin et al., 2018). Therefore, a SC joint dislocation can be life-threatening.

Both GH and SC dislocations and subluxations are serious injuries. Not only do the bones move out of normal alignment, but the ligaments, tendons, and muscles surrounding the bones are stretched and damaged.

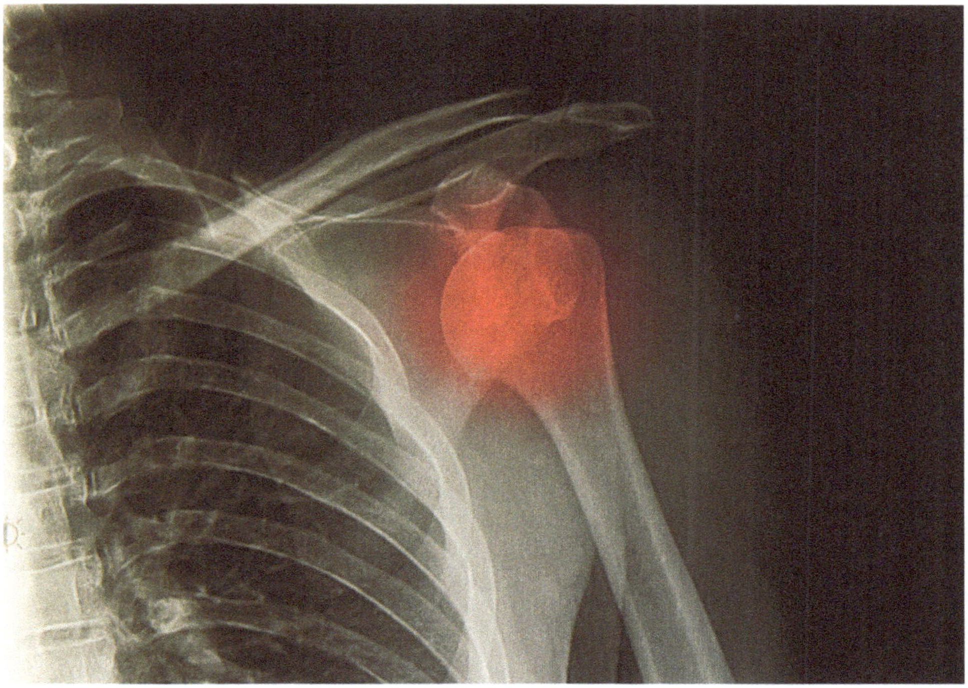

Figure 10-4 An anterior dislocation of the GH joint

Mechanism or Cause of Injury

A common mechanism of injury for a GH and SC joint dislocation or subluxation is a fall on an outstretched arm. A GH anterior dislocation can also occur when a direct blow occurs to the arm when the upper arm is abducted from the body and the elbow is in a 90-degree angle. An inferior dislocation can be caused by a direct blow down onto the tip of the shoulder while the arm is at the patient's side. A posterior dislocation can occur when the arm is outstretched and the patient falls forward, which forces the head of the humerus backwards. The GH joint can become dislocated when the hand is firmly fixed on a surface, such as the floor, and the patient's body moves and twists the GH joint. The SC joint can receive a direct blow and be dislocated or subluxed.

Signs and Symptoms

A dislocation appears physically deformed. You can see the humeral head or sternum out of normal position. The individual will complain of severe pain, inability to move the arm, point tenderness, and loss of feeling into the hand due to trauma to the brachial plexus. Signs of injury include deformity, malalignment, swelling, and ecchymosis. The individual may be in shock. Signs and symptoms for a subluxation include pain, a feeling of significant movement of the bones during injury, swelling, point tenderness, tingling or numbness in the fingers, and loss of motion. Typically, the signs and symptoms of a GH or SC subluxation are not as significant as with a dislocation.

Immediate Care

If the individual has dislocated their GH or SC joint, have them stop activity and rest in a comfortable position while you call 911. Splint the arm in the position that you find it (even for a SC dislocation), and apply ice to the injured area. Treat the individual for shock if signs and symptoms are apparent. While waiting for EMS to arrive, take their bilateral pulse at the radial artery. Compare the pulse rate and quality and determine if their arm has adequate blood flow. Give this information to the EMTs when they arrive. In the ER, the physician will **reduce** the dislocation. Because reduction of the dislocation is painful and the muscles surrounding the joint are tense, the patient is typically given a sedative or muscle relaxant before the reduction occurs. In some instances, the physician may put the patient under general anesthesia for reduction. Once in proper position, the patient's arm is immobilized for up to 3 weeks before rehabilitation begins. The patient is prescribed nonsteroidal anti-inflammatory drugs (NSAIDs) to assist in decreasing pain and inflammation.

If an individual subluxes a GH or SC joint for the first time, splint the arm and ice the area. Depending on the severity of signs and symptoms, you may need to call 911 or refer the individual to a physician for evaluation. Any time the individual is in shock, even if the injury is minor, treat them for shock and call 911. For recurrent subluxations without any secondary injuries or complications, refer them to their physician for further evaluation.

Prevention

An individual must have adequate muscular mass and strength in order to prevent the bones from moving out of alignment when force is applied. Likewise, they must have enough muscular flexibility, active range of motion (AROM), and passive range of motion (PROM) in order to prevent dislocations and subluxations. After the first dislocation or subluxation, surgery may be warranted to prevent additional dislocations and subluxations if rehabilitation alone is not effective. Athletic participants must wear proper protective gear, and be cognizant of their surroundings, body movements, and positioning to prevent falls, as noted with shoulder fractures.

Separation

A shoulder separation is the term utilized for disruption of the AC joint. The ligaments around the joint are stretched, creating a joint sprain. The injury can be minor which is referred to as a Grade 1 separation. A Grade 1 separation is a mild AC ligament sprain. A moderate sprain, or a Grade 2 separation, is a tear of the AC ligament and a sprain of the coracoclavicular ligament (Kiel & Kaiser, 2021). A severe AC separation is a Grade 3 separation. A Grade 3 separation is a complete tear, or rupture, of both ligaments. The higher grade of separation requires greater rehabilitation time to restore the patient's shoulder function.

Mechanism or Cause of Injury

The mechanisms of injury for a separated shoulder are a fall on an outstretched arm or a direct blow to the tip of the shoulder, AC joint, or clavicle.

Signs and Symptoms

A patient with an AC separation has varying degrees of signs and symptoms depending on the grade of the injury. The patient feels discomfort to significant pain. They are unable to move the arm without pain especially in horizontal adduction (across the front of the body). With higher grades, the AC joint appears deformed, as a large bump, due to the clavicle rising up above the acromion **(Figure 10-5)**. The shoulder muscles surrounding the AC joint feel weak.

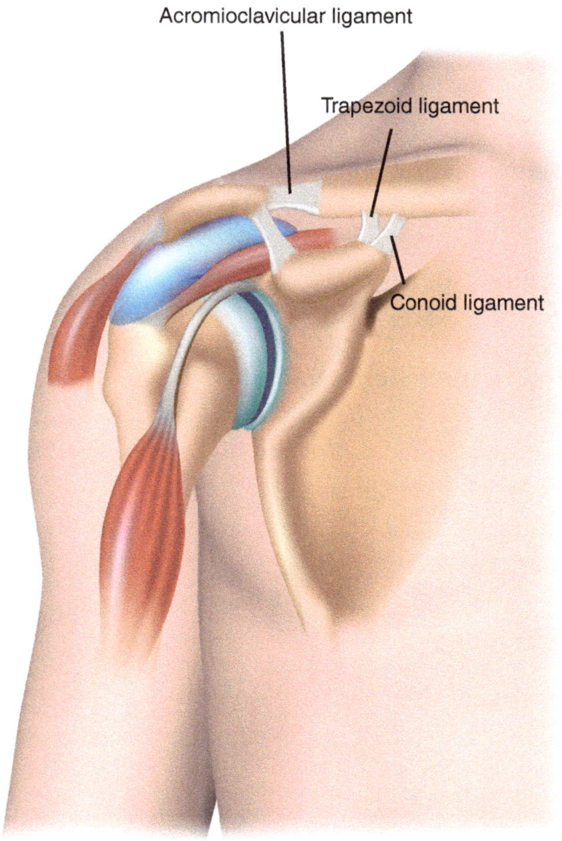

Figure 10-5 Complete tears of the acromioclavicular, trapezoid, and conoid ligaments cause the clavicle to rise above the acromion, creating a deformity.

Immediate Care

Rarely will you need to call 911 for an individual with any grade of AC separation. If the individual goes into shock, which can occur with many injuries, then call 911 immediately. The individual may go into shock due to the pain or after visualizing the deformity resulting from a Grade 3 separation. When an individual sustains a separated shoulder, first perform a secondary survey to evaluate them in attempt to determine the SINS of the injury. If the individual has mild signs and symptoms, you most likely do not need to utilize a sling. An ice bag will assist in decreasing discomfort. Even with a mild, Grade 1 AC separation, the individual should not be allowed to return to activity at your facility until they are evaluated and cleared by their physician. If the individual has moderate to severe signs and symptoms of injury, then utilize a sling to rest the area and apply ice. Refer them to their physician for further evaluation.

Typically, surgery is not necessary for a Grade 3 AC separation. Proper healing can occur by treating the AC separation with rest, ice, compression, and elevation (RICE). The individual will most likely wear a specialized immobilization brace to support and rest the arm. They can also take NSAIDs to decrease pain and inflammation. A few weeks of rehabilitation of the shoulder joint and surrounding musculature is necessary in order to regain full ROM and strength.

Prevention

Individuals must pay particular attention to their body position and proximity to other patients, equipment, etc. in order to avoid an AC separation. Athletes should also wear protective shoulder padding depending on what is appropriate for the activity. Individuals must have significant upper body ROM and muscular strength in order to prevent against AC separations.

Sprains

Sprains to the shoulder can occur to the AC joint (which was discussed in the shoulder separation section), SC joint, and GH joint. Sprains to the SC joint are not common.

Mechanism or Cause of Injury

A sprain to the SC joint is often caused by a direct blow to the sternum or end of the clavicle **(Figure 10-6)**. Both sprains to the SC and GH joints can occur due to a fall on an outstretched arm or a blow to the tip of the shoulder. A GH sprain can also be caused by a sudden movement that stretches the joint ligaments. For example, a quarterback who is ready to throw a pass has his shoulder in abduction, away from the body, with their elbow in flexion. If an opposing lineman blocks the pass and strikes the quarterback's arm, forcing it into extension, the anterior GH joint ligaments can be sprained.

Signs and Symptoms

The patient complains of pain and point tenderness. They cannot move the shoulder through a full ROM without pain. Swelling is present, as well as deformity with Grade 3 SC joint sprains.

Immediate Care

After you have performed a secondary survey, treat the affected joint with RICE. If you suspect the injury is a Grade 2 or 3 sprain, splint the arm to prevent movement, apply ice, and refer the patient to their physician. Usually Grade 3 sprains are not a medical emergency and do not

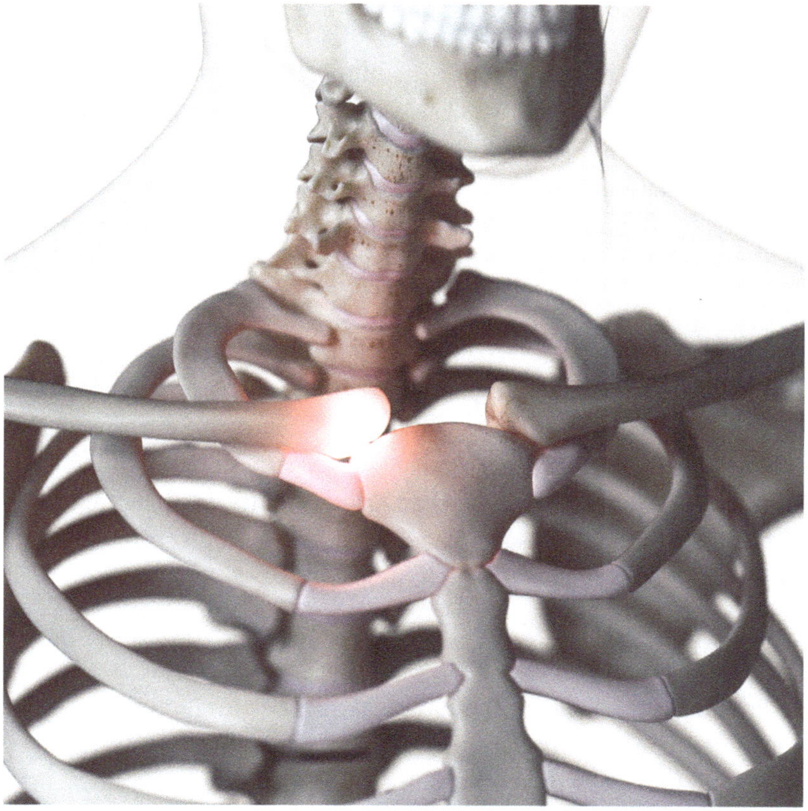

Figure 10-6 Sternoclavicular joint sprain location

warrant calling 911. The patient's physician will prescribe shoulder rehabilitation. Typically, the patient will have to perform GH shoulder ROM as well as shoulder muscle strengthening and flexibility exercises. As with all sprains, the higher the grade of injury, the longer the patient will be in an immobilized position before rehabilitation begins. Likewise, the duration of Grade 3 SC and GH sprain rehabilitation will be longer. Therefore, the patient will return to full activity with full shoulder function at a later date as compared to Grade 1 or 2 sprain.

Prevention

Entirely preventing shoulder sprains is difficult because direct blows often occur to the area and the shoulder motion is extensive. An individual must always perform proper body mechanics and skills for their activity. Upper body conditioning in order to maintain full ROM, flexibility, and strength is important. By having full ROM, flexibility, and strength, their shoulder will be healthy enough to combat any direct blows as well as **internal forces** that can cause a shoulder sprain.

Glenohumeral Joint Instability

GH joint instability is excessive movement of the humeral head out of its normal position as it sits in the glenoid fossa. The instability is classified as anterior, posterior, or inferior, which means the individual has excessive humeral head motion in these respective directions. Most often, patients have multidirectional instability, which means the individual has instability in more than one direction. Typically, an individual has inferior instability concurrently with either anterior or posterior instability. However, an individual can have instability in all three directions.

Mechanism or Cause of Injury

GH joint instabilities can occur to a person who has had a traumatic event such as a GH dislocation or subluxation. The instability can also result over time if they have had severe joint ligament and capsular sprains. Some athletes, such as swimmers and gymnasts, require significant ROM at the GH joint. Over time they have stretched the ligaments and/or capsule surrounding the GH joint. The result is significant laxity or looseness of these soft tissue structures around the joint. This laxity causes instability.

Signs and Symptoms

The individual complains of "looseness" and joint laxity. They may complain that during motion they feel the humeral head sliding or moving out of joint, along with clicking, popping, or crepitus. The individual may have pain, especially in the area corresponding to the instability during motion (i.e. if they have posterior instability, they will have posterior pain). They will most likely have a decreased AROM due to joint pain, and muscular impingement, especially with an anterior GH joint instability (Prentice, 2021).

Immediate Care

The individual should stop activity if they feel GH joint instability so they do not injure themselves further. If they are experiencing pain, provide them with an ice pack to apply to the injured area. Refer them to a physician for further evaluation. They may or may not need surgery, depending on the extent of instability and how much the condition affects their activities including ADLs. Their physician may prescribe a conservative treatment approach at first, which includes strengthening the musculature surrounding the joint.

Prevention

In order to prevent GH joint instability, individuals must abide by the prevention strategies for GH dislocations, subluxations, and sprains. They must make sure they have full ROM, flexibility, and most importantly muscular strength around the joint. Muscle strength is important to help the humeral head maintain its position during motion.

Strains

Shoulder muscle strains typically occur to the biceps brachii, triceps brachii, and rotator cuff muscles. Among these three muscle groups, the biceps brachii is most commonly ruptured **(Figure 10-7)**.

Mechanism or Cause of Injury

As with any other strain, shoulder strains are caused by a forceful concentric or eccentric muscle contraction. A strain can also be caused by a passive muscular stretch. Most often, the biceps brachii and rotator cuff muscles are strained during overhead activities, including throwing and swimming. The muscles are typically strained during the eccentric contractions that occur in the follow through phase of throwing.

Signs and Symptoms

The patient complains of pain with AROM, especially when mimicking the overhead throwing motion. The pain may not appear immediately; instead, the pain may appear hours after the activity has stopped. They may also complain of a dull ache in the muscles while at rest. Weak and point tender muscles are evident. For Grade 3 strains (ruptures), the individual cannot contract the injured muscle if the origin or insertion tendon is ruptured. If the tendons are intact but some muscle fibers are ruptured the individual may be able to partially contract the muscle. A bulge and/or divot in the muscle indicate the tendon and/or muscle belly fibers are ruptured. The muscle looks deformed **(Figure 10-8)**.

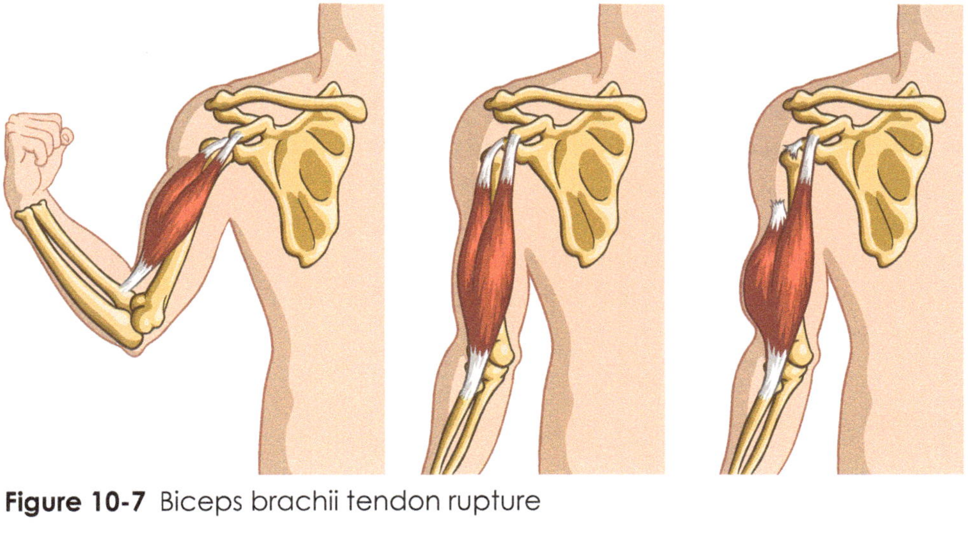

Figure 10-7 Biceps brachii tendon rupture

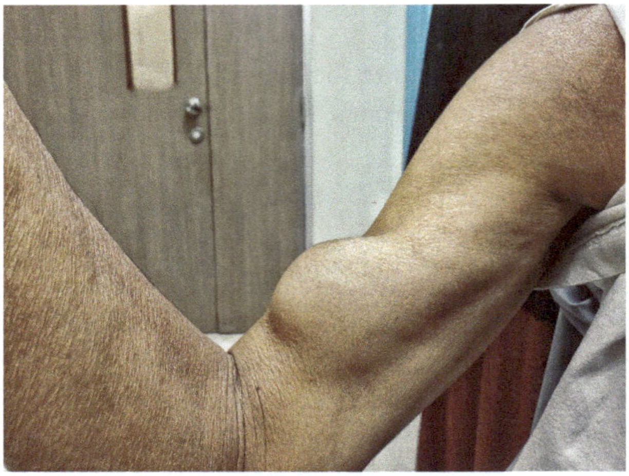

Figure 10-8 A biceps brachii muscle rupture exhibits deformity.

Immediate Care

To care for all shoulder muscle strains, apply the RICE principle. Intermittent ice application and rest from the causative activity is effective for treating Grade 1 strains. Referral to a physician for these mild strains may not be necessary; however, the individual should be referred to a physician for any strain that causes muscular weakness, loss of function, moderate pain, and tingling into the arm and the hand. If you suspect the individual has sustained a muscle or tendon rupture, has numbness into the arm and hand, or severe pain then call 911 to summon advanced medical care. The individual most likely will experience shock when they have sustained a muscle rupture. Treat them for shock while you simultaneously splint the injured area and wait for EMS to arrive.

Prevention

In order to prevent shoulder strains, an individual must have adequate muscle flexibility. They need adequate muscle strength without one muscle group stronger than the opposing muscle group (e.g., the biceps brachii should not be significantly stronger than the triceps brachii). This muscular strength balance allows for proper co-contractions during movement. Athletes must properly perform the activity skill (e.g. proper overhead throwing) and a proper warm-up and cool-down.

Impingement Syndrome

Impingement **syndrome** occurs most often with the supraspinatus tendon, but can also involve the subacromion bursa and long head tendon of the biceps brachii. The extremely small space underneath the acromion process, which is called the subacromial space, is where these soft tissue structures are located. When the humerus is raised away from the body in abduction, the acromion presses upon, or impinges, the supraspinatus tendon. Three stages of rotator cuff impingement syndrome exist (Neer, 1972). The first stage occurs in individuals under the age of 25. The individual experiences signs and symptoms of an acute inflammatory response at the tendon. Stage 2 impingement affects the 25- to 40-year-old population. The individual's tendon is fibrotic, which means excess connective and scar tissue has formed. In addition to having a fibrotic tendon, the individual is classified as having supraspinatus tendinitis. Stage 3 impingement affects individuals over the age of 40. In stage 3, due to the long period of time the syndrome has existed, the acromion has osteophytes, or tiny bone spurs, formed along its arch. At this point, the rotator cuff tendon is significantly weakened and may rupture.

Mechanism or Cause of Injury

The cause of rotator cuff impingement syndrome includes a variety of factors. The patient may be participating in an activity where overhead throwing or arm motion occurs in a repetitive manner **(Figure 10-9)**. Direct trauma to the area can cause impingement. Muscular

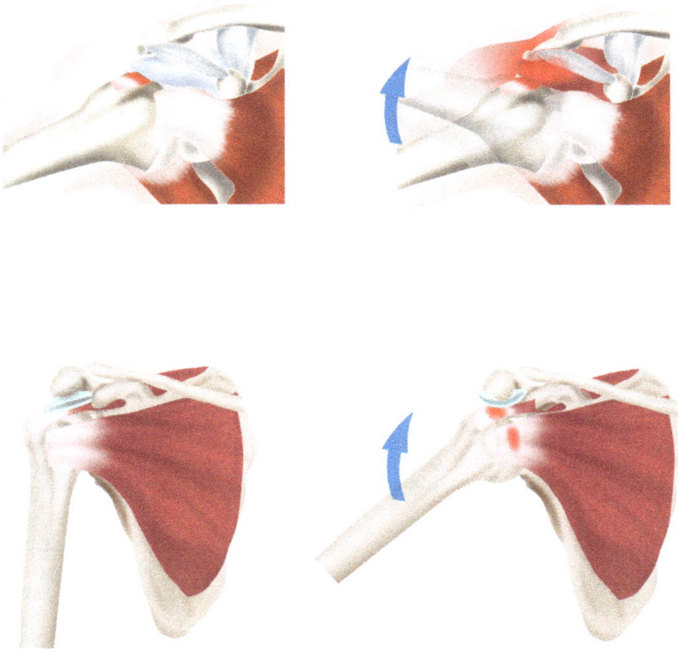

Figure 10-9 Shoulder impingement syndrome is often caused by elevation of the shoulder with concurrent compression of the bursa and tendons under the acromion process.

imbalance, rotator cuff weakness, GH instability, AC joint arthritis, abnormal acromion structure (especially if the acromion is hooked anteriorly), a thickened or calcified coracoacromial ligament, and a thick subacromial bursa are all causes of impingement syndrome (Consigliere et al., 2018).

Signs and Symptoms

Because rotator cuff impingement syndrome is more of a chronic condition than an acute injury, the signs and symptoms appear slowly. As an individual continues to utilize the GH joint in an overhead position, the supraspinatus tendon continues to be impinged. Over time, the tendon develops microtears and becomes seriously inflamed. The individual complains of pain, which may even exist at rest and at night while sleeping. They also are unable to raise the arm into a cocked, overhead, abducted, and externally rotated position due to pain and muscle weakness.

Immediate Care

If an individual has impingement syndrome, have them stop all upper body activities with the affected arm and refer them to a physician for evaluation. Fortunately, Stage 1 impingement can be treated in most cases with RICE, **therapeutic modalities,** and rehabilitation. Stage 2 and stage 3 impingement can only be treated with surgery. After surgery is performed, the patient participates in lengthy rehabilitation. With their physician's consent, the patient can participate in lower body exercise activities during the course of treatment for during any stage of impingement.

Prevention

An individual must listen to their body in order to prevent impingement syndrome. When performing upper extremity overhead activities, if they begin to feel discomfort, the individual should immediately apply ice and refrain from activities that cause the discomfort until the discomfort subsides. If they do not take preventative measures, they may develop impingement syndrome in the near future. Athletic participants need good flexibility and muscular strength for all muscles that move the shoulder joint.

TIPS FROM THE FIELD

Tip 1 When performing a secondary survey for a patient who has a chronic shoulder injury, determine if the injury is impingement syndrome by asking the patient to point with one finger where the pain is the most. If they point at the GH joint from the lateral or anterior sides and states that the pain is coming from deep inside, then suspect the patient has supraspinatus impingement. If the patient points anteriorly and is very point tender superficially, then the biceps brachii is most likely impinged.

Tendinitis

The rotator cuff and biceps brachii muscles are commonly inflamed. The tendons can become acutely or chronically inflamed, but most often tendinitis of these muscles occur in a chronic state because the injury occurs over a long duration **(Figure 10-10)**.

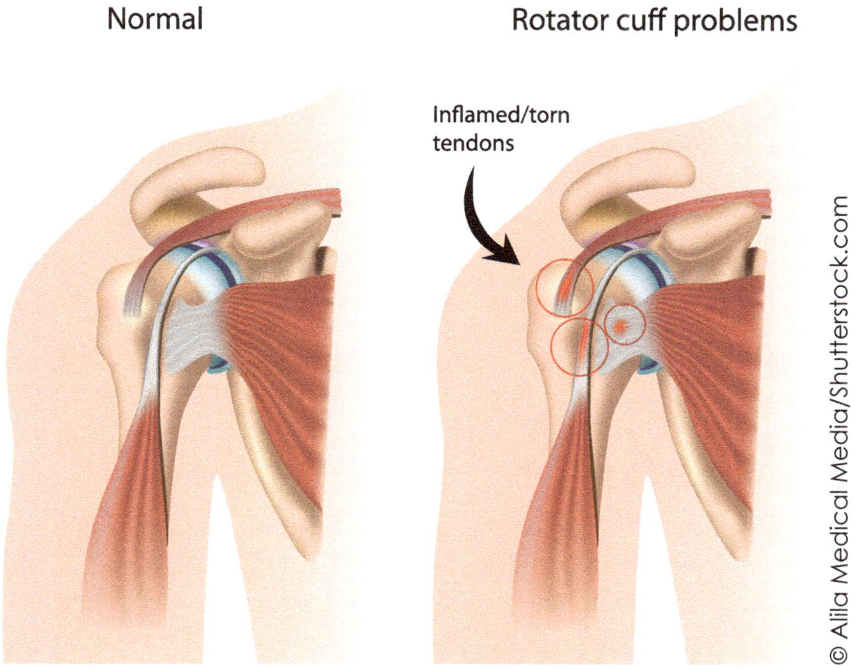

Figure 10-10 Rotator cuff and biceps tendinitis location at the shoulder

Mechanism or Cause of Injury

Shoulder tendinitis can occur due to repetitive, low-intensity contractions, a sudden, violent muscle contraction, acute trauma to the muscle or tendon, and poor upper body posture (Medline Plus, 2021b). If the individual maintains their arm in a stationary position for a period of time (e.g., when sleeping), the tendons can be stressed. As with impingement syndrome, athletes who perform repetitive overhead activities, such as a baseball pitcher or swimmer, is more susceptible to tendinitis.

Signs and Symptoms

The individual feels pain and crepitus. The biceps brachii tendon may subluxate from its position in the bicipital groove. The individual has point tenderness and loss of function. Over time, the tendon thickens and appears larger than the contralateral side. This thickening causes tendon inflexibility.

Immediate Care

Have the individual utilize RICE in attempt to make the signs and symptoms of injury subside. If the signs and symptoms do not subside within a few days, then they should be evaluated by a physician. The physician will most likely prescribe NSAIDs, rest, and rehabilitation.

Prevention

The individual must concentrate on strengthening the affected and opposing muscles (e.g., the triceps brachii muscles oppose the biceps brachii). Avoiding overhead activities and resting the shoulders after strenuous activity can help avoid shoulder tendinitis. The individual needs to continue to stretch and strengthen the musculature to allow for full ROM and avoid muscular weakness.

Contusion

Because the biceps brachii muscle is an anterior shoulder and upper arm structure, it is very susceptible to contusions.

Mechanism or Cause of Injury

As with any other contusion, the mechanism of injury for a biceps brachii contusion is a direct blow to the muscle. Typically, an implement, such as a bat or stick; part of another person's body, such as an arm or fist; or an object, such as a ball, strikes the biceps brachii and causes the contusion.

Signs and Symptoms

A biceps brachii contusion results in various signs and symptoms including pain, muscular weakness, loss of function, transitory paralysis, muscle spasm, ecchymosis (**Figure 10-11**), swelling, tingling into the hand, and point tenderness.

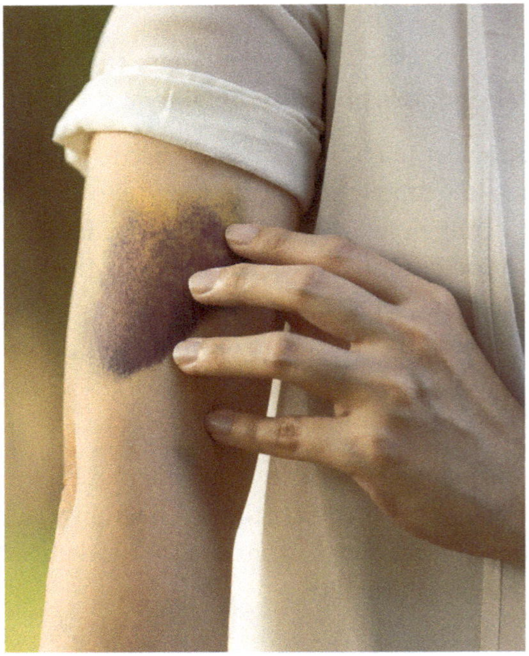

Figure 10-11 Biceps brachii contusion exhibiting ecchymosis (bruising)

Immediate Care

When an individual notifies you of their injury, perform a secondary survey to rule out a humerus fracture. If they do not appear to have sustained a humerus fracture, immediately apply ice and compression to the contused area. If they have significant pain, splint them by utilizing a sling. Instruct them to apply RICE to the area. With a biceps brachii contusion, aggressive stretching should be avoided, and heat should not be applied for the first 72 hours.

A complication that can arise from a deep tissue biceps brachii contusion is myositis ossificans, which is a bony growth that forms in the muscle. Typically, myositis ossificans forms where the hemorrhage exists. Although the exact cause of myositis ossificans has not been determined, aggressive muscle stretching and heat application while the injury is in the inflammatory phase are two predisposing factors for acquiring myositis ossificans.

If after utilizing RICE the signs and symptoms do not subside within a few days, refer your client to a physician for evaluation. If at any time you are unsure whether or not the injury is more extensive, treat the injury as if it is a fracture and summon EMS.

Prevention

Individuals should be aware of their surroundings at all times. They can prevent accidental contusions, such as walking into a barbell in the gym, by being cognizant of their actions. Athletic participants should wear upper extremity protective gear and padding as appropriate for their activities.

Adhesive Capsulitis

Adhesive capsulitis is also referred to as frozen shoulder. The patient is not able to move the shoulder due to joint capsule inflammation.

Mechanism or Cause of Injury

The actual cause of adhesive capsulitis is unknown; however, it may result from direct or indirect trauma and repetitive motion. The inflammation makes the individual unable to move the GH joint through a ROM. Other factors which predispose an individual to have adhesive capsulitis are shoulder surgery, cervical disc disease, open heart surgery, hyperthyroidism, and diabetes (Medline Plus, 2021a).

Signs and Symptoms

Adhesive capsulitis is painful, and due to the significant pain, the individual is unable to move the shoulder. The shoulder becomes very stiff and, even when pain subsides, the individual cannot move their GH joint.

Immediate Care

If your patient has frozen shoulder with a significant amount of pain, have them evaluated by a physician immediately. Use RICE to make the symptoms subside. Further care for adhesive capsulitis includes NSAIDs, rehabilitation, and possibly steroid injections to alleviate pain and inflammation **(Figure 10-12)**. The physician may decide that surgery, followed by

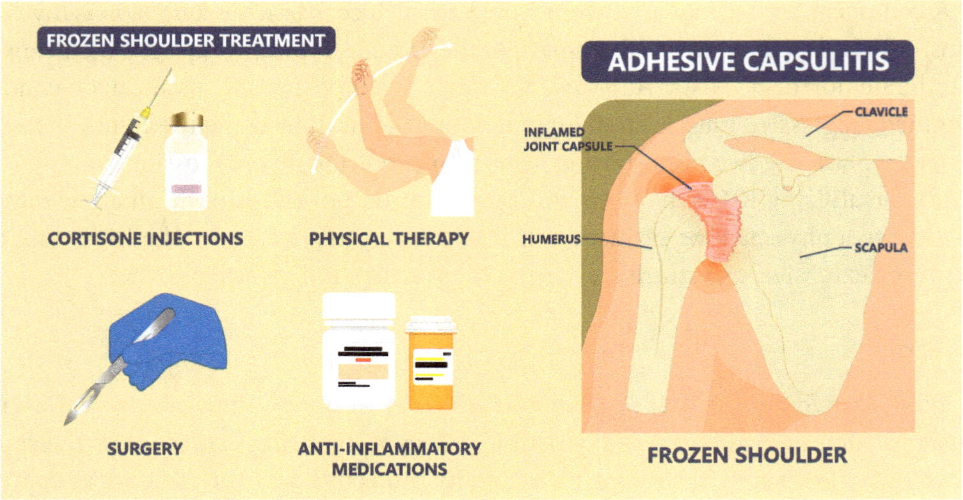

Figure 10-12 Adhesive capsulitis treatment

rehabilitation, is the patient's only option. Even with treatment, it may take up to a year for a patient with adhesive capsulitis to have normal shoulder function. Without any treatment, the patient's shoulder should return to normal function within 2 years (Medline Plus, 2021a).

Prevention

If your client has any conditions such as diabetes and hyperthyroidism, these conditions must be under control in order to prevent adhesive capsulitis. Also, if they begin to feel shoulder pain accompanied by stiffness, they must utilize RICE, ROM, and flexibility exercises immediately to avoid the condition progressing to frozen shoulder.

Brachial Plexus Stretch Injury

The brachial plexus is a pathway of nerves located in the neck and shoulder region on both sides of the body (**Figure 10-13**). A brachial plexus stretch injury is also called a stinger or a burner. These injuries typically occur in contact sports, most often in football and wrestling.

Mechanism or Cause of Injury

A brachial plexus stretch injury occurs when the shoulder is depressed, and the neck is either rotated away or tilted laterally from the depressed shoulder. The shoulder can be depressed by an object or another person pressing upon the top of the shoulder (e.g., blocking in football), or by an individual grabbing another individual's wrist and pulling their arm down (e.g., in wrestling).

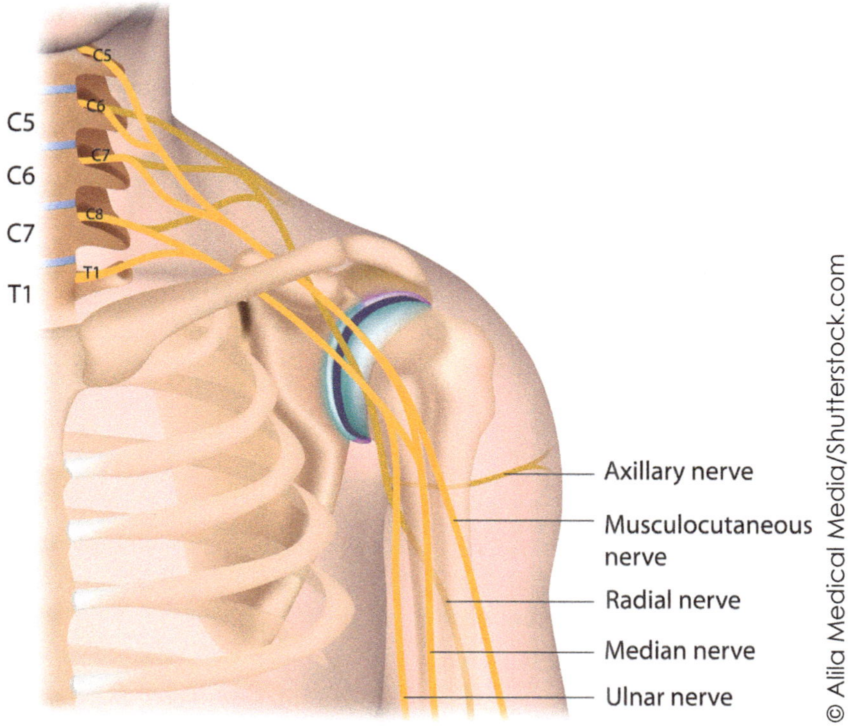

Figure 10-13 The brachial plexus

Signs and Symptoms

A person who sustains a brachial plexus stretch injury will feel burning, tingling, or numbness down their arm to the fingers. They will have temporary loss of function for up to a few minutes. In more severe cases, they have abnormal sensations that linger for days after the injury occurred. As time progresses, these sensations subside. When sensation has been restored, function will also be restored; however, they may also have residual muscular weakness through the entire arm.

Immediate Care

Immediately after the injury, instruct the individual to regain sensation to their hand by flexing and extending their fingers by making a fist, fully opening their hand, moving the wrist in all directions, and flexing and extending their elbow. As they are doing these ROM activities, complete a secondary survey in order to determine if they have any other injuries that warrant immediate treatment. Within a few minutes, they should have full function, including sensation. The individual cannot return to play if they do not have full sensation, ROM, and strength in the affected upper extremity and neck, as compared to the contralateral side. If the symptoms do not subside quickly, they should go to see their physician as soon as possible. The physician may prescribe pain medication and therapeutic modalities to alleviate pain. Surgery is rarely performed. If the individual has sustained multiple brachial plexus stretch injuries and nerve damage has occurred, then surgery with rehabilitation following the procedure may be the only option to restore function.

Prevention

Preventing brachial plexus stretch injury is difficult, but the risk of injury can be minimized by performing daily arm and neck ROM, flexibility, and strengthening exercises. Instruct your patient on how to properly perform all activities, while utilizing proper form and skills at all times.

Thoracic Outlet Syndrome

The thoracic outlet is the area at the neck between the clavicle and the first rib. Nerves and blood vessels run through this area. Thoracic outlet syndrome (TOS) is a condition when these nerves and/or blood vessels become compressed in this space.

Mechanism or Cause of Injury

Although the specific mechanism of TOS is not often determined, it can be caused by direct trauma or repetitive injuries to the thoracic outlet area. A patient may have an extra rib, which is an anatomical abnormality. This extra rib can compress on the structures in the thoracic outlet space. The nerves and blood vessels can also be compressed by the clavicle and neck muscles (i.e. scalenes and pectoralis minor) **(Figure 10-14)**.

Signs and Symptoms

TOS causes pain in the area, along with tingling or numbness down the arm and into the fingers. The patient may experience pain in the neck and shoulders, and a dull, weak feeling in the injured arm and hand. The patient's grip is weakened on the affected side. The pulse on the affected side is slower and weaker, or perhaps nonexistent by palpation, as compared to the uninjured arm.

Immediate Care

Treatment for TOS consists of medication and therapeutic modalities for pain relief and muscle relaxation, along with rehabilitation. In some instances, the physician may perform surgery on the patient to restore function. Rehabilitation will follow surgery. If TOS is not treated, then permanent injury to the nerves and blood vessels can result.

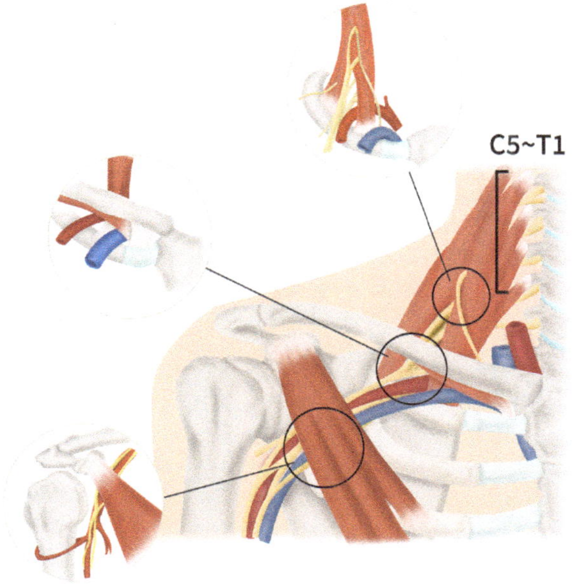

Figure 10-14 TOS can be caused by nerve and blood vessel compression by the scalenes, clavicle, or pectoralis minor.

Prevention

TOS can be prevented. Individuals should not carry heavy objects, such as boxes, bags, or purses, over the same shoulder repetitively. They should stretch the anterior shoulder and neck muscles, including the scalenes and pectoralis muscles. If the individual is overweight, they must lose weight to prevent or decrease symptoms of TOS. By losing the weight, compression and stress on the nerves and blood vessels in the thoracic outlet space will decrease (Mayo Clinic, 2019).

Injuries to the Elbow and Forearm

The elbow consists of the humerus, radius, and ulna bones. The forearm is considered the area between the elbow and the wrist where the radius and ulna lie. Elbow and forearm injuries can occur alone or in conjunction with other injuries to the upper extremity. As with shoulder injuries, elbow and forearm injuries can be acute or chronic, with some injuries necessitating emergency care.

Fractures

Radius and ulna fractures can occur separately when only one bone is fractured, or both bones can be fractured simultaneously **(Figure 10-15)**. When a significant forearm injury occurs, such as a fracture, or a dislocation occurs to the elbow, you must determine if the

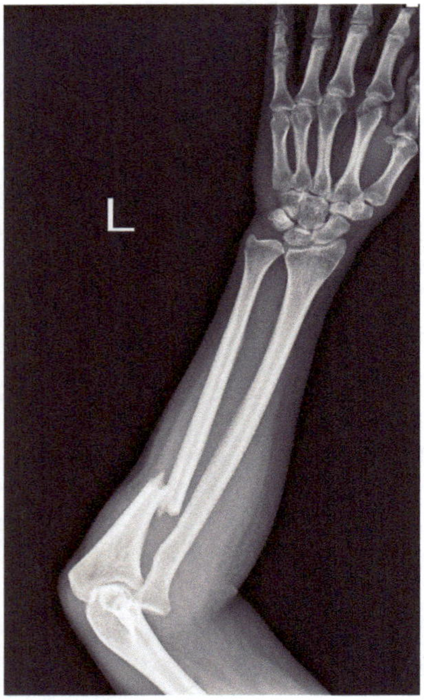

Figure 10-15 Ulna fracture at the elbow

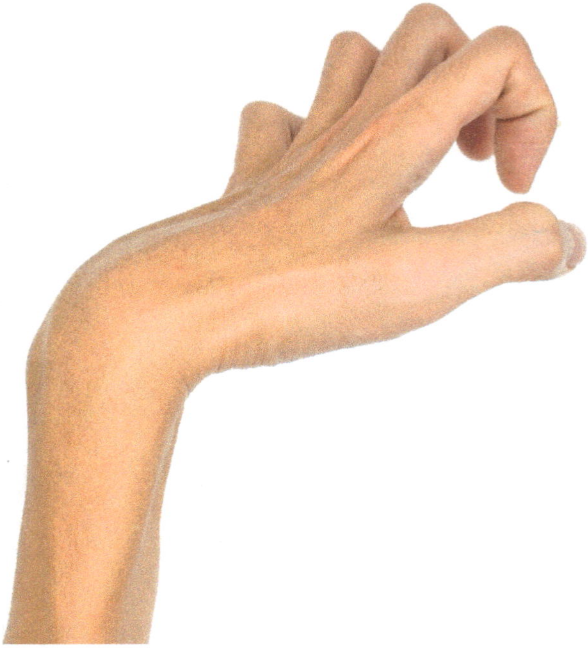

Figure 10-16 Volkmann's contracture

individual is experiencing Volkmann's contracture. Volkmann's contracture is a result from a traumatic injury to the upper extremity, particularly at the elbow, humerus, and forearm, which causes significant swelling. The edema presses on the blood vessels. Consequently, the blood vessels cannot deliver oxygenated blood to the distal upper extremity. If lack of blood flow to the distal extremity continues, then the nerves and soft tissues become damaged, which could be permanent. The insufficient blood flow and oxygen causes the hand to take on a claw-like appearance **(Figure 10-16)** due to muscle contracture from lack of oxygen to the tissues. The muscles in the forearm and hand are contracted in a flexed position. The patient cannot passively extend the fingers. Volkmann's contracture is a medical emergency.

As a first responder, there is not much first aid that you can perform for Volkmann's contracture, other than to call 911 and treat for shock. Check the individual's radial pulse. Touch their fingers and hand on the affected side and ask them if they can feel your touch. When the EMTs arrive at the scene, inform them of your findings. If the individual's blood flow to the distal extremity is not restored immediately, via addressing the causative factor such as the fracture or dislocation, then the possibility of losing distal extremity function exists. In cases of Volkmann's contracture, surgery may be necessary.

Mechanism or Cause of Injury

Acute elbow and forearm fractures can occur from a fall on an outstretched arm. Fractures can also be caused by a direct blow to the area, which most often occurs in contact sports, especially when equipment such as sticks are involved (i.e. in lacrosse and field hockey). An individual can also be in a weight-bearing position where the hand is fixed on an immovable surface, such as the ground or a mat. In this position, they may twist their body while their hand remains fixed, resulting in a fracture. Due to twisting of the radius and ulna, a spiral fracture would most likely result with this weight bearing mechanism of injury. This mechanism of injury could occur in gymnastic events, such as floor and vault apparatus.

Signs and Symptoms

The individual experiences severe pain, point tenderness, and loss of function. If the nerves in the elbow and forearm are affected, they will also have loss of sensation. Other signs and symptoms include muscle spasm, swelling, ecchymosis, and deformity. If they have deformity, then the fractured bones are displaced.

Immediate Care

Treat the person as you would for any other fracture. Have them keep their arm still, make sure they are comfortable, and call 911. Splint the area using boards, SAM splints (www.sammedical.com/sam_splint.html), or any other stabilizing materials **(Figure 10-17)**. Apply ice on the injured area, while taking care not to apply an ice bag too heavy, which would cause an increase in symptoms or complications. Watch for Volkmann's contracture and shock to arise. Once the individual is at the ER, the physician will evaluate the injury, take x-rays, and cast or

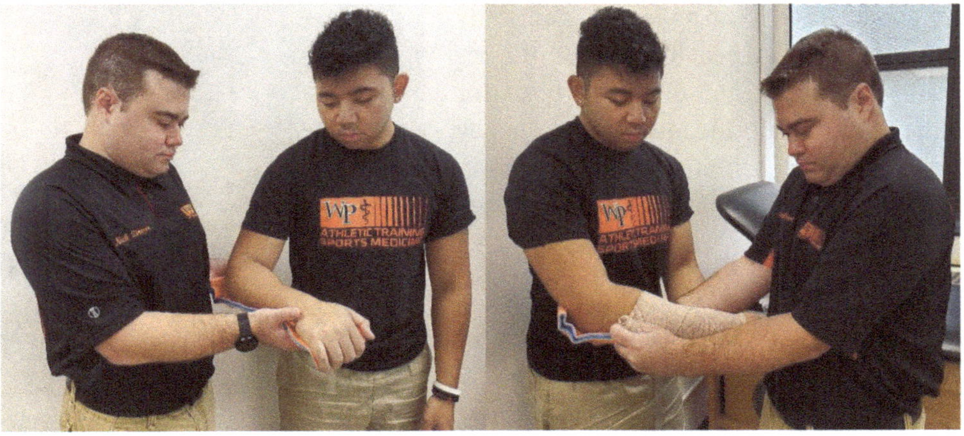

Figure 10-17 Splinting for a radius and ulna fracture

splint the area. After the cast or splint is removed, the patient will have to undergo rehabilitation for the entire upper extremity in order to restore full function.

Prevention

Athletic participants must wear appropriate protective equipment and padding in order to prevent elbow and forearm fractures. They should also have adequate ROM, flexibility, and muscular strength at the forearm, as well as muscular coordination and balance, especially if they perform upper extremity weight-bearing activities. Weight-bearing activities help keep bones strong as well as having an adequate supply of calcium and vitamin D in their diet. If an individual has strong bones, the potential for fractures can be minimized.

Dislocations

Elbow dislocations occur to the ulna. The ulna is forced out of its alignment with the humerus, most commonly into a posterior position relative to the joint **(Figure 10-18)**. As with any other dislocation, an elbow dislocation is a medical emergency, and the possibility of Volkmann's contracture exists. Likewise, dislocations often occur along with elbow and forearm fractures.

Mechanism or Cause of Injury

An elbow dislocation occurs with significant trauma. A direct blow can dislocate the elbow. Also, a fall on an outstretched arm with the elbow in a slight degree of flexion will force the ulna out of alignment and dislocate posteriorly.

Signs and Symptoms

An individual with a dislocated elbow most likely will be in shock. The elbow appears significantly swollen and deformed. Their forearm on the injured side appears shortened due to its posterior displacement. Severe pain and loss of function may exist, as well as loss of sensation from their forearm to fingers due to **neurovascular compromise**.

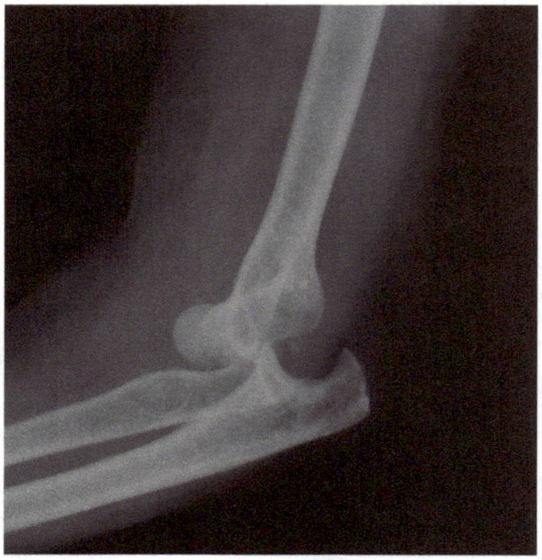

Figure 10-18 An elbow dislocation can occur when the ulna is forced posteriorly.

Immediate Care

Treat an individual who has sustained an elbow dislocation as you would for any other medical emergency. Immediately call 911. Make sure they are in a comfortable position and supporting the injured elbow. Splint the elbow in the position that you find it and apply ice to help decrease pain. Take their radial pulse and determine their hand and fingers sensation as you would for an elbow fracture and Volkmann's contracture. Most importantly, treat them for shock until EMS arrives.

In the ER, the physician will reduce the elbow and put the ulna back into normal alignment. X-rays will determine whether a fracture also exists. The patient will be splinted with their arm in a sling. The patient must apply ice frequently to the injured area with the splint removed, as per the physician's orders. Within a few weeks, rehabilitation begins. Eventually the splint is no longer utilized.

Prevention

Falling on an outstretched arm is a common mechanism of injury, so your client should attempt to avoid falling in this manner. If your client falls, they should have their body positioned to roll on the ground as they strike the surface. They must take care when exposing themselves to any situation where they could fall. Good muscular strength around the elbow helps to prevent an elbow dislocation.

Sprains

Sprains to the elbow typically occur to the ulnar collateral ligament (UCL) or the radial collateral ligament (RCL). These ligaments support the medial and lateral sides of the elbow, respectively.

Mechanism or Cause of Injury

The UCL and RCL can be injured by a fall on an outstretched arm, a fixed hand with twisting of the arm, or a direct blow to the elbow. The UCL is injured by a force applied to the elbow's lateral side, compressing that area, which results in a traction force on the elbow's medial side where the UCL is located. This force, called a valgus force, stretches and sprains the UCL **(Figure 10-19)**. Likewise, the RCL is injured by a force applied to the elbow's medial side, compressing that area, which creates a traction force on the elbow's lateral side causing a RCL sprain. This force is called a varus force. UCL injuries often occur when the arm is in a cocked position and an athlete throws a ball with the elbow with an improper side-arm position. Repetitive side-arm throwing motions cause UCL tears because the athlete's arm is in a valgus position during the motion.

Signs and Symptoms

Signs and symptoms of elbow sprains include all inflammation signs and symptoms such as pain, redness, swelling, point tenderness, ecchymosis, redness, increased skin temperature at the injured area, loss of function or function with pain, and joint instability.

Figure 10-19 An ulnar collateral ligament sprain due to repetitive side-arm throwing

Immediate Care

If you suspect the athlete has sustained an elbow sprain, have the athlete discontinue activity and rest. Rule out any other serious injuries such as a fracture or dislocation. Have them apply ice and compression to the elbow. Elevate the elbow by applying a sling. Depending on the severity of the injury, you may need to refer the athlete to a physician for evaluation. The physician will prescribe NSAIDs and possibly have the athlete wear a splint or sling until signs and symptoms of injury decrease. Surgery is not performed for a common, uncomplicated elbow sprain.

Prevention

Athletic participants must wear protective elbow padding as required by their activity. They must be aware of their surroundings including opponents, implements, immovable structures, and the like when participating in activities in order to prevent sprains to the elbow.

Little League Elbow

Little league elbow is an overuse injury that occurs to the medial elbow of throwing athletes, especially pitchers. This injury is a syndrome, which includes growth complications at the medial epicondyle, medial epicondylitis (which is discussed in this chapter), and **apophysitis**. The syndrome is considered to be chronic inflammation of the medial epicondyle.

Mechanism or Cause of Injury

Athletes can succumb to little league elbow from repetitive overhead throwing. Usually, it occurs to younger pitchers who throw too many hard, fast pitches, during practices and games. Because the growth plates on children and adolescents are not yet fused, the stress from constant throwing causes weakness at the medial epicondyle, and little league elbow results. The primary force causing this syndrome is a valgus force to the elbow.

Signs and Symptoms

The main symptom of little league elbow is pain at the medial elbow. This pain worsens if the athlete continues to throw, and becomes most painful when the athlete attempts elbow extension. Also, the pain remains for days after the last throwing day. The athlete complains of muscular weakness, loss of coordination, control, and function. The elbow may be swollen and point tender at the medial epicondyle.

Immediate Care

Explain to the athlete the cause of little league elbow, and have them stop the causative factor, which is throwing and/or throwing improperly. If the causative factor is not removed or corrected, then the injury will get worse. Rest is very important for little league elbow. The area needs sufficient time to heal. Have the athlete apply RICE and see how the injury responds to treatment. If the injury heals well, then the athlete should begin muscle strengthening around the elbow. A slow return to throwing, called a throwing progression, can begin once ROM, strength, and coordination at the elbow have been regained. If the athlete does not respond to RICE, then they should see their physician for further evaluation. In severe cases where part of the medial epicondyle is avulsed from the humerus, surgery is necessary to secure the fractured bony pieces.

Prevention

The athlete must be aware of how much they throw. Baseball pitch counts are helpful to keep track of how many times the athlete has thrown in one practice or game. The athlete must throw properly, and not subject the elbow to undue valgus forces. Very young athletes should not be throwing breaking balls, such as curve balls and sliders, as these pitches put excessive amounts of stress on the immature medial elbow. Once the athlete reaches adolescence, then they can learn the proper way to throw these pitches without predisposing their elbow to little league elbow. A variety of information regarding training and pitch count for little league players can be found at www.littleleague.org.

Strains

Muscle strains at the elbow most often occur at the biceps brachii, triceps brachii, and anterior forearm muscles. Forearm muscle strains are often referred to as forearm splints, which often occur to individuals who repetitively utilize their wrist in flexion or extension activities. Gymnasts who are pommel horse specialists and keep their wrists in extension for the majority of their routine, and weightlifters who perform wrist curls are two examples of athletes who could sustain forearm splints.

Mechanism or Cause of Injury

The mechanism of injury is a repetitive overuse of the muscles. The muscles can also be stretched for an extended period of time, which can cause the fibers to tear. A one-time forceful muscle contraction or stretch can also cause a muscle strain.

Signs and Symptoms

Elbow and forearm muscle strains are similar in signs and symptoms as shoulder muscle strains, especially because some of the same muscles are involved. The patient experiences pain which may appear immediately, hours, or days after injury; loss of function; and point tenderness. The area may be swollen, red, and warm. Ecchymosis may appear. A Grade 3 biceps brachii tendon sprain or rupture at the insertion appears like a large bulge in the middle of the humerus **(Figure 10-20)**. A divot or depression would also be present. This divot indicates that the tendon is no longer attached to the bone.

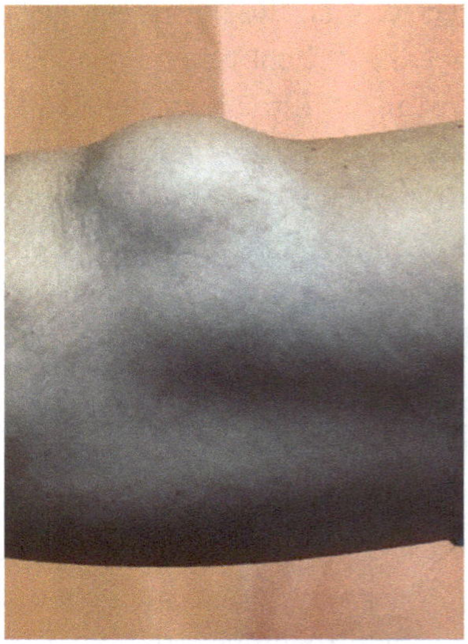

Figure 10-20 A biceps brachii rupture appears as a bump at the upper arm.

Immediate Care

Care for an elbow and forearm strain includes RICE. If the patient is in severe pain, has no muscle function, and/or has any signs or symptoms that indicate a Grade 3 strain, call 911 for advanced medical care.

Prevention

Muscular strength and flexibility are extremely important to prevent and minimize muscle strains. The patient should strengthen the muscles around the elbow and forearm regularly, which protects them against excessive stress and resultant injury.

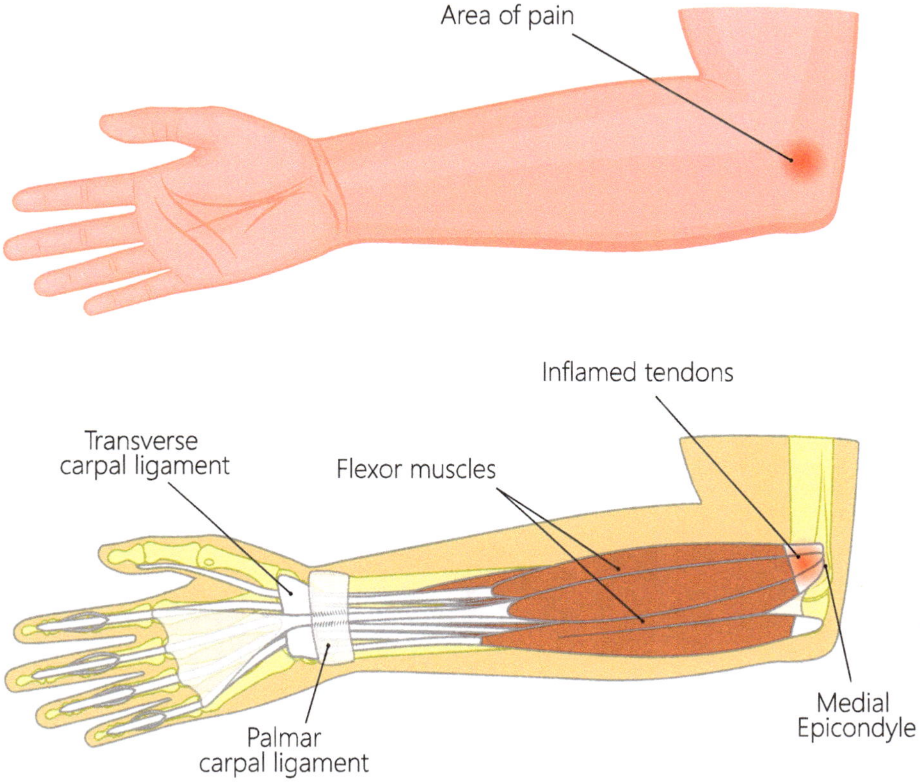

Figure 10-21 Medial epicondylitis (golfer's elbow)

Lateral and Medial Epicondylitis

Epicondylitis is chronic overuse injury, which is a type of a muscular strain. It is an inflammation of the tendons that attach to the epicondyles of the humerus at the elbow's bony prominences. Medial epicondylitis is often referred to as "golfer's elbow" **(Figure 10-21)**, while lateral epicondylitis is often referred to as "tennis elbow" **(Figure 10-22)**.

Mechanism or Cause of Injury

Medial epicondylitis is caused by repetitive, forceful wrist flexion. The injury is called "golfer's elbow" because during the golf follow-through swing, some golfers incorrectly perform the skill and flex the wrist. Lateral epicondylitis, or "tennis elbow", is caused by repetitive forceful wrist extension. A tennis player performs an incorrect backhand and extends the wrist instead of keeping it straight. Over time, lateral epicondylitis develops. Both of these injuries most often do not occur from sport activities, but rather from other daily, repetitive, physical activities, such as computer work, gardening, and construction.

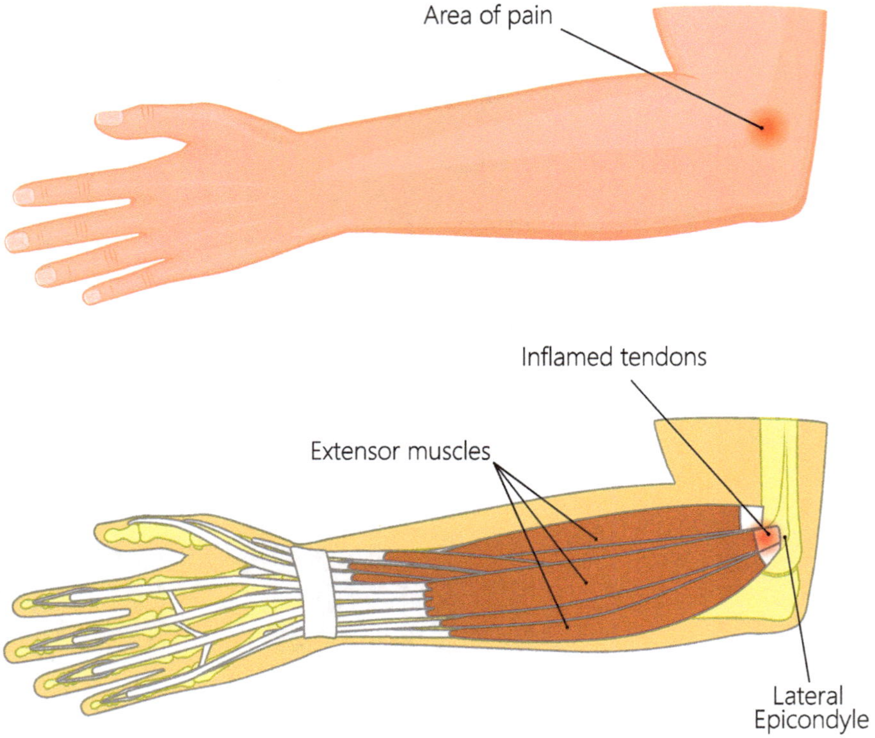

Figure 10-22 Lateral epicondylitis (tennis elbow)

Signs and Symptoms

Signs and symptoms of medial and lateral epicondylitis are the same. Pain at the epicondyle, along with muscular weakness are the prominent signs and symptoms of epicondylitis. Grip strength is weak. Therefore, performing ADLs such as opening a can with a manual can opener, turning a doorknob, and holding a cup are difficult and uncomfortable. The patient is point tender at the epicondyle and swelling may be visible. The pain may eventually occur during all activities utilizing the elbow, wrist, and fingers. Without treatment, over time the pain may perpetuate as a dull ache throughout the day at rest.

Immediate Care

In order to stop any further exacerbation of signs and symptoms, have the individual stop the causing activity and utilize RICE to decrease signs and symptoms. If the signs and symptoms persist throughout the day, then the individual must see a physician for evaluation. The physician may prescribe NSAIDs to decrease pain and inflammation. The patient may wear a brace, called a counterforce brace, distal to the epicondyles. This brace decreases stress on the injured tendons as the muscles contract, and also provides compression. In some cases, the physician may provide a **corticosteroid** injection to promote healing and decrease pain to the injured tendons and muscles. Rehabilitation must follow the corticosteroid injection. The muscles and tendons around the epicondyle must be strong to prevent recurrence. Even with treatment, epicondylitis may take many months to subside. If after a year, the patient continues to have significant signs and symptoms of epicondylitis that affect their ADLs and conservative treatment has not proven to be effective, then surgery most likely will be performed.

Prevention

Individuals must always use proper form when participating in physical activities to avoid epicondylitis. If a person does not know how to perform a skill properly, assist them in learning proper skill execution. Elbow muscles and tendons must be strong enough to minimize the potential for epicondylitis.

Olecranon Bursitis

The olecranon bursa sits on the olecranon between the bone and the skin. Olecranon bursitis is an inflammation of the bursa. Normally you cannot feel the bursa. Fluid collects in the bursa when it is inflamed, and you can easily palpate and visualize it in this condition.

Mechanism or Cause of Injury

Olecranon bursitis can be acute or chronic. Acute bursitis is caused by a direct blow to the olecranon when the elbow is flexed. Chronic bursitis is caused by constant rubbing of an object on the olecranon, such as an improperly fitted elbow pad.

Signs and Symptoms

The patient feels pain and has loss of ROM, especially in elbow flexion. Acute bursitis often makes the elbow appear deformed because the swelling is very localized. The bursa is swollen and resembles a ping pong ball inside the elbow at the olecranon **(Figure 10-23)**. The chronic bursitis swelling is more diffuse than for acute bursitis. Ecchymosis and point tenderness will most likely be present, as well as red and warm skin.

Immediate Care

The force required to cause acute olecranon bursitis is hard enough to potentially cause an olecranon or proximal ulna fracture. Therefore, apply ice, wrap the arm with an elastic bandage, and put it in a sling. Refer the patient to a physician to have x-rays taken to rule out a fracture. For chronic bursitis due to friction, advise the patient to remove the causative factor.

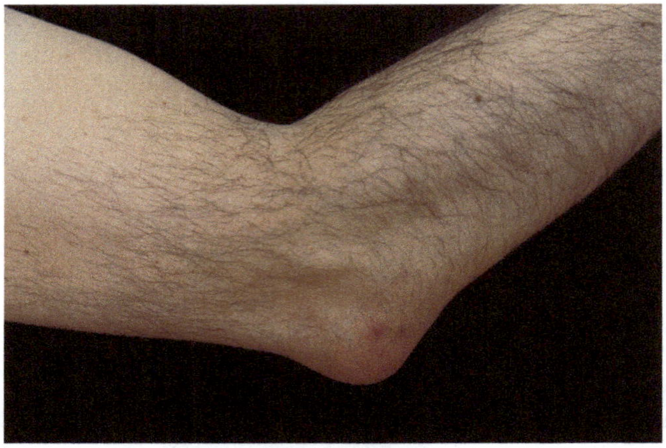

Figure 10-23 Acute olecranon bursitis

Apply ice and a compression wrap. They may be able to continue limited participation if they wear a compression sleeve, applies ice intermittently, and takes over-the-counter NSAIDs. If the patient's signs and symptoms do not decrease, then refer them to a physician for evaluation. For both acute and chronic olecranon bursitis, the physician will prescribe NSAIDs, therapeutic modalities, compression, and rehabilitation. In some cases, the bursa may need to be drained to relieve the accumulated fluid. Also, corticosteroids may be injected into the bursa.

Prevention

Individuals must wear well-fitted elbow pads whenever participating in activities where the potential for the olecranon to receive a direct blow exists. Likewise, the elbow pads must fit properly in order to prevent rubbing of the pad on the skin.

Ulnar Nerve Injury

The ulnar nerve runs along the elbow's medial side. Because the nerve sits very superficial to the skin and is lodged between the medial epicondyle of the humerus and the ulna, it is often predisposed to injury.

Mechanism or Cause of Injury

The ulnar nerve can be injured by a direct blow to the medial elbow. When this injury occurs, the individual may say that they hit their "funny bone". Continual pressure on or stretching of the nerve can lead to cubital tunnel syndrome **(Figure 10-24)**. If a person sleeps with their arm flexed, they may awaken to a tingling forearm and fourth and fifth fingers. The nerve may

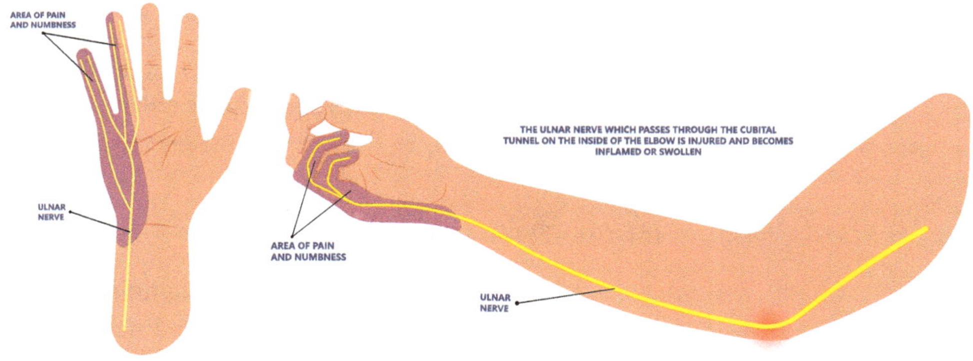

Figure 10-24 Ulnar nerve injury can cause cubital tunnel syndrome.

also be compromised if another elbow injury exists, such as medial epicondylitis, little league, elbow, a UCL sprain, a fracture, or a dislocation. The edema from the other injury compresses the nerve and create signs and symptoms of an ulnar nerve injury.

Signs and Symptoms

Signs and symptoms of ulnar nerve injury include transient pain at the injury site, and tingling and numbness down the elbow to the fourth and fifth fingers. The hand is also weak, especially when attempting to grip with the fourth and fifth fingers. Over time, if the injury is not treated, the individual will have visible atrophy of some hand and forearm muscles.

Immediate Care

To care for an ulnar nerve injury that occurs due to a direct blow to the ulnar nerve, have the individual move their fingers, hand, and wrist as much as possible until feeling is restored. Feeling should be restored within a few seconds to minutes. Typically after a direct blow to the elbow, the individual does not experience any other complications and can return to activity if they have full elbow, wrist, and hand ROM and strength. Ice should not be applied directly on top of the nerve since the nerve is very superficial. Direct ice on the nerve can damage it if the ice is left on too long.

For other ulnar nerve injuries not caused by a direct blow, or if sensation, ROM, and strength at the elbow does not return to normal, the individual should be evaluated by a physician. Rehabilitation, and perhaps occupational therapy, for the elbow and hand will be warranted. Specialized splints can be utilized to wear during the day and while sleeping to assist in keeping the elbow at a comfortable position and avoiding full flexion. The physician may inject corticosteroids into the area to decrease pain and minimize inflammation. Other medications such as over-the-counter or prescription NSAIDs may be prescribed.

Prevention

Preventing ulnar nerve injury includes having individuals wear properly fitted and worn elbow pads, splints, and other equipment for their activity. Individuals should also avoid holding the elbow in a flexed position for long periods of time during the day and while sleeping, if possible.

Injuries to the Wrist, Hand, and Fingers

Although the wrist, hand, and fingers are small body areas, they make a significant contribution to body function and activity. The hand and fingers provide grip and dexterity. Full function of each joint is truly important. Many wrist, hand, and fingers injuries are not medical emergencies; however, the significance of the injuries and importance of proper treatment cannot be underestimated.

Fractures

Fractures can occur to any of the wrist, hand, and finger bones. However, the most common fractures are to the distal end of the radius (Colles' fracture) **(Figure 10-25)**, the fifth metacarpal (boxer's fracture) **(Figure 10-26)**, and the base of the first metacarpal (Bennett's fracture) **(Figure 10-27)**. Metacarpal, scaphoid, hamate, and phalange fractures are common as well.

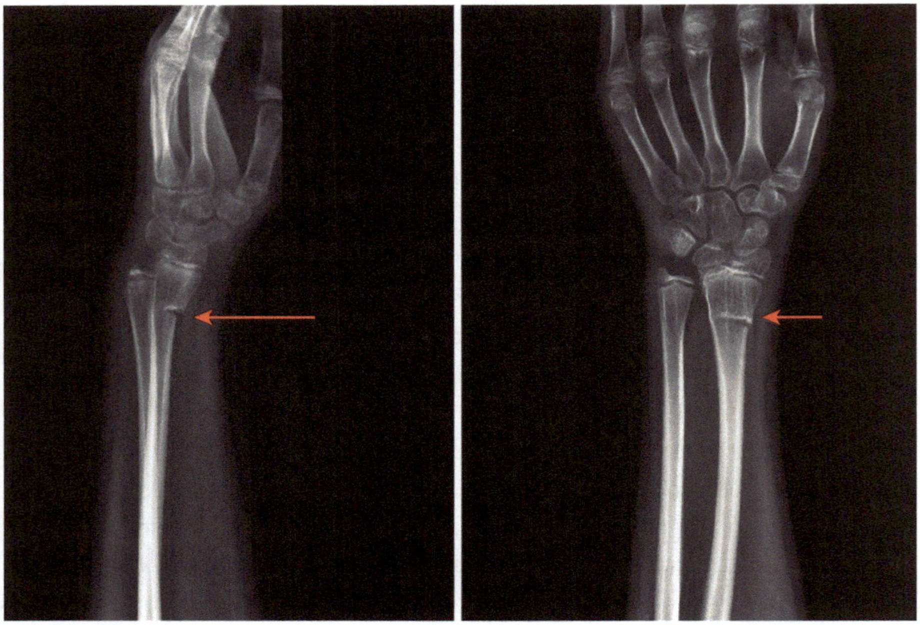

Figure 10-25 A Colles' fracture is a fracture to the distal radius.

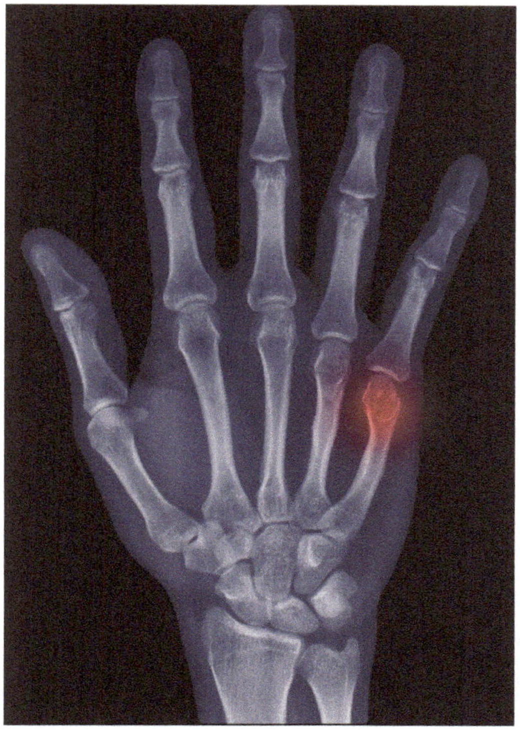

Figure 10-26 A fracture to the distal 5th metacarpal is a "boxer's fracture".

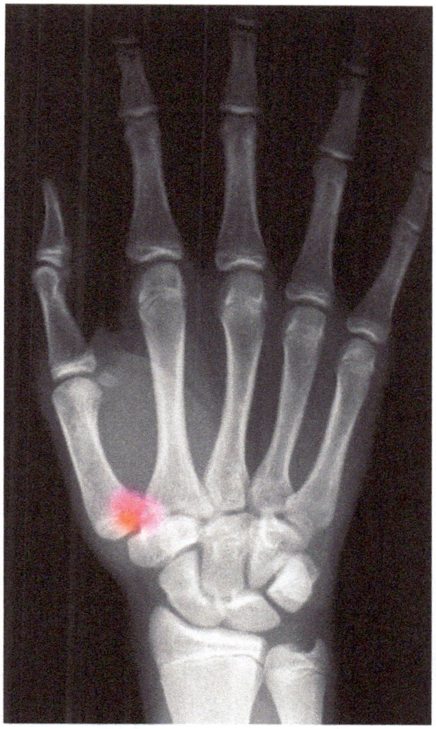

Figure 10-27 A Bennett's fracture is a fracture to the base of the first metacarpal.

Mechanism or Cause of Injury

Fractures to the bones mentioned are most often injured by a direct traumatic force. A Colles' fracture typically occurs when a patient falls on an outstretched arm/hand (FOOSH mechanism of injury). A boxer's fracture can occur when a patient strikes a hard, immovable object with a closed fist. A Bennett's fracture can occur when an object strikes or a patient falls on the tip of the thumb when in slight flexion. A scaphoid fracture can occur by falling on an outstretched arm. Due to the location of the hamate, it is fractured most often when a patient is holding an implement, such as a field hockey stick or a baseball bat, and a traumatic force occurs with the implement in hand. Any metacarpal and phalange can be fractured by getting hit on the tip of the finger, or when a person's hand is stepped on. Stress fractures can also occur to the scaphoid. Repetitive lower intensity forces over time with the wrist in extension can put undue stress on the scaphoid and eventually lead the bone to break down. This bone does not have a good blood supply. Therefore, without blood to assist in healing, the scaphoid becomes necrotic and dies.

TIPS FROM THE FIELD

Tip 2 One simple way to splint a fractured or sprained finger is to "buddy tape" the finger **(Figure 10-28)**. Have the patient support the injured finger as you prepare the athletic tape. Take two to three strips of athletic tape that is approximately ½ to 1-inch width and rip or cut them into approximately 3-inch length (or longer if the individual's fingers are large). Place the injured finger next to the adjacent, uninjured finger and have the individual hold them still. Place the strips of tape around the fingers securely, but not so tight where circulation would be disrupted. The tape should not be directly over the injured area, but should be placed proximally and distally to support the injury. If the injury is to the third or fourth fingers, you can buddy tape the injured finger in between the two adjacent, uninjured fingers.

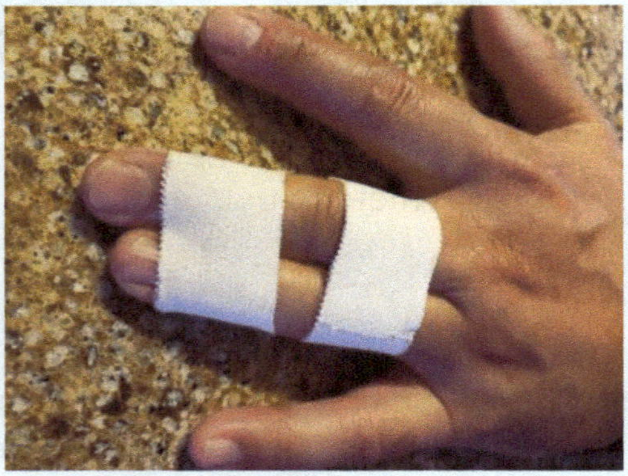

Figure 10-28 An injured finger is buddy taped to the neighboring finger for support.

Signs and Symptoms

Fractures of the wrist, hand, and fingers cause pain, point tenderness, loss of function, and muscular stiffness. Swelling and ecchymosis may be present. The area may or may not exhibit deformity.

Immediate Care

Treat a suspected fracture of the wrist, hand, and fingers as you would any other fracture. Begin with RICE and splint the area. Call 911 if the person is experiencing severe signs and symptoms of injury, has an open fracture, loss of feeling or function, or is in shock. Instances when you may not need to call 911, but should refer the person to the ER for x-rays are for a closed phalangeal fracture, a non-displaced metacarpal fracture, or any closed wrist, hand, and finger fracture that results in only mild signs and symptoms of injury. The x-rays identify whether a fracture exists. The physician will determine whether a splint or hard cast is necessary, as well as if surgery is required to facilitate proper healing.

Prevention

Individuals must learn how to correctly perform activities in order to prevent fractures to the wrist, hand, or fingers. They should wear proper protective gear for the area. Vitamin D and calcium ingestion, along with weight-bearing activities, are important for the individuals in order to keep their bones strong.

Dislocations

Lunate and phalangeal dislocations are very common dislocations which occur at the wrist, hand, and fingers. Lunate dislocations are often assumed to be a wrist sprain until an x-ray confirms the dislocation.

Mechanism or Cause of Injury

When a direct traumatic force strikes the palm of the hand at the lunate, such as when a patient falls on an outstretched arm, a lunate dislocation can occur. Phalangeal dislocations occur from being stepped on, or from a direct blow to the tip of the finger, such as when attempting to catch a basketball.

Signs and Symptoms

The patient experiences the typical signs and symptoms of common dislocations, including pain, loss of function and sensation at the dislocation site. Deformity is present along with swelling and ecchymosis, especially for phalangeal dislocations **(Figure 10-29)**.

Immediate Care

Always be prepared to treat for shock if necessary when a traumatic injury such as a dislocation occurs. Splint the injury, apply ice, and summon EMS. An individual may want to reduce their own phalangeal dislocation. Do not allow them or anyone else to reduce the dislocation, because reduction without training can cause further injury or complications.

Prevention

Individuals must be careful not to fall on an outstretched arm. They must be cognizant of their surroundings when participating in activities, especially activities that utilize equipment, implements, and balls that could strike the tip of the finger.

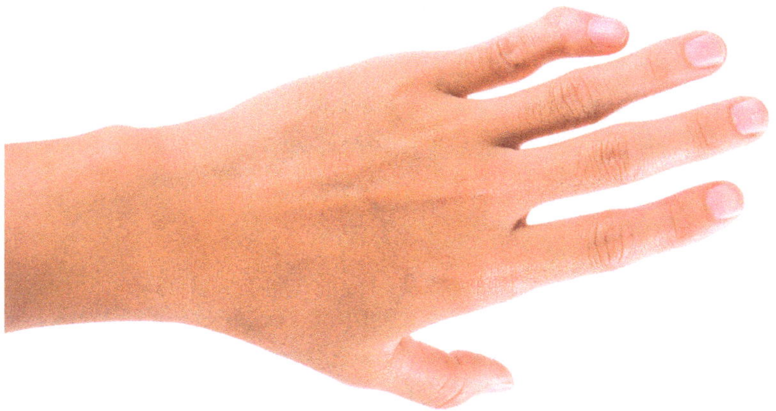

Figure 10-29 A finger dislocation at the DIP joint shows significant deformity.

Sprains

Collateral ligaments exist not only at the elbow, but also at the wrist and fingers. The wrist joint and every joint in the fingers, including the distal, proximal, and metacarpal phalangeal joints, all have a medial collateral ligament (MCL) and a lateral collateral ligament (LCL).

Mechanism or Cause of Injury

The wrist can be sprained by a fall on an outstretched arm. The phalangeal joints can be sprained by a blow to the tip of the finger. Similarly to the elbow, a valgus force applied to the wrist and phalangeal joints can result in a sprained MCL, whereas the LCL can be sprained by a varus force.

Signs and Symptoms

Sprains to the wrist and fingers result in signs and symptoms of pain, especially during motion, swelling, stiffness, ecchymosis, point tenderness, and increased tissue temperature.

Immediate Care

The first course of action to care for the patient is to apply RICE. The patient can also take over-the-counter NSAIDs to decrease pain and inflammation. Once the signs and symptoms of inflammation subside, the patient can slowly progress to perform AROM and muscle strengthening. With Grade 1 and Grade 2 sprains, physician evaluation may not be necessary. If the signs and symptoms indicate a more significant Grade 2 or a Grade 3 sprain, then refer the patient to a physician for evaluation. Grade 3 sprains can also occur in conjunction with an avulsion fracture; consequently, when you suspect a Grade 3 sprain, the patient must be referred to a physician for x-rays. Anti-inflammatory medication, RICE, and a removable splint, followed by rehabilitation, are necessary to return to normal function.

Prevention

Individuals should avoid falling on an outstretched arm with the wrist in extension. Also, precaution should be taken to prevent valgus or varus forces to the wrist and fingers in order to minimize trauma to the MCL and LCL.

Carpal Tunnel Syndrome

The carpal tunnel is an area on the anterior wrist that contains the median nerve and nine wrist and finger flexor tendons. Carpal tunnel syndrome is a chronic condition that involves median nerve compression **(Figure 10-30).** This condition occurs three times more commonly to women than men (U.S. Department of Health and Human Services Office of Women's Health [OASH], 2019), and often to people between the age of 30 and 60 years (Medline Plus, 2022).

Mechanism or Cause of Injury

Carpal tunnel syndrome can occur to anyone who utilizes the hand in repetitive motion, especially in conjunction with wrist flexion. Individuals who participate in racquetball and handball or other activities that require them to grip an implement and perform wrist flexion are most prone to carpal tunnel syndrome. Other people who participate in long periods of computer use, writing, sewing, and driving also can succumb to carpal tunnel syndrome. Rheumatoid arthritis, diabetes, hypothyroidism, obesity, and menopause are conditions that predispose people to carpal tunnel syndrome.

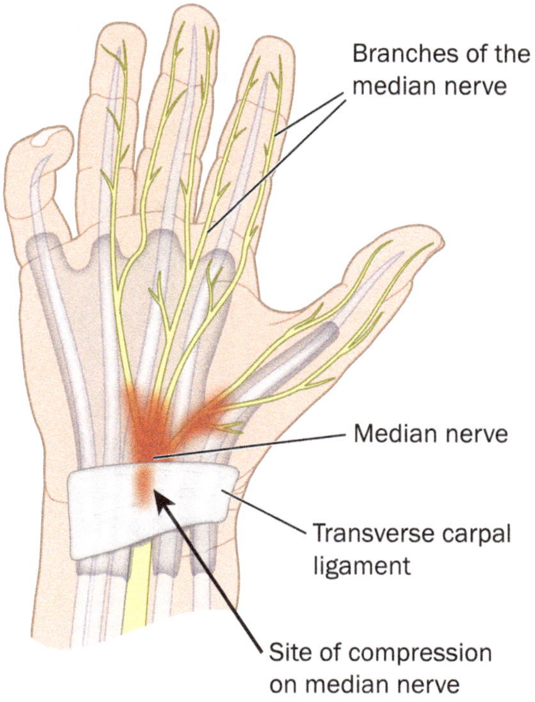

Figure 10-30 Median nerve compression site at the anterior wrist

Signs and Symptoms

Signs and symptoms of carpal tunnel syndrome include tingling and numbness in the thumb, index, and third fingers, and the palm of the hand. The individual has pain with wrist flexion, which can radiate to the elbow and down into the fingers. Their wrist, finger, and grip strength are weak, and function and coordination (including dexterity) are decreased. Over time, the individual's thenar eminence, located at the palm side of the first metacarpal, will slowly atrophy.

Immediate Care

Because this condition is not caused by acute trauma, the patient would state that the signs and symptoms have worsened over time. Perform a secondary survey that includes a special test, called Tinel's sign, to determine if the patient has carpal tunnel syndrome. With the patient's wrist facing up, gently tap over the wrist area where the median nerve is located **(Figure 10-31)**. If the patient feels tingling into the wrist and fingers, then the test is indicative of carpal tunnel syndrome.

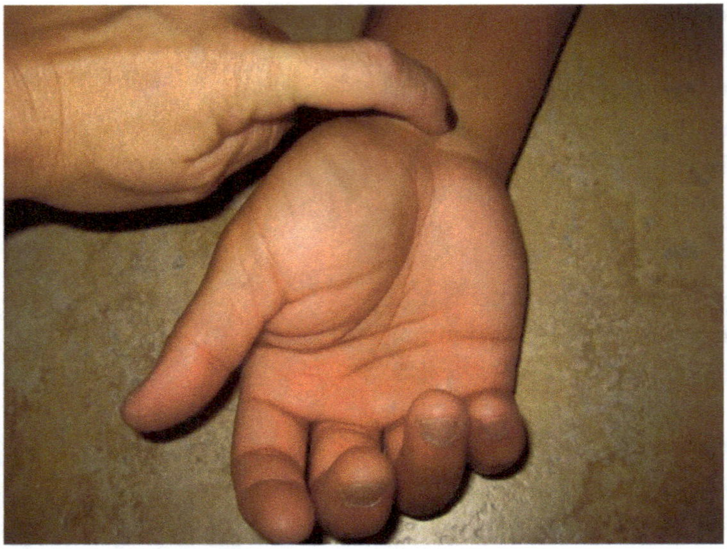

Figure 10-31 Tinel's sign being utilized to identify carpal tunnel syndrome

Your patient should see a physician, but in the meantime, they can utilize RICE or moist heat on the area to eliminate pain and inflammation. Moist heat is acceptable to utilize for carpal tunnel syndrome because the condition is not acute. The patient should discontinue any activity that causes pain or aggravates symptoms. They can also take over-the-counter anti-inflammatory medication such as ibuprofen or naproxen.

The physician may prescribe NSAIDs and a splint to wear during the day and perhaps at night. The splint assists the patient in maintaining some wrist extension, which alleviates median nerve pressure. If the carpal tunnel syndrome is caused by improper wrist positioning when utilizing a computer, the patient can purchase **ergonomic equipment**, such as ergonomic keyboards and mouse pads. This equipment assists in placing the wrist in a more comfortable, extended position while typing. Rehabilitation to strengthen the hand and forearm musculature is necessary. If this conservative approach to treatment does not decrease the signs and symptoms, then the physician may choose to give the patient a corticosteroid injection. Surgery is another option to decrease pressure on the median nerve.

Prevention

In attempt to prevent carpal tunnel syndrome, individuals should refrain from keeping the wrist in flexion for long periods of time. Whenever ergonomic equipment is available, individuals should utilize the equipment to keep the wrist in a comfortable, less stressful position of slight extension.

De Quervain's Tenosynovitis

De Quervain's tenosynovitis, which is also referred to as de Quervain's syndrome, is a condition when the synovial sheath of the tendons that abduct and extend the thumb become inflamed. Consequently, the tendons cannot move properly inside the sheath.

Mechanism or Cause of Injury

Similarly to carpal tunnel syndrome, de Quervain's tenosynovitis is caused by repetitive movements. When the thumb is constantly gripping or in a fist, such as when utilizing an implement like a hammer, a racket, or dumbbell, the individual can irritate the thumb tendons. A repetitive wringing motion, as with wringing out a towel, can also cause inflammation. In particular, people who have rheumatoid arthritis are prone to de Quervain's syndrome.

Signs and Symptoms

The individual experiences pain at the base of the thumb especially when gripping objects or making a fist. Swelling, crepitus, and loss of function are also apparent.

Immediate Care

If the patient complains of chronic pain at the thumb tendons, perform a secondary survey. At the end of the examination, perform the following special test called the Finkelstein test. Have the patient make a fist with the thumb inside, then passively move the wrist medially to apply a stretch to the thumb tendons **(Figure 10-32)**. Pain on the wrist area by the thumb indicates

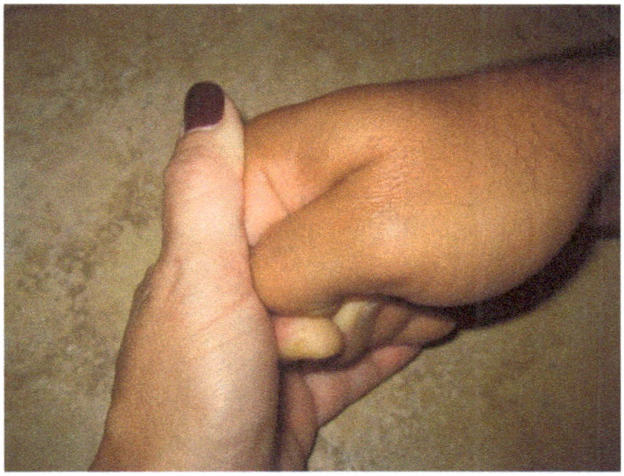

Figure 10-32 Finkelstein test being utilized to identify de Quervain's syndrome

de Quervain's tenosynovitis. Treatment for de Quervain's syndrome is similar to carpal tunnel syndrome. Have the patient apply RICE or heat to the area if the tendons are not acutely inflamed. The patient should see a physician, who will probably prescribe NSAIDs and rehabilitation. The physician may also have the patient wear a splint to keep the thumb in a rested, straightened position. The patient should see progress and a decrease in signs and symptoms in about a month. If conservative approach to treatment does not work, then the physician may perform surgery.

Prevention

Individuals should attempt to avoid repetitive gripping and wringing activities, and perform AROM of the thumb to decrease the incidence of de Quervain's syndrome. As with carpal tunnel syndrome, ergonomic equipment can assist in preventing de Quervain's syndrome. Finger, hand, and wrist muscles should also be strengthened to prevent injury due to repetitive stresses.

Ganglion Cyst

A ganglion cyst is a fluid-filled sac that develops at the wrist and carpal bones. The cyst is **benign**; however, it may be unsightly and cause functional problems for your client.

Mechanism or Cause of Injury

The cause of ganglion cysts is unknown. It is speculated that synovial fluid in the joint spaces among the carpal bones and the wrist joint becomes encapsulated over time and forms the cyst. The individual states that the cyst has developed and increasingly increased in size over time.

Signs and Symptoms

The cyst is not painful; however, it appears like a large bump **(Figure 10-33)**. Upon palpation, the cyst can range from very hard to soft. Palpation of the cyst does not cause point tenderness. No signs of inflammation exist, and the patient has full function and sensation.

Immediate Care

Perform a secondary survey to determine that the cyst is not something else. Ganglion cysts typically do not require any treatment. If your client is unsure if the bump is in fact a cyst, pain or loss of function exists, or they believe it is unsightly and want it removed, then your client should see their physician. To remove the cyst, the physician must remove the fluid with a needle and syringe. Then your client's wrist will be compressed with a compression wrap or

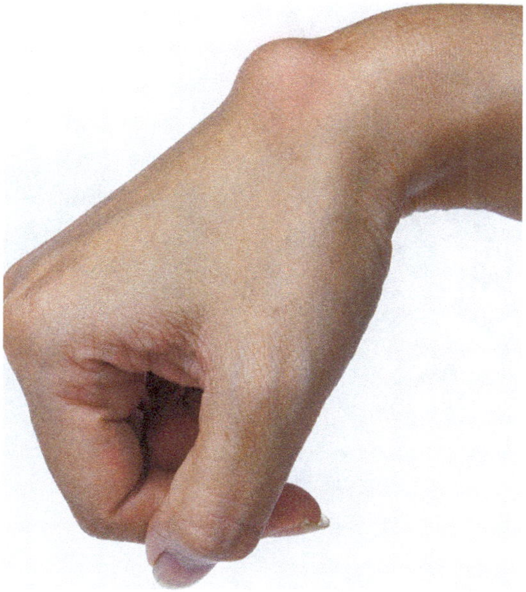

Figure 10-33 Ganglion cysts can occur on the anterior or posterior sides of the wrist.

tape. At no point should your client try to burst the cyst. If an individual attempts to burst the cyst, they may cause further injury.

Prevention

Unfortunately, there is no way to prevent a cyst from developing. Individuals who have had wrist injuries are predisposed to cysts more than others who have not. Consequently, individuals should attempt to avoid wrist injuries.

Gamekeeper's Thumb

Gamekeeper's thumb is a sprain and resultant chronic ulnar collateral ligament (UCL) laxity of the thumb's metacarpophalangeal (MCP) joint. An acute variation of this injury is called skier's thumb.

Mechanism or Cause of Injury

The cause of gamekeeper's thumb is a repetitive valgus force to the thumb when it is in extension and abduction **(Figure 10-34)**. This repetitive force is placed on the thumb, as it is in the position furthest away from the second finger, creating a forward or backward "L" appearance

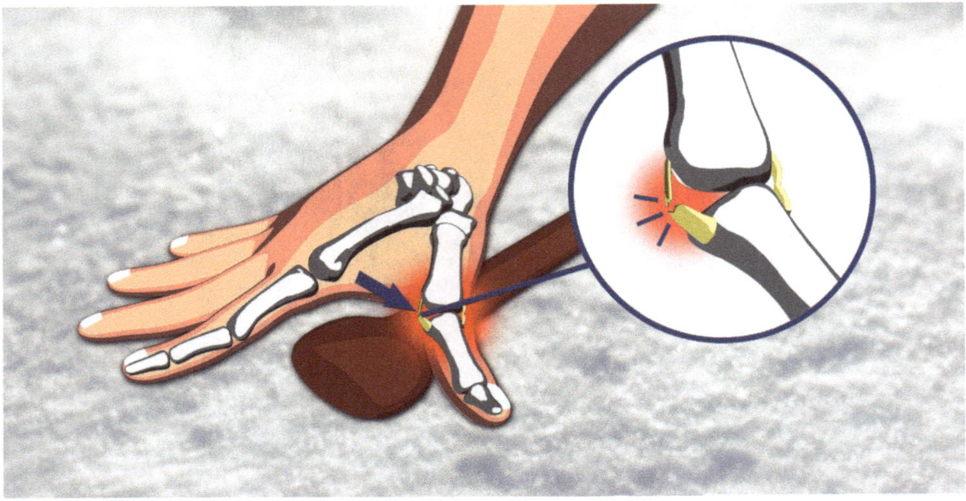

Figure 10-34 Gamekeeper's thumb

with the second finger. When a skier falls with the ski pole in hand, a valgus force is placed on the thumb, which causes the injury.

Signs and Symptoms

The individual has pain and a deficit in grip strength. The pain occurs most often when the individual makes a pinching motion with the thumb and index finger. Swelling and ecchymosis is present along with joint laxity.

Immediate Care

If the injury is acutely inflamed, the individual should apply ice to the area and splint the thumb. The individual should take NSAIDs to decrease pain and inflammation. If the individual has an increase in symptoms or significant joint laxity, refer them to a physician. If the UCL is ruptured, they may have to wear a splint for approximately 1 month or surgery may be warranted. Thumb musculature rehabilitation is necessary regardless of whether surgery has or has not been performed.

Prevention

Athletes should be careful when falling on an outstretched arm or when blocking an opponent with the hands. If their activity requires utilizing an implement or object in the hand, they should be aware not to fall with the thumb in a hyperextended and abducted position.

Mallet Finger and Boutonnière Deformity

Mallet finger is a rupture of the finger's extensor digitorum tendon at the distal interphalangeal (DIP) joint (the joint closest to the tip of the finger). Boutonnière deformity is a rupture of the finger's extensor digitorum tendon at the proximal interphalangeal (PIP) joint (the joint closest to the metacarpal). Avulsion or other fractures can occur with either acute injury.

Mechanism or Cause of Injury

Mallet finger and boutonnière deformity are caused when a force is placed on the tip of the finger and forcefully flexes the finger at the joint. As a result, the extensor tendon ruptures. An individual can also cut the tendon with an implement, such as a saw or knife, which leads to tendon rupture.

Signs and Symptoms

The individual has pain and loss of finger extension at the joint by the ruptured tendon. Finger deformity is visible. With mallet finger, the DIP joint appears in slight flexion because the tendon that holds the distal phalange in a normal position is ruptured **(Figure 10-35)**. The remainder of the tendon is intact, so the other finger joints remain in a normal position. With boutonnière deformity, the DIP is in slight extension and the PIP is in flexion due to the

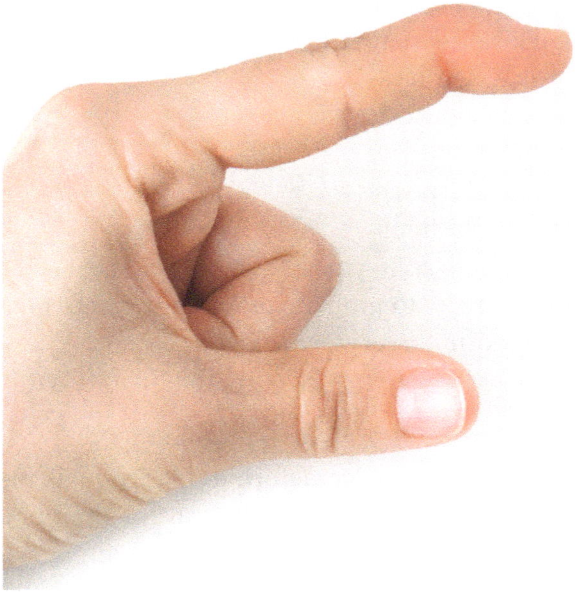

Figure 10-35 Mallet finger

ruptured tendon (**Figure 10-36**). Swelling, redness, ecchymosis, and point tenderness is present. The patient may say that they heard or felt a pop or a snap at the time of injury.

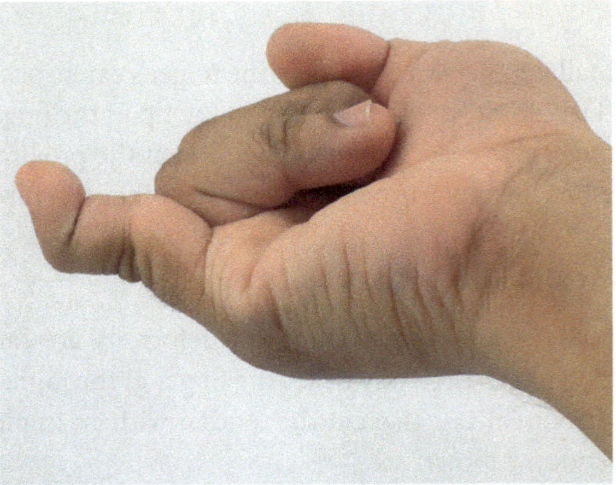

Figure 10-36 Boutonnière deformity

Immediate Care

These finger injuries are not medical emergencies unless the individual goes into shock or is bleeding severely. In these cases, treat the individual appropriately and call 911. If the individual is not in shock or severely bleeding then you do not need to summon EMS; however, they need to see a physician right away. Evaluate the injury by performing a secondary survey. Test to see if the tendon is intact. Hold the uninjured joints so they are stable. Have the individual move the affected joint in extension. If the patient cannot move the phalange, then they may have a ruptured tendon. Before the individual leaves your facility to see their physician, apply a splint with the injured joint in extension and apply ice. Finger splints made with bendable plastic or thin aluminum pieces covered with foam can assist you in creating a splint appropriate for the injury (**Figure 10-37**). Put the patient into a sling to keep the area elevated and rested. The physician will take x-rays and splint the finger to promote proper healing. Depending on the patient's activity, the physician may perform surgery.

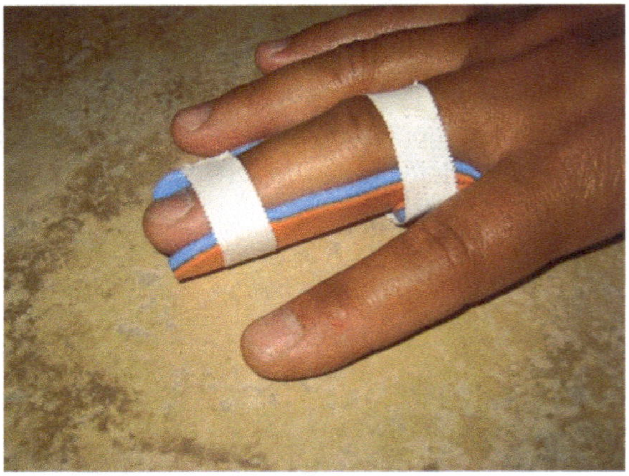

Figure 10-37 Finger splint

Prevention

To prevent mallet finger and boutionnière deformity, individuals must be careful when catching equipment, such as balls, by utilizing the pads of the fingers and the palm of the hand. Proper catching skills should be used to avoid having the ball hit the tip of the finger. Also, individuals should take care when utilizing sharp objects to avoid cutting themselves.

Jersey Finger

Jersey finger is similar to mallet finger because the finger DIP tendon is torn or ruptured. However, the ruptured tendon is the flexor digitorum profundus, which commonly occurs at the fourth finger DIP **(Figure 10-38)**. Tears can be partial tears or complete ruptures.

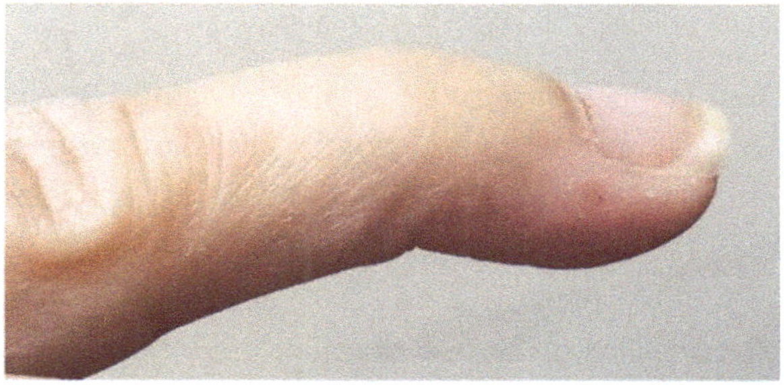

Figure 10-38 Jersey finger

Mechanism or Cause of Injury

Jersey finger was given its name because when an athlete attempts to grab an opponent's jersey, in sports such as rugby and football, they forcefully contract the finger's flexor tendon, which results in a tendon rupture. An individual can also cut their flexor tendon with a sharp implement, such as a saw or knife.

Signs and Symptoms

The individual feels pain and has loss of finger flexion. They may say they heard or felt a pop or a snap at the time of injury. Because the flexor tendon is ruptured at the DIP, the individual cannot flex the finger at this joint. The injury can occur with an avulsion or another phalangeal fracture. The individual is point tender at the injury site and may complain of numbness at the tip of the finger. Swelling, redness, and ecchymosis are visible.

Immediate Care

Always treat the individual for shock and call 911, if necessary. Perform a secondary survey if you do not need to summon EMS. As with mallet finger, test to see if the tendon is intact. Hold the uninjured finger joints so they are stable. Have them move the injured joint into flexion. If they cannot move the phalange then they may have a ruptured tendon. Refer the individual to a physician. Apply ice and splint the injured joint in slight flexion. The injured finger joint must be splinted, and the arm placed in a sling until he is evaluated by a physician. The physician will take x-rays, prescribe NSAIDs, splint the finger in flexion, and prescribe rehabilitation. Unlike mallet finger, which tends to heal without surgery, surgery is performed for a flexor tendon rupture; otherwise, proper healing cannot occur. Splinting and rehabilitation follows surgery to promote full function.

Prevention

Individuals must use caution when using sharp implements that can cut through soft tissue. Also, to prevent jersey finger, athletic participants should perform athletic activity skills properly.

Dupuytren's Contracture

Dupuytren's contracture is thickening of tissue underlying the skin in the palm of the hand. Men are more commonly affected than women. The condition can be unilateral or bilateral, with any finger having the contracture. Interestingly, the ring finger is most commonly affected.

Mechanism or Cause of Injury

The cause of this condition is unknown. Dupuytren's contracture is not caused by an athletic activity. It may have some hereditary predispositions. Diabetes, alcoholism, smoking, and age have shown to be risk factors for this condition.

Signs and Symptoms

The individual first feels and then visualizes a bump or nodule on the palm of the hand. This bump is the contracture forming, which eventually forms into a cord-like band. Over time, the individual's finger become contracted into a flexed position, and they cannot straighten it.

Immediate Care

The individual should see a physician for evaluation. They can utilize heat and ROM exercises in an attempt to loosen the contracture and restore some function. The physician may feel that surgery is warranted to release the contracture, followed by rehabilitation to restore full function. However, the International Dupuytren's Society (2020) notes the most recent treatment for the condition is for the patient to have an enzyme, *Clostridium histolyticum* collagenase, injected into the contracture. This enzyme causes the collagen scar tissue bonds to weaken. With ROM exercises, the contracted tissue can be mobilized, which breaks the bonds.

Prevention

The only means to attempt to prevent Dupuytren's contracture would be to avoid the controllable risk factors. Make sure the patient takes care of themself physically to avoid Type 2 diabetes, does not drink excessive alcohol, and does not smoke.

Summary

Injuries and conditions to the upper body vary in regard to severity, but often many mechanisms or causes of injuries are the same. Many upper extremity injuries do not require summoning EMS, but do require the individual to see a physician for evaluation. Even though most people do not weight bear on the upper extremity, upper extremity injuries should be taken seriously. Without shoulder, elbow, forearm, wrist, hand, and finger ROM, flexibility, and strength, individuals may not be able to perform a variety of activities including ADLs.

Keywords

Reduce To relocate the dislocated bone into proper, normal alignment. Reduction must only be performed by a qualified health care provider.

Internal forces Forces that the body creates due to motion and muscle contraction. These forces can cause injury by moving the bones, joints, and soft tissue into a position to which they are not accustomed.

Syndrome A group of signs and symptoms that, when put together, indicate a particular injury, illness, condition, or disease.

Therapeutic modalities Mediums and interventions which can be utilized to assist in treating the injury or illness. Electrostimulation, ultrasound, and massage are types of therapeutic modalities.

Neurovascular compromise The body's nerves and blood vessels are detrimentally affected due to trauma. Consequently, the nerves and blood vessels will not be able to perform their actions as they should.

Apophysitis Inflammation of a bony outgrowth. Common areas of apophysitis include the medial epicondyle (Little League elbow) and tibial tubercle (Osgood Schlatter's disease).

Corticosteroid A medication used to minimize inflammation. Corticosteroids prevent detrimental chemical mediators from being produced after injury during the inflammatory phase of healing. They can be given to a patient by mouth, injection, or intravenously. The medication also comes in eye solutions and topical creams.

Ergonomic equipment Equipment, chairs, keyboards, etc. which place the body in a proper position for optimal performance and to avoid injury.

Benign Noncancerous.

Discussion Questions

1. Which upper extremity injuries warrant you to call 911 immediately?
2. Which upper extremity injuries do not necessitate emergency care, but require referral to a physician?
3. Which upper extremity injuries are considered chronic injuries?
4. What are common mechanisms or causes of upper extremity injuries?
5. Which injuries require surgery followed by rehabilitation in order to restore full function?

CASE STUDY: KICKBOXING SHOULDER STRESS

Lorraine is a married, 45-year-old professional and mother of a 6-year-old boy. Aside from being slightly overweight she is in good health. Lorraine realizes that in order to improve her quality of life she needs to lose weight. She also wants to gain muscle tone, particularly in her arms and legs. She begins to exercise regularly at We R Fit Gym for 2 months by jogging on a treadmill and lifting weights. She has been doing well with her weight loss and muscle tone, but she is becoming bored with performing the same exercises. A trainer at the gym suggests that she try the classes that the gym offers. They suggest that Lorraine try the most popular class which is impact kickboxing.

Immediately after the first class Lorraine is hooked on kickboxing. The next day she is sore from head to toe, but feels that she is getting a great workout. She is excited to continue the kick boxing classes three times per week. She jogs on a treadmill and performs weightlifting on the alternate two days. At the end of the first week, Lorraine notices she has pain at her left anterior shoulder whenever she flexes it. Also, she is unable to raise her arm without discomfort, and has weakness past 90 degrees of abduction or flexion. In the past she has experienced post-exercise soreness for an hour or so after the workouts, so she figures the soreness decrease in a day or so.

At the beginning of the following week, Lorraine's discomfort in her left arm is gone. She starts the next kickboxing class. During class she decides to increase her intensity when striking the bag with her fists. A few hours after the session, she feels a dull pain and significant weakness not only in her anterior shoulder and down her humerus, but also on her lateral shoulder. As the day progresses, she is not able to perform ADLs which requires her arm to be raised into flexion or abduction more than 45 degrees. As nighttime came and Lorraine goes to bed, she begins to feel tingling "pins and needles" down into her hand and fingers. The dull aching persists throughout the evening.

Lorraine does not continue with kickboxing or upper body weightlifting the remainder of the week, but continues to jog on the treadmill. The simple motion of her shoulder and arm moving forward and back when jogging is painful. The dull pain in her left shoulder and arm does not subside. The pain continues to affect her daily activities, such as washing her hair, reaching up in her closet to get her clothes, and putting groceries in her cupboard. She is extremely frustrated and does not know what to do. She is ready to quit working out altogether.

1. What structure(s) do you believe is (are) injured?
2. What was the mechanism or cause of the injury?
3. What should Lorraine have done as soon as she felt discomfort at the shoulder and arm to provide immediate care for the injury?
4. What advice would you give Lorraine to care for her shoulder injury? Should she be evaluated by a physician? Why or why not?
5. What should Lorraine have done to prevent this injury?

References

Abrams R, & Akbarnia H. (2021, August 13). Shoulder dislocations overview. In StatPearls [Internet]. StatPearls Publishing; Available from: https://www.ncbi.nlm.nih.gov/books/NBK459125/

American Society of Surgery of the Hand (ASSH) (2018). 3 Types of shoulder fractures. Retrieved October 29, 2021 from https://www.assh.org/handcare/condition/shoulder-fracture

Consigliere P, Haddo O, Levy O, Sforza G. (2018). Subacromial impingement syndrome: management challenges. *Orthopedic Research and Review*,10, 83-91. doi: 10.2147/ORR.S157864

Edwin, J., Ahmed, S., Verma, S., Tytherleigh-Strong, G., Karuppaiah, K., Sinha, J. (2018). Swellings of the sternoclavicular joint: review of traumatic and non-traumatic pathologies. *EFORT Open Reviews*, 3(8), 471-484. doi: 10.1302/2058-5241.3.170078

International Dupuytren Society (2020). Enzyme (collagenase) injection to treat Dupuytren's contracture. Retrieved July 21, 2021 from, http://www.dupuytren-online.info/dupuytren_collagenase.html

Kiel. J. & Kaiser, K. Acromioclavicular joint injury. (2021, August 27). In: StatPearls [Internet]. StatPearls Publishing; 2021; Available from: https://www.ncbi.nlm.nih.gov/books/NBK493188/

Mayo Clinic. (2019). *Thoracic outlet syndrome: prevention.* Retrieved July 21, 2021 from, http://www.mayoclinic.com/health/thoracic-outletsyndrome/DS00800/DSECTION=prevention

Medline Plus (2022). *Carpal tunnel syndrome.* Retrieved on January 10, 2022 from, https://medlineplus.gov/ency/article/000433.htm

Medline Plus (2021a). *Frozen Shoulder.* Retrieved on July 21, 2021 from, https://medlineplus.gov/ency/article/000455.htm

Medline Plus. (2021b). *Rotator cuff problems.* Retrieved on July 21, 2021 from, http://www.nlm.nih.gov/medlineplus/ency/article/000438.htm

Neer, C. S. (1972). Anterior acromioplasty for the chronic impingement syndrome in the shoulder: a preliminary report. *Journal of Bone and Joint Surgery, American Edition*, 54, 41–50.

Prentice, W.E. (2021). *Principles of athletic training: a competency-based approach* (17th ed.). Champaign, IL: McGraw-Hill.

U.S. Department of Health and Human Services Office of Women's Health [OASH]. *Carpal tunnel syndrome.* Retrieved on January 10, 2022 from, https://www.womenshealth.gov/a-z-topics/carpal-tunnel-syndrome

Chapter 11

The Spine, Abdomen, & Thorax

Chapter Objectives

After you have read this chapter, you will be able to understand:

- Acute traumatic injuries that occur to the cervical spine.
- The similarities and differences between cervical and thoracic spine injuries.
- The mechanisms of injury for chronic lumbar spine injuries.
- The various injuries and illnesses that can occur to the lungs, heart, and other abdominal organs.
- The spine, abdomen, and thorax injuries and illnesses that warrant summoning EMS.

The Spine

The spine consists of the cervical, thoracic, lumbar, sacral, and coccygeal vertebrae. The spinal cord, which is part of the central nervous system (CNS), and the peripheral nerves pass through the vertebrae and provide motor function and sensation to all parts of the body. The vertebral disks located in between each of the cervical, thoracic, and lumbar vertebrae provide cushioning and act as shock absorbers against forces applied to the spine. As a whole, the spine gives the head and body support, maintains the body's shape, provides movement, and protects the spinal cord. Although the spine is well supported by many ligaments and muscles, acute and chronic injuries to the spine frequently occur.

The Cervical Spine

The cervical spine consists of seven vertebrae, with eight pairs of cervical nerves exiting from the intervertebral foramen. The spinal cord starts at the base of the skull, travels through the cervical vertebrae, and continues down to the sacrum. The first two vertebrae, the atlas and the axis, cannot be palpated since they are at the base of the skull. These two vertebrae, along with the articulation of the atlas and the occiput of the skull, contribute to significant of movement of the head, including flexion, extension, and rotation. The remaining cervical joints allow for these motions including **lateral flexion**. The cervical spine has a lordotic curve, which is an inward curve, or anterior concavity, of the spine when looking at the patient from a lateral view. Many cervical spine injuries are serious, and potentially limb-threatening; therefore, immediate proper care is crucial.

Fractures and Dislocations

Cervical fractures and dislocations are among the most serious and damaging injuries to the body. The cervical vertebrae can fracture, dislocate, or have a concurrent fracture-dislocation. Vertebral body compression fractures, and transverse and oblique fractures to the spinous and transverse processes, laminae, and pedicles are common fractures that occur to the cervical spine. Dislocations can occur between any two vertebrae. Cervical fractures and dislocations that occur at the atlas **(Figure 11-1)** or axis **(Figure 11-2)** can

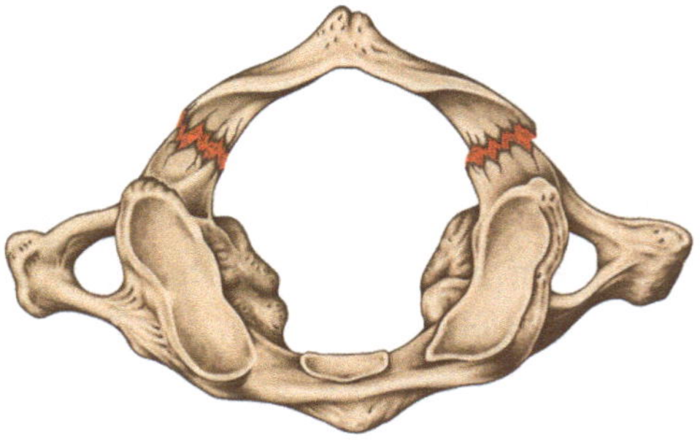

Figure 11-1 Fracture of the atlas (C1) can occur bilaterally.

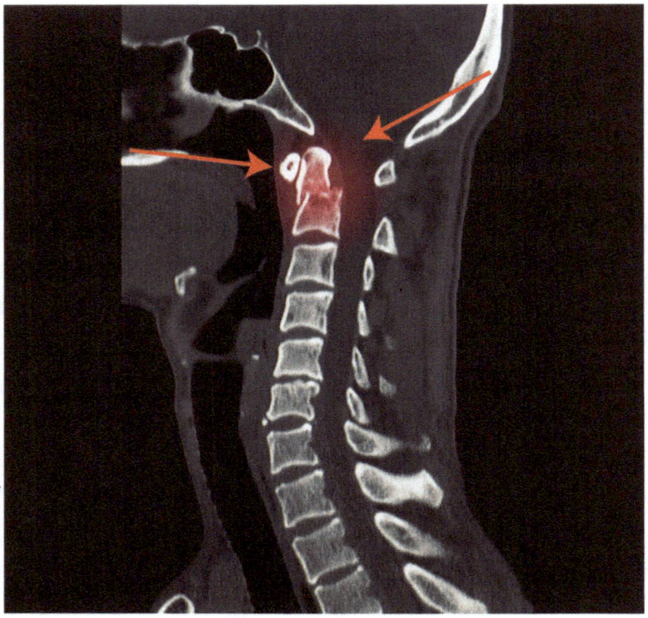

Figure 11-2 A fracture with displacement of the axis (C2)

be life-threatening if the spinal cord is severed in conjunction with the fracture. In this case, the nerves affecting heart function and breathing can be affected and a person can die immediately. When cervical fractures or dislocations injure the spinal cord, the injury can render the patient **paraplegic** or **quadriplegic**.

Mechanism or Cause of Injury

A mechanism of injury for cervical fractures and dislocations is a direct impact to the top of the head when the neck is in approximately 30 degrees of flexion. When the neck is in slight flexion, the cervical spine's lordotic curve is straightened. This straightened spine facilitates force transmission, and compresses and crumples the spine. This injury could occur when a football player has their head down while attempting to tackle an opponent, which is called spearing. A cervical fracture or dislocation can also occur when a person dives into a shallow end of a pool with their neck in the same position. A forceful flexion-extension that snaps the neck, as with whiplash in a car accident, can also cause these cervical injuries.

Signs and Symptoms

The individual complains of bony spinal pain, especially with palpation, the inability and unwillingness to move the head and neck, and loss of function and/or sensation within the arms and legs. The individual may say they are unable to move any part of their body, which indicates paralysis. They also may show signs of shock.

Immediate Care

The first priority is to see if the individual is conscious, check their airway, breathing, and circulation, and immediately apply in-line cervical spine stabilization. Tell the individual not to move and summon someone to call 911. If the patient is in shock, treat them accordingly but do not move their body. Determine the extent of their consciousness by talking to them. Ask history questions, including those focusing on the extent and location of pain. Also, without having the individual move their head and spine, determine if they have feeling in their arms and legs. Ask them if they are able to wiggle their fingers and toes. Carefully and lightly touch the extremities while asking them if they can feel your touch. When emergency medical services (EMS) arrive on the scene, the emergency medical technicians (EMTs) may ask you to assist them to spine board the patient **(Figure 11-3)**. Listen to the EMTs' directions carefully as they instruct you how to assist. At the hospital, the physician will give the patient pain medication, and take spinal images to visualize the injury. Surgery is immediately necessary for the patient's recovery.

Prevention

To prevent cervical spine fractures and dislocations, athletic participants should learn proper techniques for their athletic activity, including diving and tackling. Individuals should always

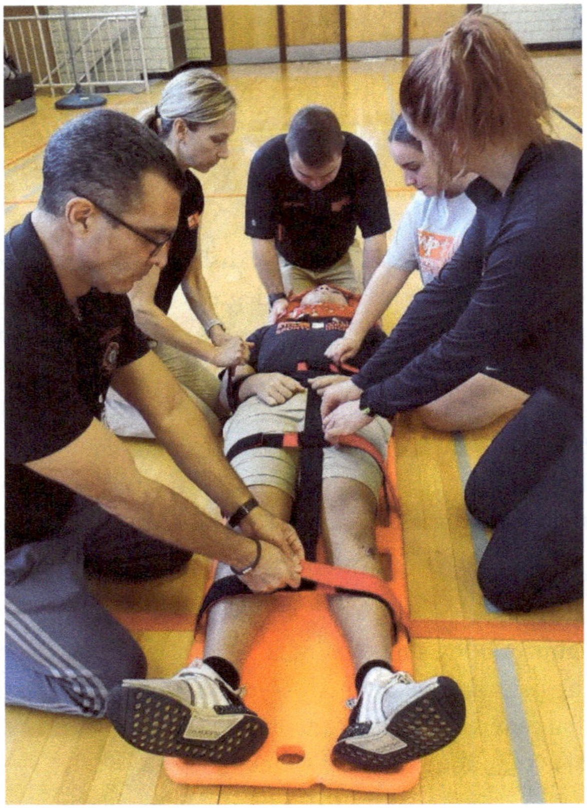

Figure 11-3 If a patient has a possible cervical spine injury, the athlete must be placed securely on a spine board.

abide by activity and facility rules, such as not diving in shallow ends of pools. Also, individuals must always wear seatbelts when riding in motor vehicles.

Spinal Cord and Nerve Injuries

Spinal cord and nerve injuries can be traumatic, such as with a severed or contused spinal cord, or chronic, such as a vertebral disk compressing on the spinal cord and/or nerve root.

Mechanism or Cause of Injury

Traumatic spinal cord injuries, including a severed and contused spinal cord, typically occur in athletics (for example in football) by a blow to the top of the head secondary to a cervical spine fracture or dislocation (**Figure 11-4**). These injuries can also occur due to falls onto the head. However, a fracture or dislocation does not need to occur to cause significant spinal cord

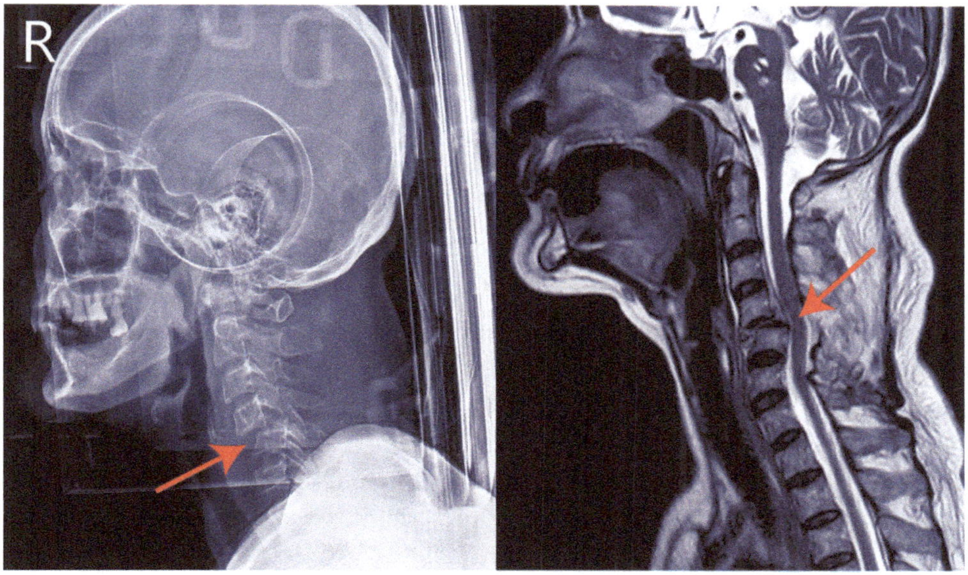

Figure 11-4 A fracture-dislocation of the cervical vertebrae can sever the spinal cord.

damage. The spinal cord can be contused and swell (called *spinal cord shock*). With this injury, the swollen spinal cord presses on the vertebrae in the spinal canal. Also, the spinal cord can be compressed by blood and fluid from inflammation from a traumatic event. Spinal cord and nerve injuries can also occur from a patient having a small vertebral foramen (called *spinal stenosis)*, which causes compression on the spinal cord.

Signs and Symptoms

An injury to the spinal cord can be life-threatening, especially if it occurs at cervical vertebrae 1 or 2 (atlas or axis) level, which affects the breathing centers. Spinal cord and nerve injuries are more often limb-threatening, which means that an injury to cervical 3 through 7 affects motor function and sensation from the arms to the legs. An individual with a severed spinal cord may be not breathing, in cardiac arrest, or deceased if the spinal cord is severed up at the atlas or axis levels. The individual may be conscious and breathing, but they may have paralysis in the extremities. They may experience pain, incontinence, and muscle spasm. With spinal cord shock, the spinal cord swells and a temporary loss of function and sensation results. Once the spinal cord swelling decreases, then the individual's function and sensation gradually return. Unlike with acute spinal cord injuries, with chronic spinal cord and nerve injuries, the patient is conscious. Chronic spinal cord and nerve injuries cause pain, temporary loss of function and sensation, as well as burning, tingling, and numbness throughout all extremities. These signs and symptoms of injury may last for a few minutes or weeks.

Immediate Care

An acute, traumatic spinal cord injury that exhibits loss of motor function and sensation is a medical emergency and must be treated as a spinal fracture or dislocation. Maintain in-line stabilization, monitor airway, breathing, and circulation, and call 911 to summon EMS. Make sure you tell the patient to lie still. The EMTs will spine board the person for transfer to the emergency room (ER). At the ER, the physician will determine the extent of injury. The physician can utilize computed tomography (CT), magnetic resonance imaging (MRI), x-rays, or a **myelogram**. Typically, the patient is given medication to relieve swelling. The physician may perform surgery to fuse vertebrae or remove fluid that may be causing the signs and symptoms. The patient is put on bed rest for a period of time.

For chronic spinal cord and nerve injuries, complete a secondary survey of the patient's injury, and determine the severity, irritability, nature, and stage (SINS) of their injury. Ultimately, refer them to a physician to determine the underlying cause of the injury. The physician can address this cause of injury by prescribing nonsteroidal anti-inflammatory drugs (NSAIDs), corticosteroid injections, and rehabilitation. Lifestyle modification will most likely be necessary to prevent recurrence.

Prevention

Traumatic spinal cord injuries can be avoided if when an individual participates in activities they perform the skills properly and abide by activity rules (as with prevention of cervical fractures and dislocations). Sometimes chronic spinal cord injuries cannot be avoided, such as if spinal stenosis exists.

Herniated Disk

A disk is made up of the annulus fibrosus and nucleus pulposus. The annulus fibrosus is the disk's tough, outer portion and the nucleus pulposus is the disk's jelly-like, softer portion. A herniated disk refers to a protrusion of a disk between the vertebrae, which can occur at the cervical, thoracic, or lumbar spine as pictured in **Figure 11-5**. The disk can actually rupture and the nucleus pulposus can protrude through the annulus fibrosus **(Figure 11-6)**. Most often, herniated disks occur to people who have occupations that require heavy lifting, pushing, pulling, or twisting, which puts pressure on the disks, people who are middle-aged, due to disk degeneration, and individuals who are overweight, due to the stress placed on the disks (Mayo Clinic, 2019).

Mechanism or Cause of Injury

Herniated disks typically do not have an acute, traumatic mechanism of injury. As a person gets older, disks lose their water content and degenerate. Because the disks are not as strong as when the person was young, the disks are prone to tearing and rupturing with spinal

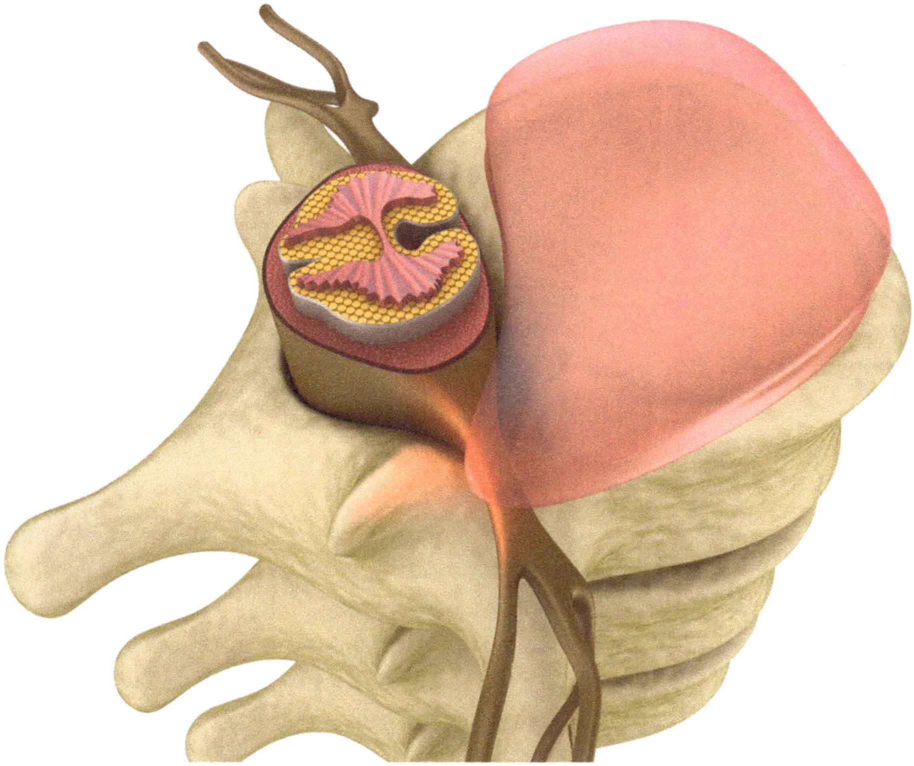

Figure 11-5 A herniated disk protruding on the spinal nerve

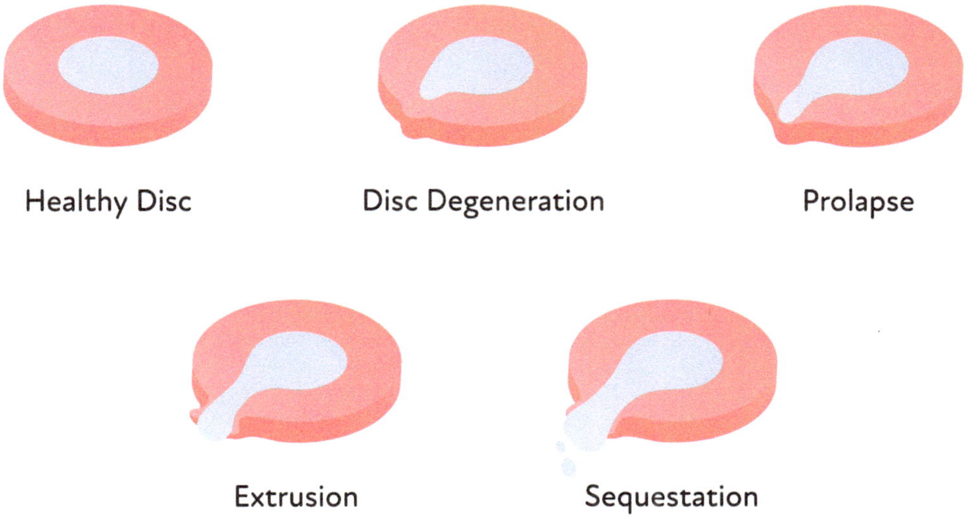

Figure 11-6 A disk can herniate and the nucleus pulposus can rupture through the annulus fibrosus.

movements. Spinal movements typically are not traumatic or exceptionally forceful, but over the years, they will further weaken and damage the disks. For example, patients who continually lift heavy objects improperly, by utilizing their back muscles, are prone to herniated disks (Mayo Clinic, 2019). As a result, the herniated disks can compress upon the spinal cord and nerves.

Signs and Symptoms

Some individuals do not know that they have a herniated disk because they do not have any signs or symptoms. In many cases, a herniated disk can cause pain, loss of function and sensation, numbness, tingling, or burning down the arms and legs, depending on the site of herniation.

Immediate Care

If your patient has any of the above signs or symptoms, they must see their physician immediately to rule out any other injuries or conditions. The physician will prescribe various medications, such as over-the-counter or prescription medications including NSAIDs, narcotics, nerve pain medications, muscle relaxants, and cortisone injections. The patient will participate in rehabilitation, including the utilization of therapeutic modalities to decrease signs and symptoms of the condition, traction, and exercises to decrease the pain and increase the strength at the cervical spine. Surgery is rarely needed. If conservative treatment is not improving the patient's condition, or if a portion of the disk must be removed to allow for the patient to perform activities of daily living (ADLs) and decrease the signs and symptoms, then surgery is an option.

Prevention

In order to prevent a herniated disk, an individual must have good posture, including utilizing proper mechanics when lifting, pulling, and pushing heavy objects; have strong core muscles, and maintain a healthy, normal weight.

Sprains and Strains

Cervical sprains and strains tend to occur concurrently. Determining whether the injury is a sprain or a strain is difficult.

Mechanism or Cause of Injury

A sprain or strain to the cervical spine is caused by forceful motions of the neck. Whiplash, which often occurs in motor vehicle accidents, is a common cause of cervical sprains. This mechanism of injury entails a forceful hyperextension of the neck followed immediately by a forceful hyperflexion. These forceful movements along with sudden twisting or rotation motions can also cause cervical strains.

Signs and Symptoms

Cervical sprains and strains have the same signs and symptoms of injury as any other sprain or strain. The patient complains of neck pain and stiffness, which result in a loss of range of motion (ROM). The area is point tender and localized swelling is evident. The patient may be holding their head and neck very still and have to turn their body to look around. They do not have nerve dysfunction; consequently more serious injuries can be ruled out.

Immediate Care

If you suspect your patient has a cervical sprain or strain, have them apply ice to the area. Have them lie on their stomach with their head in a comfortable position to apply the ice pack. The patient can take over-the-counter NSAIDs to alleviate pain and inflammation. If the patient cannot move his neck and is in noticeable pain, then the injury is significant enough for them to be evaluated by a physician. The physician will prescribe NSAIDs and perhaps muscle relaxants to alleviate pain, inflammation, and spasm. The patient rests the area by wearing a Philadelphia or cervical collar **(Figure 11-7)**, which is a soft foam neck brace that assists in stabilizing and resting the neck musculature. The patient performs rehabilitation including ROM and strengthening exercises, and also has regular application of therapeutic modalities and soft tissue massage. Throughout the rehabilitation process, the patient should maintain cardiorespiratory fitness levels without putting the neck in further danger of harm.

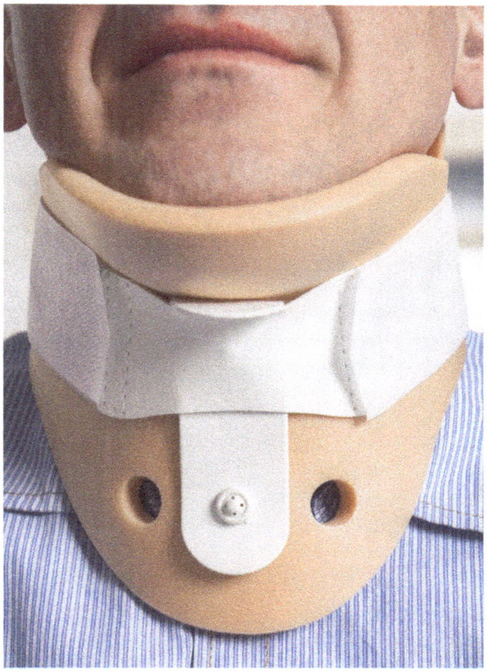

© Monika Wisniewska/Shutterstock.com

Figure 11-7 A cervical collar supports your patient's neck after a cervical sprain or strain.

Prevention

The patient must avoid any forceful cervical spine movements in order to prevent sprains and strains. The patient must have full neck ROM, adequate muscular strength, and flexibility to prevent injuries.

Acute Torticollis (Wryneck)

Acute torticollis of the neck is also called *wryneck*. The injury is a sudden, painful neck muscle spasm.

TIPS FROM THE FIELD

Tip 1 If you need to apply an ice pack onto a patient's cervical spine, do not secure it with a compression wrap or any other securing bandage, as you may asphyxiate the patient. Instead have the patient lie on their stomach, prone, on a table or mat. To make the patient's neck and head comfortable, you can make a temporary face cradle. Take a towel from the longest side and roll it up. Place the ends of the towel together, leaving a hole large enough for the patient to place their face in. Place the towel rolled up into a circle, underneath the patient's face on the table, with the patient's forehead and chin on the towel material. Make sure the patient can breathe normally. If not, then you may need to adjust the towel roll or place the patient in another position.

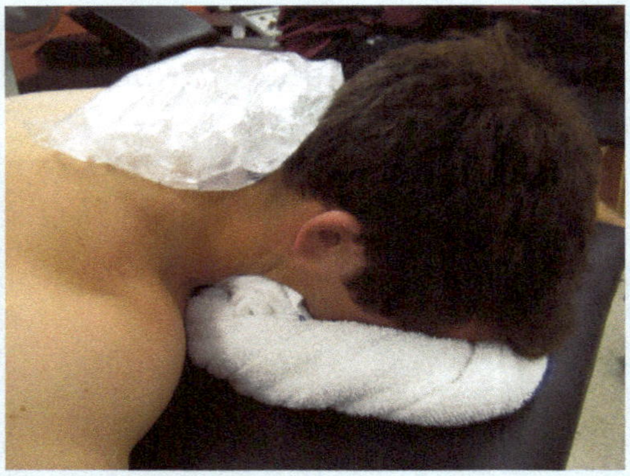

A towel roll used as a face cradle can make the patient more comfortable when they are lying on their stomach during cervical spine ice application.

Mechanism or Cause of Injury

Acute torticollis can be caused by acutely bending or twisting the neck, stress, muscular tension, and sleeping in an unusual position for hours in a cold, drafty room.

Signs and Symptoms

The individual complains of neck pain and stiffness, which occurs typically on one side. They hold their head to the opposite side of the pain. The individual may state that they went to bed and woke up with discomfort and stiffness that became worse throughout the course of the day. They may feel that their neck is "stuck".

Immediate Care

The individual should see a physician in order to rule out any other significant cervical spine injuries. Therefore, if they approach you and are in severe pain, and/or holds their head still unable to move it, summon EMS immediately. The physician will evaluate the patient and take x-rays in order to rule out other cervical injuries. The physician will prescribe medication and therapeutic modalities, including moist heat, to alleviate pain and spasm. Massage, gentle ROM, and stretching exercises will assist in resolving wryneck.

Prevention

Prevention of acute torticollis includes maintaining normal posture, even when sleeping. For some individuals, maintaining normal posture may require various ergonomic equipment. For example, pillows are available that can help prevent wryneck that occurs during sleep. Individuals should maintain a low level of stress and participate in stress reduction activities. If the patient works regularly at a desk or computer, they should take frequent breaks and perform active range of motion (AROM) movements and easy, manual neck muscle stretching exercises.

The Thoracic Spine

The thoracic spine includes the 12 thoracic vertebrae, along with the intervertebral disks, spinal cord, and nerves. Unlike the cervical spine, the thoracic spine has a **kyphotic** curve versus a lordotic curve **(Figure 11-8)**. The thoracic spine does not have the mobility as the cervical spine does due to the shape and configuration of the vertebrae, in particular the spinous processes, as well as the fact that the ribs attach to the thoracic vertebrae.

Thoracic spine injuries have similarities to cervical spine injuries. Thoracic fractures, dislocations, spinal cord injuries, herniated disks, sprains, and strains occur to the thoracic spine as they do to the cervical spine. The same mechanisms of injury and signs and symptoms that occur with cervical spine injuries occur to the thoracic spine with few variations. Instead of reiterating each injury in this section, the differences between these cervical and thoracic injuries are discussed.

Traumatic thoracic injuries, such as fractures and dislocations, do not often occur when a person is participating in athletic activities. These injuries typically occur with high impact forces to the spine, such as in an automobile accident or fall from a height onto the head or

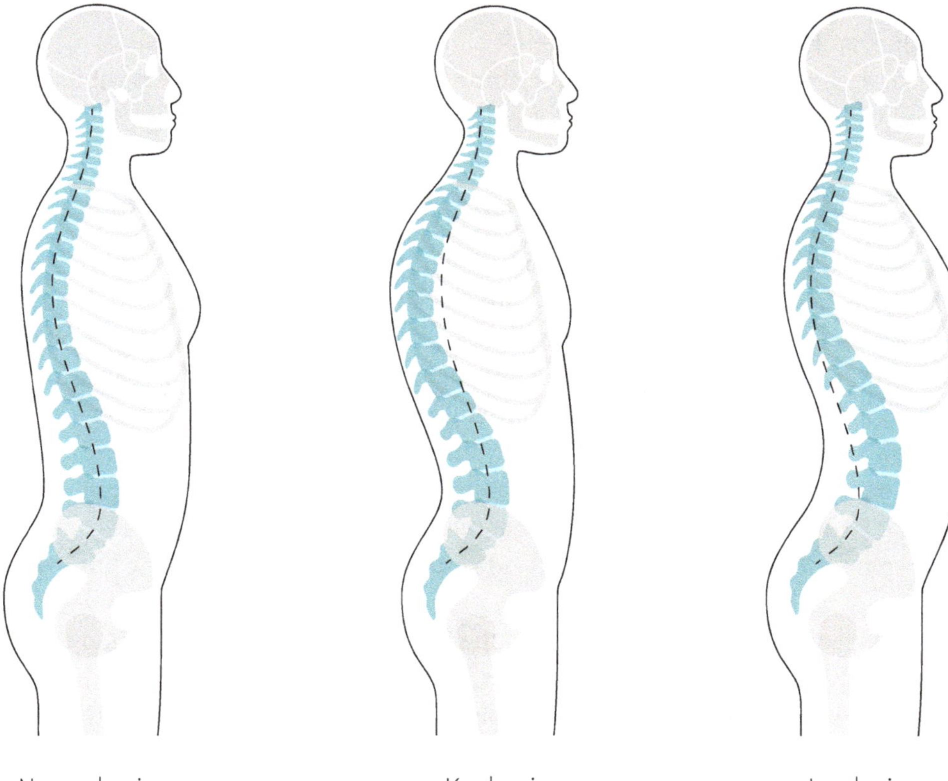

Figure 11-8 Normal, kyphotic, and lordotic spines

feet. Thoracic spinal cord injuries are similar to cervical spinal cord injuries, except for the area of the body that is affected. Loss of motor function and/or sensation from a thoracic spinal cord injury occurs into the chest, abdomen, and legs with a severed spinal cord. Herniated disks compressing on the spinal cord and/or nerve root also produces abnormal sensation in the chest and abdomen.

The ligaments that run through the cervical vertebrae also exist at the thoracic vertebrae. Ligamentous sprains produce the same signs and symptoms of inflammation as with cervical sprains, but since the thoracic area cannot create a lot of motion, loss of motion due to spasm is minimal as compared to the loss of motion that occurs with a cervical sprain. Thoracic spine muscle strains occur frequently and exhibit similar signs and symptoms of injury as cervical muscle strains. The muscles attaching to the thoracic spine move the neck, shoulder, and scapula. Therefore, loss of function is noticeable in regard to these structures versus at the actual thoracic spine. Deep muscles that attach to the thoracic spine, such as the erector spinae and rhomboids, can be strained with forceful muscle contraction or sudden stretch. Superficial muscles attaching to the thoracic spine, such as the latissimus dorsi and trapezius, are as susceptible to muscular strains as any other muscle in the thoracic spine area.

Immediate care of these injuries is the same for cervical injuries. Care for traumatic injuries include calling 911, maintaining in-line spinal stabilization, monitoring airway, breathing, and circulation, and treating for shock. Care for chronic or non-traumatic injuries is the same as the respective cervical spine injuries. Prevention of thoracic spine injuries is similar to prevention of cervical spine injuries.

The Lumbar Spine

The lumbar spine consists of five large vertebrae, intervertebral disks, spinal cord, and nerves. The lumbar spine has a lordotic curve and a notable amount of ROM, similar to the cervical spine. As with thoracic traumatic injuries, such as fractures and dislocations, lumbar fractures and dislocations occur mainly with high impact trauma, such as motor vehicle accidents and falls from a significant height, typically when landing on the feet. The lumbar vertebrae are considerably larger and are stronger than the other spinal vertebrae; therefore, enormous trauma must occur to fracture or dislocate the bones. Lumbar spinal cord injury can occur, but the spinal cord is not often severed at the lumbar region during athletic activity as compared to the cervical spine. Herniated disks, sprains, and strains occur frequently at the lumbar spine, however.

The human body's center of gravity lies at the lumbar spine and the upper body weight is borne on the lumbar spine. The lumbar spine performs flexion, extension, rotation, and lateral flexion as the cervical spine does. These motions predispose the lumbar spine to herniated disks, sprains, and strains. These lumbar injuries exhibit similar signs and symptoms of the respective cervical spine injuries. Immediate care and prevention of these injuries are the same as with cervical and thoracic spine injuries.

Spondylolysis and Spondylolisthesis

Spondylolysis and spondylolisthesis are chronic injuries that occur over a period of time. Spondylolysis is a lumbar vertebrae stress fracture which occurs most commonly at the fifth lumbar vertebrae (L5), and next commonly at the fourth lumbar vertebrae (L4) (American Academy of Orthopaedic Surgeons [AAOS], 2016). The stress fracture occurs at the base of the spinous process, which is called the pars interarticularis. If the stress fracture completely breaks through the bone, the vertebrae become unstable. As a result the vertebral body begins to slide forward on the surrounding vertebrae. This complication of spondylolysis is called spondylolisthesis **(Figure 11-9)**. If the L5 vertebrae is affected by spondylolysis, then L5 slips forward on the sacrum. If L4 is fractured, then it slips anteriorly on L5. If the vertebra continues to move out of position, it may press on the spinal cord and nerves and cause loss of motor function and sensation into the pelvis and lower extremity.

Mechanism or Cause of Injury

Hyperextension of the lumbar spine predisposes the individual to spondylolysis and spondylolisthesis. Many of these injuries are found in individuals who participate in sports that require a constant loading of and stress on the low back, such as gymnastics, wrestling, and football (linemen in particular). Genetics can also play a role in creating spondylolysis and

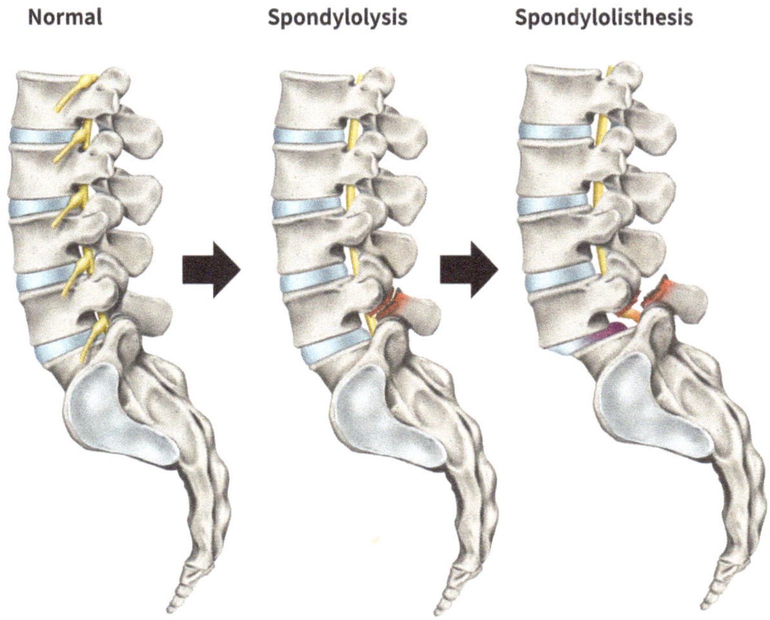

Figure 11-9 The progression of a normal spine to spondylolysis to spondylolisthesis

spondylolisthesis. Some patients are born with thin pars interarticularis, which make the bone susceptible to stress fracture.

Signs and Symptoms

The most common symptom of spondylolysis and spondylolisthesis is diffuse pain across the low back. Due to lack of pain localization, the patient may think they have a low back strain. Spasm of the low back muscles can occur, which alters posture and gait (AAOS, 2016). Pain may radiate, and the individual may have burning, tingling, or numbness down the legs if the vertebra has slipped forward enough to press on the spinal cord and nerves.

Immediate Care

Begin caring for the individual by performing a secondary survey to determine the SINS of injury. If they complain of diffuse pain across their lower back, and has a mechanism of injury that would precipitate spondylolysis and spondylolisthesis, then have the individual rest from any activity that aggravates the low back, apply an ice pack and an elastic bandage for support. Refer them to a physician. X-rays will show whether a fracture exists and if the vertebra has slipped anteriorly. If the individual has either condition, the physician may attempt conservative, non-surgical treatment first, which includes rest from activities that exacerbate low back pain, NSAIDs, bracing if necessary, and rehabilitation. The core body muscles must be strengthened and stretched in order to attempt to realign the vertebra and decrease symptoms. If rehabilitation does not decrease the pain, and the symptoms begin to affect performing ADLs, then surgery may be the only option to treat the injury. Surgery entails fusing the lumbar vertebra to prevent future slippage.

Prevention

Prevention of spondylolysis and spondylolisthesis includes having strong, flexible muscles around the core body. The individual should avoid continual hyperextension exercises that predispose them to these injuries.

Myofascial Pain Syndrome

Myofascial pain syndrome is a chronic pain syndrome. Although it can occur in the cervical spine area, the lumbar spine is often affected.

Mechanism or Cause of Injury

Myofascial pain syndrome can affect any area of the body that is overused. These muscles are repeatedly contracted during ADLs, hobbies, work duties, and athletic activities. **Trigger points** form in the muscles and refer pain throughout the entire muscle.

Signs and Symptoms

The patient experiences trigger point pain. The pain is a deep, aching pain that is more severe than normal muscular pain. The pain travels throughout the muscle in which the trigger point lies, and worsens over time.

Immediate Care

Usually, muscular soreness and pain resolve quickly when the muscle is treated for inflammation and pain by utilizing rest, ice, and NSAIDs. If your client complains of chronic low back pain that does not subside within a few days, especially after rest from activity and utilizing ice packs frequently, then refer them to their physician. A physician can inject corticosteroid medication into the trigger points **(Figure 11-10)**, and prescribe NSAIDs and muscle relaxants. Rehabilitation, massage, stretching, and relaxation techniques assist in decreasing signs and symptoms.

Prevention

To avoid myofascial pain syndrome, explain to your patients the importance of exercising and stress management. Exercise, including ROM, flexibility, and strengthening exercises, assist your patients in promoting healthy, strong, pain-free muscles. Your patients must also find enjoyable ways to relax in order to control stress.

Contusions

Low back musculature contusions are similar to any other muscle contusion.

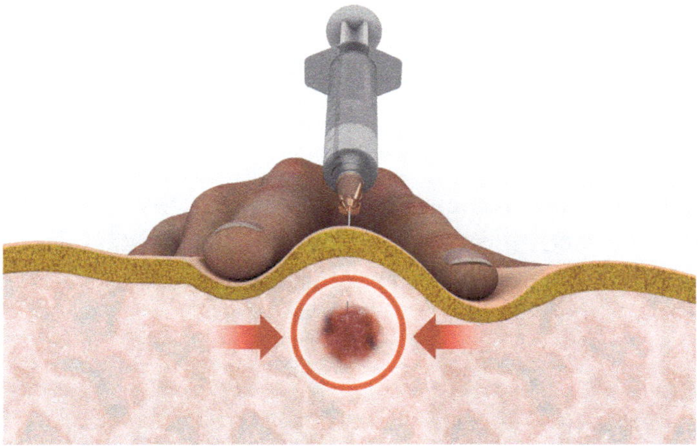

Figure 11-10 Physicians can inject medication into the trigger points if necessary to relieve symptoms.

Mechanism or Cause of Injury

Contusions to the lumbar spine and surrounding musculature occur due to a direct blow to the area.

Signs and Symptoms

Pain with motion, point tenderness, swelling, and ecchymosis are the common signs and symptoms of any contusion. Muscle contusions cause spasm, stiffness, and inability to fully contract the muscle.

Immediate Care

Most often, lumbar contusions do not warrant EMS care. Assist the individual by applying ice, compression with an elastic wrap or lumbar brace, and telling them to rest from any activity that causes pain. If the signs and symptoms do not subside within a few days, or if they worsen causing persistent pain, then refer them to their physician.

Prevention

Low back contusions can be avoided if the athletic participants wear appropriate protective equipment. The low back musculature should be strengthened in order to protect against, or at least minimize, injury due to blunt force trauma.

The Thorax

The thorax, also referred to as the thoracic cavity, is the area of the body between the neck and the abdomen. The sternum, ribs, thoracic vertebrae, and diaphragm create the thoracic cavity boundaries. Circulatory and respiratory system structures, including the heart, great blood vessels, trachea, bronchi, lungs, and nerves, are located in the thorax, as well as the thymus (an immune system structure) and esophagus (a digestive system structure).

The Ribs

The ribs are located in an area of the body called the thorax. They give the thoracic cavity its shape and protect the heart and lungs. Twelve pairs of ribs, the costal cartilage, sternum, and spine make up the rib cage. The external and internal intercostal muscles are in between each rib and assist respiration.

Fractures

The fifth through ninth ribs are most prone to fractures because they are rigidly secured to the rib cage (Schultz, Houglum, & Perrin, 2015). Also, these lower ribs are not as well protected by the arms, especially if the arms are not down by a person's side during activity.

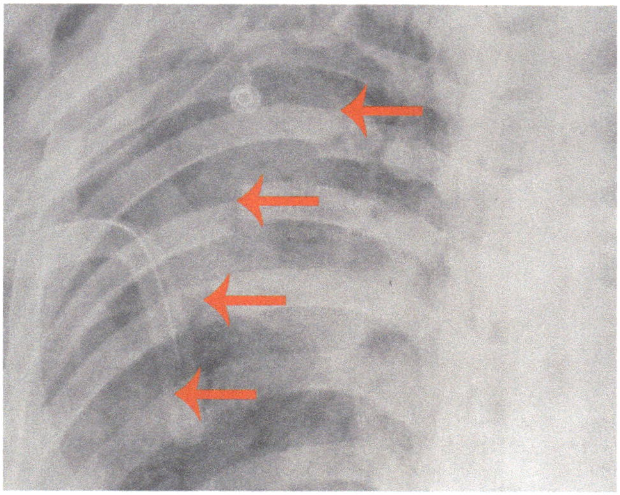

Figure 11-11 Rib fractures

Mechanism or Cause of Injury

Rib fractures occur from a direct blow to the rib cage. The direct blow can occur during contact sport activities, falls, and motor vehicle accidents **(Figure 11-11)**. Repetitive twisting of the torso or coughing spells can also fracture a rib.

Signs and Symptoms

With a fractured rib, the patient has pain on inspiration, especially when taking deep breaths. The rib is point tender and the individual may experience crepitus upon palpation. Also upon palpation, the individual may feel a false joint. A false joint is when a crack in the bone is palpable and feels like a joint space. Usually rib fractures are closed fractures.

Immediate Care

Most broken ribs heal on their own within a couple of months. In the meantime, it is important for the individual to control their pain by utilizing ice packs and NSAIDs. If the individual's pain causes breathing difficulty or significant pain along the rib, then they should see a physician. The physician will perform an evaluation and take x-rays to determine if the ribs are fractured. If a fracture exists, the physician will prescribe rest, NSAIDs, and ice packs to decrease pain and inflammation. According to the Mayo Clinic (2021), compression wraps are no longer used for rib fractures. Compression wraps can hinder deep breathing, which can increase the risk of the patient acquiring pneumonia.

Remember that various organs lie within the rib cage, and a fractured rib can lacerate one of these organs. Therefore, if you suspect an organ is lacerated, which may be the case if the individual goes into shock, then call 911 immediately.

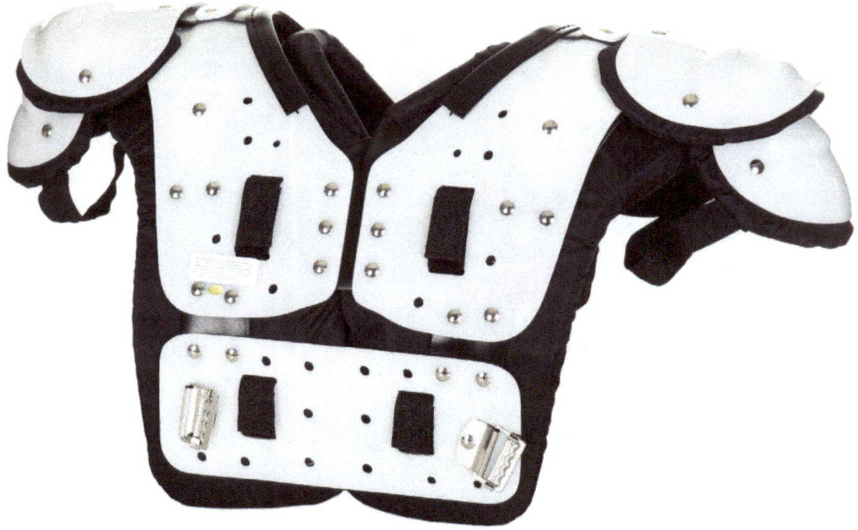

Figure 11-12 Some football shoulder pads have rib guards to help prevent rib injuries or to protect the ribs post-injury.

Prevention

As with any other measures to prevent fractures, individuals need strong bones by having an adequate intake of calcium and vitamin D. Athletic participants should wear protective rib equipment as per their activity **(Figure 11-12)**, be cognizant of their surroundings, and protect themselves from falls.

Costochondral Separation (Sprain)

The costochondral area is located between the rib and the attachment to the sternum. A costochondral separation occurs when the costocartilage is separated from the sternum. The injury is also called a separated rib, and is considered a severe, Grade 3 sprain **(Figure 11-13)**.

Mechanism or Cause of Injury

A costochondral separation is caused by a direct blow to the lateral rib cage. The injury can also be caused by an anterior direct blow to the costochondral area.

Signs and Symptoms

The individual feels varying degrees of pain, especially upon deep breathing, point tenderness, and crepitus. Ecchymosis and localized swelling may be present.

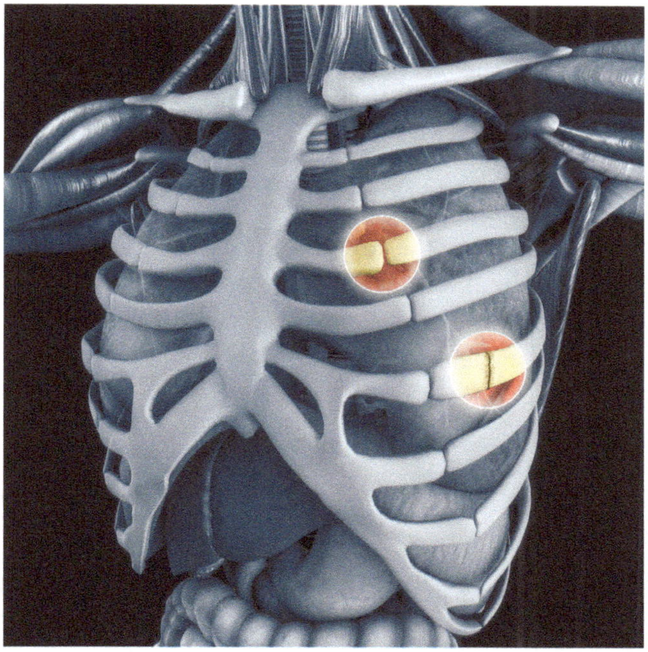

© Naeblys/Shutterstock.com

Figure 11-13 A costochondral separation (top circle) occurs in a different area in rib cage as compared to a rib fracture (bottom circle).

Immediate Care

Assist the individual to rest the injured area. Ice packs assist in pain and inflammation control. Treatment should be similar to rib fracture treatment, and 911 should be called in the same circumstances (i.e., breathing difficulty, possible injury to underlying organs, or shock).

Prevention

Costochondral separation prevention is the same as for rib fractures. Individuals need strong bones by having an adequate intake of calcium and vitamin D. Athletic participants should wear protective rib equipment as per their activity, be cognizant of their surroundings, and protect themselves from falls.

Contusions

Rib contusions may be mistaken for a rib fracture due to the similar mechanism and signs and symptoms of injury.

Mechanism or Cause of Injury

Rib and surrounding muscle contusions occur from a direct blow to the rib cage. Even if an athlete is wearing rib protective equipment, a traumatic blow can still contuse the ribs.

Signs and Symptoms

Rib contusions are painful, even when the athlete is not breathing deeply. Swelling, ecchymosis, and point tenderness are present. Unlike rib fractures, rib contusions do not exhibit crepitus nor a false joint on the rib. The absence of crepitus will assist you in differentiating whether the athlete has a rib fracture or a contusion.

Immediate Care

The athlete should immediately apply ice, and rest from activity. They can take NSAIDs to decrease pain and inflammation. If the athlete has notable pain when breathing or difficulty breathing, then summon EMS immediately.

Prevention

Prevention of contusions includes wearing protective rib equipment as appropriate for the activity. Individuals must be aware of their surroundings to avoid trauma to the area (e.g., not walking or running into equipment, other people, etc.). The facility should be free from objects that the individual may walk or run into during activity.

The Lungs

Pneumothorax

A pneumothorax is a collapsed lung. Air collects around the lung in the pleural cavity, which is the space around the lung in the thoracic cavity **(Figure 11-14)**. This air causes improper lung functioning, and the lung cannot take in normal amounts of air (Medline Plus, 2019).

Mechanism or Cause of Injury

A pneumothorax occurs when an object punctures a lung. A rib can be fractured, and the fractured bone punctures a lung. A lung can also be punctured by a knife, gunshot, archery arrow, or any penetrating object. Sometimes a collapsed lung occurs spontaneously. Air in the lung escapes and enters into to the pleural cavity. This injury is called a *spontaneous pneumothorax*. Patients who have lung-related illnesses, such as chronic obstructive pulmonary disease (COPD) and asthma, are more prone to having a pneumothorax (Medline Plus, 2019).

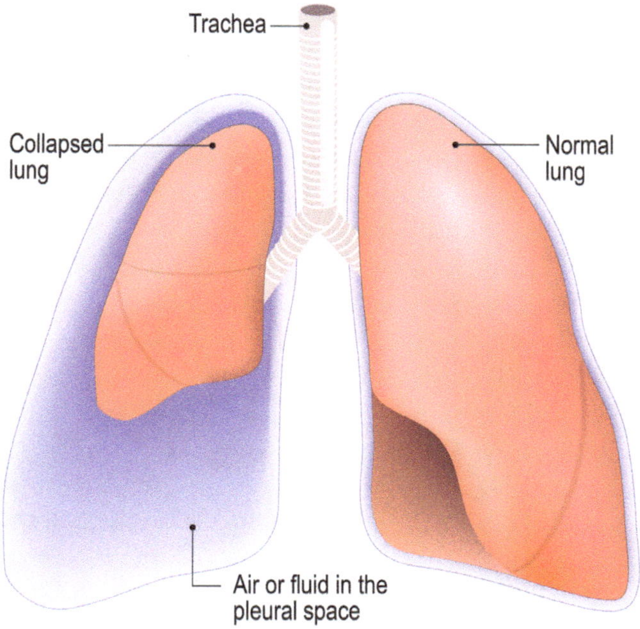

Figure 11-14 Pneumothorax

Signs and Symptoms

A patient with a pneumothorax has shortness of breath, pain when breathing (especially when breathing deeply), chest pain, and lightheadedness. The patient's heart rate is rapid, and blood pressure is low. With prolonged breathing difficulty and without immediate treatment, the patient can become cyanotic. When listening to the lungs with a stethoscope, breath sounds are nonexistent on the injured side. The patient most likely exhibits signs of shock.

Immediate Care

A pneumothorax is a medical emergency. Call 911 immediately while monitoring the patient's airway, breathing, and circulation. Treat the patient for shock if they exhibit signs and symptoms. If the patient is not treated immediately, then air pressure can build up in the pleural cavity and cause a tension pneumothorax. This air pressure moves toward the heart and healthy lung and compresses them. This tension pneumothorax inhibits heart and lung function, and causes significant respiratory distress, **hypoxia**, and death.

A minor pneumothorax, which is a small opening in the lung, often resolves on its own, once the lung is able to inflate with continual breathing. For a minor pneumothorax, the physician may remove some air via a needle inserted into the pleural cavity. The physician can also choose to prescribe rest and supplemental oxygen. A major pneumothorax requires a tube inserted into the chest to pull out air and drain any fluid that has accumulated in the plural space. Surgery may be necessary, especially if this pneumothorax is not the first pneumothorax that the patient has sustained.

Prevention

A pneumothorax can be prevented by protecting the rib cage as should be done to prevent rib fractures and contusions. In order to keep their lungs healthy, individuals should not smoke. An asthmatic individuals must abide by their physician's orders to treat their asthma accordingly.

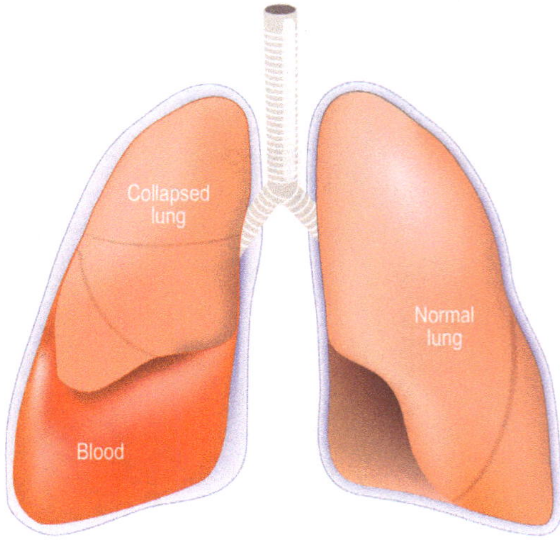

Figure 11-15 Hemothorax

Hemothorax

A hemothorax is similar to a pneumothorax in regard to mechanism and signs and symptoms of injury. However, a hemothorax is when the pleural space fills with blood instead of air **(Figure 11-15).**

Mechanism or Cause of Injury

A hemothorax is caused by the same mechanism of injury as a pneumothorax. Blunt trauma from an object (fractured rib, knife, gunshot, archery arrow, etc.) penetrates the lung and results in hemorrhage. The blood fills the pleural cavity. An individual can also be predisposed to a hemothorax if they have tuberculosis, lung cancer, and previous lung conditions and surgery.

Signs and Symptoms

Signs and symptoms of a hemothorax include rapid, shallow breathing and shortness of breath, rapid pulse, low blood pressure, and chest pain. The individual will be anxious and exhibit signs of shock.

Immediate Care

A hemothorax is a medical emergency; therefore, you must summon EMS immediately. Treat the individual for shock while monitoring their airway, breathing, and circulation. At the hospital, the physician will perform numerous tests including a chest x-ray, a CT scan, pleural tests, etc. in order to determine if the patient has a hemothorax. The physician's first objective is to stop the bleeding. If the bleeding does not stop, then the physician will perform surgery. Fortunately, it is typical for the bleeding to stop, consequently, surgery is often unnecessary.

Prevention

Prevention of a hemothorax includes wearing protective chest protection equipment as required by the activity. In cases where the person has predispositions for hemothorax as mentioned above, the injury may not be preventable.

Asthma

Asthma is a potentially life-threatening condition in which the respiratory tract airways become inflamed. The airways become swollen and decreased in size. Consequently, not enough air enters the airways, and the individual has serious difficulty breathing.

Mechanism or Cause of Injury

Asthma is caused when an individual breathes in an allergen or trigger. When a trigger affects someone, they have an exacerbation (previously referred to as an *asthma attack*). Triggers can be various substances including smoke, pet dander, pollen, mold, dust, fragrances, and chemicals in the air. Exacerbations can also be caused by stress, emotions, environmental changes, especially in cold weather, respiratory infections, including colds, and exercise. Asthma triggered by exercise is called exercise-induced asthma (EIA). Many individuals who have EIA also have regular asthma. Some individuals have EIA and not asthma, which renders the EIA cause as unknown.

Signs and Symptoms

The asthmatic person experiences shortness of breath, wheezing, anxiety, coughing, chest tightness, and rapid pulse. The signs and symptoms can last for minutes to days, and tend to worsen in cold weather and with exercise. Severe signs and symptoms also include chest pain, an abnormal breathing pattern, or cessation of breathing for any period of time.

Immediate Care

The first course of action is to remove the person from the trigger or vice versa, whichever is safer. Assist them in administering their prescribed rescue inhaler if they have one available **(Figure 11-16)**. Never give the individual another person's inhaler, even if the medication on the label appears to be the same. Try to calm the individual down, have them sit in a comfortable position, and take slow controlled breaths. If you do not see that the individual is beginning to breathe normally within a few minutes, then phone 911. Monitor their airway, breathing, and circulation until EMS arrives and treat for shock if necessary. At the ER, the physician will take many tests to determine what triggers the patient's asthma, along with the extent of the condition. The physician will take the patient's chest x-rays as well as lung function and breathing tests. The physician will also give the patient medication

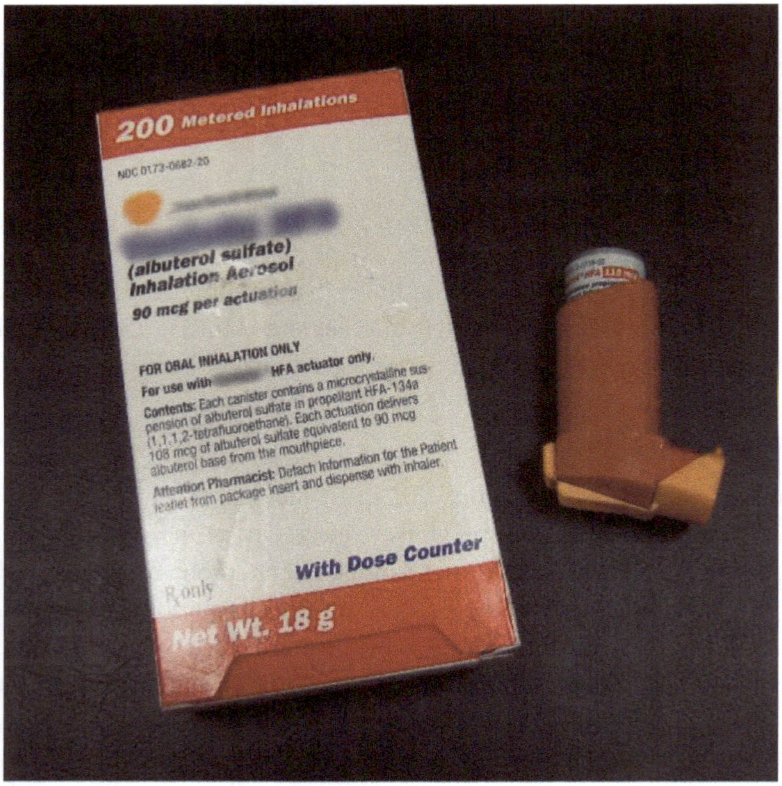

Figure 11-16 A rescue inhaler assists an asthmatic patient during an exacerbation.

to make the asthma exacerbation subside. The patient will have to take prescription medication to decrease the potential for exacerbations, including long and short duration (or "rescue") inhaled corticosteroids. The long duration corticosteroids assist in preventing exacerbations, while the short duration corticosteroids relieve signs and symptoms if an exacerbation begins.

Prevention

Preventing asthma is not always possible, because people cannot necessarily change how their bodies respond to allergens. However, to prevent exacerbations, asthmatic individuals should always take their prescription asthma medication as directed by their physician. They should also avoid their asthma triggers. The individual's home should be clean and free of dust, smoke, and any allergen that triggers their exacerbations. For patients who have EIA, they should exercise in warm, moist environments, such as in a swimming pool, because this environment tends to decrease the incidence of exacerbations.

Hyperventilation

Hyperventilation is when the blood contains low levels of carbon dioxide.

Mechanism or Cause of Injury

Hyperventilation occurs when a patient breathes quickly and deeply for a period of time. The quick, deep breathing typically occurs when the patient is panicking, anxious, angry, or depressed. It can also occur if the patient has an infection, lung or cardiac disease, stress, and severe bleeding. This type of breathing causes excessive oxygen and low levels of carbon dioxide in the blood (MedlinePlus, 2022).

Signs and Symptoms

The individual who is rapidly breathing, may experience panic, lightheadedness, dizziness, and confusion. They may have chest pain, heart palpitations, and dry mouth.

Immediate Care

In most cases when a person is hyperventilating, you can care for them without needing to call 911. Comfort and console the person by talking to them in a relaxed tone of voice while reassuring them that they will be okay. Help the individual accumulate more carbon dioxide in their blood to normalize the levels by having them breathe in and out through pursed lips, or have them close their mouth and breathe through only one nostril. Breathing into a paper bag is no longer recommended because the individual could then become hypoxic. Direct them to breathe slowly and in a regulated manner. The person's breathing rate should slowly return to normal within approximately a minute. If the patient's breathing does not quickly return to normal rate and depth, or if they have severe chest pain, then call 911 immediately. The physician will evaluate the patient and perform many tests, including a chest x-ray and breathing tests, to identify any underlying illnesses that may have triggered the hyperventilation.

Prevention

Preventing hyperventilation begins with stress reduction exercises. These exercises can assist in controlling emotions and panic attacks. The individual may need to see a professional counselor to assist them in controlling these emotions. The individual should have annual physicals to make sure they are healthy and free of illness, including lung or cardiac disease.

The Heart

Sudden Cardiac Death Syndrome

Sudden cardiac death syndrome (SCD) is when an individual dies unexpectedly from cardiac arrest. They may or may not experience any signs or symptoms of illness and succumb to cardiac arrest with no warning. Individuals who experience signs and symptoms of cardiac problems and succumb to SCD die within an hour after the signs and symptoms first appear.

Mechanism or Cause of Injury

SCD is most often caused by cardiac disease and illnesses such as hypertrophic cardiomyopathy **(Figure 11-17)**, atherosclerosis, viral myocarditis, aortic valve stenosis, and drug-induced electrolyte imbalance (Markwerth et al., 2021). Less common causes of SCD include conditions such as idiopathic ventricular fibrillation, sick sinus syndrome, atrioventricular node tumor, and Wolff-Parkinson-White syndrome. Some patients who die of SCD do not have any underlying cause and are classified as having sudden arrhythmia death (SAD) syndrome (Al-Khatib et al., 2017).

Signs and Symptoms

The individual may experience chest pain, breathing difficulty, confusion, sweaty skin, and unsteadiness immediately prior to cardiac arrest. The individual loses consciousness, stops breathing, and has no pulse.

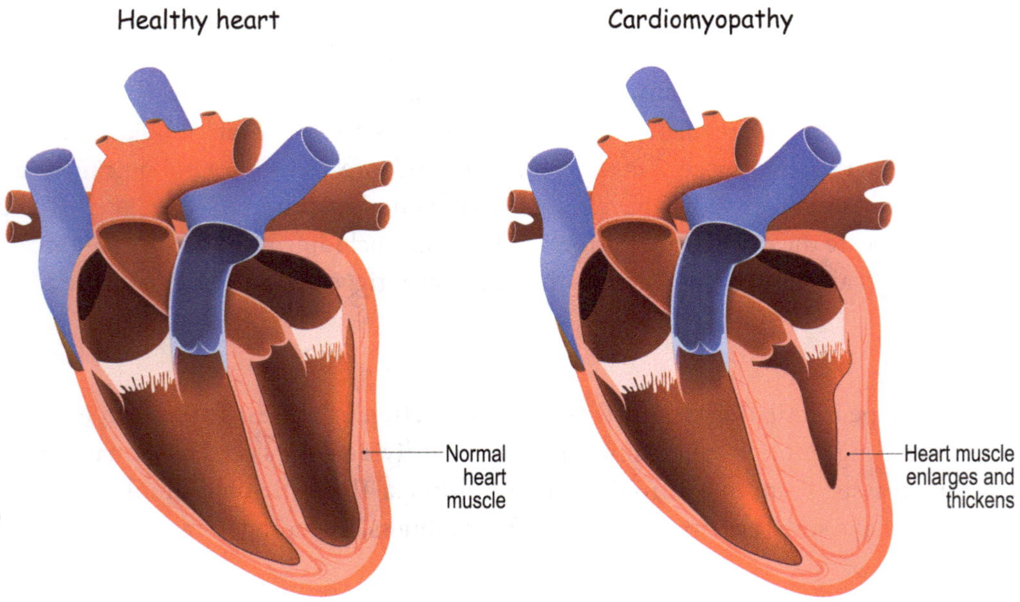

Figure 11-17 A normal heart versus one that suffers from hypertrophic cardiomyopathy (HCM). One cause of sudden death is HCM, which is the thickening of the left ventricular wall. The ventricle cannot pump sufficient amounts of blood to the body.

Immediate Care

Call 911 immediately and check the individual's airway, breathing, and circulation. Perform cardiopulmonary resuscitation (CPR) and utilize and automated external defibrillator (AED) in attempt to resume a normal heartbeat. Do not to stop CPR until EMS arrives and the EMTs take over for you, another trained person takes over, the environment becomes unsafe, or you are too tired to continue.

Prevention

SCD may not be entirely preventable; however, underlying risk factors can be identified. Individuals must have annual physicals with electrocardiograms taken to determine if they have any heart rhythm abnormalities. Individuals should take care of themselves, consume proper nutrients, and maintain normal body weight. They must avoid smoking or drinking excessive alcohol. Participation in physical and wellness activities in order to avoid cardiac disease is imperative. Individuals should gradually progress activity intensity to prevent undue stress to the heart, especially when beginning a new activity or after a long duration of inactivity.

Commotio Cordis

Commotio cordis is sudden death due to a disruption in the heart's electrical conductivity. The person may or may not have an underlying cardiac issue.

Mechanism or Cause of Injury

Commotio cordis occurs when a person is struck by an object at the sternum, which overlies the heart. The person may be wearing chest protective equipment, but the propelled object's force is so great that the equipment cannot entirely protect the heart.

Signs and Symptoms

Individuals with commotio cordis are unconscious, not breathing, without a pulse, and cyanotic. Ecchymosis appears at the impact point on the chest, which indicates a contusion.

Immediate Care

Call 911 immediately, check for airway, breathing, and circulation, and then immediately start CPR. According to experimental data, AED utilization within 1 minute of loss of pulse gives the patient 100% chance of survival (Yabek, 2016). As each minute goes by, the chance of survival decreases significantly. Unfortunately, CPR with AED use is not usually initiated within 1 minute of a patient with commotio cordis.

Prevention

Athletic participants must wear properly fitted chest protection equipment for the activity. However, protective equipment is not fool-proof in preventing commotio cordis. The equipment is utilized in attempt to protect the body and dissipate force from the striking object. When participating in activities where the possibility of receiving a direct blow to the chest exists, the individual must always be aware of their surroundings.

Heart Murmur

Many people have heart murmurs. Heart murmurs are extra or unusual sounds that occur when the heart beats. The murmurs can be harmless and not a cause for concern, or may indicate an underlying cardiac problem.

Mechanism or Cause of Injury

The National Heart, Lung, and Blood Institute (2020) notes that "harmless" or "innocent" heart murmurs have an unknown cause. It is speculated that extra blood flow, such as when an individual is pregnant, may cause a murmur. Abnormal heart murmurs are typically congenital in children. Various portions of the heart may be damaged which leads to valve problems and murmurs. In adults, murmurs are usually indicative of heart valve disease, which can be caused by infection, disease, and aging.

Signs and Symptoms

Individuals with harmless heart murmurs may experience no signs and symptoms, and may not even know they have a murmur. Some people may experience shortness of breath during exertion, excessive sweating without cause, cyanosis, dizziness, fainting, and chest pain.

Immediate Care

If your client exhibits signs and symptoms of a heart murmur, have them stop activity and rest, and refer them to a physician for evaluation. If they are in distress, which is not typical, then call 911. First aid is not provided to the individual if they have an innocent heart murmur. If they have an abnormal heart murmur, their physician will address the cause. If they have another illness or disease that could be causing the murmur, such as hyperthyroidism and anemia, the physician will treat the underlying cause. Once the underlying cause is addressed, the murmur should stop. If the cause is a congenital heart defect, surgery may be warranted.

Prevention

Innocent and abnormal congenital heart murmurs cannot be prevented. However, in attempt to prevent heart valve disease, individuals should lead a healthy lifestyle, maintain proper nutrition, and participate in physical activity and exercise on a regular basis.

The Breasts

Breast Cancer

Breast cancer is the most common form of cancer in the U.S. in biological women after skin cancer; however, breast cancer can also occur in biological men. The cancer forms in the ducts of the breast cells.

Mechanism or Cause of Injury

No definitive cause of breast cancer has been identified. The disease occurs when breast cells grow abnormally. Various risk factors predispose a person to breast cancer, such as being a biological female, having familial history of breast cancer, beginning menstruation at a young age, beginning menopause at a young age, taking postmenopausal medications, having the first child at age 35 or older, alcohol consumption, and obesity (CDC, 2021).

Signs and Symptoms

An individual with breast cancer experiences a lump in the breast that feels unusual as compared to the other tissue. The lump is not necessarily painful, and remains in the same area. The nipple may be inverted, bleeding, or dimpled. The breast may change shape or size, and the skin may appear wrinkled.

Immediate Care

If the individual has any signs or symptoms of breast cancer, they should see a physician to be evaluated, even if they have had a recent mammogram. The physician will order a variety of tests including a mammogram, MRI, ultrasound, and a biopsy. A biopsy involves removing some of the abnormal breast tissue mass and testing it to see if it is cancerous. If the patient has breast cancer, then they can have surgery to remove the mass, the cancerous breast, and/or the lymph nodes. Chemotherapy and/or radiation are prescribed regardless of whether surgery is performed.

Prevention

Mammograms identify abnormal breast tissue. Biological females should have an annual mammogram beginning at the age of 40 years, and frequently perform breast self-exams

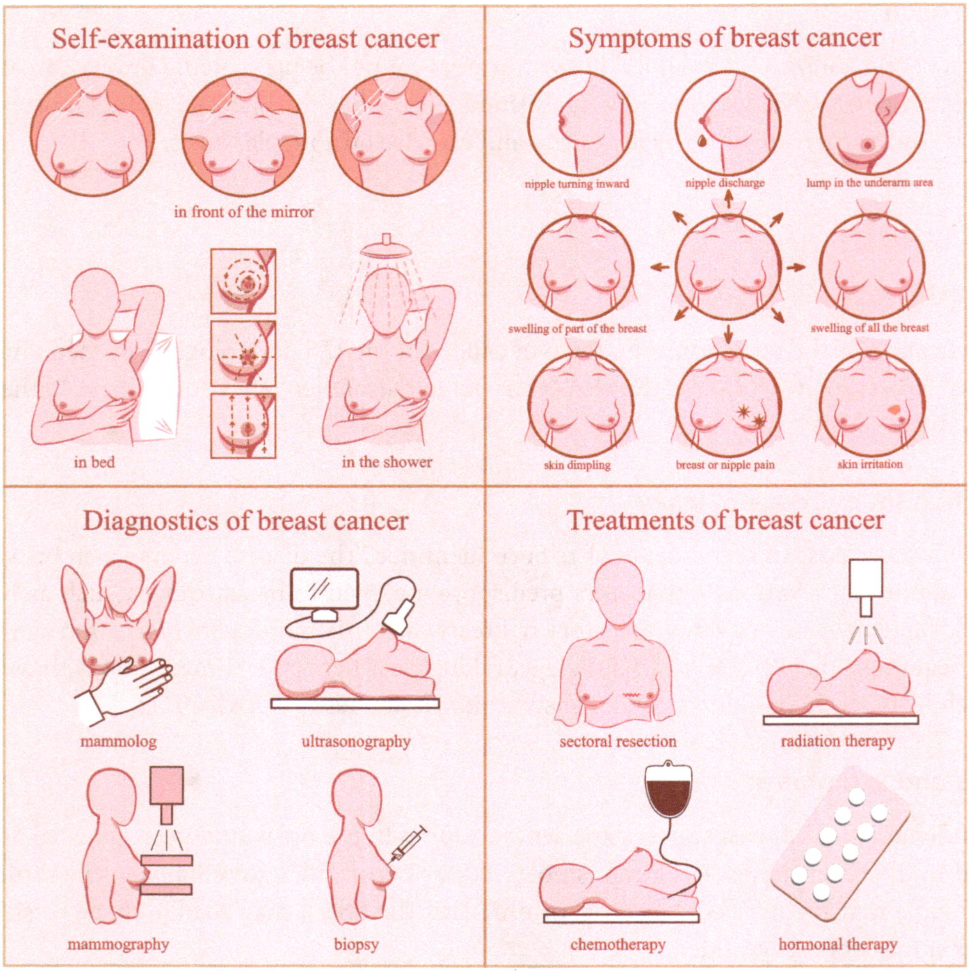

Figure 11-18 Breast cancer self-examination, symptoms, diagnostics, and treatments

(**Figure 11-18**). Individuals should exercise, eat nutritious foods, and avoid smoking and alcohol consumption. Biological females should consider whether postmenopausal hormone therapy is appropriate because it increases the chance of acquiring breast cancer.

The Abdomen

The abdomen, which is commonly referred to as the *belly*, is the area below the diaphragm and above the pelvis. The abdomen contains the stomach, small and large intestines, liver, gallbladder, pancreas, kidneys, and spleen. The aorta and inferior vena cava also descent from the thorax to the abdomen.

The Kidneys and Urinary System

Kidney Contusions

A kidney contusion is a serious injury. If the kidney does not have adequate time to heal and sustains another injury, complications may occur. Kidney function may deteriorate, or the kidney can fail.

Mechanism or Cause of Injury

Blunt force trauma is the cause of kidney contusions. If the force is strong enough, the kidney can actually be lacerated, which is a more significant injury.

Signs and Symptoms

The patient complains of pain in the back by the kidney (called the *flank*) and possibly in the abdomen. They also complain of nausea and difficulty breathing. The patient may vomit and may have some blood in the urine (hematuria), but often this blood is not visible to the naked eye. Ecchymosis and swelling may be at the impact site.

Immediate Care

If your client has sustained blunt force trauma to the flank area, and signs and symptoms indicate that they have sustained a kidney contusion, then refer them to a physician. In the meantime, your client must apply ice to the area, rest, and discontinue any contact activities. They can take over-the-counter NSAIDs to reduce pain and inflammation. The physician will perform a urinalysis to check for blood in the urine and will order a CT scan, an ultrasound, and other tests that evaluate the kidney's function. The individual should wear padding or a brace over the affected area to protect the area from additional direct trauma until the kidney has healed. Rarely is surgery needed. If the kidney is lacerated or the blood supply to the kidney is damaged, then surgery will be an option to save the kidney.

Prevention

Athletic participants should wear flank protective gear if they participate in contact activities. They should strengthen the musculature that will help protect the kidney from blunt force trauma.

Kidney Stones

Kidney stones can be found anywhere in the urinary tract, but are formulated in the kidneys. Kidney stones are formed over a period of weeks or months.

Mechanism or Cause of Injury

Kidney stones can form due to urine containing too much calcium or uric acid. Oxalate, which is found in foods such as spinach, beets, almonds, and sesame seeds, can combine with calcium and form the kidney stones. Kidney stones can be hereditary, and caused by medications, such as acyclovir, which treats herpes outbreaks.

Signs and Symptoms

The individual experiences back pain, nausea, vomiting, chills, fever, and hematuria or abnormal urine color.

Immediate Care

If the individual believes they have kidney stones, they should be evaluated by their physician. The physician will perform various tests including blood tests, ultrasounds, CT, MRI, x-rays to determine if a kidney stone is present and, if so, its location. Treatment for kidney stones is conservative at first because the stones usually pass through the urinary tract on their own. When kidney stones pass through the urinary tract, the patient may be in a lot of pain and should take NSAIDs. The physician may prescribe narcotics for the pain. If the patient believes he is passing a stone when urinating, they should strain the urine to collect the stone **(Figure 11-19)**. Once the stone is collected, the patient should give it to their physician for evaluation, in order to determine what caused the stone. If the stone cannot be passed or

Figure 11-19 Kidney stones

other complications exist, the physician may need to perform surgery or other procedures to eliminate the stone.

Prevention

Individuals should drink about eight glasses of water per day to make sure adequate urine is being produced and any substances within the urine are diluted.

Urinary Tract Infections

Urinary tract infections (UTIs) occur in both males and females, with the infection occurring more often in biological females.

Mechanism or Cause of Injury

UTIs occur due to bacteria getting into the bladder and causing cystitis, which is an inflammation of the bladder. A UTI can also occur due to urethritis, which is an inflammation of the urethra. This inflammation can also be caused by bacteria entering the urethra or sexually transmitted diseases (STDs), otherwise known as sexually transmitted infections (STIs).

Signs and Symptoms

The individual experiences pelvic pain, as well as severe pain and burning with urination. They constantly feel the need to urinate, and the urine is pink or cloudy.

Immediate Care

A person with a suspected UTI must see their physician for a urinalysis to confirm the UTI and treatment. Approximately a 7-day course of antibiotics is necessary to eliminate the infection. Rarely does a patient have a severe UTI that needs to be treated by intravenous antibiotics and hospitalization.

Prevention

UTIs can be prevented by drinking plenty of water each day and emptying the bladder as soon as the urge to urinate exists. Individuals should pay attention to pelvic area hygiene, especially after utilizing the bathroom.

The Digestive System

Peptic Ulcer

Peptic ulcers are sores that are located in the lining of the esophagus, stomach, and upper small intestines **(Figure 11-20)**. Ulcers can become open sores that can hemorrhage.

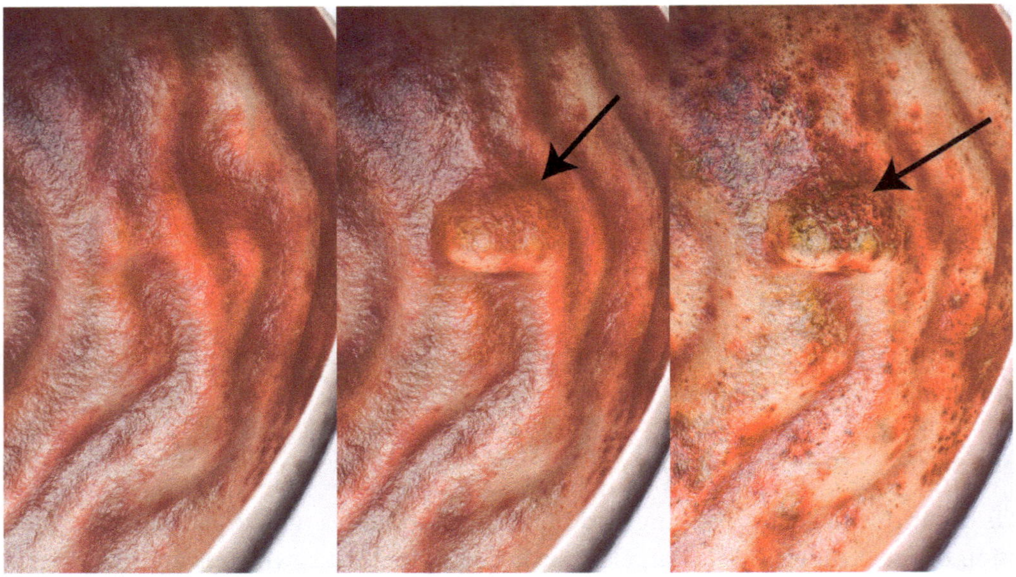

Figure 11-20 A peptic ulcer forming in the upper digestive tract

Mechanism or Cause of Injury

Bacterial infections, especially *H. pylori*, are the most common cause of peptic ulcers. Stomach acid and overuse of aspirin and other NSAIDs can cause wearing away of the lining of the upper digestive tract. Chemicals from smoking tobacco can also cause the lining to be worn away. When the lining is worn away, an ulcer is formed. Physicians now recognize that stress and food do not cause ulcers.

Signs and Symptoms

Newly formed peptic ulcers exhibit a burning pain at the upper digestive tract, especially when the patient has an empty stomach or at night. The pain may come and go for weeks at a time. More severe ulcers cause bleeding, and as a result, the patient may vomit blood that is very red in color. The patient's stools, however, are dark black in color from the blood traveling through the entire digestive tract before being eliminated. The patient does not have an appetite and most likely loses weight.

Immediate Care

If the signs and symptoms are not significant, the patient can take over-the-counter antacids. If the patient has consistent signs and symptoms, then they should see their physician. Through testing, the physician will determine the cause of the ulcer. *H. pylori* can be treated by antibiotics. Various medications can be prescribed to prevent stomach acid production and promote ulcer healing. Antacids can be taken to neutralize acid production.

Prevention

Individuals should not overuse NSAIDs. If continual pain occurs that requires NSAIDs, an individual should consult a physician to determine what can be done to modulate the pain. Proper hand washing practices should be practiced regularly to prevent spread of bacteria. Smoking should also be avoided.

Gastroenteritis

Gastroenteritis is stomach and small intestine inflammation. When the illness is caused by eating contaminated food, it is referred to as *food poisoning*.

Mechanism or Cause of Injury

Gastroenteritis occurs when bacteria, viruses, or parasites enter the digestive tract. This infection can occur if these contaminants are contained in poorly prepared or uncooked food. The contaminants can be found in water that is ingested or that is used in food preparation. A person can also pass the contaminants to another person. Noncontagious causes of gastroenteritis are chemicals and other toxins; certain substances found in foods, such as seafood and dairy products; and medications.

Signs and Symptoms

The individual has abdominal pain, nausea, vomiting, and diarrhea. Flu-like symptoms, including fever if the individual has an infection, and chills are evident.

Immediate Care

Gastroenteritis commonly relieves itself in a short amount of time. Usually, the body rids the contaminant within a day to a week. In the meantime, the individual must treat the signs and symptoms. Ingestion of electrolyte fluids is imperative in order to avoid dehydration. The individual must ease into eating normal foods after having gastroenteritis.

Prevention

An individual should practice frequent hand washing with soap and water in order to prevent gastroenteritis. They should inform their physician if they have any intolerance or stomach upset with any foods, medications, or toxins.

Vomiting

Vomiting is the body forcing out the stomach contents. Vomiting has many causes. If a person vomits, an underlying cause needs to be identified.

Mechanism or Cause of Injury

Many causes for vomiting exist. Vomiting can be caused by illnesses and infections, such as ulcers, gastroenteritis, appendicitis, and the flu. A person can vomit when they are in shock, have a migraine, or are in severe pain. Medications, allergens, chemicals, food, and alcohol can also cause someone to vomit.

Signs and Symptoms

The person feels nauseous, has abdominal pain, and perhaps begins to sweat prior to vomiting. They may become pale, disoriented, and weak.

Immediate Care

To care for a person who is or has vomited, immediately rule out any life-threatening injuries or illnesses by performing a primary survey. Then perform a secondary survey and determine the SINS of illness. If you can readily determine the cause of vomiting and the person is not in a life-threatening situation, then have them vomit into a receptacle, rest, and take slow sips of an electrolyte drink. Remember, if blood is in the vomit, bloodborne pathogens may exist; therefore, wear personal protective equipment (PPE) when assisting the patient. If vomiting does not stop within 24 hours after it has begun, blood is in the vomit, the underlying cause cannot be identified, or the cause is life-threatening or serious, then immediately call 911. Also if the person is in severe pain or becomes dehydrated, EMS must be summoned. In the ER, intravenous fluids, medication to stop the vomiting, and pain medication will be prescribed. Once the underlying cause is identified, then the physician will determine if it is safe for the patient to go home or if hospitalization is necessary.

Prevention

Individuals should avoid all substances that may cause them to vomit. They should also refrain from being around others who knowingly have a contagious illness such as the flu or gastroenteritis.

Diarrhea

Diarrhea is a loose, watery, frequent bowel movement. If a person has three of more of these bowel movements per day, then the illness is classified as diarrhea.

Mechanism or Cause of Injury

Diarrhea can occur by the same mechanisms of illness as vomiting. Bacteria, viruses, and parasites, as well as illnesses, infection, contaminated food and water, food intolerances, and medications can cause diarrhea.

Signs and Symptoms

The signs and symptoms include abdominal cramping, bloating, nausea, and the urge to defecate. The stools appear extremely watery and loose. Blood, which appears as very dark red or black, may be in the stool.

Immediate Care

To treat the patient's diarrhea, remove the causative factor, if you are able to identify it after performing a secondary survey. The patient should rest in a comfortable place and take slow sips of an electrolyte drink. If the causative factor is not an underlying illness or infection, then the patient can take over-the-counter antidiarrheal medication. If the causative factor is an underlying illness or infection, the patient becomes dehydrated, you are not able to identify the cause, or the diarrhea does not stop within 2-3 days, then refer the patient to a physician.

Prevention

Individuals should practice frequent hand washing. They should refrain from being around others who knowingly have a contagious illness, such as the flu or gastroenteritis.

Gastroesophageal Reflux Disease (GERD)

Gastroesophageal reflux disease (GERD) is also called peptic esophagitis and dyspepsia. Some people refer to it as indigestion or heartburn. When a person eats or drinks, the substances travel through the esophagus, through a sphincter, and into the stomach. The sphincter prevents food and drink from coming back up into the esophagus. If the sphincter is not able to keep the food and drink in the stomach, then reflux, or leaking back into the esophagus, occurs. If the reflux also includes stomach acid, which is created and used for digestive purposes, then the individual feels a burning sensation or heartburn.

Mechanism or Cause of Injury

GERD can be brought on by drinking alcohol, smoking, obesity, and pregnancy. Various medications, including some high blood pressure, depression, and asthma medications, can cause GERD.

Signs and Symptoms

The individual with GERD has heartburn, which is a burning sensation into their esophagus. They may have indigestion when they regurgitate their food, or has the sensation that food is stuck in their esophagus by the lower portion of the breastbone. The burning worsens at night and when lying down and sitting.

Immediate Care

The individual can take a variety of over-the-counter acid reflux medications to prevent, decrease, or neutralize the stomach acid. They should begin to lose weight if they are obese, and quit smoking and drinking excessive alcohol. If the problem persists for weeks to months after self-treatment, then the individual should be evaluated by a physician. The physician may prescribe medication to assist in decreasing the signs and symptoms of GERD, as well as lifestyle changes to minimize the effects of the illness.

Prevention

Individuals should maintain a healthy weight, not smoke or drink excessive alcohol, and eat slowly at meals in order to prevent GERD. Any foods that aggravate the individual's digestive system as well as oral anti-inflammatory medications should be avoided.

Irritable Bowel Syndrome (IBS)

Irritable bowel syndrome (IBS) is a common condition of the large intestine. Unlike some other lower intestine illnesses, such as Crohn's disease and colitis, IBS does not produce inflammation. Biological women are more likely to have IBS than are biological men.

Mechanism or Cause of Injury

IBS has no known cause. Individuals may have triggers that exacerbate IBS, such as gas, certain food, stress or other emotions, medications, and hormone changes in biological females. IBS can also be hereditary.

Signs and Symptoms

IBS causes abdominal pain, cramping, gas, bloating, diarrhea, and constipation (**Figure 11-21**). Mucus is visible on the patient's stools. Most often, these signs and symptoms are minor. In rare cases, they can be disabling, and the patient must readily see a physician.

Immediate Care

Since IBS has no definitive cause, the patient must treat their symptoms. The patient should control their diet by eliminating gas-producing foods, including broccoli and cabbage, as well

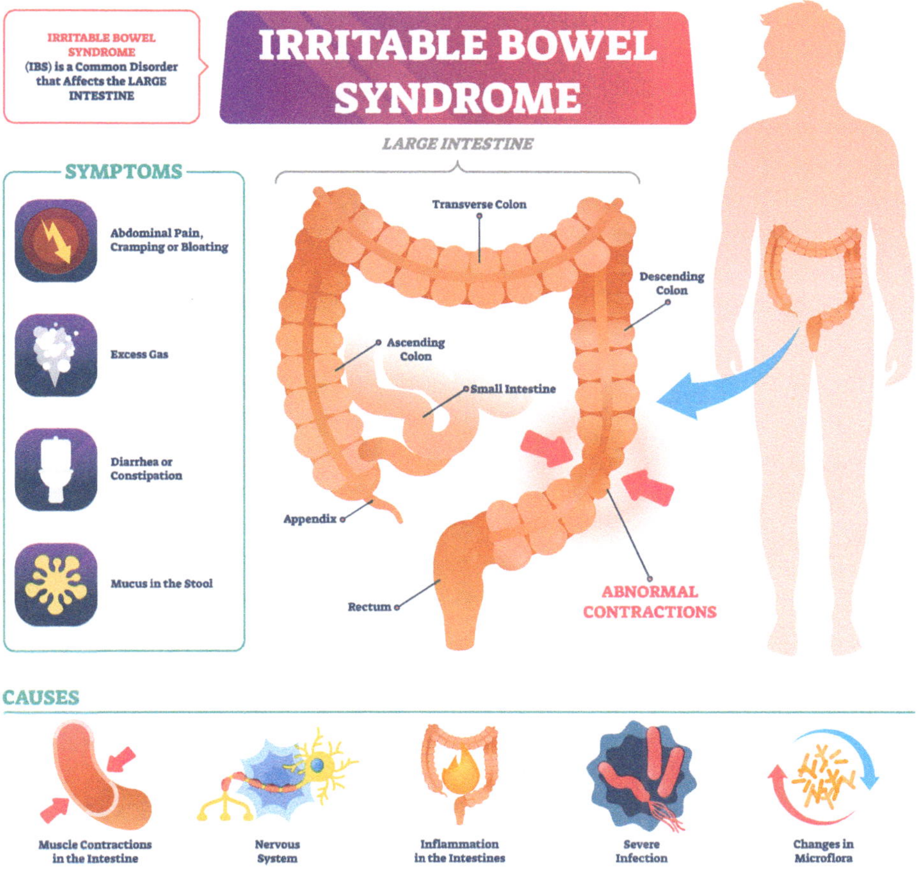

Figure 11-21 Irritable bowel syndrome symptoms and causes

as foods that can increase signs and symptoms of IBS, such as sugar-free sweeteners, caffeine, carbonated beverages, and dairy products. The patient should eat fiber-filled foods or take fiber supplements to control constipation. They must manage their stress and exercise frequently. If the patient has diarrhea, antidiarrheal medications are necessary. If the patient has stress, anxiety, or depression, they should participate in relaxation techniques, speak with a professional counselor, or see a physician for medication addressing the issue. If the patient's signs and symptoms are disabling, then refer them to a physician for evaluation. The doctor can prescribe medication specific to treat IBS, along with recommending lifestyle changes to decrease the incidence of signs and symptoms.

Prevention

A person can prevent IBS by participating in physical activity. They should regularly participate in relaxation activities. Eating small meals throughout the day, including fiber in the diet, drinking eight glasses of water per day, and avoiding foods that cause IBS signs and symptoms helps prevent IBS.

Constipation

Constipation is a common GI problem for individuals. When a person is constipated, their stools are hard and difficult to pass.

Mechanism or Cause of Injury

Constipation may occur from a lack of fluid or fiber in the diet. The waste products move too slow through the GI tract and lose fluid. This keeps the waste products hard and difficult to pass. Constipation can also occur due to an underlying condition or disease such as diabetes, thyroid conditions, and stroke.

Signs and Symptoms

A person with constipation passes less than three stools per week. The stools are hard and difficult and perhaps painful to pass. They feel like the rectum is being blocked, and they strain to produce a bowel movement.

Immediate Care

The individual can take over-the-counter medications including fiber supplements and laxatives to assist in softening and eliminating the stool. They can also use an enema. Any of these remedies should not be utilized too frequently, because they can irritate the colon and cause complications. If the individual continues to pass stools infrequently, then an underlying cause for the constipation may exist and they should see a physician.

Prevention

To avoid constipation, the patient must include high fiber in their diet. They can include fiber-filled foods, such as fruits, vegetables, whole grains, and beans, and/or take fiber supplements. The individual must drink approximately eight glasses of water per day to assist in moving the stool through the colon. Exercise also has shown to promote colon function.

The Reproductive System

The reproductive system can be affected by systemic disease or injury.

Testicular Cancer

Testicular cancer is not very common, but is highly treatable.

Mechanism or Cause of Injury

As with breast cancer, no definitive cause of testicular cancer has been determined. Abnormal cells begin to grow in the testes, which create a hard, unusual mass. Risk factors for testicular cancer include undescended or abnormal testicles and family history. Caucasians are more prone to testicular cancer than other races, and approximately half of the cases of testicular cancer occur to biological men ages 20-34 years old (American Cancer Society, 2018).

Signs and Symptoms

A testicular cancer mass feels like a lump in the testicle. The patient has dull pain in the abdomen and significant pain in the testicle. The scrotum may be swollen due to fluid collecting in the area.

Immediate Care

The individual should see their physician if they have any signs and symptoms of testicular cancer that persist and do not resolve within a week or two. If the individual has severe pain, refer them immediately for medical evaluation. Testicular cancer is treated with chemotherapy, radiation, and/or surgery.

Prevention

Testicular cancer is not preventable. However, testicular self-exams should be performed regularly to feel for any abnormalities in the scrotum and testicles.

Scrotal Contusion

A scrotal contusion is similar to any other body contusion in regard to mechanism of injury and signs and symptoms.

Mechanism or Cause of Injury

Scrotal contusions occur due to a direct blow to the scrotum. A person could run into an object or be struck by an object in the scrotal area to cause the injury.

Signs and Symptoms

With a scrotal contusion, the individual has immediate disabling testicular pain. They are typically bent over at the waist due to excruciating pain and feels like they cannot breathe. They may also feel nauseous and vomit. Testicular swelling, ecchymosis, and hematuria may be present.

Immediate Care

Immediate treatment is for the individual to relax and wait for the pain to subside. An ice pack can be applied to the area, and they can take NSAIDs to decrease pain and inflammation.

If they have swelling at the scrotum that does not decrease within a few days of rest and ice application, then they must see a physician. The individual may have another injury such as a hydrocele or spermatic cord torsion (which are discussed in the following sections). The individual should wear supportive underwear during the healing phases.

Prevention

To avoid scrotal contusions, athletic participants in sports such as baseball, ice hockey, and football should wear protective equipment for the genitalia.

Hydrocele

A hydrocele is an accumulation of fluid in the scrotal sac around the testicles **(Figure 11-22)**.

Mechanism or Cause of Injury

Similarly to scrotal contusions, hydroceles are also caused in adults by direct trauma to the scrotum and testicles. Testicle or epididymis infection can also cause a hydrocele.

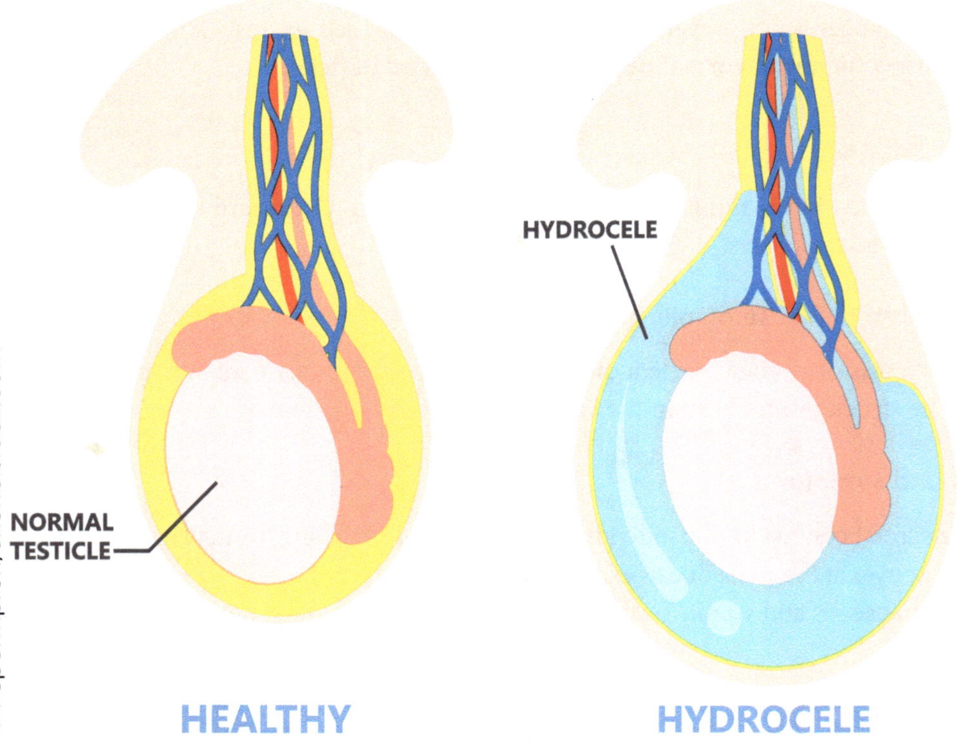

Figure 11-22 A hydrocele is an accumulation of fluid in the scrotum.

Signs and Symptoms

The individual rarely feels pain, but sees a significant amount of scrotal sac swelling. They may complain of scrotal sac heaviness.

Immediate Care

Often a hydrocele does not need treatment, but it is prudent for the patient to be evaluated by their physician to rule out any other conditions such as spermatic cord torsion. A hydrocele typically resolves itself within 6 months or so. If the hydrocele does not resolve then the physician may aspirate the fluid from the scrotum.

Prevention

Hydroceles are not entirely preventable. Athletic participants should wear protective equipment for the scrotum to avoid injury due to direct trauma.

Spermatic Cord Torsion

Spermatic cord torsion, also called testicular torsion, can occur to biological males of all ages. The condition occurs when the spermatic cord and testicle twists around and then are contracted in this position. Because the spermatic cord is twisted, blood supply to the testicle is inhibited or completely cut off **(Figure 11-23)**. The testicle can become hypoxic and die.

Mechanism or Cause of Injury

Spermatic cord torsion can be caused by a direct blow to the scrotum or can occur during strenuous exercise. The condition can also occur due to an anatomical abnormality where the testes are loose within the scrotal sac, which causes the scrotum to twist easily, during sleep, or for no apparent reason.

Signs and Symptoms

The individual complains of a sudden onset of severe scrotal pain on the torsion side and in the abdomen. They feel nauseous, vomit, and have a fever. The scrotum may be red, swollen, and point tender.

Immediate Care

Spermatic cord torsion necessitates immediate care. If the individual feels like they have a spermatic cord torsion, they should attempt to reverse the torsion manually. Even if they are able to reverse the torsion, they should see a physician immediately. If they are not able to reverse the torsion, call 911 to have them transported to the ER immediately for care. The physician

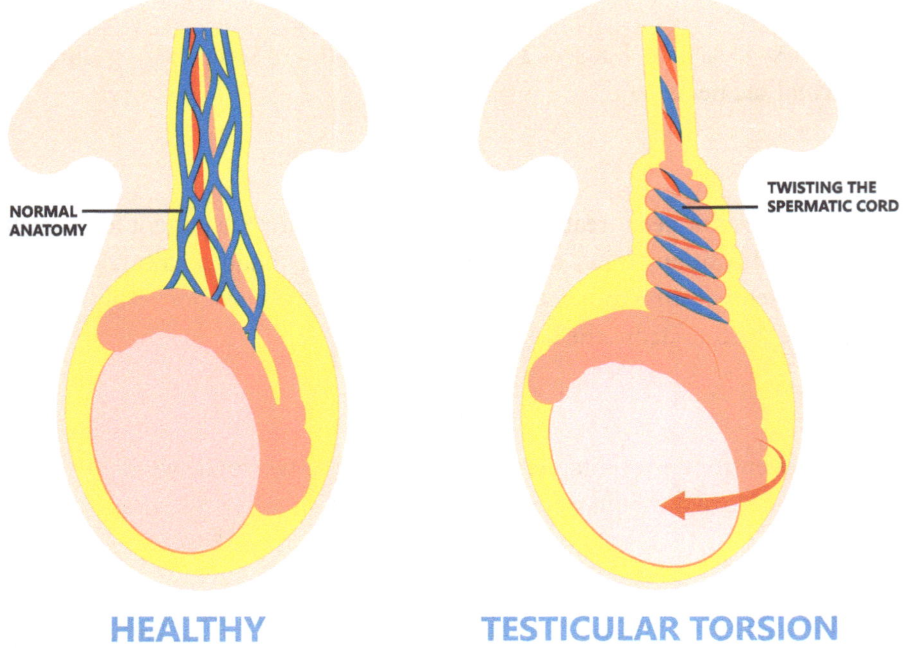

Figure 11-23 Testicular torsion is twisting of the spermatic cord.

may need to perform immediate surgery in order to return blood supply to the testicle. After surgery, the patient must rest for proper healing and so the condition does not recur.

Prevention

Spermatic cord torsion is not entirely able to be prevented. Athletic participants should wear protective equipment for the scrotum to avoid injury due to direct trauma.

Other Abdominal Conditions

Appendicitis

Appendicitis is an inflammation of the appendix, which can occur to individuals of all ages **(Figure 11-24)**. Pus accumulates in the appendix and causes significant signs and symptoms of illness. The appendix can burst, which allows pus to enter into the abdominal cavity. The pus is toxic to the body and a person can die.

Mechanism or Cause of Injury

Appendicitis does not have a definitive cause. The inflammation may be caused by an obstruction of fecal material in the colon by the appendix, or GI tract infection

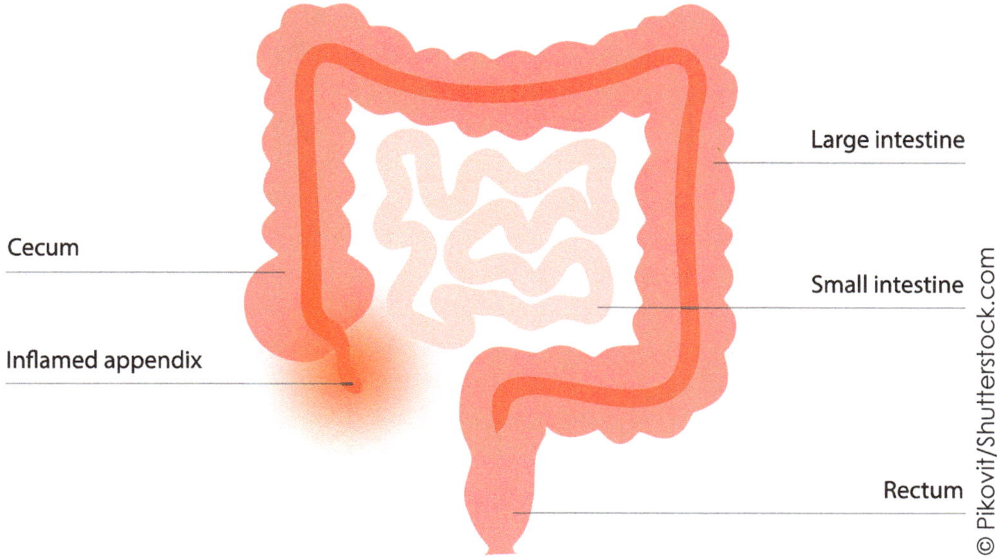

Figure 11-24 An inflamed appendix (appendicitis)

Signs and Symptoms

From the onset, the patient complains of an increase in signs and symptoms over the course of the day, which eventually becomes severe. The patient feels pain at the lower right abdomen at McBurney's point, especially when coughing, walking, or making sudden twisting movements. McBurney's point is a landmark located midway between the umbilicus and anterior superior iliac spine **(Figure 11-25)**. The area is very point tender. The patient has rebound tenderness, which is absence of pain when pressure is applied to the area, but significant pain when the pressure is released. The patient may have a low-grade (99° F) fever, feel nauseous, and vomit.

Immediate Care

If you suspect your patient has appendicitis due to the existing signs and symptoms, then refer them to their physician immediately. Call 911 if your patient has severe abdominal pain that does not subside despite the attempt to get into a comfortable position. The physician will perform an examination and imaging tests to determine if the illness is appendicitis. If your patient has appendicitis, the physician will perform surgery to remove the appendix. After the surgery, rest and abdominal support to promote healing is necessary.

Prevention

Appendicitis cannot be prevented. Signs and symptoms of appendicitis must be recognized immediately in order to seek medical care and avoid a ruptured appendix.

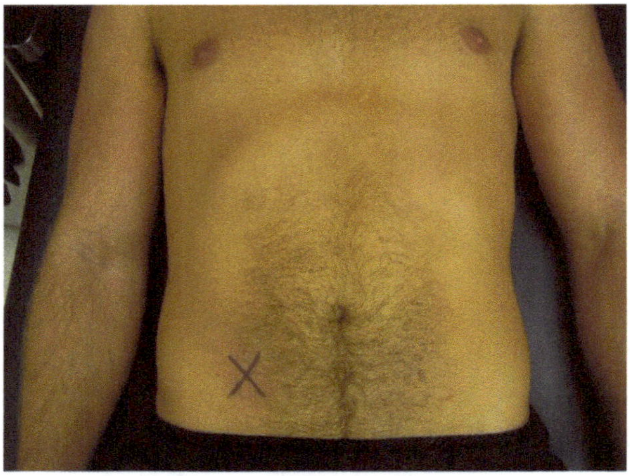

Figure 11-25 Location of McBurney's point marked with an X at the lower right quadrant of the abdomen

Spleen Injury

Contusions and lacerations of the spleen do not occur very often. However, since the spleen has a vast blood supply, if it is injured then it can severely hemorrhage. This severe spleen hemorrhage is life-threatening.

Mechanism or Cause of Injury

A spleen injury is caused by blunt force direct trauma to the upper left quadrant of the abdomen where the spleen is located. This trauma can occur due to a direct blow by another person's body, an implement or piece of equipment, falling hard on the ground onto the area, or a motor vehicle accident (**Figure 11-26**).

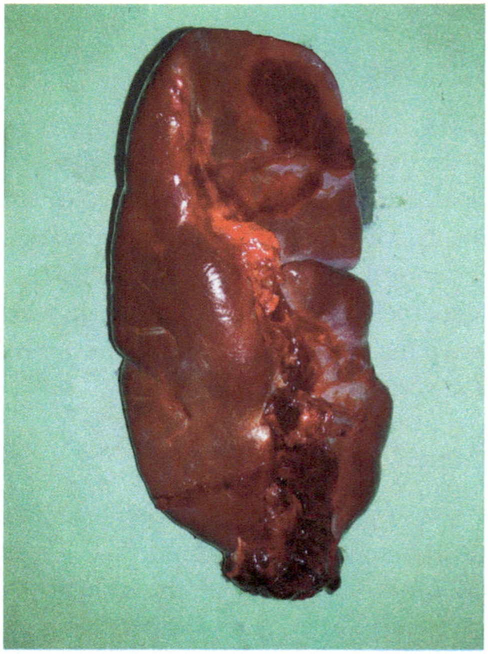

Figure 11-26 Lacerated spleen due to blunt abdominal trauma

Signs and Symptoms

Typical signs and symptoms of spleen injuries include severe pain at the upper left portion of the abdomen, left shoulder pain (called *Kehr's sign*), nausea, vomiting, shock, abdominal muscle guarding and rigidity, difficulty breathing, and faintness.

Immediate Care

An injury to the spleen is a medical emergency. Call 911 immediately, since the individual needs immediate medical care. Monitor their airway, breathing, and circulation while treating them for shock until EMS arrives. For spleen contusions, the physician will have the patient rest and avoid any contact with others. The patient cannot come in bodily contact with other people because another less traumatic blow can cause the spleen to rupture. For severe spleen contusions or lacerations, the spleen most likely will need to be repaired or removed surgically.

Prevention

Athletic participants must wear properly fitted protective equipment to prevent against a spleen injury. They should always be cognizant of their surroundings while participating in activities. Individuals should always wear seatbelts in motor vehicles.

Mononucleosis

Mononucleosis, or *mono* as it is often called, is a viral infection.

Mechanism or Cause of Injury

Mononucleosis is caused by the Epstein-Barr virus, which is passed through saliva.

Signs and Symptoms

The individual with mono exhibits flu-like symptoms including a fever, extreme fatigue and weakness, sore throat, headache, and loss of appetite. They may have night sweats, swollen lymph nodes, especially in the posterior neck, and swollen tonsils. Mono can also cause an enlarged, swollen spleen.

Immediate Care

The individual who has this or any other potentially infectious illness must not be allowed into your facility until their physician verifies that they are not contagious. The individual must see their physician to be tested. If diagnosed with mono, they need to have significant rest, to eat healthy foods, and drink fluids to become well. The physician may prescribe antibiotics to treat other bacterial infections, such as tonsillitis, that occur along with mono. The individual should avoid close proximity with others because they can transmit the virus to others. Likewise, they should not participate in any activity that allows for close physical proximity with athletic participants, implements, equipment, or the like due to the swelling of the spleen. When the spleen is swollen and engorged with blood, a seemingly insignificant direct blow to the upper left abdominal quadrant can cause the spleen to rupture and create a life-threatening situation for the individual.

Prevention

Since mono is spread through saliva, sharing drinks, utensils, toothbrushes, etc. should be avoided. Proper hand washing can also prevent virus transmission.

Blow to the Solar Plexus

The solar plexus, or celiac plexus, is located between the sternum and the umbilicus. A blow to this area causes a temporary paralysis of the diaphragm, which is a crucial structure involved in respiration. When this injury occurs, the individual may say they "got the wind knocked out" of them.

Mechanism or Cause of Injury

A direct blow to the solar plexus by an object or another person, or a fall onto the area can cause a temporary paralysis of the diaphragm.

Signs and Symptoms

When the diaphragm is paralyzed, breathing stops for an extremely short amount of time. The individual feels an inability to breathe, gasps for breaths, becomes anxious, and begins to panic.

© Linda Gazzillo Diaz

Figure 11-27 A comfortable position for a patient who has sustained a blow to the solar plexus

Immediate Care

To assist the individual, attempt to calm them down. Have them sit comfortably with their knees bent and their body slightly leaning forward (**Figure 11-27**), and loosen any tight clothing, including equipment. Assist the person in regulating their breathing by having them perform short inhalations and long exhalations. Within minutes, their breathing should be restored to normal rate and depth. If normal breathing does not occur quickly, and the patient is in distress then call 911.

Prevention

Athletic individuals should wear properly fitted protective equipment that covers the solar plexus area, and should be aware of their surroundings during activities. They should take precautions to avoid falls. All objects and equipment at the facility must be stored away properly so a person does not run or walk into the object, causing a blow to the solar plexus.

Stitch in the Side

The phrase a *stitch in the side* describes pain and/or cramping on the side of the body, between the flank and abdomen.

Mechanism or Cause of Injury

No definitive cause has been identified as to why a stitch in the side occurs. Various theories include improper conditioning, overeating, intestinal gas, spasm of or lack of oxygen to the diaphragm and intercostal muscles, and constipation.

Signs and Symptoms

The individual complains of cramping and pain during activity that occurs below the ribs on the lateral side of the body between the flank and the abdomen. The cramping and pain usually are significant enough for them to stop their activity.

Immediate Care

The individual should stop activity and rest. They should raise the arm on the affected side and stretch the muscles by leaning away from the injured area **(Figure 11-28)**. Usually the stitch in the side subsides with stretching in minutes. If the individual continues to have a stitch in the side during subsequent activities, then they should be evaluated by a physician, because an underlying condition or lifestyle practice may be the cause.

Figure 11-28 The patient should lean away from the side of the pain if a patient has a "stitch in the side."

Prevention

Because the exact cause of a stitch in the side is unknown, prevention is not entirely possible. However, the individual must stretch the body before exercise, progress the exercises in an appropriate manner, not overeat immediately before exercise, practice proper eating habits and proper nutrition, and go to the bathroom before exercise.

Hernia

Hernias are very common and occur to people of all genders and ages. Various types of hernias exist. An abdominal hernia is a bulging of an internal organ, most often the intestines, through the abdominal wall. A hiatal hernia is an opening in the diaphragm that allows part of the upper stomach to move into the chest. An inguinal hernia occurs in the groin, a femoral hernia occurs in the upper thigh, and an umbilical hernia occurs around the navel **(Figure 11-29)**.

Mechanism or Cause of Injury

A hernia may not have a direct cause. Continual heavy, improper lifting may cause some hernias. If an action, such as constant coughing, creates significant pressure on the abdominal wall and the abdominal muscles are weak, then these conditions promote an abdominal hernia. Interestingly, hernias seem to have a familial relationship.

Signs and Symptoms

Signs and symptoms of a hernia include a visible bulge at the site. Usually, the individual does not have pain, but some people complain of discomfort. The hernia bulge may appear to enlarge when the patient lifts objects, bends, or strains their abdomen.

Immediate Care

The individual should see a physician as soon as the hernia is identified. The only course of treatment for a hernia is surgery. The hernia can get bigger over time. If the hernia is not

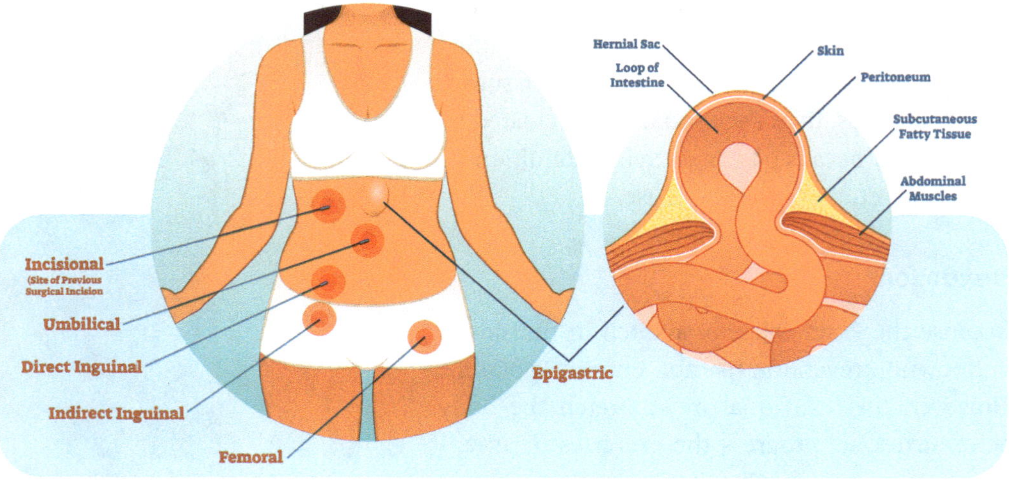

Figure 11-29 Various sites of hernias

surgically repaired then the hernia can strangulate, which means blood flow is cut off to the area. Hernial strangulation is a medical emergency.

Prevention

Although not all hernias can be prevented, an individual can strengthen their abdominal muscles and avoid continual lifting of heavy objects, bending, and straining the abdomen.

The Pelvis

Stress Fractures

Stress fractures of the pelvis typically occur to the femoral neck and the pubic ramus **(Figure 11-30)**. Long distance biological female runners are most commonly affected by pelvic stress fractures. Also, athletes who are not physically conditioned and begin an intense running program are more prone to pelvic stress fractures.

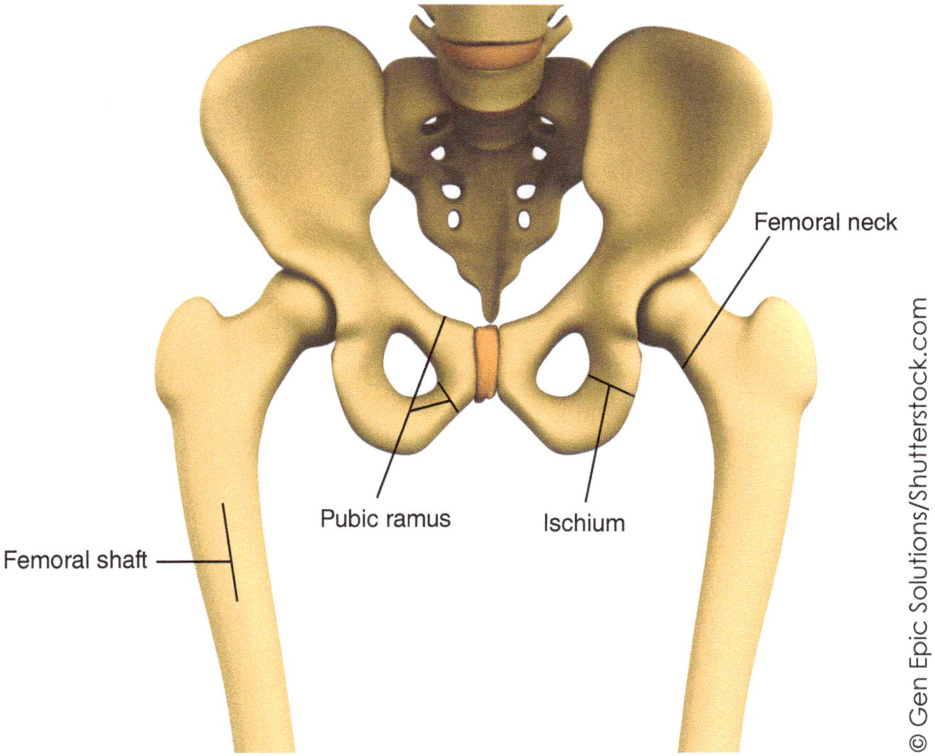

Figure 11-30 Pelvic and femoral stress fractures can cause groin, hip, and thigh pain.

Mechanism or Cause of Injury

The repetitive bounding and overload on the pelvic area when running is cause for pelvic stress fractures. Individuals who tend to have less muscle tissue to protect the bones, have osteoporosis, utilize an improper running technique, or have a leg length discrepancy are more prone to pelvic stress fractures.

Signs and Symptoms

Pain exists and increases with activity and resolves with rest. If the causative activity continues, then pain increases and becomes persistent even at rest. The individual is point tender at the stress fracture site. Eventually, the pain causes loss of function. Groin pain is indicative of a pelvic stress fracture, whereas pain down the lateral hip and thigh may indicate a femoral neck stress fracture.

Immediate Care

At the onset of pain, the individual should rest, apply ice, and compress the area with an elastic wrap. They can take NSAIDs to alleviate pain and inflammation. If the individual's signs and symptoms do not decrease with rest, ice, compression, and elevation (RICE) and anti-inflammatory medication, then refer them to a physician for further evaluation. If the injury has an **insidious onset**, or the signs and symptoms worsen with treatment, then they must see a physician immediately. The physician will take x-rays, rule out any other injuries, and treat the stress fracture conservatively with rest, minimal weight bearing with the use of crutches or a cane, and NSAIDs. The stress fracture will heal in approximately 1 to 3 months, and then activity can gradually resume.

Prevention

An individual can prevent a pelvic stress fracture by progressing the intensity of weight-bearing exercise in an appropriate, safe manner; increasing muscle mass and strength around the pelvis, ingesting calcium and vitamin D to promote strong bones, and providing the body with sufficient rest periods between lower extremity weight-bearing exercise sessions.

Sacroiliac Joint Dysfunction

The sacroiliac (SI) joints are relatively immovable joints that are created by the articulation between the sacrum and the ilium at the posterior pelvis. SI joint dysfunction is a term used to describe pain around the SI joints that then causes functional deficiencies and other signs and symptoms of injury around the low back, pelvis, and hip.

Mechanism or Cause of Injury

The most common cause of SI joint dysfunction is a wearing away of the cartilage located in the joint between the sacrum and the ilium. Degenerative arthritis results at the SI joint. Other causes for SI joint dysfunction include leg length discrepancy or lower extremity pain that cause improper ambulation and biomechanics, pregnancy due to pelvic expansion, improper low back posture, and landing on the buttocks or on a single, extended leg. A direct blow to the SI joint can also cause SI joint dysfunction.

Signs and Symptoms

SI joint dysfunction exhibits signs and symptoms of pain and stiffness at the joint **(Figure 11-31)**, especially when weight-bearing on the affected side. Pain can also occur in the lower back, hip, groin, and thigh. The irritation may be severe enough to affect the sciatic nerve, which runs over the SI joint. If the sciatic nerve is affected, the patient feels a burning and/or aching pain down the back of their thigh. The aching pain in this area may mimic a hamstring strain.

Immediate Care

The patient must first stop any activity that increases the signs and symptoms of SI joint dysfunction, and rest in the most comfortable position. They should apply ice to the area and take NSAIDs to help decrease pain and inflammation. If the signs and symptoms do not subside, then the patient should see a physician for evaluation. The physician will take x-rays, a MRI, and/or CT scan to diagnose the condition. The physician may prescribe pain and anti-inflammatory medication, corticosteroid injections, and/or oral steroids such as prednisone.

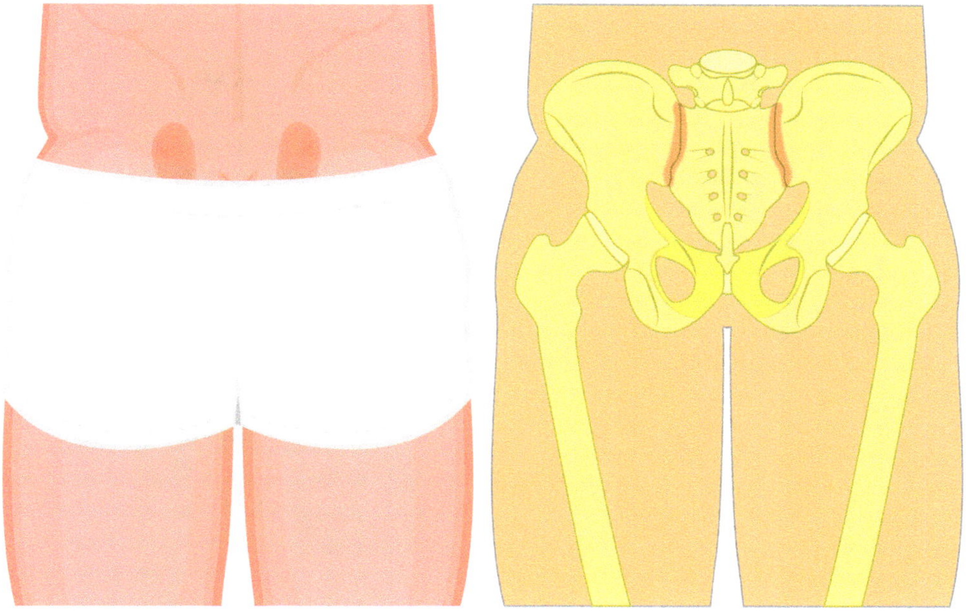

Figure 11-31 Site of SI joint pain

The patient will have to perform rehabilitation exercises to strengthen and stretch muscles surrounding the SI joints. Manual therapy such as joint mobilization and massage can assist in decreasing signs and symptoms of SI joint dysfunction.

Prevention

SI joint dysfunction can be avoided by maintaining proper low back posture, strengthening and stretching the muscles surrounding the SI joints, and utilizing proper lower extremity biomechanics during activity.

Hip Pointer

A hip pointer is a contused iliac crest. The injury can be disabling for the individual.

Mechanism or Cause of Injury

A hip pointer is caused by a direct blow to an unprotected iliac crest. Objects that can bruise the iliac crest include a helmet, another person's body, or an implement. The person can also fall on the iliac crest causing the hip pointer.

Signs and Symptoms

A hip pointer causes pain, ecchymosis, and swelling at the area **(Figure 11-32)**. The area is very point tender. Side bending toward the affected side exacerbates pain.

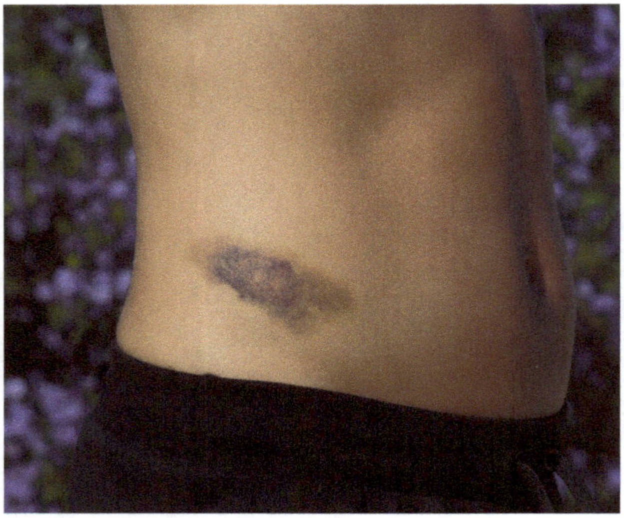

Figure 11-32 A hip pointer can cause significant ecchymosis, pain, and disability.

Immediate Care

The individual should immediately rest the area, apply an ice pack, and wrap the injury with a compression wrap. They can take anti-inflammatory medication. The signs and symptoms should decrease in approximately one week, and then the individual can slowly begin to participate in activity. They should wear padding over the iliac crest to protect the area **(Figure 11-33)**. If the pain persists, then the individual should see his physician for evaluation. They will have to participate in rehabilitation exercises, which can help regain motion and strength.

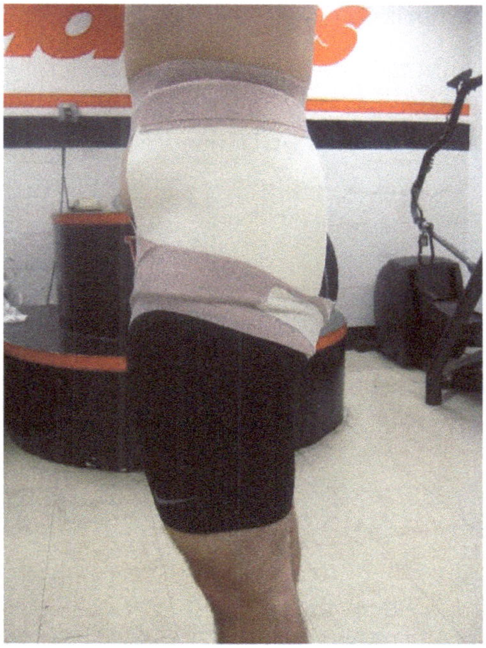

Figure 11-33 Padding secured with an elastic wrap can protect the patient's contused iliac crest.

Prevention

Any individual who participates in contact activities which puts the iliac crest at risk for a contusion should wear proper equipment or padding to protect the area. Avoiding falls and being aware of the surroundings can assist a person in preventing a hip pointer.

Osteitis Pubis

Osteitis pubis is a chronic inflammation of the pubic symphysis and the surrounding adductor muscles. The inflammation occurs most often to biological female long distance runners.

Mechanism or Cause of Injury

The exact cause of osteitis pubis is unknown, but it is apparently caused by overuse and microtrauma to the pubic symphysis. The inflammation can also be caused by muscular imbalance, improper biomechanics, and SI joint dysfunction.

Signs and Symptoms

The athlete complains of groin pain and point tenderness at the pubic bone. Activity increases the pain, but the pain is relieved with rest. The adductor muscles are inflexible. Contracting or stretching these muscles also elicit pain.

Immediate Care

The athlete must rest the area. They must discontinue participation in aggravating activities that overuse the adductor muscles or bear significant weight on the lower extremity. Ice application and NSAIDs are used to alleviate pain and inflammation. Any biomechanical problem, such as improper ambulation, leg length discrepancy, or SI joint dysfunction must be addressed and corrected.

Prevention

Osteitis pubis can be prevented by strengthening and stretching the adductor muscles. If an individual must participate in activities that cause a shearing force across the pubic symphysis, assist them in gradually progressing the activities' intensity and duration to avoid osteitis pubis.

Summary

Individuals commonly sustain injuries and illnesses to the spine, thorax, and abdomen. It is evident that many injuries and illnesses to these bodily areas have similar signs and symptoms. These similarities are often perplexing when attempting to determine the nature of the injury or illness that the individual has sustained. It is also sometimes difficult to determine whether or not the injury is life-threatening. As with any other injury and illness, if you are unsure of what care to provide, at minimum monitor the patient's airway, breathing, and circulation, treat for shock, and summon EMS.

Keywords

Lateral flexion When an individual bends their neck to the side by moving their head toward their shoulder.

Paraplegic An individual who has paralysis of the lower body including the legs. Paralysis usually involves loss of motor function and sensation.

Quadriplegic An individual who has paralysis of the legs, arms, and torso.

Myelogram An imaging test used to determine if an individual has a spinal cord injury. The physician injects dye into the spinal column and then takes an x-ray.

Kyphotic An outward, posterior curvature of the spine when viewing the individual from the side. This curve is found normally at the thoracic and sacral spines.

Trigger points Hypersensitive, hyperirritable nodules in muscle tissue. They are also referred to as *knots* in the muscle.

Hypoxia When tissues in the body are deprived of oxygen. If the oxygen deprivation continues for a period of time, then the tissues will die.

Insidious onset A slow and gradual development of signs and symptoms of injury without any definitive mechanism of injury.

Discussion Questions

1. What are the various head injuries that can occur to an individual? Which injuries warrant EMS?
2. Name some life-threatening injuries or illnesses that occur to the thorax and abdomen.
3. What injuries to the spine, thorax, and abdomen are considered chronic injuries?
4. What spine, thorax, and abdomen injuries and illnesses exhibit similar signs and symptoms despite the area affected?
5. Which spine, thorax, and abdomen injuries require surgery followed by rehabilitation in order to restore full function?

CASE STUDY #1: ON COLLISION COURSE

Alyssa is a senior, third baseman for her softball team at Village High School. Today, her team is competing in the county championship game against their biggest rival. During the top of the fourth inning, a short fly ball is hit to shallow left field. Alyssa turns and runs full speed to try and catch the ball. Jennifer, the left fielder, charges in at full speed, also in an attempt to catch the ball. Neither player realizes that they are approaching each other at full speed. They both call for the ball at the last minute, but it is too late. They collide hard and fall to the ground. Jennifer gets up rather quickly and goes over to her teammate to see how she is. Alyssa remains on the ground clutching her abdomen in pain. The coach runs out to the field to assess his two players' condition. Jennifer says that aside from a sore left hip she is fine. Alyssa is still lying on the ground complaining that her abdomen hurts. The coach asks her if she has any other symptoms and Alyssa says "no". The coach allows Alyssa a minute to gather herself. Alyssa says that the pain is subsiding, and she wants to stay in the game. Because Alyssa said that she does not have any other symptoms of injury and is able to move her body normally, the coach allows her to continue playing.

At the end of the inning, the players return to the dugout and the coach immediately asks Jennifer and Alyssa how they feel. Jennifer says she is fine, but has a bruise on her hip where she hit Alyssa, which is sore and tender to the touch. Alyssa says her abdomen is still painful, but she wants to continue playing. She is still clutching her abdomen with her arm and is leaning over slightly, but the coach allows her to get up to bat. Alyssa is up at bat and gets a hit. She advances each base as her teammates get hits and walks. When she returns to the dugout, Alyssa tells her coach that she feels lightheaded. The pain in her abdomen is persistent and increasing. The coach looks at her, notices that she is slightly pale and clammy, and decides to check her pulse, which is rapid but weak.

1. What possible injury(ies) could Alyssa have?
2. What possible injury(ies) could Jennifer have?
3. Should the coach call EMS? Why or why not?
4. What immediate treatment should the coach give to both Jennifer and Alyssa?

CASE STUDY #2: WORK IS A PAIN

Nathan is a 35-year-old businessman who recently changed jobs. Whereas he used to be traveling from client to client as a salesperson, he now spends his entire workday behind his desk. He is either on the phone or working on his computer the entire day.

Nathan is in relatively good shape since he regularly goes to We R Fit Gym to perform cardiovascular exercise. Recently, Nathan has been experiencing some low back discomfort and stiffness on and off throughout the day. He figures that the discomfort and stiffness is a result of his hard gym workouts, and believes the symptoms will eventually go away. As a few weeks pass, the discomfort and stiffness turn into pain. The pain in his low back starts to creep down into his right buttock area. One day, Nathan is at his desk for a few hours without rising. He attempts to stand up and immediately feels pain shoot down the back of his right leg, which stops above his knee. The pain feels like a burning sensation, but it disappears after a few minutes. For the remainder of the day Nathan tries sitting in different positions to alleviate the pain. He even gets up every few minutes to walk around, but the pain persists.

The pain continues to affect him the most while seated at his desk. Sitting for short periods of time becomes impossible due to the burning pain down the back of his leg. The pain begins occurs at home and during his daily activities. He cannot sleep without feeling the dull pain in his low back. Driving has become unbearably painful. Working out in the gym on the stationary bike and stair machine is painful, and this pain prevents him from having full function and strength to complete the exercises.

Nathan finally decides to treat his pain. He decides to take some time off from his cardiovascular exercise and rest his low back and leg. For a week, he rubs a menthol balm on his low back and hamstring to see if it decreases the pain, but the counter irritant brings little, temporary relief. He decides to stretch his hamstrings daily to see if that helps decrease his symptoms, but the stretching makes his pain worse. Despite his efforts, the pain persists and nothing he is doing is making the pain go away. Nathan realizes that he needs advice regarding his pain. Nathan goes to We R Fit Gym and asks one of the personal trainers what he should do.

1. What do you think is the primary cause of Nathan's pain?
2. As Nathan's personal trainer, what would you suggest Nathan do in regard to his condition and pain?
3. Did Nathan take the appropriate course of self-treatment for the pain? Why or why not?
4. Is there anything Nathan can do to change his working conditions at his desk in order to prevent the low back pain in the future?

References

Al-Khatib, S. M., Yancy, C. W., Solis, P., Becker, L., Benjamin, E. J., Carrillo, R. G., ... & Varosy, P. D. (2017). 2016 AHA/ACC clinical performance and quality measures for prevention of sudden cardiac death: a report of the American College of Cardiology/American Heart Association Task Force on Performance Measures. Circulation: Cardiovascular Quality and Outcomes, 10(2), e000022. doi: 10.1161/HCQ.0000000000000022

American Academy of Orthopedic Surgeons (AAOS). (2016). *Spondylolysis and spondylolisthesis.* Retrieved on August 4, 2021 from http://orthoinfo.aaos.org/topic.cfm?topic=a00053

American Cancer Society. (2018). *Risk factors for testicular cancer*. Retrieved on February 7, 2022 from https://www.cancer.org/cancer/testicular-cancer/causes-risks-prevention/risk-factors.html

Center for Disease Control (CDC). (2021). *What are the risk factors for breast cancer?* Retrieved February 2, 2022 from https://www.cdc.gov/cancer/breast/basic_info/risk_factors.htm

Markwerth, P., Bajanowski, T., Tzimas, I., Dettmeyer, R. (2021). Sudden cardiac death—update. *International Journal of Legal Medicine,* 135, 483–495. doi: 10.1007/s00414-020-02481-z

Mayo Clinic. (2021). *Broken ribs: Treatments and drugs.* Retrieved August 4, 2021, from http://www.mayoclinic.com/health/broken-ribs/DS00939/DSECTION=treatments-and-drugs

Mayo Clinic. (2019). *Herniated disks.* Retrieved on August 4, 2021, from http://www.mayoclinic.com/health/herniated-disk/DS00893/

MedlinePlus. (2021). *Collapsed lung (pneumothorax).* Retrieved on August 4, 2021, from https://medlineplus.gov/ency/article/000087.htm

MedlinePlus. (2022). *Hyperventilation.* Retrieved on February 1, 2022, from https://medlineplus.gov/ency/article/003071.htm

National Heart, Lung, and Blood Institute. (2020). Heart murmur. Retrieved August 4, 2021, from https://www.nhlbi.nih.gov/health-topics/heart-murmur

Schultz, S. J., Houglum, P. A., & Perrin, D. H. (2015). *Examination of musculoskeletal injuries* (4th ed.). Champaign, IL: Human Kinetics.

Yabek, S. M. (2016). *Commotio cordis treatment and management.* Retrieved on August 4, 2021, from http://emedicine.medscape.com/article/902504-treatment

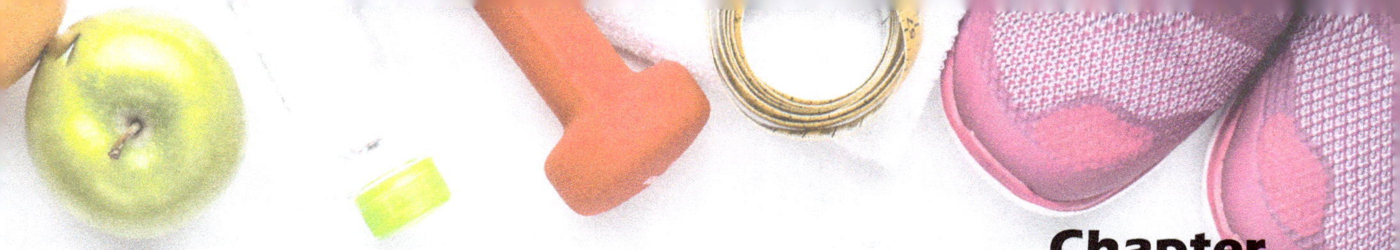

General Medical Conditions

Chapter 12

Chapter Objectives

After you have read this chapter, you will be able to understand:

- The differences among various general medical conditions.
- The conditions which are highly contagious.
- Signs and symptoms of each condition.
- How to treat general medical conditions.
- When referral to a physician is necessary for an individual with a general medical condition.

General medical conditions occur frequently to individuals, and some people are more prone to these conditions. Individuals who are young or old, as well as those who have immune or other disorders, such as human immunodeficiency virus (HIV) or diabetes, tend to be afflicted more often by various general medical conditions than the general, healthy population. Depending on the person's characteristics, the type of pathogen, the body part affected, and the duration the pathogen is on the body or in the bloodstream, some general medical conditions can be very troublesome.

Local and Systemic Infections

General medical conditions include bodily infections. Bacteria, viruses, and parasites and can cause local or systemic infections. Local infections can also be caused by fungi. Individuals acquire these infections in a variety of ways. The pathogens can enter the skin through a cut or mucous membrane. An individual can consume pathogens which reside in food or water. Some pathogens are transmitted through the air, saliva, blood, skin contact, and animal and insect bites. Pathogens can be found on surfaces such as tables, floors, and mats, and are transmitted to an individual when touching the contaminated surface.

Systemic infections affect the entire body. These infections are caused when a virus or bacterium enter into the patient's body. Once in the body, the pathogens spread via the bloodstream. The resulting infection affects a large portion of the body. Signs and symptoms of a systemic infection become apparent throughout the body and not at one particular site. Some classic systemic infection signs and symptoms include nausea, vomiting, fever, aches, weakness, and chills. Even though systemic infections are spread through the bloodstream, they are not necessarily more severe than local infections. Some examples of systemic infections include mononucleosis, the common cold, influenza, strep throat, mumps, measles, Human Immunodeficiency Virus (HIV), hepatitis B (HBV), and syphilis. Common minor infections, such as the common cold and influenza, can be treated at home. Other serious infections, such as HIV and measles, require a physician's care. Some systemic infections, such as **septicemia,** are medical emergencies. Septicemia spreads through the body quickly, and can cause septic shock and death. Treatment for systemic infections may include rest, **antipyretics**, fluid intake, and intravenous and other medications.

Unlike systemic infections, local infections affect only a small area of the body and are concentrated at a specific site. These infections do not enter into the bloodstream. Local infections include fungal infections, cellulitis, conjunctivitis, genital chlamydia, and herpes. With the exception of fever, signs and symptoms of local infections are different as compared to systemic infections. Local infections exhibit signs and symptoms of inflammation including redness, warmth and point tenderness at the site, pus, swelling, pain, and a pungent odor with edema drainage. Usually local infections can be treated at home by cleaning the area with soap and water, applying a disinfectant, such as povidone-iodine, applying appropriate antifungal or antibacterial ointment depending on the causative pathogen, and dressing and bandaging the area. The individual should observe the local infection to make sure the signs and symptoms are decreasing and not remaining the same or worsening. In general, if the local infection does not go away within 4 days, or if the signs and symptoms of infection increase, then refer the individual to a physician. Some local infections, such as cellulitis and sexually transmitted diseases, are very serious and the patient should see a physician immediately. A few local infections, such as gonorrhea, may become systemic if they are not treated, and will exhibit signs and symptoms of a systemic infection. Therefore, if an individual has obtained a serious local infection or a local infection that has become systemic then they must be readily evaluated by a physician.

Individuals can avoid infection by practicing cleanliness and good hygiene. Frequent hand, body, and clothes washing with soap and water is crucial to eliminate pathogens from the skin's surface. Sharing toothbrushes, razors, cups, or utensils should be avoided. Continuously wiping down equipment with an appropriate commercial disinfectant after each of your client's use, and frequent cleaning restroom and shower areas is crucial to prevent infection at your facility.

Common infections can be classified into five categories. The first category includes common respiratory infections, which is further broken down into upper and lower respiratory system infections. The other four categories include the following: skin infections, viral infections, bacterial infections, and sexually transmitted diseases (STDs), respectively.

Respiratory Infections

Upper Respiratory System

The upper respiratory system (also called the upper respiratory tract) (**Figure 12-1**) includes the sinuses, nose, mouth, throat, larynx, and trachea. An upper respiratory infection (URI) is a general term for an infection of the upper respiratory system. With these URIs, inflammation exists along with a variety of signs and symptoms.

Acute Rhinitis (Common Cold)

Acute rhinitis is the common cold. Over 100 rhinoviruses exist that can invade the body and cause a cold. A person obtains a cold through various means including contact with nasal secretions from an infected person during hand shaking, water molecules in the air containing the virus transferred by a sneeze, or saliva from sharing a drinking cup. The contagious period is 1 to 2 days after symptoms arise (Tesini, 2021). The person first has a sore throat, a feeling of malaise, and a loss of appetite. A low-grade fever may develop. Then a runny nose and a cough,

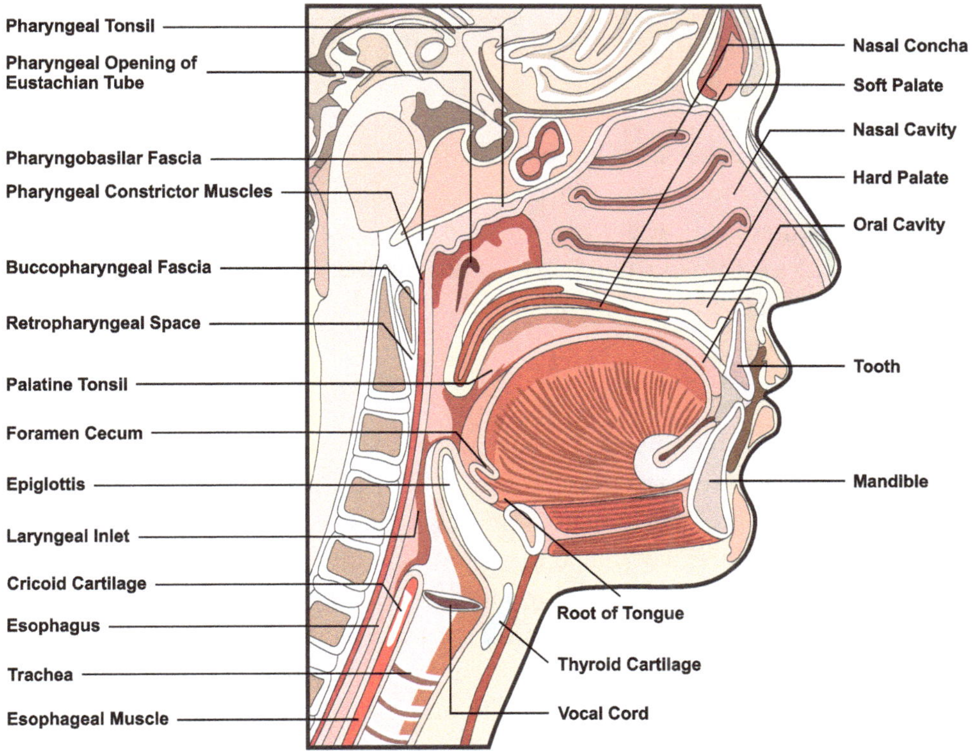

Figure 12-1 The upper respiratory tract

Figure 12-2 Symptoms of and treatment for the common cold

accompanied by sneezing develops **(Figure 12-2)**. The nasal mucous is clear and thin at first and may turn thick and yellow-green. The cough is dry and hacking, and then may produce mucus. Over-the-counter medications can decrease signs and symptoms. These medications include decongestants which thin nasal mucus, antihistamines that dry out the nasal passages, expectorants to expel mucus when coughing, and suppressants to quiet the cough. The cold will last about 4 to 10 days.

Allergic Rhinitis (Hay Fever)

Allergic rhinitis, commonly referred to as hay fever, affects the nose and eyes. Allergic rhinitis is not truly an infection; however, it is included in this section because it is an upper respiratory condition which exhibits extremely similar signs and symptoms as acute rhinitis. Hay fever is often a hereditary infection that is passed down by the person's parents' genetics, especially the mother (Henochowicz, Zieve, & Conaway 2020). Exposure to an allergen such as dust, pollen, mold, or pet dander triggers histamine release. The histamine causes the signs and symptoms of hay fever. Signs and symptoms include sneezing and nasal discharge, which is usually thin. The patient may have clear, watery, and itchy eyes, nose, and throat **(Figure 12-3)**. As the

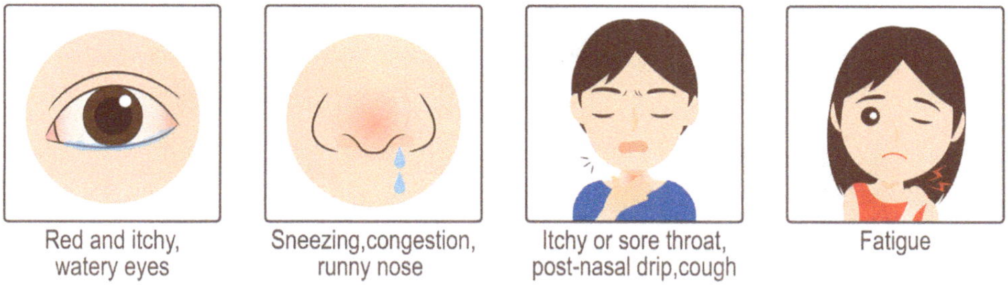

Figure 12-3 Common signs and symptoms of allergic rhinitis

allergic rhinitis progresses, the patient may feel fatigued and irritable, along with having a headache, cough, stuffy nose, **postnasal drip**, and puffy eyes.

In order to treat allergic rhinitis, the individual must avoid any exposure to the allergens. Over the counter and prescription antihistamines can help the patient treat and avoid signs and symptoms of allergic rhinitis. Oral medications include first- or second-generation antihistamines. First-generation antihistamines (e.g. Benadryl Allergy, Chlor-Trimeton) cause drowsiness, whereas second-generation antihistamines (e.g. Zyrtec, Allegra, Claritin) maintain wakefulness. Decongestant and corticosteroid nasal sprays, the latter of which must be prescribed by a physician, also help alleviate signs and symptoms of allergic rhinitis.

Sinusitis

Sinusitis is inflammation of the sinuses, which is caused by a virus, bacteria, or fungus. Sinusitis is classified as acute, sub-acute, and chronic depending on the length of the infection. Acute sinusitis is caused by bacteria as a result of a prolonged URI and lasts up to a month. Sub-acute sinusitis lasts 1 to 3 months. Chronic sinusitis, which is caused by bacteria or fungus, lasts 3 months or more.

If a patient has a cold and the nasal passageways are blocked, which prevents the mucus from draining, air cannot flow through the sinuses. As a result, bacteria forms in the sinuses and creates an infection. People who have a deviated septum, allergic rhinitis, or are smokers are prone to sinusitis. Signs and symptoms of sinusitis include fever, congestion, sinus pain and pressure, sore throat and bad breath from postnasal drip, cough, fatigue, and weakness **(Figure 12-4)**.

Most acute sinusitis infections can be treated at home and clear up within 2 weeks. Treatment includes nasal sprays, including prescription, over-the-counter, and saline sprays; antipyretics; **analgesics**; and decongestants. A warm or cool mist humidifier utilized while sleeping can assist in moistening air passageways and loosening existing mucus. Flushing the sinuses with a **neti pot** solution helps loosen and remove stagnant mucus in the sinuses. The patient will require antibiotics to clear up the infection if self-treatment does not alleviate the signs and symptoms within a few days.

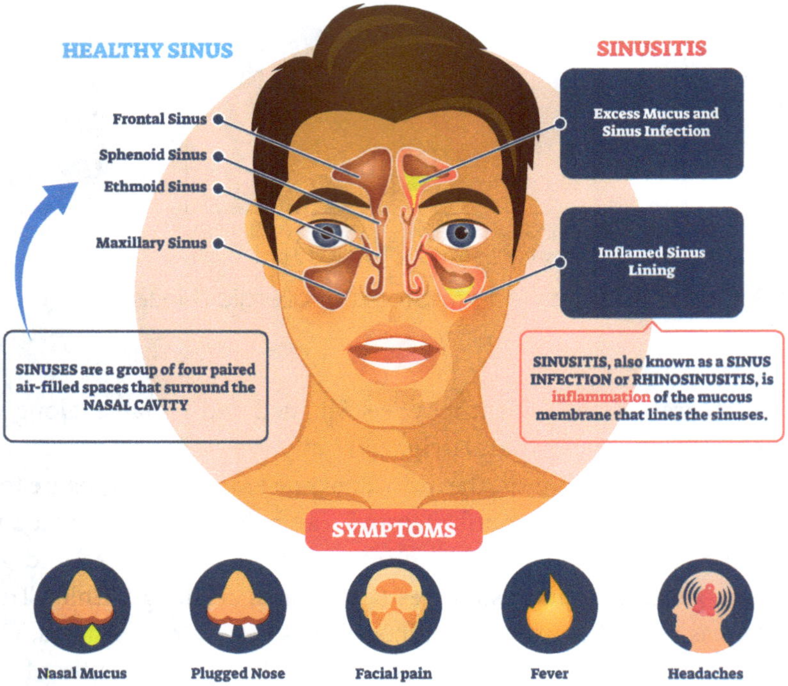

Figure 12-4 Common signs and symptoms of sinusitis

Pharyngitis

The pharynx is the area between the tonsils and the larynx in the back of the throat. Inflammation of the pharynx, or pharyngitis, is also commonly called a sore throat. Pharyngitis is caused by a viral or bacterial infection, as well as continuous postnasal drip or cough, allergies, and smoking. Viral pharyngitis occurs with a common cold or flu. Bacterial pharyngitis infections are caused by Group A *Streptococcus* bacterium. This bacterium is the most common cause for strep throat. Strep throat is a painful inflammation of the throat that most often occurs in children **(Figure 12-5)**. Antibiotics are necessary to treat the infection.

Strep throat can cause an individual to come down with an inflammation of the tonsils, or tonsillitis. Tonsils are lymph nodes located in the throat that normally filter out bacteria; however, with a significant infection such as strep throat, the tonsils become infected and inflamed. Tonsillitis caused by strep throat or other bacteria is treated with antibiotics.

Signs and symptoms of pharyngitis include fever, joint pain, muscle aches, headache, swollen lymph nodes in the neck, and nasal congestion. Simple pharyngitis often goes away without antibiotics or other medication. The patient can lessen the aggravating signs and symptoms by taking oral and topical analgesics (e.g., acetaminophen and sore throat sprays,

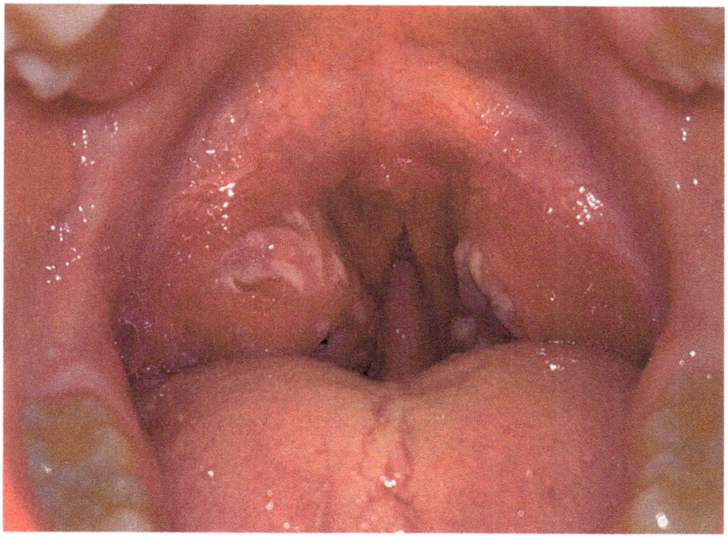

Figure 12-5 Strep throat can result from a bacterial pharyngitis infection.

respectively), utilizing a humidifier and saltwater gargles, ingesting fluids, and getting enough rest. If the signs and symptoms do not readily decrease or if they worsen, refer the patient to a physician. The patient may need antibiotics to get rid the infection.

Laryngitis

The larynx, also referred to as the *voice box* or *vocal cords*, is located at the upper portion of the trachea or *windpipe*. The larynx is a passageway to the lungs and functions to produce vocal communication. Laryngitis is classified as acute or chronic. Acute laryngitis is an inflammation of the larynx, most commonly from a viral infection or by overuse, such as yelling **(Figure 12-6)**. A bacterial infection can also cause laryngitis. Acute laryngitis often occurs with or as a result of an URI. Chronic laryngitis occurs due to work- or habit-related overuse (e.g., singing or continuous talking), smoking, inhaling allergens or pollutants, gastroesophageal reflux disease (GERD), or chronic sinusitis. Signs and symptoms of acute laryngitis last approximately 1 week, whereas chronic laryngitis signs and symptoms can last a couple of weeks. The signs and symptoms include hoarseness and change in sound of voice; a sore, dry, and painful throat; and coughing.

Treatment for laryngitis includes ingesting plenty of fluids to moisten the area, taking analgesics, and resting the throat by decreasing voice communication, singing, and other activities that utilize the vocal cords. If the cause of the laryngitis is a URI, recommend to the patient to take a decongestant that assists in alleviating symptoms. If the patient exhibits a fever over 103° F, makes high pitched sounds, has trouble breathing, drools excessively, or has difficulty

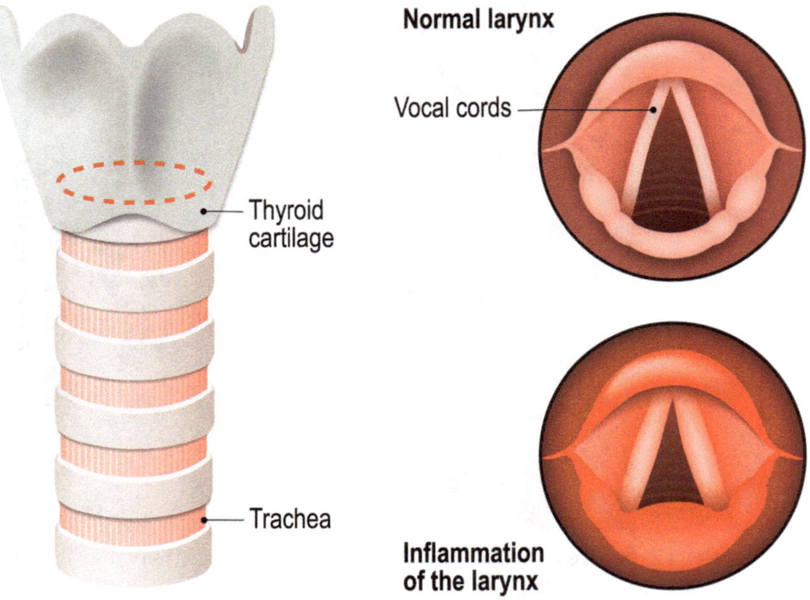

Figure 12-6 Inflammation of the larynx (laryngitis)

swallowing, then refer the patient to his physician or the emergency room (ER) immediately. These signs and symptoms indicate either croup or epiglottitis, which are two severe, potentially life-threatening infections.

Lower Respiratory System

The lower respiratory system (also called the lower respiratory tract) includes the trachea, bronchi, and lungs. Infections in this area can be severe because they affect the lungs, which function to receive oxygen and distribute it to the body. When the lower respiratory system is infected, the oxygen cannot be delivered appropriately to the body and severe secondary illness or death can occur.

Influenza

Influenza is commonly called the *flu*. Viruses cause this highly contagious and potentially deadly infection. The flu affects the nasal passageways to the lungs. The viruses spread through water molecules when an infected patient sneezes or coughs. The flu viruses can also thrive on surfaces, such as tables, equipment, and mats. When a person touches the contaminated surface, then puts their hand by their mouth, nose, or eyes, they may become infected. Patients are contagious a day before flu signs and symptoms are apparent, and approximately 5 to

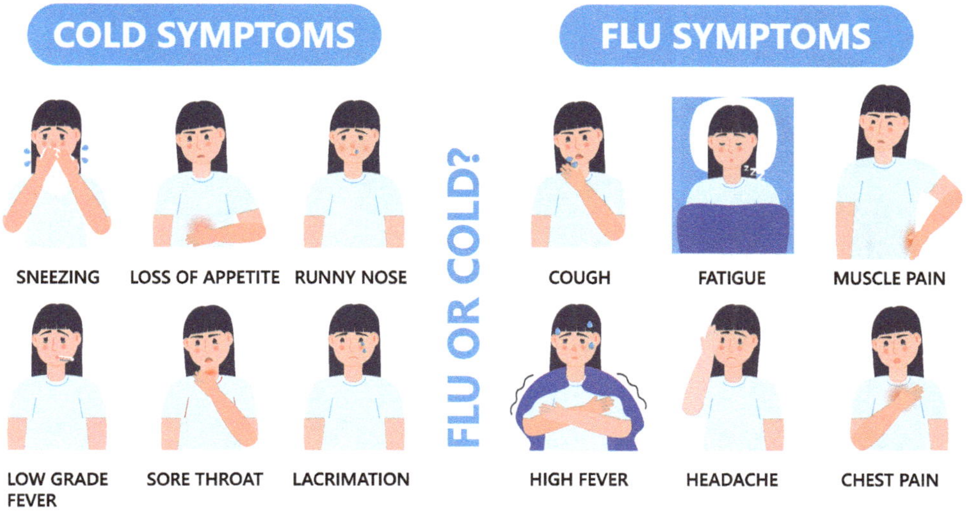

Figure 12-7 The differences in signs and symptoms between the flu and the common cold

7 days afterwards (Center for Disease Control [CDC], 2021d). Signs and symptoms of the flu include fever over 100° F, fatigue, weakness, muscle aches, cough, nasal congestion, and headache **(Figure 12-7)**.

The CDC notes on its website that "the best way to prevent flu is by getting a flu vaccine each year" (CDC, 2021c). The flu season predominantly occurs in the winter months. Individuals who are particularly at risk for acquiring the flu, including older individuals, young children, and pregnant women, should be **inoculated** each year before the winter season. People who have diabetes, asthma, or heart disease should be vaccinated. Because viruses mutate, the flu virus strain changes each year. Consequently, the vaccination required changes each year, and a person must be vaccinated annually to protect against the flu. The flu vaccination is injected typically into the deltoid muscle. The vaccine causes the body to create antibodies, which protect the patient from the potential flu viruses most likely to affect individuals during the upcoming flu season. If an individual is not inoculated and is infected with the flu then they must rest and drink fluids. The flu must run its course, but over-the-counter and prescription antiviral medications (e.g. Tamiflu and Relenza) can help to reduce flu signs and symptoms.

Bronchitis

The bronchi are two air passageways, or bronchial tubes, that arise from the trachea. One passageway attaches to the right lung and the other to the left lung. When the bronchi lining is inflamed, the illness is called bronchitis **(Figure 12-8)**. Bronchitis is categorized as acute or

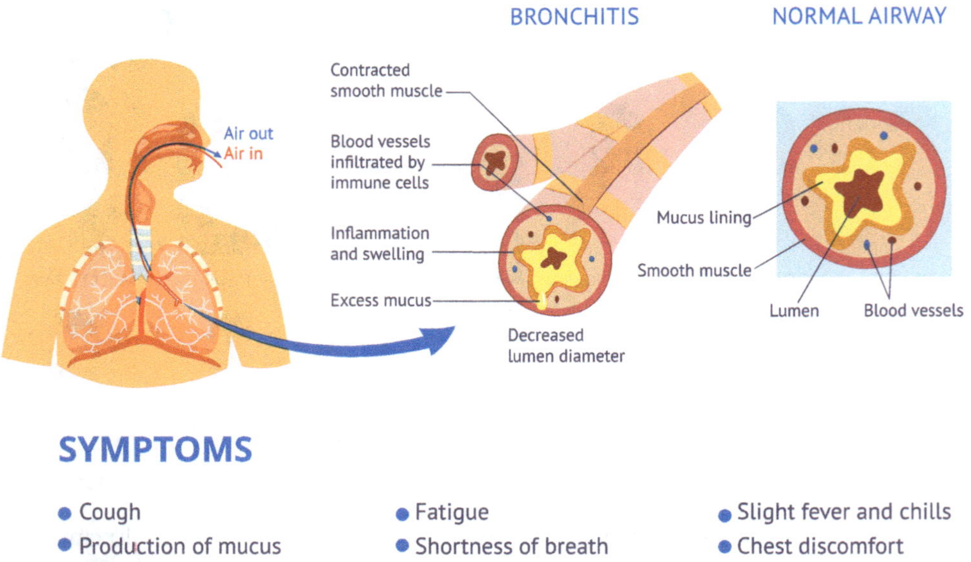

Figure 12-8 Bronchitis versus a normal airway

chronic. Similarly to influenza or a cold, viruses cause acute bronchitis. Acute bronchitis lasts a short duration, only 1 to 3 weeks, as compared to chronic bronchitis. Chronic bronchitis lasts months or years. Chronic bronchitis is most commonly caused by smoking. Air toxins, including pollutants, chemicals, and gases, can also cause bronchial irritation.

Chronic bronchitis is one of the two illnesses that comprise chronic obstructive pulmonary disease (COPD). Along with chronic bronchitis, COPD also includes emphysema, which is lung tissue degeneration that occurs over a period of years **(Figure 12-9)**. No treatment exists for COPD. The condition is life-threatening because it causes severe breathing difficulty, lack of oxygen transport, and cardiac **arrhythmias**. Signs and symptoms of bronchitis and COPD include fatigue, chest discomfort, especially when deep breathing and coughing, low grade fever; chills, and mucus production when coughing. COPD signs and symptoms are more severe and prolonged than acute and chronic bronchitis alone.

People who have chronic bronchitis have a productive cough with yellow to green colored mucus. The cough can continue for years. Self-treatment for acute bronchitis is often effective and includes rest, fluid consumption, cough medicine, and analgesics. Utilizing a warm mist humidifier moistens the air passageways and eases breathing. Chronic bronchitis is a serious illness that commonly requires long-term medication and treatment prescribed by a physician. For chronic bronchitis, the physician may prescribe antibiotics to prevent a secondary bacterial infection.

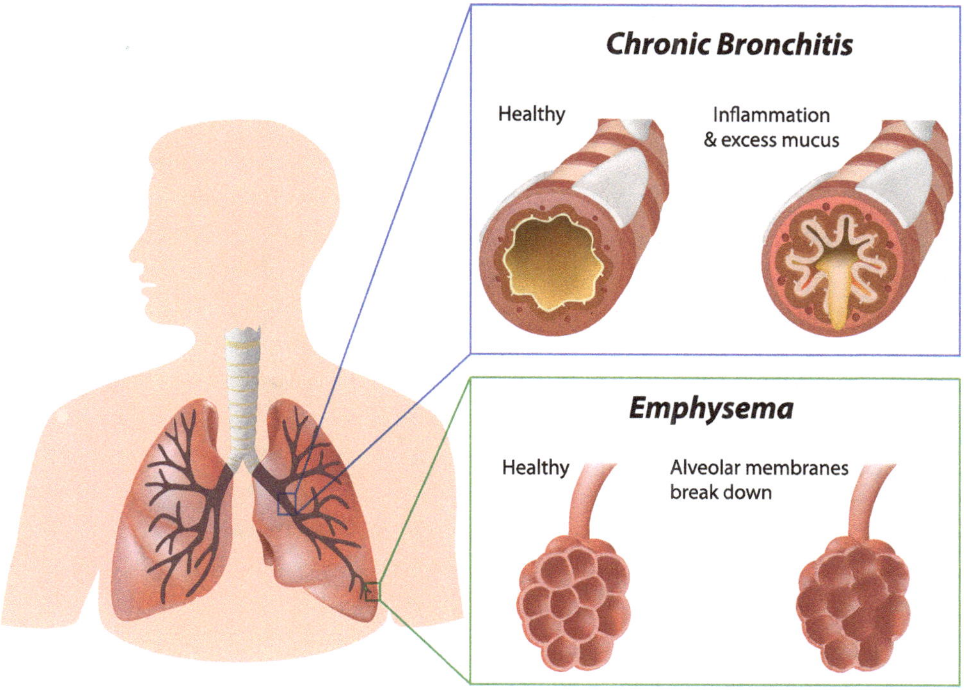

Figure 12-9 Chronic obstructive pulmonary disease (COPD) includes chronic bronchitis and emphysema.

A person with COPD is continually under a physician's care and needs various medications, including corticosteroid inhalers, to facilitate breathing by reducing inflammation and opening the bronchi. Respiratory therapy is also crucial for a person with COPD. The therapy does not heal the damaged tissue, but instead teaches the patient to breathe more effectively in order to perform activities of daily living (ADLs) and other activities. If the cough lasts for more than 3 weeks or produces blood or discolored mucus, refer the individual to a physician. If they have a 100° F fever or above, along with pain, wheezing, or difficulty breathing, then they must see a physician immediately or call 911 for emergency medical services (EMS).

Pneumonia

Pneumonia is an inflammation of one or both lungs caused by viruses, bacterium, fungi, or parasites. *Streptococcus pneumonia* is the bacterium that most commonly causes pneumonia. Pneumonia is mild to life-threatening. If left untreated, other illnesses, such as the flu and bronchitis, can progress to pneumonia. Pneumonia can affect patients of all ages, but is a significant concern when a patient aged 65 years and older acquires pneumonia. Patients who smoke, have COPD, a weak immune system, diabetes or heart disease, have had a recent cold or flu, or had recent surgery are at risk for pneumonia **(Figure 12-10)**.

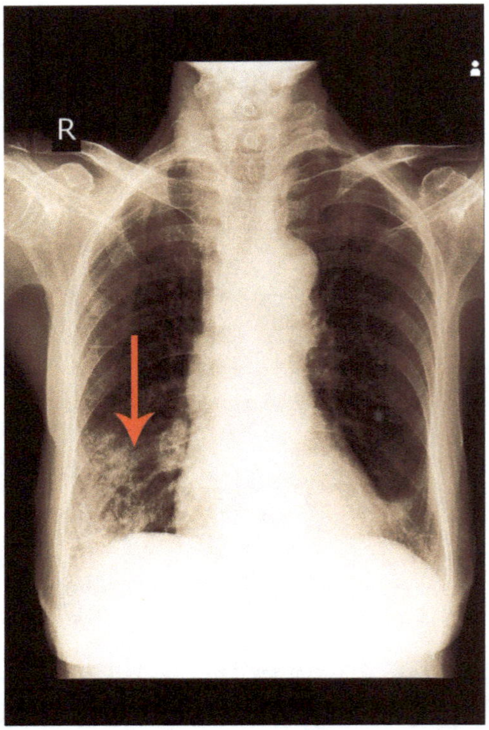

© Jarva Jar/Shutterstock.com

Figure 12-10 X-ray of a patient with pneumonia in the lungs' right lower lobe

Pneumonia is classified based upon how the person acquired the infection. Community-acquired pneumonia occurs when a person comes in contact with a pathogen during regular contact with an infected patient, surface, or object. These pneumonia cases are typically mild. Individuals in hospitals or health care centers, in particular kidney dialysis and cancer treatment centers, acquire healthcare-acquired pneumonia. These cases are more serious because the pathogen strains are typically more resistant to treatment than are strains involved with community-acquired pneumonia. Inhalation or aspiration pneumonia occurs when a patient breathes in a pathogen found in their own vomit, food, or fluid from their mouth into their lungs. Opportunistic pneumonia occurs when a person has a weak immune system, as a result of issues such as acquired immune deficiency syndrome (AIDS) or an organ transplant.

Signs and symptoms of pneumonia include fever, chills, fatigue, weakness, headache, breathing difficulty including shortness of breath, chest pain, and cough. The individual should see a physician if they have a fever 102° F or higher, chills, chest pain, muscular weakness, and continual cough. Refer your client to a physician if they have a cold or flu that does not resolve in a timely manner or worsens. Because bacterial pneumonia is most common, treatment includes antibiotics, antipyretics, and cough suppressants. If a virus causes the pneumonia, antibiotics are not effective. Antiviral and over-the-counter medications to reduce symptoms may help until the infection runs its course. Depending on the patient's age and severity of symptoms, the patient may be admitted to the hospital for treatment.

Skin Infections

The skin is made up of three layers, which include the epidermis (outer layer), dermis (middle layer), and hypodermis (deep subcutaneous layer) **(Figure 12-11)**. The skin protects and deters pathogens from entering it. However, at times the skin becomes infected. Skin

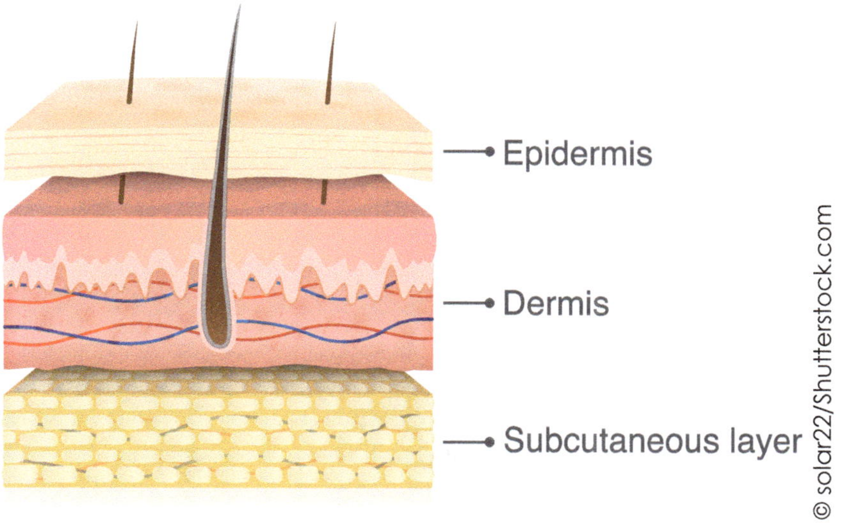

Figure 12-11 Layers of the skin

infections are local infections caused by bacteria, viruses, and fungi. Most skin infections are mild, but some can be severe. If severe skin infections are left untreated, life-threatening sepsis can occur.

Folliculitis

Folliculitis is an inflammation of the skin's hair follicles due to viruses, bacterium, and fungi, with bacteria being the most common pathogen causing the infection (**Figure 12-12**). Cases can be mild to severe. Folliculitis occurs when a pathogen enters a damaged follicle. This infection occurs from shaving, excessive sweating, abrasions and other skin wounds, and inflammatory skin conditions such as acne and dermatitis. Blocked follicles can also promote bacterial growth. The folliculitis appears as pus-filled or red pimples around a hair that may look like a rash. The folliculitis may be unsightly, especially if many pimples exist in groups on the face or unexposed areas of the body. The pimples are itchy, tender to the touch, or painful.

The pimples may also ooze and crust over. Deep folliculitis exhibits these signs and symptoms along with a large mass that appears as a lump under the skin. Most often the folliculitis is superficial, and with treatment can be cured in a few days. Have the patient keep the area clean by washing often with soap and water. Warm, moist compresses promote clearing and draining of the pus in the follicle. Deep folliculitis must be treated by a physician. If the folliculitis spreads or does not resolve within a few days, refer the individual to a physician. Topical, oral antibiotic, or antifungal medication may be necessary to clear the infection.

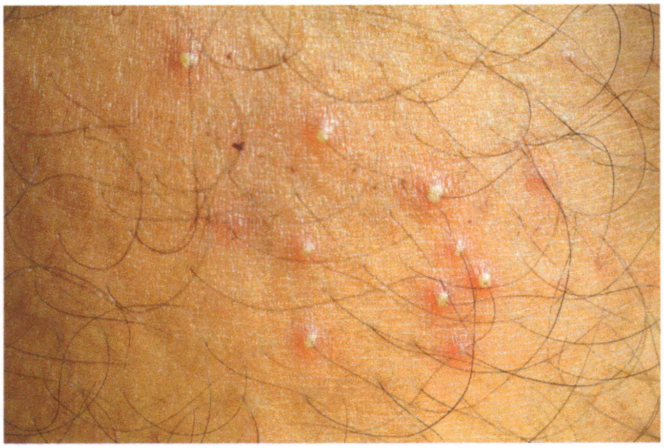

Figure 12-12 Folliculitis

Contact Dermatitis

Contact dermatitis is a non-contagious infection that occurs when an object or substance comes in contact with the skin and causes an allergic reaction on the skin's surface. Irritant and allergic contact dermatitis exist. Irritant contact dermatitis affects the epidermis and occurs often to the face and hands. Soaps, cosmetics, and chemicals are common irritants. Allergic contact dermatitis is a hypersensitivity to a substance, and can be caused by poison ivy **(Figure 12-13)**, perfume, cosmetics, detergent, latex, and chemicals. These allergens trigger an immune response in the skin. Certain substances, such as cosmetics, can cause both irritant and allergic dermatitis.

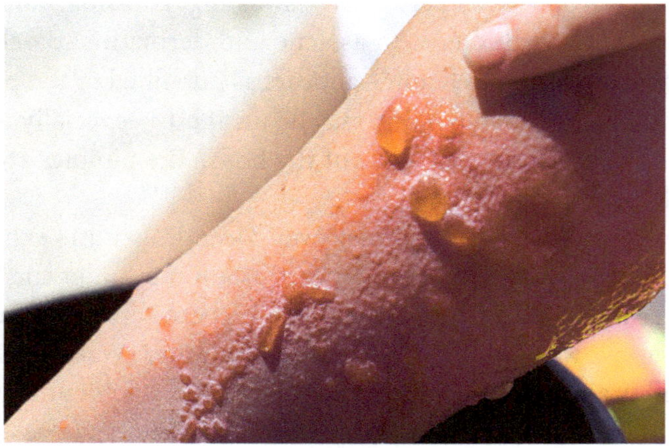

Figure 12-13 Poison ivy commonly causes contact dermatitis.

The signs and symptoms of dermatitis vary in severity depending on the strength of the irritant or allergen and the length of time the allergen is in contact with the skin. Signs and symptoms of contact dermatitis include red, itchy, blotchy skin that may appear as a rash. Irritant contact dermatitis is most often dry, whereas allergen contact dermatitis creates blisters that ooze fluid. The fluid dries with a crusty appearance. Both types of contact dermatitis may cause tenderness and pain. The irritant or allergen can leave a distinctive red rash, mark, or shape on the skin that identifies the actual object that caused the contact dermatitis. For example, a person can be irritated by costume jewelry or belts that contains nickel. For example, if a person is wearing a necklace made with nickel and develops irritant contact dermatitis, the rash appears around her neck in the shape of the necklace **(Figure 12-14)**.

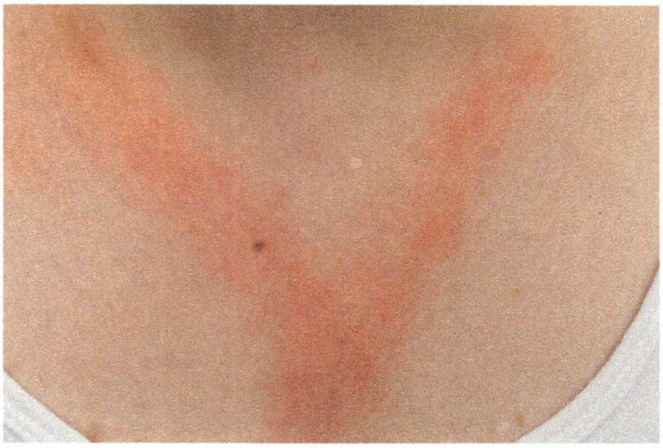

Figure 12-14 Contact dermatitis from a necklace containing nickel

To treat contact dermatitis, assist your patient in identifying the allergen that caused the contact dermatitis, and promptly remove the allergen. Washing the area with soap and water to eliminate the irritant or allergen is crucial. Patients can use over-the-counter topical medications, such as hydrocortisone creams, to dry the blisters and decrease itching. If the contact dermatitis spreads to other parts of the body or does not improve after 2 weeks of treatment, then the patient must see a physician. For example, poison ivy can become systemic for some patients and appear at areas other than the contact site. The physician may prescribe oral corticosteroids to clear up the contact dermatitis.

Cellulitis

Cellulitis is a local bacterial infection that typically occurs at the skin of the lower extremity; however, cellulitis can affect any portion of the body **(Figure 12-15)**. If cellulitis is left untreated, the infection can become systemic and life-threatening. The most common bacteria that cause cellulitis are *Staphylococcus* and *Streptococcus*, which enter through an open wound, break, or crack in the skin surface. Risk factors for cellulitis include people who have athlete's foot, open wounds, a weak immune system, other skin conditions, and swollen extremities. People who are obese or who have had recent surgery are also at risk. Once infected, the skin is very inflamed, red, swollen, hot, and point tender. The person may have a fever and other general infection signs and symptoms including illness, fatigue, muscular ache and pain, sweating, and chills. The infection can spread rapidly, and the skin appears stretched. The individual must see a physician immediately for treatment to avoid the infection becoming systemic.

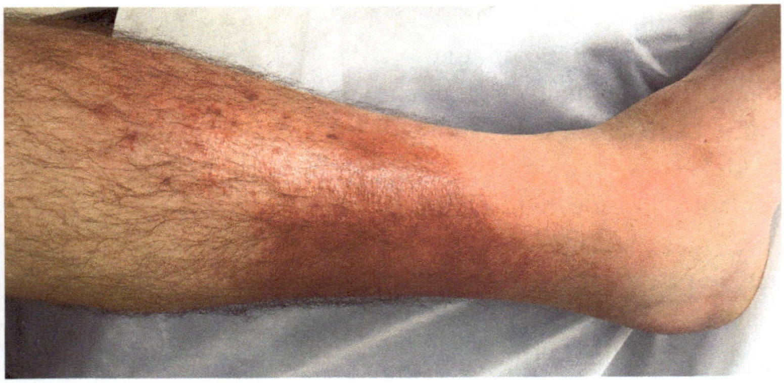

Figure 12-15 Cellulitis is a serious infection that can occur on any part of the body.

If the infection is not treated immediately, the bacteria can go deeper into the skin surface and into the bloodstream. An individual must take oral antibiotics for up to 14 days in order to clear up the infection. If the signs and symptoms do not subside after taking antibiotics for a few days, then they may need hospitalization in order to introduce intravenous antibiotics to the body. If the signs and symptoms of cellulitis and the rash is quickly changing shape or expanding in size, then call 911.

Verruca (Common Warts)

Verruca is caused by human papillomavirus (HPV) that enters the body through a crack in the skin. Common warts can be located anywhere on the body, but most commonly on the feet and hands **(Figure 12-16)**. Warts can spread on the body from one area to another, and less commonly, from one person to another.

The signs and symptoms include raised bumps that may be light gray or brown in color with a scaled surface. Some warts on the bottom of the feet are flat and painful due to weight bearing. These plantar warts may appear to have black dots within them. These dots are blood vessels that have grown into the wart. Warts are typically unsightly, especially if they are located on the face and hands.

Individuals can treat the warts at home with over-the-counter wart removal preparations (e.g., Compound W® or Dr. Scholl's® Dual Action Freeze Away®). These preparations

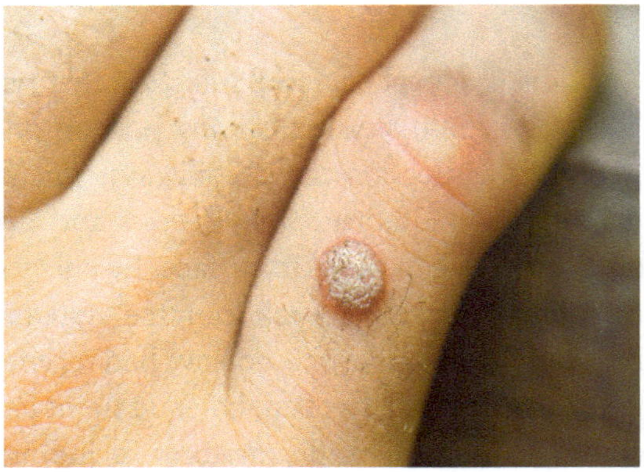

Figure 12-16 Warts most commonly affect the hands and feet.

should not be used on the face or genitals. If the wart removal preparations do not cure the infection, then they should see a physician who will treat the wart in a different manner. A physician can utilize electrocautery (burning the wart), cryotherapy (freezing the wart), laser treatment, or stronger prescription topical medication to remove the wart.

Tinea

Tinea is a fungal infection that occurs on the body (tinea corporis, also commonly known as ringworm), the head (tinea capitis), the groin (tinea cruris, also commonly known as jock itch), and the feet (tinea pedis, also commonly known as athlete's foot). Fungi live and flourish in warm, dark, moist areas. Tinea is highly contagious. Therefore, your client with tinea must not be allowed to participate in any activity that requires utilization of equipment or contact with other clients or employees at your facility until cleared by a physician. People are more prone to fungal infections if they sweat frequently, have poor hygiene, and/or have minor skin wounds. People who come in contact with contaminated surfaces, such as shower floor and a pool deck, clothing, or other objects which have the pathogen on it can obtain an infection when the fungi enter the skin through a crack or break. The person's fungal infection can also spread on the person's own body.

The tinea infection appears different depending on the affected area. On the body, ringworm first appears as a red, bumpy, scaly rash that then develops into a red ring with raised edges **(Figure 12-17)** On the other hand, with tinea pedis the skin appears scaly and peeling **(Figure 12-18)**. The skin may be red and cracked, especially in between the toes. The infection

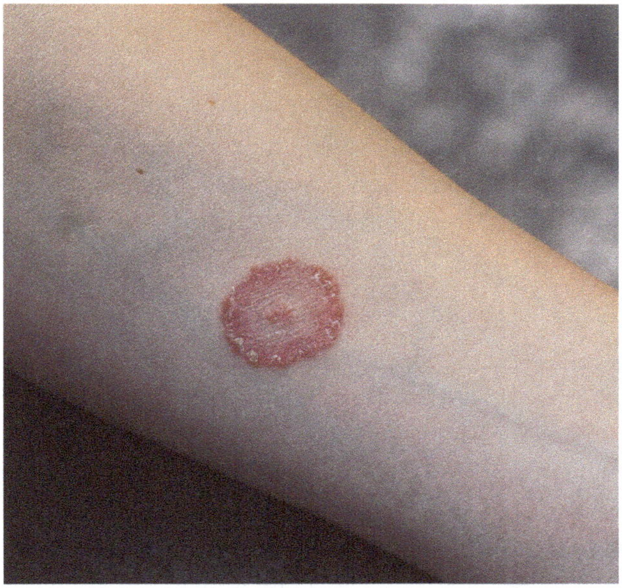

Figure 12-17 Ringworm on the forearm

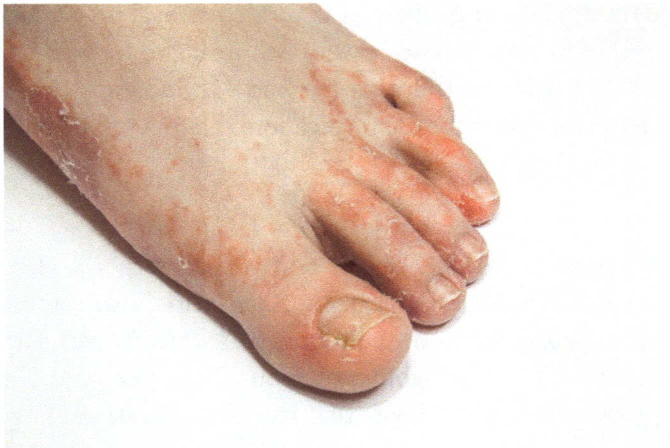

Figure 12-18 Tinea pedis appears as scaly and peeling infection on the foot and toes.

may spread to the toenails, which make them dry, brittle, cracked, and discolored. Tinea capitis may be itchy, and appear red and scaly with loss of hair and pus-filled sores at the affected area. The individual may also have a low grade (100° F or so) fever with swollen neck lymph nodes. Tinea cruris appears as red, scaly skin at the groin, which may have blisters that ooze. The area is uncomfortable and itchy.

Treatment of tinea pedis and tinea cruris involves self-treatment with antifungal medications (e.g., Tinactin® and Desenex®), which are available in sprays, powders, and creams. Tinea corporis and tinea capitis are typically treated under a physician's care with oral or topical prescription antifungal medication (e.g., Diflucan® and Nizoral®, respectively). A medicated shampoo is also used for tinea capitis. Along with these medications, the individual must thoroughly wash their clothing, practice good hygiene, and keep the skin dry and clean in order to destroy the fungi. The infection should lessen and completely resolve within a few weeks. If self-treatment does not improve the infection soon after treatment begins, or the individual has tinea corporis or tinea capitis, then refer them to a physician.

Impetigo

Impetigo is most often caused by the *Staphylococcus aureus* (staph) bacteria, and secondly by *Staphylococcus pyogenes (strep)* bacteria. This infection can occur to people of any age, but most commonly in children and adults who have skin-to-skin contact with other children or adults. Impetigo is a highly contagious infection. It is spread through physical contact with an infected person. The bacteria do not have to enter through a break or cut in the skin in order for it to be transmitted. Therefore, as with tinea infections, individuals with impetigo must not participate at your facility until cleared by a physician. Impetigo has shown to be associated with a URI since the *Staphylococcus aureus* bacterium is also the bacteria associated

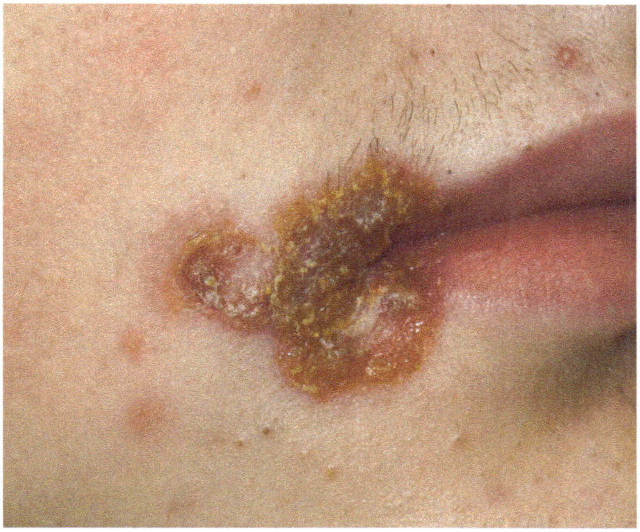

Figure 12-19 Impetigo can be identified by its honey yellow crusted lesions that can occur anywhere on the body.

with strep throat (CDC, 2020a). Signs and symptoms of impetigo include pustules that enlarge into blisters, which secrete a yellowish liquid. The secretion becomes crusty and honey colored when dry (**Figure 12-19**). The affected area itches and appears red, but is not painful. The individual must see a physician for topical, prescription antibacterial medication, and oral antibiotics to treat impetigo. Also, the individual must practice good hygiene, which includes gently washing the area with soap and water. With proper treatment, the impetigo easily heals.

Herpes Simplex (Cold Sores)

Herpes simplex virus (HSV) is classified into two types. Type 1 (HSV-1) is responsible for producing cold sores, also called fever blisters, around the mouth, while Type 2 (HSV-2) produces genital sores. HSV-1 and HSV-2 are highly contagious. The virus is transmitted via close contact with an infected person, or touching objects that have the virus (e.g., surfaces, clothing, razors, towels, etc.). Once a person is afflicted with HSV, the virus is in their body for life. HSV can remain dormant in the facial nerve tissues for a long period of time, and outbreaks can occur where a cold sore erupts on the lip. Usually these outbreaks occur due to ultraviolet and direct sunlight, fever, trauma, and hormonal changes in women.

Herpes simplex cold sores are painful blisters on the lip (**Figure 12-20**). Signs and symptoms appear a few weeks after infection and can be mild to severe. The first signs and symptoms include tingling, burning, or itching at the area where the outbreak will occur. The individual may have a fever, sore throat, and swollen glands. The blisters erupt and are visible on the lips, mouth, gums, and/or throat and leak a clear, yellowish fluid. These blister outbreaks can

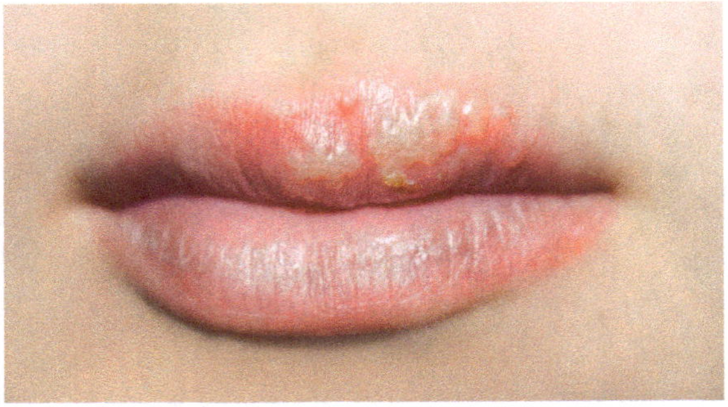

Figure 12-20 HSV-1 sores commonly erupt on the lips.

occur numerous times throughout the year. When herpes simplex affects the area around the eyes, the infection can cause blindness. Outbreaks over a large portion of the body can be life-threatening if the individual has a weakened immune system as a result of contracting other illnesses such as cancer or HIV.

Because a virus causes herpes simplex, no medication exists to destroy the virus. Treatment is symptomatic, and prescription medications (e.g., Zovirax™ and Valtrex™) can decrease the number and severity of outbreaks. Individuals should frequently wash the area with soap and water, utilize salt-water rinses, take over-the-counter pain-relieving medication, and apply an ice pack to the area if pain exists. If an individual has blisters form around the eyes, or signs and symptoms that persist for more than 2 weeks, then they must be examined by a physician.

Methicillin-Resistant Staphylococcus Aureus (MRSA)

Methicillin-resistant Staphylococcus aureus (MRSA) was first identified as a significant pathogen in the 1960s. MRSA causes a serious bacterial infection. Staph bacteria are often found on 25% to 30% of people's bodies, in particular in the nose (Sakr, et al., 2018); however, these bacteria do not harm or cause signs and symptoms of infection. This type of staph bacterium is considered colonized, which means that it is not infectious. Presently, only 1.5% of people have the MRSA bacteria on their bodies. The bacteria are asymptomatic; however, they can enter the body via an open wound or mucosa and cause a life-threatening situation. Risk factors for death due to MRSA infection include age (an older person has an increased chance of death), organ impairment, and nursing home residents (Rasmussen et al., 2021).

MRSA is resistant to the methicillin antibiotic, which is similar to penicillin and amoxicillin. Therefore, MRSA is not easily treated in all cases. When the infection first was viable, patients in hospitals acquired the pathogen due to invasive surgical procedures. This type of MRSA is called health-care associated MRSA (HA-MRSA). In 1990, community-associated MRSA (CA-MRSA) developed and was first acquired by athletes. Skin-to-skin contact with an infected athlete, in activities such as wrestling, can cause MRSA transmission. MRSA has also been transmitted in overcrowded or unclean settings, such as childcare facilities and military training camps. The bacteria enter the body through open wounds, cracks, or breaks in the skin surface, as well as mucous membranes. Once the bacteria are in the body, it spreads throughout the bloodstream, organs, bones, and joints.

Signs and symptoms of MRSA include fever, chills, and other flu-like symptoms, the presence of a wound that does not heal, or a lesion, pimple, boil, or rash that erupts on the skin **(Figure 12-21)**. The lesion may look like a spider bite and turn into a painful **abscess**. Regardless of the infection's severity, a physician should treat MRSA. Mild cases of MRSA may only require lesion draining. Severe cases require a long course of antibiotics to fight the infection. If a patient has signs and symptoms resembling MRSA that do not decrease, and the wound or lesion does not readily heal, then refer the patient to a physician for evaluation. To prevent the possibility of spreading MRSA, all equipment, tables, and the like that are utilized by one patient must be immediately disinfected prior to use by another patient.

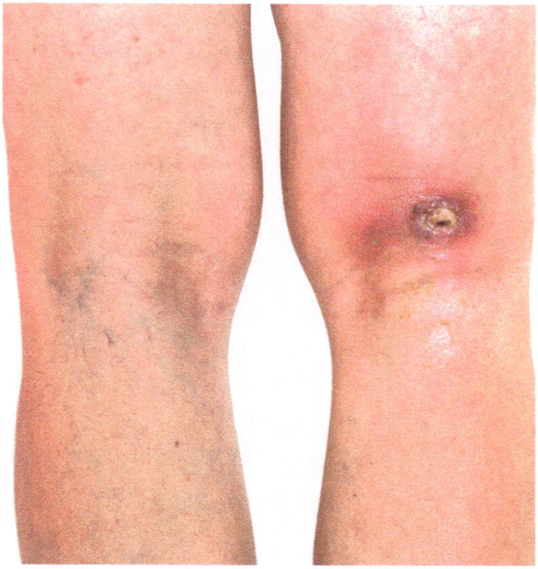

Figure 12-21 MRSA that has turned into an abscess

Viral Infections

Viruses are small microorganisms that cause illness. Once in the body, viruses take over the body's healthy cells. Viruses live in the cells, replicate, and eventually kill the cells. Some viruses are stronger than others and are highly contagious. Consequently, if your client has these infections, they must not be allowed to continue participating at your facility until they are no longer contagious and has been cleared by a physician. Likewise, the facility must be thoroughly and regularly cleaned with appropriate disinfectant to avoid spreading the infection to other clients and employees. Viral infections do not respond to medications such as antibiotics, consequently these infections are difficult to treat. Vaccines exist for some viral infections which can help protect patients from obtaining the infections in the first place.

Measles

Measles is a viral respiratory infection that most often affects children. Signs and symptoms of measles include an itchy, red rash from head to toe **(Figure 12-22)**, fever, sneezing, coughing, sore throat, runny nose, muscle pain, fatigue, conjunctivitis, white spots in the mouth, and sensitivity to light. According to the CDC (2020b), 10% of children with measles also

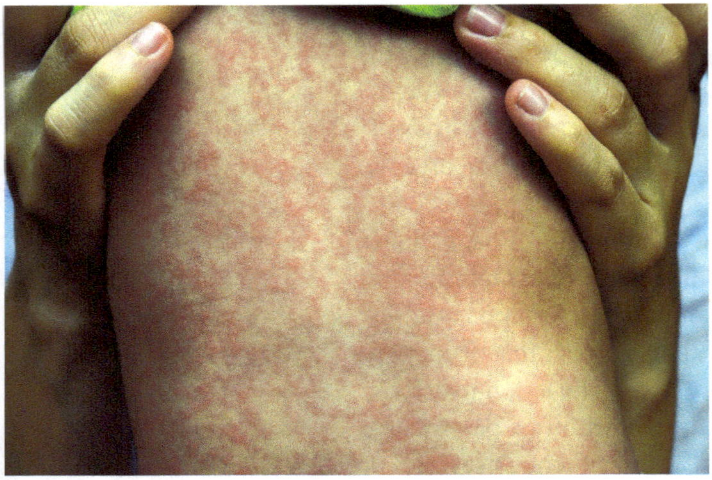

Figure 12-22 Measles rash

sustain an ear infection, and 5% come down with pneumonia, which most often causes death in children.

A vaccine for measles exists, which is given in conjunction with a vaccine for mumps and rubella (referred to as the measles, mumps, rubella or MMR vaccine). Inoculated individuals are immune to the disease. Some adults do not have their children inoculated due to fear that the MMR vaccine may cause **autism**; however, many research studies have shown that no link between the MMR vaccine and autism exists (CDC, 2021a) . Measles is so highly contagious that 90% of people who are not inoculated and in contact with the contagious individuals will become infected. An individual is contagious 4 days before and 4 days after the rash appears. If a person suspects that they have measles, they must see a physician immediately. No medication can cure measles, so the infection must run its course. The individuals can take acetaminophen for aches and pain, utilize a humidifier to moisten the air passageways, and get plenty of bed rest to combat fatigue.

Mumps

Mumps is an uncommon viral infection that, like measles, most often affects children. The infection thrives in the parotid glands, which are salivary glands below and in front of the ears. The virus is transmitted by saliva when an infected person sneezes or coughs and another person breathes in the droplets in the air. A person can also be infected if they drink out of a cup that an infected person has used. The person is contagious for 1 week after signs and symptoms are evident. Signs and symptoms of mumps do not always appear when the patient first obtains the virus. The signs and symptoms, which can appear 2 to 3 days after infection, include swelling of and painful parotid glands, which appears as if the patient has apples in his cheeks, fever, fatigue, weakness, and pain with chewing or swallowing **(Figure 12-23)**. The only

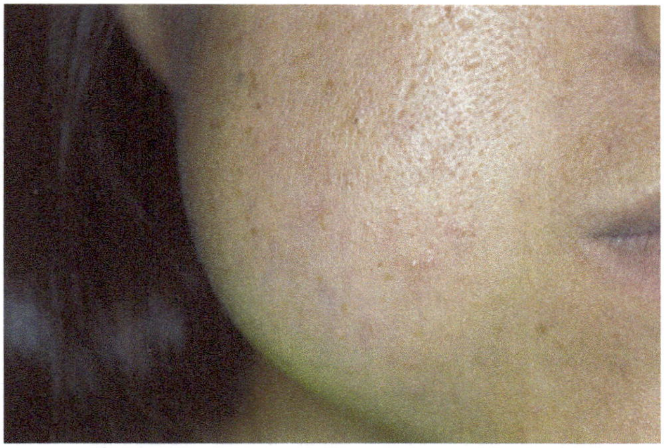

Figure 12-23 The signature sign of mumps is swelling of the parotid glands.

treatment for mumps is acetaminophen, ice or heat packs on the neck, fluids, warm salt-water gargles, and rest. The infection usually clears in 2 weeks. An individual with suspected mumps must be evaluated by a physician. The MMR vaccination creates immunity for mumps.

Rubella (German Measles)

Rubella, or German measles, is a contagious disease caused by a virus spread through close contact with an infected person or through the air. Children are mostly affected by rubella. As with measles, rubella also causes a rash **(Figure 12-24)**. A person is contagious 1 week prior to the rash eruption and 1 to 2 weeks afterwards. Other signs and symptoms of rubella

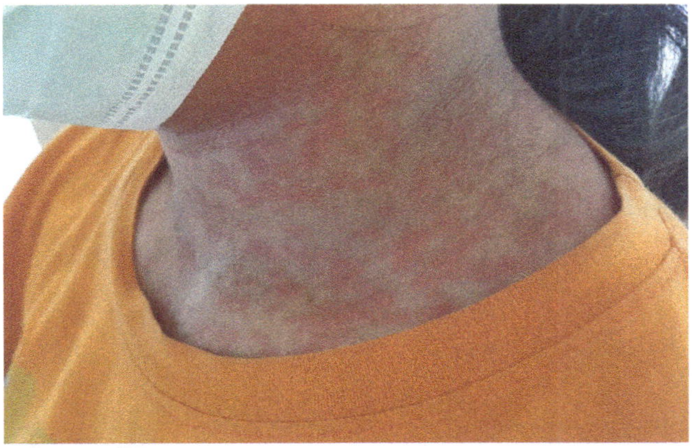

Figure 12-24 Rubella produces a similar red rash as measles.

are similar to measles. Fatigue, weakness, joint pain, runny nose, and headache may exist, although children have few signs and symptoms. No treatment exists for rubella. The individual can take acetaminophen to decrease aches and pains. Individuals should receive the MMR vaccine as children to be immune to rubella. MMR booster inoculations may be necessary for older adults and pregnant women, since the vaccine may decrease in effectiveness as the patient ages.

Varicella (Chicken Pox)

Varicella, or chicken pox, is caused by the contagious varicella-zoster virus, which affects mostly children. In the past, most children were infected by chicken pox and as a result became immune to the varicella virus as an adult. However, now a chicken pox vaccination exists and is given to children. Chicken pox is spread through droplets in the air from an infected individual who sneezes or coughs, or direct contact with the infected person's rash. The infection creates various signs and symptoms resembling the flu, such as fever, aches and pains, fatigue, weakness, headache, dry cough, and loss of appetite. The individual has an itchy, red rash over the body, including in the eyes, throat, and genitals **(Figure 12-25)**. The rash first appears like pink or red bumps, which turn into fluid filled blisters. These blisters break and crust over. The infected individual is contagious 2 days before the rash appears and until all blisters have crusted over. If you suspect a person has chicken pox, refer them to a physician. The physician can prescribe an antihistamine to lessen the itching. For severe infections, the individual may be prescribed antiviral medications to decrease the duration and signs and symptoms of the infection. These antiviral medications are only effective if taken within 24 hours after the rash appears. After chicken pox infection, the varicella-zoster virus remains dormant in the body's

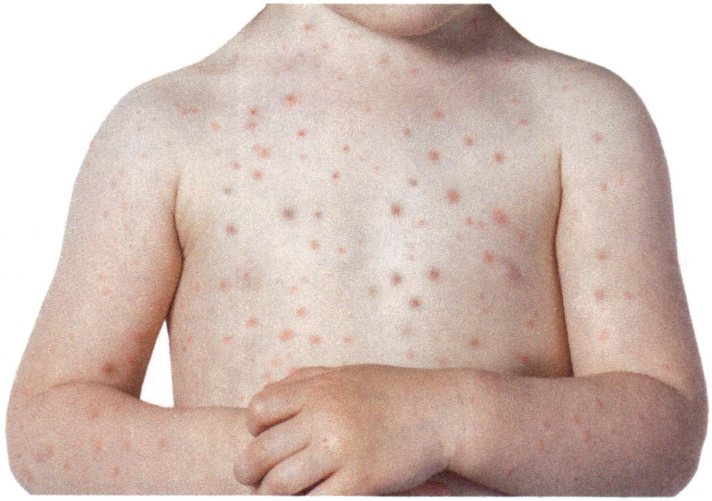

Figure 12-25 Chicken pox

nerve roots. If an individual, in particular an older adult, has a weakened immune system, the virus can become active and cause shingles. Shingles appears as a localized, blistering skin rash. A person with shingles may complain of itchiness and pain at the rash site, headache, visual changes including sensitivity to light, and flu-like symptoms (Pathak, 2021). Shingles is treated with antiviral medication, and usually resolves within a few weeks.

Coronavirus 2019 (COVID-19)

Coronavirus 2019 (COVID-19), also called SARS-Cov-2, is a highly contagious respiratory virus that can affect people of all ages. While it has similar signs and symptoms to the flu, it is more highly contagious. Individuals with COVID-19 can take longer before they show symptoms, and be contagious longer than if they had the flu. COVID-19 spreads when an infected person breathes out very small droplets and particles into the air and these droplets come in contact with another person. These droplets and particles can be breathed in or land on a person's eyes, nose, or mouth, and result in transmission. Transmission may also occur by a person coming in contact with a surface that has been contaminated by the virus, and then a person touches their eyes, nose, or mouth. Healthcare professionals who work in hospitals or clinics that see a high volume of infected patients are high-risk for being infected with COVID-19 if they are not wearing proper personal protective equipment (PPE). Also, people who are closer than 6 feet from an infected person for a cumulative total of 15 minutes or more over a 24-hour period (close contact) are more likely to be infected. When there is a high level of transmission in a specific area, community spread can occur. Community spread is when people have been infected with the virus in a specific location. In this case, many individuals will not be certain how or where they became infected. Each health department determines community spread differently based on local conditions (CDC 2021b).

Individuals with COVID-19 have reported a wide range of symptoms from mild symptoms to severe illness. Signs and symptoms may appear 2 to 14 days after exposure to the virus. If a person has fever, chills, cough, shortness of breath, fatigue, muscle or body aches, headache, loss of taste or smell, sore throat, congestion or runny nose, nausea or vomiting, or diarrhea, they might have COVID-19 and should get tested (**Figure 12-26**). The health department may contact the individual to begin contact tracing. Contact tracing assists in determining who the infected individual has come in close contact with and may have potentially infected. The health department contacts the individuals who were in close contact with the infected individual. At this point, these individuals need to get tested and quarantine as per the current CDC protocols. Anyone who has trouble breathing, persistent pain or pressure in their chest, unexplained confusion, the inability to wake or stay awake, and pale, gray, or blue-colored skin, lips, or nail beds should seek medical attention immediately. These signs and symptoms constitute a medical emergency, and you must call 911 for the individual to be transported to the ER for treatment.

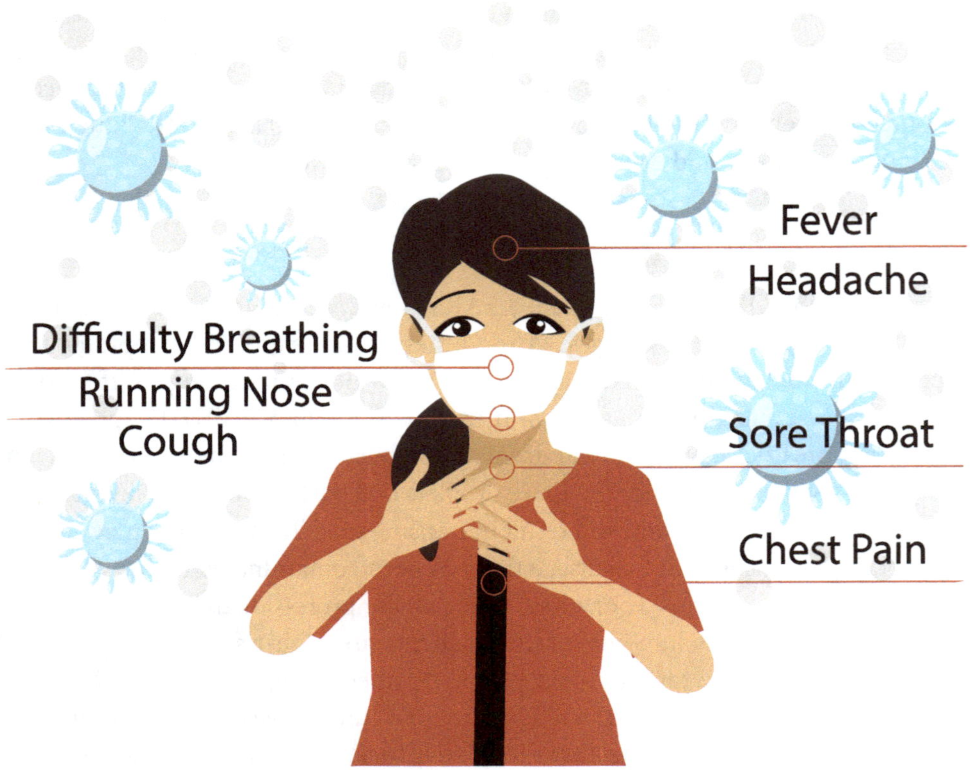

Figure 12-26 Signs and symptoms of COVID-19

Most people with COVID-19 have mild symptoms, but some people can become severely ill and require hospitalization. Older people, individuals who are immunocompromised, and those with underlying medical conditions, like heart or lung disease or diabetes, are most likely at higher risk for developing serious complications from COVID-19 illness. If a person is sick with COVID-19 and has mild symptoms, they should stay at home, quarantine from other people based on the current CDC guidelines, and monitor their symptoms. If any signs and symptoms worsen or become severe, the person should go to the ER and seek immediate medical care.

Since COVID-19 has been viable in the United States, CDC has changed the guidelines for quarantine numerous times. The changes have occurred due to various factors including, but not limited to, research data, individual vaccination status, and transmission rate. The the most updated COVID-19 guidelines can be found on the CDC website https://www.cdc.gov/coronavirus/2019-ncov/index.html (CDC, 2021b).

In some people, the signs and symptoms of COVID-19 may become chronic after their recovery from mild, moderate, or severe cases of COVID-19. Post-COVID symptoms are a wide range of new, returning, or ongoing health problems patients can experience more than 4 weeks after first being infected with the virus that causes COVID-19 (CDC, 2021b). These post-COVID conditions may also be known as long COVID, long-haul COVID, post-acute COVID-19, long-term effects of COVID, or chronic COVID. These conditions can present as different types and combinations of health problems for different lengths of time. An individual that suffers from post-COVID symptoms should be monitored by their physician.

Currently, there are no cures for COVID-19. For individuals with mild symptoms, taking over-the-counter medication, such as acetaminophen, can help alleviate a fever and muscle or body aches. If they have gastrointestinal symptoms, anti-nausea or anti-diarrheal medication if they are nauseous and/or have diarrhea, respectively, can decrease these symptoms. For individuals who are admitted to the hospital with a severe case, monoclonal antibody treatment or antiviral drugs (e.g., Paxlovid™) may help hospitalized patients suffering the effects of COVID-19. If a patient's breathing is severely compromised and lung function is deteriorating, they may be placed on a ventilator. Once placed on a ventilator, there is an increased risk of complications from other respiratory issues, such as pneumonia, and death (Lim et al. 2021).

To aid in the prevention of severe cases of COVID-19 and decrease community spread of the disease, the CDC recommends that all eligible people get vaccinated and receive a booster shot when qualified to do so. Vaccination can reduce the ability for the virus to mutate to create more variants of the virus that may be resistant to the vaccine. If an individual is not able to get vaccinated due to severe medical illness or autoimmune disease, they should wear a proper mask whenever in public and adhere to the CDC guidelines for unvaccinated people. People who have been vaccinated and are immunocompromised should also wear a mask in public to limit their risk of being infected. Wearing a mask properly **(Figure 12-27)**, especially

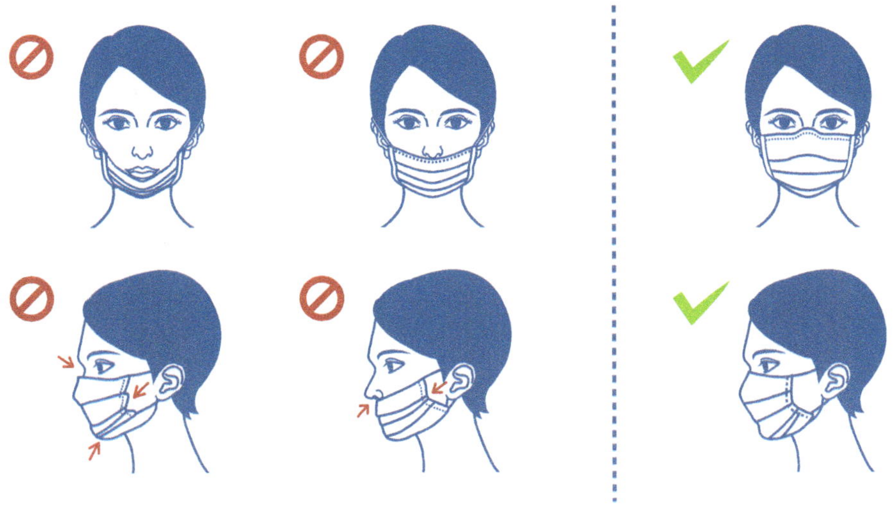

Figure 12-27 How to wear a face mask properly

indoors in public in an area of substantial or high transmission is also best practice for people, regardless of vaccination status until transmission rate in their area has decreased.

Bacterial Infections

Bacteria are single-celled organisms. Some bacteria live on or in our bodies and promote body system function (e.g., bacteria in the intestinal tract help with digestion). Very few bacterial strains cause infection, but the infections that bacteria cause can be fatal. Bacteria reproduce and thrive in the body. They emit a toxin that in some cases causes an individual to become extremely ill. Antibiotics are utilized to rid the body of bacteria; however, over years of being exposed to antibiotics, some bacteria have become resistant to the medications.

Lyme Disease

The *Borrelia burgdorfer* bacteria cause Lyme disease. This type of bacteria is spread by deer ticks, which ingest the blood of animals and humans. These small ticks attach to a human's skin and transfer the bacteria **(Figure 12-28)**. This method of transmission is the sole means of infection. People cannot spread the infection to others. Individuals who live or participate in activities in wooded or grassy areas (e.g., hiking or hunting) are more prone to acquire Lyme disease.

The signature sign of Lyme disease is a red, bull's-eye pattern rash which develops from a red bump at the tick bite **(Figure 12-29)**. Although this sign is indicative of the disease, many infected people do not exhibit this bull's-eye rash. The rash may form approximately 1 month prior to other signs and symptoms, which include flu-like symptoms, joint pain that occurs bilaterally

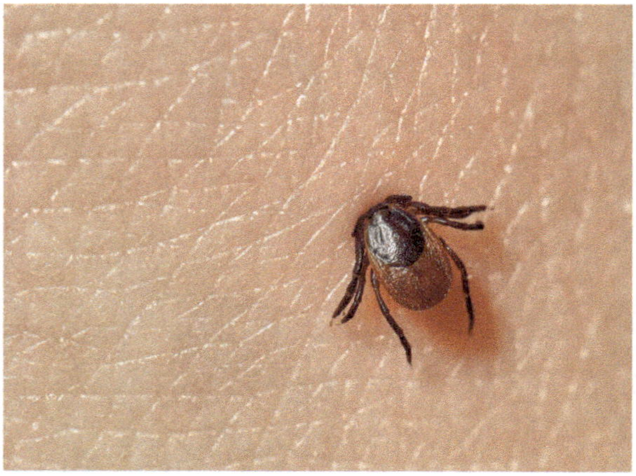

Figure 12-28 Deer ticks are very small organisms that are responsible for transmitting Lyme disease to humans.

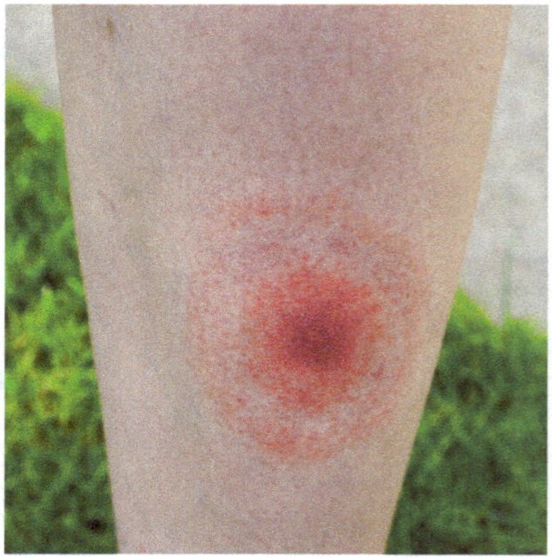

Figure 12-29 Bull's-eye rash associated with Lyme Disease

and at various body joints, and loss of extremity sensation and function. The individual's joint pain may appear at first to be a musculoskeletal injury. Consequently, take a thorough secondary survey to rule out any musculoskeletal injury. If your client has a deer tick on them, remove it immediately to hopefully avoid bacterial transmission (see Tip from the Field Tip #1). If your client exhibits signs and symptoms of Lyme disease and has been in a wooded or grassy area recently, refer them to a physician. Lyme disease is treated with oral and intravenous antibiotics. How long the individual has had the disease before treatment affects the treatment duration. Fortunately for most individuals the treatment destroys the bacteria and rids the infected individuals from Lyme disease.

TIPS FROM THE FIELD

Tip 1 A tick that is grasping onto an individual's skin with its mouth must be removed properly and as soon as possible. Proper tick removal is important, so the person does not become injured during the process. Likewise, you want to properly remove the entire tick, including its head, so it can no longer cause harm. It is difficult for a person to remove a tick that is located on their back or scalp. Consequently, when the tick is imbedded in these areas you must assist the individual. Locate the tick and brush aside any hair that is in the way of clearly visualizing the tick. Use fine tipped, clean tweezers to remove the tick. Grab the tick near its head with the tweezers. Try not to grasp the tick's body because it may release more bacterial toxins into the individual. Make sure the tweezers are as close as possible to the skin's surface. Grasp the tick firmly with the tweezers and slowly pull upward on the tick without twisting it or pulling its body from its head. The tick should release its grasp from the skin. If a part of the tick's mouth stays on the skin, remove the mouth with the tweezers. Once the tick has been removed, clean the area and your hands with soap and water or an antiseptic. If you cannot remove the mouth, or the tick's head is imbedded in the skin, leave the tick and have the individual consult their physician immediately, because the longer the tick is attached to the skin, the longer it transmits harmful bacteria. Never place petroleum jelly or soap on a tick and wait for it to detach itself from the skin. This method is ineffective. Never burn the tick with a match or other flame because you may burn the individual's skin. For additional information on how to properly remove a tick, refer to the CDC's website https://www.cdc.gov/ticks/removing_a_tick.html.

Meningitis

Meningitis is an inflammation of the meninges that surround the brain **(Figure 12-30)**. Meningitis can be caused by a virus or bacteria. Viral meningitis is typically mild, and the patient gets well without treatment. However, bacterial meningitis is a serious, potentially life-threatening infection that must be treated immediately. Bacterial meningitis is transmitted from person to person through saliva (e.g., sharing a cup or kissing an infected individual) or from respiratory secretions when the infected person coughs or sneezes. *Listeria monocytogenes* is bacteria that cause meningitis that can be transmitted when a patient eats contaminated food.

Signs and symptoms of meningitis can develop rapidly and last up to a week. The signs and symptoms include severe headache, a stiff neck, fever, chills, nausea, vomiting,

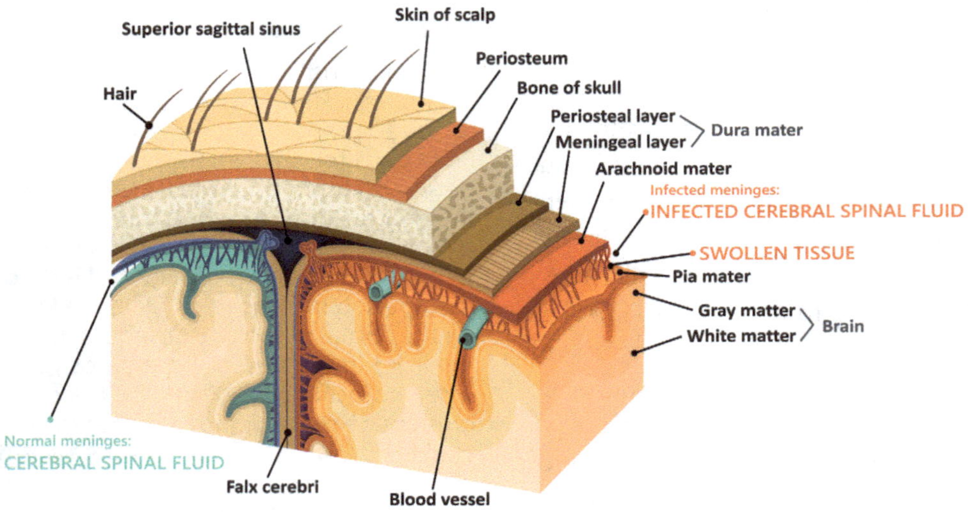

Figure 12-30 Areas of the brain affected by bacterial meningitis

confusion, and sensitivity to light. Bacterial meningitis is a medical emergency, so you must call 911 immediately. Your client must be treated in a hospital with intravenous antibiotics. Anyone who has been in close physical contact with an infected person must also be treated with oral antibiotics. A meningococcal vaccine to prevent bacterial meningitis is routinely given to patients who are 11 to 12 years old. A booster is given at 16 years old. The CDC (2019) states that the vaccine prevents infection for four types of bacterial infections, including two out of the three most common bacterial meningitis infections in the United States.

Sexually Transmitted Diseases

Sexually transmitted diseases (STDs), also called sexually transmitted infections (STIs), are caused by viruses, bacteria, or fungi. Some STDs can be treated and cured, while others cannot. The best STD prevention is to refrain from unprotected sexual contact with another individual. Sexually active individuals must practice safe sexual intercourse and utilize condoms in attempt to prevent STDs. Various STDs that individuals may acquire are discussed in the following sections.

Genital Herpes

Genital herpes is caused by the herpes simplex virus type 2 (HSV-2). The virus is highly contagious and transmitted by genital-to-genital contact. HSV-1 can cause genital herpes if mouth-to-genital contact occurs. Biological women are more often affected by genital herpes than are biological men. A pregnant woman can pass HSV-2 to their baby during childbirth. The signs and symptoms of genital herpes occur from 2 days to 1 week after infection and are present before an outbreak of genital sores. These signs and symptoms include flu-like symptoms, fever, muscular aches, fatigue, swollen lymph glands, painful urination, and vaginal discharge. Before the sores erupt, the person may feel tingling in the area, which indicates an outbreak will occur. The genital sores are painful, clear, or yellow fluid-filled blisters **(Figure 12-31)**. These blisters break and crust over. The skin tissue heals in 1 to 2 weeks. Sometimes the individual does not have an outbreak of sores, or the sores are mild and look like pimples or insect bites. In these cases, the individual may not realize they have been infected with HSV-2. Even if they do not have sores, they are still contagious. After the first outbreak, the subsequent outbreaks are usually less severe and shorter in duration.

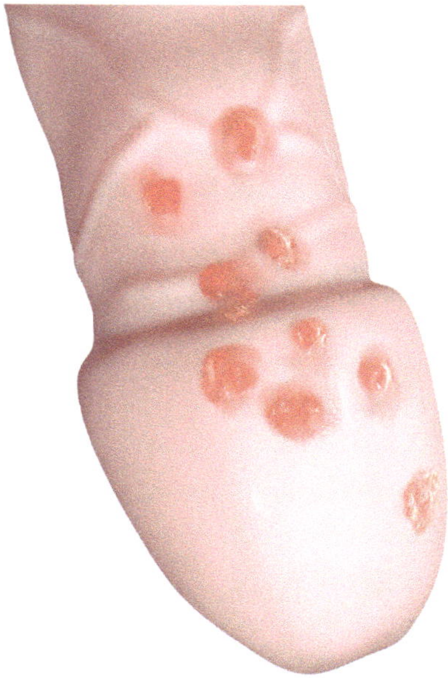

Figure 12-31 HSV-2 sores on male genitalia

An individual with herpes must see a physician for evaluation. Treatment is similar to HSV-1 infections, with antiviral medications and good hygiene. Infected people should refrain from unprotected sexual activity. Many people who have genital herpes do not seek treatment due to the mildness and infrequency of outbreaks, perhaps not recognizing they have the STD. People with suspected HSV-2 infection should always seek medical evaluation and treatment, because unfortunately the virus can spread to other parts of the body including the brain, lungs, and other organs.

Chlamydia

Chlamydia is a common disease found in sexually active teenagers and young adults who do not utilize condoms. The bacterial infection is passed from one person to another during sexual intercourse, including vaginal, anal, and oral sexual activity, as well as through childbirth. In both biological men and women, the infection produces mild or nonexistent signs and symptoms, and as a result the person may not know they have been infected. Some signs and symptoms of chlamydia are fever, lower abdominal and back pain, and pain during sexual intercourse. Biological males may have a discharge from the penis, swollen testicles, and burning during urination. Fortunately, chlamydia can be cured with treatment. The person who exhibits signs and symptoms of chlamydia must see a physician immediately to be screened for chlamydia. Chlamydia often occurs with other STDs, as well as HIV. Oral antibiotics are

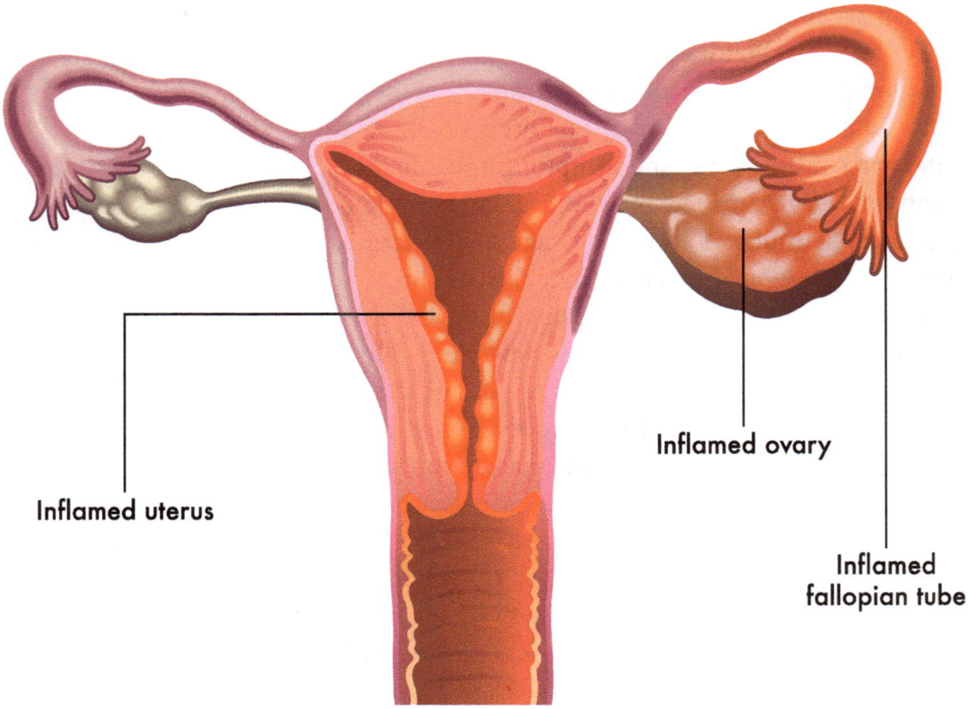

Figure 12-32 Pelvic inflammatory disease that can result from an untreated chlamydia infection

prescribed to resolve the chlamydia infection. If early treatment is not obtained, then the infection can cause a biological woman to have serious complications including **pelvic inflammatory disease (PID) (Figure 12-32)** and infertility. Untreated chlamydia can cause urethral infection and painful testes in biological males.

Trichomoniasis

Trichomoniasis is a very common, curable STD that is caused by a parasite **(Figure 12-33)**. The organism is transmitted between sexual partners during intercourse. Biological men typically have no symptoms, other than possible painful urination. Biological women may have painful urination, vaginal itching, and foul-smelling, discolored discharge. Signs and symptoms appear between 5 and 28 days after infection. Individuals with suspected trichomoniasis must see a physician for screening. Both sexual partners need to be examined and treated by a physician, especially because biological men do not often have any signs or symptoms of infection. The physician will most likely prescribe the oral antibiotic metronidazole (e.g. Flagyl®), which cures the infection in approximately 1 week.

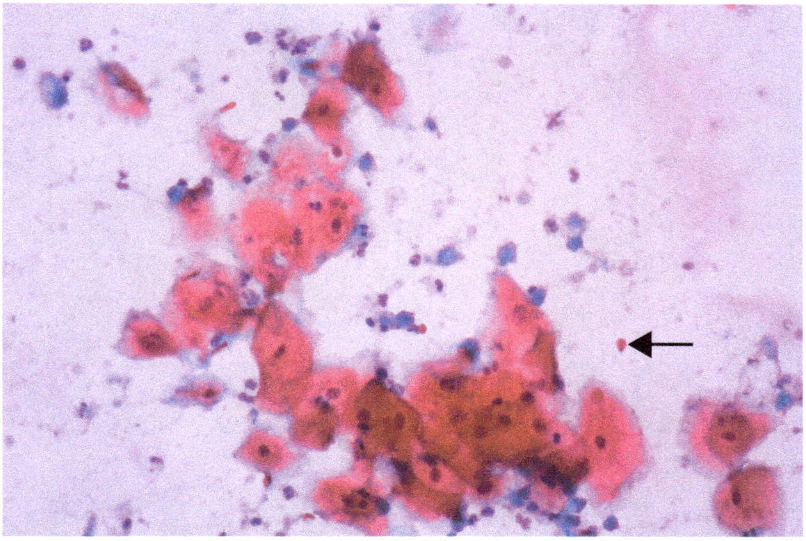

Figure 12-33 Trichomoniasis is caused by a parasite as identified in this vaginal discharge by the arrow.

Human Papillomavirus (HPV)

Human papillomavirus (HPV) is the most common STD in the United States (CDC, 2022). HPV is the virus that causes genital warts. Some types of HPV can cause cervical and other cancers. In approximately 90% of HPV cases, the infection is cleared by the body's immune system in 2 years (CDC, 2022). Individuals can develop the warts months after infection; however, most biological women may not know that they are infected because most warts develop inside the vagina or on the cervix. The warts can be flat and flesh colored, or raised with a cauliflower-like appearance **(Figure 12-34)**. A physician must treat an individual with HPV. The individual must not use over-the-counter wart removal medications to treat genital warts. A physician prescribes wart removal treatment, which includes topical medications, electrocautery, cryotherapy, or laser therapy. At times, the physician may use surgery to excise the warts.

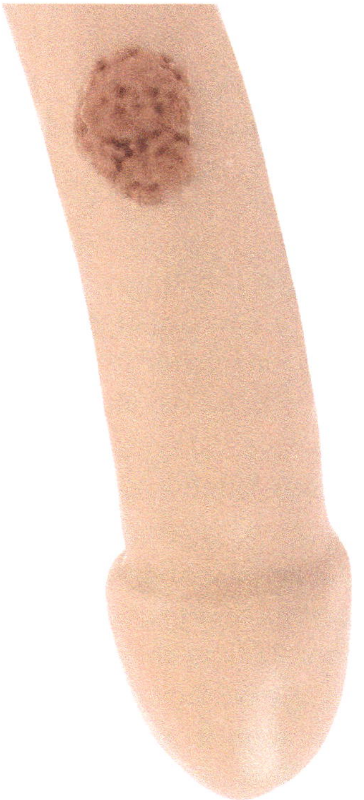

Figure 12-34 Genital warts are caused by the human papillomavirus.

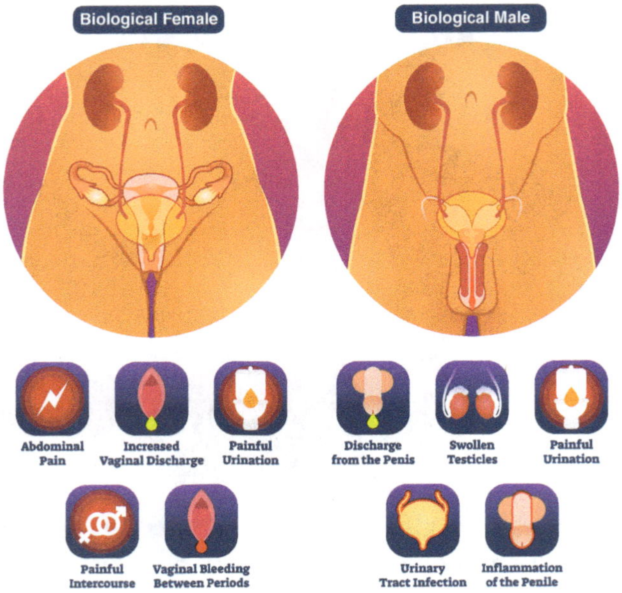

Figure 12-35 Common signs and symptoms of gonorrhea

Both biological men and women ages 9 to 26 years can become inoculated for HPV with vaccines such as Gardasil®9 and Cervarix®.

Gonorrhea

Gonorrhea is a common, highly contagious STD that is caused by bacteria. The infection affects the reproductive organs as well as the eyes, mouth, and throat. Transmission occurs through sexual intercourse and childbirth. Signs and symptoms may appear days to months after infection; however, often individuals do not always exhibit signs and symptoms of infection. Some signs and symptoms biological men may experience include discolored discharge from the penis, painful, burning urination, and swollen testicles. Biological women may experience very mild symptoms including discolored discharge, painful urination, painful sexual intercourse, and bleeding in between periods **(Figure 12-35)**. Individuals who suspect that they have gonorrhea must be examined by a physician. Fifty percent of biological women who have gonorrhea have chlamydia, which are treated simultaneously. The physician prescribes antibiotics to treat the infection. Untreated gonorrhea can cause PID and ectopic pregnancy in biological women, and inflammation of the epididymis in biological men, which can lead to infertility. Gonorrhea can become systemic and cause arthritic joints and skin lesions on all areas of the body **(Figure 12-36)**.

Syphilis

Syphilis is a STD that is caused by the bacteria *Treponema pallidum*. Biological men and women are both affected by this STD. The infection can affect the genital and anal area, as well as the lips and mouth. Syphilis is transmitted when a person comes in contact with an infected person's open sore. As with most other STDs, syphilis can be passed to a fetus while in utero and through childbirth if the pregnant mother is infected.

Signs and symptoms of syphilis may not appear for years, but the average time they appear after infection is approximately 3 weeks. An early sign of syphilis is a painless, open sore, called a chancre **(Figure 12-37)**. The chancre

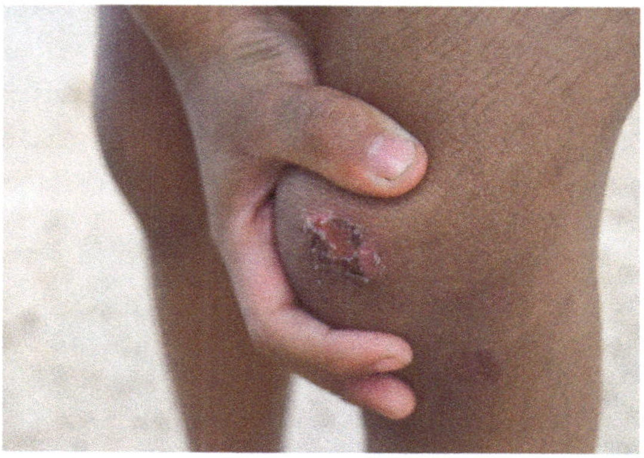

Figure 12-36 If left untreated, gonorrhea can become systemic and affect the entire body, causing pelvic inflammatory disease, infertility, joint arthritis, and skin lesions.

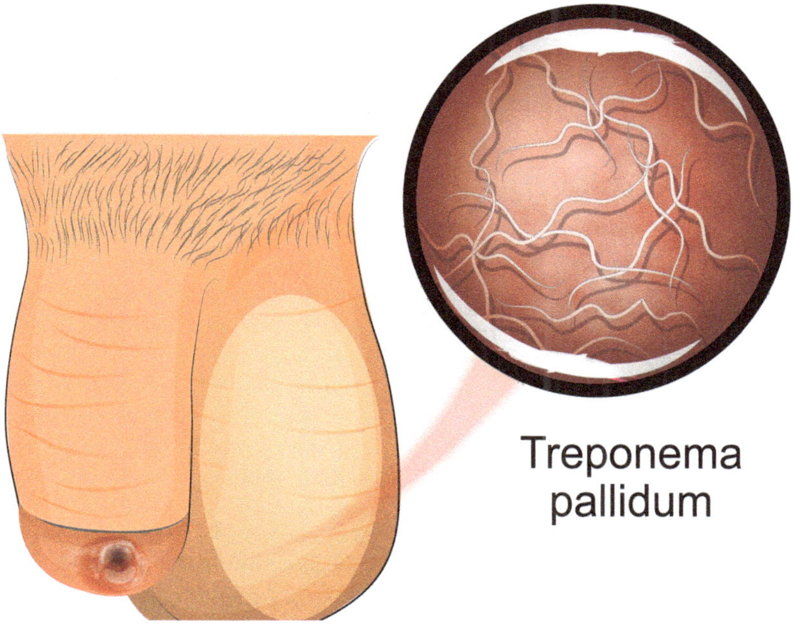

Figure 12-37 In the early stages of infection, syphilis produces chancres on the genitals.

eventually heals. However, without treatment the infection produces a rash that can be located anywhere on the body, must most often on the hands and feet **(Figure 12-38)**. The rash will disappear, but the individual may be asymptomatic, yet contagious, for years. The last stage of syphilis may cause chancres on the body, numbness, paralysis, blindness, dementia, and death **(Figure 12-39)**. A person with syphilis must be under a physician's care. With early treatment, syphilis can be cured by injectable penicillin, or other antibiotics if the individual has a penicillin allergy.

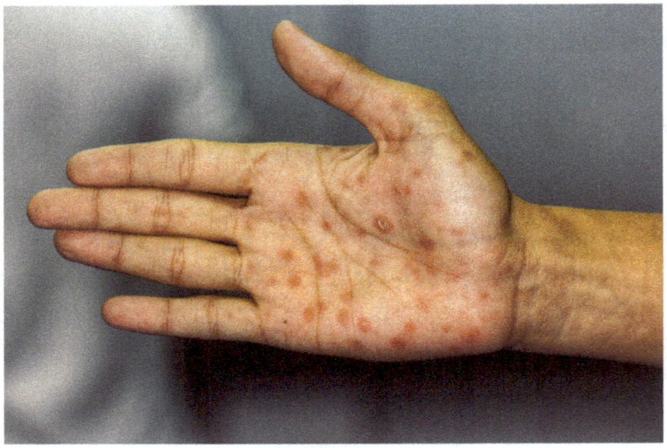

Figure 12-38 In the second stage of a syphilis infection, a rash erupts on the body.

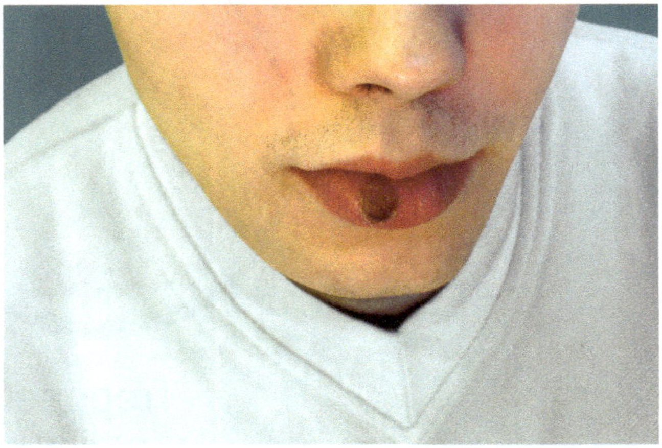

Figure 12-39 In the tertiary stage of a syphilis infection, chancres erupt elsewhere the body. A chancre is visible on this person's mouth.

Summary

General medical conditions are numerous, and undoubtedly at one time or another, our athletes, clients, and patients will be infected by a pathogen. The severity and duration of the infection varies according to the type and strength of pathogen, the individual's characteristics and health, and the treatment available. Educate your athletes, clients, and patients about the various infections that exist. They should be aware of the signs, symptoms, and treatment of general medical conditions. The incidence of transmission among your athletes, clients, and patients, as well as your employees can be lessened if not prevented at your facility. Therefore, require everyone at your facility to take proper steps to prevent the transmission of general medical conditions.

Keywords

Septicemia A life-threatening infection that typically occurs in the body along with another systemic infection. Septicemia spreads through the bloodstream very quickly, and the individual must be hospitalized and treated immediately. The mortality rate for the infection can be more than 40% (Mayo Clinic, 2021).

Antipyretics Fever-reducing medications such as acetaminophen, ibuprofen, and aspirin.

Postnasal drip Mucus that drains from the nose to the air passages and then to the throat.

Analgesics Pain-reducing medications such as acetaminophen, ibuprofen, and aspirin. These specific medications are also antipyretics (decreasing fever). Ibuprofen and aspirin are also anti-inflammatory medications; however, acetaminophen is not.

Neti pot A nasal irrigation device that utilizes a saline solution to clear congested nasal passages.

Inoculated A person who has been vaccinated in order to produce immunity against a pathogen.

Arrhythmias Abnormal heart rhythms including irregular heart rate (tachycardia), which is a fast heart rate, or a slow heart rate (bradycardia).

Abscess A collection of pus within the skin's superficial and deep layers due to a pathogen. The abscess causes swelling and inflammation at the affected area.

Autism A developmental disorder of the brain that affect children under 3 years old. An autistic child lacks proper communication and social skills.

Pelvic inflammatory disease (PID) An inflammation of the pelvis including the uterus, fallopian tubes, and other reproductive organs. PID can cause severe pelvic pain, infertility, ectopic pregnancy, and formation of an abscess.

Discussion Questions

1. What are general medical conditions? What is the difference between a local and systemic infection? How can local infections become systemic infections?
2. What are common methods of transmission for URIs? skin infections? viral infections? bacterial infections? STDs?
3. Which infections can the patient treat at home? Which infections require immediate referral to and treatment by a physician?
4. Which URIs can become severely complicated for the patient if infection remains untreated?
5. What are some common signs and symptoms of the various skin infections?
6. Which viral or bacterial infections can become life-threatening?
7. Which STDs are caused by bacteria? viruses? parasites?
8. Which STDs cannot be cured with treatment?

CASE STUDY #1: *ICE HOCKEY FEVER*

Ryan is a 16-year-old varsity hockey player at Vegas High School. With Ryan's hockey talent, the season has been very successful. The team is tied for first place in the conference, and Ryan is one of the top scorers. Over the past 3 days, Ryan has been battling an annoying, intermittent dry cough, but otherwise he has felt fine. Today, Ryan woke up with a stuffy nose and a sore throat. He was tired and generally did not feel well. He went to school feeling very weak and fatigued. At after school practice he told his coach how he felt. The coach told Ryan that he probably had a cold. The coach said that the cold would probably go away within a few days. The coach asked Ryan if he was able to practice today, and Ryan said he could. Ryan put on his gear and skated onto the ice. During practice, Ryan skated slow and was always a step behind his teammates. He had difficulty catching his breath and, on a few occasions, asked a teammate for a substitution due to his fatigue.

At the end of practice, the coach pulled Ryan aside and told him to go home, eat a nutritious dinner, drink fluids, and go to bed early to rest his body. Ryan took the coach's advice, but at home he did not eat much due to his lack of appetite. He went to bed early, but had trouble falling asleep because of his frequent cough, which was now producing a light green, thick mucus. At one point during the night, Ryan broke out in a sweat, so he got up and took his temperature which was 100° F. Ryan thought it was strange to have a fever because during the night he was also having frequent chills.

The next morning when he woke up, Ryan was exhausted. He was congested and had a headache. Ryan felt weak despite eating a small, nutritious breakfast. The team's conference game was in 2 days, so Ryan had to attend school in order to be eligible to practice and compete in the game. At practice, Ryan did not perform well. Each time he skated, he felt worse. He continued to cough up the mucus, began to have breathing difficulty due to the congestion, and experienced some chest discomfort when he exerted himself.

When Ryan went home after practice he told his parents how he felt. They took his temperature which was 101.5° F. Since Ryan had been ill for 5 days and his signs and symptoms were getting worse, his parents decided to take him to his physician. Ryan's parents made an appointment for Ryan to see his physician early in the morning, and Ryan went right to bed to rest.

1. What advice should the coach have given Ryan the first time Ryan went to him complaining of symptoms?
2. What possible infections could Ryan have?
3. If left untreated, what could happen to Ryan if the illness progresses?
4. What do you think the physician will prescribe to treat the infection?

CASE STUDY #2: *UNIDENTIFIED LESION*

Alexandra has been working out at We R Fit Gym for approximately 6 months. She has been using treadmills and stair machines to increase her cardiorespiratory endurance, and weight machines and yoga to tone her muscles. One day after a workout, she was showering and felt what seemed to be a pimple on the back of her right leg. She was not concerned about the pimple, because she frequently got them from excessive sweating. Alexandra washed the area thoroughly and figured that the pimple will go away on its own in a few days as the other pimples normally did.

Three days later while dressing for work, Alexandra looked in the mirror and noticed that her pimple increased in size and was swollen. The pimple was red and contained what appeared to be pus under the skin. When she touched the pimple it was very tender to the point of being almost painful. Alexandra attempted to pop the pimple in order to relieve the pressure. A small amount of pus oozed out, but the pimple was now more inflamed. She was going to be late to work so she put some acne medicine on the area and covered it with a bandage.

When Alexandra returned home from work, the pimple was now the size of a dime. The area around the pimple was very red and now painful to the touch. More pus was evident within the pimple. Some pus oozed out and left dried yellowish crusts around the area and on the bandage. Alexandra was now concerned because the pimple did not look like a normal pimple anymore. After she bathed, she put antibiotic ointment and a bandage on the pimple. The area was still sore when Alexandra went to bed.

The following morning as Alexandra was getting ready to go to the gym, she removed the bandage and looked at the pimple. The pimple was extremely inflamed and had increased in size. Alexandra was worried and wondered what she should do.

1. What type of skin lesion could Alexandra have? What led you to make this determination?
2. How do you think she acquired the lesion?
3. How must Alexandra treat the area?
4. Should Alexandra seek medical attention? Why or why not?
5. Can Alexandra continue to participate in exercise and fitness activities at We R Fit Gym? Why or why not?

References

Center for Disease Control (CDC). (2022). *Genital HPV infection—fact sheet.* Retrieved January 14, 2022, from http://www.cdc.gov/std/HPV/STDFact-HPV.htm

Center for Disease Control (CDC), (2021a). *Autism and vaccines.* Retrieved October 31, 2021, from https://www.cdc.gov/vaccinesafety/concerns/autism.html

Center for Disease Control (CDC). (2021b). *COVID-19.* Retrieved October 8, 2021, from https://www.cdc.gov/coronavirus/2019-nCoV/index.html.

Center for Disease Control (CDC). (2021c). *Key Facts About Influenza (Flu).* Retrieved October 6, 2021, from https://www.cdc.gov/flu/about/keyfacts.htm

Center for Disease Control (CDC). (2020a). *Impetigo.* Retrieved January 6, 2022, from https://www.cdc.gov/groupastrep/diseases-hcp/impetigo.html

Center for Disease Control (CDC). (2020b). *Transmission of Measles.* Retrieved October 8, 2021, from http://www.cdc.gov/measles/about/transmission.html

Center for Disease Control (CDC). (2019). R*esources for Healthcare Professionals.* Retrieved October 8, 2021, from https://www.cdc.gov/meningitis/clinical-resources.html

Henochowicz, S. I., Zieve, D., Conaway, B. (2020). *Allergic rhinitis.* Retrieved on October 8, 2021, from https://medlineplus.gov/ency/article/000813.htm

Lim, Z.J., Subramaniam, A., Ponnapa Reddy, M., Blecher, G., Kadam, U., Afroz, A., Billah, B., Ashwin, S., Kubicki, M., Bilotta, F., Curtis, J.R., Rubulotta, F. (2021) Case Fatality Rates for Patients with COVID-19 Requiring Invasive Mechanical Ventilation. A Meta-analysis. *American Journal of Respiratory and Critical Care Medicine*, 203 (1), 54-66. doi: 10.1164/rccm.202006-2405OC.

Mayo Clinic. (2021). *Septicemia.* Retrieved October 8, 2021, from https://www.mayoclinic.org/diseases-conditions/sepsis/symptoms-causes/syc-20351214

Pathak, N. (2021). *Shingles.* Retrieved October 8, 2021, from https://www.webmd.com/skin-problems-and-treatments/shingles/shingles-skin

Rasmussen, P.U., Uhrbrand, K., Bartels, M.D., Neustrup, H., Karottki, D.G., Bültmann, U., & Madsen, A.M. (2021). Occupational risk of exposure to methicillin-resistant Staphylococcus aureus (MRSA) and the quality of infection hygiene in nursing homes. *Frontiers of Environmental Science & Engineering*, 15, 41. doi: 10.1007/s11783-020-1333-y

Sakr, A., Bregeon, F., Mege, J., Blin, O. (2018). Staphylococcus aureus Nasal Colonization: An Update on Mechanisms, Epidemiology, Risk Factors, and Subsequent Infections. *Frontiers in Microbiology*, 9, 2419. doi:10.3389/fmicb.2018.02419

Tesini, B. L. (2021). *Common Cold.* Retrieved October 8, 2021, from https://www.merckmanuals.com/home/infections/respiratory-viruses/common-cold?redirectid=427

Chapter 13

The Lower Extremity

Chapter Objectives

After you have read this chapter, you will be able to understand:

- Lower extremity injuries that occur to the hip, thigh, knee, patella, low leg, ankle, and foot.
- How to identify which lower extremity injuries necessitate calling 911.
- The lower extremity injuries that the patient can treat at home to promote healing.
- The lower extremity injuries that require surgery in order for the patient to regain full function.
- Typical lower extremity injuries the occur most often to children.

The hip, thigh, knee, patella, low leg, ankle, and foot are the anatomical structures that make up the lower extremity. The mechanisms of injury for lower extremity injuries are often different as compared to upper body injuries, due to the fact that the lower extremity is almost always weight bearing during activity. Consequently, the lower extremity is often injured when the foot is in contact with the ground. When force is applied to the foot, any portion of the lower extremity can be injured due to forces traveling up through the bones and joints. Therefore, when your patient sustains a lower extremity injury while weight bearing, always check for injuries that may have occurred from the toes to the hip. As with all other injuries, lower extremity injuries may be acute or chronic, and mild to severe. Likewise, the signs and symptoms you find during your secondary survey will assist you in determining your patient's care.

The Hip and Thigh

The hip is a ball and socket joint made up of the head of the femur and the acetabulum of the pelvis. The hip creates a lot of motion because of its configuration, and can perform flexion, extension, abduction, adduction, internal rotation, external rotation, and **circumduction**. The thigh consists of the femur and its surrounding musculature. The quadriceps, hamstrings, adductors, and iliotibial band are the thigh muscles commonly injured.

Femoral Fracture

Even though the femur is the strongest and largest bone in the body, both acute traumatic and stress fractures occur. Most acute fractures occur to the femoral shaft **(Figure 13-1)**. Common femoral fractures classifications are oblique, transverse, comminuted, and spiral. Open fractures can also occur. Stress fractures typically occur to the femoral neck. These fractures can take weeks to develop, and are not nearly as severe as acute, traumatic fractures.

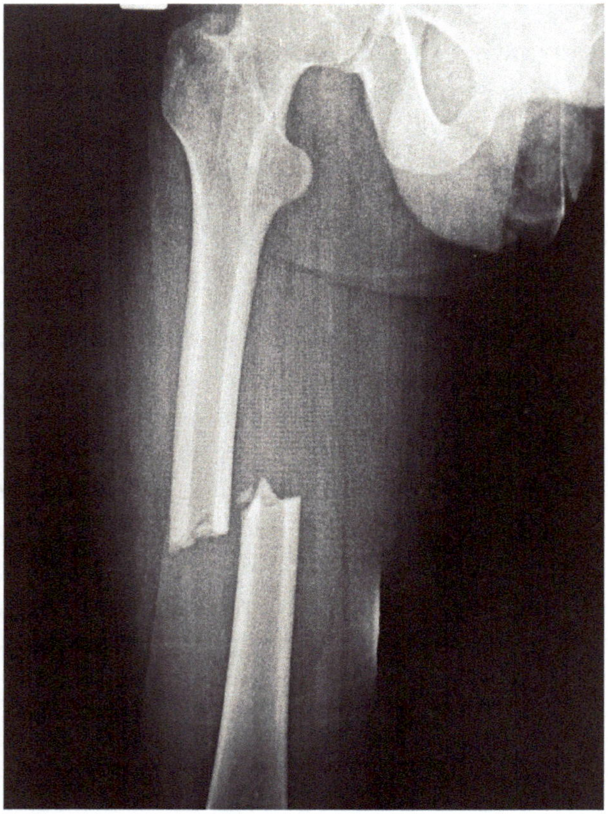

Figure 13-1 Acute femoral fractures often occur at the femoral shaft.

Mechanism or Cause of Injury

The amount of force needed to cause a femoral shaft fracture is substantial. The number one cause of acute, traumatic femoral shaft fractures is car accidents (American Academy of Orthopaedic Surgeons [AAOS], 2018). Other causes are motorcycle accidents, pedestrian-car accidents, and falls from a great height. In athletics, the femoral shaft must sustain significant force in order to break. This injury occurs in high velocity collision or contact sports such as football or mixed martial arts.

A femoral neck stress fracture is not a common injury. This stress fracture is caused by repetitive motion and forces applied to the femur during constant weight bearing. These overuse injuries occur most often to biological females who participate in endurance sports such as long distance running. Long distance runners repetitively weight bear and bound on hard surfaces, which transmits significant forces up the femur to the femoral neck. Individuals who have relatively low body weight and lack of muscle mass at the pelvis, hip, and thigh, are at risk for femoral stress fractures. Muscles assist in dissipating forces. If an individual does not have enough of muscle to dissipate force away from the bones, then stress fractures can occur. For example, an endurance athlete who participates in weight-bearing activities, has little muscle mass at the pelvis, hip, and thigh, and is complaining of groin or hip pain that increases with activity may have a femoral stress fracture (Lodge et al., 2020).

Signs and Symptoms

An individual who has sustained an acute, traumatic femoral shaft fracture feels excruciating pain. They most likely are in shock and unable to put pressure or stand on the leg. The femur may be deformed, appear crooked, and look shorter than the uninjured leg. In the case of an open fracture, deformity and visible bleeding exists. An individual who has a femoral neck stress fracture complains of groin or hip pain that increases with activity. Swelling, point tenderness, inability to fully weight bear on the leg, thigh muscle weakness, loss of hip function, and an abnormal gait may be present.

Immediate Care

When an individual has sustained an acute, traumatic femoral shaft fracture, they most likely are in shock, so treat them accordingly. Call 911 immediately. Leave the individual in the position that you find them, provided that their airway is open and they are breathing normally. Without moving the injured limb, splint the limb in the position that you find it and take care of any bleeding **(Figure 13-2)**. If you are not trained to properly splint a femoral fracture, feel uncomfortable or not confident to splint the injury, or do not have any materials accessible to do so, then keep the patient still, treat them for shock, and wait until the emergency medical technicians (EMTs) arrive. The EMTs are highly trained to splint femoral and other fractures.

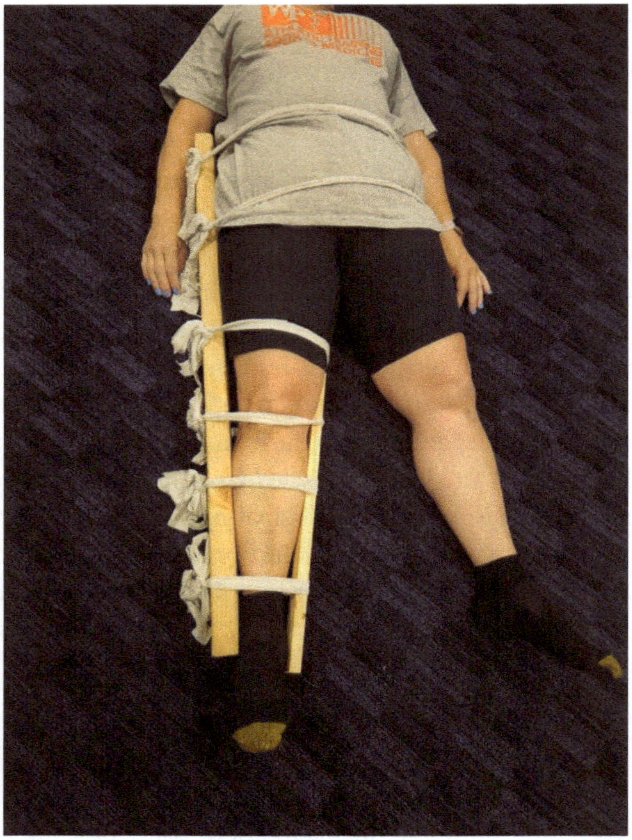

Figure 13-2 Splinting a femoral fracture

At the hospital, the physician takes x-rays and/or CT scans to determine the extent of the fracture. When a patient sustains a femoral shaft fracture, surgery may be warranted to repair the fractured bone. The patient is splinted and immobilized until the patient is physically able to have surgery. However, a patient who has an open fracture needs surgery immediately. With open femoral shaft fractures, the potential for the patient to sustain a secondary infection or significant external bleeding exists.

Other complications can arise with femoral shaft fractures. The femoral shaft has a large medullary cavity which contains fatty yellow bone marrow. The fat can escape out of the medullary cavity and cause life-threatening conditions, such as pulmonary embolism. Complications can also arise from the surgery because metal plates, rods, and other hardware are placed through the bones to promote healing. A non-union of the femoral shaft, blood clots, bone malalignment, and tearing of blood vessels and nerves can also occur (AAOC, 2018). After the patient's fracture has healed, they will participate in a thorough rehabilitation program in order to regain full extremity function.

If you believe an individual has sustained a femoral neck stress fracture **(Figure 13-3)**, have them discontinue any activity that aggravates their signs and symptoms, and apply ice

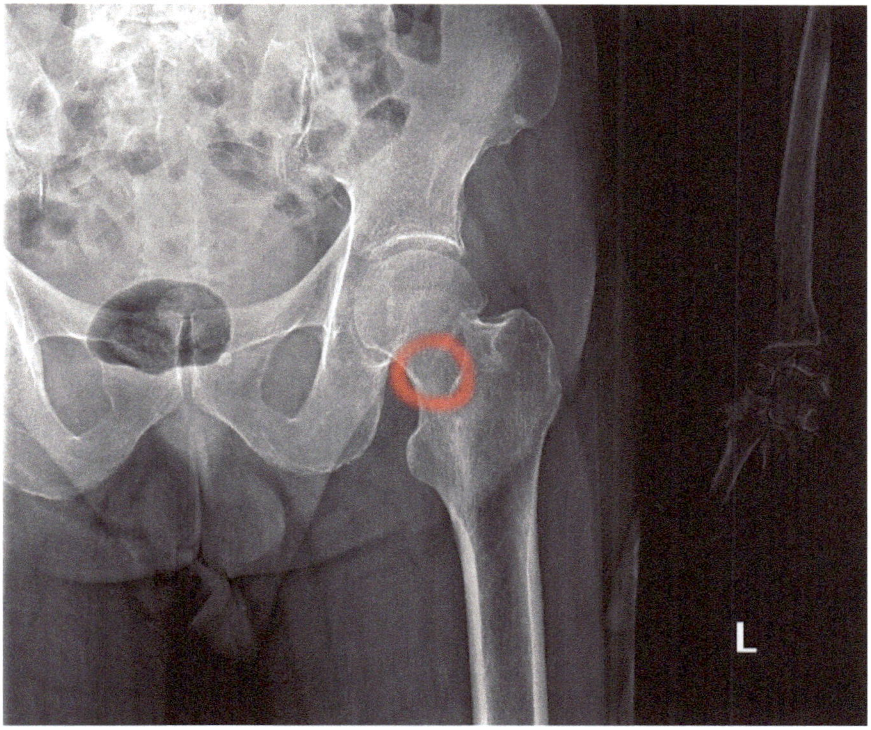

Figure 13-3 Femoral neck stress fracture

to the area. Apply a compression wrap to their hip and thigh, and fit them for crutches or a cane so they are not fully weight bearing. Anti-inflammatory medication can help decrease their pain. Although the injury is not an emergency, the individual should see their physician as soon as possible. The physician will take x-rays of the femoral neck to determine if it is fractured. If it is fractured, the physician may need to perform surgery in order to promote bone healing. Whether or not the physician performs surgery, in order to heal the patient must rest from predisposing activities, take anti-inflammatories, weight bear as tolerated, and perform rehabilitative exercises. The stress fracture can take many weeks to heal. Once the physician confirms the stress fracture has healed, then the patient is able to slowly resume activity.

Prevention

Preventing femoral shaft fractures may not always be possible. Protective sports equipment worn on the thigh is helpful to prevent acute femoral fractures, but the equipment cannot always protect the femur against high impact traumatic forces. Femoral neck stress fractures can be prevented by proper conditioning which includes muscular strengthening. Ultimately, to avoid femoral neck stress fractures, individuals should increase their intensity slowly, participate in muscle strengthening exercises, and progress activities as their bodies allow.

Hip Dislocation

A hip dislocation occurs when the femoral head becomes displaced from the acetabulum of the pelvis. The hip joint is severely disrupted and the ligaments surrounding the joint are sprained to varying degrees. Most often the hip dislocates posteriorly, whereas the femoral head is forced backwards out of the joint. Hip dislocations can occur with or without concurrent fractures.

Mechanism or Cause of Injury

A hip dislocation can be caused by a substantial traumatic direct blow to the hip, to a flexed knee with force placed upward through the femur, or to the foot sending force up the lower extremity. These traumatic blows occur most commonly in car accidents or by a moving vehicle striking an individual. They do not commonly occur during athletic activities. However, in some high impact athletic activities, such as football, rugby, and gymnastics, or in downhill skiing and snowboarding when traumatic falls occur, hip locations can occur. The hip will flex, adduct, and internally rotate, or flex, abduct and externally rotate when the foot or knee strikes the ground or another object to cause the dislocation.

Signs and Symptoms

The individual will experience extreme pain and will most likely experience shock. They cannot sit up or move their hip. A telltale sign of a hip dislocation is the lower extremity's appearance. The hip is in an adducted, internally rotated position, and the injured leg appears shorter than the uninjured leg **(Figure 13-4)**. The individual may have abnormal or loss of sensation down the leg to the foot due to a compromised sciatic nerve.

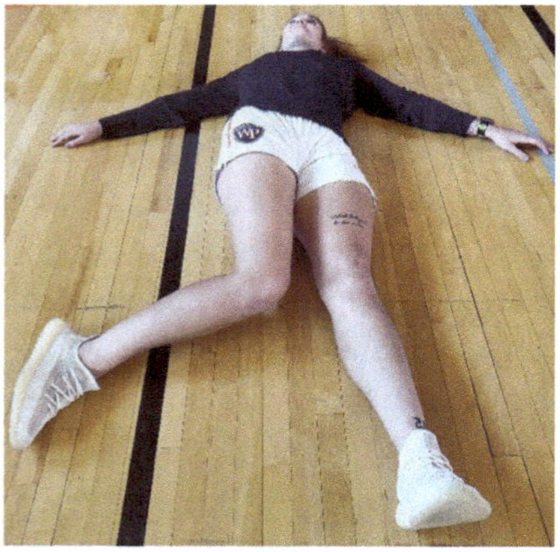

Figure 13-4 An individual with a hip dislocation appears to have a shortened, internally rotated, adducted leg on the injured side.

Immediate Care

Hip dislocations are medical emergencies, so call 911 immediately. Tell the individual not to move, treat them for shock, and splint the hip and leg in the position you find it. Similar to acute traumatic femoral fractures, if you are not trained to properly splint a hip dislocation, feel uncomfortable or not confident to splint the injury, or do not have any materials accessible to do so, then keep the patient still, treat them for shock, and wait until the EMTs arrive. Monitor their airway, breathing, and circulation. Perform quick sensory tests by asking them if they have sensation down their leg and into their foot. Give the EMTs all information regarding the individual's injury, including signs and symptoms and any other findings, when they arrive on the scene.

At the ER, the physician will order x-rays to determine the extent of injury. Then, the physician will give the patient a sedative or general anesthesia before reducing the dislocation. Afterwards, the patient must use crutches for a few weeks to rest the hip. The patient can take nonsteroidal anti-inflammatory drugs (NSAIDs) or narcotic pain medication and will need to participate in lower extremity rehabilitation as prescribed by their physician. If the patient also has a fracture or significant hip joint instability, then they will need to wear a hip stabilizing brace. With proper treatment and rehabilitation, the patient can return to full activity at approximately 3 months post-injury.

Prevention

Preventing a hip dislocation is not entirely possible. Individuals must avoid high risk activities in order to minimize the potential of sustaining a hip dislocation. All activity surfaces should be kept clean and safe, so the athletic participants do not slip and fall. As always, maintaining strong hip and thigh musculature is critical to minimizing the extent of injury.

Hip Sprain

Although the hip joint contains the three strongest ligaments in the body, acute sprains to the iliofemoral, ischiofemoral, and pubofemoral ligaments do occur **(Figures 13-5 and 13-6)**. When a hip is dislocated the ligaments are sprained to varying degrees.

Mechanism or Cause of Injury

Hip sprains are caused by a forceful stretch of the ligaments due to excessive, involuntary hip joint range of motion (ROM) during activity. The athlete may be standing or running and be hit by an opponent in the thigh. This force pushes the hip joint beyond its normal ROM, which results in sprained ligaments. The hip ligaments can also be sprained by a direct blow to the hip.

Signs and Symptoms

The athlete has hip pain, especially upon hip movement. Consequently they do not want to move the joint freely. The muscles become inflexible, the joint becomes stiff, and the athlete walks with a limp. The area surrounding the hip may be swollen and point tender.

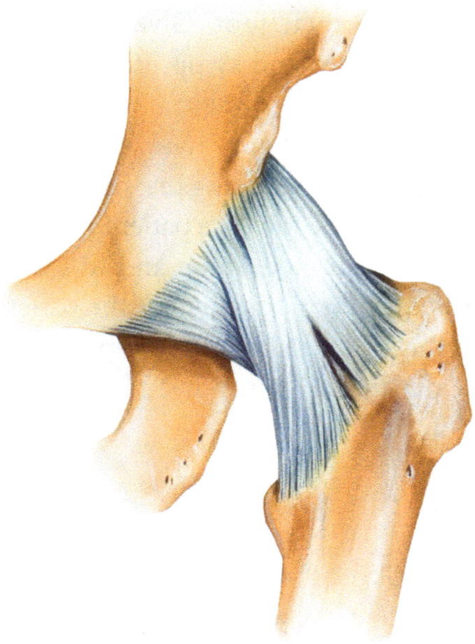

Figure 13-5 Anterior view of the hip showing the iliofemoral and pubofemoral ligaments

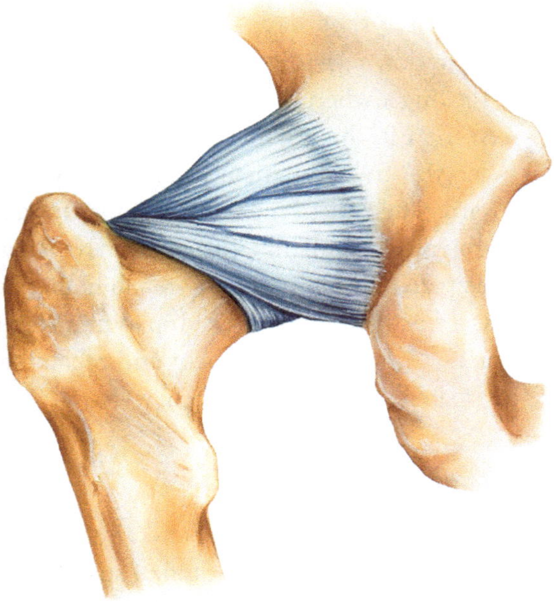

Figure 13-6 Posterior view of the hip showing the iliofemoral and ischiofemoral ligaments

Immediate Care

To care for the athlete, have them rest the hip by utilizing crutches or a cane to ambulate, apply ice packs to the area, wear a compression bandage, and elevate the lower extremity whenever possible. Anti-inflammatory medication can modulate pain and inflammation. If signs and symptoms of injury do not decrease over a few days, then the athlete should see their physician. The physician will examine the athlete's hip to determine the extent of injury and if any secondary injuries exist. Conservative treatment, including rehabilitation exercises, will be prescribed.

Prevention

Athletic participants can wear hip protective equipment and padding to avoid injury by direct blows. If the muscles surrounding the hip are strong and the athlete has good passive range of motion (PROM) at the hip, then injury to the hip ligaments can be minimized.

Hip Bursitis

The trochanteric, iliopsoas, and ischial bursae are located at the hip. These bursae assist in providing cushion between bone and soft tissue, which allows for unrestricted motion. These bursae, in particular the large trochanteric bursa, can become inflamed. Hip bursitis occurs primarily to middle-aged or older biological women.

Mechanism or Cause of Injury

Hip bursitis is typically a chronic, overuse injury. Individuals who have hip arthritis, previous hip injury or surgery, a leg length discrepancy, or **scoliosis** are prone to hip bursitis. Trochanteric bursitis can also occur if the individual has a tight iliotibial band which rubs against the bursa **(Figure 13-7)**. Iliopsoas bursitis occurs from repetitive hip flexion. Ischial bursitis can occur with prolonged sitting or moving the hip from flexion to extension repeatedly, as when riding a bicycle.

Signs and Symptoms

Hip bursitis produces severe pain at the hip (trochanteric bursitis), the groin (iliopsoas bursitis), or the ischial tuberosity at the buttocks (ischial bursitis). The severe pain becomes a dull, diffuse pain. The pain increases when pressure is applied to the area, such as when sleeping, sitting, or walking. The hip joint may feel stiff and point tenderness may exist over the bursae. When the individual moves the hip, they may feel a snapping sensation, especially with trochanteric and iliotibial bursitis.

Immediate Care

The individual should utilize rest, ice, compression, and elevation (RICE) and avoid all activities that aggravate the injury. They must see a physician if they have pain lasting for over a week despite self-treatment, severe hip joint pain which does not decrease each day, ecchymosis, swelling, or redness at the area around the joint, or any intense, shooting pain, which indicates nerve dysfunction. In these cases, the course of treatment includes NSAIDs, rehabilitation,

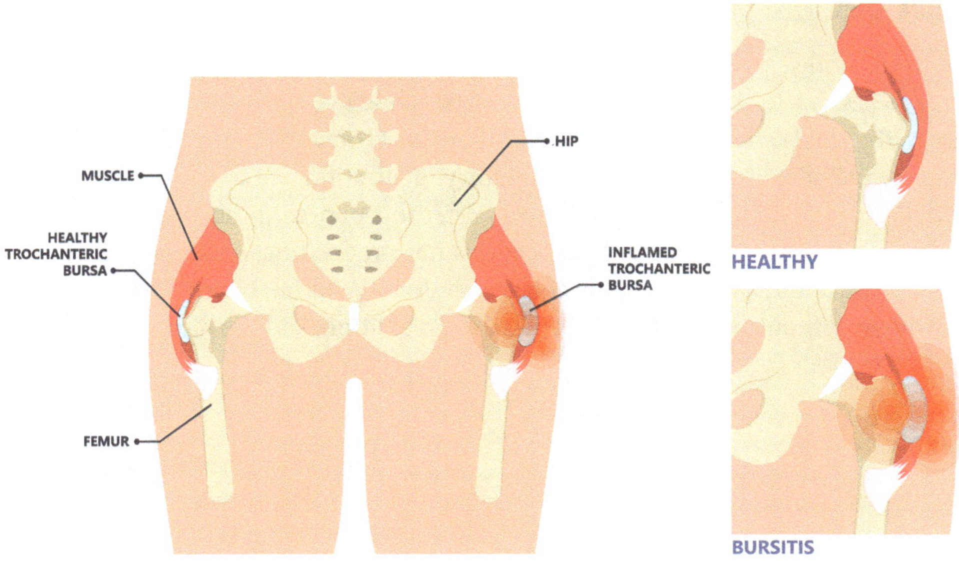

Figure 13-7 Trochanteric bursitis

and possibly corticosteroid injections. Surgery may be a possibility if the bursa needs to be drained or removed.

Prevention

Individuals must exercise, maintain a normal healthy weight, and maintain good posture when lifting or sitting in order to prevent hip bursitis.

Legg-Calvé-Perthes Disease

Legg-Calvé-Perthes disease occurs when the femoral head is deprived of blood. The bone becomes necrotic and breaks. This condition is mostly seen in children, especially toddler to pubescent biological males, and typically affects one hip.

Mechanism or Cause of Injury

The mechanism of injury for Legg-Calvé-Perthes disease is unknown. For undetermined reasons the head of the femur is deprived of blood and dies. This necrotic area of the femur is weak and becomes unstable. As a result, a piece of the femoral head fractures.

Signs and Symptoms

The child complains of hip pain, and/or pain that refers down into the groin and knee. The pain is most noticeable to the child when they are active. At rest the pain decreases or goes away entirely, until they participate in activity again. The child has stiffness, lack of ROM in the hip, and walks with a limp. Upon x-ray examination, the femoral head appears flattened (**Figure 13-8**).

Immediate Care

Speak with the child's parents or guardians and refer them to their physician for evaluation. X-rays are necessary to determine the extent of the child's condition. If the condition is detected early, the child can return to full function with good outcomes. The physician's treatment protocol may include prescribe anti-inflammatory medication, rehabilitation that focuses on hip ROM, crutches, and bracing to rest the hip. After this non-surgical approach is attempted, the child's condition is reevaluated. If the child is not progressing well, then surgery may be required to replace the femoral head in the acetabulum. With treatment, the child should be fully functional without signs and symptoms of the condition, and the femoral head healed in approximately 2 years.

Prevention

Legg-Calvé-Perthes disease cannot be prevented.

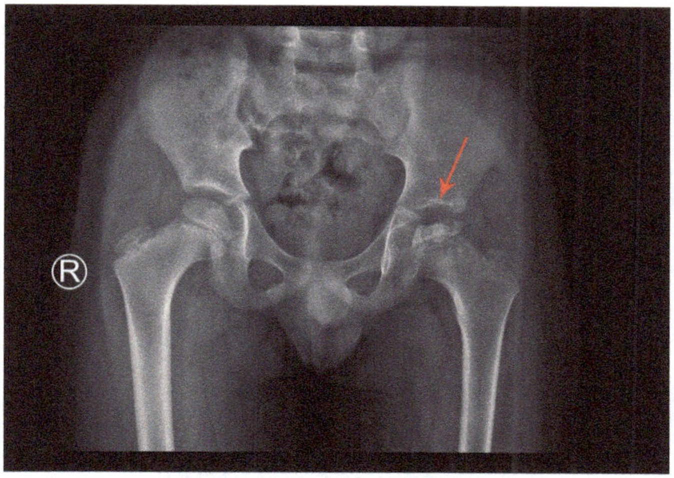

Figure 13-8 Legg-Calvé-Perthes disease of the left hip, showing the necrotic, flattened femoral head

Slipped Capital Femoral Epiphysis

A slipped capital femoral epiphysis (SCFE) is a more common condition of the hip that occurs in children, especially pubescent and adolescent biological males who are overweight for their height. The femoral head slips backwards out of the acetabulum **(Figure 13-9)**.

Mechanism or Cause of Injury

The cause of a slipped capital femoral epiphysis is unknown. The condition can occur slowly during a child's growth. The bone's growth plates are weak during puberty and adolescence, and they grow very fast during this time. As a result, the femoral head moves out of position from the acetabulum. SCFE can also result from acute trauma, such as when a child patient lands on or receives a direct blow to their hip.

Signs and Symptoms

The child experiences hip and knee pain. The pain increases when walking, which they do with difficulty and/or a limp. The child's hip feels stiff, and they may not be able to bear weight on the lower extremity. The affected leg appears shorter and turned outward.

Immediate Care

If you believe the child may have SCFE, refer them immediately to a physician. The condition must be treated within 24 to 48 hours for the best outcome. The physician will order x-rays to confirm the condition. Surgery is necessary to fixate the femoral head to secure it in the

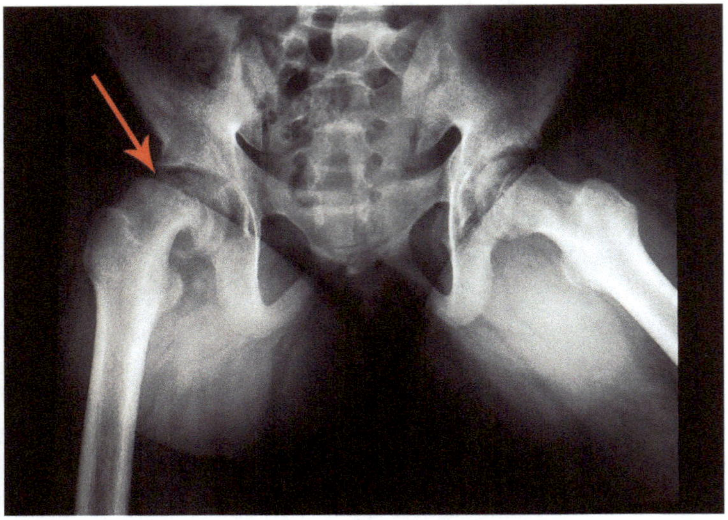

Figure 13-9 A slipped capital femoral epiphysis of the right femoral head (appears on left side of x-ray)

acetabulum. After surgery and hospitalization, the child is nonweightbearing on crutches for months. The child begins rehabilitation and weight bearing activities gradually. It may take up to 2 years for the child to return to normal athletic activities. When SCFE is treated immediately and properly, the child is able to heal, and their hip can regain normal function.

Prevention

SCFE is not preventable. Children must maintain a proper weight for their height to decrease the chance of acquiring SCFE.

Piriformis Syndrome

The piriformis is a muscle in the buttock area that attaches from the sacrum to the greater trochanter of the femur. The piriformis primarily functions to externally rotate the hip. The muscle is important in stabilizing the hip and maintaining balance when weight bearing. When the piriformis is inflamed, the sciatic nerve, which runs under and/or through the piriformis, is compressed by the muscle. Sciatic nerve pain results. This condition is called *sciatica* **(Figure 13-10)**.

Mechanism or Cause of Injury

The piriformis becomes inflamed or injured due to overuse. The piriformis is functional during any activity that involves walking, shifting weight from one extremity to another, or externally rotating the thighs. Therefore, these repetitive, continual motions cause piriformis

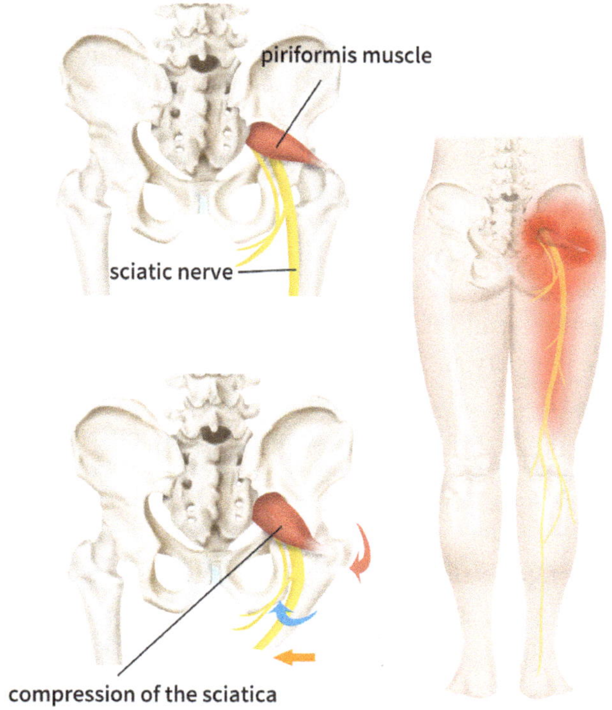

Figure 13-10 Piriformis syndrome and resultant sciatica

muscle inflammation, trigger points, tightness, and spasm. The sciatic nerve is affected secondarily to the muscular injury.

Signs and Symptoms

The patient most likely feels signs and symptoms of sciatic nerve pain before they note the signs and symptoms of piriformis injury. They feel loss of internal hip ROM, burning pain down the posterior thigh to the knee, pain in the buttocks and hamstring area, and tightness, stiffness, and point tenderness at the buttocks over the piriformis. Pain also occurs when the patient is in a seated position.

Immediate Care

The patient must treat the primary cause for the sciatic nerve pain, which is the piriformis inflammation. Have the patient rest from any activity that stresses the piriformis and irritates the sciatic nerve. The patient can take NSAIDs, and use ice and then heat after approximately 72 hours to relieve the pain and piriformis spasm. Various stretches and exercises to help the piriformis return to its normal state assists in alleviating the sciatica. If the signs and symptoms do not continually decrease after utilizing these treatments, then refer the individual to their physician. The physician may prescribe anti-inflammatory or muscle relaxant medication, as well as corticosteroid injections to decrease the signs and symptoms. Other beneficial treatment practices include use of therapeutic modalities, such as electrostimulation and ultrasound.

Prevention

Preventing piriformis syndrome and subsequent sciatic nerve pain begins with the individual gradually progressing the intensity and duration of their exercises. They should always maintain proper posture when sitting, lifting, and running. Flexibility exercises for the piriformis and surrounding muscles as well as hip ROM can help prevent piriformis syndrome.

Groin Strain

The groin muscles run along the medial thigh, and include the adductor longus, magnus, and brevis muscles, as well as the gracilis and pectineus **(Figure 13-11)**. These muscles are commonly injured in athletic activities, especially activities that require running and sudden changes in direction.

Mechanism or Cause of Injury

The groin muscles are injured when one or both of the legs are forced into abduction with or without lower extremity rotation. The foot may or may not be planted on the ground when the injury occurs. The sudden stretch to the groin tears the muscle fibers.

Signs and Symptoms

The signs and symptoms of a groin strain depend on whether the strain is a first-, second-, or third-degree. A groin strain causes significant pain and point tenderness on the inside of the thigh up to the pubis. The pain is increased as the individual contracts the muscles and actively moves the legs together (adduction), or when the legs are passively pulled apart (abduction), which stretches the muscles. The individual has loss of motion, ecchymosis, swelling, and all other signs and symptoms of injury that exist for any other strain.

Immediate Care

Groin strains typically heal with self-treatment including rest, ice, application of an elastic compression wrap, and anti-inflammatory medication. Fit the individual for crutches if weight bearing is painful. Once the muscles are in the fibroblastic repair phase of healing and signs and symptoms have decreased, have them begin gentle isometric followed by isotonic

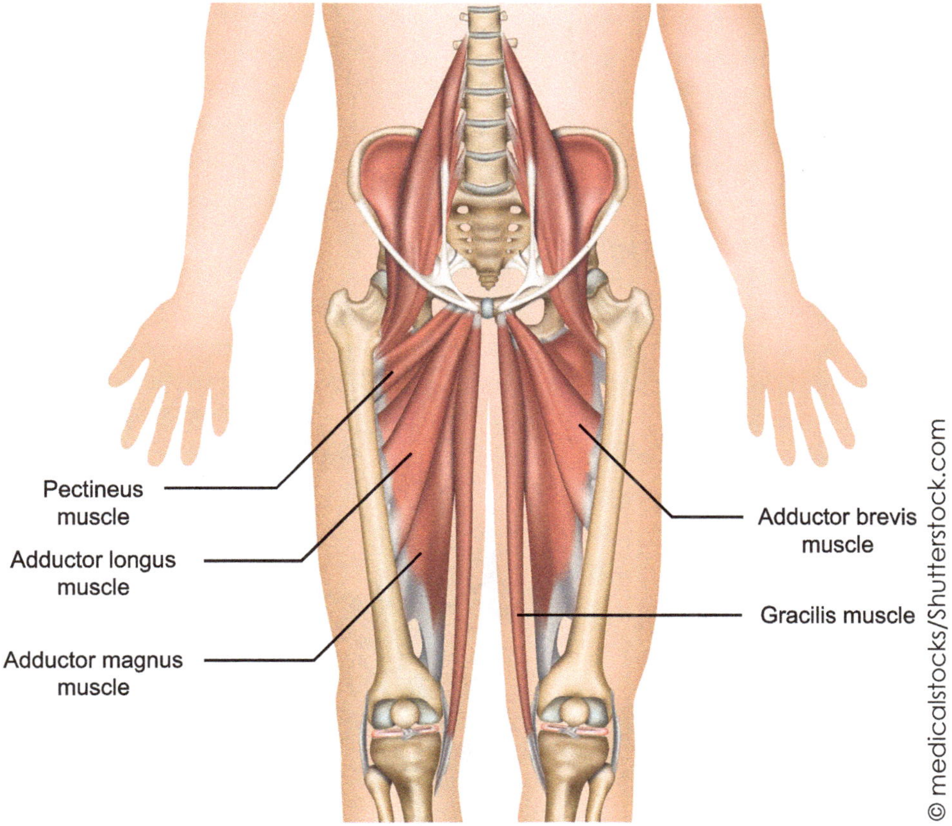

Figure 13-11 Groin muscles

strengthening exercises. The individual should see a physician if they cannot weight bear, have severe signs and symptoms of injury, or any complications arise.

Prevention

Individuals, especially those who are physically active, should have strong, flexible groin muscles in order to prevent groin strains. They should participate in a daily flexibility program for these muscles. Various agility and cutting exercises must be incorporated into regular workouts, so the muscles become accustomed to quick, forceful movements.

Quadriceps Strain

Quadriceps muscle strains most often occur to the rectus femoris muscle (Schultz, Houglum, & Perrin, 2016) (**Figure 13-12**).

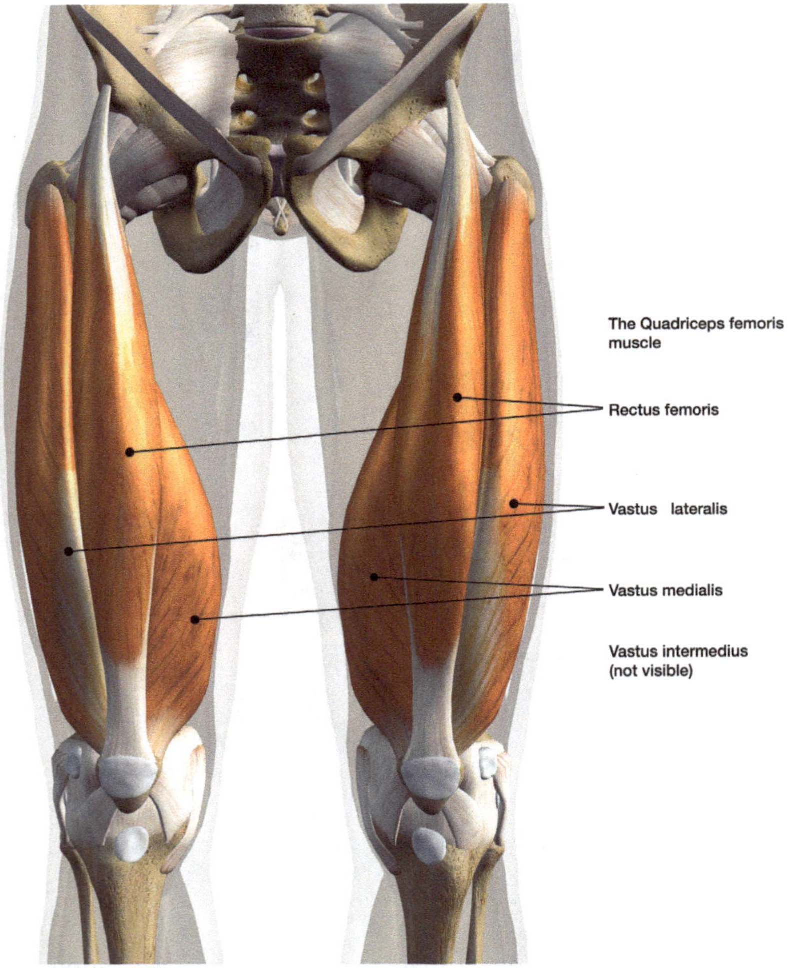

Figure 13-12 The rectus femoris is the mostly commonly strained quadriceps muscle.

Mechanism or Cause of Injury

Quadriceps strains occur when a person concentrically or eccentrically contracts the muscles during acceleration or deceleration, respectively. Running, sprinting, and jumping activities often cause quadriceps strains.

Signs and Symptoms

Depending on the degree of severity, they may have pain, muscle spasm, loss of function, and point tenderness. The pain increases when they attempt to contract the quadriceps by moving the knee into extension or the hip into flexion. The pain also increases when they passively move the knee into flexion and the hip into extension. The quadriceps may be swollen, and with a Grade 3 strain a bulge and/or divot may be present. Your client may also state that they felt a popping or snapping sensation at the muscle when the injury occurred. They may limp when walking to avoid pain.

Immediate Care

Have your client use RICE immediately to decrease the signs and symptoms of injury. If they cannot walk without a limp or are in pain, fit them for crutches to use until they are able to bear weight on the lower extremity normally. Anti-inflammatory medication assists in decreasing your client's pain and inflammation. After the signs and symptoms have subsided, they can begin ROM and strengthening exercises. Return to activity should be slow and as tolerated. Signs and symptoms of the muscle strain should not recur when your client returns to sport. If they do recur, then they have returned too soon and/or not progressed at an appropriate pace. If your client has a ruptured quadriceps muscle, then they should be evaluated by a physician to have diagnostic tests performed and to be certain that no secondary injury exists.

Prevention

To prevent quadriceps muscle strains, always have your client complete a proper warm-up and cool-down before participating in any athletic activity. Quadriceps muscle ROM, flexibility, and strengthening programs assist in minimizing potential injury. If they participate in lower extremity high intensity activities, lower extremity agility and coordination training is important to prevent injury.

Quadriceps Contusion

A quadriceps contusion can disable an individual and can keep them out of activity for a period of time.

Mechanism or Cause of Injury

As with any other contusion, a quadriceps contusion occurs from a direct blow by an object. This direct blow can occur from an object striking a person, such as a batted baseball, or the individual falling on a stationary object, such as a weight bench in the gym. If the muscle is contracted at the time of impact, the injury often is more severe than if the muscle was relaxed during impact.

Signs and Symptoms

Quadriceps contusions may produce signs and symptoms of pain, loss of motion (either when attempting to contract the muscle or passively stretching the muscle), point tenderness, spasm, increase in temperature, and ecchymosis **(Figure 13-13)**.

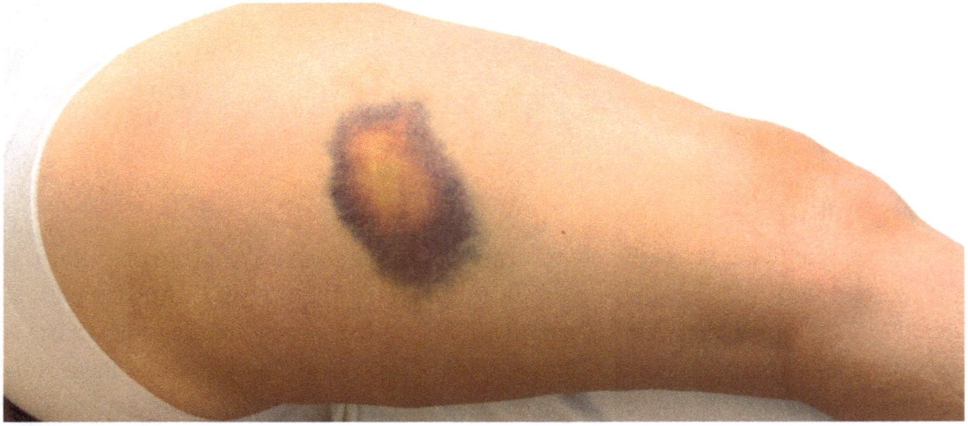

Figure 13-13 Ecchymosis is a prominent sign of a quadriceps injury.

Immediate Care

RICE is used to treat the contusion, along with NSAIDs to decrease pain and inflammation. An ice pack must be applied to the contused muscle with the knee in some degree of flexion as tolerated without pain by the individual. This position allows the muscles to slowly lengthen. This lengthening assists in increasing ROM and flexibility; however, aggressive ROM and flexibility exercises are not warranted until signs and symptoms of injury notably subside. Also, massage is **contraindicated** for quadriceps contusions in the early stages of healing because massage techniques may promote myositis ossificans (which is discussed in the next section). While the individual's muscle is healing, they should wear an elastic compression wrap around the contused muscles. The compression bandage can also hold on padding to cover and further protect the area.

Prevention

Athletic participants must wear appropriate sports protective equipment and padding as required for the activity, especially if they participate in contact or collision sports. The stronger the quadriceps muscle is the greater possibility that the muscle will not be severely injured by a direct blow. Therefore, participation in a quadriceps conditioning program, as noted for the prevention of quadriceps strains, is crucial in preventing injuries to these muscles.

Myositis Ossificans

Myositis ossificans is an **ectopic** bony growth that occurs in muscle groups particularly the quadriceps and biceps brachii. Myositis ossificans arises in approximately 9 to 17% of quadriceps contusions and strains that have significant hematomas (Saad et al., 2021). An individual

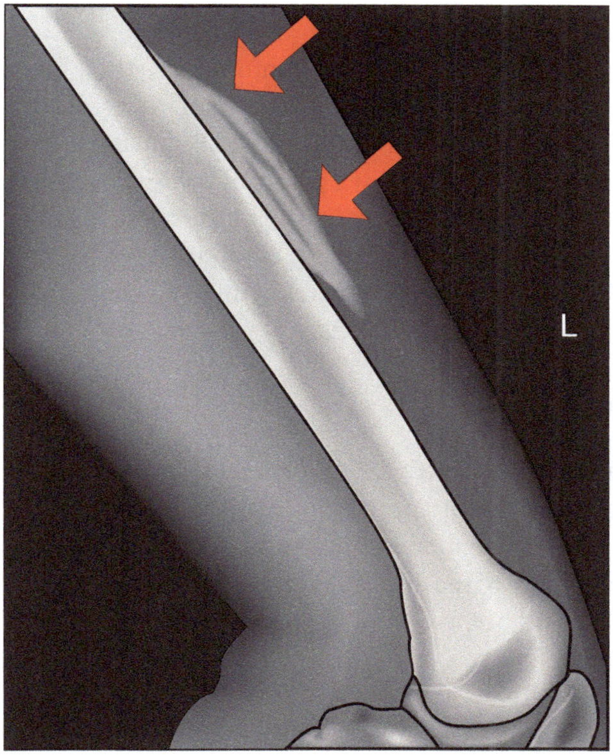

Figure 13-14 Myositis ossificans in the quadriceps muscle

who has previously sustained a quadriceps contusion and sustains another contusion at the same muscle is at risk to develop myositis ossificans within that muscle (Saad et al., 2021).

Mechanism or Cause of Injury

Myositis ossificans has no definitive cause; rather, the condition is a complication of a muscle contusion or strain. Trauma causes a hematoma within the muscle, which resorbs. As a result, bony deposits form within the muscle **(Figure 13-14)**. Myositis ossificans has also developed when heat, massage, and aggressive stretching have been utilized too soon after a muscle contusion or strain has occurred.

Signs and Symptoms

If a muscle contusion or strain does not readily heal with conservative treatment, and pain, loss of function, and other signs and symptoms of injury increase, suspect that the individual has myositis ossificans. Myositis ossificans causes pain upon motion that notably decreases when the knee is flexed. The bony formation may be palpated, depending on its size.

Immediate Care

Whether the individual has sustained a muscle contusion or strain that resulted in myositis ossificans, they should continue to treat the primary injury conservatively. These treatment techniques also treat myositis ossificans. By utilizing RICE, and increasing ROM and strength with rehabilitative exercises, the signs and symptoms of myositis ossificans can be controlled. Once the ectopic bone has been formed, it remains in the soft tissue unless it is surgically removed. Surgical removal of the ectopic bone is an option if conservative therapies do not promote healing and decrease signs and symptoms of injury. If conservative treatments do not work, then refer the individual to their physician.

Prevention

Myositis ossificans cannot be prevented since the mechanism of injury is not definitive; however, muscle strengthening is important to minimize the extent of injury if a contusion or strain occurs. Protective equipment and padding worn during contact sports can dissipate force when a direct blow occurs to the muscle. Heat, aggressive stretching, and massage should only be used in the fibroblastic repair phase of healing, when signs and symptoms of injury have noticeably decreased.

Hamstring Strain

Hamstring strains are more common than quadriceps strains (Schultz, Houglum, & Perrin, 2016), and can occur at any point within the semitendinosus, semimembranosus, or biceps femoris muscles.

Mechanism or Cause of Injury

Hamstring strains occur most often when the muscle is concentrically or eccentrically contracted during activity. For example, the muscle can be strained when a sprinter pushes off the blocks at the start of an event, or as they decelerate at the finish line. The quadriceps muscle group is stronger than the hamstring muscle group; however, if the quadriceps group exceeds the normal strength as compared to hamstrings, then a muscular imbalance occurs between the two groups. Consequently, when the quadriceps muscles contract, they can cause a forceful pull on the hamstrings and result in a strain. Also, high velocity activities, such as running and jumping, and activities that require sudden stops and starts, such as in basketball, can predispose a patient to hamstring strains. An individual who has inflexible hamstrings or a prior hamstring strain is also at risk for subsequent strains.

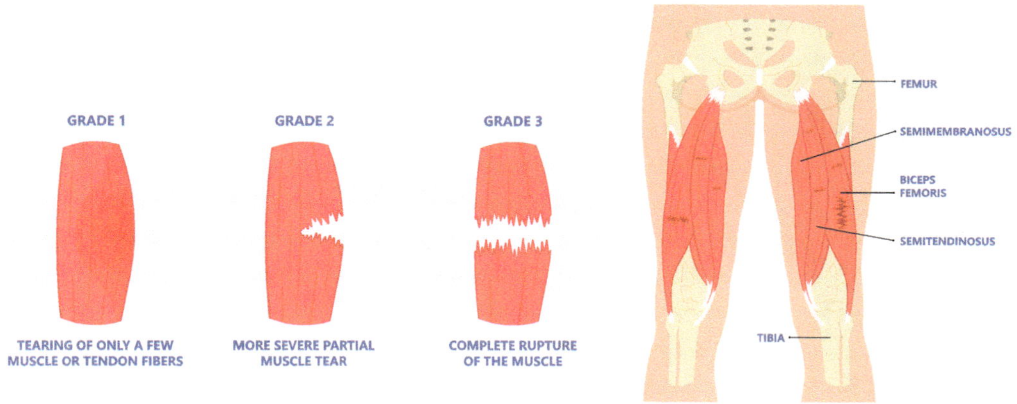

Figure 13-15 Three grades of hamstring strains

Signs and Symptoms

Signs and symptoms of a hamstring strain are similar to signs and symptoms of a quadriceps strain. The athlete may feel a snap or pop at the time of injury along with immediate severe pain. A defect, a bump, or a divot exists within the muscle at the site of the injury especially with a grade 3 strain **(Figure 13-15)**. Swelling, ecchymosis, point tenderness, and loss of ROM and strength also are evident. The athlete may not be able to ambulate normally or without pain.

Immediate Care

The individual can use RICE to treat their injury. They may need to use crutches at first in order to rest their leg. Crutches are also necessary if they cannot bear weight without limping. Anti-inflammatory medication can be helpful to decrease signs and symptoms of inflammation. Surgery typically is not utilized as an option unless an avulsion exists. The individual should see their physician if they cannot bear weight, have unusual or loss of sensation down their leg, are in debilitating pain, or are unsure of the extent of the injury.

Prevention

Hamstring strength is important to prevent hamstring strains. The hamstrings should be approximately 40% of the quadriceps group strength, otherwise a muscular imbalance exists. Hamstring strengthening should incorporate eccentric exercises that help the muscle decelerate properly. This type of training can assist in minimizing or avoiding injury. The hamstrings should have adequate flexibility in order to lengthen during activity.

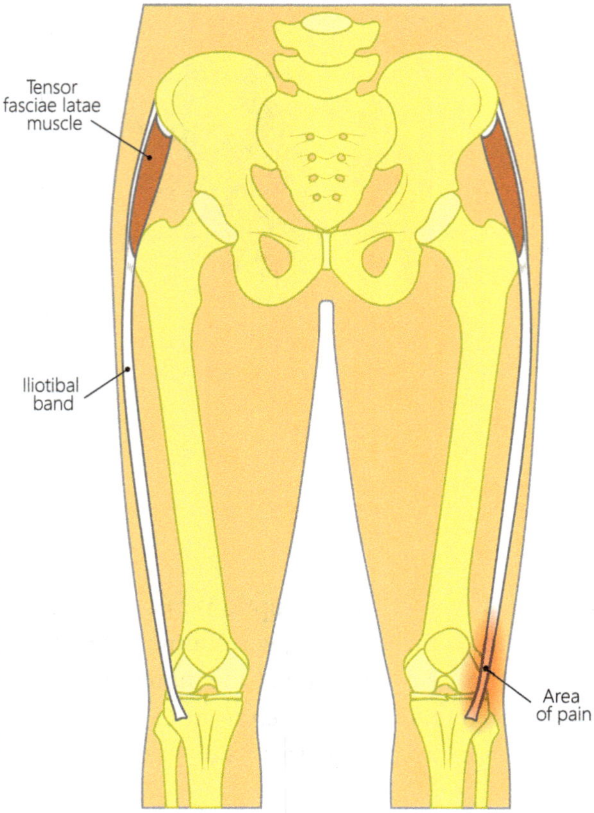

Figure 13-16 ITB syndrome causes pain at the lateral knee

Iliotibial Band Syndrome

Iliotibial band (ITB) syndrome describes an overuse, chronic ITB inflammation.

Mechanism or Cause of Injury

Repetitive, constant friction of the ITB over the lateral femoral condyle causes ITB syndrome **(Figure 13-16)**. Sometimes the ITB can become inflamed over the greater tuberosity of the femur. This friction occurs with activities which require a person's knee to repetitively move from flexion to extension, such as in long distance running and cycling. ITB inflexibility and abnormal gait promotes ITB syndrome.

Signs and Symptoms

The athlete may feel pain and a popping sensation or sound that occurs over the lateral femoral condyle or greater trochanter. This sensation happens during activities that require continual hip and knee flexion and extension. The ITB may feel tight, rigid, and point tender upon palpation. The tighter the ITB, the greater potential for friction and inflammation.

Immediate Care

ITB syndrome treatment includes rest, heat, and stretching prior to exercise, and an ice pack or ice massage after exercise. Heat can be utilized safely and effectively since ITB syndrome is a chronic condition. However, if any acute signs of inflammation arise, have the athlete use ice before and after exercise. The exercises should focus on ITB and surrounding muscle stretching and strengthening. Utilizing massage on the area can help decrease band tightness. NSAIDs can decrease inflammation. If conservative treatment is not effective to restore the athlete's full, pain-free function, then refer them to their physician. The physician may inject the inflamed site with corticosteroids, and prescribe additional rehabilitation.

TIPS FROM THE FIELD

Tip 1 Properly fitting athletic shoes (sneakers, cleats, etc.) help your client avoid many lower extremity injuries. When your client is shopping for new athletic shoes, give them advice on how to choose athletic shoes. Tell them that they should expect to pay a moderate amount for quality athletic shoes. Inexpensive athletic shoes may not have the materials and construction necessary to provide proper cushioning and adequate arch support. On the other hand, expensive shoes are often expensive due to brand or athlete endorsement. Expensive shoes may not have better quality construction than moderately priced shoes.

The individual should try on new shoes with the exact socks that they will wear during the intended activity, and should try on the shoes in the afternoon or end of the day. At these times, their feet are at their largest size due to weight bearing during the day. A shoe specialist at the store should measure the individual's foot each time they purchase a new pair of athletic shoes. Individuals who gain or lose weight, children who are still growing, and aging individuals will have shoe sizes that may vary frequently. The shoe's toe box must be large enough so all toes fit next to each other comfortably and are mobile. The front of the toe box should be about one-half inch from the front of the great toe. The heel counter should come high enough above the calcaneus and the Achilles' tendon to be supportive, but not to cause friction when walking or running. The shoes should be laced up by using equal tension from the toes to the talus. After the shoe is laced, the foot should feel secure in the shoe.

When the shoes are properly laced, the individual can determine right away if the shoe is comfortable while sitting, standing, and walking in the store. If the shoes are comfortable in the store, then they do not need a breaking in period. The individual can wear them for exercise immediately. Certain athletic shoes that have special features, such as gel inserts, mesh material to allow for better air circulation, or lightweight construction, may be valuable for your client depending on if they have any present foot conditions. Athletic shoes should be replaced whenever the materials become worn, especially on the sole of the foot, or when they no longer feel comfortable or supportive.

Prevention

Athletic participants should wear properly fitted shoes designed for their activity in order to prevent ITB syndrome. Also, participation in a daily ITB flexibility program, as well as ITB stretching before and after exercise, should be included in an individual's prevention measures.

The Knee and Patella

The knee joint is made up of the articulation between the femur and the tibia. The patellofemoral joint is made up of the articulation between the posterior patella and the femur. The patella is the largest **sesamoid bone** in the body. Various, disabling injuries occur to both the knee and patella.

Knee Dislocation

A knee dislocation occurs when the femur or tibia are displaced **(Figure 13-17)**. These dislocations are very rare, especially in athletic activities. When knee dislocations occur, other secondary injuries occur to the soft and bony tissues.

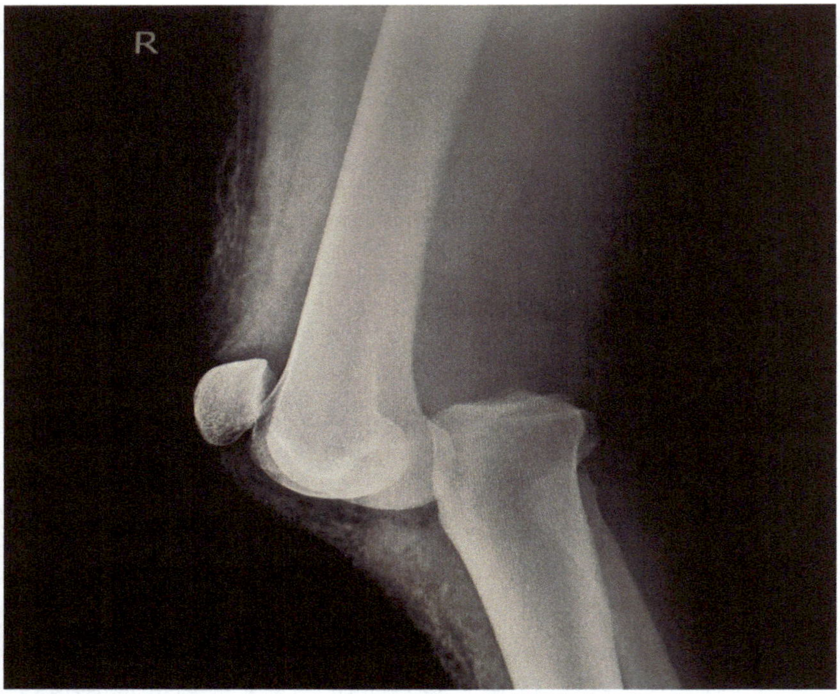

Figure 13-17 A lateral X-ray of a knee dislocation

Mechanism or Cause of Injury

Direct trauma causes a knee dislocation. An excessive amount of force is needed to separate the femur and tibia from each other. This direct trauma can occur in falls, motor vehicle accidents, and high-intensity collision athletic activities.

Signs and Symptoms

The individual exhibits shock. They may be on the ground, perhaps grabbing their knee in excruciating pain. They may state that they cannot feel their lower leg and circulation may be compromised. The knee appears severely deformed.

Immediate Care

A knee dislocation is a medical emergency. Call 911 immediately and treat the individual for shock. Stabilize the lower extremity and splint the knee as you find it without moving the lower extremity. Place an ice pack on the knee to assist in decreasing pain. Monitor the individual until EMS arrives. The physician will take x-rays, determine if any secondary injury exists such as a fracture, and relocate the knee at the hospital. Depending on the findings, the individual may need surgery to repair the tissues around the knee. The individual will participate in months of rehabilitation in order to regain full knee function.

Prevention

Knee dislocations are not entirely preventable since individuals are not able to avoid all high intensity direct trauma. Individuals must participate in strengthening exercises for the muscles surrounding the knee, while maintaining flexibility and ROM around the joint.

Anterior Cruciate Ligament Sprain

The anterior cruciate ligament (ACL) is within the knee joint. The ACL attaches the tibia to the femur and is tightest in full knee extension. The ligament limits anterior movement of the tibia on the femur, and knee rotation. More biological females have ACL injuries than biological males. A Grade 3 ACL sprain is called a *ruptured ACL* **(Figure 13-18)**. The ACL is one of the most commonly ruptured ligaments in the body. ACL ruptures most commonly occur during competition in noncontact sports. ACL injuries often occur along with medial collateral ligament (MCL) and medial meniscus injuries. These three structures have similar mechanisms of injury. Likewise, some fibers of the medial meniscus are attached to the MCL. When all three structures are injured simultaneously, the injury is referred to as an *unhappy triad* injury.

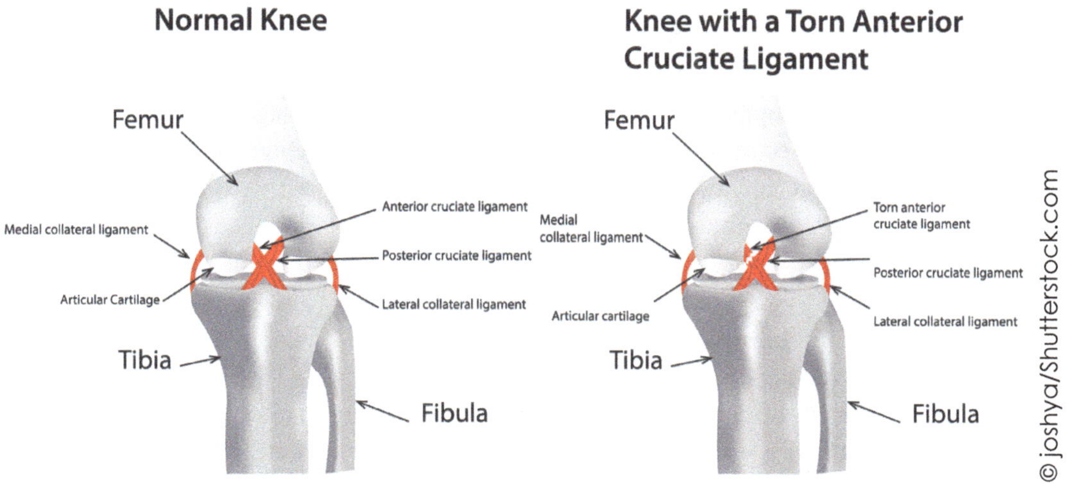

Figure 13-18 A torn anterior cruciate ligament

Mechanism or Cause of Injury

An ACL sprain can occur from noncontact or contact activities. A noncontact ACL sprain typically occurs when a person is in a weight bearing position with their foot planted on the ground. The person then cuts, twists, or changes direction of her body quickly and suddenly. These motions force the knee in a valgus position in almost full knee extension, and as a result the ligament ruptures. The person can also fall or land from a height on the foot and sprain the ACL. Contact ACL sprains occur during events in which the person's lower leg is hit by another person in events such as football, rugby, and ice hockey.

Biological females tend to have a higher incidence of ACL ruptures than biological men due to a variety of factors. Many biological females have a strength imbalance between the quadriceps and hamstrings muscles. Also hormones, tibial attachment, lower extremity anatomy, and landing biomechanics all predispose biological females to ACL injuries as compared to biological males.

Signs and Symptoms

Signs and symptoms vary depending on whether the ACL is stretched (Grade 1 or 2 sprain) or completely ruptured (Grade 3). At the time of injury, the individual hears an audible "pop", which indicates the ligament rupture. They feel immediate, severe pain and joint instability when attempting to weight bear on the leg. Consequently, they may not be able to weight bear due to pain. Swelling and edema may continue to increase hours after the injury.

Immediate Care

After the individual has sustained an ACL rupture, their pain will be unbearable, and they may be anxious. Calm them down and console them. Immediately utilize RICE to treat the injury. Have the individual lie down on their back. Wet an elastic wrap with cold water, wring it out and apply it to the knee to provide compression. Apply ice packs with an elastic wrap on all sides of the knee. While supporting the knee, have them elevate the leg onto pillows, blankets, or other comfortable objects, so the leg is higher than their heart. Once the individual is calm and treated, fit them for crutches and stabilize the lower extremity with an immobilizing brace. Although an ACL sprain is not a medical emergency, the individual needs to see a physician for evaluation shortly after the injury is sustained. If the individual is in extraordinary, severe pain that causes them to go into shock, treat them appropriately and phone 911. Also, if you do not have knee immobilizing materials or crutches readily available, then summon EMS immediately to provide the individual additional care.

ACL ruptures are most often surgically repaired. If the individual wishes to be active and/or participates in competitive activities that involve running, cutting, and jumping, then surgery is imperative to repair the ligament and restore joint function. A variety of surgical procedures are utilized. The physician will discuss the repair options with their patient, which

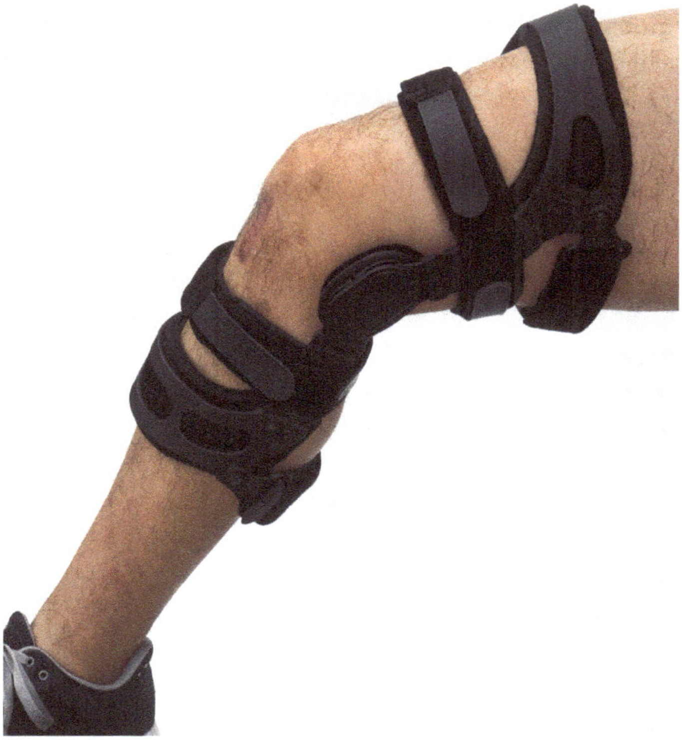

Figure 13-19 A patient may need to wear a custom brace when participating in activity after ACL surgery.

include replacing the ruptured ligament with a portion of the patient's hamstring tendon or patellar tendon, or donor (typically cadaver) tissue. Whether or not the patient decides to have the ligament surgically repaired, the patient partakes in a rigorous rehabilitation program to regain ROM, strength (especially hamstring strength), balance, agility, and the like. The physician may prescribe a custom, functional brace to assist in supporting the patient's knee during activities **(Figure 13-19)**. A gradual progression in activities assists the patient in returning to activity safely.

Prevention

Prevention of ACL sprains, especially in biological females, includes proper nutrition to reduce muscular fatigue, proper calcium intake to keep bones strong, and adequate sleep to promote mental alertness. Individuals should not abuse alcohol, which has a potential neuromuscular contribution to promote ACL sprains. Controlling stress, overtraining, and burnout are also crucial to prevent ACL sprains (Forcada et al., 2017). Other factors to prevent ACL sprains include proper quadriceps to hamstring strength ratio (3:2), core and lower extremity strength and conditioning programs, balance and neuromuscular training, agility exercises, and proper landing techniques and skill performance. The individual must also wear properly fitted shoes appropriate for the sport and playing surface.

Posterior Cruciate Ligament Sprain

The posterior cruciate ligament (PCL) crosses the ACL in the knee joint, making an *X* appearance with the ACL. The PCL also attaches from the femur to the tibia, but unlike the ACL, the PCL is tight in knee flexion. The PCL functions to control posterior tibial movement on the femur, as well as valgus and varus forces (Raj, Mabrouk & Varacallo, 2020). Biological males are more likely to injure their PCL than biological females.

Mechanism or Cause of Injury

The PCL is injured by a direct force to the anterior tibia while the knee is in approximately 90-degree knee flexion. PCL sprains most often occur in high-velocity events, such as in car accidents when the anterior tibia strikes the dashboard. The PCL can also be injured in low-velocity events. An individual can fall or be hit by an object at the anterior tibia while the knee is in flexion, which causes a PCL sprain. As an example, a football player can land on a flexed knee with the ankle in plantarflexion, and a PCL injury can result. The PCL can also be injured by a direct blow to the knee while in hyperextension (Bernhardson et al., 2019).

Signs and Symptoms

Severity of injury dictates the extent of signs and symptoms after a PCL sprain. The patient may hear a pop at the time of injury and feel severe pain if they have sustained a Grade 3 PCL rupture **(Figure 13-20)**. Swelling appears and the individual is point tender in the popliteal area. The individual has immediate loss of ROM. Knee joint instability may not be present if they have strong quadriceps muscles, which keep the tibia in a normal position while walking.

Immediate Care

Treat the individual as if they have an ACL sprain, and refer them to their physician for further evaluation and imaging. PCL ruptures are not often surgically repaired. Surgery may be an option if an avulsion or other soft tissue structures (i.e., other ligaments, meniscus, and muscle) are severely injured along with the PCL. Conservative therapy is the

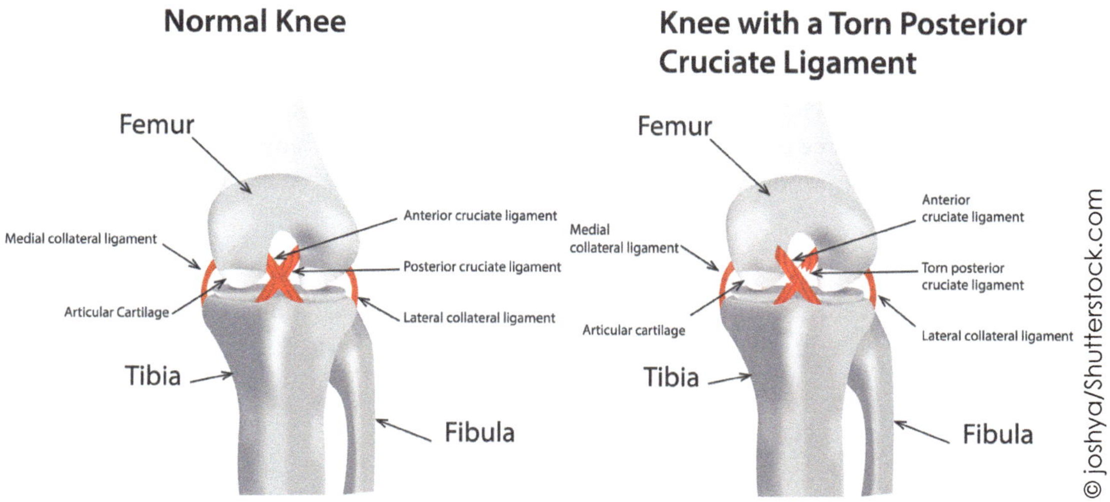

Figure 13-20 A torn posterior cruciate ligament

treatment of choice. Knee immobilization in extension for a few weeks with RICE, anti-inflammatory medication, and rehabilitation that focuses on quadriceps strengthening is prescribed. Quadriceps strengthening keeps the tibia in a normal position relative to the femur. A gradual return to activity can resume after the patient has rehabilitated the knee and lower extremity enough to have unrestricted ROM, adequate strength, flexibility, coordination, and agility.

Prevention

By having adequate quadriceps and hamstring strength and flexibility, avoiding falls on a flexed knee, and wearing protective knee equipment during contact activities an individual can attempt to prevent PCL sprains.

Collateral Ligament Sprains

The knee has two collateral ligaments on each side of the joint. The medial collateral ligament (MCL) attaches from the femur to the tibia on the inside of the knee. The deep fibers of the MCL also attach to the medial meniscus. Consequently, at times due to their anatomical attachment, both the MCL and medial meniscus are simultaneously injured. The lateral collateral ligament (LCL) attaches from the femur to the fibular head on the lateral knee. The MCL and LCL assist in limiting knee rotation and extension. The MCL limits valgus stress, while the LCL limits varus stress on the knee. The MCL is more often injured than the LCL, and the LCL is not as commonly injured as other knee ligaments.

Mechanism or Cause of Injury

The MCL is injured by a valgus force to the knee while the foot is planted, or a direct blow to the lateral side of the knee that forces the joint into a valgus position **(Figure 13-21)**. The LCL is injured by a varus force to the knee while the foot is planted, or a blow to the medial side of the knee which forces the joint into a varus position **(Figure 13-22)**.

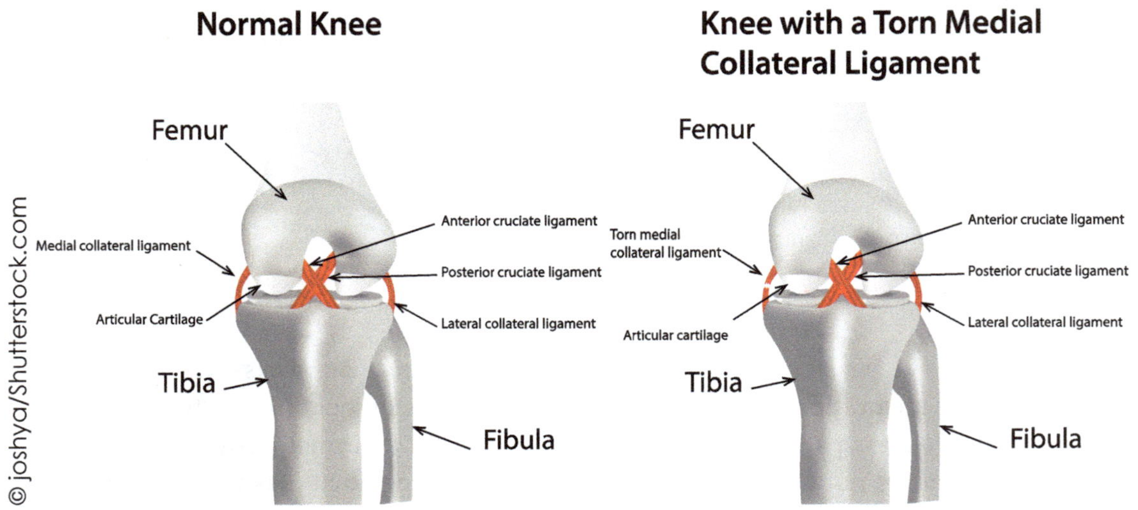

Figure 13-21 A torn medial collateral ligament

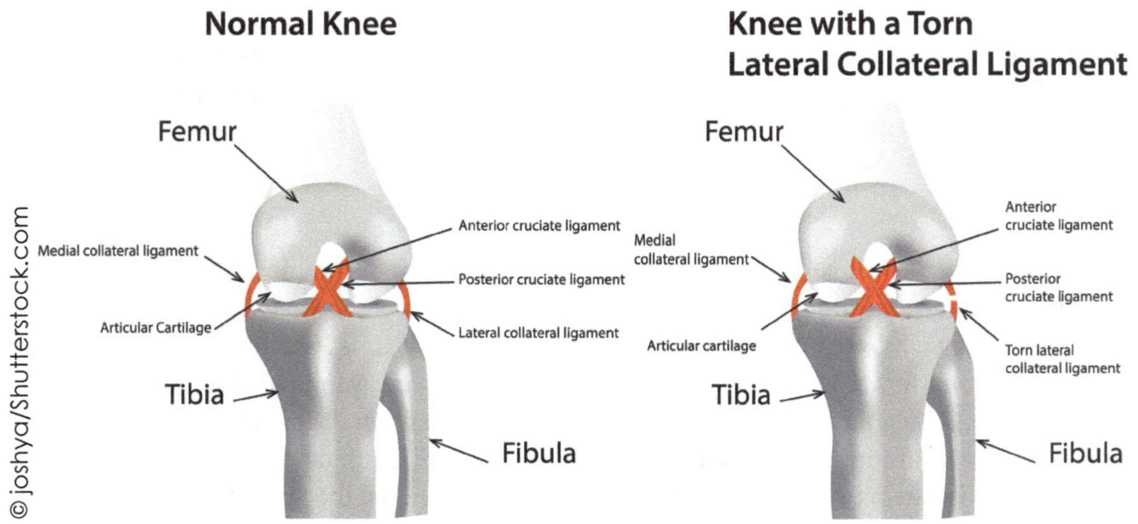

Figure 13-22 A torn lateral collateral ligament

Signs and Symptoms

With both MCL and LCL injuries, the athlete may feel pain and point tenderness at the site. Swelling and ecchymosis may be present. The athlete may complain that they feel the tibia shifting or sliding when they walk which indicates joint instability.

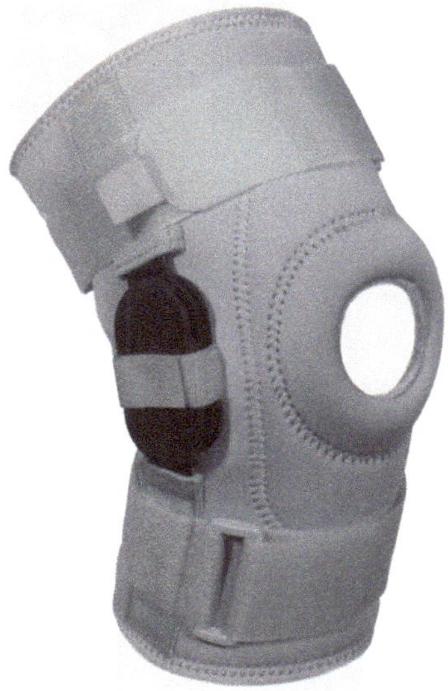

© Med_Ved/Shutterstock.com

Figure 13-23 After a collateral ligament injury, the athlete may need to wear a brace with medial or lateral support for the injured ligament.

Immediate Care

Immediate collateral ligament treatment is the same as for an ACL sprain. Likewise, as with PCL ruptures, MCL and LCL ruptures do not often require surgery. These injuries can be effectively treated with RICE, anti-inflammatories, bracing **(Figure 13-23)**, and rehabilitation with a focus on strengthening the musculature on the respective side of the knee where the collateral ligament was injured.

Prevention

MCL and LCL sprains can be prevented by having strong musculature around the entire knee. Proper strengthening and flexibility of the lateral and medial musculature is important to avoid injury due to varus and valgus forces. Athletic participants should wear protective knee equipment as required by the activity, and perform skills properly.

Meniscal Injury

The medial and lateral menisci are located on the tibial plateaus within the knee joint. They act as shock absorbers for the knee, stabilize and deepen the joint surface, and promote appropriate weight distribution when weight bearing. The menisci are one of the most common injured knee structures. Meniscal tears often occur with other knee injuries such as ACL and MCL sprains, due to similarities in mechanism of injury. The MCL is attached to the medial meniscus; therefore, simultaneous injuries can occur. The meniscus can tear at its periphery or within its body (the horn) **(Figure 13-24)**.

Mechanism or Cause of Injury

The medial and lateral menisci are injured when the knee is in some degree of flexion and then rotates while the lower extremity is weight bearing. As the knee approaches greater degrees of flexion, the femoral condyles sit on the meniscus. With tibial or femoral rotation, the femoral

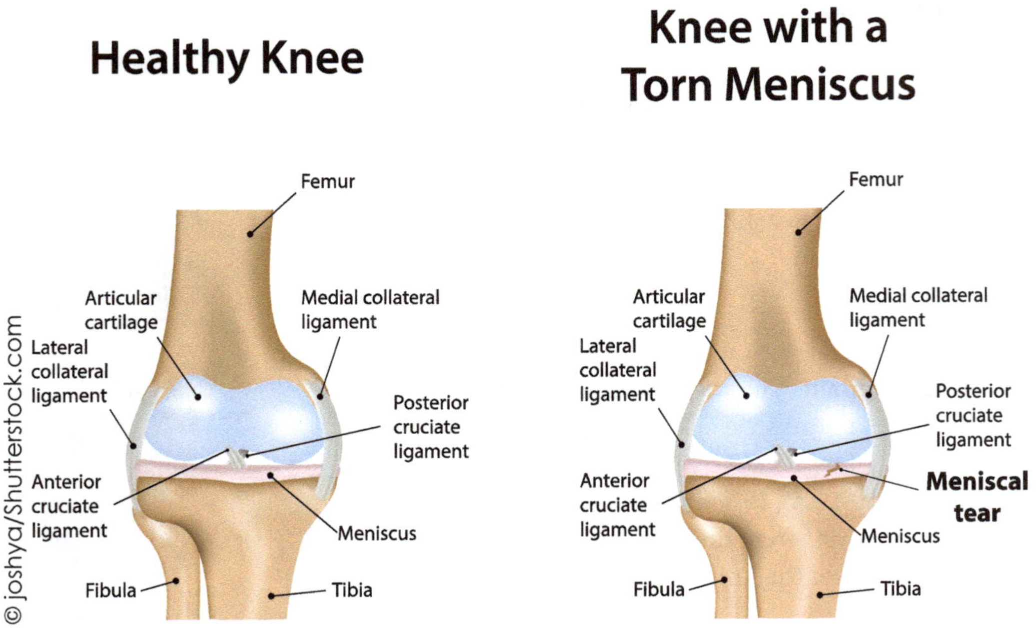

Figure 13-24 A peripheral medial meniscal tear

condyles grind on the meniscus and cause a tear. The individual can also receive a direct blow to the knee, which can cause meniscal injury. As people get older their menisci become weak and thin. Consequently, knee flexion activities that are not seemingly traumatic, such as continual rising from and sitting in a chair, can tear the menisci. In these situations, a mechanism of injury may not be evident.

Signs and Symptoms

Meniscal injuries can produce varying degrees of signs and symptoms. The signs and symptoms may be very mild, and the individual may not even realize they have sustained a meniscal injury. On the other hand, some meniscal injuries are severe which cause significant disability. A meniscal tear produces pain and a feeling of catching or locking within the knee joint. The individual may say that the knee feels like it is stuck in knee flexion. The knee joint line may be swollen and is often point tender. The individual may not be able to move the knee through its full ROM.

Immediate Care

An individual with a meniscal tear who is experiencing minor signs and symptoms of injury requires rest from knee flexion activities, including activities of daily living (ADLs) such as climbing up and down stairs. Have them apply ice packs intermittently as needed, wear an elastic compression bandage, and elevate the leg. The individual may need crutches if they cannot weight bear or walk without a limp. Although a minor meniscal injury is not a medical emergency, the individual should go to their physician to be evaluated. If the individual's tear is a minor peripheral tear and does not prevent knee function, then ROM and strengthening exercises can assist to rehabilitate the area. If the individual's knee is immovable or they are in significant pain, have them rest in a **long sitting position**, splint the knee, apply ice, and call EMS. The physician in the emergency room (ER) will evaluate the patient by performing an examination, x-rays, and/or a magnetic resonance imaging (MRI) scan.

Regardless of the type of tear, the individual may need arthroscopic surgery to repair the meniscus if the tear is creating pain or loss of function. Arthroscopic surgery is utilized to visualize the inside of a joint, such as the knee, and perform procedures within the joint to repair injured structures. The physician utilizes a camera (arthroscope) placed inside the joint that projects onto a monitor so the physician can see the inside of the joint. Other tools are also inserted into the joint in order for the physician to repair and irrigate the joint during surgery. Quadriceps and surrounding muscles that are damaged and weakened due to the surgical procedure itself must be strengthened during rehabilitation. Return to activity depends on the extent of the meniscal injury, whether or not surgery is performed, and success of rehabilitation.

Prevention

Avoiding deep knee flexion and rotation activities are beneficial in preventing these injuries; however, meniscal injuries due to tissue degeneration are difficult to prevent.

Patellar Fracture

Patellar fractures can create significant disability for an individual. When the patella is fractured, breaks occur in one or more places **(Figure 13-25)**. Because correct patellar alignment and movement are imperative for proper ambulation, a fractured patella causes improper ambulation.

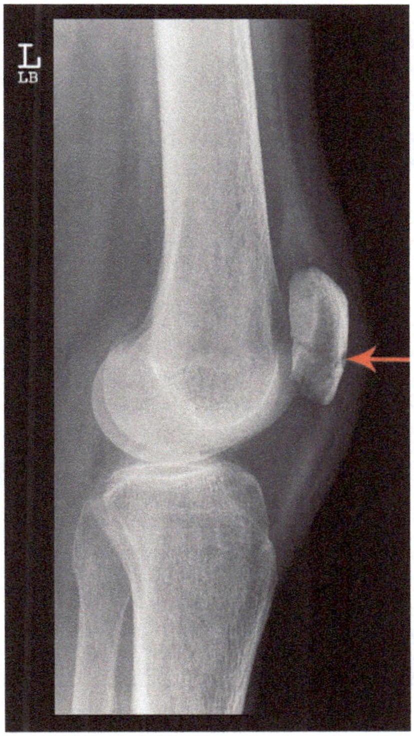

Figure 13-25 A lateral view x-ray of a patellar fracture

Mechanism or Cause of Injury

The patella can be fractured by a direct blow to the bone. An object hits or an individual falls on the patella and fractures the bone. The quadriceps can also contract forcefully enough to pull on the superior pole of the patella and cause it to fracture.

Signs and Symptoms

The individual has immediate pain, which increases if they attempt to contract the quadriceps and move the knee into extension. The knee appears in flexion, and they cannot extend the knee. Swelling, deformity, ecchymosis, and point tenderness exists.

Immediate Care

If your client has a patellar fracture, splint the leg in the position that you find it, apply an ice pack on the area, and treat them for shock. Your client needs immediate medical evaluation, so call 911. The physician will take x-rays to determine the extent of the fracture, including the type of fracture, and whether it is nondisplaced or displaced. Nondisplaced patellar fractures can be treated by splinting or casting the leg in extension, which allows the bone to heal. The individual will utilize crutches and is immobilized for a couple of months, at which time they are allowed to bear weight on the leg. Displaced fractures usually require surgery in order to approximate the patella pieces to promote proper healing **(Figure 13-26)**. Regardless whether or not surgery is needed, rehabilitation after the patella has healed includes partial to full weight bearing as tolerated, ROM exercises, and quadriceps muscles strengthening and stretching.

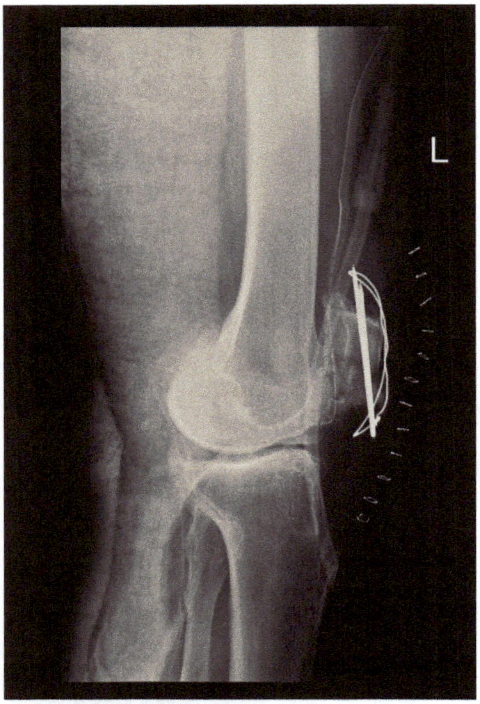

Figure 13-26 A surgically repaired fractured patella

Prevention

Patellar fractures can be prevented by wearing protective knee equipment during contact activities. Stretching and developing good quadriceps muscles neuromuscular control, along with avoidance of extreme, forceful knee flexion assists in avoiding patellar fractures.

Patellar Dislocations and Subluxations

The patella is a commonly dislocated or subluxed bone. It commonly dislocates and subluxes laterally from the femoral groove **(Figure 13-27)**.

Mechanism or Cause of Injury

Patellar dislocations and subluxations often occur due to an imbalance between the stronger vastus lateralis muscle and the weaker vastus medialis muscle of the quadriceps group. This imbalance causes the vastus lateralis pull, or track, the patella

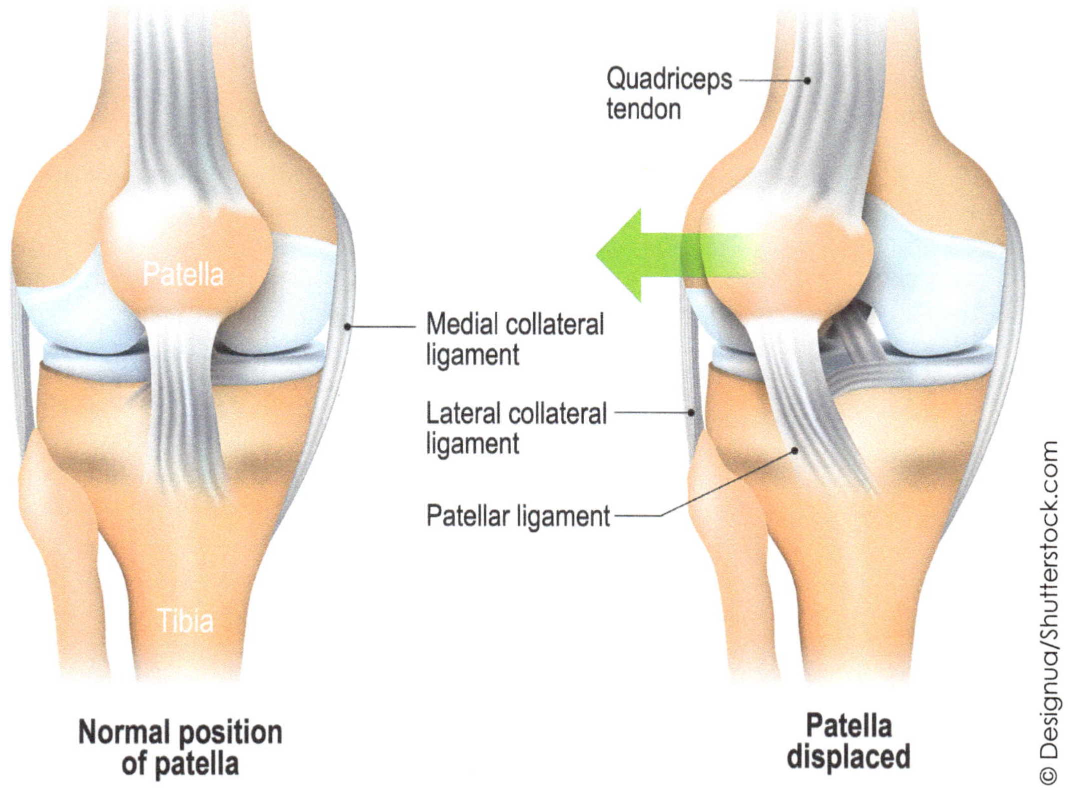

Figure 13-27 The patella usually dislocates laterally.

laterally during motion. Biological females are more prone to patellar subluxations due to their greater **Q-angle** than biological males **(Figure 13-28)**. The patella can then sublux when the athlete is running or performing other lower extremity movement activities, especially when the athlete changes direction suddenly. A direct blow to the medial patella can also causes a dislocation.

Signs and Symptoms

An athlete who has sustained a patellar dislocation or subluxation has pain, which is more severe with a dislocation. The dislocation appears deformed since the patella is out of normal alignment with the femur. Swelling and point tenderness exists. With a dislocation, the athlete cannot move the knee joint. With a subluxation, the athlete feels the patella moving out of then back into place at the time of injury. With a subluxed patella, the athlete can ambulate normally, and swelling is minimal to none.

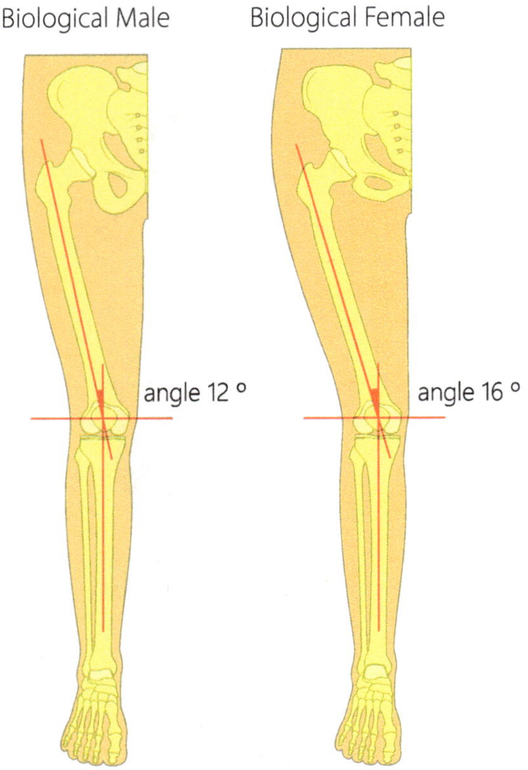

Figure 13-28 Q-angle measurement

Immediate Care

For a patellar subluxation, apply ice to the area and have the athlete rest. Apply an elastic compression wrap for support. The athlete can take anti-inflammatory medication to relieve pain and inflammation. Once inflammation has decreased, the athlete needs to begin a strengthening program for the vastus medialis and medial thigh muscles, and a stretching program for the vastus lateralis and the lateral thigh muscles. The athlete can wear a neoprene or other knee brace with a patella cut-out and lateral border to assist in keeping the patellar in its correct position. If the athlete has another subluxation or the signs and symptoms get worse with treatment, then they should be evaluated by their physician.

Patellar dislocations are treated like any other dislocation. Have the athlete remain still in whatever position is most comfortable for them, stabilize above and below the knee by splinting the limb, apply ice to the area, treat for shock, and call 911. At the ER, the patella is reduced by a physician. The physician takes x-rays to be certain that the posterior portion of the patella or the femoral condyle did not fracture. The athlete must be nonweightbearing in a knee immobilizer on crutches for a brief time, then they begin rehabilitative exercises to strengthen medial and stretch lateral knee musculature.

Prevention

Patellar subluxations and dislocations can be avoided if good strength balance exists between the medial and lateral knee musculature. The lateral musculature should be flexible enough, so the patella is not pulled laterally.

Patellofemoral Pain Syndrome

Patellofemoral pain syndrome (PFPS) is also called patellofemoral stress syndrome. PFPS is a general term used to describe pain at the anterior knee and around the patella.

Mechanism or Cause of Injury

PFPS has an insidious onset and no definitive cause. However, it is speculated that patellar compression against the femur (especially in knee flexion), improper patellar tracking during ambulation, patellar malalignment, biomechanical issues such as flat feet or a high arch, weak quadriceps and hip muscles, tight hamstrings and calf muscles, and muscular imbalance can cause PFPS. Long distance runners and cyclists are susceptible to PFPS, as well as athletes who train on inclines and uneven surfaces. Frequent step climbing can predispose a person to PFPS.

Signs and Symptoms

The individual feels pain between the anterior knee and the posterior surface of the patella especially when running, climbing stairs, and deep knee flexion movements, such as squatting and sitting for long periods of time **(Figure 13-29)**. Pain at the patella occurring after hours of sitting is called *movie theater sign*. The individual may also complain of grinding, grating, and point tenderness around and behind the patella. Swelling is not often present with PFPS.

Immediate Care

In order to treat PFPS the individual must treat and correct the underlying cause. Therefore, assist them in identifying what is truly causing the condition. Take a secondary survey and perform a postural examination of the individual in attempt to identify the mechanism of

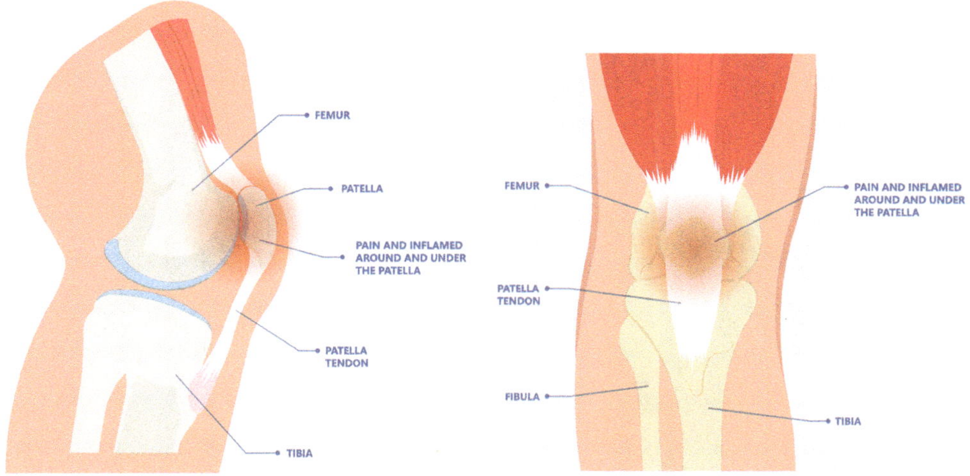

Figure 13-29 Patellofemoral pain syndrome is indicative by pain around and posterior to the patella.

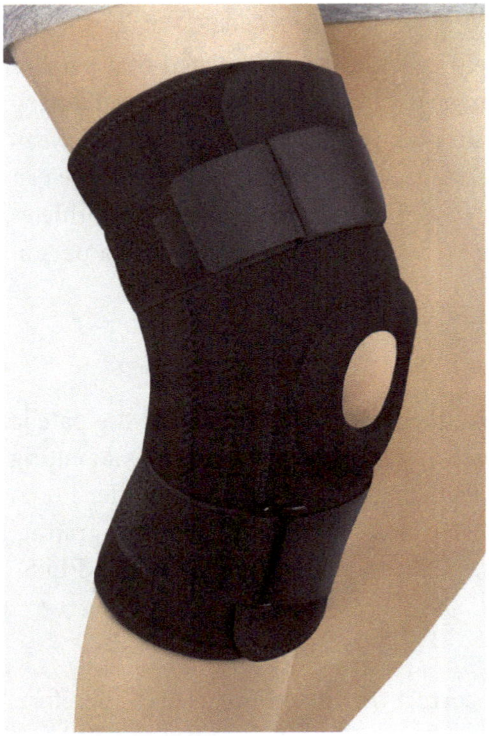

Figure 13-30 Knee braces with a patellar cutout can keep the patella in proper position during activity.

injury. If you cannot identify the cause, then refer the athlete to a physician for evaluation. To treat the athlete's immediate signs and symptoms, have them discontinue any activities that aggravate the patellofemoral area, especially knee flexion activities. Apply ice on and around the patella intermittently throughout the day and have the athlete take anti-inflammatories to alleviate pain and inflammation. Depending on the underlying cause of PFPS, the physician may prescribe a variety of treatments. A neoprene sleeve with a cut out for the patella provides some lateral stability **(Figure 13-30)**, or taping of the patella with a taping procedure called *McConnell taping* may provide some pain relief for patients with PFPS. The athlete may benefit from custom orthotics for their shoes. Custom orthotics are shoe inserts made from a mold of the patient's foot along with various foot measurements **(Figure 13-31)**. Orthotics can assist the athlete in correcting his biomechanical problems. Rehabilitation includes stretching and strengthening of knee musculature. Surgery is not typically utilized to correct PFPS.

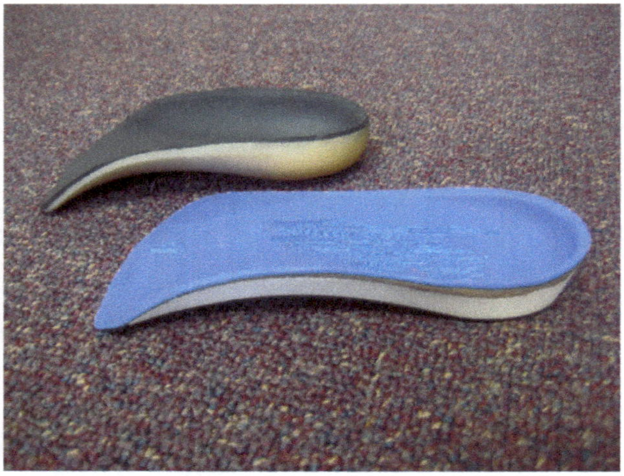

Figure 13-31 Custom foot orthotics are created to address each individual's specific foot condition(s).

Prevention

PFPS may not be entirely preventable due to a person's structural anatomy. Proper lower extremity conditioning exercises including ROM, flexibility, and strengthening should performed in order to prevent PFPS. Additionally, proper footwear that fits appropriately and is purposeful for the sport and activity must be worn.

Chondromalacia Patella

Chondromalacia patella is a type of PFPS which occurs when the cartilage on the lateral posterior portion of the patella softens and degenerates over time. The condition is an overuse injury that may first appear as generalized PFPS and with repetitive trauma can develop into chondromalacia patella.

Mechanism or Cause of Injury

Chondromalacia patella occurs from the same mechanisms of injury as PFPS. Also, repetitive knee flexion activities, lower extremity malalignments, and previous patella trauma, such as a previous dislocation which has injured the patellar articular cartilage, can cause chondromalacia patella. Individuals that participate in running and jumping activities are most at risk for chondromalacia patella (**Figure 13-32**).

Signs and Symptoms

The individual feels a dull, aching pain especially when the patella is contacting and being compressed against the femur with knee flexion. The patient may feel crepitus, grating, or grinding when walking or performing activities requiring knee flexion. Slight puffiness, indicating edema within the area, may be visible around the patella, and the area may be point tender.

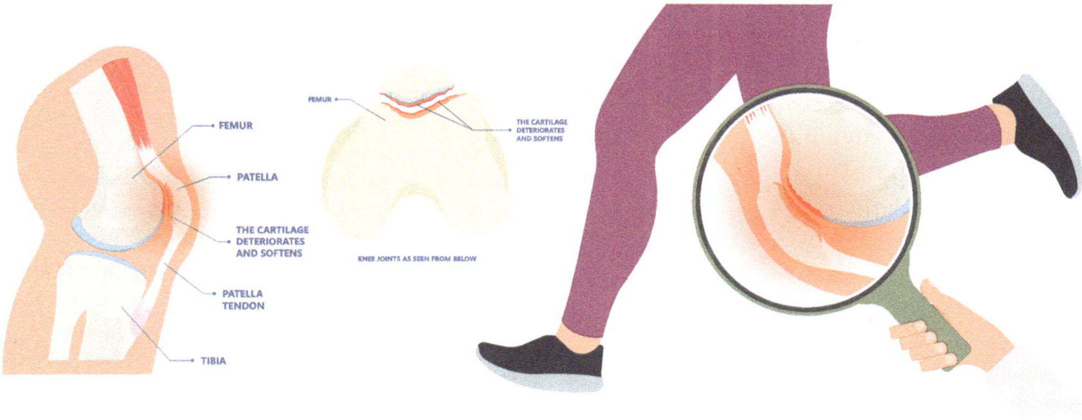

Figure 13-32 Chondromalacia patella often occurs in runners.

Immediate Care

The immediate care is the same as with PFPS. RICE, anti-inflammatories, bracing and taping, rehabilitation, and avoidance of deep knee flexion activities assists the individual in treating the injury. Refer them to a physician if these treatment methods are not successful. Surgery is not often utilized as a treatment method, but in rare cases a physician will remove damaged cartilage via arthroscopic surgery or realign the patella, so it tracks properly in the femoral groove.

Prevention

Athletic participants should take part in overall conditioning, including lower extremity strengthening and stretching exercises; wear properly fitted and appropriate shoes for the activity, utilize proper technique, and increase intensity of new knee flexion activities in a progressive manner in order to prevent chondromalacia patella.

Osteochondritis Dissecans

Osteochondritis dissecans (OCD) is another overuse condition. OCD occurs at the patellofemoral joint when the posterior patella and/or the femoral condyles become necrotic due to lack of blood flow to the area. The cartilage degrades and begins to fragment and fracture along with attached bone (**Figure 13-33**). This condition occurs most often to adolescents.

Mechanism or Cause of Injury

Although the exact mechanism of injury is unknown, OCD is caused by lack of blood flow to the femur and posterior patella. OCD may also be caused by repetitive microtraumas at the knee and patellofemoral joints that go unnoticed by an individual.

Signs and Symptoms

Because OCD is an overuse injury, the individual feels pain that occurs gradually over time. The pain occurs most often after activity has stopped. The individual may feel grating and catching if a loose bone fragment is within the joints. Some joint line point tenderness and edema may exist. The individual may have loss of knee ROM. In certain instances, they may not exhibit significant signs and symptoms of injury. If the fragmented cartilage and bone remain near the location from which it broke off, then the fracture may heal on its own. If this is the case, then signs and symptoms typical for OCD are not evident.

Immediate Care

Recommend to the individual to rest the knee and avoid all painful activities, apply ice, take anti-inflammatory medication, and perform rehabilitative exercises to promote lower extremity ROM, strength, and flexibility. If signs and symptoms of OCD continue, then refer them to

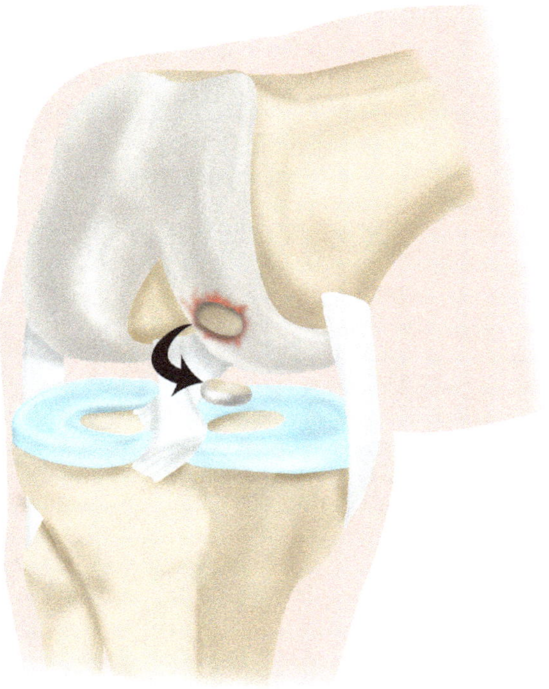

© Chu KyungMin/Shutterstock.com

Figure 13-33 Osteochondritis dissecans of the knee

a physician. If a loose piece of cartilage and bone is in the joint causing pain or loss of function, then the physician will perform arthroscopic surgery to remove the fragment.

Prevention

OCD prevention includes utilizing proper techniques when participating in athletic activities, as well as participating in lower extremity conditioning and strength training programs on a regular basis.

Patellar Tendon Rupture

The patellar tendon attaches from the inferior portion of the patella to the tibial tuberosity. When the quadriceps muscles contract, the patellar tendon assists in knee extension. Although a patellar tendon rupture is a rare injury, middle-aged people who participate in running or jumping activities are most commonly affected. The tendon can partially or completely tear (rupture), and tear at any point in the tendon **(Figure 13-34)**. When the tendon tears, an avulsion fracture of the patella's inferior pole can also occur.

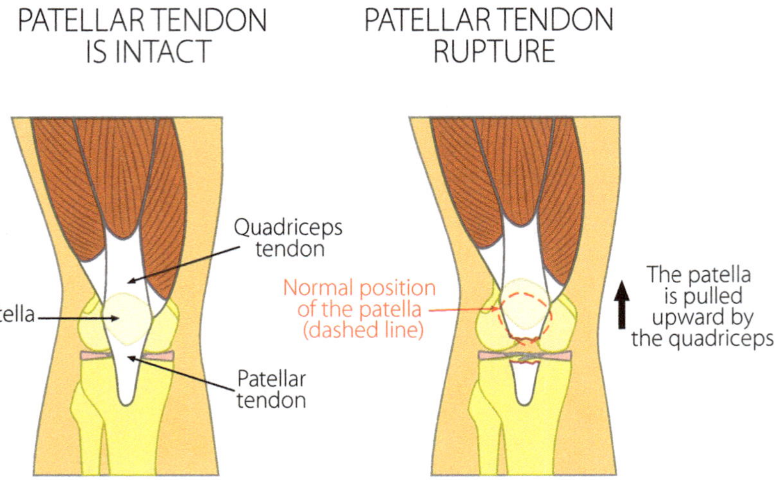

Figure 13-34 Patellar tendon rupture

Mechanism or Cause of Injury

The patellar tendon ruptures from a forceful, sudden quadriceps muscle contraction which forces the knee in extension. The tendon can also rupture from a fall when the individual lands on the area. If they land on their feet with the knees in deep flexion after jumping or falling, the patellar tendon can stretch to the point of failure. The patellar tendon can weaken due to illness that disrupts blood supply, such as diabetes, rheumatoid arthritis, infection, and metabolic disease (AAOS, 2021). A weakened patellar tendon along with a forceful stretch or contraction can cause tendon rupture.

Signs and Symptoms

The individual complains of severe pain immediately after the injury occurs, which may cause them to go into shock. They may say that they felt or heard a pop when the tendon ruptured. The individual cannot perform active knee extension. A visible defect may be present where the tendon ruptured, along with ecchymosis, swelling, and point tenderness.

Immediate Care

If the individual has ruptured the patellar tendon, they will most likely be in shock, so treat them appropriately. Apply ice, splint the area, and call 911. If the injury is a partial tear with mild to moderate signs and symptoms of injury, then utilize RICE, place the individual on crutches, and refer them to a physician for evaluation. For partial or incomplete patellar tendon tears, a nonsurgical approach is taken to treat the injury. The nonsurgical approach includes immobilization for approximately one month and rehabilitative exercises. To treat and promote healing for a completely ruptured patellar tendon, surgery must be performed to repair the tendon. Immobilization and rehabilitation begin after the procedure, with return to activity in approximately 6 to 12 months (AAOS, 2021).

Prevention

Individuals can attempt to prevent patellar tendon ruptures by performing quadriceps muscle group strengthening and flexibility exercises, and lower extremity conditioning. Avoiding unnecessary high impact, forceful contraction jumping activities is also important. If an individual's activity includes these jumping activities, as in basketball and volleyball, then a proper warm-up and cool-down are always imperative to avoid muscle and tendon injuries.

Patellar Tendinitis (Jumper's Knee)

Patellar tendinitis is an overuse injury. Repetitive stress that occurs to the tendon causes microtears, which results in tendon inflammation. Over time, if the causative stress is not removed, then further damage occurs to the tendon. The tendon becomes very weak and can fail.

Mechanism or Cause of Injury

Patellar tendinitis typically has an insidious onset. The patient is not able to specify when the tendon first became problematic. The mechanism of injury is repetitive knee flexion concurrently with a quadriceps muscle overload. This mechanism of injury occurs in activities such as weightlifting (i.e., when performing lunges and squats), and basketball and volleyball (i.e., when jumping). Due to the mechanism of injury, the name *jumper's knee* was coined.

Signs and Symptoms

The athlete experiences pain between the inferior pole of the patella and tibial tubercle (**Figure 13-35**). The pain arises at the beginning of exercise activity and again when the athlete has completed the activity. Usually pain subsides during exercise; however, as the tendinitis becomes more severe, the pain occurs at all times during exercise. As the tendinitis continues to worsen, pain is exacerbated during ADLs, including climbing stairs or any motion requiring knee flexion. The area is point tender, but little swelling exists.

Immediate Care

Treat the tendinitis by having the athlete rest and discontinue activities that cause pain. Apply ice and elevate the area. Patellar compression straps, which are similar in function to epicondylitis straps, can be utilized to decrease stress on the tendon. The athlete can take anti-inflammatory medication to reduce inflammation and pain. Once the inflammation and pain are controlled, the athlete should focus on stretching and strengthening the quadriceps

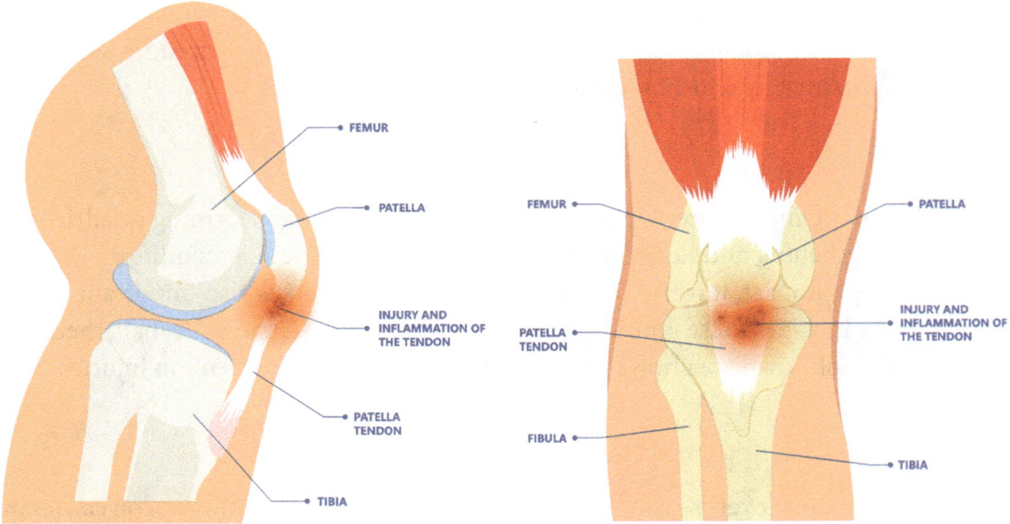

Figure 13-35 Jumper's knee (patellar tendinitis) causes pain and inflammation at the inferior pole of the patella at the patellar tendon.

muscles. If the tendinitis continues to worsen and interfere with ADLs, such as walking or climbing steps, or if the area becomes red and swollen, then refer them to their physician for evaluation. Along with rehabilitation and NSAIDs, the physician may inject corticosteroids or prescribe topical corticosteroids along with electrostimulation (iontophoresis) or ultrasound (phonophoresis) to decrease inflammation.

Prevention

Stretching and strengthening of the quadriceps group is important to prevent jumper's knee. Eccentric strengthening must be included in the individual's strengthening protocol since repetitive eccentric loads of the quadriceps muscles are a cause of patellar tendinitis. Utilizing proper biomechanics, skill, technique, and progression when exercising is also important to avoid patellar tendinitis.

Osgood-Schlatter and Sinding-Larsen-Johansson Diseases

Osgood-Schlatter's disease (OSD) is inflammation of a person's tibial tubercle apophysis where it attaches to the patellar tendon **(Figure 13-36)**. Sinding-Larsen-Johansson disease (SJLD), which is not as common as OSD, is an inflammation of the patella's inferior pole at its growth plate, where it attaches to the patellar tendon **(Figure 13-37)**. These diseases occur most frequently to adolescent biological males whose bones are rapidly growing. Athletes who

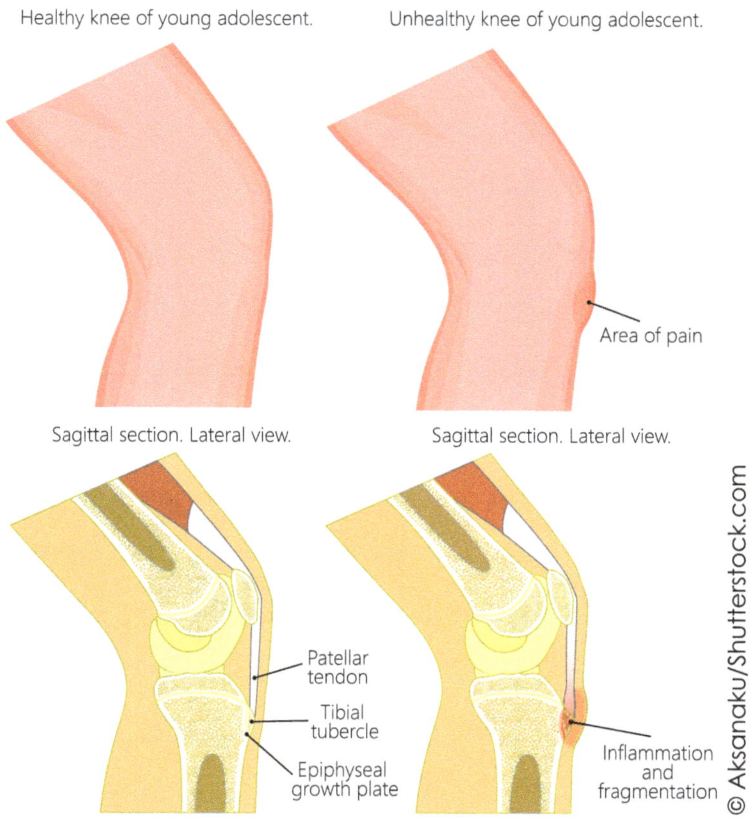

Figure 13-36 An adolescent experiencing Osgood-Schlatter's disease has patellar tendon inflammation and pain at the tibial tubercle.

participate in sports that involve jumping, running, and changes in direction are most prone to these conditions. The injuries can occur to one or both extremities.

Mechanism or Cause of Injury

The mechanism of injury for both conditions is the same. The adolescent's body is growing rapidly. The bones grow faster than the muscles and tendons. Consequently, the muscles and tendons are stressed and pulled tight, and consequently pull on the bones. Over time, this causes an inflammatory response. The injuries occur when the knee is repeatedly flexed during low or high intensity activities. Individuals do not need to participate in athletic activities to sustain either of these injuries. Any activity that requires repetitive knee flexion, such as squatting, lifting heavy boxes, gardening, or the like, can cause these injuries. Changes in intensity of activity, improper shoes, poor posture, and faulty biomechanics can also cause OSD or SJLD.

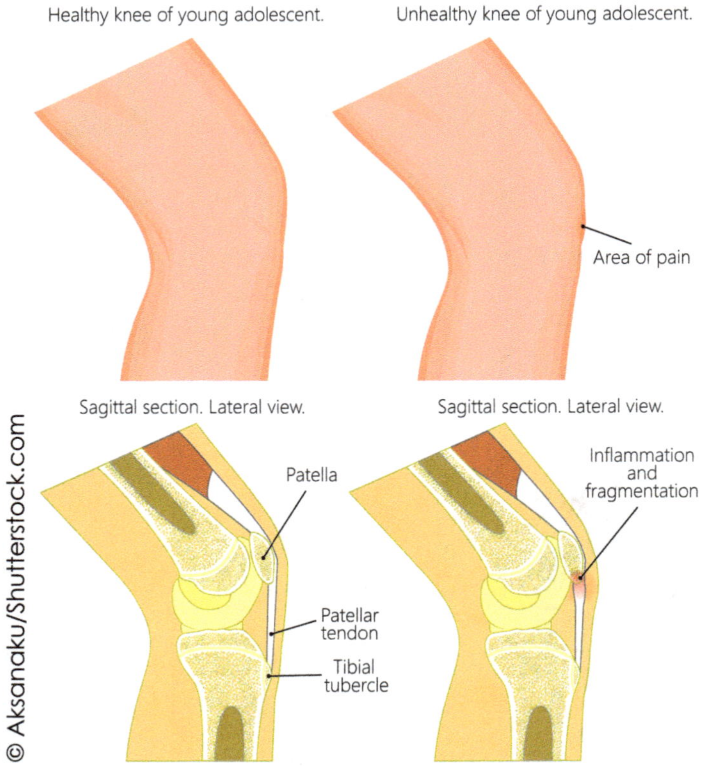

Figure 13-37 An adolescent experiencing Sinding-Larsen-Johansson disease has patellar tendon inflammation and pain at the inferior patella.

Signs and Symptoms

At first, the individual feels pain, especially with knee flexion activities, but resolves at rest. They may have point tenderness and swelling at the tibial tubercle (with OSD) or the inferior patella (with SJLD). If the stress on the patellar tendon is not eliminated, then eventually the bone stimulation causes new bone to be laid down. The bone formation causes a bump to form on the tibial tubercle. This bump may appear deformed as compared to the contralateral side **(Figure 13-38)**.

Immediate Care

Instruct the individual to apply ice packs or ice massage throughout the day to alleviate pain. Activities that cause pain and inflammation should be decreased or avoided entirely. Intensity of activities should be decreased also. The individual should take anti-inflammatory

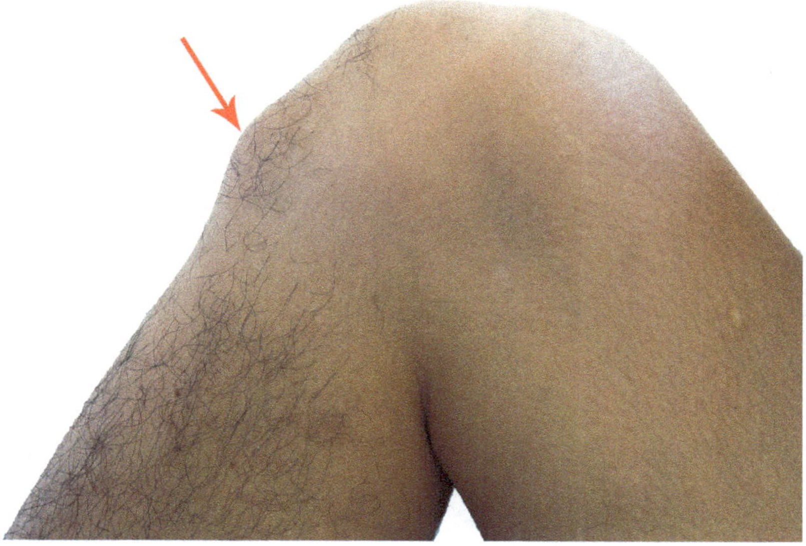

Figure 13-38 Osgood-Schlatter's disease can result in a bony formation on the tibial tubercle.

medication if possible. Both injuries may last for months, but for children the injuries will typically heal on their own when the child stops growing. If the condition worsens or does not get better within a few weeks' time, then refer the child to their physician to determine the extent of injury. The individual continues with ice application, NSAIDs, and rehabilitation which focuses on quadriceps muscles stretching. A patellar tendon strap can assist in decreasing stress on the tendon. The child does not necessarily need to stop all athletic activities during the rehabilitation process. Work with them to create a safe, progressive, low intensity, exercise activity program that allows them to continue to be active, yet heal appropriately.

Prevention

Progress activity intensity slowly for adolescents who are growing rapidly. Children participating in athletic activities should stretch and strengthen their muscles with advice from and under the supervision of a qualified, trained professional such as a sports medicine specialist.

The Lower Leg and Ankle

The lower leg consists of the area from the knee down to the ankle joint. The ankle joint is comprised of the distal tibia and the talus. The fibula borders the lateral side of the ankle. A variety of injuries occur to the low leg and ankle, ranging from insignificant minor strains to life-threatening open fractures **(Figure 13-39)**.

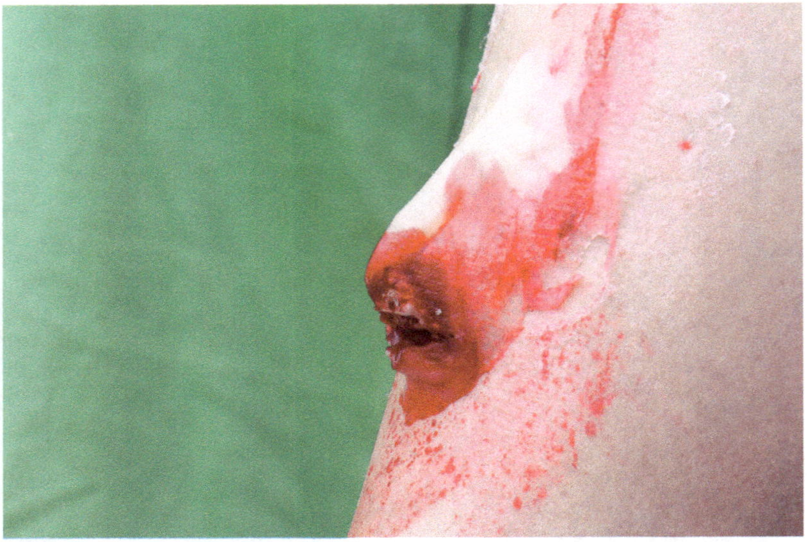

Figure 13-39 An open fracture to the lower leg is a medical emergency.

Lower Leg Fractures

In athletic activities, lower leg fractures occur to the tibia and fibula. The tibia is a weight-bearing bone, while the fibula is not. Therefore, stresses from the foot contacting the ground can cause overuse tibial stress fractures. Acute tibial and fibular fractures also occur **(Figure 13-40)**. These acute fractures may occur to only one or both bones simultaneously. The fractures can occur anywhere on the bone, but the tibial shaft is most commonly fractured. Fractures can also occur at the epiphyseal plates, tibial tuberosity, and tibial plateaus. A distal fibula fracture is called a *Maisonneuve* fracture **(Figure 13-41)**.

Mechanism or Cause of Injury

Acute fractures are caused by a fall, a motor vehicle accident, a direct blow to the bone, or a twist of the lower extremity. In athletics, a direct blow by equipment, implements, or another person is most common. Stress fractures occur due to constant, repetitive bounding of the foot on the ground. The ground reaction forces are transmitted up to the tibia. Over time, these forces weaken the tibia. The tibia cracks at the weak points and stress fractures form. Stress fractures can occur when an individual is poorly conditioned, has increased the intensity of or changed their activity too quickly, and wears shoes inappropriate for the activity.

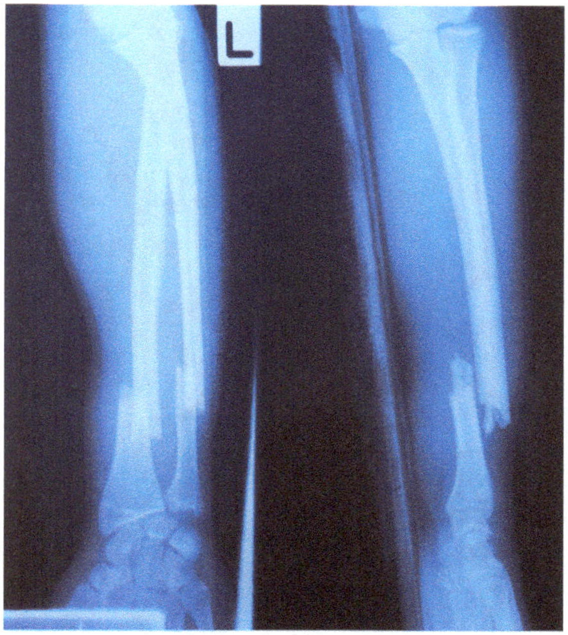

Figure 13-40 Lower leg fractures can occur to the tibia, fibula, or both simultaneously as shown in this X-ray.

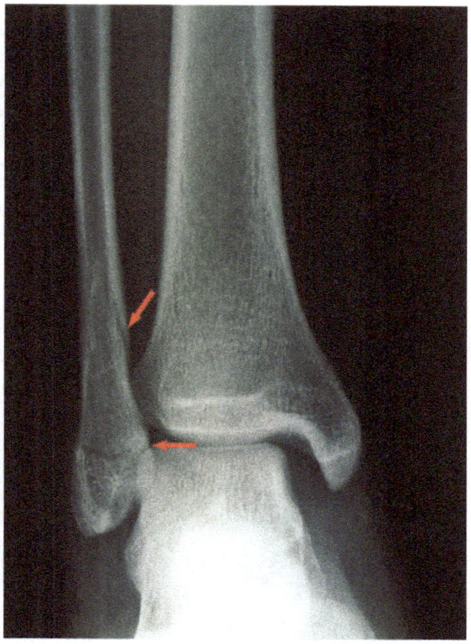

Figure 13-41 A distal fibular fracture is called a Maisonneuve fracture.

Signs and Symptoms

For acute fractures, the athlete feels pain and is unable to move the body part. They have point tenderness at the fracture site. The area may exhibit swelling, bruising, and deformity. If only the fibula is fractured, the athlete may be able to walk. Tibial stress fractures may take weeks to develop. Consequently, the signs and symptoms take some time to affect the athlete as well. The athlete begins to experience a gradual onset of localized tibial pain. The pain increases during activity and decreases at rest. As the stress fracture becomes more severe, the pain occurs at rest. The pain may wake the athlete at night. The area where the stress fracture is located point tender, and the athlete may walk with a limp.

Immediate Care

Care for an acute tibial and fibular fracture as you would for any other acute fracture. Call 911 and treat the athlete for shock. If the athlete has sustained an open fracture, control the bleeding, and carefully dress and bandage the wound without moving the leg. Splint the injured extremity in the position that you find it **(Figure 13-42)**. Apply ice to the area. Monitor the athlete until EMS arrives. If you suspect that an athlete has a stress fracture, have

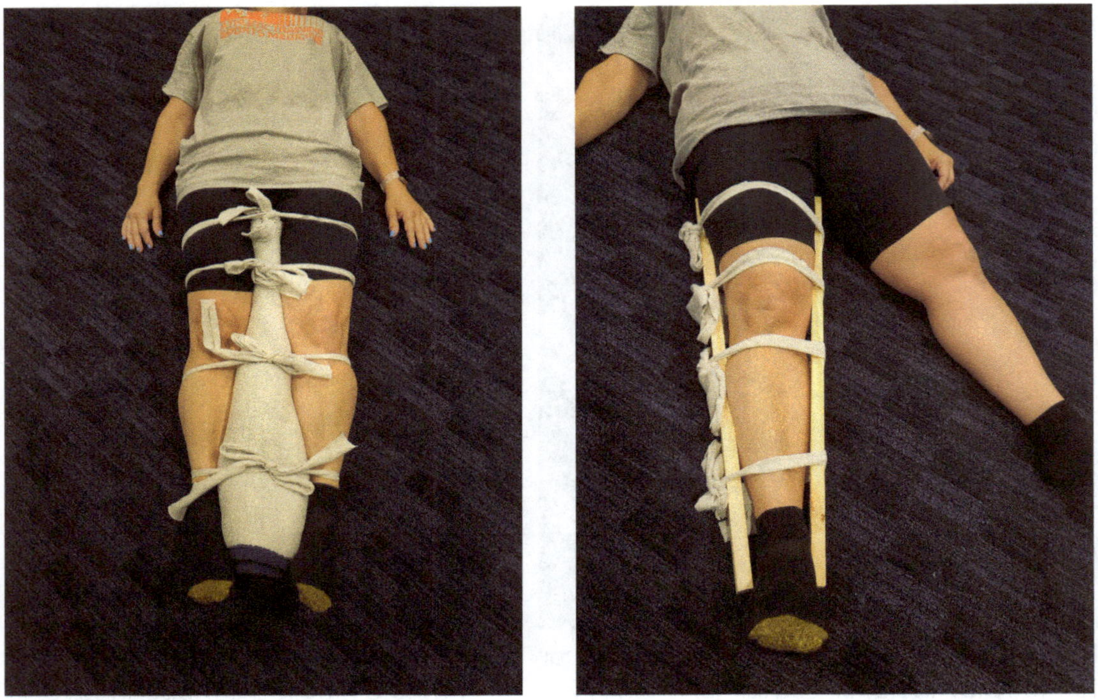

A **B**

Figure 13-42 Two methods of splinting tibia and fibular fractures: (**A**) Anatomic splint using the patient's body and blankets. (**B**) Utilizing two boards.

them discontinue all weight bearing activities until they have seen a physician. The athlete can continue to perform upper extremity exercises. The athlete should apply ice intermittently throughout the day and take anti-inflammatories to decrease pain and inflammation.

The athlete's physician takes x-rays, an MRI, or a bone scan to determine if a stress fracture exists **(Figure 13-43)**. The athlete has to rest the area, continue with ice application and anti-inflammatory medication, strengthen the anterior tibial musculature, stretch the gastrocnemius and soleus, correct training errors, properly increase training regimens, and wear proper footwear for their activity. They will gradually return to sport once the inflammation is gone, and they have regained some strength in the lower extremity. Depending on the severity of the stress fracture, they can begin to return to activity in about two months.

Prevention

To prevent acute fractures, athletic participants should wear protective equipment such as shin guards when playing soccer. Stress fractures can be prevented by strengthening and stretching low leg muscles, utilizing proper biomechanics during activity, wearing proper footwear for the activity, and gradually increasing intensity, duration, and type of training.

Medial Tibia Stress Syndrome

Medial tibia stress syndrome (MTSS) is an overuse condition commonly called *shin splints*. MTSS affects the overlying tibial muscles, of which the posterior tibialis is most commonly affected. MTSS occurs most frequently to individuals who perform running activities, especially activities that involve sudden stopping and starting. If the individual ignores the signs and symptoms of MTSS, does not take steps to treat the condition, and continues with the causative activity, then MTSS can progress into a tibial stress fracture.

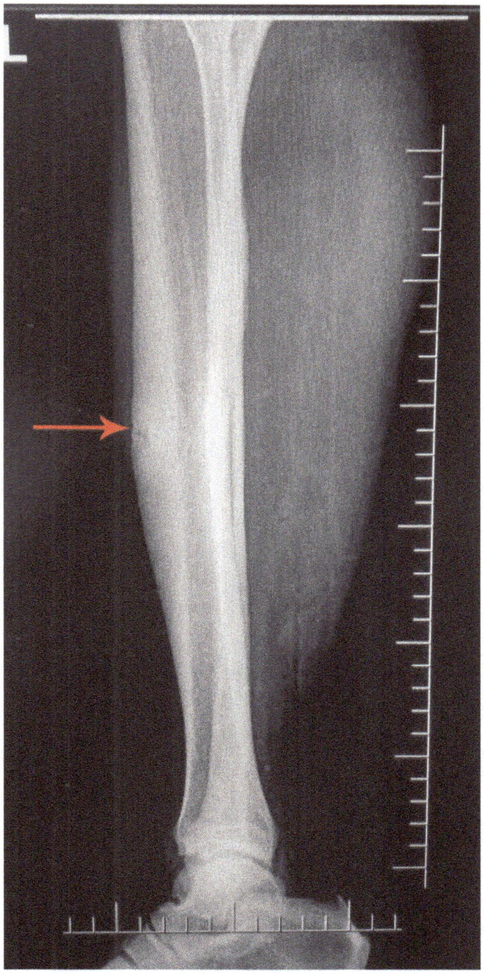

Figure 13-43 X-rays are used to determine if the individual has a stress fracture.

Mechanism or Cause of Injury

MTSS is caused by an overload of the medial musculature which lies over the tibia. The overload occurs when the individual increases intensity and duration of activity too quickly, runs on uneven, slanted, or hard surfaces, runs downhill consistently, and performs activities that require sudden stops and starts.

Signs and Symptoms

The individual has pain and point tenderness on the middle portion of the tibia **(Figure 13-44)**. The pain decreases or goes away during activity, but then returns at rest. As MTSS continues, the pain persists during rest and activity. Some mild edema may be present in the area.

Immediate Care

The individual can treat MTSS themselves by applying ice to the area and taking NSAIDs. They do not need to discontinue activity completely, but you should limit their activities that cause pain and inflammation. If signs and symptoms continue even with limited activity, then the activity needs to be limited further or discontinued. The individual should see a physician if the signs and symptoms of MTSS do not decrease or get worse with treatment. If the individual has sharp tibial pain, call 911.

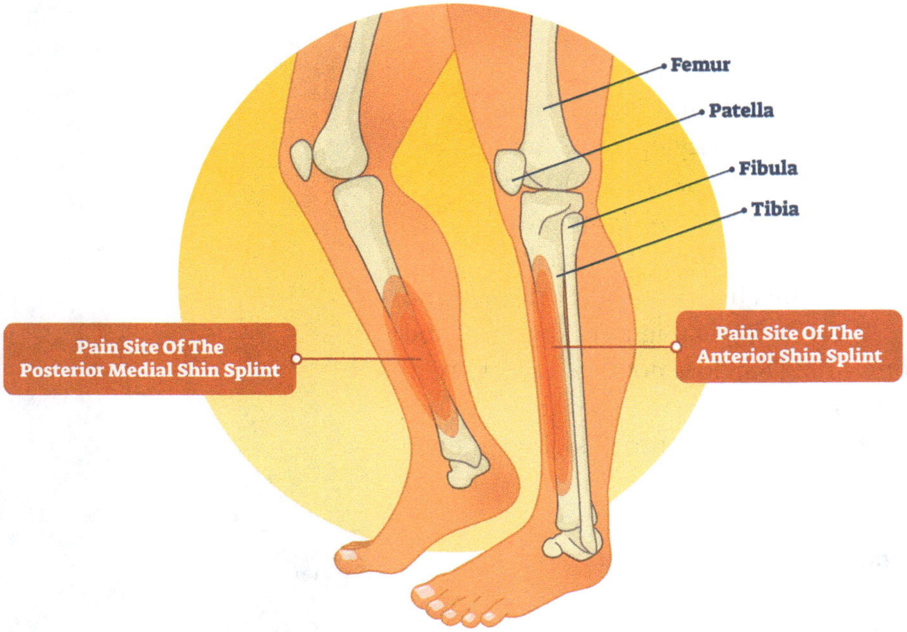

Figure 13-44 Medial tibial stress syndrome's (shin splints) location of pain.

Prevention

The individual should strengthen the low leg anterior musculature and stretch the posterior musculature in order to prevent a muscle imbalance and avoid MTSS. They should wear properly fitted shoes with arch supports. Also, the individual should seek advice from a professional in order to participate in a safe, progressive exercise activity protocol which poses no harm the anterior lower leg musculature.

Compartment Syndrome

The lower leg has four compartments that contain muscles, which move the ankle and foot, along with nerves and blood vessels. Compartment syndrome is a condition in which the pressure in the lower leg compartments increases and begins to compromise the nerve and vascular structures **(Figure 13-45)**. Two types of compartment syndrome exist. Acute compartment syndrome is limb-threatening since pressure on the nerves, blood vessels, and muscles can cause these structures to die. Exertional, or chronic, compartment syndrome occurs during exercise activity and can also be debilitating to an individual.

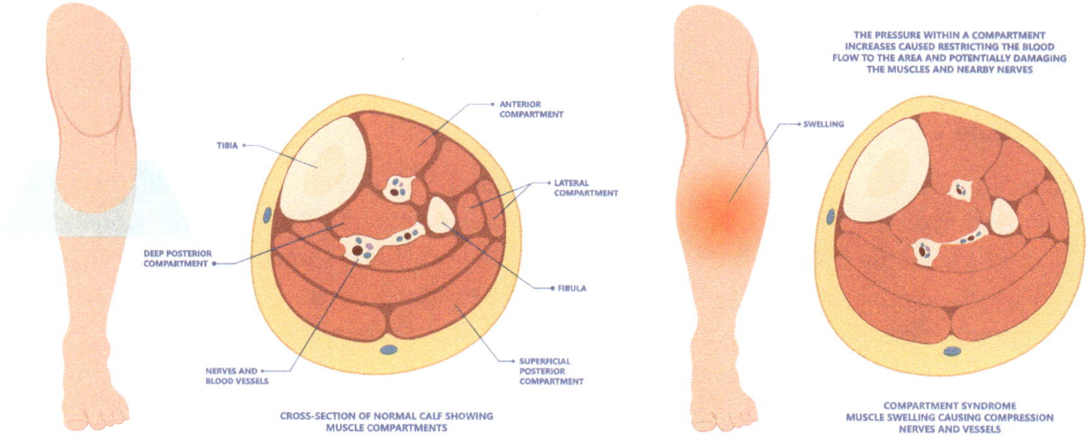

Figure 13-45 Compartment syndrome affects the lower limb nerves and blood vessels.

Mechanism or Cause of Injury

Acute compartment syndrome is caused by a direct blow or severe trauma to the low leg, such as a tibial fracture. The muscles in the anterior compartment become inflamed and swollen. The fascia, which contain the muscles in the compartment, does not expand. Consequently, as the swelling and edema increases, the pressure in the compartment increases.

Exertional compartment syndrome is caused by muscular contraction during exercise activity. The muscles fill with blood and expand as they normally should. However, with exertional compartment syndrome, excessive pressure builds up in the compartments. It is not certain why some people have exertional compartment syndrome and others do not. Large muscles, thick fascia, high venous pressure, and lower extremity biomechanics may contribute to exertional compartment syndrome.

Signs and Symptoms

You can differentiate whether your client has acute compartment syndrome or a basic contusion. If the pain does not decrease despite treatment efforts, then they most likely have acute compartment syndrome. With acute compartment syndrome the individual experiences persistent pain that develops over hours and progressively gets intense. The area may be swollen and red. Individuals with severe compartment syndrome may also have decreased sensation and muscular weakness down the leg and into the foot. An individual who has exertional compartment syndrome also feels pain come on gradually during exercise and continues to increase until exercise is stopped. The pain lasts shortly after exercise during rest. They may feel loss of sensation and muscular weakness down the leg during exercise while the compartment pressure exists.

Immediate Care

Acute compartment syndrome is a medical emergency, so call 911. The individual will have surgery immediately to release the pressure in the compartments. Although exertional compartment syndrome is not a medical emergency, the individual sometimes requires surgery to release the compartments' pressure. Conservative treatment includes stretching, orthotics, biomechanical changes, massage, and rest from activities. Surgery is more effective than conservative treatment in eliminating exertional compartment syndrome.

Prevention

Acute compartment syndrome can potentially be prevented by wearing protective shin guards for activities in which low leg injury is possible, such as soccer. Exertional compartment syndrome is not preventable, but athletic participants should participate in proper conditioning, such as a warm-up and cool down, in attempt to keep the muscles strong and flexible.

Strains

Muscle and tendon strains occur frequently to the lower leg. The gastrocnemius and the Achilles' tendon are commonly strained. The Achilles' tendon is prone to ruptures (Grade 3 strains), typically to biological men in their 40's **(Figure 13-46)**.

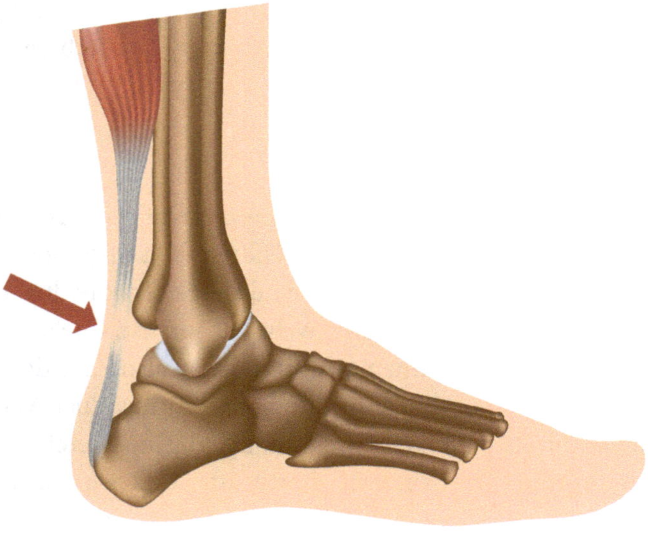

Figure 13-46 Achilles' tendon rupture

Mechanism or Cause of Injury

The causes of a low leg muscular strain are a forceful muscle contraction or a sudden stretch. Repetitive loading can also cause strains. Most Achilles' tendon ruptures occur due to a forceful gastrocnemius and soleus contraction when the person pushes off on the ball of their foot.

Signs and Symptoms

Grade 1 and 2 strains exhibit the typical signs and symptoms for strains, as previously discussed (**Figure 13-47**). When a muscle or tendon is ruptured, such as the Achilles' tendon, the tissue tears away from its bony attachment or at any other portion of the soft tissue. When an individual's Achilles' tendon ruptures, they may describe the incident as feeling like they were struck in the leg with a baseball bat. They feel a snap or pop at the time of injury. The gastrocnemius and soleus muscles roll up and create a bulge in the calf area. This bulge appears deformed as compared to the contralateral side. The individual experiences severe pain and may exhibit signs and symptoms of shock. They most likely fall to the ground immediately after the injury because they cannot weight bear on the affected leg, and have loss of function.

Immediate Care

Treat Grade 1 and 2 strains with RICE. An individual with a Grade 2 strain may also need crutches to ambulate. Whenever an individual needs crutches to ambulate for a Grade 2 strain, the injury is significant enough to warrant seeing a physician. An individual who has a Grade 3 strain probably is in shock. Consequently, call EMS for assistance. Treat the individual for shock,

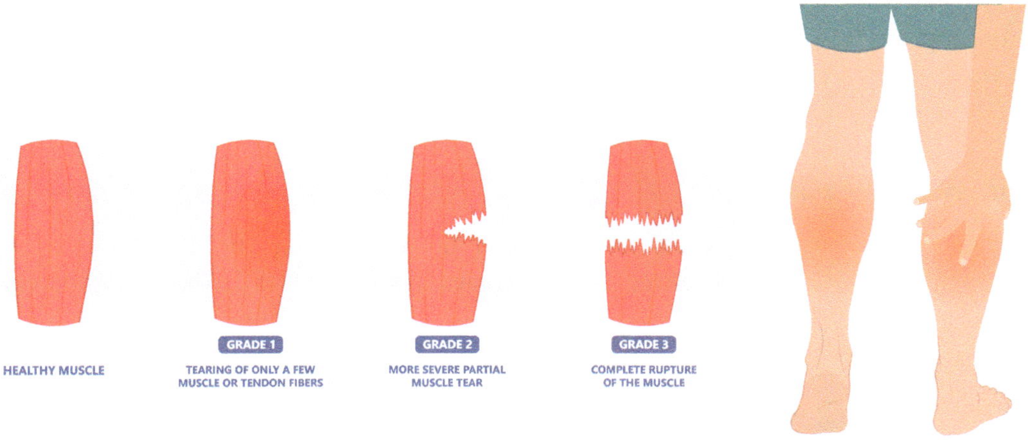

Figure 13-47 The calf muscles can sustain mild (Grade 1), moderate (Grade 2), or severe (Grade 3) strains.

use RICE, and keep them comfortable. The physician will evaluate the individual and determine the extent of injury. An individual who has sustained a ruptured Achilles' tendon typically needs the tendon surgically repaired in order to achieve full function in the future. After the surgery, utilization of therapeutic modalities and rehabilitation begin. The individual cannot return to full activity for approximately 4 to 6 months. A non-surgical, conservative approach includes wearing a cast and boot which elevates the heel and places the individual's ankle in plantarflexion, in attempt to properly align the tendon. This conservative approach is not effective if the tendon has snapped up and does not approximate the tendon or the attachment site.

Prevention

Athletic participants need to undertake a low leg flexibility program, especially the gastrocnemius and Achilles' tendon. The anterior muscles should also be strengthened so an imbalance between the anterior and posterior muscles is avoided. Athletic conditioning programs must incorporate a variety of exercises other than exercises which require a forceful push-off. Also, the exercise program should follow a safe, progressive increase in intensity and duration in order to avoid low leg strains.

Tendinitis

Tendinitis can occur in any low leg, ankle, or foot tendons. The Achilles' **(Figure 13-48)**, peroneal **(Figure 13-49)**, and posterior and anterior tibialis **(Figure 13-50)** tendons are commonly affected by inflammation. Tendinitis can be acute or chronic.

Mechanism or Cause of Injury

Tendinitis is caused by a quick stretch or contraction (acute) or repetitive loading to the tendon (chronic). The tendon can also become inflamed due to friction against an object, such as a shoe; improper lower extremity alignment; and faulty biomechanics during activity. Athletic and work-related activities, as well as hobbies and ADLs that require repetitive motions, can cause lower leg tendinitis.

Signs and Symptoms

The individual experiences pain and possibly crepitus with activity. The tendon may be point tender with mild swelling. As the tendinitis becomes chronic, the tendon noticeably thickens.

Immediate Care

Tendinitis is treated with rest, ice, and anti-inflammatories. The individual must correct or stop any activity which causes stress on the tendon otherwise the tendinitis will persist. If the tendinitis persists and the signs and symptoms interfere with the individual's ADLs, then

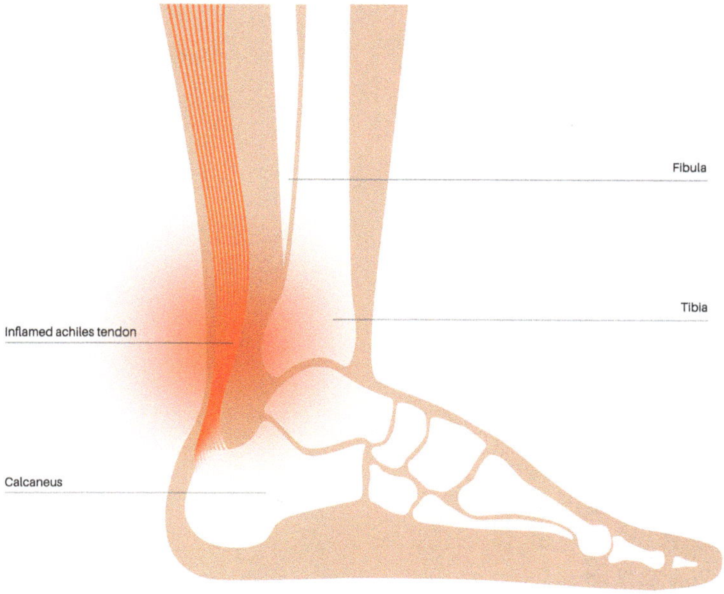

Figure 13-48 Achilles' tendinitis

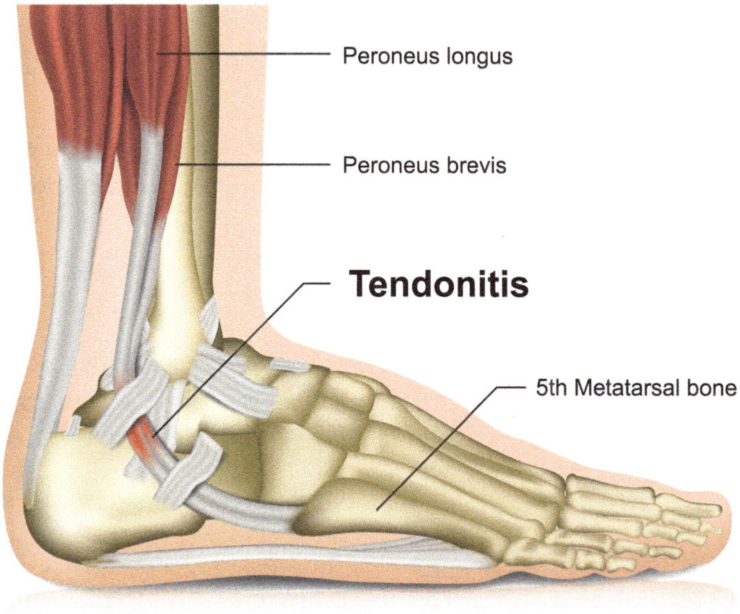

Figure 13-49 Peroneal tendinitis

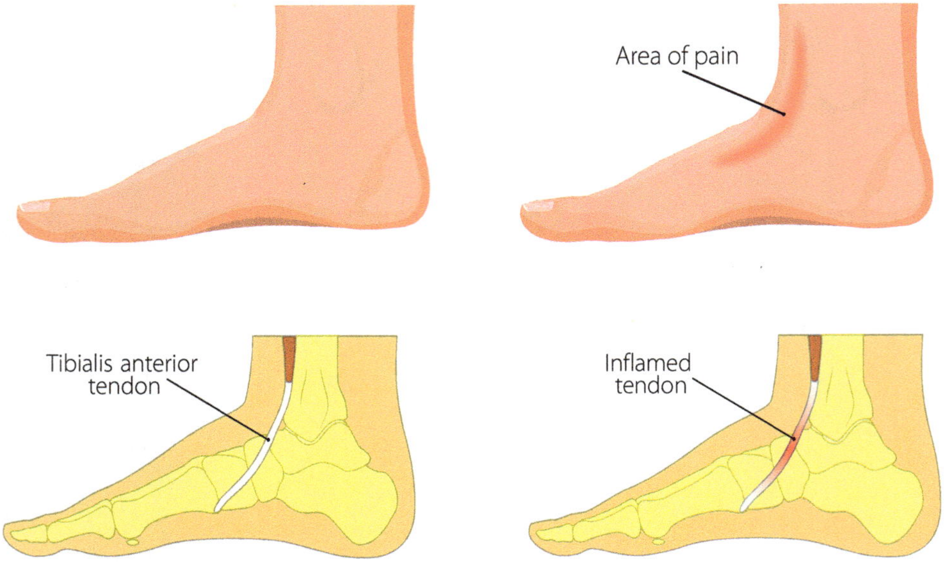

Figure 13-50 Location of anterior tibialis tendinitis

refer them to a physician. The physician may recommend treatment including corticosteroid injections, NSAIDs, and rehabilitation, including muscle and tendon stretching and strengthening.

Prevention

Preventing tendinitis includes stretching the muscles and tendons, utilizing proper technique, completing a warm-up and cool down during an exercise session, and avoiding activities that place undue stress on the tendons.

Ankle Dislocation

Similar to a knee dislocation, an ankle dislocation is rare. The ankle has a decent amount of stability due to the talus and tibia bony configuration. Therefore, a great amount of trauma is necessary to dislocate the ankle. When an ankle dislocates, it commonly has an associated fracture **(Figure 13-51)**.

Mechanism or Cause of Injury

A severe force must be placed on the joint in order to dislocate the ankle. The severe force can be from direct contact, which can occur during a high intensity collision at an athletic event, a fall from a height, or a motor vehicle accident. A person can dislocate an ankle if they twist their ankle beyond the joint's normal ROM.

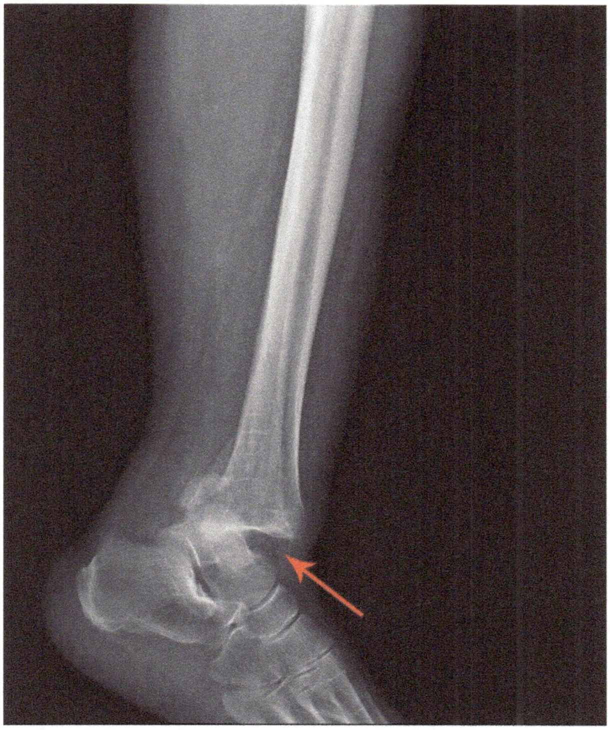

Figure 13-51 When an ankle is dislocated, a fracture often occurs simultaneously.

Signs and Symptoms

The athlete experiences the same signs and symptoms with an ankle dislocation as with a knee dislocation. They have severe pain and are in shock. Deformity, swelling, point tenderness, and abnormal or loss of sensation in the affected limb's toes is present. The athlete cannot move the joint.

Immediate Care

Treat the dislocation as you would for any other dislocation by calling 911, treating the athlete for shock, stabilizing and splinting the ankle, applying ice to the area, and monitoring them until EMS arrives **(Figure 13-52)**.

Prevention

Ankle dislocations are not entirely preventable. The athlete must keep the muscles around the ankle strong, and make sure the ankle has normal ROM. Unfortunately, unexpected direct trauma forces that cause severe injury cannot always be avoided.

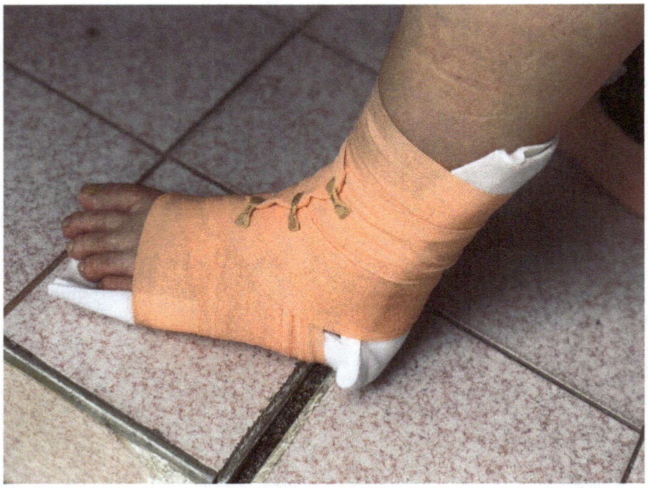

Figure 13-52 A dislocated, fractured, or severely sprained ankle should be splinted by utilizing rigid or soft materials and an elastic bandage to prevent movement.

TIPS FROM THE FIELD

Tip 2 If an athlete has a severe ankle or foot injury do not remove the shoe. The shoe assists to minimize swelling by acting as a compression mechanism. Removing the shoe allows blood and edema to enter the area, and swelling will increase. Also, if the individual has a dislocation or fracture, removing the shoe may make the injury worse. Splint the injury with the shoe on and apply ice over and around the shoe.

Ankle Sprain

An ankle sprain is one of the most common lower extremity injuries. Ankle sprains occur to the lateral, medial, and anterior tibiofibular ligaments, and the syndesmosis.

Mechanism or Cause of Injury

Ankle sprains occur when the joint is forced beyond its normal ROM. A lateral ankle sprain is caused by excessive ankle plantarflexion and inversion **(Figure 13-53)**, a medial ankle sprain is caused by forceful ankle dorsiflexion and eversion **(Figure 13-54)**, and a syndesmotic (also called a high ankle sprain) is caused by forceful dorsiflexion **(Figure 13-55)**. These excessive forces can occur during athletic activities when running or jumping, or in non-athletic activities such as stepping on an uneven surface, losing balance, or tripping.

Signs and Symptoms

As with other sprains, the severity of the signs and symptoms depends on the grade of sprain. The individual has pain and point tenderness at the site of injury. Swelling, ecchymosis, redness, joint instability, and loss of function is present. Individuals with Grade 1 sprains may be

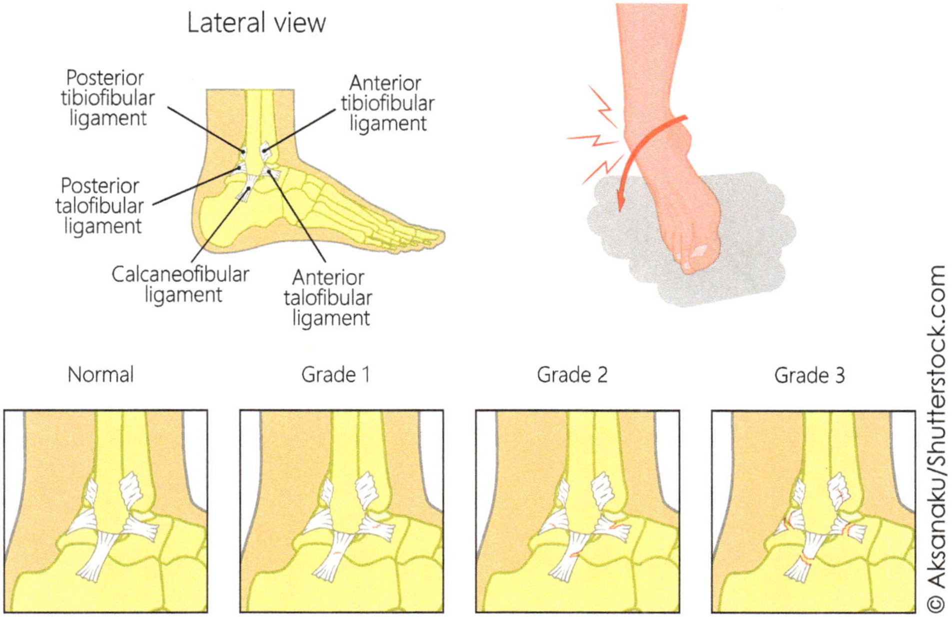

Figure 13-53 A lateral ankle sprain is caused by an inversion mechanism.

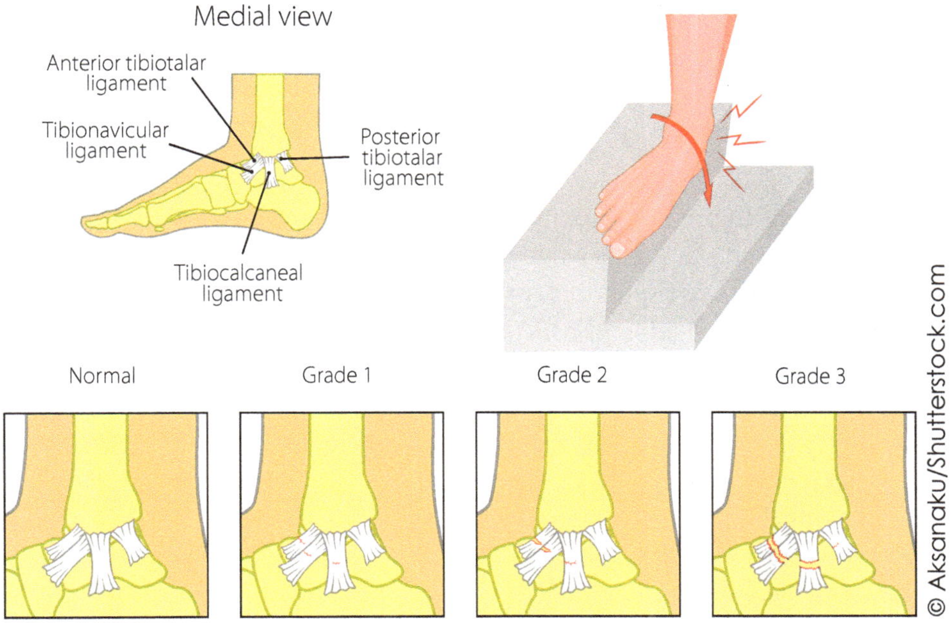

Figure 13-54 A medial ankle sprain is caused by an eversion mechanism.

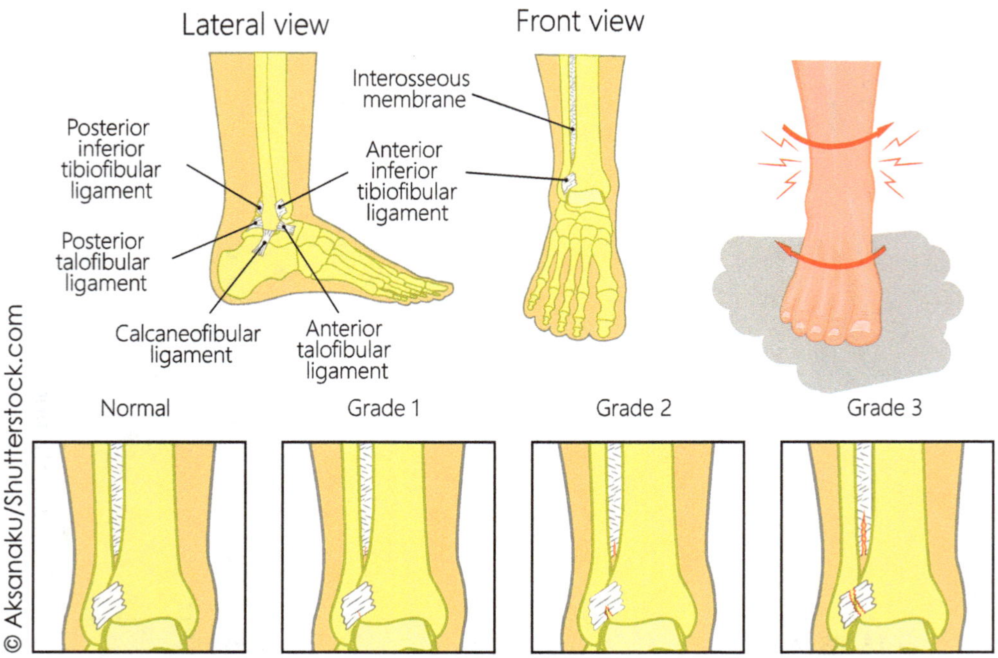

Figure 13-55 A syndesmosis ankle sprain is caused by an external rotation mechanism.

able to bear weight and ambulate normally, whereas individuals with Grade 2 and 3 sprains walk with a limp or are unable to bear any weight. The individual may state that they heard a pop at the time of injury.

Immediate Care

Immediately after the injury, apply ice to the area with a compression wrap. Have the individual lie on their back and elevate the ankle above their heart with their heel against the wall. If they have sustained a Grade 1 sprain, after the ice application and feeling to the ankle has been restored, wrap their ankle with an elastic compression wrap. They most likely can ambulate normally without pain or a limp.

If the individual has sustained a Grade 2 or 3 sprain, they may be unable to properly ambulate due to pain and loss of function. Consequently, fit them for crutches and have them ambulate without putting weight on the injured ankle.

If an individual suffers an ankle sprain and cannot walk properly, has severe pain and/or significant loss of function, or has point tenderness on the distal fibula and lateral malleolus, medial malleolus, base of the fifth metatarsal and/or the navicular bone, then they must see a physician for x-rays to determine whether or not a fracture has also occurred.

A sprained ligament can tear a piece of the bone off with the ligament during injury and cause an avulsion fracture. The excessive force with abnormal movement of the joint can cause bone to strike bone and cause a fracture on the opposite side of the sprain. Regardless of the grade of injury, the individual requires rehabilitation. They should take NSAIDs, utilize crutches as necessary, wear an ankle brace, and continue RICE for weeks depending on the severity of injury. The individual can gradually return to full function if they follow this course of treatment.

Prevention

Ankle sprains can be prevented by stretching the gastrocnemius and Achilles' tendon, strengthening the muscles that act on the ankle, improving lower extremity coordination, balance, and agility, and wearing proper shoes for the activity and playing surface.

TIPS FROM THE FIELD

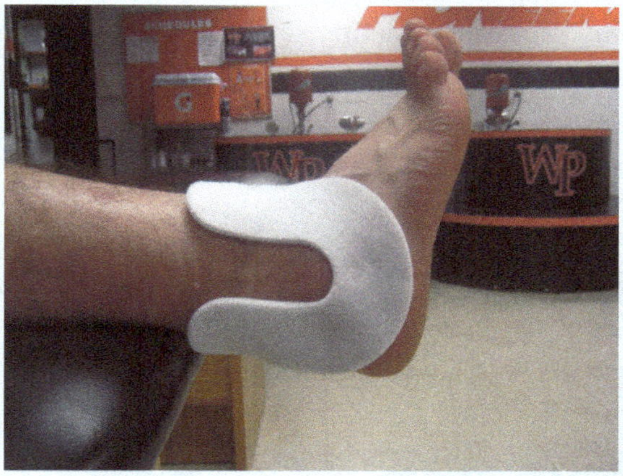

© Linda Gazzillo Diaz

Tip 3 When treating a lateral ankle sprain that has notable swelling around the malleolus, compression of the joint is important to mechanically force the edema out of the joint space. You can promote edema movement by applying a "horseshoe pad" to the ankle under the compression wrap. In order to make a horseshoe pad, you need approximately 8" x 8" foam or felt sheet which is soft, but not too compressive. You can purchase foam and felt from a medical supply store. Place the felt against the injured ankle. Take a pen and trace a U shape on the felt that goes around the tip of the malleolus, so the lateral malleolus and fibula is within the concave portion of the U. The lateral malleolus should fit snugly in the bottom portion of the U shape. Make the felt horseshoe approximately 1 inch or so wide throughout the U. The top of the U should come up approximately 4-5 inches above the malleolus. Cut out the horseshoe. Place the horseshoe on the ankle so the lateral malleolus and fibula are within the concave portion of the U. Then begin wrapping the elastic compression wrap from the toes over the horseshoe up to approximately where the Achilles' tendon meets the gastrocnemius. Along with the compression wrap, the horseshoe forces the edema out of the area underneath the horseshoe. When you remove the compression bandage and horseshoe to apply ice, the edema, including the ecchymosis, has moved out from underneath the horseshoe. Reapply the horseshoe and compression wrap after the patient has applied ice and regained full feeling of the ankle.

The Foot

Fracture and Dislocation

Foot and toe fractures occur to a variety of bones including the phalanges, metatarsals, and calcaneus. Some fractures have specific names. For example, a fracture at the base of the 5th metatarsal is called a Jones' fracture **(Figure 13-56)**, and a fracture that results in a proximal metatarsal dislocation is called a Lisfranc fracture. Stress fractures can occur to any of the bones since they are all weight bearing bones. Metatarsal stress fractures are commonly called march fractures. Foot dislocations are not common. Other than a Lisfranc fracture, which is a dislocated metatarsal due to a fracture, the phalanges are most likely to dislocate **(Figure 13-57)**.

Mechanism or Cause of Injury

The mechanism for an acute foot fracture includes direct trauma to the area. Often a person's foot is stepped on by another person, which results in a fracture, or the person drops a heavy object, such as a bowling ball or a dumbbell, on their foot. Stress fractures occur from overuse and repetitive weight bearing and bounding on the foot during activities, such as continual walking, running, and jumping. March fractures occur often to the second

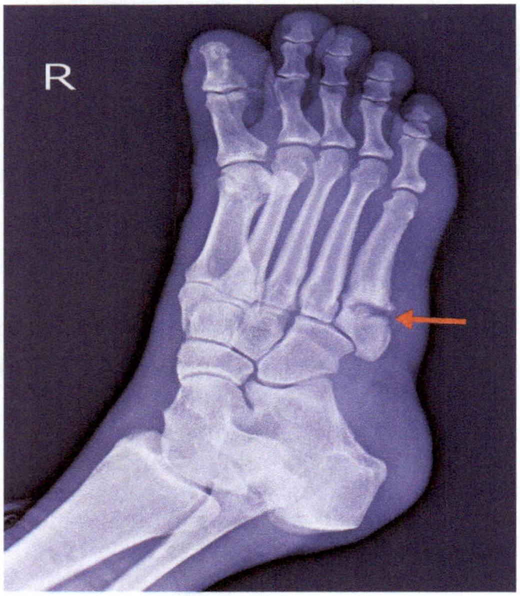

Figure 13-56 Jones fractures occur to the base of the 5th metatarsal.

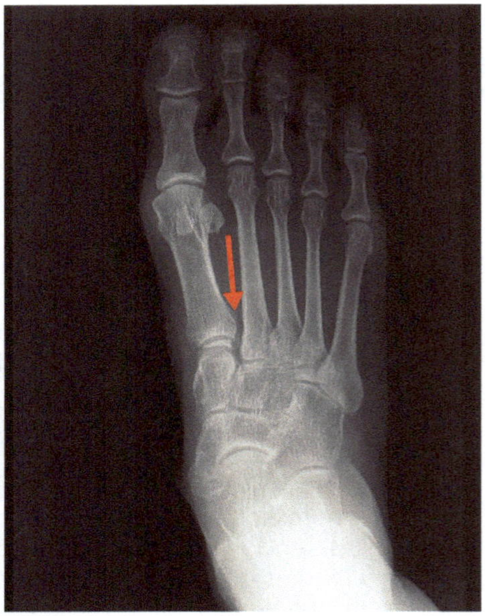

Figure 13-57 A Lisfranc injury occurs between the first and second metatarsals.

metatarsal when an individual has a condition called Morton's toe. Morton's toe is classified by the second toe appearing longer than the first toe. Usually the first metatarsal is longer than the second metatarsal; however, with Morton's toe the first metatarsal is shorter than the second metatarsal (**Figure 13-58**). Consequently, the majority of pressure is placed on the longer, second metatarsal, which is not typical. Over time, this undue stress creates a second metatarsal march fracture. Toe dislocations occur by axial loading, which is a direct blow to the tip of the phalanges. This mechanism of injury transmits force down the adjacent bones. Acute fractures and dislocations can also result from extreme foot torsion while weight bearing.

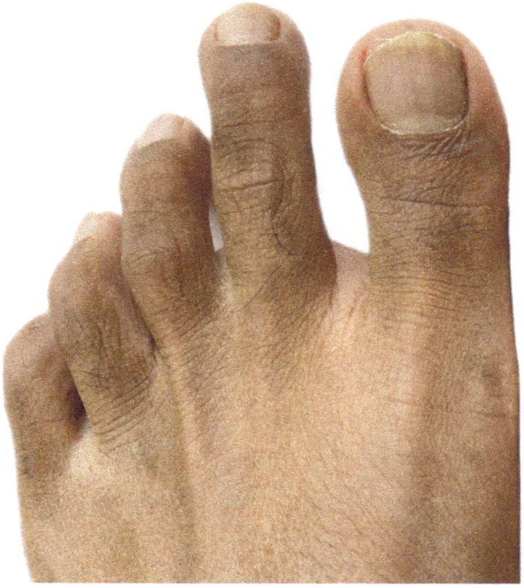

Figure 13-58 Morton's toe

Signs and Symptoms

Acute foot fractures and dislocations result in the same signs and symptoms as found with any other fracture or dislocation. Pain, point tenderness, swelling, and deformity exist. The individual may be in shock. Foot stress fractures exhibit the same signs and symptoms of other stress fractures. Pain is dull at first, then becomes sharp and persistent. Point tenderness and mild swelling may exist. The individual cannot weight bear normally.

Immediate Care

Acute foot fractures and dislocations require immediate advanced medical care and examination. Call 911 immediately. Check the individual for shock and treat them appropriately. Splint the foot and the ankle in order to rest and stabilize the injury. Apply ice to the area to decrease pain and inflammation. Monitor them until EMS arrives. The individual may or may not need surgery for the injury, depending on the bony alignment. Their foot will be placed a cast or hard walking boot, and they will utilize crutches until the area heals. Rehabilitation helps the patient gain full foot ROM and strength.

Individuals with suspected foot stress fractures should use RICE. Have them rest the foot by discontinuing weight bearing activity, and fit them for crutches until they are able to walk without pain or a limp. Apply ice to the injury and an elastic compression wrap to give the foot support and decrease any swelling. The individual should also elevate the foot above the heart whenever possible. If they continue to have pain, the inability to bear weight and walk normally, or any stress fracture signs and symptoms that increase despite treatment, then refer them to a physician for evaluation.

Prevention

Individuals cannot always prevent acute fractures and dislocations of the foot. They must be careful not to drop a heavy object on the foot or kick an unyielding object. An individual who participates in work-related activities with the potential of foot injury, such construction, should wear appropriate protective footwear. They should perform strengthening exercises for the lower leg and ankle since these muscles and tendons act on and support the foot. Supportive, appropriately fitted shoes for the activity and playing surface should be worn to prevent foot stress fractures.

Retrocalcaneal Bursitis

Retrocalcaneal bursitis is an inflammation of the bursa located between the calcaneus and the Achilles' tendon. Due to the bursa's location, the patient may mistake the condition as Achilles' tendinitis. The condition is often referred to as *pump bump*.

Mechanism or Cause of Injury

Retrocalcaneal bursitis is caused by friction on the bursa. A person who wears tight or poorly fitting shoes combined with repetitive walking, running, and jumping irritates the bursa, which causes inflammation.

Signs and Symptoms

The individual has heel pain that intensifies when walking, especially upstairs or inclines, and during running and jumping. Pain continues at rest and even at night while sleeping. Point tenderness and swelling is evident at the injured area. An apparent bump forms at the calcaneus by the Achilles' tendon attachment (**Figure 13-59**).

Immediate Care

The individual can treat the condition themselves. They should avoid any irritating activities, apply ice to the area frequently throughout the day, take anti-inflammatory medication, wear properly fitted work and exercise shoes, stretch the gastrocnemius, soleus, and Achilles' tendon, and strengthen the muscles around the ankle. They should place over-the-counter heel wedges in both shoes. These heel wedges raise the heel slightly and decrease some tension on the Achilles' tendon. If the signs and symptoms of retrocalcaneal bursitis are not resolved after several weeks of treatment, then refer the individual to a physician. The physician will recommend the same treatment protocol and perhaps prescribe a corticosteroid injection and/or immobilization to promote healing.

Prevention

Preventing retrocalcaneal bursitis is possible. Individuals should be properly fitted for work and exercise shoes by an expert in the shoe business. These shoes must not cause friction at the

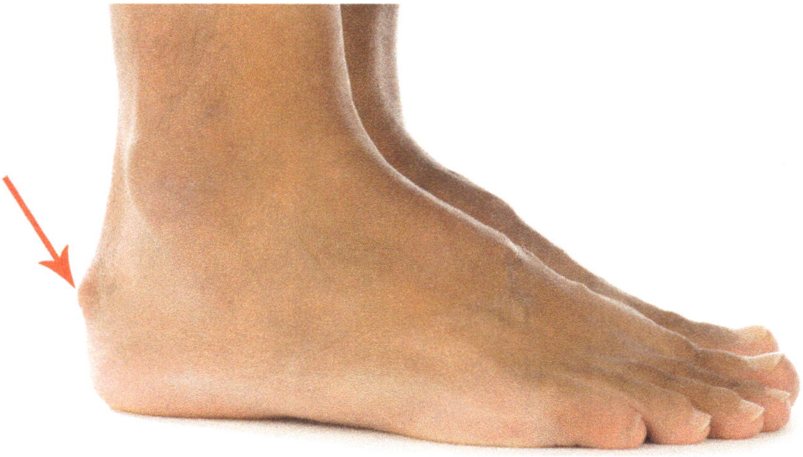

Figure 13-59 Retrocalcaneal bursitis appears as a bump at the calcaneus by the Achilles' tendon attachment.

calcaneus and Achilles' tendon. The individual should stretch the Achilles' tendon frequently, to allow for flexibility in the area. Strengthening the muscles around the ankle is also necessary to prevent retrocalcaneal bursitis.

Plantar Fasciitis

The plantar fascia is thick band of soft tissue that runs from the calcaneus to the metatarsal heads. It supports the foot's medial longitudinal arch and acts as a shock absorber during weight bearing. Inflammation of the plantar fascia commonly occurs to athletic participants.

Mechanism or Cause of Injury

When excessive tension is placed on the plantar fascia over a period of time, the tissue begins to fail and inflammation results (**Figure 13-60**). Runners are predisposed to plantar fasciitis due to the stress on the tissue during weight bearing. Also, overweight and pregnant individuals are at risk due to the extra force placed on the feet due to increased body weight. Athletic participants who wear poorly supportive shoes are commonly afflicted with plantar fasciitis.

Signs and Symptoms

Because plantar fasciitis is an overuse injury, signs and symptoms of injury develop slowly. A signature symptom of plantar fasciitis is sharp pain at the underside of the foot upon waking in the morning and stepping down. During sleep, the foot is in a relaxed, plantarflexed position, which allows the plantar fascia to shorten from lack of use. When the athlete steps down for the first time after rising, the plantar fascia is forcefully stretched, which elicits pain. As the

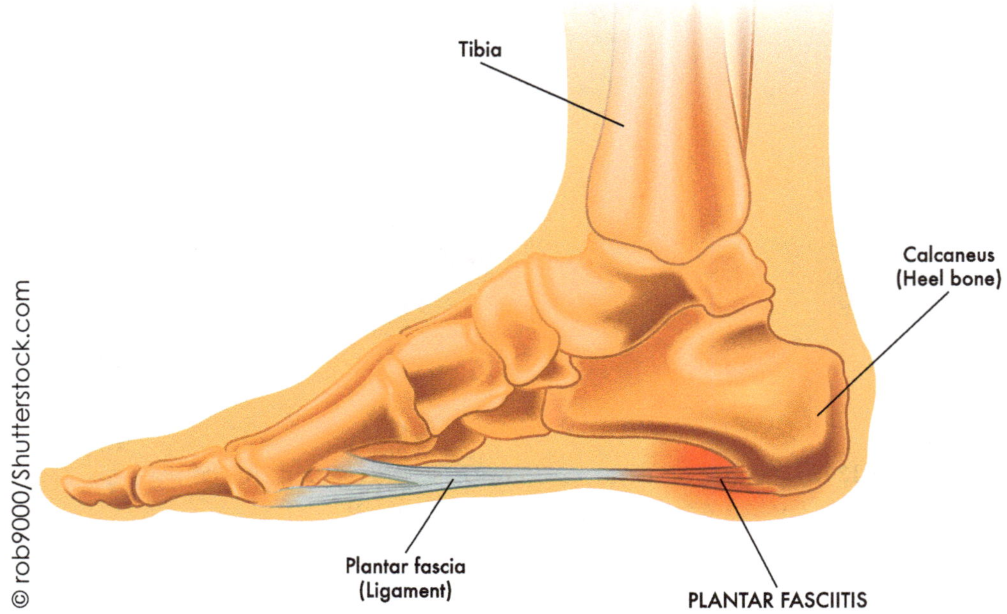

Figure 13-60 Inflammation can occur anywhere along the plantar fascia.

athlete walks, the pain decreases due to the plantar fascia becoming stretched and more mobile. Plantar fasciitis usually occurs in one foot, but can be present in both feet.

Immediate Care

A conservative treatment approach to heal the plantar fascia should begin at the onset of signs and symptoms. The treatment includes NSAIDs, rehabilitation (including stretches for the plantar fascia and Achilles' tendon), and lower leg muscle strengthening. If this treatment does not alleviate signs and symptoms of plantar fasciitis, the athlete should see a physician for additional therapies. A physician can prescribe corticosteroids therapeutic modalities, such as ultrasound, night splints (which are worn to keep the plantar fascia in a stretched position), and orthotics to help decrease stress on the plantar fascia. Usually the athlete's plantar fasciitis signs and symptoms resolve, and their foot will be at a pre-injury state within a few months.

Prevention

To prevent plantar fasciitis the patient needs to wear supportive shoes that are in good condition. Additionally, individuals need to maintain a healthy weight in order to decrease stress on the plantar fascia.

Pes Planus and Pes Cavus

Pes planus and pes cavus are conditions of the foot's medial longitudinal arch. Pes planus is a flat arch called *flat foot* **(Figure 13-61)**, and pes cavus is a high arch (**Figure 13-62**). Pes planus can be structural or functional. Both conditions can cause various lower extremity conditions and injuries.

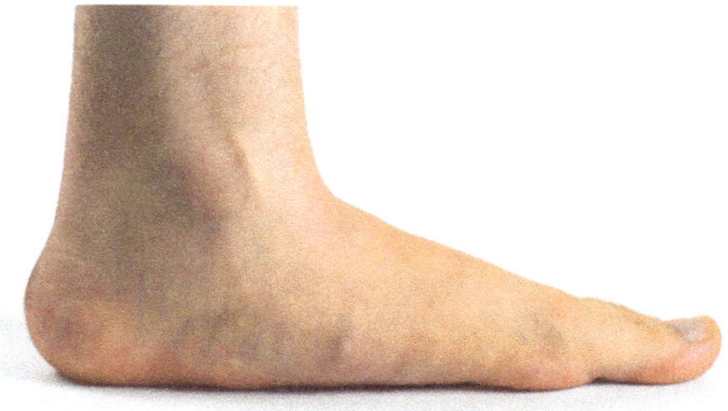

Figure 13-61 Pes planus is "flat foot" or a flat arch.

Mechanism or Cause of Injury

Structural pes planus occurs in individuals typically from birth. Infants and young children have flat feet, but as they grow older a normal arches form. For unknown reasons, the arch does not form in some children. Functional pes planus is caused by loose soft tissue structures, including the tendons and plantar fascia that comprise the plantar portion of the foot. An individual who has had a previous foot injury, or who is older may have pes planus.

Pes cavus is not as common as pes planus. Pes cavus is caused by bone malformations in the foot or nerve problems. Pes cavus can also be caused over time when an individual continually wears shoes that have a too small toe box. Tight toe boxes force the toes to passively flex and raise the arch. The soft tissue structures shorten and contract in that position, and form pes cavus.

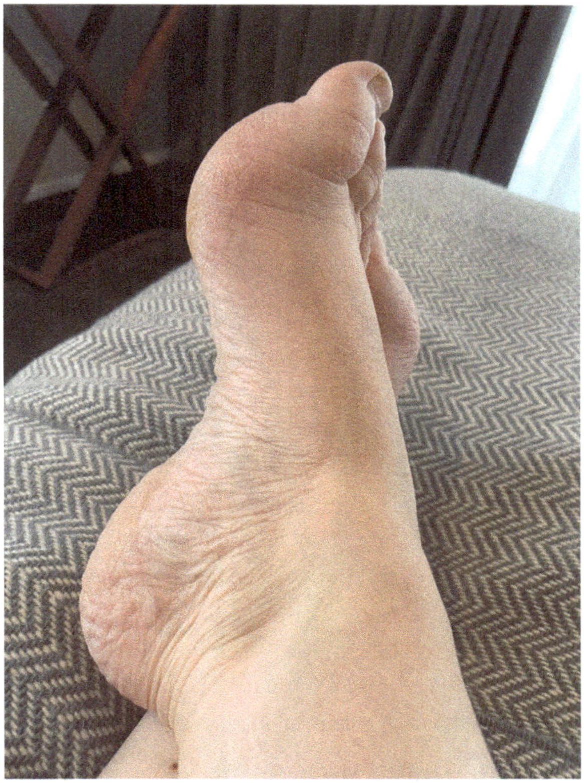

Figure 13-62 Pes cavus is a high arch.

Signs and Symptoms

When observing an individual with pes planus, the medial longitudinal arch will be flat on one or both feet. An individual with structural pes planus does not have an apparent medial longitudinal arch when weight bearing and non-weight bearing. The arch is flat in both positions. The individual who has functional pes planus has a visible medial longitudinal arch while non-weight bearing, and a flat arch when weight bearing. Pes planus does not necessarily cause troublesome signs and symptoms, especially if an adult individual has had flat feet since birth. The individual may have a tired feeling in their feet after standing, walking, or running for long periods of time due to lack of plantar fascia support.

In contrast to pes planus, pes cavus is commonly painful. If the foot is very rigid, the pain develops when the individual is on their feet standing, walking, or running. They may complain of secondary problems caused by pes planus or pes cavus, such as MTSS and plantar fasciitis, respectively.

Immediate Care

If the individual's pes planus or pes cavus does not bother them or cause secondary injuries, then they do not need to treat the condition. If the individual is experiencing pain or other secondary injury due to pes planus or pes cavus, then they need to see a physician for evaluation. The individual may need custom orthotics to assist in decreasing pain and making the foot "normal", as well as correcting any biomechanics that are causing secondary injuries.

Prevention

Flat feet cannot be prevented if the person has structural pes planus since birth. Functional pes planus can be minimized or prevented by strengthening the musculature and wearing shoes that support the medial longitudinal arch. Pes cavus can be prevented by stretching the plantar fascia and musculature that comprises the plantar surface of the foot. Also, individuals should wear shoes that fit their feet well and have adequate toe box size.

Bunion

A bunion is a bony outgrowth which occurs at the base of the medial first metatarsal.

Mechanism or Cause of Injury

A bunion forms when an individual wears shoes that have a tight and pointed toe box. The great toe is forced laterally toward the second toe. This angulation is called hallux valgus. At the same time, the angulation and the shoe causes friction on the medial side of the first metatarsal head. Eventually the bunion forms **(Figure 13-63)**. Heredity plays a role in formulating bunions, as does arthritis.

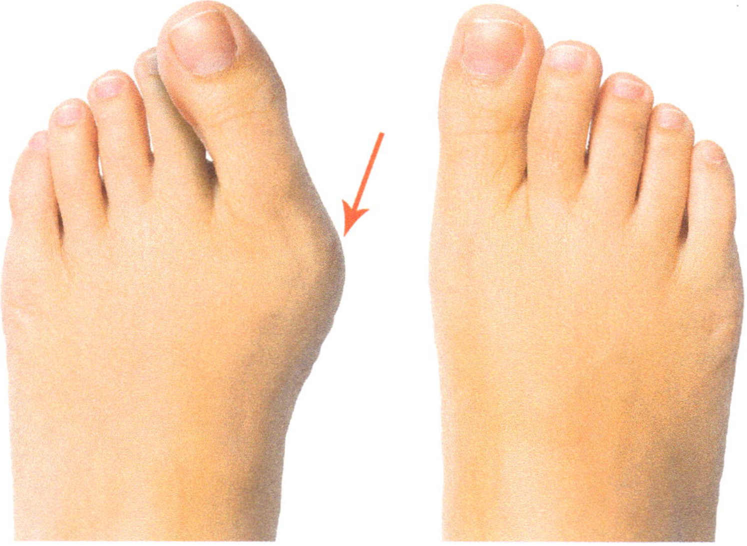

Figure 13-63 A bunion and hallux valgus of the left foot

Signs and Symptoms

The individual's great toe is angulated toward the second toe. The great toe may be severely angulated, which results in the great toe lying on top of the second toe. The individual also has a large bump (the bunion) at the medial first metatarsal head. The individual's great toe may be red and swollen at the metatarsophalangeal joint due to the inflammation. Likewise, calluses may form at the area. The individual has soreness or pain at the site of the bunion due to friction when wearing shoes. The first metatarsophalangeal joint function is compromised.

Immediate Care

If the bunion or first digit angulation does not create inflammation, pain, or loss of function for the individual, then no immediate care or treatment is needed. Individuals who have problematic, inflamed bunions should wear shoes with a wide toe box. Have the individual apply ice to the area frequently to reduce pain and inflammation. If the bunion continues to cause pain, the inflammation worsens, or has loss of function of the first digit, then they should see a physician. A bunionectomy may need to be performed. This procedure involves shaving down the bunion and realigning the angulated toe. The individual may be able to walk after the surgery, but commonly they wear a walking boot and utilize crutches until the pain and inflammation from the procedure subside. The individual should be able to return to full activity in approximately 2 months.

Prevention

Individuals should wear comfortable, well-fitted shoes with adequate space in the toe box in order to prevent bunions. Unfortunately, bunions caused by heredity and arthritis are not preventable.

Morton's Neuroma

Morton's neuroma, or metatarsalgia, is a condition that occurs at the ball of the foot. Fibrous tissue thickens around the nerve between the metatarsals and causes various signs and symptoms of nerve injury. The lateral plantar nerve runs between the metatarsals. This nerve is most commonly irritated between the third and fourth metatarsals (MayoClinic, 2021) **(Figure 13-64)**.

Mechanism or Cause of Injury

Morton's neuroma is caused by pressure or friction on the ball of the foot, or by previous injury (e.g., metatarsal fracture). Because the ball of the foot between the third and fourth metatarsals is under a lot of pressure and stress when weight bearing, the area becomes irritated. Due to the irritation, fibrous tissue builds up between these metatarsals. Individuals who wear tight

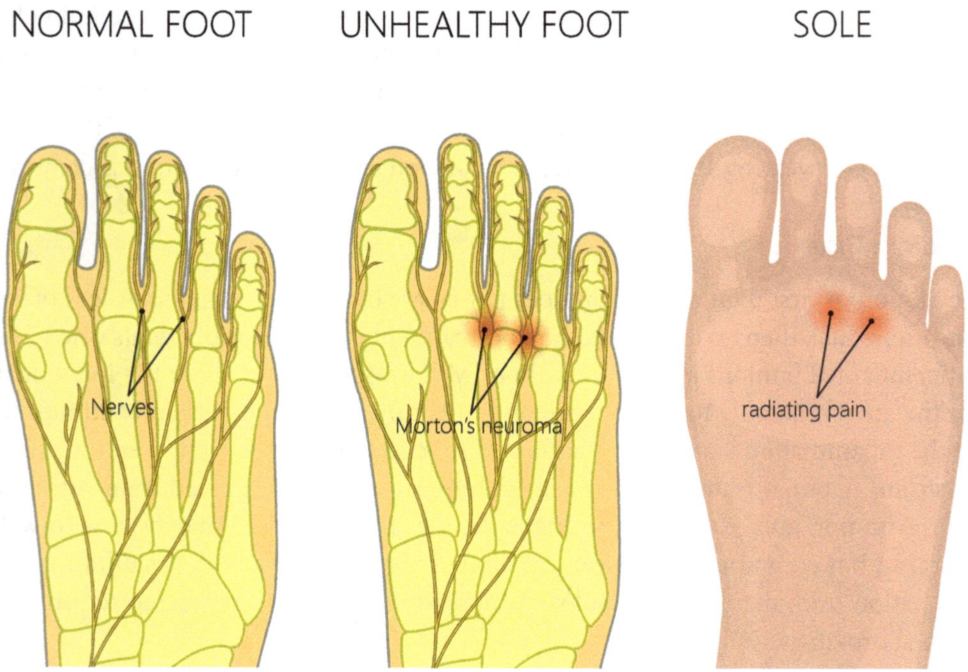

Figure 13-64 Morton's neuroma

shoes, utilize the balls of their feet to participate in sport (e.g., rock wall climbing), or who have pes cavus or hallux valgus are more prone to Morton's neuroma.

Signs and Symptoms

The individual complains of sharp, burning, shooting pain that is common with nerve injury. The radiating pain may go into their toes. They may also have tingling or loss of sensation from the ball of the foot to the toes.

Immediate Care

An ice pack or ice massage applied frequently throughout the day will help treat the injury. The individual can take NSAIDs, must wear footwear that supports the metatarsal arch, and place over-the-counter orthotics in their shoes. They should avoid any aggravating weight bearing activities on the balls of their feet. If the individual continues to have pain in their foot that does not decrease a few days after treatment, then they should be evaluated by a physician. Their physician may prescribe corticosteroid injections to decrease pain and inflammation. Surgery may be needed to either decrease the tightness of other structures that are compressing the nerve, or, in severe cases, remove the nerve.

Prevention

In order to prevent Morton's neuroma, individuals should wear properly fitting shoes that are not tight. They should also avoid constant weight bearing activities utilizing the balls of their feet.

Sprain

Toe sprains occur to the medial and lateral collateral ligaments, cartilage, and joint capsule. Sometimes you cannot specify if the toe is fractured or simply sprained. In fact, a sprain may also accompany a fracture.

Mechanism or Cause of Injury

Toe sprains are caused by hitting the end of the toe on a nonyielding object. A person can cause a sprain by kicking a wall, stubbing the toe against the ground, or striking it against another person, such as in martial arts. Stopping short or changing direction while running resulting in the toe hitting the front of the shoe forcefully can cause a sprain. The interphalangeal and metatarsophalangeal joints can also be forced into a valgus or varus position, which sprains the collateral ligaments. The great toe metatarsophalangeal joint is often sprained by forceful hyperextension when kicking. This injury is called *turf toe.*

Signs and Symptoms

The individual experiences the same signs and symptoms of injury as any Grade 1, 2, or 3 sprain. They have pain and loss of function at the injured area. The area may be stiff, swollen, and point tender. The toe may appear black and blue (exhibit ecchymosis) from internal bleeding.

Immediate Care

The individual should use RICE immediately on the toe. Support the injured toe by buddy taping the injured toe to the adjacent toes. The individual should not weight bear if they cannot do so without pain. If the individual cannot weight bear, then fit them for crutches. The individual should also take anti-inflammatory medication. Once the inflammation has subsided, they can perform toe exercises to increase ROM and strengthening exercises for the lower leg muscles that affect the toes. As always, if the individual's signs and symptoms do not decrease or get worse within a few days despite treatment, then they should see their physician to rule out a toe fracture.

Prevention

Prevention of toe sprains include having good ROM, flexibility, and strength at the toes. Supportive, comfortable shoes with an adequately sized toe box so the toes are not cramped or touching the front of the shoe should be worn during high impact activities. Avoiding kicking any nonyielding objects is also recommended for the prevention of toe fractures.

Hammer Toe, Claw Toe, and Mallet Toe

Hammer, claw, and mallet toe are deformities from tendon contractures **(Figure 13-65)**. These contractures may take years to develop. Hammer toes are distinguished by metatarsophalangeal joint hyperextension and proximal interphalangeal joint flexion Claw toes, which are common with individuals who have pes cavus, are indicated by metatarsophalangeal joint hyperextension, proximal interphalangeal joint and distal interphalangeal joint flexion. Mallet toe is characterized by flexion of the distal interphalangeal joint . The deformities can occur to one or multiple toes on one or both feet simultaneously.

Mechanism or Cause of Injury

These toe deformities are caused by wearing shoes that have a tight toe box. Consequently, the shoes do not have enough room at the front of the toe to allow for proper movement when an individual stops and changes direction. High-heeled shoes also force the toes to become crowded and unnaturally bend into these deformed positions. Nerve damage and previous injury, such as fractures and sprains, can cause hammer, claw, or mallet toe. Also, some individuals inherit the deformities from their parents.

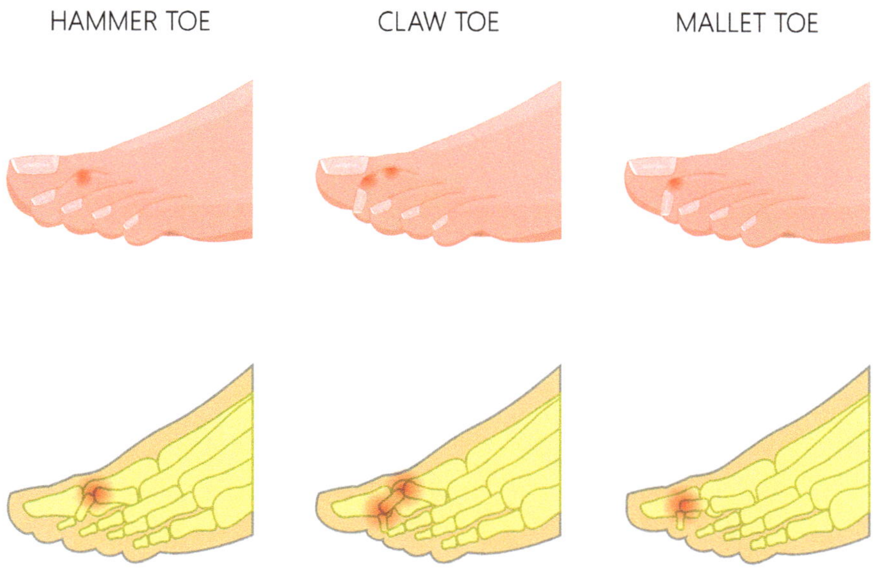

Figure 13-65 Differences among hammer, claw, and mallet toes

Signs and Symptoms

The individual's toes are deformed and contracted. They may not be able to move the toes in a normal manner, and feels pain when they try to do so. Calluses may form where the toes rub against the shoes.

Immediate Care

If the toes are still flexible, then it is possible to correct the deformities. The individual must wear shoes with larger toe boxes so the toes do not hit the front of the shoe when running. They can utilize shoe inserts to help relieve pain and pressure. The individual needs to perform ROM and flexibility exercises for each affected toe. If the individual has persistent pain or cannot walk without pain or normal toe function, then they should see a physician. If the toes are tightly contracted and inflexible, the physician may recommend surgery to correct the deformities. The surgical procedure releases the tendons and/or realign the bones.

Prevention

To prevent hammer, claw, or mallet toes, wearing properly fitting shoes with low heels and a roomy toe box is essential.

Subungual Hematoma

A subungual hematoma is blood underneath the toenail (**Figure 13-66**).

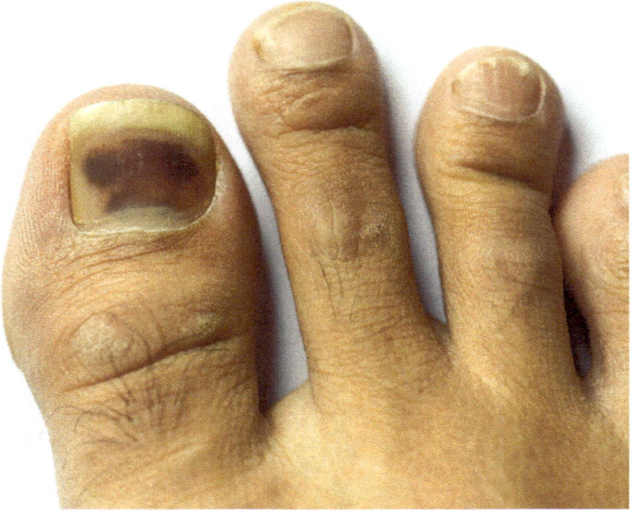

Figure 13-66 Subungual hematoma of the great toe

Mechanism or Cause of Injury

A subungual hematoma is caused by a direct blow to the nail. An individual who drops a weight on their toe, is stepped on by another person, or stubs their toe into a nonyielding object can have a subungual hematoma form.

Signs and Symptoms

The individual experiences pain as the blood accumulates under the nail due to the pressure created by the blood. The blood under the nail is red at first. As days go by, the blood turns dark purple to black. The nail is point tender. If the nail is significantly damaged, it may fall off during the healing process.

Immediate Care

A minor toe subungual hematoma does not need treatment other than ice application. If the toe is still painful after a few days of ice treatment then the individual should see a physician who will drain the blood from the toe. Draining the blood eliminates the pressure from underneath the nail. The individual instantaneously feels pain relief. The physician releases the blood by utilizing a sterile object, such as a pointy scalpel or wire. The hole created to release the blood needs to be treated as an open wound and bandaged to prevent infection and promote healing. In some instances, the nail is significantly damaged and need to be removed by the physician.

Prevention

Individuals must be careful not to drop heavy items on their toes in order to attempt to prevent subungual hematomas.

Summary

Injuries to the lower extremity vary, but many mechanisms of these injuries are the same. A traumatic, direct blow, torsion of the lower extremity, stress from repetitive, forceful weight bearing, and poorly fitted shoes are common causes for lower extremity injuries. Since the lower extremity is weight bearing during numerous activities, forces applied at the foot can be transmitted throughout the extremity and cause injuries at unexpected sites. Consequently, when you examine an individual's lower extremity, do not assume that an injury is only located where force was applied. Consider the possibility and look for secondary injuries, and treat all injuries appropriately.

Keywords

Circumduction The distal end of the extremity (the hand or foot) makes a circular motion moving freely through space while the proximal end (the shoulder or hip) remains stable or fixed.

Scoliosis A lateral curvature of the spine when you are viewing the spine from a posterior view.

Contraindicated A certain treatment, action, or rehabilitation technique must be avoided due to the particular condition, illness, or injury that an individual has sustained. If the contraindicated treatment, action, or rehabilitation technique was utilized, the individual's situation most likely will worsen.

Ectopic The formation of soft tissue, bone, an organ, or the like outside of its normal position or location.

Sesamoid bone A bone that is embedded within a tendon, which most often is located over a joint. Other than the patella, which is the largest sesamoid bone, sesamoid bones are located in the hands and feet.

Long sitting position When an individual is seated on the ground with both legs extended.

Q-angle Stands for the "quadriceps angle". The Q-angle is the relative position of the patella to the tibia, the femur, and pelvis. The Q-angle is measured by visualizing one line from the midpoint of the patella to the anterior superior iliac spine, and another line from the midpoint of the patella to the most prominent point of the tibial tuberosity. The superior angle created by the bisection of the two lines is the Q-angle . The normal Q-angle for biological women is 15° to 18°, and for biological men is 10° to 12°. Angles outside of these ranges, especially a Q-angle greater than 18° for biological women, can cause various patellar injuries and conditions including PFPS, chondromalacia patella, and patellar subluxations and dislocations.

Discussion Questions

1. Which lower extremity injuries have an acute mechanism of injury? Which injuries have a slow or insidious onset?
2. What are common areas of the lower extremity that can sustain a stress fracture?
3. What lower extremity injuries can an individual treat themselves? At what point should the individual go to see a physician?
4. What lower extremity injuries typically causes an individual to go into shock? Why do they go into shock when sustaining these injuries?
5. What lower extremity injuries must be surgically repaired and why?
6. What lower extremity injuries typically occur to biological men? biological women? children?
7. What role does improper footwear play in causing lower extremity injuries?

CASE STUDY: HALF MARATHON DREAMS

Taryn is a 22-year-old female who is active but does not exercise on a consistent basis. She decides to do something different to force herself to exercise regularly, so she begins to train for a half marathon. The half marathon will take place in a little over five months, so she has to begin to prepare now. Since she did not previously run as part of her exercise routine, she wants to take her training slow and train only 5 days per week. Taryn begins her training and completes three miles by the end of her first week. Aside from some delayed onset muscle soreness in her quadriceps and hamstrings, which is alleviated by stretching, she is not experiencing any physical problems. Therefore, after the first week she decides to increase her distance a half mile each week in subsequent weeks.

At the beginning of week four, Taryn adds another half mile to her workout routine, which has her completing 4 ½ miles. She also begins to run on a new path which includes various surfaces and slight inclines, which mimic the half marathon course. After the second day completing the new mileage and route, Taryn experiences pain at the end of her workouts on the front of both lower legs. She dismisses the pain and speculates that her body is becoming accustomed to the increased mileage and new training route terrain. As she continues her daily workouts and begins her fifth and sixth weeks of training, she feels the pain progressively earlier in her mileage. Taryn's friend suggests that new running shoes will solve her problem.

Early one morning before her run, Taryn goes to her local sporting goods store to purchase a pair of running shoes. She picks out a stylish pair, figuring that they are probably good for her since they are endorsed by a celebrity and are expensive. She tries the sneakers on, and they feel a little tight, but she figures that they will stretch out. She goes home, puts the sneakers back on, and goes for her run. In the beginning of her training, Taryn immediately realizes that the sneakers do not help alleviate her pain. The sneakers actually seem to exacerbate her shin pain, because the pain now arises within the first 10 minutes of her run. The pain becomes increasingly stronger as she progresses in mileage. She has to stop running at the 2-mile mark.

Taryn decides to take the next 3 days off from running. On the first day, she notices that her pain is present during the day while she is on her feet at work. Taryn's pain is evident when she performs normal daily weight-bearing activities, such as walking up and down stairs. When she touches her medial shins, the area is very tender to the touch. She goes to bed that evening and cannot sleep due to the throbbing pain felt at both medial shins.

Taryn has become extremely frustrated with her condition. She has not been able to complete her training and the pain is not subsiding with rest. Taryn fears that if she goes to see a physician, they will make her stop running for an extended period of time. The rest time will put her behind schedule and ruin her dream of running in the half marathon. Taryn does not know what to do.

1. What injury has Taryn sustained?
2. What is the cause(s) of her injury?
3. What should Taryn have done to treat the injury before it worsened?
4. Should Taryn go to her physician for evaluation? What treatment do you think the physician will recommend?
5. What should Taryn consider when purchasing running shoes?
6. Was the injury preventable? Why or why not?

References

American Academy of Orthopedic Surgeons (AAOS). (2018). *Femur shaft fractures (broken thighbone).* Retrieved on August 14, 2021, from http://orthoinfo.aaos.org/topic.cfm?topic=A00521

American Academy of Orthopedic Surgeons (AAOS). (2021). *Patellar tendon tear.* Retrieved on October 30, 2021, from http://orthoinfo.aaos.org/topic.cfm?topic=a00512

Bernhardson, A.S., DePhillipo, N.N., Daney, B.T., Kennedy, M.I., Aman, Z.S., & LaPrade, R.F. (2019). Posterior Tibial Slope and Risk of Posterior Cruciate Ligament Injury. *American Journal of Sports Medicine*, 47(2), 312-317.

Forcada, C., Pons, A., Seijas, R., Sallent, A., Dominguez, A., Ares, O., & Alvárez, P. (2017). Risk Factors and Prevention Strategies of Anterior Cruciate Ligament Injuries in Young Females Athletes. International Journal of Orthopaedics, 4(3), 734-739. Retrieved on October 30, 2021, from http://scholar.google.com/

Lodge, C.J., Sha, S., Yousef, A.S.E., MacEachern, C. (2020). Stress fractures in the young adult hip. Orthopaedics and Trauma, 34(2), 95-100. doi:10.1016/j.mporth.2020.01.006.

MayoClinic (2021). *Morton's neuroma.* Retrieved on February 16, 2021 from https://www.mayoclinic.org/diseases-conditions/mortons-neuroma/symptoms-causes/syc-20351935#:~:text=Morton's%20neuroma%20involves%20a%20thickening,numbness%20in%20the%20affected%20toes

Raj, M.A., Mabrouk, A., Varacallo, M. (2021). Posterior Cruciate Ligament Knee Injuries. In: StatPearls [Internet]. Treasure Island (FL): StatPearls Publishing. Retrieved August 14, 2021, from https://www.ncbi.nlm.nih.gov/books/NBK430726/

Saad, A., Azzopardi, C., Patel, A., Davies, A.M., Botchu, R. (2021). Myositis ossificans revisited – The largest reported case series. Journal of Clinical Orthopaedics and Trauma, 17, 123–127. doi: 10.1016/j.jcot.2021.03.005.

Schultz, S. J., Houglum, P. A., & Perrin, D. H. (2016). *Examination of musculoskeletal injuries* (4th ed.). Champaign, IL: Human Kinetics.

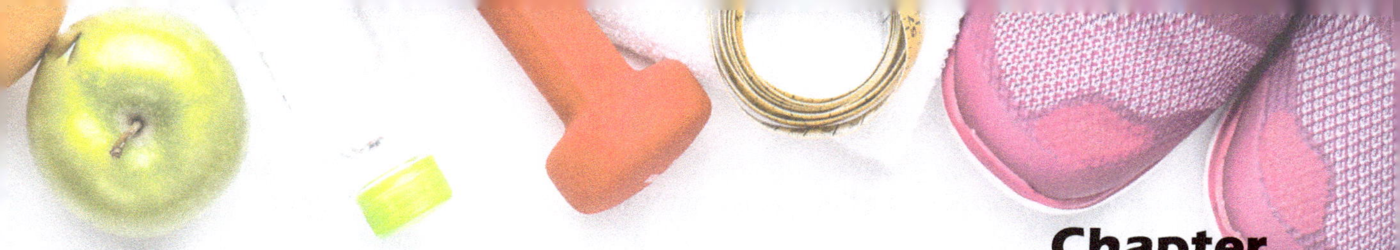

Chapter 14

Posture & Gait

Chapter Objectives

After you have read this chapter, you will be able to understand:

- The appearance of normal posture.
- The various postural abnormalities and associated injuries.
- The appearance of normal gait patterns.
- The abnormal gait patterns in injured patients, and the injuries or postural deviations that contribute to these abnormalities.
- The abnormal gait patterns which result from injury.
- The abnormal gait patterns which are congenital in origin.

Posture

When evaluating injuries, especially chronic injuries, it is imperative to evaluate the patient's posture. Posture is the positioning and arrangement of the body parts in relation to each other. If a patient has correct, normal posture, minimal stresses are placed upon their body. When a patient has incorrect posture, then a greater chance for stresses to adversely affect bony and soft tissue structures exists. The stress on the body due to incorrect posture can cause chronic injury. When a patient complains of signs and symptoms of chronic injury including pain, loss of function, stiffness, decreased flexibility, muscular weakness, and/or muscular spasm, in conjunction with an insidious onset, you should evaluate the patient's posture.

Poor posture can cause chronic injury not only to the spine, but also to the extremities. Most often the lower extremity is affected by incorrect posture. Because the lower extremity is weight bearing, postural deviations can cause chronic injury through the entire lower extremity down to the feet. Therefore, you must evaluate the patient's posture to determine if it is the cause of the patient's lower extremity problem.

If the faulty posture is causing the chronic injury, then the patient's posture needs to be corrected. Incorrect posture can be evident at birth. It can also result from incorrect body movements and positioning after injury. The patient may utilize poor sitting and standing habits, and, as they age, their posture may be affected. (Shultz, Houglum, & Perrin, 2016).

Postural Evaluation

To begin evaluating the patient's posture, you must first recognize what is considered normal posture. By reviewing anatomical pictures of the body, you can visualize what is considered normal posture. In order to evaluate the patient's posture, examine the patient from anterior, posterior, and lateral views **(Figure 14-1)**. When you examine a patient in an anterior or posterior view, visualize a line running down the patient in a sagittal plane, which divides the patient equally into right and left halves. A plumb line assists you in creating this sagittal plane. A plumb line is string suspended from the ceiling attached to a small weight, similar to a fishing pole weight, which hangs to the floor. Before you examine the patient, make sure the plumb line is steady. The patient should stand close to the plumb line during evaluation, but far enough away so they do not touch it.

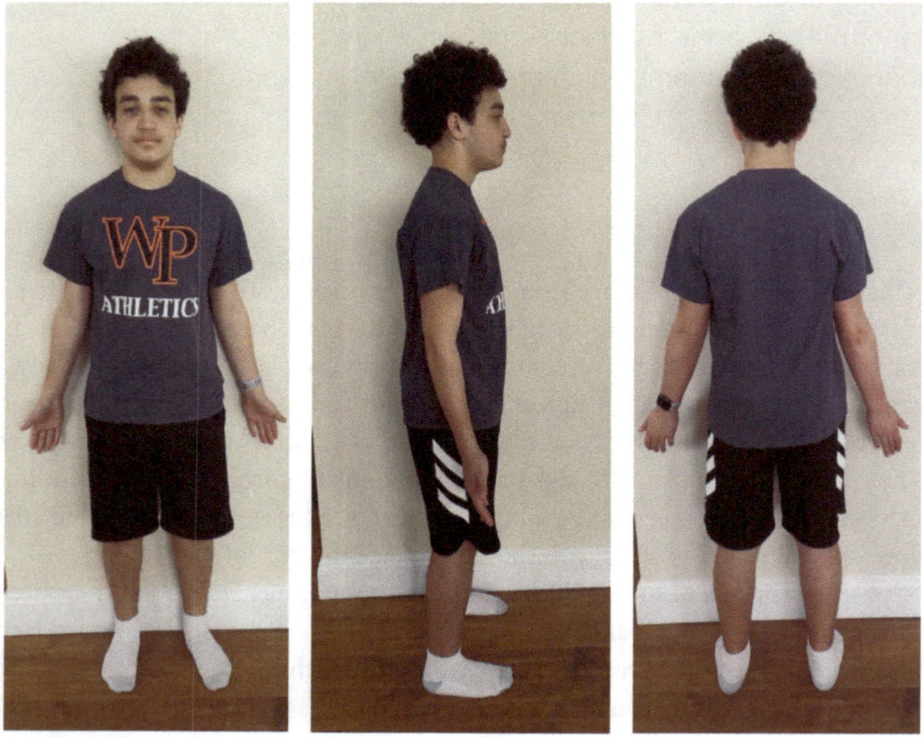

Figure 14-1 Anterior, lateral, and posterior views for assessing posture

To examine their anterior structures, have the patient stand behind the plumb line facing you. In this position, the patient's body is divided into two equal halves. The plumb line bisects the patient's nose, sternum, and umbilicus. The plumb line is lined up midway between the feet. With the plumb line in place, observe the patient's ears, eyes, acromioclavicular (AC) joints, antecubital fossa at the elbows, iliac crests, patellae, medial longitudinal arches of the foot, and great toes. Determine if each of these body parts are in alignment with the matching part on the other side. For example, determine if the AC joints on each upper extremity is aligned at the same height across the body, and if the patella are at the same height and position. Start evaluating at the head and end with the feet.

To evaluate their posterior structures, the patient must stand with their back to the plumb line, bisecting their body into right and left halves as with the anterior view. As you look at the plumb line relative to their spine, the spine should be straight. The spinous processes for each vertebrae should be in line with the plumb line. Compare the height and alignment of the following structures bilaterally: the shoulder, olecranon process, scapula, iliac crest, popliteal fossa, and calcaneus. To examine the patient from the lateral view, have them stand to the side of the plumb line. The plumb line should run through the middle of the ear's auditory meatus, the acromion process, the greater trochanter, slightly posterior to the patella, and in front of the lateral malleolus.

When comparing the contralateral side, if any anatomical landmarks are not aligned or one side of the body does not appear as it should, then the patient may have a postural deviation. These postural deviations can be the cause of acute and chronic injuries in the body and must be addressed. If you find the patient has a postural deviation potentially due to an injury, then refer the patient to their physician for evaluation.

TIPS FROM THE FIELD

Tip 1 You can make a plumb line to evaluate a patient's posture even when you do not have string or weight available. Take the end of athletic, duct, or masking tape and secure it to the ceiling. Then unroll tape from the ceiling to the floor. Unroll about 2 feet more than the distance between the ceiling and the floor, and cut the tape. Then beginning from the ceiling, roll the tape between the palms of your hands and fingers down to the floor. You should end up with a tight, rolled "string" of tape. Then secure the tape to the floor. Look at the tape string from each angle and move it so it is straight from the ceiling and the floor. This task is best accomplished with a patient standing by the tape. Once the tape plumb line is straight, then use it to evaluate your patient's posture.

Common Postural Deviations

There are a number postural deviations you should look for when performing a postural evaluation. Typically, these deviations originate from the spine; however, the lower extremities may also contribute to postural abnormalities.

Spine

The spine is divided into 5 different sections: cervical, thoracic, lumbar, sacral, and coccyx. The sections of the spine where it is more common to see deviations are at the cervical, thoracic, and lumbar spines. This potentiality of deviations is due to the increased mobility of the cervical, thoracic, and lumbar spines as compared to the sacral and coccygeal spines.

At the lumbar spine, an excessive anterior curvature can occur due to tight psoas major muscles, since these muscles attach to the anterior surface of all five lumbar vertebrae. This tightness can cause an anterior translation of the spine, also known as **lordosis**. The psoas major muscle tightness, along with other hip flexor muscle tightness, and gluteus maximus and hamstring muscle weakness can also tilt the pelvis forward. Tight anterior muscles and weak posterior muscles causes a muscle imbalance, which is referred to as **lower crossed syndrome**. Addressing the anterior tightness and posterior weakness by stretching and strengthening, respectively, can help alleviate this imbalance and return the pelvis to a more neutral position.

At the thoracic level, an excessive posterior curvature that is typically due to tight pectoralis muscles and weak upper back muscles is referred to as **kyphosis**. The tight pectoralis muscles pull the shoulders forward, due to the attachment at the clavicles (pectoralis major) and scapula (pectoralis minor). Due to decreased strength, the upper back muscles are unable to pull the shoulders back, resulting in incorrect posture. The imbalance of these muscle groups contribute to **upper crossed syndrome**. Additionally, the patient's head will also take on a more forward appearance, which will be visible during a lateral view postural evaluation. Addressing the anterior tightness and posterior weakness by stretching and strengthening, respectively, can help alleviate this imbalance and return the shoulders to a more neutral position.

During the posterior postural evaluation, determine if all vertebral spinous processes are in line with the plumb line. If there are any lateral deviations of the spine, the patient has scoliosis. Patients typically do not need referral to a physician if they have minor deviations if the deviations do not cause the patient discomfort and/or are not getting worse over time. If a patient has an extreme deviation, they should be referred to their physician or spine specialist to be treated. Until cleared by a physician, the patient should not participate in any athletic activities.

Lower Extremity

At the lower extremity, postural deviations can contribute to chronic injuries, such as medial tibial stress syndrome, patella femoral pain syndrome, and IT band syndrome.

At the feet, the patient's arch height is one contributing factor to chronic injuries. Pes planus, or flat feet, can place stress on the medial side of the leg. The increased stress typically occurs at the tibialis posterior muscle that attaches to the medial side of the foot. When a patient has pes planus, the tendon of the muscle is subjected to excessive stress that can affect the entire muscle up to its origin site on the tibia's posterior surface. This excessive stress can result in medial tibial stress syndrome, otherwise known as shin splints. If a patient suffers from pes cavus, or high arches, the same stress can be placed on this tendon, especially if the patient wears footwear with inadequate support. Proper footwear and orthotics can help alleviate stress on the lower leg, which in turn can decrease risk of chronic injury.

The knees' position in relation to the hips can contribute to postural deviations. When the knees are more medial to a straight line between the hips and feet then the patient has genu valgum. This deviation is more common in biological females, and puts stress on the lateral structures on the knee and thigh, such as the IT band. There is also a higher risk of anterior cruciate ligament (ACL) injuries in patients that have genu valgum (Samaei et al., 2012). Contributing factors to genu valgum are hip abductor weakness and/or pes planus. Addressing these weaknesses and/or wearing proper footwear can decrease the risk of injury associated with this deviation. When the knees are more lateral to a straight line between the hips and feet the patient has genu varum. This deviation is more common in biological males and is not associated with as many chronic injuries as compared to genu valgum. Patients that have genu varum may also have pes cavus. If the patient suffers from any discomfort in the lower leg from this deviation, proper footwear and orthotics can help alleviate the stress and decrease risk of chronic injury.

Gait

At one time or another, you have most likely sat in a public area and observed how people walk or run. No two people move the same way, but they are all able to complete the movement and get to their desired destination. How individuals carry themselves, hold their bodies upright, and put one foot in front of the other to walk or run can identify any postural deviations, muscle imbalances, and/or gait pattern abnormalities. These postural deviations, muscle imbalances, and/or gait pattern abnormalities can also identify an injury an individual has sustained, including the injury's severity, irritability, nature, and stage. It is critical to identify postural deviations and gait abnormalities that may be contributing to or be a result of an injury, in order to provide the patient with proper treatment and rehabilitation.

Gait is a complex activity with many different elements that contribute to the manner in which a person ambulates. Most gait activity involves lower extremity motion. However, it is important to understand how the thorax, abdomen, and upper extremity, as well as any abnormalities, contribute to type of gait (running or walking).

Components of Gait

Gait is comprised of a number of elements that make up a gait cycle. The two phases that contribute to a gait cycle are the **stance phase** and the **swing phase**. (Subcategories of each phase will be described later in this chapter.) These phases are defined by events that make up the basic fundamental components of gait. These events are described as foot strike and toe-off, and are used to define both the stance and swing phases of the gait cycle **(Figure 14-2)**.

A **step** is foot strike of one foot to foot strike of the opposite foot (i.e., making contact with the right foot and then making contact with the left foot) **(Figure 14-3)**. A **stride** is foot

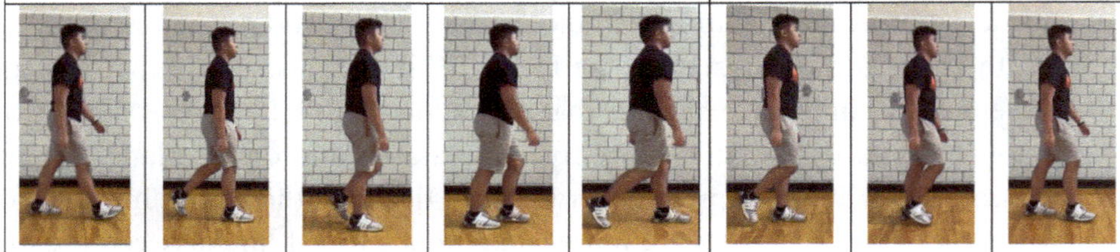

Stance Phase					Swing Phase		
Initial Contact (foot strike)	Loading Response	Mid-stance	Terminal Stance	Pre-swing (toe-off)	Initial Swing	Mid-swing	Terminal Swing
Supination	Pronation			Supination			

Figure 14-2 Phases of a normal gait cycle

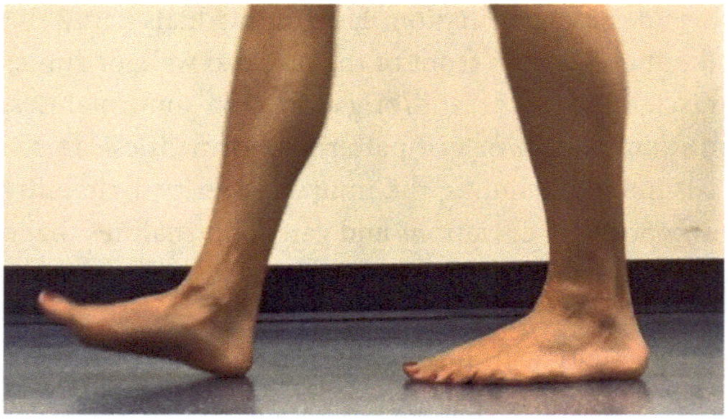

Figure 14-3 Foot strike of an individual's left foot to foot strike of their right foot is a step.

strike to the next foot strike of the same foot. A stride is made up of two steps (i.e., right step, left step). Step length is the distance covered from foot strike of one foot to foot strike of the opposite foot (i.e., right foot strike to left foot strike). Stride length is the distance covered from foot strike of one foot to the next foot strike of the same foot (i.e. right foot strike to the next right foot strike). How quickly a person takes steps is referred to as **cadence.** Cadence is typically measured in steps per minute.

Stance Phase

Stance phase is the entire time the foot is in contact with the ground. During walking, the stance phase is the gait cycle's longest phase. Approximately 60 percent of the gait cycle is the stance phase. The amount of support provided to the body depends on if only one or both feet are on the ground. Single support occurs when only one foot is in contact with the ground, and double support occurs when both feet are in contact with the ground simultaneously.

The stance phase can further be classified into four smaller sub-phases, which assist in describing the foot's positioning during its contact with the ground. The beginning of the stance phase is called initial contact, which is when the foot makes contact with the ground for the first time. During walking, initial contact is made with the heel. However, during running or in some abnormal types of gait initial contact can be made with the mid-foot or forefoot. During this sub-phase, both feet are in contact with the ground. The next sub-phase is the loading response phase, which occurs from initial contact of one foot until the opposite foot leaves the ground. During this sub-phase a person's weight is transferred from one foot to the other as the opposite leg leaves the ground. The third sub-phase is the mid-stance phase, also known as the swing phase. During this sub-phase, the opposite leg is completely off the ground, and begins to prepare for the next contact with the ground. The foot in contact with the ground is responsible for maintaining balance and posture during the opposite foot's transition. This sub-phase is the beginning of the cycle's single support phase. The final sub-stance phase is the terminal stance phase, which occurs just prior to when the foot in the swing phase makes contact with the ground. During the transition from the mid-stance to the terminal stance phases, the body is progresses forward and the transfer of weight moves from the middle of the foot to the forefoot. The final sub-phase is the pre-swing phase. In pre-swing, the foot on the ground prepares to move into the swing phase, and the foot in the swing phase makes contact with the ground (i.e., the initial contact phase for this foot). Once the foot in the swing phase makes contact with the ground, the individual is in a double supported stance again.

Swing Phase

The swing phase is when the foot makes no contact with the ground or is swinging through the air to prepare for the next foot strike. During walking, this phase makes up the other 40 percent of the gait cycle. Similar to the stance phase, the swing phase is broken up into smaller sub-phases.

The first sub-phase is the initial swing phase. During this sub-phase, the foot accelerates through the air to begin the progression towards the next contact with the ground. This phase occurs from when the foot leaves the ground to when the knee is in maximal knee flexion in swing. Following this sub-phase is the mid-swing phase. The thigh continues to progress forward while the knee is flexed to make sure the foot clears the ground, otherwise the person will trip. The final sub-phase is the terminal swing phase. During this phase, the lower leg begins to extend towards the ground to prepare for its next initial contact. Once the foot hits the ground, the stance phase begins and the cycle repeats again until the individual stops walking.

Differences Between Walking and Running Gait

Two of the major differences between the walking and running gaits are that with walking one foot maintains contact with the ground at all times, and a double leg stance phase during the walking gait cycle exists. In running, a definite flight phase where both feet leave the ground at the same time occurs, and only a single leg stance phase during the gait cycle exists. Since an individual only has a single leg stance as part of the running gait cycle, balance, coordination, and proprioception are very important to complete the action in an efficient manner. As an individual runs faster, the stance phase of running gets shorter and the swing phase (flight) gets longer. This means the runner is spending more time in the air than on the ground to complete the motion. Also the body has less time to adjust to each stance phase sub-phase to continue to propel the runner forward. Additionally, when running speed increases, stride length and cadence also increases.

Ground Reaction Force

Another important component of gait is ground reaction force (GRF). GRF is the amount of force the body absorbs and travels up the lower extremity as the person ambulates. These forces can be measured vertically, horizontally or from anterior-to-posterior. In regards to injury, the vertical GRF is the most important to focus on. This force is dependent on a number of factors such as the person's body mass, ambulation speed, foot strike characteristics, and the surface the person is ambulating on.

As an individual's mass increases as they move through the lifespan, they will produce more force during all ambulation activities. Increased production of force is completely dependant of ambulation speed, foot strike characteristics, and the surface the person is ambulating on. Additionally, when a person's mass increases as an adult, they will also have an increased GRF. The differences between an increase in body mass as a person goes from a child to an adult versus an adult that is fully developed can put different types of forces on the body. As a child matures, their bones, muscles, and tissues naturally develop and the body accommodates to these changes. As with any type of injury, if excessive stress to the bones increases, such as through increased running intensity or surface changes, they will be more susceptible to stress fractures. Likewise, certain illnesses and conditions, such as if an individual has disordered eating habits, can predispose an individual to stress fractures. If an adult increases their mass (i.e., gains fat or muscular tissue) when they are fully developed, it can put excessive stress on their joints causing pain and discomfort in the short term, and put the individual at risk for osteoarthritis over time (Lee et al., 2018).

Speed of ambulation and foot strike are other factors that determine the amount of GRF placed on the body. Walking puts the least amount of stress on the lower extremities, with about an average of 1 to 1.5 times the body weight placed on the knee joints (Elhafez et al., 2019). As walking speed increases, so does the amount of force that is placed on the lower extremity. Miller et al. (1990) published a fundamental paper about the biomechanics of running, which is the basis for most of the current gait research. The authors found that during running a person can absorb up to 3 times their body weight, depending on how fast they are running and if they are a heel striker or a mid-foot striker **(Figure 14-4)**. The way a person strikes the ground can also add excessive GRF to their body. Heel strikers put more force on the lower extremities as they come in contact with the ground since the first part of their body to strike the ground is the heel. This heel strike provides force directly to the calcaneus bone, which does not absorb GRFs as well as soft tissue. Consequently, force is driven up the leg. In contrast, a mid-foot striker makes initial contact with the ground with their more tissue dense mid-foot. Since the plantar fascia, which is located in the mid-foot, has more shock absorbing properties than bone, the amount of force that travels up the lower extremity is reduced. If a person has other structural or functional abnormalities, such as genu valgum, pes planus, or drop foot, the amount of force placed on the body may be increased.

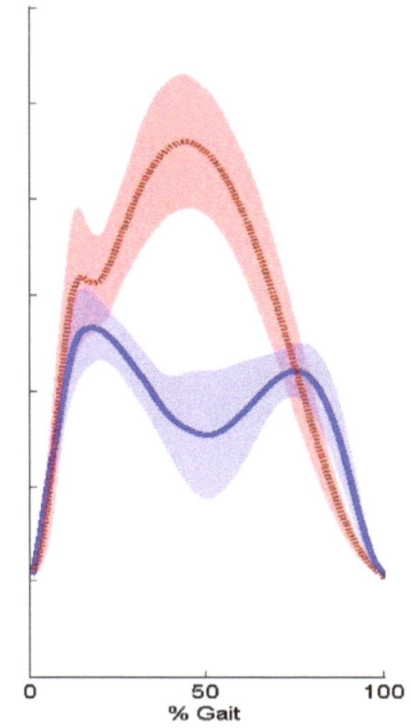

Figure 14-4 Ground reaction forces of walking (blue) and running (red). The x-axis represents the percentage of the gait cycle where the forces occur from foot strike to toe off.

Surface firmness is another contributing factor to the amount of GRF that affects the body. Hard surfaces, such as pavement or concrete, provide the most GRF to the lower extremities. Combined with a person who is a forceful heel striker, hard surfaces put additional, excess stress on the lower extremities, which can lead to stress fractures. Softer surfaces, such as grass, an all-weather running track, or sand, have more give to them and will cause less GRF stress on the body. The downside to the softer surfaces is that the hips, knees, ankles, and feet need to be very stable to have proper movement control on these softer, potentially more uneven, and/or shock absorbing surfaces.

Shoe Pattern Wear

When completing your observation, you first want to take a look at the patient's shoes. Examine the shoes that the patient wears regularly, which has some wear on the soles. Take a look at the heel and note the pattern of wear. An individual with a neutral and supinator foot has wear more towards the lateral side with a pronator being more medial. Moving to the mid-foot part of the shoe, look where the wear pattern tracks. Individuals who have a neutral foot and those who supinate will have a trajectory towards the lateral side of the foot. The individual who supinates will have even more wear on the lateral edge of the shoe due to the nature of their pes cavus arch. Individuals who pronate will have more wear on the medial side of the foot, consistent with their pes planus foot. Individuals who have extreme pronation will possibly have wear on the medial side of the shoe where the sole meets the fabric or leather part of the shoe. On the forefoot of the shoe, look to see at what point the patient toes off. Most patients will have wear under their big toe. However, if the patient has a Morton's toe there may be more wear under the second toe on the shoe as compared to under the first toe.

When you have the patient put their shoes on for the gait analysis, be sure that they lace up and tighten their shoes in the manner they normally wear them. As previously mentioned, you want to recreate the most natural conditions for the patient in order to observe for any gait abnormalities.

Gait Analysis

When analyzing a patient's gait, you want to observe them in their most natural form. Often when you tell someone you are observing them, they typically change the way they move or carry themselves, thereby not demonstrating their natural gait. If possible, watch how the patient ambulates as they approach you, whether it be for an initial evaluation or follow-up evaluations. You will then be able to determine their natural form. If you are unable to observe the patient prior to asking them to walk or run for you, have the patient to walk or run on a treadmill at a self-selected pace. You do not want the patient to walk slower or faster than their natural pace, otherwise you will not be able to observe any natural gait abnormalities they may have.

When completing a gait analysis on your patient, you want to look at and listen to the patient's gait pattern. They can be barefoot, **shod**, or you can observe them in both conditions. If you are viewing the person barefoot in both walking and running gaits, only view them walking without shoes, unless they are a barefoot or minimalist shoe runner. You want to recreate the patient's most natural gait in both conditions to provide a good gait evaluation.

When you are viewing your patient's gait, you want to observe them from posterior, lateral, and anterior views. From the posterior or back frontal plane view, first look at the patient's feet, knees, and hips **(Table 14-1)**. Observe any deviations at foot strike (i.e., does the patient land on the medial or lateral sides of their foot when they foot strike). Also observe their gait as they transfer their weight forward, and when the foot is in mid-stance and toe-off. Do you

Table 14-1 Gait Analysis Checklist

1. Check wear pattern of patient's shoes
   a. Where is most of their wear?
   b. What do these patterns say about the type of foot they have (pronator, supinator, neutral)? Keep this in mind when you watch the patient walk/run.
   c. Do their shoes look like they need to be replaced?
2. Have patient walk on treadmill barefoot (preferred) or with socks
   a. Patient **self-selects** the speed that is comfortable to their normal walking pace
   b. Once they find their comfortable pace, instruct the patient to walk as normal as possible. Wait at least 30 seconds let the patient get comfortable on the treadmill.
   c. Before you begin looking at their gait, listen for any abnormalities in their steps as the patient walks. Do this for every condition (no shoes walking, shod walking, shod running).
3. Analyze the patient's gait walking without shoes (inclusive, but not limited to the questions below)
   a. Posteriorly
      i. Look for how the patient foot strikes the treadmill. Do you see any abnormalities from R to L?
      ii. Are they a pronator or supinator? Are the shoes they are wearing appropriate for the type of foot striker they are?
      iii. Do they have an unusual swing on one side vs. the opposite side?
      iv. Is there an adequate knee gap as one leg swings forward and the other is in stance on the treadmill?
      v. Do you notice any hip drop?
      vi. Does the trunk rotate excessively?
      vii. Do the upper extremities move symmetrically?
      viii. Is there any excessive head bobbing in the frontal plane?
   b. Laterally (both R & L sides)
      i. Do all of the lower extremity joints flex, extend, plantar flex, and dorsiflex appropriately? Do you notice any differences when you compare sides (i.e. drop foot, lack of hip or knee flexion/extension, etc.)?
      ii. Do they have an unusual swing on one side vs. the opposite side?
      iii. Does the trunk rotate excessively?
      iv. Do the upper extremities move symmetrically?
      v. Is there any excessive head bobbing in the sagittal plane?
   c. Anteriorly
      i. Look for how the patient toes off the treadmill. Do you see any abnormalities from R to L?
      ii. Do they have an unusual swing on one side vs. the opposite side that you did not notice from the posterior view?
      iii. Is there an adequate knee gap as one leg swings forward and the other is in stance on the treadmill that you did not notice from the posterior view?
      iv. Do the upper extremities move symmetrically that you did not notice from the posterior view?
      v. Is there any excessive head bobbing in the frontal plane that you did not notice from the posterior view?
4. Analyze the patient's gait walking with shoes
   a. Have patient put shoes on and complete the analysis again
5. Analyze the patient's gait jogging/running with shoes
   a. Have patient jog/run at a self-selected pace and complete the analysis again
   b. Do any of the symptoms you saw during walking increase, decrease, or remain the same compared to when the patient is running?
6. Review the findings with your patient
   a. Use of 2D camera in slow motion can help patient understand what you are explaining
   b. What type of intervention or treatment would they need to correct any abnormalities, if applicable?
   c. Are there any other recommendations you can provide the patient?

TIPS FROM THE FIELD

TIP 2 When evaluating a patient's gait, it can be difficult to see all of the abnormalities with the naked eye. Utilizing a 2D camera, such as cell phone camera, can help you with the patient's overall gait evaluation. As the evaluator, you should take video of the patient from the posterior, right and left lateral, and anterior views. Before you record, be sure that the patient is comfortable on the treadmill with the gait you are doing the analysis on, either walking or running. Record for at least 10 seconds or 10 strides, depending on how fast the patient is ambulating. You can use the video to help with your comprehensive gait evaluation if you have difficulty identifying any abnormities by observing in present time. You can also utilize the slow motion features of the camera to assist with your analysis.

Once the analysis is complete and you provide recommendations to your patient, you can share the video with your patient. If the patients requests, you can also provide a written report on your findings and time stamps of the video so the patient can observe what you found for themselves. This can be important in having the patient understand what is contributing to any issues they are having during ambulation.

hear any differences when their right foot strikes the treadmill as compared to when the left foot strikes the treadmill? Look at the swing leg. Do you notice any abnormalities while the lower extremity is in the swing phase? You also want to observe if the medial sides of the knees are touching or if there is a noticeable gap. If the knees are touching, there is mostly likely a weakness in the hip abductors on the weight bearing side that is causing the non-weight bearing hip to drop. This is more evident during the running gait than walking gait. After observing the lower extremities, you want to look at the spine, shoulders, arm swing, and head. Notice any excessive trunk rotation or lean to one side, symmetry in the arm swing, and if the head is bobbing excessively in the frontal plane.

The lateral (sagittal) plane view should be completed on both right and left sides. Observe for lower extremity joint angle differences. These differences could range from a decrease in ankle, knee, and/or hip range of motion of one side compared to the other. These differences could contribute to the way the patient foot strikes, toes off, or swings their lower extremity during the gait cycle. At the trunk, observe for any excessive forward trunk sway, excessive trunk flexion, or any unnecessary trunk rotation compared to the opposite side. Lastly, observe the upper extremities and head for any asymmetries in movement or excessive bobbing or neck flexion, respectively.

In the anterior (frontal) plane view, look at the same differences and abnormal movements as you did in the posterior view. Compare what you saw in the anterior view with the posterior view. Some abnormalities are best seen posteriorly, such as knee gapping, and other abnormalities are best seen from the anterior view, such as arm swing. You can also visualize if the patient is experiencing any pain or discomfort by looking at their face while they are ambulating. Their facial expressions can indicate where in gait pattern they are the most uncomfortable and provide more insight to your evaluation.

When comparing the contralateral side during the analysis, you must consider that any abnormalities noted from one side to the other could potentially be from an injury, muscle weakness, or muscle imbalance the patient may have. These gait deviations can be caused from both chronic or acute injuries, and must be addressed. If you find the patient has a gait deviation potentially resulting from an injury or pathology, refer the patient to their physician for further evaluation.

Abnormal Gait Patterns

Many gait abnormalities are identified by the pathology that results in the abnormal gait (Loudon et al., 2013). Whether patient has an abnormal gait pattern due to an injury or a congenital cause, it is important to understand the fundamentals of normal gait before examining a patient's abnormal gait pattern.

Antalgic Gait

An antalgic gait is the result of pain in at least one lower extremity that causes the patient to walk with a limp. The stance phase of this type of gait will be shorter on the affected side. The patient will not want to weight-bear for a long period of time on the affected side due to the patient being in pain or discomfort. This pain and unwillingness to ambulate normally on the affected side results in a shorter step length, a longer swing time, and a slower cadence. Patients who walk with this type of a gait for a long period of time could cause long-term gait issues once the pain subsides. Ideally, the patient should be fitted for crutches until they able to fully weight bear and walk normally.

Arthrogenic Gait

An arthrogenic gait is the result of stiffness in a patient's lower extremity joints. This gait is characterized by a forward lean (i.e., excessive trunk flexion), decreased range of motion of the knee or hip, and/or circumduction of the affected leg to accommodate the decreased range of motion at the knee and hip. Identifying the source of the stiffness is the best way to devise a treatment plan for the patient. If the issue is functional, or muscle related, strengthening the weak musculature and stretching the tight musculature is the best intervention. If the issue is structural, or more related to bone or intervertebral disc, referral to a physician to identify the source of the problem is the appropriate intervention.

Gluteus Maximus (Lurch) Gait

This type of abnormal gait is characterized by weakness in the gluteus maximus muscle **(Figure 14-5)**. As a result, the patient will lurch backward, or extend the trunk excessively, to compensate for the lack of hip extension to maintain balance and control during walking. Strengthening the posterior chain muscles, the gluteus maximus and hamstrings, and stretching the hip flexors can help normalize this posture if the issue is functional, or due to

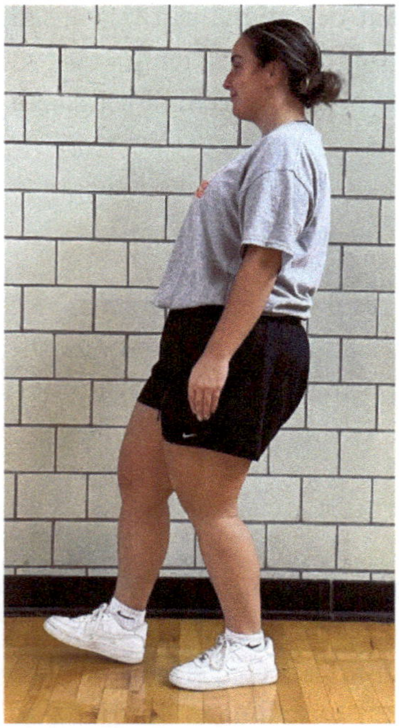

Figure 14-5 Lurch Gait

a muscle imbalance issue. If the issue is structural, you may need to refer the patient to an orthopedic specialist for further evaluation.

Gluteus Medius (Trendelenburg) Gait

This gait is a frontal plane gait deviation that results from weakness in one or both of the hip abductor muscles. During the stance phase, the ipsilateral gluteus medius muscle helps keep the pelvis parallel to the floor to stabilize the pelvis while the contralateral leg is in the swing phase. If the gluteus medius is weak, the contralateral hip that is in the swing phase will drop and cause the contralateral knee to move towards the knee that is in the stance phase **(Figure 14-6)**. This abnormal gait places stress on the leg, mostly on the knee, in stance phase. If both gluteus medius muscles are weak, the patient will walk with a wobbling gait and be more prone to falls. Strengthening the muscle, taking smaller steps, and walking with a cane are ways to correct this gait.

Steppage (Drop Foot) Gait

The steppage, or drop foot, gait typically occurs in patients who have weak dorsiflexors or peripheral neuropathy of the deep peroneal nerve that may or may not be a result of a lumbar disc injury at L4. If the deep peroneal nerve has been injured, the dorsiflexor muscles will not be able to fire to bring the foot closer to the shin during mid-swing to foot strike. This abnormal movement can cause a patient to trip because they are unable to clear their toes from the ground. As a result, the patient may compensate by increasing the amount of knee and hip flexion during the swing phase to avoid tripping. Identifying the cause of the drop foot is the key to correcting this type of gait abnormality.

Ataxic Gait

A patient who walks with this type of gait is most likely suffering from a cerebellar issue that is affecting their balance. They will walk with a wide base of support and hold their hands out to their sides for stability. Identifying the source of the issue is critical in providing the appropriate intervention for this gait. If the patient has suffered brain damage, there may be no treatment to correct the ataxic gait other than having the patient walk with an ambulatory aid (crutches, cane, or walker) and do balance training. Communicating with the patient's physician is important to confirm that any interventions are appropriate so the patient reduces their risk of falling and further injuring themselves.

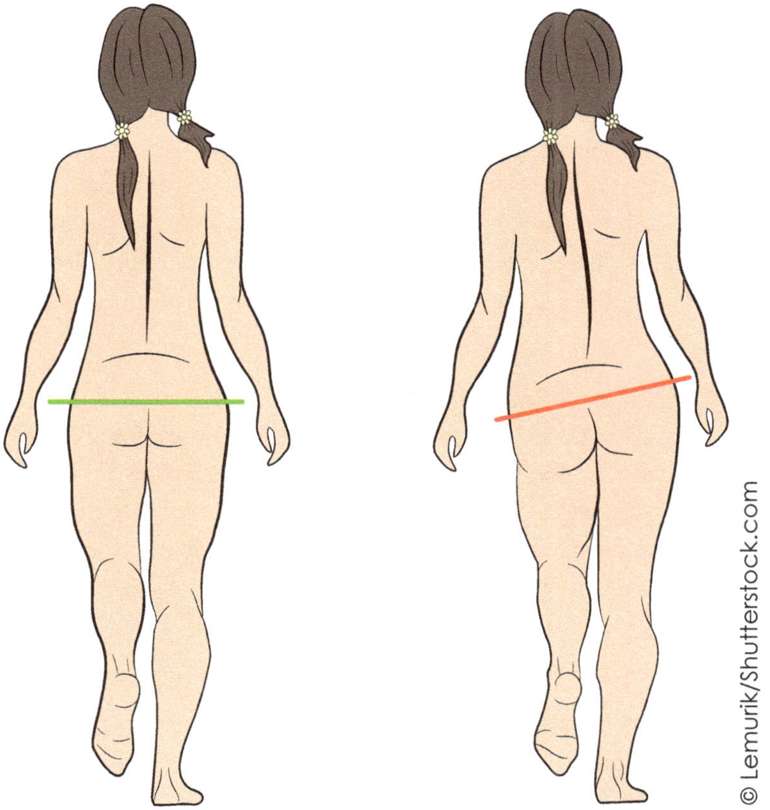

Figure 14-6 Trendelenburg gait with the pelvis dropped (right picture)

Contracture Gait

When a patient has a contracture gait, they will have limited mobility in one or more of the lower extremity joints. A contributing factor to this gait is sitting for long periods of time (i.e., desk job, truck driver, and other occupations which require sitting for long periods of time). If there is a contracture at the hip, the patient will walk with an increased lumbar lordosis, or anterior pelvic tilt, and knee flexion to compensate. Additionally, the patient may have an increase in trunk flexion due to the shortening and/or tightness of the hip flexors that do not allow for upright posture. If the patient has a knee flexion contracture, the patient will walk with increased dorsiflexion on the affected side. At the ankle, a plantar flexion contracture will create excessive extension or hyperextension at the knee and increased flexion of the trunk. Identifying the cause of the contracture, in addition to increasing range of motion through stretching the contracted muscles and strengthening the antagonist muscles, can allow the patient to walk with a more normal gait pattern. If a patient has a congenital disease, such as cerebral palsy or muscular dystrophy, they should work with their physician to come up with a plan for what treatments, surgical or non-surgical, will work best for them to reduce the gait abnormality.

Hemiplegic (Spastic) Gait

A hemiplegic, or spastic, gait results after a patient has had a stroke and one side of their body has paralysis. This will result in the patient shuffling on the involved side to ambulate. Additionally, the upper extremity is held close to the body with the shoulder in adduction, and the elbow, wrist and fingers are in a flexed position. This position is also known as a tonic position, which typically occurs after a stroke. Patients should work with their physician to come up with a plan for treatments that will reduce the gait and upper extremity abnormalities.

Parkinsonian Gait

As described in the name, this type of abnormal gait affects individuals with Parkinson's disease. It is characterized by the patient decreasing their stride length and shuffling their steps with a wider than normal walking base of support. In most cases, the patient will also hold their arms out for balance with little to no swinging occurring during walking. They will also have difficulty stopping suddenly, which can cause them to bump into objects or other people accidentally. Patients should consult with their physician to devise a treatment plan to reduce the gait abnormality.

Scissor (Diplegic) Gait

The scissor, or diplegic, gait is characterized by hip adduction and forceful propulsion of the limb forward to keep the patient advancing forward during walking. Patients who have had lower extremity spastic paralysis typically present with this type of gait abnormality. Patients should consult with their physician to devise a treatment plan to reduce the gait abnormality.

Summary

Posture and gait are important aspects of a patient's evaluation. The evaluations can provide you with information regarding your patient's static and dynamic abnormalities that demonstrate an overall picture of a patient's postural health. If the patient has any abnormalities, addressing the contributing factors can help decrease risk of injury. If a postural abnormality issue is unable to be corrected with rehabilitation, referral to a physician will be necessary to help manage the deviation.

Keywords

Lordosis Excessive anterior curvature of the lumbar spine.

Lower crossed syndrome The result of an excessive anterior tilt of the pelvis contributed by tight anterior hip musculature, and weak posterior hip and spine musculature.

Kyphosis Excessive posterior curvature of the thoracic spine.

Upper crossed syndrome The result of an excessive forward rounding of the shoulder contributed by tight pectoralis musculature, and weak upper back and spine musculature.

Scoliosis Excessive lateral curvature of the spine that can make the spine form an 'S' shape curve.

Genu valgum Increased lateral deviation of the knees. Also known as knock knees.

Genu varum Increased medial deviation of the knees. Also known as bow-leggedness.

Pes planus A decrease in arch height giving the appearance of flat feet.

Pes cavus An increase in arch height.

Ambulate How an individual walks or runs.

Step Foot strike of one foot to foot strike of the opposite foot.

Stride Foot strike of one foot to the next subsequent foot strike of the same foot.

Stance phase Phase of gait where the foot is in contact with the ground.

Swing phase Phase of gait where the foot has no contact with the ground and is moving through the air.

Cadence The number of steps taken in a certain amount of time. This is typically measured in steps per minute.

Shod When an individual is wearing shoes.

Discussion Questions

1. What are some anatomical landmarks you must observe when evaluating a patient's posture from the anterior, posterior, and lateral views?
2. What injuries can occur as a result of postural deviations at the spine and lower extremities?
3. Would you look at the same anatomical landmarks during a patient's postural evaluation as compared to a gait evaluation?
4. When looking at a patient's shoes, what can the wear pattern of the shoe tell you about how the patient ambulates?
5. Which gait abnormalities are associated with injury and which ones are associated with a pathological condition? For the abnormalities that are due to injury, what treatments can help the patient return to a normal gait pattern?

CASE STUDY: RUNNING PAINS

Katie is a 14-year-old freshman runner for the Village High School cross country team. It is the day before the big county cross country meet, for which she has been training all season. Over the past few weeks, Katie has been having some lateral knee pain that started as a mild pain towards the end of her training runs. Now she is experiencing pain during her entire training run. Sometimes it even hurts when she walks to and from her

(continued)

CASE STUDY: RUNNING PAINS (CONTINUED)

classes. She decides to go see her athletic trainer because she is very worried about running in the meet tomorrow.

After taking a thorough history, the athletic trainer begins doing a comprehensive physical examination. During the physical exam, the athletic trainer notices Katie has pes planus and does not have any corrective orthotics in her shoes. She also has some genu valgum, which increases when she takes off her shoes and stands barefoot. The athletic trainer takes a look at the bottom of Katie's shoes and notices significant wear. Consequently, the shoes do not offer her much support for her feet. To continue the examination, the athletic trainer asks Katie if she could walk and run on the treadmill in the fitness room to evaluate her gait.

As Katie walks on the treadmill, the athletic trainer notices Katie has some hip drop in the leg that is in the swing phase. The athletic trainer asks Katie to run at a self-selected pace that is similar to her warm-up pace for training. Upon inspection, the athletic trainer notices that the hip drop is more significant and that the space between her knees is minimal during running.

1. What possible factor(s) are contributing to Katie's knee pain?
2. If you were Katie's athletic trainer, what treatment would you recommend to help alleviate her pain?
3. Do you think Katie waited too long to be evaluated? Why or why not?
4. What type of physician(s) would you recommend Katie go see to help her manage her issue? Why?

References

Elhafez, S.M., Ashour, A.A., Elhafez, N.M., Elhafez, G.M., Abdelmohsen, A.M. (2019). Percentage Contribution of Lower Limb Moments to Vertical Ground Reaction Force in Normal Gait. *Journal of Chiropractic Medicine, 18*(2), 90–96. doi: 10.1016/j.jcm.2018.11.003

Lee, J. Y., Han, K., McAlindon, T. E., Park, Y. G., & Park, S. H. (2018). Lower leg muscle mass relates to knee pain in patients with knee osteoarthritis. *International Journal of Rheumatic Diseases, 21*(1), 126–133. doi: 10.1111/1756-185X.12896

Loudon, J. Manske, R. Reiman, M. (2013). *Clinical Mechanics and Kinesiology*. HumanKinetics. Champaign, Illinois.

Miller, D. I. (1990). Ground reaction forces in distance running. In P. R. Cavanagh (Ed.), *The Biomechanics of Distance Running* (pp. 203–224). Human Kinetics.

Prentice, W. (2021). Principles of Athletic Training: A Guide to Evidence-Based Clinical Practice, 17th ed. McGraw-Hill.

Samaei, A., Bakhtiary, A. H., Elham, F., Rezasoltani, A. (2012). Effects of Genu Valgum Deformity on Postural Stability. *International Journal of Sports Medicine*, 33(6), 469–473. doi: 10.1055/s-0031-1301331.

Shultz, S. Houglum, P. Perrin, D. (2016). Examination of Musculoskeletal Injuries, 4th ed. Human Kinetics. Champaign, Illinois.

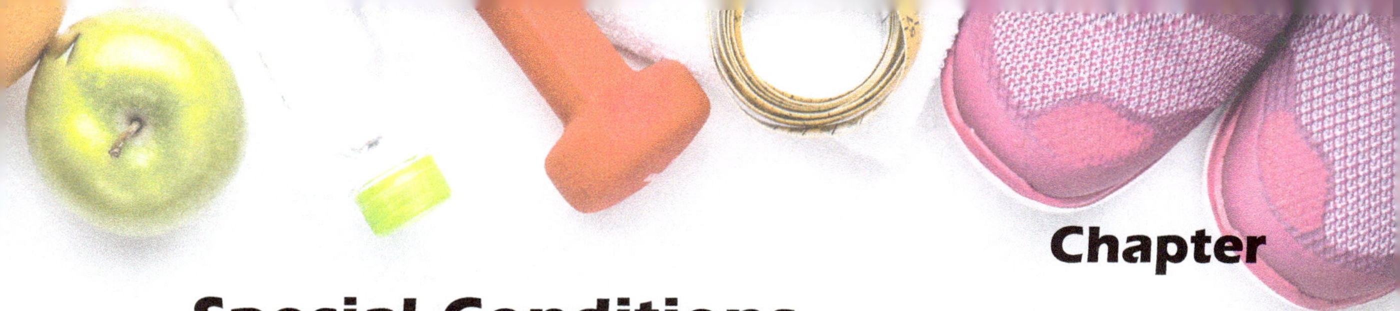

Chapter 15

Special Conditions

Chapter Objectives

After you have read this chapter, you will be able to understand:

- The physical activity, exercise, and nutritional considerations for youth athletes, masters athletes, and older adults.
- Specific needs that individuals with cardiovascular, immunological, metabolic, neuromuscular, orthopedic, respiratory, and other conditions have when participating in physical activity and exercise.
- Limitations affecting an individual's participation in physical activity and exercise.
- How to modify and vary an individual's exercise protocol based on their condition in order to facilitate safe and purposeful participation.

Adults and children alike should participate in physical activity and exercise programs, and practice proper nutrition in order to promote and maintain a healthy, good quality of life. Unfortunately, many individuals are afflicted with cardiovascular, immunological, metabolic, neuromuscular, orthopedic, respiratory, and other conditions. These conditions may place limitations on an individual's participation in physical activity and exercise. In many cases these individuals are not able to participate in physical activity and exercise at the same level as compared to an individual unaffected by these conditions. Physical activity and exercise program modification is necessary so the individual can participate in an effective, safe manner. Proper nutrition is also a key for promoting an individual's health. As a sports medicine professional, you must have in depth knowledge of your client's specific conditions, physical capabilities, and limitations. With this knowledge, you can create appropriate, safe physical activity and exercise programs, and effective nutritional programs aiming to facilitate your client's positive quality of life.

Age: Youth Athletes, Masters Athletes, and Older Adults

A child who is in the prepubescent through adolescent age group is considered a youth athlete. Masters athletes are over the age of 35 (World Masters Athletics, n.d.). Older adults are considered by most organizations and researchers to be 65 years old and older. All age group populations have special needs that you must identify and consider when devising and implementing a physical activity, exercise, and nutrition program.

© Linda Gazzillo Diaz

Figure 15-1 A youth athlete

Youth Athletes

Youth athletes are growing physically and emotionally **(Figure 15-1)**. Their bodies are constantly changing. Their bones are growing during the pubescent and adolescent years. The epiphyseal plates, or "growth plates" at the ends of long bones, are delicate during the youth years. Consequently, these areas are susceptible to fractures. A youth athlete's muscles do not grow as quickly or in the same proportion as their bones. When bones grow, they create tension on the muscles and tendons causing stretching of the soft tissues. When a young athlete creates joint movement, the bones pull the muscles which can cause microtears, or the tendon can pull off its attachment causing apophysitis (i.e. Osgood-Schlatter's disease).

A youth athlete can be injured while participating in activities including sports and conditioning exercise due to a number of factors. Youth athletes do not tolerate the heat as well as average-aged masters athletes. They tend to take in more heat from the environment and sweat less. Consequently, in a hot, humid environment, youth athletes should not participate as long or intensely. These athletes should acclimatize for a period of 10 to 14 days (Cuppett & Walsh, 2017). Many youths today are obese and sedentary, and do not participate in physical activity, which make them at risk for injury. Youth athletes often do not participate in proper conditioning or may condition their bodies too much. Too much or intense conditioning along with incorporating powerful and ballistic movements, and forceful, repetitive muscular contractions can cause injuries throughout the youth's body. Youth athletes must be properly fitted with helmets and other equipment appropriate for the sport. For example, too often pee wee athletes are poorly fitted with notably loose football helmets and shoulder pads. This poorly fitted equipment can predispose the youth athlete to severe injury.

Conditioning and strength training youth athletes was considered harmful in the past due to their skeletal immaturity. When properly executed with correct progression and intensity, conditioning and strength training exercises can be beneficial for youth athletes (Papson et al., 2018). The American Academy of Pediatrics (AAP) states that young athletes can perform weight training successfully with adult supervision and proper training techniques (Stricker et al., 2020). Likewise, lower injury rates have been reported among youth who participate in strength training programs. However, youth athletes must avoid high weight explosive repetitions until skeletal maturity, to avoid injury. Also, aerobic capacity in youth athletes is lower than adult athletes. Youth athletes are not as capable to determine exercise intensity and calculate heart rate properly, especially among children under 8 years old. Therefore, sports medicine professionals may have difficulty determining a youth's intensity during exercise, and when it is appropriate to progress the program's intensity.

As for nutritional requirements, youth athletes require more protein than masters athletes due to growing tissues. Likewise, youth athletes have a higher resting metabolism and energy expenditure than masters athletes. Therefore, their caloric intake will be higher than masters athletes', especially in regard to carbohydrate intake (Desbrow et al., 2018).

Masters Athletes

When devising masters athletes' physical activity and exercise programs you must consider any mind-body issues that may exist. As with athletes of all ages, masters athletes must have a thorough preparticipation examination prior to participating in physical activity and exercise programs to determine their current health status and readiness for regular physical activity and exercise. Many older adults are not able to handle high intensity physical activity and exercise demands. Consequently, aerobic exercise for these adults should start gradually and at a very low intensity (Lee et al., 2017). **(Figure 15-2)**. Progression of activities can be as tolerated. Masters athletes are not as able to handle hot, humid environments as when they were young. Unlike young athletes, they may have chronic diseases and take prescription medication to address these diseases. These factors affect their body's ability to tolerate environmental heat and dissipate body heat through sweat. Consequently, masters athletes should use caution when exercising in the heat. They should drink plenty of fluids, acclimatize appropriately, shorten the exercise duration, and decrease work out intensity in hot, humid environments.

Many of the conditions masters athletes experience occur due to aging. Some of these conditions include balance difficulties, cognitive decline, and musculoskeletal discomfort (Lee et al., 2017). Since resting metabolic rate and lean muscle mass also decrease with age, masters athletes have different nutritional requirements than younger athletes (Strasser et al., 2021). If these athletes consumed the same amount of total calories as when they were in their 20's or 30's, they would undoubtedly gain weight. Consequently, their caloric intake must be less. Also with age, masters athletes must increase vitamin D, calcium, magnesium, and omega-3

Figure 15-2 Masters athletes should begin aerobic activity at a low intensity.

fatty acid intake to maintain optimal nutrition (Strasser et al., 2021). However, iron requirements decrease as women become postmenopausal and the intake becomes similar to men's iron requirements. Consider these nutritional needs when you develop a masters' physical activity and exercise program in order to obtain optimal results.

Older Adults

Older adults desiring to begin a physical activity and exercise programs who have never been active before will have the same conditions as masters athletes due to age. Likewise they will also have similar nutritional requirements. However, unlike masters athletes who have been participating in physical activity and exercise regularly, older adults may have additional concerns. For example, inactive older adults may have a negative attitude toward exercise. Since they are not active, older adults may be afraid of injury, and lack of self confidence in completing physical activity. Often, older adults are set in their daily habits and routines, and are uncomfortable changing their schedule. In order to make an inactive older adult become comfortable with physical activity and exercise, first assist them by thoroughly discussing and setting their goals. Discuss how to best fit physical activity and exercise into their daily routine. Learn the intricacies of their personality and determine their motivation level toward physical activity and exercise. The individual will be more willing, motivated, and compliant if they participate in physical activities in which they find most interesting and enjoyable. Therefore, develop their program to include the individual's primary interests.

Cardiovascular Conditions

Adults who have cardiovascular (CV) conditions can significantly benefit from physical activity and exercise. Exercise benefits include increases in heart and lung efficiency and maximum oxygen consumption, along with decreases in body weight, fat stores, LDL-cholesterol and triglycerides, heart rate, blood pressure, and symptoms of angina (Nystoriak & Bhatnagar, 2018). Fortunately, these benefits are applicable not only to adults that have CV conditions, but all individuals who participate in physical activity and exercise.

All individuals with CV conditions should be under the supervision of a physician. Ask the individual if they will sign a Health Insurance Portability and Accountability Act (HIPPA) release for you to be allowed to communicate with their physician in order to obtain their medical history and discuss your client's exercise considerations. This information is imperative for devising and executing a safe, effective physical activity and exercise program for your client. Work closely with the physician to determine your client's needs. Consult with their physician to discuss if your client has any **contraindications** to exercise. All adults with CV conditions should be stress tested by a trained sports medicine professional prior to the individual's exercise participation. The stress test is one objective means to assist you and your client in designing their exercise program within their physical activity capabilities.

Angina, heart attack, and hypertension are three very common CV conditions for masters athletes and older adults. Consider these conditions, the individual's capabilities, and their physical limitations when developing a safe physical activity and exercise program.

Angina

Angina is chest pain created due to a lack of oxygenated blood flow to the heart **(Figure 15-3)**. Often this lack of blood flow is due to plaque buildup, from high LDL cholesterol and triglycerides, within the coronary arteries. Stable angina is diagnosed when the pain occurs in a predictable manner during physical activity and exercise. The pain can also spread to the neck, shoulders, and arms. Exercise can help decrease coronary artery plaque, which decreases the individual's CV risk. Exercise also helps increase oxygenated blood supply when they are at rest, which can reduce the incidence of angina.

Adults with angina must follow a warm-up and cool-down protocol, as well as all other conditioning principles. When you assist an individual in beginning a physical activity and exercise program, begin by setting achievable goals. For example, one goal could be for your client to perform 20 minutes of physical activity, gradually progressing in intensity, for a minimum of 3 days per week. Then once this goal is reached, your client can set another goal to exercise for a longer duration, the progress to more days per week. Aerobic, full body physical activity should be performed, which may include walking and household activities including cleaning and gardening. Adults with angina can safely perform resistance training two days a week for 15-minute sessions. The strength training should focus on circuit training with

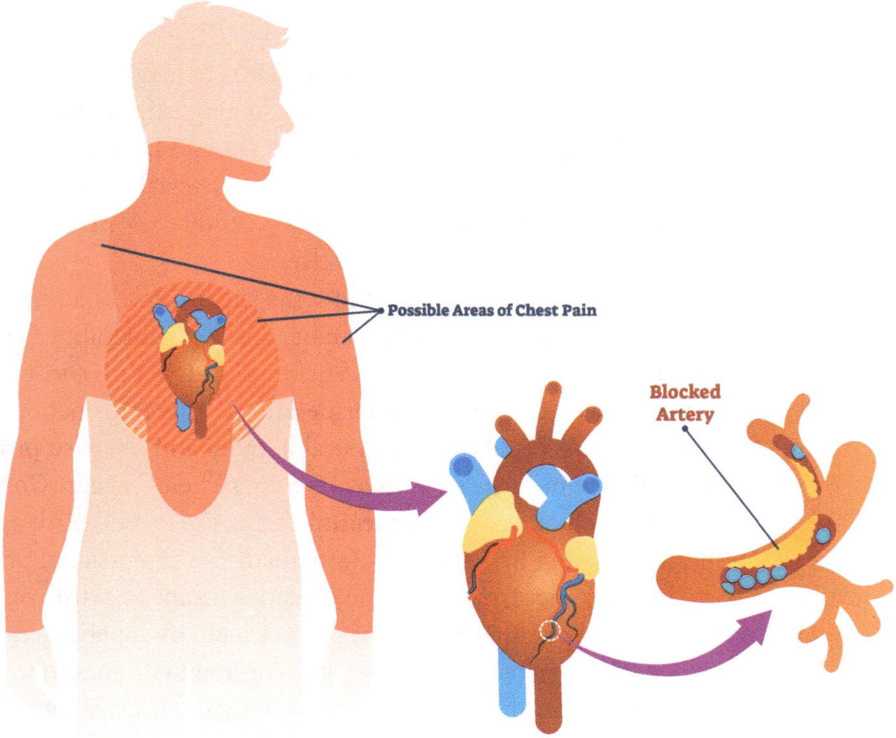

Figure 15-3 Angina is chest pain created due to a lack of oxygenated blood flow to the heart.

light and body resistance. Flexibility exercises are beneficial for the client's upper and lower body. Gentle stretching of the individual's muscles 2 to 3 days per week can help decrease the risk of musculoskeletal injury.

During the individual's program orientation, educate them on the importance of communication. They must inform you immediately when they are experiencing symptoms of angina during exercise. Be aware of any medication that they take for angina. The medication must be on hand during the exercise sessions in case your client experiences symptoms. For example, if your client is prescribed nitroglycerin and experiences angina during exercise, they must take the medication immediately. Before and after exercise evaluate and record your client's heart rate (HR) and blood pressure (BP). They must take their HR throughout an aerobic exercise session. During strength training activities, individuals must avoid performing a **Valsalva maneuver** so that BP, blood volume, and HR are not detrimentally altered during exercise. If at any time the individual's angina symptoms change or increase during or due to the physical activity and exercise sessions, then you must immediately stop the exercise and inform their physician.

Heart Attack

A heart attack, or myocardial infarction, occurs when one of the coronary arteries is blocked due to plaque **(Figure 15-4)**. As a result, not enough oxygenated blood is delivered to a portion of the heart, and consequently that portion dies. Individuals who have sustained a heart attack complete three phases of cardiac rehabilitation, which includes physical activity and exercise (Tessler & Bordoni, 2022). Phase I Clinical Phase exercise includes simple exercises such as moving from a standing to a sitting position and back again, and other nonstrenuous exercises. These exercises make the body accustomed to changes in stress on the heart due to various positions and movements, as well as ADLs. Phase II Outpatient Cardiac Rehab involves more rigorous exercise utilizing both upper and lower body movements, while Phase III Post-cardiac Rehab helps promote continued exercise, flexibility training, and strengthening (Tessler & Bordoni, 2022).

As with individuals suffering from angina, individuals who have sustained a heart attack must avoid performing a Valsalva maneuver during exercise, which often occur during isometric exercises or lifting greater resistance than accustomed. Individuals with any CV condition should not participate in physical activity in extreme environments, both hot and cold, due to circulatory changes that can detrimentally affect their condition. Adults who are on medication, such as beta-blockers, can have a decreased HR and exercise capacity while

Figure 15-4 Signs and symptoms of a heart attack

exercising. Any medications that affect the CNS may cause the athlete to become dizzy or faint. Each of these factors must be seriously considered when the individual is commencing a physical activity and exercise program.

Hypertension

Hypertension is high blood pressure (HBP). When all individuals exercise, their systolic blood pressure (BP) rises. When individuals who have HBP exercise, their systolic BP increases more dramatically than an individual without HBP. Therefore, the individual needs to make every attempt to lower BP on a daily basis.

Many individuals who have HBP are overweight. A primary goal should be for the individual to lose weight and eat nutritious foods such as vegetables, fruits, and low-fat and low-cholesterol foods. Adults with HBP should also make lifestyle changes to assist in decreasing BP. These lifestyle changes include quitting smoking, limiting alcohol consumption, and reducing salt intake.

Low intensity exercise is effective in decreasing BP. Adults with HBP must progress to a goal of completing 30 minutes of low intensity aerobic physical activity or exercise such as walking as many days per week as possible (MayoClinic, 2021). Eventually the individual should be performing physical activity or exercise 7 days per week. The hypertensive individuals should monitor their heart rate during exercise and work up to 40% to 60% maximum HR for positive effects. HBP athletes can also benefit from strength training utilizing light resistance and stretching 2 to 3 sessions per week. Monitoring BP is important before and after exercise **(Figure 15-5)**.

Some individuals with HBP may be taking medication comparable to individuals with other CV conditions, such as beta-blockers and diuretics. These medications can lower HR and BP respectively and must be considered when devising and implementing the individual's exercise program.

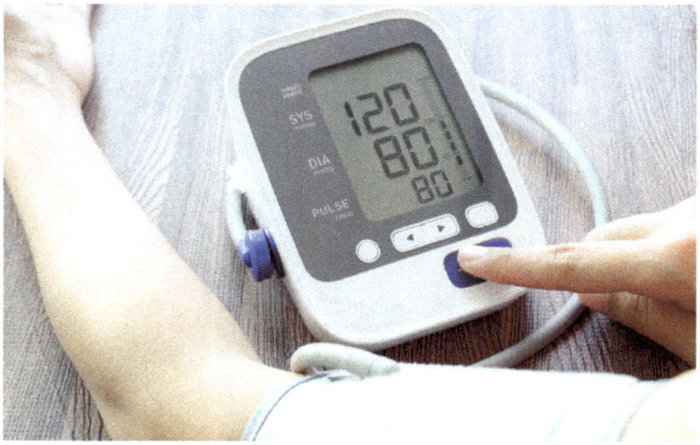

Figure 15-5 Monitor your client's blood pressure before and after exercise.

Immunological Conditions

When a pathogen has entered and adversely affects the body, sometimes the immune system cannot destroy the pathogen. Also, diseases can cause the individual's body to attack itself. These diseases are called autoimmune diseases. In either case, individuals with these immunological conditions can participate in physical activity and exercise. Physical activity and exercise can hopefully make the individual's body stronger in attempt to fight off pathogens and promote a healthy lifestyle.

Cancer

Cancer is an uncontrolled, abnormal growth of cells in the body. The cancer cells can stay localized in one part of the body or it can spread to distant sites. At this time, cancer cannot be readily prevented since no vaccine or cure exists. However, some cancers are more easily treated than others. For the most part, all individuals with cancer can benefit from exercise. Exercise for cancer patients produces many benefits including maintenance of body weight, increased body image, quality of life, and positive outlook, and decreased depression. Studies have shown that physical activity has increased energy balance, decreased fatigue, and increased survival rates for an adult with breast cancer (National Cancer Institute, 2019).

When designing an exercise program for an individual with cancer, consider each individual's specific situation. As individuals with CV conditions, communication with the individual's physician and exercise testing by a sports medicine professional are necessary before the individual begins a formal physical activity and exercise program. Some history questions to ask the individual include the following: What type of cancer do you have, where is it located, and is it localized or **metastatic**? What treatment are you undergoing and what are the side effects? Are you in **remission**? Individuals with cancer may have exercise limitations. An individual with lung cancer, for example, has decreased respiratory capability and shortness of breath. They are especially tired and weak after chemotherapy and radiation treatments. Individuals with cancer may have loss of ROM and muscular weakness due to inactivity. Often cancer patients have other conditions, such as hypertension, obesity, previous myocardial infarction, and angina, which may affect their exercise capabilities. Consider these secondary conditions and any additional limitations when developing an exercise program for individuals with cancer.

Explain to the individual that depending on their cancer treatment sessions the physical activity sessions will vary in duration and intensity. Communicate with them and their physician to gain a thorough understanding of the treatments' side effects. Some cancer treatment side effects include diarrhea, vomiting, nausea, severe fatigue, and pain. If at any time the individual has these side effects, postpone exercise for the day until the they feel well.

In general, the individual should participate in aerobic exercises comprised of large muscle activity. This activity includes walking, cycling, and water aerobics. Incorporating a daily flexibility program is important because cancer patients typically lose ROM and flexibility due to lack of motion and a sedentary lifestyle. Strength training, including light resistance free weights and bands, can be utilized to help maintain muscle mass and strength. Circuit training is also beneficial. By incorporating ADLs into the program, the individual can improve daily living and promote their sense of individuality and independence. These ADL activities include walking up and down stairs, reaching for high objects, and moving from a seated to standing position and vice versa.

Chronic Fatigue Syndrome

Chronic fatigue syndrome (CFS) is a condition which affects mostly middle-aged biological women. The individual who has CFS is continually tired, which interferes with ADLs (MayoClinic, 2020). The individual may also have headaches, sore throat, low grade fever, difficulty concentrating, confusion, and memory loss. Rest does not relieve the symptoms. The condition is not caused by illness or disease. Although no specific cause of CFS has been determined, CFS is thought to result from an improperly working immune system. No cure exists for CFS, but the symptoms of depression and mental anguish can be treated. One means to treat these psychological symptoms is exercise.

Mild to moderate, low exertion physical activity can be beneficial for individuals with CFS. Although exercise does not dramatically decrease the individual's CFS signs and symptoms, research has shown that exercise facilitates positive changes by increasing their perceived quality of health, improving sleep, and decreasing fatigue (Larun et al., 2017). Before beginning exercise, inform your patient that it is normal for them to be more tired than usual after the first few exercise sessions. Your patient may become discouraged after exercise due to fatigue caused by physical exertion. Explain that the post-exercise fatigue will decrease over time as exercise sessions are continued. Determine the time of the day when your patient typically feels least fatigued, and schedule this time for their exercise.

Encourage and support your patient. Have them begin with low intensity and short duration exercises including aerobic, strength training, flexibility, and functional exercises. Allow the patient to exercise at their own pace and progress as tolerated. Some valuable, self-paced exercises include walking, yoga poses, and gentle stretching. Keep in mind that an individual with CFS will not be able to progress as quickly as individuals without CFS. Completion of mild to moderate intensity exercises most days of the week without an exacerbation of CFS symptoms is a primary goal. High intensity exercises are contraindicated. Reiterate to the individual that the exercise program's purpose is to maintain strength, CV endurance, and flexibility with a goal to facilitate ADLs.

Explain to your patient that exercise progression will be a slow process, and not to be concerned with progressing the exercise intensity quickly. The individual's **rate of perceived exertion (RPE)** dictates when to increase time and frequency of exercise. A RPE of approximately 9 (very light) to 12 (light to somewhat hard) is the goal for each exercise session **(Table 15-1)**. Mild physical activity can also increase their self-image. As the individual

Table 15-1 Exercising individuals can use Borg Rating of Perceived Exertion (RPE) scale to effectively monitor their progress.

Borg RPE	Description
6	No exertion at all
7	
7.5	Extremely light
8	
9	Very light
10	
11	Light
12	
13	Somewhat hard
14	
16	Hard (heavy)
17	
18	
19	Extremely hard
20	Maximal exertion

Created using information from Borg, G. (1998). *Borg's perceived exertion and pain scales*. Human Kinetics.

becomes in control of their exercise program, they will eventually realize that they can be in control of their body and her life. When an individual has "good days" and feels that they can perform more exercise during the session, encourage them not to do so. The sudden increase in exercise intensity may make them have a relapse or exacerbate CFS symptoms.

Fibromyalgia

Fibromyalgia is a chronic condition that most often affects middle aged biological women twice as much as biological men (Center for Disease Control and Prevention [CDC], 2020). The condition causes many signs and symptoms including joint pain and stiffness, inflexibility and contracture of soft tissues, anxiety, depression, and sleep disturbances. **(Figure 15-6)**. No specific cause for the condition exists and it has been associated with CFS. Exercise can decrease fibromyalgia pain, joint stiffness, depression, anxiety, and fatigue symptoms. Exercise also increases health-related quality of life, muscle and tendon flexibility, and physical function (Bidonde et al., 2017).

Adults with fibromyalgia typically are more hesitant to exercise than normal adults due to fear of increased pain. They may experience exacerbated symptoms when in cold or hot environments. Therefore it is important to begin the exercise and progress the individual slowly

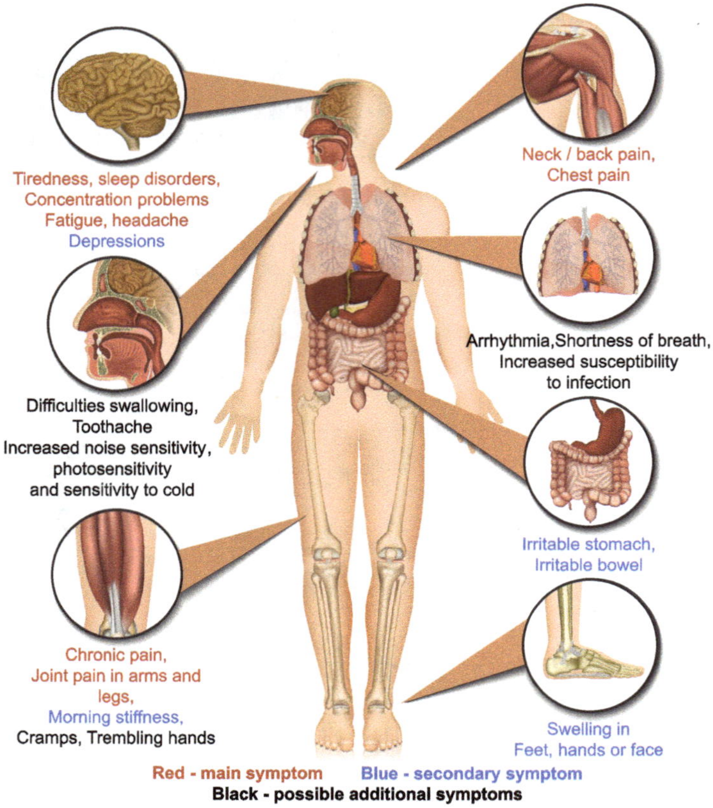

Figure 15-6 Signs and symptoms of fibromyalgia

in a neutral temperature environment. Inform your patients that fibromyalgia symptoms may possibly increase after the first few exercise sessions, until their body adapts to the activities.

Your encouragement and support, as well as exercise in a group or with a partner, can improve the individual's compliance to physical activity. Have your patient minimize any movements or exercises, including eccentric activity, which can increase symptoms. Also consider the time of day that the individual should exercise in order to minimize symptoms and promote purposeful activity. For example, they may have greater loss of ROM due to joint stiffness and muscle inflexibility in the morning. Therefore, the exercise sessions should take place in the early afternoon once the individual has been moving around and these symptoms decrease.

In order to promote adherence to exercise, begin with easy exercises such as walking or utilizing the UBE without resistance. Their aerobic exercise program should progress and continue to incorporate large muscle aerobic activity, such as biking and aquatic therapy. For example, the individual can begin with 20 minutes of exercise, 2 days per week, and can progress toward completing 40-minute exercise sessions, 3 days per week. The exercise program must move very slowly for these adults in order to address the individual's physical and psychological considerations. Flexibility and functional exercises are also incorporated. The functional activities should mimic the individual's ADLs. Therefore, in order to make these activities useful for your patient, ask them about their typical daily activities. It is important to determine what ADLs your patient cannot perform due to the fibromyalgia, in order to set goals to improve their function while decreasing their symptoms. Stress management and relaxation exercises are also beneficial for an individual with fibromyalgia.

Metabolic Conditions

Metabolic conditions develop when the body's normal **metabolism** is disrupted by abnormal chemical reactions, including decreased or loss of vital organ function. Diabetes and obesity are two very common and related metabolic conditions that affect children and adults worldwide.

Diabetes

As previously discussed, diabetes is a disease in which high levels of sugar exist in the blood. All diabetic individuals can benefit from exercise. These benefits include an increased insulin sensitivity (i.e. insulin can be utilized more effectively), a decrease in body fat, and an increase CV health. A Type 2 diabetic individual can have decreased blood glucose levels with exercise. Unfortunately, this decrease does not readily occur with Type 1 diabetics.

When your diabetic client exercises, they utilize glucose as an energy source. They must have a simple CHO snack available during exercise, such as orange slices or juice, or their glucose becomes depleted and may experience insulin shock. Normal fasting blood glucose levels are under 100 mg/dl. The individual should take their blood glucose before exercise **(Figure 15-7)** and should not exercise if their blood glucose is over 250 mg/dl or below 90 mg/dl. In these cases their blood glucose levels should be reduced with insulin or increased with glucose ingestion (respectively) prior to exercise (Colberg et al., 2016).

Utilizing the FITT principle, a diabetic individual can perform aerobic and anaerobic activities at levels that an individual without diabetes

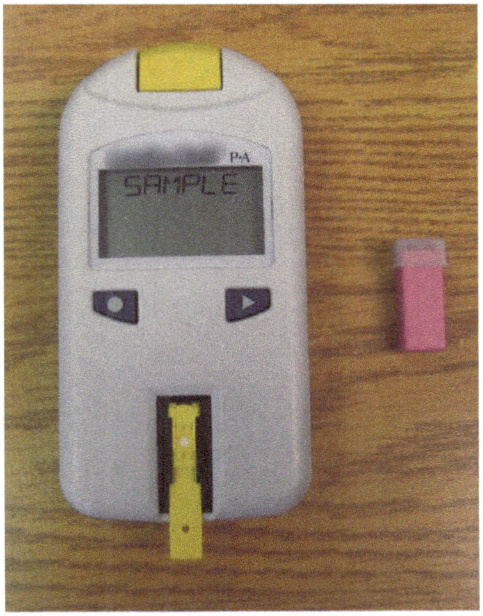

Figure 15-7 Blood glucose monitoring equipment

would. Aerobic activities should begin with walking and progress to more vigorous activities for at least 150 minutes per week. Strength training activities focus on muscular endurance training with low resistance and high repetitions. Exercise performed for a long duration, as well as strenuous exercise creates hormones that combat the effects of insulin. Diabetic individuals have progressively poor circulation in their extremities. Consequently, they need to wear properly fitted, cushioning sneakers during exercise to protect their feet when weight bearing.

Obesity

As previously discussed, obesity is an excessive amount of body fat. An adult that has a BMI over 30 is considered obese **(Figure 15-8)**. Obesity detrimentally affects the individual's health due to numerous factors. One of these factors is that obese individuals are usually inactive and do not participate in regular physical activity. Fortunately, even a small amount of physical activity and exercise can improve the individual's condition. Along with caloric modification, obese individuals must become physically active and perform regular exercise in order to lose body fat. Likewise, with regular exercise, their energy expenditure increases which facilitates weight loss. Weight reduction can also eliminate many of the other conditions (i.e. hypertension, Type 2 diabetes, high blood pressure) that an obese individual may have, as well as promote a healthy lifestyle. Before beginning the individual's program, communicate with them and their physician to determine if the individual has any other medical conditions which may affect their ability to exercise.

Figure 15-8 Obese individuals must participate in physical activity to lead a healthy life.

When initially working with an obese child or adult, consider that they most likely are sedentary relative to other normal weight adults. Their program must begin with low intensity activities. Depending on the extent of inactivity and individual's weight, lower extremity activities may need to include both weight bearing and non-weight bearing exercises. Incorporate simple exercises such as AROM, gentle stretching, and isometric activities into the program and progress the individual as tolerated. Have them participate in devising their exercise program. Have your client describe the activities they enjoy, and then integrate these activities into their exercise sessions. Sessions do not have to consist of one long session per day. Rather, obese, sedentary individuals may prefer and better tolerate two shorter sessions per day. The individual can obtain optimal effects with 5 to 6 days of exercise per week. Motivation is the key for the exercise program to be successful. They will be more motivated and compliant if they see progress. The individual must continually hydrate before, during, and after exercise since obese individuals lose a lot of water through sweat due to increased body heat production. The individual should be wearing clothing that allows the sweat to dissipate from their body, and they should be exercising in cool temperatures. Eventually when your client begins to see progress, they will develop a sense of well-being and appreciation for a healthy lifestyle.

Neuromuscular Disorders

Neuromuscular disorders are conditions when the nerves in the body improperly function. This improper functioning affects communication between nerves and muscles. Consequently, the muscles do not function as they should.

Cerebral Palsy

Cerebral palsy (CP) is a brain and nervous system condition that develops in utero or within the first 2 years of life. CP occurs during brain development. Suspected causes for CP include in utero brain hypoxia, bleeding, or injury, a genetic condition, or neurological disorder. Damage and abnormal development occur to the portion of the brain which is responsible for the spinal nerves and motor control. Consequently, CP causes problems with a child's motion, motor control, reflex capability, balance, muscle tone, and posture. CP can also affect oral motor function, including swallowing and speech. CP affects children and adults in very individualized ways. Consequently, one individual may have different needs than another. Signs and symptoms range from mild to severe which include contracted joints and resultant loss of ROM, shortened musculature and resultant flexibility, lack of coordination, deficiencies in fine and gross motor skills, and delays in motor and speech function while growing from infant to child.

Individuals with CP can obtain the same benefits from physical activity and exercise as any able-bodied individual would. Most importantly, for CP individuals, exercise can decrease condition's signs and symptoms, which includes reducing muscle spasticity and contractures, while increasing mobility. Physical activity can also promote the individual's well-being, independence, and social interaction with others. Before your client begins the exercise program, determine if the client is taking any medications and how the drugs affect their ability to perform exercise. Obtain the individual's permission to speak with their physician to gain this information prior to developing their exercise protocol.

Individuals with CP may need to use a wheelchair to mobilize. Wheelchair bound individuals may have increased lower extremity symptoms as compared to an ambulatory CP individual, since wheelchair bound individuals are more sedentary due to continual sitting. Include flexibility, aerobic, and strength training exercises in order to facilitate performing ADLs. The exercises should focus on gaining muscular endurance in order for the to withstand the stresses of ADLs. The specific aerobic exercises depend upon whether your client is ambulatory, or wheelchair bound. If the individual is ambulatory, then they can perform aerobic weight-bearing exercises. However, if they are in a wheelchair, they can participate in a variety of nonweight-bearing activities. Both ambulatory and wheelchair bound CP individuals can participate in nonweight-bearing activities including utilizing an UBE, hand weights, and resistance bands. They should perform upper and lower extremity stretching exercises, for which they may need assistance. Individuals can play sports such as basketball **(Figure 15-9)** and badminton, as well as participate in dance. Many individuals with CP are able to perform aquatic exercise including swimming using flotation belts and vest. The specific activities incorporated into the exercise program

Figure 15-9 A wheelchair-bound individual with CP can participate in many of the same exercise activities as able-bodied individuals.

greatly depend on the severity of the individual's CP and their function. The American Academy for Cerebral Palsy and Developmental Medicine has published thorough guidelines for exercise for individuals with CP (https://www.aacpdm.org/UserFiles/file/fact-sheet-fitness-083115.pdf).

Multiple Sclerosis

Multiple sclerosis (MS) is a disease that affects the CNS. Nerve damage occurs due to inflammation of the myelin sheath which covers the nerves. The nerves themselves can also be damaged. In either case, scar tissue develops around the nerve. The nerve damage and scar tissue cause the nerves to malfunction. Although MS is a neuromuscular disease, it is also considered an autoimmune disease. The cause of MS has not been determined, but autoimmune responses, the environment, genetics, and pathogens are currently being studied in order to determine an exact cause (National Multiple Sclerosis Society, 2022). Signs and symptoms of MS can be mild to severe and include loss of sensation in the extremities, muscle tremors, spasm, weakness, incoordination, and paralysis, and fatigue. MS individuals may also be sensitive to heat and have loss of bladder control **(Figure 15-10)**.

Exercise benefits individuals with MS in the same manner as individuals without MS. However, before implementing a physical activity and exercise program for your patient,

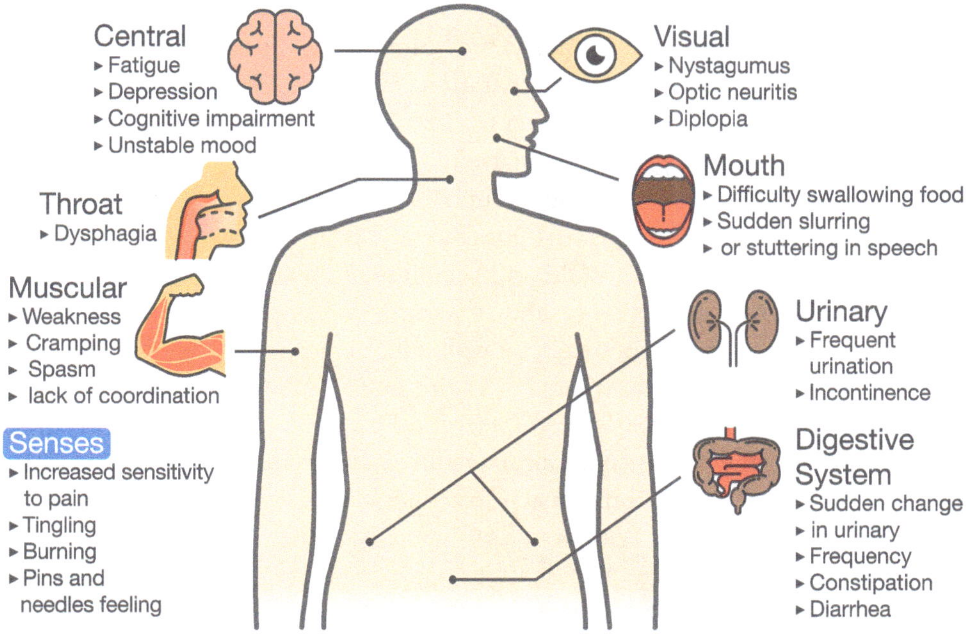

Figure 15-10 Signs and symptoms of multiple sclerosis

discuss the medications they take and if they experience any side effects. Some MS medications cause muscle weakness, decreased sweating, fatigue, or shortness of breath. Many individuals have decreased or no sweat production. Consequently, the exercise environment is maintained at a normal or slightly cooler temperature. Hydration is important for the individual to avoid heat illness before, during, and after exercise. In attempt to avoid heat illness, the individual can also cool themself by utilizing cold therapy to decrease core body temperature prior to aerobic exercise. As with CP, some individuals with MS may be wheelchair bound and modification of their activities is imperative. As a sports medicine professional, you may need to assist them with completing the physical activities if their mobility is limited (Kalb et al., 2020).

Participation in a minimum of 150 minutes of physical activity per week can assist the individual with MS by increasing their mobility, flexibility, strength, endurance, and well-being, while decreasing spasm, stiffness, fatigue, and depression (Kalb et al., 2020). Aerobic, strength, and flexibility training should be incorporated into the individual's exercise program. Although no specific regimen exists, MS individuals can perform aerobic and strength training activities utilizing the FITT principle, but progressing in a slow, gradual manner. Flexibility exercises should be performed each day. Since MS progresses over time, and symptoms may become exacerbated due to the condition's progression, you may need to frequently modify their program.

Spinal Cord Injury

When a child or adult has spinal cord injury, they can experience a multitude of signs and symptoms, in particular loss of function and sensation. An individual with a severe spinal cord injury has partial or complete loss of function in the torso and all extremities (quadriplegia) or the lower extremities (paraplegia). The spinal cord injury causes the person to have reduced or complete inability to perform gross motor function. A quadriplegic individual has lower cardiac output than a paraplegic individual. Exercise assists them in decreasing muscle contracture and spasm, while increasing ROM and flexibility of the movable limbs. The physical activity facilitates a decrease in depression and an increase in self-worth and independence.

Before you devise your patient's exercise program, determine if they have any special considerations due to the spinal cord trauma including any additional noteworthy conditions. Always supervise the individual closely during exercise. Quadriplegic individuals in particular do not adapt well to extreme heat or cold. Consequently, they need to exercise in a comfortable, controlled environment. Since the individual is in a wheelchair for prolonged periods of time, they may develop pressure sores. With your assistance, have them change positions during exercise to relieve the pressure. You must learn the proper way to perform lifts and transfers from equipment to the wheelchair and vice versa. If your patient has core body deficiency or paralysis, utilize belts and straps to make sure they are safely stabilized while exercising. If the individual has hyper or hypotension, monitor BP before and after exercise. Have them empty their bladder, bowel, and urine or and colostomy bag prior to exercise. If your patient has any signs or symptoms of fainting, change in color, dizziness, nausea, or extreme weakness, then stop the exercises immediately.

The exercise program should include activities within the individual's capabilities. Recommendations include 20 minutes of aerobic exercise 2 times per week and strength training for all muscle groups an additional 2 times per week (Martin Ginis et al., 2018). Some beneficial activities include utilizing a UBE, mobilizing the wheelchair (wheelchair cranking), and utilizing parallel bars to ambulate. Manual resistance exercises, neck AROM, and extremity PROM should be performed with your assistance **(Figure 15-11)**. Aerobic exercises can also include swimming with the individual wearing a flotation device, seated aerobic classes utilizing arm movements only. The paraplegic individual can participate in aerobics class instruction with able-bodied individuals, performing upper and core body activities, in order to promote social communication. Strength training exercises include free weights, bands, and tubing. Begin the patient's aerobic and strength training exercises slowly, using the FITT principle. Flexibility exercises are performed daily and before and after exercise. Always provide encouragement and explain to the individual that they will notice small but beneficial improvements each week.

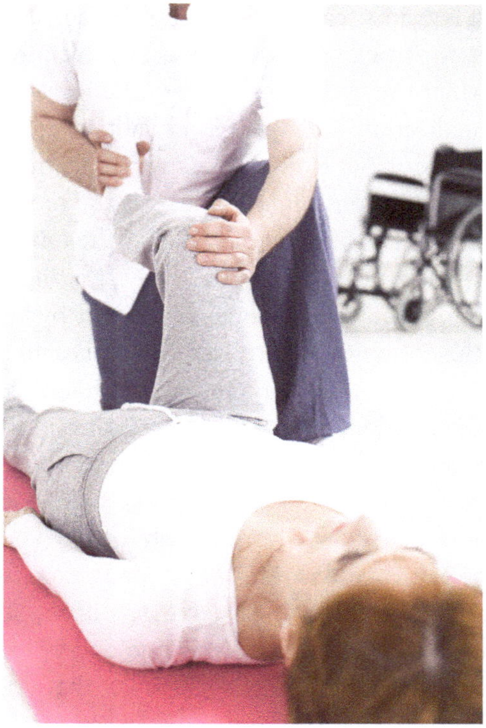

Figure 15-11 Assist your spinal cord injury patient with PROM exercises.

Orthopedic Conditions

Orthopedic conditions can affect any individual at any age. Unfortunately as people age, their bodies cannot adapt to stress in the same manner as when they were young. Two common orthopedic conditions which appear with age are arthritis and osteoporosis. Exercise assists in decreasing the signs and symptoms of these often debilitating conditions.

Arthritis

A chronic condition which involves inflammation of the joints is called arthritis. Arthritis typically begins to appear during the middle-age. The condition is caused by cartilage breakdown within the joints. The decrease of cartilage causes the bones comprising the joint to rub against each other. The rubbing causes inflammation, joint pain, swelling, and stiffness. Arthritis can also be caused by infection, injury, or an autoimmune condition, which occurs when the body breaks down the joints for unknown reasons. If the arthritis is treated with medication, therapeutic modalities, and exercise, then the arthritis may heal or become asymptomatic. However, many people have chronic arthritis. Osteoarthritis, otherwise known as degenerative joint disease, is the most common type of chronic arthritis. Osteoarthritis is caused by the wearing down of the joint's bone surface which occurs with the aging process. Osteoarthritis cannot be healed, but the symptoms can be treated. Rheumatoid arthritis is an autoimmune disease characterized by synovial membrane inflammation around the joints. This inflammation causes eventual cartilage and joint surface breakdown **(Figure 15-12)**.

The American College of Rheumatology (2020) states that exercise is beneficial for arthritic adults. Typically an arthritic individual is deconditioned due to inactivity and joint pain. Consequently, they may be hesitant to exercise. Educate the individual and explain how moderate exercise can improve their quality of life. Improvements in cardiovascular status, neuromuscular control, flexibility, aerobic capacity, and muscular strength and endurance can be gained with low intensity daily exercise. AROM and flexibility exercises performed at the arthritic areas help to decrease stiffness and increase ROM during ADLs. The individual can increase their activity level and energy expenditure on a daily basis. Arthritic individuals can participate in almost any activity that does not put undue stress on the joints. Safe activities

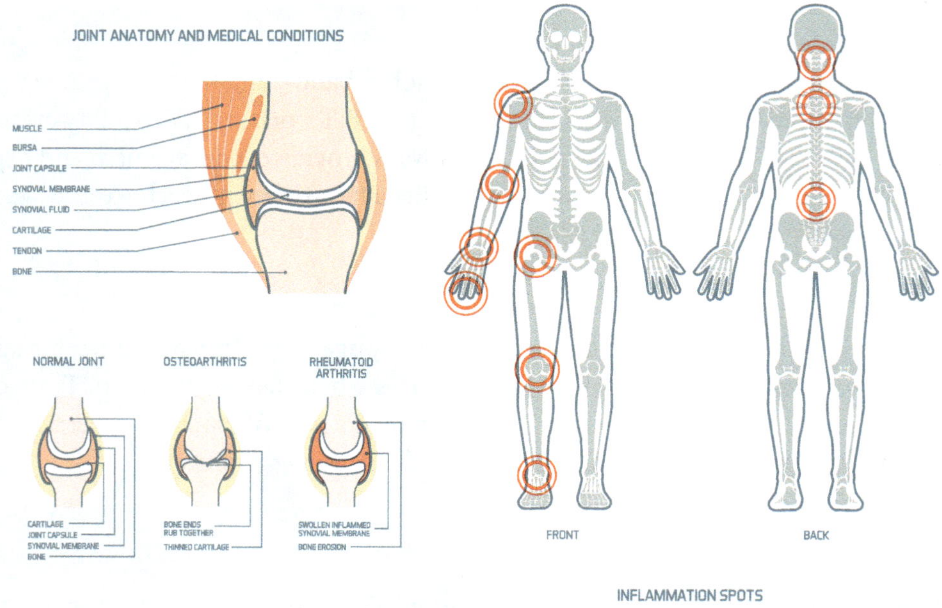

Figure 15-12 Osteoarthritis and rheumatoid arthritis can affect various joints in the body.

include walking, cycling, and swimming. Running, jumping, and any high impact activities are contraindicated.

When developing your patient's program, begin the exercises at a low intensity and duration. Swimming and water exercise are excellent activities for arthritic individuals due to the buoyancy property of water. Buoyancy helps decrease stress on the upper and lower extremities. Flexibility exercises are incorporated daily, but the individual should not overstretch the tendons surrounding the joints because further irritation can occur. Strength training can include any activity that a non-arthritic individual can perform including circuit training, dumbbells, weight machines, bands, and tubing. Proper footwear that cushions the soles of the feet are extremely important to reduce any unnecessary ground reaction forces and stress on your patient's lower extremity joints. Inform them that some discomfort may occur at first during the beginning stages of exercise and when new exercises are introduced. Discomfort may also occur at the end of the exercise session or 24 to 48 hours post-exercise until the individual becomes accustomed to the exercise program. At any time when pain or swelling develops, have your patient stop the causative exercise and modify their program.

Osteoporosis

Osteoporosis is when bones become thin, brittle, and weak with age due to hormonal issues (in biological women) or deficiency in calcium and/or vitamin D (in both biological men and women). The condition is more pronounced in biological women aged 50 years and older than biological men. When osteoporosis occurs, the body does not create bone to replace lost bone. Also, the body may resorb too much bone, which decreases bone density and causes them to be at risk for fracture. Osteoporosis may not exhibit significant signs and symptoms in its beginning stages. In later stages, the individual may have pain and point tenderness at and around the area of decreased bone density, which can also indicate a fracture.

Exercise, especially weight bearing exercise, is crucial for adults to minimize the signs and symptoms of osteoporosis. Weight bearing exercise assists the bones in maintaining their density and strength, and assist in slowing down the osteoporotic progression. The individual can perform the exercises as per the FITT principle. The type of exercise depends on their motor and cognitive function, and previous physical activity. Weight bearing activities include walking, jogging, aerobic classes, and playing organized sports such as racquetball and tennis. Strength training activities can incorporate any type of resistance equipment. Flexibility and functional activities are also included to improve ROM and the ability to perform ADLs. The individual's diet must consist of calcium supplementation as well as high calcium foods, such as dairy products, green leafy vegetables, and calcium fortified foods, in order to maintain bone density and strength. Increased vitamin D is also important because it assists the body in absorbing calcium **(Figure 15-13)**.

Adults with osteoporosis may have a fear of falling and breaking a bone. Assist your client to control anxiety and fear by having them begin with simple, low to the ground exercises, Have

Figure 15-13 Means to prevent the incidence of osteoporosis

your client perform two-foot weight bearing exercises with a wide stance to promotes increased balance. Also teach your client stress management exercises to assist in alleviating anxiety.

Respiratory Conditions

Respiratory conditions are problematic for individuals who exercise because their lung function is compromised. Consequently, they may not be able to exercise as easily as another person without a respiratory condition due to the decreased oxygen provided to the body. However, with continued exercise the respiratory condition can be improved, as well the individual's overall health.

Asthma

As previously discussed, asthma is a condition that causes the bronchi to swell and become narrow. Since the passageways are not their normal diameter, an inadequate amount of oxygen is transported to the lungs. This inadequacy of oxygen can gravely affect asthmatic individuals when they exercise. Exercising in warm, moist environments versus cold, dry environments tends to decrease in the likelihood of asthma's triggers and symptoms. Swimming is a beneficial activity due to the individual being in this warm, moist environment. Shorter duration exercises with intermittent bouts are better tolerated by asthmatic individuals than long duration strenuous activities. Aerobic activities such as walking, aerobics, hiking, and biking are good activities which lessen the possibility of asthma attacks (American Academy of Allergy, Asthma, and Immunology, 2020).

Over time, aerobic activity produces more efficient lung efficiency, less breathing complications, a decrease in attacks, a decrease in wheezing, an increase in general overall fitness and cardiorespiratory endurance, and easier and better ADL performance. The type, intensity, and duration of exercise depends on the severity of the individual's asthma. Strength training should include utilization of dumbbells, tubing and band exercises, and isotonic machines. Flexibility exercise should always be incorporated into the individual's exercise program.

If prescribed by the individual's doctor, have the individual utilize their bronchodilator prior to exercise. Make every attempt to have the individual exercise in an environment free of any triggers and allergens. Although, avoiding potential triggers is not always avoidable. For example, if the individual must exercise in a cool environment or an environment with allergens (i.e. they are skiing or running outdoors in the midst of high pollen season), then have them wear a scarf or material which covers the nose and mouth. This item warms the air as it enters the respiratory tract. The facial covering also assists to keep allergens out of the passageways which decreases the risk of attacks. The individual must have their rescue inhaler medication at all times during exercise in case they experience symptoms **(Figure 15-14)**.

COPD

Chronic obstructive pulmonary disease (COPD) is a respiratory disease involving chronic bronchitis and/or emphysema. COPD most often affects men and women over the age of 65 with symptoms first appearing at age 40. Smoking is the primary risk factor for COPD. A person with COPD cannot be cured. However, signs and symptoms can be treated and decreased

Figure 15-14 Individuals with asthma must have their fast-acting rescue inhaler with them at all times while they exercise in case they experience symptoms.

through medication and exercise, which includes respiratory therapy. Signs and symptoms of COPD include a persistent cough, wheezing, inability to breathe at a normal rate, decreased lung volume, and shortness of breath especially with exertion. Along with typical exercise benefits, individuals affected with COPD benefit from exercise by promoting increased efficiency of the functional lungs and cardiovascular system, decreased wheezing and shortness of breath with everyday activity, decreased respirations and oxygen necessary to perform ADLs, and a better quality of life (Spruit et al., 2016).

When devising a physical activity and exercise program for an individual with COPD, you must consider how the disease affects the individual. Individuals with COPD have similar bronchodilator medication as asthmatic individuals. Make sure they have immediate access to their medication at all times during exercise. Always consult with their physician prior to devising an exercise program to determine the effects of the disease and medications on the individual's ability to exercise. For example, some medications may produce hypotension, muscle weakness, cardiac palpitations, and tachycardia.

Individuals with COPD may have difficulty maintaining lean muscle mass. Strength exercises along with proper nutrition including lean meats and fish, fruits, vegetables, assist the athlete's body to build and maintain lean muscle mass. Also, COPD is correlated with obesity (Verberne et al., 2017). Loss of weight will assist these individuals to breathe better. Consequently, aerobic activity assists in this endeavor.

Some individuals may need supplemental oxygen during exercise. Therefore, learn about the equipment, how it is utilized, and any mobility constraints affecting them during exercise **(Figure 15-15)**. Since COPD is a progressive disease, many adults are also treated for

Figure 15-15 If your patient needs supplemental oxygen during exercise, be certain to know how their equipment operates.

depression. Group exercise, for example a yoga or tai chi class with peers, can promote social activity and assist in relieving depression symptoms.

Cystic Fibrosis

Cystic fibrosis (CF) is a hereditary, life-threatening disease. CF is characterized by an abnormal quantity of thick, salty mucus that exists in and clogs the air passageways and other body organs such as the lungs and pancreas. The mucus can cause lung infections and digestion complications. Children with CF are usually diagnosed before the age of 2 years. The gene that causes CF is inherited by both parents. Signs and symptoms of CF include constipation, nausea, loss of appetite, discolored stools, fatigue, nasal congestion, coughing, recurrent pneumonia, and pancreatitis **(Figure 15-16)**.

Individuals with CF can particularly benefit from exercise by increasing cardiorespiratory efficiency. Increasing cardiorespiratory efficiency assists in clearing mucus from the air passageways, which in turn increases oxygen consumption. Aerobic and

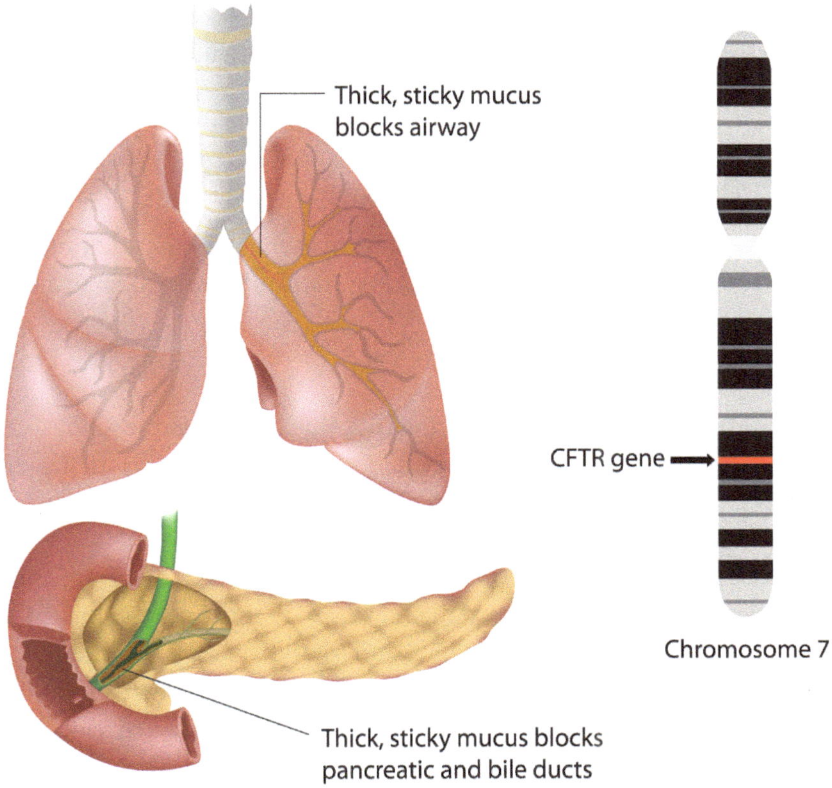

Figure 15-16 Cystic fibrosis affects not only the lungs, but also the pancreas and digestive system.

strength training exercises have shown to benefit the CF individual by increasing lean body mass, maximum oxygen consumption, respiratory muscle endurance, and health-related quality of life.

Aerobic activities should include large muscle group exercises such as swimming, walking, jogging, and bicycling. Many CF individuals can tolerate high intensity prolonged exercise, which has been shown to be highly beneficial. However, exercise sessions should be approximately 10 minutes for 5 days per week when the individual begins an exercise program, and progress very slowly (Cystic Fibrosis Foundation, n.d.). The individual should be able to eventually perform 30-minute moderate intensity sessions for 3 to 4 days per week. Keep in mind that some individuals with severe CF may have lower extremity joint pain which hinders their capability to perform lower body weight bearing exercise. Therefore, passive stretching exercises should be performed daily. Strength training activities should involve large muscle groups, and functional activities should focus on ADLs.

As with other respiratory conditions, individuals with CF are prescribed bronchodilators. Some CF individuals need to utilize the bronchodilator prior to exercise. They may also be taking additional medications for their condition. These medications, as well as the bronchodilators, may cause side effects which may affect how you devise their exercise program. These side effects include tachycardia, muscular weakness, and increased BP. The individuals can tolerate exercise in the heat even though they lose excessive salt when sweating, as long as they have adequate fluid replacement during exercise.

Other Conditions

Individuals with many other conditions can benefit from exercise. These additional conditions include anemia, mental deficiencies, pregnancy, and vision and hearing impairment.

Anemia

Anemia is a condition when an individual's blood contains insufficient red blood cells, which results in decreased oxygen to the body. Anemia is caused by lack of iron and vitamins in the diet, especially B12 and folate, decreased RBC production, the body's breakdown of RBC's, blood loss due to gastrointestinal bleeding or injury, and chronic disease. Signs and symptoms of anemia include fatigue, cold extremities, headaches, dyspnea, and dizziness **(Figure 15-17)**. Various types of anemia exist, and some are more severe than others. Common anemia conditions include iron deficiency and vitamin deficiency anemia, which are easily controlled. Most individuals affected by iron deficiency anemia are biological women. Sickle cell anemia is a hereditary condition which typically occurs to African-American biological men. With this type of anemia the individual's RBCs are a sickle or crescent shape instead of a normal circular shape. Consequently, oxygen carrying capacity is diminished.

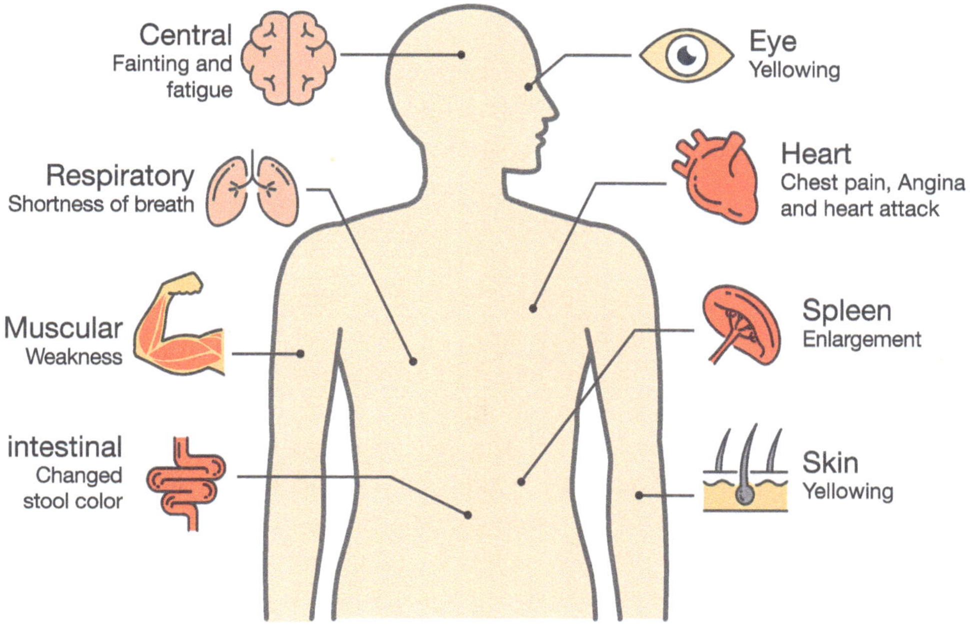

Figure 15-17 Symptoms of anemia

Also due to the RBCs' sickle shape, the RBCs can become lodged in small blood vessels and then block blood and oxygen flow to the tissues.

Anemic individuals have decreased oxygen to the muscles at rest because iron, which is the oxygen binding site in hemoglobin, is not sufficient in the body. When the individual exercises, oxygen to the muscles is increased and is comparable to non-anemic individuals. Sickle cell anemic individuals can participate in aerobic exercise most often without any issues. However, to decrease any risk of illness, keep their exercise at a low intensity, have them take frequent rest breaks, and make sure they are hydrated. Various aerobic activities following the FITT principle and progression are appropriate for the anemic individual. With regular exercise, anemic individuals can improve their cardiorespiratory endurance significantly.

Individuals who have iron deficiency anemia must supplement their diet with iron rich foods including red meat, chicken, turkey, fish, spinach, beans, broccoli, and any iron fortified foods. Iron supplements may be necessary for individuals with severe cases of iron-deficiency anemia. To treat vitamin-deficiency anemia, their diet must contain vitamin B12 and folate rich foods. Good sources of B12 vitamins include fish and shellfish, cheese, beef, and eggs. An individual may safely ingest B12 supplements. The body eliminates excess B12 vitamins since they are water soluble. Good sources of folate include nuts, beans, spinach and leafy green vegetables, eggs, broccoli, and squash. An individual can take a daily prenatal vitamin which combines iron, B12, and folate together, even if the individual is not pregnant.

Mental Illness

Mental illness includes a variety of conditions such as depression, stress, panic, and anxiety disorders, obsessive compulsive disorder (OCD), and posttraumatic stress disorder. Individuals with these illnesses should be under a physician's and/or mental health specialist's care. If not, refer the individual to the appropriate physician or mental health specialist for evaluation and treatment before devising an exercise program for the individual.

Individuals with mental illness commonly take daily prescription medication, which may cause side effects. With the individual's permission, communicate with the individual's physician or mental health specialist to determine any effects of the medication on exercise. Some side effects of mental illness medications include dizziness, weight gain, fatigue, or insomnia. Discuss how the individual deals with these side effects on a daily basis. This information is imperative to create an appropriate, successful exercise program for the individual.

Exercise has been shown to increase the individual's mood, balance emotions, decrease depression, stress, and anxiety, increase social communication, and increase well-being. When devising the individual's exercise program, utilize the same principles as with an individual without a mental illness. If the individual has a secondary illness, such as diabetes or asthma for example, then modify the program to address those conditions as well. Aerobic activity should begin at a low intensity (40% max HR) and duration (20 minutes) for first-time participants, and progressively increase as with any individual. Individuals with mental illness typically respond well to structure, so plan their activities well in advance. Giving the individual an advance copy of the daily program and recording the activities in a log (see **Tips from the Field**) may make them feel more comfortable. By utilizing these tactics, the individual knows the daily exercise expectations and sees his progress. As a result, the individual may exhibit decreased mental illness signs and symptoms during exercise. Individuals with social anxiety issues most likely need to begin an exercise program with individual versus group exercises. Hopefully, with your encouragement and as time progresses, the individual develops a social connection to others in the facility and chooses to exercise with a partner or in small groups.

Pregnancy

Although pregnancy is not an illness or disease, it is a condition which affects a person's ability to exercise. Pregnant individuals greatly benefit from exercise, provided the exercise is performed within the physician's recommendations. Benefits of exercise during pregnancy include all cardiorespiratory benefits, maintenance of healthy weight, decrease in back pain during later pregnancy stages, decrease risk of gestational diabetes, increase in energy, and increase in muscle endurance. The individual's physician must approve exercise throughout the pregnancy. The physician may not clear them for exercise if they have been bleeding or spotting, had previous miscarriages, previous premature births, a low placenta, and a weak cervix. With the individual's written consent, develop a relationship with their physician to regularly discuss their status in regard to exercise. Knowing the individual's and the baby's, current health status as well as any exercise limitations throughout each of the trimesters is necessary to develop a safe exercise program.

Pregnant individuals can benefit from at least 30 minutes of moderate exercise as tolerated as many days per week as possible. Exercises focus on aerobic, flexibility, and low intensity strength training exercise **(Figure 15-18)**. If they were previously sedentary, they should perform 5 minutes of exercise and increase each session as tolerated working to complete 30-minute sessions. Individuals who were exercising regularly prior to pregnancy can probably continue at their pre-pregnancy level of exercise with their physician's approval, until the second and third trimester.

Aerobic activities such as walking, aerobics classes, bicycling, and swimming are best for pregnant individuals. Stretching and relaxation activities such as yoga and tai chi are beneficial. The individual should exercise on a flat surface, wear comfortable supportive shoes, and eat a nutritious meal or snack at least an hour or two before exercise. As they enter their second and third trimester, the individual gains weight. Consequently, their balance may change while ambulating and moving from various positions. They must be careful when utilizing and getting on and off machines (i.e. treadmill and stationary bike) and up from the floor (i.e. during a yoga session). After pregnancy, the individual can begin low intensity exercises approximately 2 weeks after a vaginal birth, and approximately 4 weeks after a cesarean birth.

Figure 15-18 Pregnant individuals can participate in various aerobic, strength training, and flexibility exercises through much of their pregnancy.

Pregnant individuals are more prone to iron deficiency anemia because the iron must adapt to the increased blood volume, which occurs due to the pregnancy as well as the addition of the fetus' blood volume. Pregnant individuals need iron, B12, and folate supplementation from sources previously mentioned. They also must avoid dehydration and exercise in the heat. The environment must be comfortable, and they need to maintain hydration during exercise. Activities that predispose the individual to falls, high altitudes, or forceful contact with another individual or implement resulting in trauma must be avoided. Any activity that requires jumping, hopping, bouncing, twisting, and deep knee or trunk bending should not be incorporated into the pregnant individual's exercise program. If they have any signs or symptoms of dizziness, fatigue, uterine cramping, vaginal bleeding, or dyspnea during exercise, stop the exercise immediately. Have the individual cool down briefly to restore CV and respiratory function to normal values, then have them sit down and hydrate. If uterine cramping and vaginal bleeding occurs, refer the individual to their physician immediately or call 911.

Vision and Hearing Impairment

Individuals who have visual and hearing impairments can exercise similarly to any other sighted or hearing individual. They can perform and be self-sufficient in carrying out their individualized exercise programs. When dealing with visually impaired individuals you have to complete many tasks to assure a safe and effective exercise program. Be certain the exercise area is safe for them. Familiarize the individual with the facility's layout and physical surroundings. Have them "see" the equipment with their hands. They should carry a **white cane** if they normally utilize one. Make sure as they are seeing the equipment you verbalize what structures they are touching.

If an individual is hearing impaired or deaf, they may be able to read your lips. Regardless, some words may be difficult to comprehend due to how they are pronounced. Communicate with a hearing-impaired individual by facing them while talking and speaking slowly. Some deaf individuals may have speech difficulty. If they are unable to read lips, a sign language translator, who can also pose as a workout companion may be necessary. The individual can also communicate via specialized electronic devices for the hearing impaired. If communication is a problem, then they may have less social interaction during exercise. Therefore, take an active role in determining how to involve your client in group exercise. For example, aerobics, kick boxing, and other classes require little to no communication. The individual is able to see the instructor performing the motions, and they can feel the gym floor vibrate from audio system music. Also, if they are versed in American Sign Language (ASL), you can learn and utilize this method of communication. Ultimately, ask your client what they prefer in regard to mutual communication. Utilizing facial expressions, eye contact, and visual cues are important for communication.

Prior to exercise, explain the exercises thoroughly and clearly, and record your explanation so your client can revisit it. If they are able to read large lettering or braille, have the instructions also available to them in these forms. Make sure the sound in your facility is not disruptive when you give your client verbal instructions, in order for them to hear you clearly. For the hearing-impaired individual, provide written directions, manuals, and signage on equipment. Then demonstrate each exercise activity. Visually impaired individuals can touch your arm, leg, etc. during your demonstration to visualize the activity.

The visually impaired individual may need to use touch for spatial awareness during exercise. For example, when a visually impaired person jogs, they can do so on a treadmill holding the handrail, or touching a companion jogger's bent arm while exercising outside. Hearing impaired individuals must remove any hearing devices before swimming or participating in any contact activity. An individual with hearing loss may have balance issues, so begin their exercise program on a flat surface with a wide base of support stance.

Aerobic, strength training, and flexibility exercises follow the FITT principle for both visual and hearing-impaired individuals. All benefits of exercise are applicable to visual and hearing-impaired athletes. Progress these clients as you would any other.

TIPS FROM THE FIELD

Tip 1 Many individuals regardless of their special condition require structure to maintain motivation and compliance to continue their exercise programs. Individuals may prefer to know what to expect prior to each exercise session. Likewise, most individuals want to monitor their progress. Therefore, have a written activity schedule or log with various planned activities that you and your client create. The activity log is a weekly schedule, which can be easily modified if necessary. The schedule includes the day, various exercises, exercise intensity, and length of time for the individual exercises and session. The activity log has an area available for exercise session notes such as their BP, HR, comments, limitations, progress, etc. The individual can keep an exercise journal to write in prior to and after the exercise session, as well as any other time that the individual wishes. This journal is useful for the individual to record all of their emotions regarding the exercise sessions and their "new" lifestyle. This journal provides the individual another outlet to express their thoughts and perhaps critically think about their activities and lifestyle.

Summary

Exercise is beneficial for all individuals with the aforementioned special conditions. As a sports medicine professional working with individuals having special conditions, you must research these special conditions and discuss the individual's capabilities and limitations with them, their physicians, and their health care providers, after obtaining the individual's written consent to do so. This knowledge and discussion is crucial in order to set up their safe, effective physical activity, exercise, and nutritional program.

Keywords

Contraindications Reasons or conditions why a technique, exercise, etc. should not be used.

Valsalva maneuver When an individual holds their breath and attempts to forcefully expire through their closed mouth and nose.

Metastatic Cancer cells moving from one site in the body and spreading to another.

Remission When a disease has decreased or become absent in the body. In regard to cancer, if a physician cannot detect cancer cells within an individual's body via imaging and other diagnostic tests, then the individual is in remission.

Rate of perceived exertion (RPE) The individual's opinion of how hard they are working during exercise. The method was developed by Gunnar Borg, a Swedish psychologist. The RPE is rated by the athlete on a scale of 6 to 20 with 6 being no exertion at all and 20 being maximal exertion. See the CDC website http://www.cdc.gov/physicalactivity/everyone/measuring/exertion.html for more information on RPE and the RPE scale individuals can use during exercise.

Metabolism How the body ingests food, breaks it down, and creates energy to utilize.

Dyspnea Shortness of breath.

White cane A long stick that individual's with visual impairments utilize to navigate and avoid obstacles.

Discussion Questions

1. Can individuals with special conditions obtain the same exercise benefits as healthy individuals? If yes, what are those benefits? If no, then why not?
2. What special conditions may an individual have that requires daily medication? How can this medication affect exercise performance?
3. When creating an exercise program for an individual who has any of the three respiratory conditions mentioned, what are your major concerns?
4. What special conditions require you to take utmost caution with the exercising individuals and why? What special conditions, if any, do not have exercise limitations?
5. What are some tactics can be utilized to assist a visual or hearing-impaired individual to perform safe exercise?

CASE STUDY: A DIRE SITUATION

Gil is a 62-year-old male who has been advised by his physician to improve his lifestyle immediately, or serious illness could result. Gil is sedentary. He sits behind a desk all day at work and leads a very inactive lifestyle. He has poor nutritional habits and consumes too many calories. Consequently, Gil is obese. Gil also suffers from asthma, and is on various medications to prevent exacerbations. His blood pressure is on average 150/95. He takes beta-blocker medication and diuretics in order to keep his hypertension under control. In addition, due to his weight, Gil has acquired Type II diabetes. However, at this point, he is not insulin dependent. Gil's physician advised him to control his sugar intake by monitoring his diet. Gil has not been successful with this task. He smokes about a half of a pack of cigarettes daily and occasionally has an alcoholic drink.

After his physician informed Gil about his health, Gil realizes his situation is dire. He decides to watch his food intake and eat healthier. He vows to quit smoking someday. In the meantime, he is determined to go to the gym tomorrow and start exercising with the help of a personal trainer. Although self-motivation has not been a strong personal characteristic, Gil realizes he needs to change his lifestyle to live longer and have a good quality of life.

1. What are the various conditions that Gil has acquired?
2. If you were Gil's personal trainer, what special considerations do you need to consider when devising Gil's physical activity and exercise program?
3. How would you begin Gil's physical activity and exercise program? What parameters would you utilize?
4. What can Gil do to increase his motivation and compliance toward exercise?

References

American Academy of Allergy, Asthma, and Immunology (2020, September 28). *Asthma and exercise.* https://www.aaaai.org/Tools-for-the-Public/Conditions-Library/Asthma/Asthma-and-Exercise

Bidonde, J., Busch, A.J., Schachter, C.L., Overend, T.J., Kim, S.Y. Góes, S.M., Boden, C., Foulds, H.J.A. (2017). *Aerobic exercise training for adults with fibromyalgia.* Cochrane Databser of Systematic Reviews. https://doi.org/10.1002/14651858.CD012700

Center for Disease Control and Prevention (CDC). (2020, January 6). *Fibromyalgia.* https://www.cdc.gov/arthritis/basics/fibromyalgia.htm

Colberg, S.R., Sigal, R.J., Yardley, J.E., Riddell, M.C., Dunstan, D.W., Dempsey, P.C., Horton, E.S., Castorino, K., & Tate, D.F. (2016). Physical activity/exercise and diabetes: A position statement of the American Diabetes Association. *Diabetes Care, 39*(11): 2065–2079, https://doi.org/10/2337/dc16-1728.

Cuppett, M., & Walsh, K. M. (2017). *General medical conditions in the athlete, 3rd Ed.*, Champaign, IL: Human Kinetics.

Cystic Fibrosis Foundation (n.d.). *Creating a fitness plan that works for you.* Accessed on March 5, 2022, from https://www.cff.org/managing-cf/creating-fitness-plan-works-you

Desbrow, B., Burd, N.A., Tarnopolsky, M., Moore, D.R., & Elliot-Sale, K.J. (2018). Nutrition for special populations: Youth, female, and masters athletes. *International Journal of Sport Nutrition and Exercise Metabolism, 29*(2): 220–227. https: doi.org/10.1123/ijsnem.2018-0269

Kalb, R., Brown, T.R., Coote, S., Costello, K., Dalgas, U., Garmon, E., Giesser, B., Halper, J., Karpatkin, H., Keller, J., Ng, A.V., Pilutti, L.A., Rohrig, A., Van Asch, P., Zackowski, K., & Motl, R.W. (2020). Exercise and lifestyle physical activity recommendations for people with multiple sclerosis throughout the disease course. *Mult Scler, 26*(12):1459–1469. https://doi.10.1177/1352458520915629

Larun, L., Brurberg, K. G., Odgaard-Jensen, J., & Price, J. R. (2017). Exercise therapy for chronic fatigue syndrome. *The Cochrane database of systematic reviews, 4*(4), CD003200. https://doi.org/10.1002/14651858.CD003200.pub7

Lee, P.G., Jackson, E.A., & Richardson, C.R. (2017). Exercise prescriptions in older adults. *Am Fam Physician, 95*(7):425–432.

Martin Ginis, K.A., van der Scheer, J.W., Latimer-Cheung, A.E. *et al.* (2018). Evidence-based scientific exercise guidelines for adults with spinal cord injury: an update and a new guideline. *Spinal Cord, 56,* 308–321. https://doi.org/10.1038/s41393-017-0017-3

Mayo Clinic. (2021, May 18). *Exercise: A drug-free approach to lowering high blood pressure.* https://www.mayoclinic.org/diseases-conditions/high-blood-pressure/in-depth/high-blood-pressure/art-20045206

Mayo Clinic. (2020, September 24). *Chronic fatigue syndrome.* https://www.mayoclinic.org/diseases-conditions/chronic-fatigue-syndrome/symptoms-causes/syc-20360490#:~:text=Chronic%20fatigue%20syndrome%20(CFS)%20is,doesn't%20 improve%20with%20rest

National Cancer Institute. (2019, November 12). *Prescribing exercise as cancer treatment: A conversation with Dr. Kathryn Schmitz.* https://www.cancer.gov/news-events/cancer-currents-blog/2019/cancer-survivors-exercise-guidelines-schmitz

National Multiple Sclerosis Society. (2022). *What causes MS?* Retrieved March 4, 2022, from https://www.nationalmssociety.org/What-is-MS/What-Causes-MS

Nystoriak, M.A., & Bhatnagar, A. (2018). Cardiovascular effects and benefits of exercise. *Front. Cardiovasc. Med. 5*:135. https://doi.org/10.3389/fcvm.2018.00135

Papson, A., Osmak, J., Chag, T., Matsuzaki, Y., & Molony, J.T. (2018, November 26). *Strength and conditioning for the young athlete.* Hospital for Special Surgery. https://www.hss.edu/conditions_strength-conditioning-kids.asp

Richardson, R.W. (2020). *Exercise and arthritis.* American College of Rheumatology. https://www.rheumatology.org/I-Am-A/Patient-Caregiver/Diseases-Conditions/Living-Well-with-Rheumatic-Disease/Exercise-and-Arthritis

Spruit, M.A., Burtin, C., De Boever, P., Langer, D., Vogiatzis, I., Wouters, E.F., Franssen, F.M. (2016). COPD and exercise: Does it make a difference? *Breathe*, 12(2):e38-49, https://doi.org/10.1183/20734735.003916.

Strasser, B., Pesta, D., Rittweger, J., Burtscher, J., & Burtscher, M. (2021). Nutrition for older athletes: Focus on Sex-differences. *Nutritients*, *13*(5), 1409. https://doi.org/10.3390/nu13051409

Stricker, P.R., Faigenbaum, A.D., McCambridge, T.M., LaBella, C.R., Brooks, M.A., Canty, G., Diamond, A.B., Hennrikus, W., Logan, K., Moffat, K., Nemeth, B.A., Pengel, K.B., & Peterson, A.R, (2020). *Resistance training for children and adolescents.* 145(6), e20201011. https://doi.org/10.1542/peds.2020-1011

Tessler, J., & Bordoni, B. (2022 Feb 8). *Cardiac rehabilitation.* https://www.ncbi.nlm.nih.gov/books/NBK537196/

Verberne, L., Leemrijse, C. J., Swinkels, I., van Dijk, C. E., de Bakker, D. H., & Nielen, M. (2017). Overweight in patients with chronic obstructive pulmonary disease needs more attention: a cross-sectional study in general practice. *NPJ primary care respiratory medicine*, *27*(1), 63. https://doi.org/10.1038/s41533-017-0065-3

World Masters Athletics. (n.d.). *FAQ and contact.* https://world-masters-athletics.com/faq-and-contact/